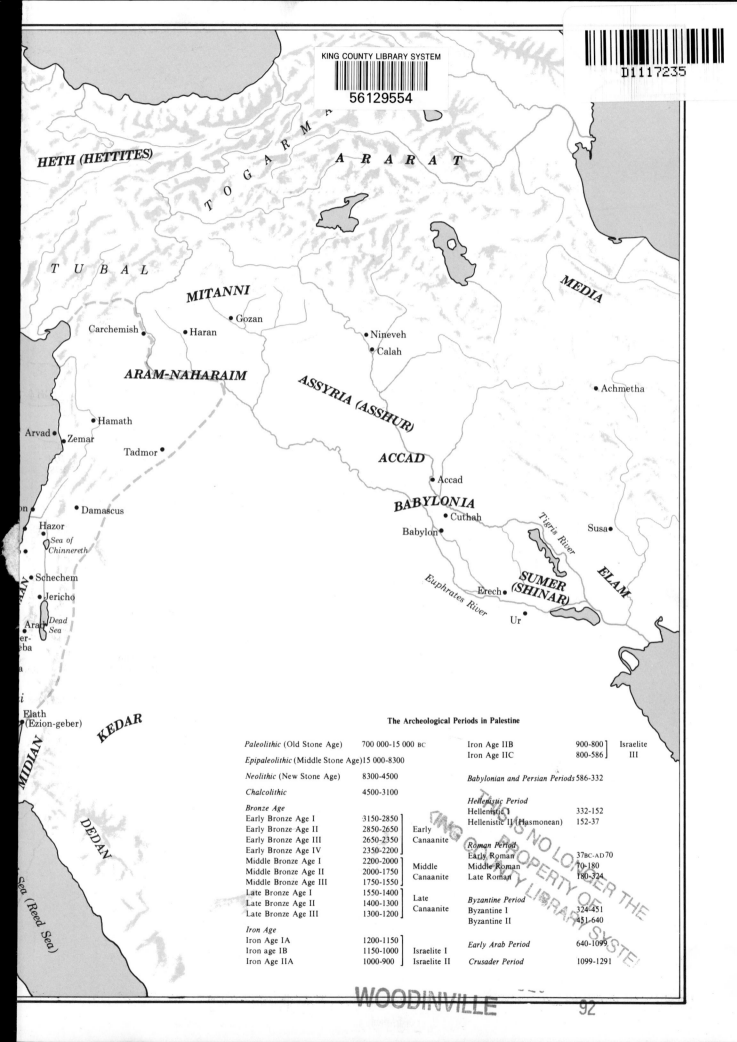

HETH (HETTITES)

A R A R A T

T O G A R M A

T U B A L

MITANNI

MEDIA

Carchemish • • Gozan
• Haran

ARAM-NAHARAIM

• Nineveh
• Calah

ASSYRIA (ASSHUR)

• Achmetha

• Hamath

Arvad • • Zemar

Tadmor •

ACCAD

• Accad

BABYLONIA

on •

• Damascus

• Cuthah

Tigris River

Susa •

Hazor
Sea of
Chinnereth

Babylon •

ELAM

• Schechem

SUMER
(SHINAR)

• Jericho

Euphrates River

Erech •

Ara•
Dead
Sea

Ur •

-eba

Elath
(Ezion-geber)

KEDAR

MIDIAN

DEDAN

Sea (Reed Sea)

The Archeological Periods in Palestine

Paleolithic (Old Stone Age)	700 000-15 000 BC		Iron Age IIB	900-800]	Israelite
			Iron Age IIC	800-586]	III
Epipaleolithic (Middle Stone Age)	15 000-8300				
Neolithic (New Stone Age)	8300-4500		*Babylonian and Persian Periods*	586-332	
Chalcolithic	4500-3100		*Hellenistic Period*		
Bronze Age			Hellenistic I	332-152	
Early Bronze Age I	3150-2850]		Hellenistic II (Hasmonean)	152-37	
Early Bronze Age II	2850-2650]	Early			
Early Bronze Age III	2650-2350	Canaanite	*Roman Period*		
Early Bronze Age IV	2350-2200]		Early Roman	37BC-AD 70	
Middle Bronze Age I	2200-2000]		Middle Roman	70-180	
Middle Bronze Age II	2000-1750	Middle	Late Roman	180-324	
Middle Bronze Age III	1750-1550	Canaanite			
Late Bronze Age I	1550-1400]		*Byzantine Period*		
Late Bronze Age II	1400-1300	Late	Byzantine I	324-451	
Late Bronze Age III	1300-1200]	Canaanite	Byzantine II	451-640	
Iron Age					
Iron Age IA	1200-1150]		*Early Arab Period*	640-1099	
Iron age IB	1150-1000	Israelite I			
Iron Age IIA	1000-900]	Israelite II	*Crusader Period*	1099-1291	

Almanac of the
BIBLE

Almanac of the
BIBLE

GEOFFREY WIGODER, Ph.D.
SHALOM M. PAUL, Ph.D.
&
BENEDICT T. VIVIANO, O.P.

Prentice Hall

New York   London   Toronto   Sydney   Tokyo   Singapore

PRENTICE HALL GENERAL REFERENCE
15 Columbus Circle
New York, New York, 10023

Copyright © 1991 by G.G. The Jerusalem Publishing House Ltd.,
39, Tchernichovski Street, Jerusalem, Israel.

Library of Congress Cataloging-in-Publication Data

Wigoder, Geoffrey, 1922–
   Almanac of the Bible / Geoffrey Wigoder.
      p.   cm.
    Includes index.
    ISBN 0-13-026899-2
    1. Bible—Handbooks, manuals, etc.   I. Title.
    BS417.W48   1991
    220'.02'02'—dc20   91-13229
                                       CIP

Designed by Techiya Rosenthal
Manufactured in the United States of America

10 9 8 7 6 5 4 3 2 1
First Prentice Hall Edition

CONTRIBUTORS

David Bivin
Fiona Gibson
Rivka Gonen
Jean-Marie Guillaume
Wayne Horowitz
Daryl Kibble
Malcolm Lowe
Chaim Mayerson
Stephen Notley
Ephraim Orni
Lilach Peled
David Pileggi
Stephen Roth
Gabriel Sivan
David Solomon
Julie Stahl
Geoffrey Wigoder
Clarence Wagner
Dany Wool

Project Manager and Picture Researcher: *Georgette Corcos*
Managing Editor: *Rachel Gilon*
Production Assistant: *Avinoam Gat*
Copy-editor and Indexer: *Suzy Shabetai*

CONTENTS

INTRODUCTION

Although called the Book of Books, the Bible is far more than a book. It is even far more than a literature. It is the world's greatest fount of inspiration and the source of Western civilization. It is religion, ethics, law, history, poetry, story-telling, all in one. It is the best-loved of all writings and its dramatis personae are not distant figures but well-loved friends. Its phrases figure in our everyday speech, its images accompany us from early childhood. An early rabbi said of it 'Keep on turning it – for it contains everything,' and indeed it is endlessly illuminating and exciting.

The Bible is turned to by countless multitudes for many reasons. First and foremost, it is the foundation of faith, but it is also eagerly sought after and studied by scholars of history and literature, as well as by the ordinary reader, in search of enthralling drama. This "Almanac" has been designed to enhance and deepen the understanding and enjoyment of the Bible by all who turn to it. Features such as the guide to persons and places mentioned in the Bible will help all readers. Descriptions of the ancient peoples, the flora and fauna of the Bible, and its musical instruments throw light on intriguing details; while in a lighter vein, famous quotations, or the sections on the Bible as depicted in art and on stamps bring unexpected aspects. A glance at the table of contents will show the wide variety of subjects covered, succinctly and authoritatively. The whole work is lavishly illustrated with pictures drawn from many sources — paintings and sculptures on biblical themes, photographs of sites and archeological discoveries, maps and tables.

The "Almanac" is the work of an international team of scholars, supervised and edited by Professor Geoffrey Wigoder, editor-in-chief of the classic "Encyclopedia Judaica", Professor Shalom Paul, Professor of Bible at the Hebrew University, Jerusalem and Benedict T. Viviano, O.P., Professor of New Testament, at the Ecole Biblique, Jerusalem

ABBREVIATIONS

Acts	*The Acts of the Apostles*
Amos	*The Book of Amos*
Ant.	*The Antiquities of the Jews (Josephus)*
I Chr	*The First Book of the Chronicles*
II Chr	*The Second Book of the Chronicles*
Col	*The Epistle of Paul the Apostle to the Colossians*
I Cor	*The First Epistle of Paul the Apostle to the Corinthians*
II Cor	*The Second Epistle of Paul the Apostle to the Corinthians*
Dan	*The Book of Daniel*
Deut	*The Fifth Book of Moses called Deuteronomy*
Ecc	*The Book of Ecclesiastes*
Eccl	*Ecclesiasticus*
Eph	*The Epistle of Paul the Apostle to the Ephesians*
Est	*The Book of Esther*
Ezek	*The Book of Ezekiel*
Ezra	*The Book of Ezra*
Ex	*The Second Book of Moses Called Exodus*
Gal	*The Epistle of Paul the Apostle to the Galatians*
Gen	*The First Book of Moses Called Genesis*
Hab	*The Book of Habakkuk*
Hag	*The Book of Hagai*
Heb	*The Epistle to the Hebrews*
Hos	*The Book of Hosea*
Is	*The Book of Isaiah*
James	*The Epistle of James*
Jer	*The Book of Jeremiah*
Job	*The Book of Job*
Joel	*The Book of Joel*
John	*The Gospel According to John*
I John	*The First Epistle of John*
II John	*The Second Epistle of John*
III John	*The Third Epistle of John*
Jonah	*The Book of Jonah*
Josh	*The Book of Joshua*
Jude	*The Epistle of Jude*
Judg	*The Book of Judges*
I Kgs	*The First Book of the Kings*
II Kgs	*The Second Book of the Kings*

KJV	*King James Version*
Lam	*The Book of Lamentations*
Lev	*The Third Book of Moses Called Leviticus*
Luke	*The Gospel According to Luke*
Macc	*Maccabees*
Malachi	*The Book of Malachi*
Mark	*The Gospel According to Mark*
Matt	*The Gospel According to Matthew*
Mic	*The Book of Micah*
Nah	*The Book of Nahum*
Neh	*The Book of Nehemiah*
NKJV	*The New King James Version*
NT	*New Testament*
Num	*The Fourth Book of Moses Called Numbers*
Obad	*The Book of Obadiah*
OT	*Old Testament*
I Pet	*The First Epistle of Peter*
II Pet	*The Second Epistle of Peter*
Phil	*The Epistle of Paul the Apostle to the Philippians*
Philem	*Philemon*
Prov	*The Book of Proverbs*
Ps	*The Book of Psalms*
Rev	*The Revelation of Jesus Christ*
Rom	*The Epistle of Paul the Apostle to the Romans*
RSV	*Revised Standard Version*
Ruth	*The Book of Ruth*
I Sam	*The First Book of Samuel*
II Sam,	*The Second Book of Samuel*
Song	*The Song of Solomon*
I Thes	*The First Epistle of Paul the Apostle to the Thessalonians*
II Thes	*The Second Epistle of Paul the Apostle to the Thessalonians*
I Tim	*The First Epistle of Paul the Apostle to Timothy*
II Tim	*The Second Epistle of Paul the Apostle to Timothy*
Titus	*The Epistle of Paul the Apostle to Titus*
Zech	*The Book of Zechariah*
Zeph	*The Book of Zephaniah*

I. THE ANCIENT NEAR EAST

I.1 PEOPLES

While focusing on the Holy Land and the Israelite/Jewish people, the Bible story ranges over many lands and nations, from Rome to Persia. The modern terms "Middle East" and "Near East" do not fully coincide with the broader locale which forms the background of biblical history.

Intertwined with the Old Testament are the so-called Fertile Crescent, the great Syrian-Arabian Desert, the river valleys of Egypt and Mesopotamia, the Sinai peninsula, and the eastern Mediterranean coastline. Other countries further away, such as parts of Asia Minor and the Arabian peninsula, make peripheral appearances. The Median-Persian Empire is important in the early Second Temple period, as is reflected in the later books of the Old Testament.

By New Testament times, the area is even wider. Roman rule over Palestine and the scattered Jewish Diaspora bring new links with far-off lands and the extent of these new interests is vividly illustrated by Paul's travels to Asia Minor, Greece, Mediterranean islands, and Rome.

The many lands involved in the Bible story mean that a multitude of people appear in the chronicle. The strategic position of Palestine at the meeting place of three continents and on two great international highways attracted foreign armies, many of them moving across to further destinations. The country fell under a succession of invaders and rulers (apart from the original Canaanite inhabitants) such as the Philistines, Egyptians, Arameans (Syrians), Assyrians, Babylonians, Persians, Greeks, and Romans, all of whom left an indelible imprint. Some of the important peoples are profiled in the following section.

AMALEKITES. An ancient nomadic tribe who roamed the northern Sinai desert and the Negeb. According to biblical tradition, they are the descendants of Amalek the son of Eliphaz, firstborn son of Esau by his concubine Timna (Gen 36:12,16). They were the first enemy to attack the Israelites in the Sinai after the crossing of the Red Sea, and were defeated at Rephidim in a battle led by Joshua under the inspiration of Moses, Aaron, and Hur (Ex 17:8-13). The people of Israel were commanded to remember forever what the Amalekites had done to them on their way out of Egypt, and not to fail to blot out the memory of the Amalekites from under the heaven (Deut 25:17-19); and indeed, the Israelites had a continuous war "from generation to generation" (Ex 17:14-16) with the Amalekites.

During the period of the Judges, the Amalekites, in alliance with the Ammonites and Moabites, were defeated by the judge Ehud (Judg 3:13ff). Subsequently, they were again defeated, this time in alliance with the Midianites and the eastern tribes, by Gideon in a battle in the valley of Jezreel (Judg 6:33; 7:12). Saul attacked the Amalekites in a war that commenced with a divine command, conveyed by Samuel, to utterly destroy them (I Sam 15:1-3). Saul annihilated the people but spared their king Agag. Samuel, angry over Saul's disobedience, personally "hacked Agag to pieces" (I Sam 15:10-33) and took away the kingship from the house of Saul.

David's revenge over the attack in Ziklag in which the Amalekites burnt the city and captured women and children, including David's wives Ahinoam and Abigail (I Sam 30:1-5), was the final blow to the Amalekites; he killed them with the exception of 400 men who escaped (I Sam 30:8-20). In the days of Hezekiah, the Simeonites defeated the Amalekites and settled their territory (I Chr 4:43).

In Jewish tradition, the Amalekites symbolize the enemies of Israel and this may be the explanation for the epithet "the Agagite" (Est 3:1) applied to Haman, who was regarded as a descendant of Agag.

AMMONITES. Ammon, the land of the Ammonites, is situated east of the river Jordan, on the north bank of the river Jabbok. At the sources of the Jabbok is situated the royal city of Rabbah (II Sam 12:27), whose central status was due to its location on the main route of international trade. According to archaeological evidence, the Ammonites settled on their land at the beginning of the 13th century BC. A few Ammonite inscriptions have been discovered. Their language was akin to Hebrew.

The name Ammon, referring to an ethnic-geographic unit, appears in the Bible only twice (I Sam 11:11; Ps 83:8). The usual term is Sons of Ammon (*Benei Ammon*). Excavations from the 8th-7th centuries BC show that Ammonite culture was eclectic and influ-

Left: Ammonite warriors on horseback; late 7th century BC. Right: Head of an Ammonite king. Sculpture from Rabbath Ammon; late 7th century BC.

enced by the cultural centers of its time, especially Egypt, Syria, and Assyria. The artistic motifs are adopted from Phoenicia, Egypt, Aram, and Assyria. The Ammonites' chief god was Milcom (Molech). However, in the story of the war of the Ammonites against Israel at the time of Jephthah, Chemosh, the chief god of the Moabites, is mentioned as their god (Judg 11:24). According to Jeremiah, the people of Ammon were circumcised (Jer 9:24-25).

According to biblical tradition, the origin of the Ammonites was the incestuous union of Lot with his younger daughter who bore him Ben-Ammi, "the father of the people of Ammon to this day" (Gen 19:38). Their land was not included among the countries promised by God to the people of Israel; instead, it was promised to the sons of Lot (Deut 2:19, 37; Judg 11:15, etc.).

Like the Moabites, the Ammonites were excluded from "the assembly of the Lord," i.e., from among the Israelites, already in the days of Moses (Deut 23:3). The Bible tells of continuous enmity between the Israelites and the Ammonites. Although Jephthah defeated them (Judg 11:31-33), during the reign of Saul, the Ammonite king Nahash conquered Israelite territories and attempted to take Jabesh in Gilead. He besieged the city, proclaimed that its people could have peace only on condition that the right eye of all the people of Jabesh be gouged out (I Sam 11). However, during the reign of David, relations with the Ammonites appear to have improved and following the death of Nahash, the Ammonite king, David sent men to comfort his son Hanun; but the messengers were humiliated and this prompted a long war (II Sam 10-11:1). The Ammonites sought military assistance from the Aramean states (II Sam 10:6; I Chr 19:6), but were repulsed. After defeating Aram (II Sam 8:5-6; I Chr 18:5-6), Joab succeeded in taking Rabbah, the Ammonite capital (II Sam 11:1, 22-24; 12:26-29; I Chr 20:1).

In King Solomon's days, peace was established and the ties became even stronger (I Kgs 14:21; I Chr 12:13).

The king married an Ammonite, Naamah, and had Ammonite women among his loves. He built a sanctuary to the Ammonite god Milcom (Molech) on the mountain east of Jerusalem (I Kgs 11:7). Until the days of Jehoshaphat, when the Ammonites regained their independence, they were tributaries of Israel. They joined the Moabites and the inhabitants of the mountainous region of Seir in fighting Judah, but they all suffered a crushing defeat (I Chr 19:1-14, 16-19). An Ammonite rebellion was subdued by Jotham (II Chr 27:5).

For most of the 7th century BC, after the Assyrian drive into Palestine under Tiglath-pileser III (743-732), Ammon remained an Assyrian province. When Nebuchadnezzar attacked Ashkelon in 604 BC, Ammon became a Babylonian province and paid tribute like "all the kings of Heth." The Ammonites joined the Chaldeans (Babylonians) in suppressing Jehoiakim's rebellion (II Kgs 24:1-2). Ezekiel describes the king of Babylon standing at a crossroads, one road leading to Rabbah, the capital of Ammon, the other to Jerusalem (Ezek 21:19-22), and choosing to march on Jerusalem. Upon returning from the Babylonian exile, Nehemiah forbade the Jews to marry Ammonites and Edomites (Neh 13:23). At that time Ammon was ruled by Tobiah, possibly an appointee of the Persian rulers (Neh 2:19; 6:14). By then many Jews had settled in this area. Under the Ptolemies, it became a Jewish political entity, called Ammonitis. Its capital was Birta or Tyros. The other important city was Rabbath Ammon, renamed Philadelphia. At the end of the Seleucid period the whole region was known as Peraea.

AMORITES. The Amorites were one of the Semitic peoples of northern Syria and Mesopotamia from about 3000 BC. They inhabited the land of Canaan before the Israelites. Their name derives from Martu ("west"), and is mentioned already in Sumerian inscriptions early in the mid-3rd millennium. Some identify the Martu with the Amu of Egyptian sources, the wanderers who overran Syria and Palestine and reached the Egyptian borders. In Akkadian and Assyrian sources of the end of the 3rd millennium they are referred to as Amurru, which is very close to the biblical name. During the 2nd millennium BC, the Amorites spread over large areas in Mesopotamia and east to the Jordan, pressing southwards and westwards. They reached their zenith in the middle of this millennium and then declined rapidly, later merging with newly arriving elements, the Horites, Hittites, Canaanites, Hebrews, Arameans, and other peoples. From the 15th century, the name Amurru refers to a country situated in the area of Lebanon, and central and southern Syria. As described in the El Amarna letters, this country was an integral part of the Egyptian province of Canaan on the border of the Hittite kingdom. At the beginning of the 14th century BC, the state of Amurru shook off Egyptian domination, but shortly afterwards it became a vassal area of the Hittites, and was again conquered by Egypt at the beginning of the 13th century. It was finally taken over by the Hittites after the battle of Kadesh-on-the-Orontes in 1297 BC. At that time the Amorites possessed a culture that was influenced by that of Mesopotamia, with local Canaanite affinities.

In the Bible. The name Amorites refers to the original inhabitants of the area before the Israelite conquest and to one of the "nations" on both sides of the river Jordan, some of whom were destroyed during the conquest and some of whom surrendered to the Israelites and mingled with them. The Amorites are mentioned in the stories of the patriarchs. During the 18th-17th centuries BC, they dwelt in several areas in Palestine. According to Genesis 14, Abram the Hebrew (Abraham) was living by the oaks of Mamre the Amorite, and the Amorites were his allies (Gen 14:13). Jacob took the city of Shechem from the Amorites with his sword and his bow (Gen 48:22). According to Deuteronomy 1:7,20 the Amorites occupied mountains which were sometimes known as "the hill country of the Amorite."

In the period of the Israelite conquest, Adoni-Zedek, king of Jerusalem, and his allies, the four kings of Hebron, Jarmuth, Lachish, and Eglon, were kings of the Amorites (Josh 10). The non-Israelite inhabitants of the domain of the Danites were Amorites, who paid tribute to the house of Joseph (Judg 1:34-35). According to II Samuel 21:2, the Gibeonites were a remnant of the Amorites. The Amorites dwelt as far south as Akrabbim (Judg 1:36). To the east, the realm of Sihon, king of the Amorites, extended from the Arnon river to the Jabbok river (Num 21:21-23; Josh 12:2, etc.). Another Amorite kingdom, farther to the north, was ruled by Og, king of Bashan (Deut 3:8; 4:47), which was also conquered by the Israelites (Josh 12:4-5). In the days of Samuel, there was peace between the Amorites and the Israelites (I Sam 7:14). The Amorites were among the peoples who remained after the Israelite conquest and paid tribute to Solomon (I Kgs 9:20ff).

Ezekiel referred to the Amorites as the "fathers" of Jerusalem (Ezek 16:3, 45).

ARAMEANS. The name of a group of nomadic and semi-nomadic western Semitic tribes. During the last quarter of the 2nd millennium and the early 1st millennium BC, they spread over the lands of the Fertile Crescent, from Elam in the east to Transjordan in the west, and from the southern parts of the Amanus mountains in the north to the Arabian desert in the South.

Various traditions concerning their origin are found in the Bible. The Table of Nations in Genesis (10:22-23) mentions Aram (together with Elam and Asshur) as a descendant of Noah from his son Shem. The Bible regards Aram as the eponymous ancestor of the Arameans. However, according to the genealogical table of the Nahorites (Gen 22:20-24), Aram was the grandson of Nahor. According to Amos (1:5; 9:7) the Arameans originated in Kir which may have been located on the border between Babylonia and Elam (II Kgs 17:9; Is 22:6). These contradictions may be explained by the fact that during various periods different tribes known as Arameans were either wandering or settling permanently in the area. Support for this view may be found in Assyrian sources (the earliest are of the 12th century) which mention dozens of Aramean tribes but say nothing of their origin. The actual origin of the Arameans is obscure, but they seem to have been among the nomadic tribes that moved northward through the west margins of the Syrian Desert towards Egypt, Canaan, and the banks of the Euphrates.

In the Bible. Biblical narratives make the Arameans close kinsmen of the patriarchs: Abraham is the brother of Nahor, and it was from his Aramean kinsmen that he drew the Aramean Rebekah as a wife for his son, Isaac (Gen 24; 25:20). The granddaughter of

Relief from Gozan showing an Aramean charioteer; late 7th century BC.

Hazael, king of Aram-Damascus. Ivory figurine from Arslan Tash; 9th century BC.

Nahor, Rebekah was "daughter of Bethuel the Aramean and sister of Laban the Aramean." Later, she instructs Jacob, "the wandering Aramean," cf. Deuteronomy 26:5, to depart in search of a wife (Gen 28:2–5). Jacob marries the daughters of Laban the Aramean (Gen 31:47). The ancestral home of the patriarchs in the Haran district is "Padan Aram" (Gen 25:20; 28:2), the "country of Aram" (Hos 12:13), or "Aram-Naharaim" to which Egyptian and Akkadian sources of the 15th-12th centuries BC referred simply as Naharaim.

The relations between the Israelites and the Arameans later found expression in various areas including matrimonial connections. Maacah, the daughter of Talmai, king of Geshur, was given to David and bore him Absalom (II Sam 3:3; 13:37). The first extrabiblical mention of the Arameans is found in the annals of Tiglath-pileser I, king of Assyria (1116–1076 BC). During the 11th century BC the Arameans played a leading role in Mesopotamia. They spread in Babylonia, mainly in the southeastern areas. While Assyria managed to control its own territories, it could not prevent the Arameans from taking over lands it had conquered

earlier. At the end of the 2nd and at the beginning of the 1st millennium BC, independent Aramean states arose in Syria: Aram-Zobah (I Chr 18:8); Aram-Beth-Rehob situated near the border of Hamath (Num 13:21), which was allied with Zobah and Maacah in the war against David (II Sam 10:8); Aram-Maacah and its capital Abel-beth-Maacah (II Sam 10:6); and Aram-Damascus. Independent states also arose in Mesopotamia: e.g., Bit-Adini (Amos 1:5). So long as the Aramean states were powerful, they challenged the very existence of the Assyrian kingdom. At the same time, however, they had to defend themselves against David who defeated Hadadezer, king of Aram-Zobah, and brought him and his allies into vassalage. Later, powerful Assyrian kings overcame Aramean resistance and ultimately converted their states into parts of Assyrian provinces. In 856 BC, Bit-Adini fell to Shalmaneser III; Tiglath-pileser III conquered Arpad of Yamhad in 740 BC; Zobah and Damascus capitulated in 732 BC; Hamath was taken by Sargon II in 720; and, in keeping with Assyrian policy, people from the Kingdom of Israel, who fell to the Assyrians in 722 (II Kgs 17:5–6), were exiled to Aramean lands. Aramean political power was gone, never to be restored.

The Aramean expansion did not create a political or cultural unity. They assimilated cultural elements of their neighbors and, except for their language and script, they left no manifest traces of their culture among other people. They borrowed the alphabet from the Phoenicians, developed their own forms of it and transmitted it to others everywhere they went. The widespread diffusion of the Aramaic language was accelerated by extensive shifts in populations and mass exiles. It was the language spoken in Palestine in New Testament times.

ASSYRIANS. The people of Assur (or Asshur), a word which, according to the context, may refer to (1) the son of Shem and eponymous father of the Assyrian people (Gen 10:22), (2) the chief god of the Assyrians, to whom he gave his name, (3) the first capital of the Assyrian empire, sacred to the god Asshur, (4) the country or empire of Assyria. This latter term sometimes includes Babylon.

Assyria, situated in northern Mesopotamia, was always a militant country. Throughout its history, it knew varying borders as its power waxed and waned, often in connection with its continual rivalry with its southern neighbor Babylon, the other mighty empire of Mesopotamia. The two warring empires had to withstand the constant pressure of neighboring nations: the hill people of Kurdistan to the north, Syrian kingdoms to the west, Aramean kingdoms to the south. The Assyrian kings were known for their bold military campaigns. Their kingdom spread at times from Asia Minor and Armenia in the north to Egypt in the south, from the Mediterranean in the west to the Persian Gulf

THE NEO-ASSYRIAN EMPIRE (890-609 BC)?

Tukulti-ninurta II (890-884)	Fought against tribes threatening Assyria.
Ashurnasirpal II (883-859)	Conquered northern Babylonia, Lebanon, and the Philistines.
Shalmaneser III (858-825)	Extended empire. Fought coalition of twelve kings led by Ben-Hadad I of Damascus and including Ahab king of Israel. The battle at Karkar (853 BC) was inconclusive. Shalmaneser later received tribute from Jehu king of Israel.
Samsi-Adad V (823-811)	Fought Babylonia. His wife, Semiramis served as regent 810-805 BC.
Adad-Nirari III (810-783)	Fought Hazael of Damascus, releasing Israel and Judah from a spate of Aramean attacks. Joash king of Israel was subsequently able to recover territory lost to Hazael (II Kgs 13:25).
Shalmaneser IV (782-773)	Continued battle against Hazael, allowing Jeroboam II of Israel to expand northern boundary to Hamath (II Kgs 14:25-28).
Tiglath-pileser III (745-727)	Proclaimed king of Babylonia. Collected a tribute of 50 silver shekels from the wealthy men of Israel during the reign of Menahem (II Kgs 15:20). Exiled the tribes of Trans-Jordan during the reign of Pekah of Israel (II Kgs 15:29), and established Hoshea on the throne of Israel (II Kgs 15:30). At the bid of Ahaz king of Judah, attacked Israel and Aram, but under his influence, Ahaz erected a pagan altar in the Temple compound (II Kgs 16).
Shalmaneser V (726-722)	Conquered the Northern Kingdom of Israel (722 BC), deposed King Hoshea, and exiled the inhabitants (II Kgs 17:1-6). He then repopulated Samaria with conquered peoples from other provinces (II Kgs 17:24).
Sargon II (722-705)	Completed conquest of Israel. According to the biblical account, he also crushed the rebellion of the king of Ashdod (711 BC), and his own inscriptions describe his subjugation of Judah.
Sennacherib (704-681)	Attacked Babylonia. Babylonia's request for help from Hezekiah king of Judah was turned down on the advice of Isaiah (II Kgs 20:12-19). Assyria turned on Judah and crushed Lachish, while still collecting tribute from Hezekiah (II Kgs 18:13-16). Sennacherib laid siege to Jerusalem (701 BC), but the siege was lifted after a plague broke out in his encampment (II Kgs 18-19). Sennacherib returned to Nineveh, where he was assassinated by his two eldest sons, Adrammelech and Sharezer (II Kgs 19:37).
Esarhaddon (680-669)	Imprisoned Manasseh of Judah in Nineveh (II Chr 33:11). He continued his father's policy of population transfer (Ezek 4:2), and required his vassals, including Manasseh, to swear allegiance to Ashur, chief god of Assyria (II Kgs 21:2-9).
Ashurbanipal (668-627)	Restored Manasseh to the throne of Judah. His attacks on the Persians to the east, allowed for Judah to exercise greater freedom. Ashurbanipal continued settling foreigners in Samaria (Ezek 4:10).
Sin-shar-ishkun (626-612)	Under his reign, Assyria fell to the Babylonians led by Nabopolassar (612 BC).
Asshur-uballit (612-609)	Last king of Assyria.

Bronze head from Nineveh, thought to be Sargon II, king of Assyria.

in the east. The contact with nations near and far stimulated the Assyrians to create a widespread culture and gave rise to new types of writings, languages, and civilizations.

Assur, the first capital of the Assyrian empire, was located on the western bank of the Tigris river, in the southern part of that country. In various periods, however, Assyrian kings moved their capital also to Calah, a city identified with present-day Nimrud, and to Nineveh, which was situated on the eastern bank of the Tigris in the northern part of the country. It is identified with present-day Kalat Sharkat, 50 miles (80 km) south of Mosul. With its destruction in 612 BC by a Babylonian-led coalition, the Neo-Assyrian empire came to its end.

Up to the middle of the 19th century, little was known of the Assyrians and their history. The first excavations took place in 1842 and uncovered remnants of the capital of Sargon II. That same year, the remains of the famous library of Asshurbanipal were discovered in Nineveh. Since then, archaeological digs have been undertaken in various parts of the area. See also II.9, Digging up the Bible: Nineveh.

In the Bible. Assyria is mentioned very early, in the second chapter of Genesis: "Now a river went out of Eden to water the garden, and from there it parted and became four riverheads... the name of the third river is the Tigris, it is the one which goes towards the east of Assyria. The fourth river is the Euphrates" (Gen 2:10).

According to the biblical account, Assyria was settled by Nimrod, Noah's great-grandson, "a mighty hunter before the Lord" (Gen 2:10,14): "He went to Assyria and built Nineveh, Rehoboth Ir, Calah, and Resen between Nineveh and Calah" (Gen 10:11).

In the 8th-7th centuries BC the kingdoms of Israel and of Judah clashed with the last great Assyrian empire, whose kings relentlessly pursued a policy of conquest to the south which was to lead them to the Mediterranean and to Egypt. At the beginning of his reign, Tiglath-pileser III (745-727 BC), like his predecessors, engaged in widespread campaigns in order to secure his borders with the Babylonians, and then went on to the west and achieved glorious conquests. He conquered the whole of Syria and the border of the Philistines and reached Gaza. To placate him, King Menahem of Israel consented to be his vassal and assembled an enormous tribute (738 BC): "So the kings of Assyria turned back, and did not stay there in the land" (II Kgs 15:20). Possibly in consequence of non-payment of taxes, Tiglath-pileser returned during the reign of Pekah the son of Remaliah, and in 733 he devastated Israel. In keeping with the Assyrian policy of carrying entire nations into captivity in far lands of the empire, Tiglath-pileser exiled many of the people of Israel (II Kgs 16:29) (732 BC). King Ahaz of Judah managed to seal an alliance with Tiglath-pileser and thus saved his kingdom (II Kgs 16:7).

During the reign of the son of Tiglath-pileser III, Shalmaneser V, which lasted only five years (727-722 BC), Hoshea the son of Elah allied himself with Egypt and did not send the annual tribute to Assyria. Shalmaneser led a new campaign against the kingdom of Israel and lay siege to Samaria (II Kgs 17:1-6), but died during the siege. The next Assyrian king, Sargon II, another son of Tiglath-pileser III, conquered Samaria. He captured 27,000 of the people of Israel and carried them to Assyria, then resettled Samaria with people from all over his vast empire (II Kgs 17:24).

Sargon was known for his brutal attitude towards his captives. The nations were in such awe of him that he sometimes achieved victories with no battles at all. With Israel disposed of, the kings of Assyria turned to Judah. Towards the end of the 8th century, Sennacherib (704-681 BC), son of Sargon, returned to the west in order to fight the alliance of Egypt and Judah led by Hezekiah king of Judah. Hezekiah fortified himself in Jerusalem but was unable to hold out, and in a vain bid to conciliate Sennacherib, he stripped the Temple of its treasure and gave him "all the silver that was found in the house of the Lord... stripped the gold from the doors, and from the doorposts" (II Kgs 18:15-16), and thus saved himself and Jerusalem. Sennacherib resumed his war with Babylonia, and Hezekiah took advantage of the hiatus to reorganize the alliance in the west. When Sennacherib returned to Judah, he sent delegates to King Hezekiah, demanding his surrender. According to biblical record, the Assyrians were defeated through the intervention of the

Tiglath-pileser II, king of Babylonia, and attendants, shown on a wall painting from his palace at Til Barsip, Syria.

angel of the Lord, and Sennacherib went back to his capital, Nineveh, where he was killed a few years later by his sons Adrammelech and Sharezer (II Kgs 19:36-37). Although the king's hasty retreat was probably due to the news of a rebellion in Assyria, and the circumstances of his death are obscure, this episode was to be the last time Assyria threatened Judah.

Even though the Assyrian kings after Sennacherib brought Assyria some great successes and expanded the empire, it was the beginning of the end. Once again Mesopotamia was thrown into turmoil: only a few years after the death of the greatest of the Assyrian kings, Asshurbanipal, Asshur, the capital, was destroyed (614 BC). Babylon was on the march and its armies, with their foreign allies, destroyed Nineveh in 612, and Haran in 610.

The Assyrian empire did not rise again. However, the destruction of Israel by the Assyrians and their devastation of Judah were to be mentioned repeatedly by the prophets who interpreted these attacks as a sign of the Lord's anger against his nation. Nevertheless, they continued to prophecy retribution: "And he will stretch his hand against the north, destroy Assyria and make Nineveh a desolation as dry as the wilderness" (Zeph 2:13). Assyria, the great empire, was divided among Egypt, Babylon, and the Medes.

Assyrian cavalryman depicted on a stone relief.

BABYLONIANS. The people of a country situated in the fertile alluvial region of southern Mesopotamia, "between the two rivers" created out of the Persian Gulf by the successive deltas of the Tigris and the Euphrates Rivers. The country came to be known as Babylonia due to its central city Babylon which was located on the eastern bank of the Euphrates. Originally, it was mentioned under several other names, the first of which was "the land of Shinar," which represents the name of Sumer. Another name commonly used in Scriptures is Chaldea, Abraham's place of origin, "Ur of the Chaldeans" (Gen 11:31). In Akkadian, the name Babylon is derived from *bab-ili* ("gate of god"); the etymology given in Genesis 11:9 derives it from the root *bll* ("to confuse"). According to biblical tradition, Babel is associated with Nimrod: "And the beginning of his kingdom was Babel, Erech, Accad and Calneh in the land of Shinar" (Gen 10:10). Indeed, Babylon began its history as a provincial capital in Mesopotamia and gained strength until it became, along with Assyria, one of the two mighty empires in Mesopotamia. The two, Assyria in the northwest and Babylon in the southwest, fought for control over Mesopotamia. Babylon, with access to the sea routes of the Persian Gulf and its better climate, had a distinct advantage over its rival.

Some scholars believe that the inhabitants of Babylon were of a pre-Sumerian origin; others think the Babylonians were a semi-nomadic people of Sumerian and Semitic origin who settled in the area over the centuries. The first mention of Babylon is in a cuneiform text dated c.2500 BC. Babylon exerted a great influence over most of southern Mesopotamia during the days of Hammurabi (1792-1749 BC), of the first Babylonian dynasty, who promulgated the famous collection of laws bearing his name. After the fall of the first Babylonian dynasty and the destruction of its capital, Babylon (c.1550 BC), a long period of Assyrian supremacy ensued during which Babylon was partially destroyed (1244-1208 BC). It regained its strength in the days of Tiglath-pileser III (745-727 BC) who gave it the status of an independent kingdom united to Assyria by a personal union. From then on the history of the two empires was intertwined: Assyrian kings ruled over Babylon, employing different names from those they used as rulers of Assyria. An independent kingdom of Babylon was proclaimed in the days of Merodach-Baladan but was overthrown by Sargon II (722-705 BC). In 689 the city of Babylon was destroyed by Sennacherib (704-681 BC), but was rebuilt by his son Esarhaddon (680-669 BC). Around the end of the latter's reign, the empire was divided between his two heirs: Ashurbanipal in Assyria and Shamash-shumukin in Babylon. The Assyrian kingdom was finally overthrown in 612 BC with the conquest of its capital Nineveh by a coalition of Babylon and the Medes. This led to the establishment of the Neo-Babylonian empire ruled over by Chaldean kings, chief of whom was Nebuchadnezzar II (605-562 BC). The fall of Babylon in 539 BC to the Persian king, Cyrus, marked the end of their empire.

In the Bible. There is no mention of Babylon in the Bible

KINGS OF BABYLONIA

Merodach-Baladan (721-710)	Chaldean king who revolted against Assyrian domination. He unsuccessfully sought the assistance of Hezekiah king of Judah, who rejected his overtures at the instigation of the prophet Isaiah (II Kgs 20:12-21). Merodach-Baladan was defeated by Sargon II of Assyria.
Nabopolassar (626-606)	Chaldean governor of the Persian Gulf region. He rebelled against Assyria and proclaimed Babylonia independent, capturing Nineveh in 612 BC. He was succeeded to the throne by his son, Nebuchadnezzar.
Nebuchadnezzar (606-563)	Waged war against Egypt, extending his control to the River of Egypt (II Kgs 24:7). Nebuchadnezzar waged war against the Egyptians in 601 BC. Jehoiakim of Judah supported Pharaoh Necho II despite the warnings of the prophet Jeremiah (II Kgs 24:1; Jer. 27:9-11). He laid seige to Jerusalem, plundering the Temple, and leading members of the aristocracy, including Daniel, into exile in Babylonia (Dan 1:1-2). He captured Jerusalem in 597 BC and established Zedekiah on the throne instead of Jehoiachin (II Kgs 24:10-17). Following Zedekiah's revolt against Babylonia, Jerusalem was captured, the Temple was destroyed, and the populace was exiled (586 BC) (II Kgs 25). Nebuchadnezzar appointed the ill-fated Gedaliah as governor of Jerusalem (II Kgs 25:22-26).
Evil-merodach (562-560)	Heir to Nebuchadnezzar, noted for his fair treatment of the exiled King Jehoiachin of Judah (II Kgs 25:27). He was assassinated by his brother-in-law, Nergal-sharezer.
Nergal-sharezer (560-556)	Son-in-law of Nebuchadnezzar (Jer 39:3) who fought against the Lydians.
Labasi-merodach (555)	Son of Nergal-Sharezer, deposed after nine months.
Nabonidus (556-539)	Seized throne from Labasi-Merodach. During a ten years sojourn in the South Arabian oasis of Tema, his son, Belshazzar, served as co-regent. During his reign, Babylonia fell to Darius, king of the Persians.

for a period of over a thousand years, from the days of Abraham up to the destruction of the Kingdom of Israel by the Assyrians, when the latter, in keeping with their policy, deported the inhabitants of the conquered Kingdom and settled in their stead people from Babylon, at the time a vassal of Assyria (II Kgs 17:24). Jerusalem and the Kingdom of Judah welcomed Babylon. The rise of the new powerful kingdom was at first greeted with relief since it meant the end of the pressure which had been exerted upon them by the rulers of Assyria over the previous decades. Indeed, according to the biblical record (which does not always coincide with the historical record), good relations between Babylon and Judah endured for a century, from the reign of King Hezekiah through the reigns of Kings Manasseh, Amon, Josiah, Jehoahaz, Jehoiakim, and Jehoiachin. Nebuchadnezzar, the second king of the neo-Babylonian Empire, captured Jerusalem, which had rebelled against Babylonian suzerainty, and made Judah a vassal. He appointed Zedekiah as its king (II Kgs 24:10, 12–13, 17–18). However, Zedekiah tried to rebel against Babylon, thus causing the return of the Babylonian armies to Jerusalem and the retaking of the city. This conquest followed a long, bitter siege, in the 19th year of the reign of Nebuchadnezzar: "Nebuzaradan the captain of the guard, a servant of the king of Babylon, came to Jerusalem; he burned the house of the Lord and the king's house; all the houses of Jerusalem, that is all the houses of the great men he burned with fire, and all the army of the Chaldeans who were with the captain of the guard broke down the walls of Jerusalem all around" (II Kgs 25:8–10). Thus ended the First Temple period. A section of the population of Judah was taken in captivity to Babylon in 586 BC and this was the beginning of the "Babylonian Exile." According to the Bible, this small community was settled along the canals of Babylon (Ps 137:1) and in places such as Chebar (Ezek 1:1), Tel Abib (Ezek 3:15), Tel-Melah, and Tel Harsha (Ezra 2:59; Neh 7:61). The feelings of this diaspora are reflected in Psalm 137.

Twenty-five years after the death of Nebuchadnezzar, whose victory over Jerusalem marked the end of the Kingdom of Judah, his country was conquered by the armies of Cyrus, king of Persia, who swept across Mesopotamia and ended the Babylonian empire. According to Isaiah 44:28, 45:1, the prophet identified Cyrus as the anointed of the Lord, who would execute the Lord's plans.

Reconstruction of the Gate of Ishtar, Babylon, belonging to the time of Nebuchadnezzar II.

Gold helmet, hammered out of one piece of metal, found in a tomb at Ur; 25th century BC.

CANAANITES. The peoples who inhabited the region of the eastern coast of the Mediterranean Sea, between Egypt in the south and Mesopotamia in the north. The Canaanites occupied Palestine west of the Jordan at the time of the Israelite invasion. Although they shared a common language, religion, and material culture, they never combined to form a political unity and were at all times fragmented into small political kingdoms, with changing frontiers as each sought to conquer land from the surrounding unit. In Genesis 9:18; 10:6, Canaan is said to be the son of Ham. The subsuming of Canaan under Hamites is most probably to be understood in geographic and political connections rather than in ethno-linguistic relations. The list of the sons of Canaan in Genesis 10:15ff, including Sidon, Heth, the Jebusite, the Amorite, the Girgasite, the Hivite, and the Hamathite, may reflect a certain geographical order of subdivisions of the Canaanites.

From early times, the Canaanites were a group of peoples speaking a northwestern Semitic language. Since Canaanite was spoken over a vast area, it was composed of many local varieties and dialects. Canaanite history spans the 3rd and 2nd millennia BC. Throughout, southern Canaan was strongly influenced by Egypt, while northern Canaan inclined more towards the influence of its northern neighbors, the Mesopotamian and Hittite Empires. The whole region of Canaan was eventually shaken around the end of the 2nd millennium by political changes, with the penetration of various Semitic tribes including the Edomites, Moabites, Ammonites, Philistines, and Israelites. The Philistine and Israelite settlement effectively marks the conclusion of the Canaanite period. Although Canaanite culture remained from that time on in certain of the northern coastal cities, such as Sidon and Tyre, the Israelite nation began to emerge and the Canaanites merged with the Israelites who became their political and cultural heirs.

The material culture of the Canaanites has come to light through a number of archaeological excavations, primarily in Ras Shamra and Byblos. The Canaanites tried to develop an independent culture, but this never became homogenous because of the fragmented nature of the Canaanite kingdoms which included various Semitic peoples, such as the Phoenicians and the Amorites, as well as peoples of other origins, such as the Horites. Texts dating from the early 14th century BC were found in Ras Shamra written on clay tablets with a script invented by the Canaanites on the basis of the Mesopotamian cuneiform system of writing. The Canaanites' greatest gift to the world is in the intellectual sphere: their invention of an alphabetic system of writing. This innovation occurred some time in the second half of the 2nd millennium BC. In southern

Glazed brick figure of a captive Canaanite noble. Egypt, 12th century BC.

Canaan, the alphabet was written in a script which, succeeded by its immediate descendants, Hebrew, Phoenician, and Aramaic, gave rise to all the alphabetic script used in the world today.

Society. The Canaanites, like all the ancient Near East, were organized according to a feudal or semifeudal society system in which the king was the head of the society and the owner of the largest properties. The royal lands were divided among his subordinates. The temples also possessed large properties. Knowledge of the Canaanites' material culture is largely confined to urban life. The settlements lacked orderly planning and the inhabitants lived in poorly constructed houses. The few larger and better-built houses were presumably palaces of local rulers. Three social groups existed: freemen, traders, and slaves; the last were, mainly, war captives and foreign slaves but also natives who sold themselves or their children into slavery to obtain their livelihood. Household goods consisted to a large extent of typical pottery food vessels which served for storage, preparation, cooking, and serving. Of the wooden furniture, the little that has survived indicates expertise in manufacture of low tables, stools, and beds from wood and reeds. The metal used by the Canaanites was initially copper, replaced later by bronze. Glass was considered a luxury material and came into use towards the end of the Canaanite period. Jewelry, usually of bronze, has been found. While the nomadic classes, both men and women, wore multicolored wool dresses, the upper classes, mainly the merchants, wore a sari-like white cloth, often with colored fringes.

Their towns and cities were surrounded by defensive systems of walls, built of stones or bricks, and massive earth ramparts around the settlements. The gates leading into the towns were well protected with towers and guard rooms. Weapons were initially forged of copper and later of bronze. Arrow heads, spear and javelin heads, daggers and swords of different shapes were most common. In the second half of the 2nd millennium the war chariot, drawn by a pair of horses, came into general use.

Most of the information concerning the Canaanite religion and mythology derives from the rich library discovered in the north Canaanite city of Ugarit (in Syria). This library also included legal and commercial material as well as heroic tales. The Canaanite pantheon consisted of numerous gods, loosely arranged in pairs. The heads of the pantheon, El and Asherah, the parents of the gods, were replaced by the young Baal, god of storm and weather, and his sister, Anath, who was also his wife. Canaanite religion was predominantly preoccupied with fertility, and its main myth centers around the kingship of Baal, who cast his protection over vegetation and fertility and defended them anew each year against drought and sterility.

The Canaanites buried their dead communally in caves outside their settlements, supplying them with

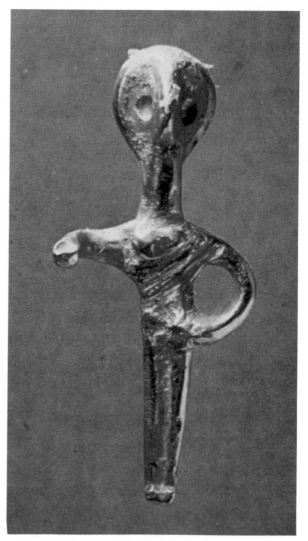

Gold-plated bronze Canaanite figurine from Hamath; late 13th century BC.

pottery vessels containing food and drink. No attempt was made to preserve the body. The bones were scattered about the cave or heaped around the walls. In the first half of the 2nd millennium BC it became common to bury babies and young children in jars under floors of houses. Individual burial of adults in pits outside settlements became general practice in the second half of the 2nd millennium BC.

The Canaanites were actively involved in international trading, specializing in the export of their well-known purple-dyed textiles. They also sold agricultural products such as cattle and oil. In prophetic and Wisdom literature, the word "Canaanite" is at times used to denote a merchant (Is 23:8; Prov 31:24; Job 40:30).

CHALDEANS. The name of a people situated in southern Mesopotamia. According to the Bible, the eponym of the Chaldeans was Chesed, the fourth son of Nahor, brother of Abraham (Gen 22:22).

In the Bible. The name "Chaldeans" may refer to a nation or a people (Job 1:17; Is 23:13), or a land (Is 23:13; Jer 24:5; 25:12; 50:1,45). It is employed in four ways: (1) as Ur of the Chaldeans, the city of Abraham in the south of Babylon (Gen 11:28, 31; 15:7), a combination that could have developed at the time when Chaldeans settled near Ur and established a population center of their own; (2) as the name of a nomadic marauders' tribe (Job 1:17) which, like other Aramean nomadic tribes, roamed along the Euphrates and the Tigris, between the Persian Gulf and the Arabian desert; (3) as synonymous with Babylon and the Babylonians (Ezek 1:3; 23:14-15, etc.) especially during the last Babylonian dynasty (625-539 BC); (4) as an epithet, in the Aramaic sections of Daniel, for magicians and astrologists (Dan 2:10, 4:4, 5:7,11).

Assyrian documents starting with the 9th century BC provide details concerning the Chaldeans. They are first mentioned in the annals of King Ashurnasirpal II of Assyria (895-883 BC). The Chaldean tribes were organized on patriarchal lines and lived in a loosely structured tribal society, loyal only to their clans. According to the annals of Shalmaneser III (859-825 BC), their leading tribes were organized in state-like structures. They were completely integrated in Mesopotamian culture and at the same time enriched it with their own distinctive elements. Their appearance and clothing caused the prophet Ezekiel to identify them with the Babylonians (Ezek 23:14-15). On bronze gates dating from the time of Shalmaneser III, they are dressed in Babylonian fashion.

According to Daniel 2:4, the spoken language of the Chaldeans was Aramaic, but scholars disagree over their original language (whether Aramaic or a dialect of Akkadian), since the Bible and extrabiblical sources distinguish them from the Arameans (II Kgs 24:2). They worshiped Bel and Nebo, deities known extensively from Babylonian literature.

Astronomy and astrology were highly respected in Chaldean culture. The astrologists occupied a central position in political life (Is 47). Chaldean language and letters, including the special language of astronomy and astrology, were taught in a school located in the palace of Nebuchadnezzar (Dan 1:3) and the king consulted his astrologists and astronomers (Dan 2:10-12).

The Chaldeans were a constant threat to the Babylonian city dwellers. Firmly opposing Assyrian efforts to subdue them, they developed their own political policy. The independent Chaldean state was subdued by Tiglath-pileser III who exiled many of the Chaldeans to Assyria. The reigns of Sargon and Sennacherib marked periods of Chaldean revolts. Merodach-Baladan II, the head of the Chaldean state, seized the throne in Babylon (721-710 BC). He found allies among other states and his messenger to King Hezekiah (II Kgs 20:12; Is 39:1) may have been trying to persuade the king to join the rebellion against Assyria. Sennacherib exiled the Chaldeans from the main Babylonian cities to Nineveh and to Israel (II Kgs 17:24). Some who fled across the Tigris established new Chaldean settlements near the mountains of Elam and the Persian Gulf. In the 7th century BC, the Chaldeans consolidated their position in the Babylonian cities and Nabopalassar became the king of Babylon (626-606). In his days and during the reign of his son Nebuchadnezzar (606-563 BC), Babylon was considered a Chal-

The standard of Ur. Mosaic panel depicting the victory of the king over his enemies; c.2500 BC.

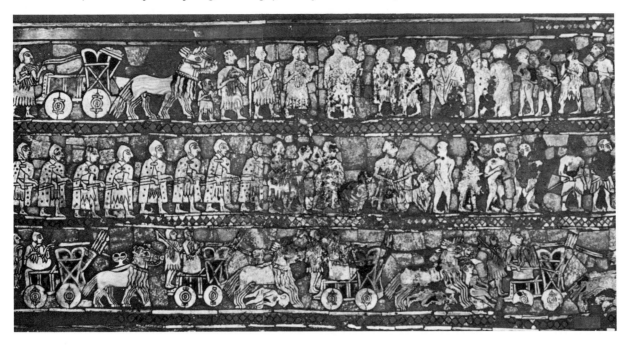

dean state. Judah was one of its vassal states, while Jerusalem was destroyed and the people of Judah were exiled by Nebuchadnezzar in 586 BC.

EDOMITES. A people of Semitic origin living in Edom, a country to the east of the Arabah. The land of Edom is bordered by Ammon to the north, the Dead Sea and the Arabah to the west, and the desert to the south and east. It is also called Seir. According to biblical tradition, the people of Edom are related to Esau, son of Isaac, who was identified with Edom (Gen 36:1). Information about the Edomites is derived largely from the writings of their neighbors and enemies, such as the Israelites, Egyptians, Assyrians and Babylonians. Archaeological investigations have shown that the area of Edom was inhabited from the 23rd to the 20th century BC, after which it was uninhabited until the 13th century BC. The Book of Genesis lists the Edomite kings "who reigned in the land of Edom, before any king reigned over the Israelites" (Gen 36:31) but the chronology is not clear. In an Egyptian list of Sethos I (c.1215 BC) the Edomites are mentioned together with Moab and the Negeb. They are also mentioned in the records of a punitive campaign organized by Rameses III (1198-1166 BC).

In the Bible Both the Book of Genesis and allusions in the prophetic books emphasize the close racial relationship between the Israelites and the Edomites. The strong hatred between Israel and Edom is attributed by the Bible to the sale of Esau's birthright to Jacob (Gen 25:29-34).

During the period of the Israelite conquest and the judges, there was no contact between the Israelites and the Edomites. Later, according to I Samuel 14:47, the Edomites were defeated by Saul. The first Israelite king to conquer Edom was David, who stationed garrisons all over the country and "won a name for himself" (II Sam 8:14; I Kgs 11:15-16). Solomon used the Edomite port in Ezion-geber (II Chr 8:17-18; I Kgs 10:26-28). Edom revolted in the days of Joram and the Edomites crowned a king of their own (II Kgs 8:20-22). About 100 years later Amaziah took Sela in Edom and renamed it Joktheel (II Kgs 14:7). King Amaziah of Judah completed the reconquest of Edom (II Kgs 14:22; II Chr 26:1-2) but in the days of Ahaz, Edom finally regained its independence (II Kgs 16:6).

Most of the Judean prophets are hostile towards the Edomites (Is 11:14; 34:5-17; Amos 1:6, 9,11; Obadiah; Malachi 1:2-4; Jer 49:7-22; Ezek 35).

While the Edomites practiced agriculture to some extent, their chief wealth came from their trade. The list of tribute which Edom paid to the Assyrian king Esarhaddon suggests that it was richer than other countries in the vicinity. It apparently owed its wealth to the copper and iron which was mined in the hills and could be exchanged for the products of Arabia, Egypt, Syria, and Babylonia. The fact that the Israelites could not use the roads passing through Edom on their way to Canaan (Num 20:17-21) shows that the country was strongly fortified at an early stage. The Edomites' religion seems to have been polytheistic and their language is cognate to Hebrew.

In the 6th century BC Edom was conquered by the Babylonians. Later, the Edomites were pressed westward into Judah by new nomadic tribes who penetrated the country and by the first half of the 2nd century BC established their kingdom on the former land of Edom. Pushed back by the Nabateans, the Edomites occupied southern Judea which became known, after them, as Idumea. They were conquered by John Hyrcanus (135-105 BC) who forcibly converted them to Judaism; henceforth, they were part of the Jewish people. One of the best-known Idumean generals was Antipater, grandfather of Herod.

EGYPTIANS. The people of a land in northwest Africa, situated along the southeastern shores of the Mediterranean, bordered by the Red Sea on the east and Libya on the west. The territory falls naturally into two parts: Lower Egypt, which included the Nile Delta, and Upper Egypt, from Cairo southwards. The Egyptians called their country the "Two Lands" or the "Black Land" in contrast to the "red" desert. The economy of the country depended on the Nile which was the sole source of water for drinking and irrigation. In the rainless northeastern desert, only the flow of the Nile and its annual floods made it possible to live in that area. Ancient Egyptian civilization was therefore confined to the Nile Valley and its delta. The prosperity of Egypt depended upon inundation, giving it widespreading waters in August and September. The annual floods brought much silt, replenishing the fertility of the soil. The water was distributed over the fields by an intricate system of dams and channels. Irrigating waters, fertilizing silt, and a warm climate, made Egypt one of the richest agricultural countries in the world. The main crops were barley and spelt, from which the staple food and drink (bread and beer) were made, as well as beans, lentils, cucumbers, and onions. Among the fruits grown were grapes and figs. Pigs, lambs, and cows were slaughtered for meat. Fowl, wild and domesticated, fish, geese, and ducks completed the diet. Livestock were important in the Egyptian economy. The most common beast of burden was the ass, the camel being unknown until late; horses were introduced c.1700 BC and were used only to draw war chariots. Flax made the linen of Egypt prized in the ancient world. Writing material was of papyrus of which Egypt had the monopoly, and it served them as a valued export.

Egyptian hills offered a variety of building stones, from hard granite to soft alabaster, and gigantic monuments were built of stone. Egypt was rich in mineral deposits: copper and turquoise were mined in the Red

Left: Statues of Rameses II, Egyptian pharaoh, in his temple at Abu Simbel. Right: An Egyptian scribe. Detail from an Egyptian wall painting; 19th century BC.

Sea hills and in west Sinai, and gold was found in the Red Sea hills and in the east and southeast of the country, though both copper and gold had also to be imported from abroad. The Egyptians had to import timber and tin for the production of bronze and iron tools, but in most basic commodities Egypt was self-sufficient. Luxury items were imported; gums, rare skins, ivory and incenses from Africa, and lapis lazuli, metalwork, and obsidian from Asia.

The valley of the Nile forms one of the most ancient cradles of civilization. It was populated from the Lower Paleolithic period. The Egyptians belonged to the Mediterranean race; they were physically like the Hamites and the South Semites. Ancient Egyptian was a member of the Hamitic family of languages.

In the time of the 1st Dynasty (c.3000 BC), Upper and Lower Egypt were unified by the semi-legendary King Menes, to whom the foundation of Memphis is attributed. Ancient Egypt was one of the earliest and most powerful nations throughout the biblical period, and was one of the great empires of the Middle East, whose only rival was in Mesopotamia (Sumeria, Assyria, Babylonia). Very early in its history, Egypt took an interest in Asia, and Egyptian rulers established rela-

tions with Byblos, which supplied Egypt with timber from Lebanon. Archaeological finds, such as jewelry and artifacts of Egyptian origin unearthed in Ai and Lachish, prove the presence of Egypt in Palestine. Peaceful expeditions were dispatched during the 3rd Dynasty (c.2686-2613 BC) to the mines of Sinai as well as military expeditions to Asia. At the end of the Old Kingdom (c.2100 BC) the frontiers of Egypt were threatened by nomads. Shortlived victories were gained against Asia and Canaan but they also marked the end of the Old Kingdom. Egypt entered a period of anarchy in which foreign enemies invaded the Delta. The country was ruled by a large number of local princes and disorder reigned for about a century.

Order was restored in Egypt by the rulers of the 11th Dynasty (c.2133-1991 BC) who unified the country. Egypt reached one of its peaks during the reign of the 12th Dynasty (c.1991-1786 BC) under Ammenemes I who, in order to pacify the turbulent population of the desert and Canaan, built a chain of fortresses blocking the road from Asia to Egypt, and under Sesostris III (1878-1843 BC), who led armies against the cities of Palestine, culminating in the conquest of Shechem in Mt. Ephraim. The wealth of Egypt attracted strangers such as the Semites. A series of infiltrations weakened the Middle Kingdom, and its prosperous period was put to an end by the Hyksos invasions (c.1674 BC). The Hyksos, who came from Asia, established themselves in the Delta, making Avaris their capital. This intermediate period lasted for about 550 years. The Hyksos were defeated by Ahmose, the founder of the 18th Dynasty (c.1567–1320 BC), in two battles (c.1570 BC). Under the reign of various rulers of the 18th Dynasty, Egypt attained a new prosperity and its borders expanded as far as Syria and Mesopotamia. A victory in Megiddo in the year 1468 BC assured Egyptian supremacy of the region and turned Palestine into a vassal state, leaving the local rulers autonomy in ruling their city states under close Egyptian supervision.

The Canaanite princes revolted against Egypt one after another and it was not until the beginning of the 19th Dynasty that the land of Canaan was reconquered under the leadership of Horemheb, an Egyptian general who usurped the throne and founded the 19th Dynasty (c.1320–1200 BC). For a short time an equilibrium reigned between Egypt and the newly rising Hittite empire. Sethos I and Rameses II fought the Hittites but without bringing about any substantial change. A long period of tranquility, made possible by a treaty with the Hittites, enabled Rameses II to undertake the immense construction works at Karnak and Luxor and to found his new capital, which bore his name (Rameses). The end of the rule of Rameses III (1198–1166 BC) of the 19th Dynasty, the last of the great Pharaohs of Egypt, marks the beginning of the decline of Egypt.

Under Rameses XI the 20th Dynasty (c.1200–1085 BC) collapsed and the north of Egypt was dominated by the priests. With the rise of the 22nd Dynasty (c.935–730 BC), Egypt came under the rule of Pharaohs of Libyan descent. The first ruler, Sheshonk I (c.935–914 BC), biblical Shishak, attacked Palestine and destroyed some of its cities. Not much is known of the histories of the 23rd (established c.820 BC) and 24th (c.730–715 BC) Dynasties. During the reign of Teharqa (c.689–664 BC) Egypt assisted Palestine and Syria against Assyria; the latter attacked Egypt in 671 and 667 BC, and in 663 BC, under Ashurbanipal, penetrated beyond Memphis and destroyed Thebes. Egypt revolted and gained independence for a short time. Cambyses defeated Egypt in the battle of Pelusium (525 BC). Persian rulers are listed as the kings of the 27th Dynasty (525–404 BC). Kings of the 30th Dynasty attempted to free Egypt from Persian rule. In 332 BC it was conquered by Alexander the Great.

In the Bible. Egypt plays a central part in biblical history and throughout the biblical period the relationship between Egypt and Israel remained unique and contradictory. Though Egypt was often hospitable to the Israelites, offering refuge and sanctuary in time of need, food during famine (Gen 12:19; 42:2), and a haven in periods of crisis, Egypt was also the country which held the children of Israel in bondage until their escape through the Red (Reed) Sea. The Bible is full of details and information concerning the life of the Egyptians. Several Egyptian words and customs found their way into the Bible: the name Moses, for example, is derived from the Egyptian verb "to be born"; Joseph is given the Egyptian name "Zaphnath-Paaneah" (Gen 41:45), and after his death, like his father, was embalmed according to Egyptian custom (Gen 50:2, 26).

It was Abraham who began the tradition of searching for food in Egypt during periods of famine. When he returned to Canaan, after his sojourn in Egypt, he was very rich (Gen 12). The tradition was continued by Jacob's sons who went there following his advice: "I have heard that there is grain in Egypt; go down to that place and buy for us there, that we may live and not die" (Gen 42:2). Later he joined his sons in Egypt and settled there with his whole family under the protection of Joseph who had been kindly received by Pharaoh after his brothers sold him into slavery. Pharaoh "set him over all the land of Egypt" (Gen 41:43) and gave him the daughter of a high priest for wife. Joseph's death marked the end of the prosperity and expansion of the Children of Israel in Egypt. A new Pharaoh, "who had not known Joseph," said to his people: "Look, the Israelite people are much too numerous for us. Let us, then, deal shrewdly with them, lest they increase and, in the event of war, join our enemies in fighting against us..." (Ex 1:9–10). The subsequent period, up to the escape from Egypt, is of crucial importance in the history of Israel. It marks long years of bondage and suffering, the emergence of Moses as a leader, the ten plagues, the hurried meal of lamb and unleavened bread which was to form the basis of the Passover ceremony (Ex 12:3–20), and the exodus from Egypt by way of the Red (Reed) Sea (Ex 14). The dramatic escape and the defeat of the Egyptians during the Exodus did not lead to lasting enmity between the Hebrews and the Egyptians. Indeed, when Moses set up the statutes which were to rule the Israelites, they were commanded "not to abhor an Egyptian, for you were a stranger in his land" (Deut 23:8). Later, during the Israelite monarchy, relations between Egypt and Israel fluctuated. For long periods they were friendly: King Solomon married a daughter of Pharaoh who brought the town of Gezer as her dowry (I Kgs 9:16); Jeroboam, King Solomon's arch-rival, found refuge in Egypt (I Kgs 11:40). Later, the first ruler of the 22nd Dynasty, Sheshonk I (935–914 BC), biblical Shishak, attacked Palestine in the fifth year of the reign of Rehoboam and destroyed numerous cities in the southern kingdom (I Kgs 14:25; II Chr 12).

After the fall of the kingdom of Israel, Judah was increasingly drawn into the power struggle between Egypt and the Assyrian-Babylonian empires. King Hezekiah joined the Egyptians against the Assyrian king Sennacherib despite the warning of Sennacher-

HISTORY OF EGYPT

PERIOD	DYNASTIES	DATE	NOTABLE PHARAOHS	BIBLICAL
Early Dynastic	1-2	3100-2800 BC		
Old Kingdom	3-6	2800-2250 BC		
First Intermediate	7-9	2250-2000 BC		Abraham goes to Egypt
Middle Kingdom	9-12	2000-1786 BC		Joseph and Jacob go to Egypt
Second Intermediate	13-17	1786-1575 BC	Hyksos	
New Kingdom	18-20	1575-1085 BC	Thutmose I	Persecution of Israelites begins
			Thutmose III	Moses raised in royal court
			Amenhotep II or Rameses II	Exodus
Third Intermediate	21-25	1085-663 BC		Solomon marries Pharaoh's daughter; Shishak invades Judah and plunders the Temple
Late	26-31	663-332 BC	Necho	Paraoh defeated by Babylonians; Jewish refugees flee to Egypt in face of Babylonian onslaught
Ptolemaic		332-30 BC		

Groups of people taking goods to Egypt. From a tomb wall painting; 19th century BC.

ib's general, Rabshakeh of Lachish: "You are trusting in the staff of this broken reed, Egypt..." (Is 36:6). King Josiah was defeated and killed in 609 BC at Megiddo when Egypt, under the reign of Pharaoh Necho II (610–595) of the 24th Dynasty, fought the Babylonians. Necho II attempted to restore Egyptian rule over Palestine and Syria, but was defeated in 605 BC by Nebuchadnezzar at Carchemish. Josiah's successor, Jehoahaz, was deported by the Egyptians who enthroned Jehoiakim in his place (II Kgs 23:34). In 589 BC when Nebuchadnezzar besieged Jerusalem, Zedekiah, king of Judah, allied himself with Pharaoh Apries (Hopra) who invaded Syria in an attempt to relieve Jerusalem, but the Egyptian support proved ineffectual once again. Egypt was conquered by the Persians under Cambyses in 525 BC, and became a vassal of the Persians.

HITTITES. An ancient people who lived in central Anatolia. The official language of their empire was cuneiform Hittite, an Indo-European language in which the historical annals, proclamations, laws, and treaties were written, from about 1600–1200 BC. Their second most important language was hieroglyphic Hittite, also an Indo-European language, which was spoken in the empire from about 1600 to 700 BC. The information concerning the Hittite language derives from the Cappadocian tablets which were discovered in Boghazkoy, Asia Minor. These tablets comprise legal and commercial letters, written by Assyrian merchants who established commercial colonies in Asia Minor in about the 19th century BC. Hittite literature attributes the foundation of their kingdom to Mursilis I. Labarnas, his heir, conquered Babylon (16th century BC). Shuppiluliumas the Great, who reigned in 1380–1350 BC, founded the Hittite Empire. He established Hittite rule over Asia Minor and waged war against northern Syrian city-states. He made his sons kings at Carchemish and Aleppo. When Rameses II was ruling Egypt, the Hittites signed a treaty of "eternal friendship" with Egypt which was engraved on the walls of Egyptian palaces and written on tablets. The Hittite empire fell apart under the invasion of waves of people from across the Aegean, "the Sea Peoples." The Hittite cities were ruined and for some time, the history of Anatolia is covered by darkness. The subsequent Late Hittite period was one of decline. The whole area once occupied by the Hittites was now divided into small kingdoms and principalities, but no great state emerged comparable in size and power with the Hittite Empire. The conquest of Carchemish by the Assyrian King Sargon II in 717 BC marks the end of the independence of the last Hittite states.

The term Hittite refers to three different groups: (1) The "Hattians," a non-Indo-European people who lived in central Anatolia; (2) a people who lived around Hattusas (modern Boghazkoy) who used an Indo-

Hittite relief from Gozan showing a warrior aiming a slingshot; 10th–9th century BC.

European language preserved in cuneiform writings; (3) a people who lived in the south of the empire and used a hieroglyphic language. However, in the Bible, the term refers to all the inhabitants of the Hittite empire. Several individual names and several stories in the Bible make it clear that Hittites living in Palestine were a group of people fully assimilated to the surrounding Semitic population.

In the Bible. According to biblical tradition, the Hittites were the offspring of Heth, Canaan's second son (Gen 10:15; I Chr 1:13; cf. Gen 23:3). They are listed among the peoples who dwelt in Canaan before the Israelite conquest (Gen 15:20; 26:34; Ex 3:8; Deut 7:1; Josh 3:10, 9:1; Judg 3:5; I Kgs 9:20; II Chr 8:7; Ezra 9:1; Neh 9:8). Ephron the Hittite sold a burial ground, Machpelah, situated near Hebron, to Abraham (Gen 23). Esau, while staying in Beersheba, married Judith, the daughter of Beeri the Hittite, and Basmath, the daughter of Elon the Hittite (Gen 26:34). Rebekah and Isaac discouraged Jacob from marrying a Hittite woman (Gen 27:46).

The Hittites lived in the mountains (Num 13:29; Josh 11:3) and joined King Jabin of Hazor in his battle against Joshua (Josh 11:1–12). God ordered the destruction of the Hittites together with the other Canaanite nations (Deut 20:17). After the conquest of Canaan, the Israelites dwelt among the local peoples, including the Hittites, and close relations were established. Some of the Israelites intermarried with them and other members of foreign nations (Judg 3:5-6). Bathsheba, the wife of Uriah the Hittite, one of David's 30 warriors, was taken by David to be his wife (II Sam 11:3ff.; 12:9-10; 23:39; I Kgs 15:5). When David was still in the wilderness, Ahimelech the Hittite was one of his soldiers (I Sam 26:6). King Solomon's numerous alien loves included Hittite women (I Kgs 11:1). The Bible mentions Hittite kings as Solomon's contemporaries (I Kgs 10:29; II Chr 1:17). When the king of Israel waged war against the Arameans, Hittites were his allies (II Kgs 7:6).

The Hittite pantheon consisted of numerous gods and goddesses, headed by the god of thunder and the sun goddess; their children and grandchildren were stormgods. There were also gods of mountains, rivers, springs, heaven and earth, clouds and winds. The stormgod assumed the form of a bull and later still was given a human likeness. Other gods were symbolized by lions, stags, and horses.

The Hittite kingdom was a divine establishment, the king and queen ministering side by side at religious ceremonies. Hittite ritual included solemn feasts and the sacrifice of animals. Divination was common and well organized with questions submitted to an oracle whose answers were recorded on tablets. Hittite literature included myths and epics, Sumerian-Akkadian-Hittite dictionaries; prescriptions for divination by hour of birth and by examination of the liver, kidney, facial features, and the constellation of the stars. Some materials such as lists of temples, incantations, medical texts, hymns, prayers, and renderings of the Gilgamesh Epic were translated from Mesopotamian literature. The Hittite legal code was composed of 200 laws, dealing with assault and violence, slavery, marriage, theft, adultery, etc. Capital punishment was confined to special offenses such as sorcery and defiance of the king.

HIVITES. One of the seven peoples who inhabited the land of Canaan at the time of the conquest by the Israelites. The Hivites are first mentioned in the Bible as the son of Canaan (Gen 10:17) but although they are listed among the Canaanites, they are not always identified with them. In some biblical writings and in the Septuagint it appears that the Hivites are distinct from the Canaanites: "the cities of the Hivites and Canaanites" (II Sam 24:7). The Hivites do not appear in any ancient Near Eastern records besides the Bible. Some scholars identify the Hivites with the Hurrians, one of the most important peoples in the ancient Near East: Zibeon the Hivite (Gen 36:2) is also called "son of Seir the Horite" (Gen 36:20). Most Septuagint manuscripts read Hurites instead of Hivites in Genesis 34:2.

According to the story of Dinah, the daughter of Jacob (Gen 34:2), the leading family in the town of Shechem in those days was Hivite, and the people of Gibeon are referred to as Hivites. However, in other contexts, the people of Shechem and the Gibeonites are called Amorites (Gen 48:22; II Sam 21:2). The Hivites are specifically associated with the towns of Shechem, Gibeon, Chephirah, Beeroth, and Kiriath Jearim (Josh 9:17) in the land of Israel, and with Mount Lebanon (Judg 3:3) and the region called Mizpah at the foot of Mount Hermon (Josh 11:3, in which the Septuagint reads Hittite rather than Hivite). Since the ethnic identity of the Hivite is unclear, it remains questionable whether the name is of a Semitic or non-Semitic origin.

HORITES. A non-Semitic people who, according to the Bible, were the early inhabitants of Seir, the land later occupied by the Edomites, and who were defeated by Chedorlaomer (Gen 14:6; Deut 2:12,22). In extrabiblical sources, they are first mentioned in an Akkadian document of the 24th century BC, when they already had a kingdom beyond the Tigris from where they began a slow penetration along the valleys of the Mesopotamian rivers southward. Along the way they encountered some Semitic elements and subsequently the two groups constituted the bulk of the population in Syria and Palestine.

Towards the 14th-13th centuries BC, they were among the ruling classes in that area. Some scholars believe that their arrival in Palestine coincided with the Hyksos arrival and conquest of Egypt in the 18th century BC. Others date it later. The Horites and the Hyksos introduced the horse and chariot into warfare. It was the Horite people together with other elements, such as the nomadic Habiru, whom the Israelites and Philistines had to face when they arrived in the land of Canaan in the 13th century BC. According to the Book of Genesis they remained in the area (Gen 36:20) until they were destroyed by the descendants of Esau (Deut 2:12, 22).

The Bible and the Septuagint sometimes interchange the names Hivites and Horites (Gen 36:2,20; and compare Septuagint "Horites" for Hebrew "Hivites" in Gen 34:2).

HYKSOS. A dynasty of Asiatics who ruled Egypt from c.1674 to 1570 BC and most of the Syro-Palestinian area in c.1800-1550 BC. It is clear from archaeological evidence that they were not an ethnic unity and did not have a specific culture of their own. Philologists have identified Semitic, Hurrian, and Indo-European elements, mainly in the names of the Hyksos. The word "Hyksos" is a rendering of two Egyptian words meaning "rulers of foreign lands," and was applied to Asiatic princes by Pharaohs of the Middle Kingdom. The beginnings of their control over Egypt are not clear, but it appears that their infiltration into the Nile Valley from the northeast over a period of several centuries took place during the chaotic period of anarchy and political dissolution which followed the reign of the 12th Dynasty (c. 1991-1792 BC) and ended the Egyptian Middle Kingdom. They established the first Hyksos dynasty (the 15th, according to Egyptian accounts) and their capital at Avaris in the eastern part of the Delta c.1674 BC.

The last Egyptian ruler of the 17th Dynasty, Kamose, succeeded in driving the Hyksos from Middle Egypt. Pharaoh Ahmose, the first ruler of the 18th Dynasty (c.1567-1320 BC) accomplished their expulsion from Egypt, destroyed their capital at Avaris, and pursued them to southern Palestine. He besieged them at Sharuhen (Tel el-Far'ah) for three years and then defeated them.

Archaeological finds of Hyksos sites are characterized by elements of military warfare. Their centers were constructed with a unique system of large fortifications of beaten earth with sloping revetments surrounded by a moat. The use of horse and chariot is associated with the Hyksos invasion of Egypt. Not having a specific culture of their own, the Hyksos attempted to adopt various cultural and religious elements of their surroundings. They quickly assimilated Egyptian culture. Their chief god was the Egyptian god Seth, but they also worshiped deities of the Canaanite-Horite pantheon, such as Ashtoreth and Anath. In *Contra Apionem*, the 1st-century Jewish historian Josephus quotes the priest-historian Manetho (c.280 BC), as the first to apply the term Hyksos, which he translated as "shepherd kings," to the Asiatic invaders. Josephus identified the Hyksos with the patriarchal Jews and connected their appearance in Egypt with the story of Joseph in the Book of Genesis. As a result, some scholars mistakenly thought that the Exodus from Egypt took place during the Egyptian 18th Dynasty, but this assumption is not supported by biblical or extrabiblical sources. The Hyksos are not mentioned at all in the Bible. Some characteristics of their rule have been found in Palestine, mainly in the fortification systems, in Megiddo, Jericho, and Hazor.

MEDES. A people of Indo-Iranian origin (similar to the Persians) who inhabited the mountainous area of Iran, between the Elburz Mountain range, the Salt Desert, Persia, and the eastern region of Mesopotamia called Media, known in Akkadian as Madai. Their capital was Ecbatana. Information concerning the history of the Medes is contained in Assyrian, Babylonian, Persian, and Greek sources. They are first mentioned in Assyrian inscriptions of the 9th century BC, reporting the invasion of the Assyrian king Shalmaneser III (858-824 BC) into the land of the Medes. At that time the Medes began to settle in towns administered by local rulers without any central authority. The Assyrians fought the Medes but failed to subdue them. Tiglath-pileser III (745-727 BC) subdued the Medes

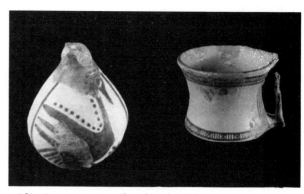

Midianite pottery vases found in the 13th-century BC temple at Tell Batashi (Timna).

and deported 65,000 of them. During the reign of Sargon II (721-705 BC), the Medes revolted against Assyria. According to a tradition reported by the Greek historian Herodotus, Deioces founded the Median kingdom, succeeded in uniting the seven Median tribes, and ruled for 53 years (699-646 BC). Herodotus further states that the kingdom was consolidated under Phraortas (646-624 BC), who headed a league that endangered the Assyrian hold over the Zagros mountains, and was killed when advancing on Nineveh. During the reign of his successor, Cyaxeres (625-585 BC), a serious threat to the Medes was posed by the Scythians. Eventually the Medes repulsed them and allied themselves with Nabopolassar, king of Babylonia, in the campaigns (620-605 BC) which led to the downfall of the Assyrian power. In 553 BC, the last king of the Medes, Astyages, was defeated by Cyrus the Great and the kingdom became part of the Persian empire.

In the Table of Nations in Genesis 10:2, and in I Chronicles 1:5, Madai is listed as the third son of Japheth. Later in the Bible, Media and the Medes are often mentioned together with Persia (Est 10:2; Dan 5:28; 8:20, etc.). The Bible depicts Media as the enemy of Babylon (Is 21:1-10) and the possibility of a Median attack upon Babylon is envisaged in Isaiah 13:17-18 and Jeremiah 51:11,28.

MIDIANITES. People of the land of Midian, which was situated in the northwestern part of the Arabian peninsula, east of the Gulf of Elath. According to biblical and later sources, Midian was bordered by Edom to the north and Arabian kingdoms to the south (the name Midian is not mentioned in extrabiblical sources). At various epochs, the Midianites occupied the Negeb, the Arabah in the area of Moab (Gen 36:35), and Sinai. It was in Sinai that Moses met Jethro, the priest of Midian, whose daughter, Zipporah, he married (Ex 2:15-3:1). Jethro himself gave Moses advice concerning Israel's juridical system (Ex 18:17-23). In some biblical sources the names Cush or Cushan (Hab 3:7) replace the name Midian. Like the Ishmaelites, the Midianites engaged in international trade (Gen 37:28) and trafficked in slaves. In some passages the Midianites are mentioned as camel riders (Judg 6:5; Is 60:6). This afforded an advantage in their activities as warriors and traders, and indeed they were the chief agents in the trade in gold and incense from Arabia (Is 60:6). According to another tradition they served as guides in the desert (Num 10:31). In the time of the Judges they marauded the settled areas (Judg 6:1-70), where they were soundly defeated by the Israelites under Gideon (Judg 6-8).

The history of the Midianites is not clear. Their relations with the Israelite tribes who came out of Egypt were usually friendly but, according to Numbers 22:4-7, some Midianite families joined the Moabites against Israel. The Midianite leaders are referred to as kings (Num 31:8; Judg 8:5) or princes (Josh 13:21; Judg 7:25). In later periods the Midianites are still mentioned as nomadic herdsmen (Judith 2:26).

MOABITES. According to biblical tradition, the Moabites were descended from Moab, who was born of the incestuous union of Lot with his elder daughter (Gen 19:30-37). Their country lay to the east of the Dead Sea, between Edom and Ammon. The early inhabitants of the area were the Rephaim, Zuzim, and Emim (Gen 14:5; Deut 2:10). During their wanderings, the Israelites passed close to the borders of Moab, but were not allowed to pass through the land (Num 22:2ff.). The

The first appearance of the name Moab inscribed in front of the temple of Luxor, Egypt; 13th century BC.

A Persian soldier from the royal guard. Carving on the wall beside a staircase of one of the royal buildings in Persepolis; 5th-6th century BC.

Reubenites and the Gadites conquered parts of the country of the Amorites that had formerly belonged to Moab (Num 21:25-31; Josh 13:15-21).

In the time of the Judges and the early monarchy, there was a constant state of war between Moab and Israel, and the judge, Ehud, saved the people of Israel from Eglon, king of Moab (Judg 3:12ff.). Saul fought Moab (I Sam 14:47) and David completed its conquest (II Sam 8:2), but there were intermediate periods during which the relations between the Moabites and the Israelites were friendly (II Sam 22:3ff.; I Kgs 11:1, 7). The Book of Ruth describes times in which the economic and social relations were good and families even intermingled. According to tradition, David was descended from the Moabite, Ruth (Ruth 4:17-22), a convert to the Israelite people and religion. The chief god of the Moabites was Chemosh, to whom Solomon built a hill-shrine on the height to the east of Jerusalem for his Moabite women (I Kgs 11:1,7). After the division of the kingdom of Israel, Moab regained its independence (I Kgs 1:1), but Omri, king of Israel, conquered the country and settled Israelites there. The Moabites regained their freedom 40 years later, after Ahab's death (I Kgs 3:4ff.). This is confirmed by the stele of the king of Moab, Mesha (the Moabite Stone, erected in his capital city Dibon and discovered in 1868, now in the Louvre), which sheds light on Moab's history and religion. Sargon II speaks in his annals of the conquest of Moab, and of the Moabite soldiers who helped the Assyrians in their wars against the Arabs. After Judah's defeat by Babylonia, Moab apparently joined in the plunder and seized some of its territory. During the Babylonian and Persian periods, Moab was incorporated in these kingdoms. In about the 4th or 3rd century BC the Nabateans penetrated Moab after gaining control of Edom. The prophets denigrated the Moabites and oracles against them were uttered by Isaiah (chaps. 15-16); Jeremiah (48), and Amos (2:1).

PERSIANS. The people of the country situated in Western Asia, between the Caspian Sea and west Turkistan in the north, the Persian Gulf and the Gulf of Oman in the south, the lower and middle Indus Basin in the southeast and Mesopotamia in the southwest. In about the middle of the 2nd millennium BC the Indo-Iranian peoples migrated, apparently from Southern Russia, to Iran (Persia) and India. By the 10th century BC numerous Iranian tribes had settled on the plateau. They seem to have wandered in different parts of the plateau until finally settling in the region of Pars before the 6th century BC. The Achaemenian period in Persia began with the establishment of the empire in 550 BC, following the revolt against the Medes under the leadership of Cyrus II, who defeated their king, Astyages, and conquered his country. In 547 BC Cyrus attacked the powerful kingdom of Lydia and conquered its capital, Sardis. His crowning success was the capture of Babylon in 539 BC (Is 44:28; 45:1), thus making Persia a universal empire, replacing the former empires of Assyria and Babylonia. When he died in 529 BC, his son and heir Cambyses continued his work. He annexed Egypt to the Persian empire in 525 BC and conquered the Greek islands of Cyprus and Samos. Cambyses enthroned himself as a pharaoh, and as the legal heir of the Egyptian rulers. He died in 522 BC and was succeeded by Darius I, a distant relation who founded a new dynasty. Under his leadership, Persia reached its zenith. He organized the administration of the huge empire, dividing it into satrapies and expanding it to the east, and built the palaces in Susa, the ancient Elamite city, and in his own capital at Persepolis. He fought the Scythians in Southern Russia and on his way back conquered the Greek coastal cities of Asia Minor. He was defeated at the battle of Marathon in 490 BC, and the Persian expansion finally came to an end with his failure to conquer Greece. Darius I died in 486 BC and was succeeded by his eldest son Xerxes, who in

King Darius of Persia seated on his throne. Behind him, Crown Prince Xerxes. Detail from a relief on one of the royal buildings at Persepolis.

480 BC defeated the Greeks at Thermopylae but in the following year was overcome in a maritime battle at Salamis, where the Persian fleet was destroyed. He was murdered in 465 BC. His successor, Artaxerxes I (464-423 BC), faced uprisings in a few satrapies, and a revolt which was supported by the Athenians in Egypt (459-454 BC). Under the next ruler, Artaxerxes III Ochus (359/8-338/7 BC), Persia subdued some of the rebellious satraps, conquered Phoenicia and renewed Persian rule over Lower Egypt. He was murdered, and his successor, Darius III (336/3-330 BC), from another branch of his family, lost the empire to Alexander the Great in the battle at Issus (333 BC).

Cyrus and his heirs used Aramaic along with Persian as the language of administration throughout the Persian Empire. The Persian script, borrowed from the Babylonians, was cuneiform.

In the Bible. Persians and Persia are frequently mentioned in the later books of the Old Testament. Persia first appears in Ezekiel, who refers to Persian mercenaries in the Tyrian army (Ezek 27:10), and links Persia to his prophecy on Gog, king of Magog (Ezek 38:5).

Some information concerning the practices of the Persian court can be derived from Daniel 6:9, Ezra 7:14, and Esther 1:13. The Persian Empire was divided into administrative units, satrapies, headed by satraps. Judah belonged to the satrapy Abar-Nahara, "Beyond the River" (Ezra 5:3). Each satrapy had to raise tribute to the king, to pay various taxes, sometimes heavy ones (Ezra 4:13; 7:24; Neh 5:4), and to maintain the troops, the administration, and the viceroy (Neh 5:17).

The Bible's favorable view of Persia stems from the fact that Cyrus permitted the deportees from Judah to return home and rebuild the Temple (II Chr 36:23) to "the God who is in Jerusalem" (Ezra 1:3). Cyrus' policy was continued by his heirs (Ezra 9:9). Darius I ratified the permission to rebuild the Temple, whose construction was completed in the sixth year of his reign. A positive attitude towards Persian religious tolerance finds expression in Ezra 6:14. The Book of Esther is set in Shushan, i.e., Susa, during the reign of Ahasuerus, who is identified with Xerxes.

PHILISTINES. A people of Aegean origin, who joined other "Sea Peoples" displaced from their original homelands. They appeared at the end of the Late Bronze Age in the southeastern sector of the Mediterranean. These "Sea Peoples" are listed among those who collaborated with the Libyans in their revolt against Egypt during the reign of Pharaoh Merneptah (1236–1223 BC). The Philistines are specifically mentioned during the reign of Rameses III (1198–1166 BC), and are vividly depicted in reliefs in his temple at Medinet Habu in Thebes. They appear as tall men, shaven, and wearing feathered headdresses fastened by chinstraps. The Bible (Gen 10:14) mentions the Philis-

Philistine pitcher with geometrical designs and reprsentations of birds, the characteristic motifs of Philistine pottery.

Glazed brick figure of a captive, probably a Philistine, dressed in the style customary in Syria and Palestine in that period; 12th century BC.

Philistine sarcophagus lid, shaped like a man, from Beth-Shean.

tines alongside the Caphtorim (Cretans). This has been interpreted to mean that the Philistines and the Cretans were kindred people (Ezek 25:16; Zeph 2:5). Moreover, Jeremiah (47:4) and Amos (9:7) both state that the Philistines originated in Caphtor (Crete).

In the Bible. According to the Bible, the Philistines were in the Negeb (southern Israel) at the time of the patriarchs, and their king, Abimelech, dwelt at Gerar (Gen 26:1), but this tradition was set down in writing when the Philistines had already settled in Canaan, in the 12th or 11th century BC. They figure very prominently in the Bible, especially in the territories of Dan and Judah, during the period of the Judges (Judg 13-16: the Samson saga), when there was an almost constant state of war between them and the expanding Israelite tribes. Open hostilities began at Ebenezer (I Sam 4) in the course of which they captured the ark of God and destroyed Shiloh (I Sam 5). They established garrisons in Judah and Benjamin (I Sam 10:5; 13:3) and took steps to prevent the use of iron weapons (I Sam 13:19). In the latter part of the 11th century BC, there was a change of fortune, and the Philistines were defeated and driven out of Israelite territory (I Sam 13:4; 14-20ff.) Another clash between the Philistines and the Israelites occurred in the Valley of Elah, where David slew Goliath (I Sam 17:49-50). This decisive battle spelled the beginning of the decline of the Philistines. David was later provided with shelter by Achish, king of Gath, who gave him the town of Ziklag (II Sam 27:6). At Mount Gilboa in the Jezreel Valley, King Saul and his sons fell in battle to the Philistines (I Sam 31:1-6). It was only after David became king of Israel that he was

finally able to defeat the Philistines (II Sam 8:1; I Chr 18:1) and even employed them as mercenaries (II Sam 8:18). Uzziah, king of Judah, pushed the Israelite conquest further into Philistine territory, taking Gath, Jabneh (Jabneel), and Ashdod (II Chr 26:6-7). During the period of the Assyrian campaigns the Philistines several times joined Egypt in alliances against the Assyrians.

The five main Philistine cities in the Bible are Gaza, Ashkelon, Ashdod, Ekron, and Gath, each with its own independent ruler. Some smaller Philistine towns are also mentioned, such as Ziklag (I Sam 27:6), Timnath (Timnah) (Judg 14:1), and the fortified town of Jabneh (II Chr 26:6). It is also recorded that during their expansion further west and north the Philistines established garrisons at Geba (I Sam 13:3) and Beth Shean (I Sam 31:12). Archaeological finds show that many other towns were also under Philistine influence or direct rule.

The Bible contains much information about the internal organization of the Philistines. At the head of each Philistine kingdom stood a lord (I Sam 5:11), or sometimes a king (I Sam 27:2), who was probably also the commander-in-chief of the army. At the head of these states was a military aristocracy which, since it was supported by an advanced military organization and superior arms, could impose its rule over a much larger local population. The army consisted of archers (I Sam 31:3), cavalrymen, and charioteers (I Sam 13:5), and was divided into military units of hundreds and thousands (I Sam 29:2). The Philistines carried the images of their gods with them into battle (II Sam 5:21). The chief of these was Dagon (Judg 16:23), and there were temples dedicated to him at Gaza, Ashdod, and Beth Shean. Their principal goddess was Ashto-

Phoenician pottery jugs and mask from Achzib.

Figurines of Phoenician goddesses; 8th-7th century BC.

reth, whose temple, the house of Ashtoreth, was at Beth Shean (I Sam 31:10).

Remains of the Philistine material culture have been found from the 12th and 11th centuries BC on many sites in the coastal plain south of the Yarkon River. These consist mainly of pottery, the most typical being bowls and jugs with a white wash and painted with a great variety of geometric patterns, birds, and fishes. From the similarity of shape and decoration it is obvious that these had their origin in the sphere of the Mycenean culture, though local features and some Egyptian elements are also identifiable.

Peculiar to the Philistines was their disposal of the dead in anthropoid clay coffins. In their cemeteries at Beth Shean, Lachish, and Tel el-Far'ah (southern Israel), as well as in some places in Egypt, clay coffins of this type were discovered with a cylindrical, elongated body and a cover made in the form of a human head framed by hands.

No written material of the Philistines has so far been found.

PHOENICIANS. Inhabitants of the land extending along the coast of Lebanon and the northern part of Palestine, from Arvad in the north to Acco (Acre) in the south. From early times maritime trade played a major part in Phoenician economy. Other relatively important elements were fishing and the extraction of purple dye from the murex, a shellfish that abounded on the coast. The Greek word for this purple dye is *phoinix*, from which is derived the word Phoenicia. The

earliest traces of human occupation on the Phoenician coast go back to the Paleolithic Age. In the Mesolithic period crops were cultivated and animals domesticated. During the Neolithic period man began to leave his caves and temporary dwellings to build villages with houses made of mud. During the last quarter of the 5th millennium BC pottery made its first appearance. Trade relations with Egypt were well-established. These relations, however, were disturbed during the period of anarchy that prevailed in Egypt in the 22nd century BC, and Egypt's hold over Phoenicia was temporarily interrupted.

By the middle of the 20th century BC Phoenicia had once again come under Egyptian control. The 19th and a great part of the 18th centuries BC were a period of great prosperity, but this was disrupted by the arrival of Hyksos, who ruled over Phoenicia from about 1730 to 1580 BC. Egyptian rule over Phoenicia was renewed with the rise of the 18th Dynasty (1567 BC). The influence of Egypt on Phoenicia was predominant, even influencing Phoenician art.

During the period between 1150 and 883 BC, the golden age of Phoenicia, the Phoenician cities enjoyed independence. Tyre and Sidon, along with some other cities, began a lively maritime trade, and Phoenician colonies were established along the Mediterranean coast, a process which culminated in the foundation of Carthage in North Africa about 814 BC. The Phoenician alphabet and script also found their way to Greece. Hiram, king of Tyre, made a treaty with Solomon (I Kgs 5:12) and helped him in building the Temple. Ties continued to be closely knit in the 9th century BC when Ahab, king of Israel, married Jezebel, daughter of Ethbaal, king of Sidon (II Kgs, 16:31).

During this period Assyria was gradually expanding towards the Mediterranean. Ashurnasirpal II (884–860 BC) invaded Phoenicia in 883 BC and imposed a heavy tribute on Tyre, Sidon, Byblos, and Arvad. During the remainder of the 8th and 7th centuries BC Phoenicia paid a heavy tribute to Assyria while some Phoenician cities attempted from time to time to break the Assyrian yoke. One revolt instigated by a confederacy of Phoenician cities, under the leadership of Tyre, was severely crushed by Sennacherib (705–681 BC). As a result Sidon was destroyed and its inhabitants were replaced by others who had been brought from far away. Further revolts by the Phoenician cities were no more successful.

After the defeat of Assyria by the Babylonians and the Medes in 612 BC, the Phoenician cities regained their independence for a few years, but after the defeat of Pharaoh Necho II, with whom the cities were allied in 605 BC, Phoenicia was brought under direct Babylonian rule. Another revolt, in which Judah and Tyre took part, resulted in the destruction of Jerusalem in 586 BC and the conquest of Tyre by Nebuchadnezzar after a 13-year siege. With the capture of Babylon by

Cyrus of Persia in 539 BC, Phoenicia became part of a Persian satrapy. A large Phoenician navy took part in the wars of Cambyses, Darius, and Xerxes against Egypt and Greece.

Early in the 4th century BC, Tyre, weary of the oppressive rule of the Persian satraps, joined the rebel Greek tyrant of Cyprus, while Tabnit, king of Sidon, rebelled later in the same century against the Persians. Artaxerxes III, king of Persia, besieged Sidon and set the city on fire in 351 BC. After the Battle of Issus in 333 BC the way was open for the conquest of Phoenicia by Alexander the Great. In the 3rd century BC, Phoenicia was under Seleucid rule.

By 112 BC all the Phoenician cities had regained their autonomy. In 64 BC Phoenicia was conquered by Pompey and turned into a Roman province, although it retained full autonomy in internal affairs. Under Roman rule Phoenicia enjoyed no less prosperity than in former times. Glass-blowing was invented at Sidon, and brought additional wealth to the city. The arts and letters flourished both in Tyre and in Sidon. By the middle of the 1st century AD a Christian community was already in existence at Tyre.

SABEANS. The inhabitants of Sheba (Gen 10:7, 25–8), a land in southwest Arabia identified with present-day Yemen. It was renowned in the Bible as an exceedingly rich region. The Sabeans were merchants and traders who made the most of their country's strategic position between the Far and Near East. "The merchants of Sheba traded for your wares the choicest spices, all kinds of precious stones and gold" (Ezek 27:22). Frankincense (Is 60:6; Jer 6:20) and myrrh, two perfumes much valued in biblical times, originated from Sheba. The Queen of Sheba, who went to Jerusalem to see Solomon's wealth and to test his wisdom, brought gold, precious stones, and spices (I Kgs 10:1ff.). The Sabeans also traded in slaves (Joel 4:8) and did not refrain from marauding (Job 1:15).

The history of the Sabean kingdom is still not well known. Sheba is mentioned in inscriptions of Tiglath-pileser III, Sargon, and Sennacherib, kings of Assyria, which refer to luxurious commodities brought by camels from Sheba. The names of some of the Sabean kings are noted in the records of kings of Assyria, such as Sargon II and Sennacherib, while other names are known from pre-Islamic inscriptions found since the second half of the last century. After 1950 serious archaeological explorations were undertaken in the area. Of special interest are the excavations in the temple of the moon god at Marib, the capital of the Sabean kingdom. From the scanty literary evidence it is known that by the beginning of the Christian era most of the arabian peninsula was ruled by the Sabeans.

I.2 RELIGIONS

The peoples of the ancient Near East were polytheists, believing that the universe was inhabited and ruled by a multitude of deities. The more powerful deities served as kings of the pantheon, or controlled forces of nature, while lesser deities served in the courts of higher gods, or as personal gods who watched over even the lowliest of human beings. As in the modern world, religious beliefs were expressed in both temple services and private worship. As no single universally accepted pantheon existed in the ancient Near East, separate cults flourished in different religious centers, many of which worshiped gods unknown in other centers. Nonetheless, attempts were made by ancient priests and religious scholars to synchronize the pantheons of different nations and cities. Gods who served a certain function in one pantheon were equated with the gods who served the same function in others. Despite the wide diversity of religious beliefs and practices, a number of common features can be identified among all ancient Near Eastern peoples including a belief in gods, a belief that the gods built the physical universe and created man, a belief that man could influence the behavior of the gods through sacrifice and prayer, and a belief in life after death.

The Gods. Gods were non-human beings believed to control the destinies of the world, nations, cities, and individuals. Gods appeared to ancient Near Eastern man in many forms. In the cult, the gods were present as statues, in the sky as the sun, moon, and stars, in nature as the forces that brought clouds, wind, and rain, in the bounty of the harvest, and in everyday life as beings that could be appeased or angered with direct consequences for mankind. Unlike the God of Judaism, Christianity, and Islam, ancient Near Eastern gods were not necessarily immortal or omnipotent. In creation epics, gods are put to death and their corpses used to build the physical universe and create mankind. Other "dead" deities included those whose temples and statues fell into disrepair and whose names were forgotten. Likewise, events could occur without the knowledge of all gods. It was believed throughout the ancient Near East that the gods of the historical pantheon were descended from pairs of primordial deities who no longer wielded influence in the day-to-day affairs of the universe.

The Pantheon. Surviving god-lists and other texts preserve the names of countless numbers of gods. Myths or other works throw light on some of them, but little or nothing is known about many others. Consequently, no full description of any ancient Near Eastern pantheon is possible. The most important of the gods in the Sumerian pantheon of 3rd millennium BC Mesopotamia numbered seven. The highest ranking were the kings of the Heavens (An), Earth (Enlil), and the underground ocean Apsu (Enki). Next in order of importance were the moon-god (Nannar), the sun-god (Utu), the goddess Venus (Inanna), and the weather-god (Ishkur). In addition to universal or national functions, these gods and others served as city-gods for Sumerian city-states, each of which had its own patron god or goddess. Two important groups of gods were the Igigi and the Anunnaki. In older materials the identity and function of the Igigi and the Anunnaki vary, but by the end of the 2nd millennium BC the Igigi are identified as the host of heaven and the Anunnaki as the host of the underworld. In a 1st-millennium mystical work, the Igigi are said to number 300 and the Anunnaki 600.

The Semitic Akkadian-speaking people of ancient Mesopotamia who emerged in the early 3rd millennium BC accepted the Sumerian pantheon more or less intact. However, many gods were known in Akkadian by Akkadian, rather than Sumerian, names.

God	Sumerian Name	Akkadian Name
Heaven-god	An	Anum
Earth-god	Enlil	Enlil/Illil
Moon-god	Nannar	Sin
Sun-god	Utu	Shamash
Venus	Inanna	Ishtar
Weather-god	Ishkur	Adad

In the 2nd millennium BC, following the conquest of the Mesopotamian city-states by western Semitic Amorite groups, and the unification of Babylonia under the rule of the Amorite king Hammurabi, the god of Babylon, Marduk, also known as Bel, "The Lord," rose to preeminence in the Mesopotamian pantheon. At first, Marduk ruled with the acquiescence of An and Enlil, as is described in the prologue to the famous Law Code of Hammurabi. Later, by the beginning of the 1st millennium BC, Marduk attained the kingship of the gods in the Babylonian pantheon, replacing An and Enlil. To the north, in Assyria, the Assyrian national god Assur was accepted as king of the gods in place of the Babylonian Marduk to the south. Outside Mesopotamia, important gods included the western Semitic gods El and Baal who occur in Ugaritic literature. In the Bible, Baal appears as the chief god of the Canaanites. Gods belonging to the national pantheons of the non-Semitic Hittites, Hurrians, and Elamites are also known from cuneiform texts.

Myths. Myth, for ancient man, served to answer both great and small mysteries of human existence in the universe, such as: "How was the universe created?", "What is the purpose of man in the universe?", "What is the nature of the human-divine relationship?", "Why do people speak different languages?". Sumerian myths indicate that the primordial universe was a dark place where heaven and earth were not yet separated. The formation of the universe as known to man was believed to have begun with the separation of heaven and earth. The Sumerian myth *Enki and Ninmah* relates that the junior gods bore the brunt of the hard labor of digging the rivers as mankind had yet to be

Deity seated upon a throne and a row of stelae; on one are carved two arms stretched out in prayer to symbols of the sun and moon.

Left: Bone sculpture representing a man in an attitude of prayer. From Beth Shean, 1600–1200 BC. Right: Astarte figurine; late Canaanite period.

created in this early universe. Later, following a divine cessation of work, mankind was created through a joint effort of Enki, the mother-goddess, and birth-goddesses, as a replacement workforce. Mankind was created to labor on behalf of the gods and provide them with all their needs, including food (offerings and sacrifices), clothing (ritual garments on statues of the gods), and shelter (temples). A parallel account of the creation of man occurs in the Akkadian *Atrahasis Epic* followed by a flood-myth. Still other Sumerian literary works preserve a Sumerian account of the Great Flood, and recount how Enki distributed divine tasks to lesser gods including the patron deities of weaving, brick-making, and agriculture (*Enki and the World Order*). Yet another text, *Enmerkhar and the Lord of Aratta*, preserves a short myth that parallels the account of "The Tower of Babel" in Genesis 11. Here, Enki ordains that human beings should speak a variety of languages rather than a single tongue.

The earliest surviving Akkadian myths date to the time of Hammurabi (1792–1750 BC), although a few mythological fragments are known from the 3rd millennium. These early Akkadian myths for the most part represent translations or adaptations of traditions also known from Sumerian sources. By the second half of the 2nd millennium BC, new Akkadian traditions emerge. In Babylon, Marduk is elevated to the kingship of the gods. The Babylonian creation epic, *Enuma Elish*, which is believed to date to the late 2nd millennium, describes the defeat of Tiamat at the hands of Marduk,

the subsequent creation of the heaven and earth from Tiamat's corpse, and the building of Babylon to house Marduk's temple. It ends with a recitation of Marduk's 50 names and a short epilogue instructing fathers to teach their sons of the great deeds of Marduk. This instruction may be compared with the Jewish commandment of fathers to teach their sons of the exodus from Egypt at the time of the Passover holiday. In Babylon itself, *Enuma Elish* was recited in Esagil, the temple of Marduk, as part of the services for the New Year's festival on the third day of the New Year, the 3rd of Nisan, thereby fulfilling the Babylonian commandment.

By the middle of the 1st millennium BC, the age of writing new mythological texts had come to an end in Babylonia and Assyria. Instead, Mesopotamian religious experts undertook the task of writing commentaries and mystical works relating to mythological traditions.

Many motifs from Sumerian and Akkadian myths are reflected in biblical materials. For example, the biblical flood narrative in Genesis 6–9 parallels the Sumerian account of the flood in "The Sumerian Flood Story," and Akkadian accounts in *The Atrahasis Epic* and *The Epic of Gilgamesh*. The discovery of a fragment of the Akkadian Gilgamesh Epic at the site of Megiddo in northern Israel has even prompted some scholars to speculate that the biblical flood tradition first reached the Land of Israel by way of the Gilgamesh Epic. Canaanite mythological traditions attested in the epic

Stele from Ugarit showing the Baal of Lightning. In his right hand he brandishes a club, and in his left hand he holds a thunderbolt.

literature of Ugarit find echoes in the Book of Psalms.

The Temple Cult. Throughout the ancient Near East, as in ancient Israel, the temple served as the center of official religious activities. In polytheistic cultures, these activities were intended to provide sustenance to the gods in accordance with the belief that man was created to serve his divine overlords. In their temples, gods were served two main meals and two light meals a day. Foods served to the gods included meats, breads and other baked goods, eggs, beer and other beverages, and dairy products. A few recipes survive explaining how to prepare fowl and beef-type dishes for the divine palate. At the conclusion of meals, leftover foods were removed from the gods' tables and could then be eaten by the priests. In addition to regular meals, special foods could be offered to gods on certain occasions. For example, a middle-2nd millennium BC ritual accompanying a request for an oracular decision required that gods be seated at a table where they were served a meal. The cultic calendar included a number of annual festivals, among them the New Year's festival in the spring, and harvest festivals, as well as monthly New and Full Moon festivals. The temple cult also required regular ceremonies outside the temple premises. These included processions of divine statues through city streets and, in Mesopotamia, divine journeys by barge along the intercity canal system. A number of special "once in a lifetime" events such as the building or restoration of temples required extra cultic preparedness. In addition to sacrifices and offerings, cultic ser-

vices included hymns and prayers to be recited before divine statues. Many such hymns were collected by ancient scholars in anthologies and have been recovered. They include Sumerian collections of penitential psalms and Akkadian magical series used to ward off witches and other malevolent forces. Outside the domain of the temple and official cults, religious texts were utilized in a number of settings. For example, "prayers to the gods of the night" (the stars) were recited to divine stars and constellations in city squares, or on rooftops beneath the open night sky, by priests on behalf of clients wishing to obtain oracles after temples had closed for the night.

Personal Religion. Ancient Near Eastern man believed that gods influenced the life of mankind. Proper human behavior was rewarded by the gods, while improper behavior was punished. Personal gods were entrusted with the protection of individuals from bad luck, while city and national gods protected society as a whole from natural catastrophes or conquest. The divine-human relationship was a symbiotic one. Men cared for their gods and kept their gods' commandments. In turn, the gods showed their gratitude by providing for the welfare of their human wards during their lifetimes, and finally by accompanying deceased humans to the threshold of the underworld. Misunderstandings between man and god resulted in divine punishment or even abandonment, but humans could humbly repent and thereby bring about reconciliation with their gods. On a personal level, penitential psalms were meant to appease the wrath of gods, while city and national laments served the same purpose for the city and state. Although no mechanism for assigning personal gods to individuals is evident in surviving materials, it may be presumed that personal gods were passed from father to son and mother to daughter, a phenomenon which may have led to the development of family or clan gods and goddesses. In the ancient

The great ziggurat of Choga-zanbil in Khuzestan, built in the 13th century BC by the Elamite king Untash Gal.

King Akhenaton and Queen Nefertiti making an offering to the sun-god Aton. Painted relief at El-Amarna; 14th century BC.

Near East, personal gods could be called upon to intercede with greater gods on behalf of their human wards. Relationships between humans and personal gods need not have been permanent as is implied by an omen which reveals that two personal gods could have a claim on a single human being. The nature of the triangular relationships between humans, lesser personal gods, and great gods, is explored in the Akkadian Wisdom Text *Ludlul Bel Nemeqi*, which is commonly known as the "Babylonian Job." In this text, the wrath of Marduk causes the personal gods of a Babylonian noble to abandon him, allowing all sorts of social disabilities and diseases to bring the noble to the brink of the grave. At the very last instant, Marduk saves the noble. Later, the personal gods and goddesses of the noble return to him in light of his reconciliation with Marduk. In "The Babylonian Job," it is Marduk who first torments and then saves the noble. The noble's own personal gods are helpless before the power of the national god, Marduk, despite their own vested interest in the noble's welfare. Another Babylonian Wisdom Text, an acrostic poem called *The Babylonian Theodicy*, similar to the Book of Job, employs dialogues to examine the nature of the divine-human relationship.

The Realm of the Dead. As in the Judeo-Christian tradition, ancient Near Eastern man believed in some form of life after death. With the rare exception of a limited number of humans, including the flood hero, who are granted divine status, humans were believed to descend to an underworld beneath the earth's surface following their demise. The dead were buried, and after traveling along a road from the earth's surface to the underworld, crossing an underworld river, and/or passing through a series of underworld gates, were judged and granted admittance to the underworld. However, there is no clear evidence in ancient Near Eastern materials of divine reward or punishment after death based on previous human behavior during one's lifetime. Conditions in the underworld vary from text to text, but a tradition that is repeated in three Akkadian epics describes the underworld as a dark, dreary, dusty place where the dead are garbed in robes of feathers and dine on clay. A more optimistic view is

presented in the Sumerian Gilgamesh tale, *Gilgamesh, Enkidu, and the Underworld*. Here various categories of human beings are accorded different fates in the hereafter in accordance with the number of sons they produced during their lifetimes. Men with only one or two sons go without in the underworld, while those with as many as seven sons are well provided for. This tradition reflects a practice of providing deceased relatives with funerary goods and grave offerings to ensure a happy afterlife. This same text also provides clear evidence for the existence of a "human soul" after death. The disembodied spirit of Enkidu issues forth as a breeze from the underworld and rises to the earth's surface through a crack in the earth. On earth, the spirit of Enkidu addresses Gilgamesh. Similar disembodied human spirits were believed to wander among the living as ghosts or demons, and could be exorcized and sent back to the underworld. There is no evidence

Philistine goddess seated, her body merging with a four-legged throne.

whatsoever for a belief in reincarnation of the dead, nor for their return to the earth's surface. Likewise, cremation was frowned upon since this denied the body the opportunity to be present beneath the earth's surface where both graves and the underworld were located.

In addition to deceased humans, the underworld also housed a full pantheon of underworld gods who were meant to keep the deceased under lock and key so as to prevent their return to earth. Most underworld gods were themselves forbidden to leave the underworld, although messengers pass freely between the heavenly and underworld pantheons in the Akkadian epic *Nergal and Ereshkigal* along a stairway called "The Stairway of Heaven," and the sun- and moon-gods are said to be present in the underworld at times when they are not visible in the sky above the realm of the living.

I.3 LANGUAGES

Both Genesis 10–11 and Ancient Near Eastern sources recount the spread of language groups throughout the biblical world. In Genesis 10, the nations and languages are divided into three groups (the sons Shem, Ham, and Japheth) while Genesis 11 recounts that God confounded the speech of mankind in the aftermath of the destruction of the Tower of Babel. In ancient Near Eastern mythology, all of mankind, too, speaks a single language at the dawn of time before different languages are created by divine fiat. Although the anthropological-linguistic models proposed by Genesis 10–11 and ancient Near Eastern myth are no longer accepted by modern scholars, it is possible to divide the spoken language of the biblical world into family groups.

Biblical Hebrew belongs to the Semitic family, a group of languages based on roots consisting of three consonants where the root is modified through the use of vowels, prefixes, suffixes, and infixes so as to produce individual words and verb forms. For example, the three consonants *ktb* "to write" are the basis for the words *katab* "he wrote," *yiktob* "he will write," and *miktab* "letter," as well as many more words all relating to the activity of writing.

The Semitic language family can be divided into three branches: northwest Semitic, southwest Semitic, and east Semitic. It has been conjectured that all three branches derive from a common ancestor, known as Proto-Semitic, which may have been spoken in prehistoric times by related tribal groups. Over time, according to this theory, the individual Semitic languages evolved as various Semitic-speaking groups migrated to different parts of the Near East. Recent research suggests that Proto-Semitic itself might belong to an even larger extended language family now known as Afrasian languages.

Sumerian pictographic writing.

Fragment of the Epic of Gilgamesh in cuneiform Akkadian script.

Hebrew itself can be classified as a northwestern Semitic language. Its sister northwestern Semitic languages include Aramaic, Ammonite, Amorite, Canaanite, Edomite, Moabite, Phoenician, Ugaritic, and perhaps also Eblaite, over which there is still a debate as to which language group it is to be associated. Eblaite, the language of the 25th-24th century archives of the city of Ebla in Syria, is written in cuneiform (wedge-shaped writing) script which was the Mesopotamian form of writing. Since most words in these texts are written as Sumerian pictograms, it is very difficult to know at times which language they are meant to represent. Ugaritic, which is closely related to biblical Hebrew, is known from the archives of Ancient Ugarit (the archaeological site Ras Shamra) on the coast of Syria. The Ugaritic texts date to the 14th-13th centuries BC and are written in an alphabetic form of cuneiform script. Aramaic was the international language of Israel's neighbors during the First Temple period and later became the daily language of Israel during the Second Temple period. It still survives in several isolated villages today in Iran. Ammonite, Edomite, and Moabite are attested in several inscriptions and are contemporary to Hebrew, Phoenician, and Aramaic. Amorite, the language of western Semitic Amorite tribes who appeared during the late 3rd millennium, is known only from personal names.

Bilingual inscription in Greek and Aramaic from Tell Dan; Hellenistic period.

Egyptian hieroglyphic writing; second millennium BC.

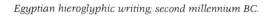

Cousins to Hebrew and the northwestern branch of the Semitic language family are the southwestern Semitic languages, of which Arabic is the sole surviving member, and the eastern Semitic language, Akkadian, the Semitic language of ancient Mesopotamia. It is attested in written documents from the middle of the 3rd millennium onwards. The first large corpus of Akkadian documents dates to the reign of the Old Akkadian dynasty of Sargon of Akkad and his successors in the 24th and 23rd centuries. The language, which is documented from the end of the 3rd millennium BC until the 1st century AD, is divided into two main dialects: a southern Babylonian dialect and a northern Assyrian dialect. In addition, regional dialects of Akkadian existed in sites outside Mesopotamia proper. During the 2nd millennium BC, Akkadian was the lingua franca of the entire ancient Near East from Egypt to Iran and from Anatolia to the Persian Gulf. Akkadian documents and literary materials have been recovered throughout the Near East. Akkadian tablets excavated in the land of Israel include economic documents, omen texts, and a fragment of the Akkadian Gilgamesh Epic.

Sumerian, a non-Semitic language, is the oldest attested language in the ancient Near East. Sumerian documents appear in the late 4th millennium BC both within Mesopotamia at sites such as Uruk and Nineveh and outside Iraq in archives from Susa (biblical Shushan) in Iran. Sumerian belongs to no known language family, but is categorized as an agglutinative language. This means that Sumerian words and sentences are formed by combining basic blocks of meaning as a child might build a toy house and city by manipulating toy blocks. For example, the Sumerian noun *e* "house" and adjective *gal* "big" can be modified by adding prefixes and suffixes or combined with other words to yield a wide variety af meanings. Together *e.gal* "big house" is the king's palace, but *gal.e* means "the house is big." Reduplication, *e.gal e.gal* yields the plural "palaces." Sumerian was used in daily discourse and business transactions, as well as literature and liturgy, throughout the 3rd millennium. The fall of the Sumerian-speaking Ur III dynasty just before the year 2,000 BC marked the end of Sumerian as a vernacular, but Sumerian continued on as a language of scholarship, religion, and culture alongside Akkadian as long as cuneiform was written. A few Sumerian words have entered biblical Hebrew and even modern languages. One such word, Sumerian *abzu* "the underground cosmic waters," may be the ultimate source of the English "abyss."

Other important languages of the ancient Near East include Hittite, Elamite, Old Persian, and ancient Egyptian. Ancient Egyptian, which was written in hieroglyphs rather than cuneiform, remained isolated from the languages of southwest Asia. Hittite, the language of the Hittite kingdoms of 2nd-millennium Ana-

The Siloam Inscription in Hebrew; 3rd century BC.

tolia, is an Indo-European language like Greek, Latin, Sanskrit, and English. It is written in cuneiform and hieroglyphic scripts and is well known from the royal archives of the Hittite kings which yielded thousands of Hittite and Akkadian texts. Elamite, the language of Elam (Ancient Iran), like Sumerian, is known from 4th-millennium tablets. It is written in cuneiform script and survives well into the 1st millennium where it appears as one of the three official languages of the Old Persian Empire of Cyrus and Darius alongside Old Persian and Babylonian Akkadian. It is non-Semitic and bears no direct relationship to any known Near Eastern language. Old Persian is the oldest form of the living Indo-European language Modern Persian. With the spread of Hellenism following the conquests of Persia by Alexander the Great in the 4th century BC,

Greek spread throughout the Ancient Near East and Levant. In Babylonia, a few examples of transcriptions of Babylonian texts into Greek letters have been recovered.

One of the Dead Sea Scrolls in Hebrew; c.1st century AD.

One of the ostracon from Tell ed-Duweir (biblical Lachish), c. 589 BC

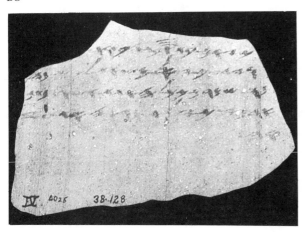

II. THE WORLD OF THE BIBLE

II.4 GEOGRAPHY OF THE HOLY LAND

The Holy Land's area is small but contains an extraordinary variety in relief, rocks, soils, climatic conditions, vegetation, and wildlife. The country lies at the intersection of the continents of Asia, Africa, and Europe, and has access to the Mediterranean and the Red Sea. It stretches from the Mediterranean shore east to the Syrian-Arabian Desert, and from Mount Hermon south to the Negeb (Negev) and the Gulf of Elath (Eilath). Marginal are the Sinai Peninsula and the Land of Midian, which the Bible does not expressly include in the Holy Land.

REGIONS AND THEIR RELIEF

The Land's singular topographic feature is the deep Jordan and Arabah (Arava) Rift Valley, a section of the 4,000 miles (6,200 km) long Syrian-East African Rift. Running north-south, it divides the country into Cisjordan and Transjordan. Deepest in it is the Dead Sea, whose water table, more than 1200 ft. (400 m). below sea level, constitutes the lowest spot on the earth's continents.

Of the Cisjordan lowlands, the narrow Mediterranean Coastal Plain is the westernmost part. Its central section bears the name Sharon while its somewhat larger south is sometimes named by the Bible Philistia, domain of the Philistines. Further inland are some intermontane valleys, of which the largest is the Jezreel Valley (Plain of Esdraelon).

In the Cisjordan hills, the Bible distinguishes between Galilee in the north, Samaria south of the Jezreel Valley, and Judea farther south. Part of these hills present, despite their moderate altitude, a pronounced mountainous relief. Hard rock slopes are steep; narrow gorges or wider valleys are deeply incised. Such landscapes characterize Upper (northern) Galilee and parts of Samaria. The Judean Hills, whose crest, running from north to south, is of a rather even height, descend abruptly to the Shephelah (foothills) in the west and even more steeply, as the Desert of Judah, to the Rift in the east.

South of the Judean Hills lies the Beersheba Plain and beyond it rise the Negeb Hills. Their southernmost section, today named Eilath Hills, differs in landscape and rocks from the rest of the Cisjordan hills.

The Rift comprises, in the Holy Land, the Huleh Valley of the upper Jordan, in biblical times mostly covered by a shallow lake; the Sea of Galilee (Lake Kinneret, Sea of Genezareth), with adjoining narrow land strips and small valleys; the Beth Shean (Beisan) and Lower Jordan valleys; the Dead Sea; and the long Arabah Valley.

In northern Transjordan rises the Bashan region, whose western section is the Golan; in the center are the Gilead Hills and the Ammon and Moab highland; in the south, the Land of Edom. Except for Bashan, all of Transjordan tilts eastward.

ROCKS AND SOILS

The country's rocks are mostly "marine," formed on the bottom of an ancient ocean called Tethys by geologists. It flooded large expanses whenever the continent to the east and south subsided. These rocks comprise hard limestones and dolomites and softer chalk. Still softer marls were mostly formed in inland lakes. Most stones have light hues, from whitish yellow to gray or reddish brown. Only Edom and the southernmost Negeb have Nubian sandstones, often of strong colors, and a variety of igneous crystalline rocks like granites, porphyries, and quartzes. On the Bashan and in small

Rock formations of various shapes have become landmarks in the Negeb.

Granite mountains in the southern part of the Sinai peninsula near the traditional site of Mount Sinai.

Rain in the Negeb does not sink into the ground, but runs off the surface in raging torrents.

parts of eastern Galilee black basalts testify to volcanic activity in the country's recent geologic past.

Among the country's arable soils, the red-brown *terra rossa*, better preserved in biblical times than at present, covers rock slopes and terraces that in the hills run horizontally or are slightly inclined. There are, however, also lighter "rendzina" and marl soils. The Coastal Plain has red sands, dark swamp soils or whitish-yellow dune sands. Dark swamp soils also cover part of the interior valleys. Dark basalt soils can be found on the Golan and in stretches of eastern Galilee, while the northern Negeb has yellowish-brown loess, typical of desert outskirts.

CLIMATE

The Holy Land's decisive climatic feature is the sharp division of the year into a moist winter and a completely rainless summer. This is the result of its position on the border of two of the globe's major climate belts, the Cyclones Zone of Europe and North America and the arid belt of Passate Winds to which most of the world's hot deserts belong. With the seasonal shift of the two belts, the country comes alternately into the reach of the one and the other.

The country's position on the earth grid results in seasonal variations in the length of day and night that are smaller than in countries nearer the North Pole: the longest day is sunlit for 14 and the shortest for 10 hours, but sunlight intensity is very strong. Temperatures are comparatively high but vary strongly from place to place according to altitude, exposure to marine influence, and wind directions. Cooling from summer to winter is abrupt in November and the warming in April-May is also quite rapid. Fall and spring, therefore, do not constitute defined periods.

A persistent day wind during summer is the sea breeze which cools the Coastal Plain and the western hill slopes. When descending east into the Rift it heats up and becomes oppressive. In winter, wind directions are more irregular, with cells of low and high pressure alternately passing over the country. East winds or high-pressure windless conditions may in May-June or in September-October let temperatures soar and sometimes carry fine dust. They adversely affect humans and animals, but in early summer hasten the ripening of grain and fruit and aid the farmer in combating weeds and pests.

A modest shower is enough to cause a flood in the Paran Valley. A river will flow here for a few hours and then disappear.

Rainfall is irregular. The country has to reckon with frequent drought years. In the prehistoric past, the country had certain moister and sometimes warmer periods than in the present, but in the biblical period conditions are assumed to have differed only slightly, if at all, from the present.

Rainfall, together with farming prospects, augments from south to north, but topography causes sharp local differences. Jerusalem's average annual rainfall of 20 in. (500 mm) is seven times larger than that of the Dead Sea shore which is only 15 miles (25 km) away. As a result of high evaporation, grain crops may fail where less than 12 in. (300 mm) of rain fall in a year.

The Coastal Plain and the hill slopes facing west toward the rain-bringing winds enjoy medium to high precipitation, while the slopes descending to the east, and the Rift bottom, lie in the "rain shadow" and remain much drier. The ascent to Transjordan is again blessed with more rain, but on the plateau dipping eastward rainfall diminishes rapidly. In the south, the Negeb ("dry land"), the Dead Sea, the middle and lower Jordan Valley, and the Arabah Valley have desert climate and contrast with the moister regions to the west and north. The rainfall map thus shows extreme differences. Mount Meron in Upper Galilee receives an annual average of 40 in. (1,000 mm) and more, and the top of Mount Hermon even up to 60 in. (1,500 mm), but Beersheba measures only 6–8 in. (150–200 mm) and Elath not even 1.2 in. (30mm).

"FRUITLAND," "DESERT," "DESOLATION"

In history, a sharp borderline separated the western so-called fruitland from the desert, the domain of nomadic shepherds. This belt provided food to grazing animals and was therefore not identical with "total desolation." The border between fruitland and desert vacillated even without climatical change, when agriculturist and shepherd endeavored to enlarge their respective domains on the other's account. Their competition in most cases impoverished the plant cover. The Bible reports how the tribes of Israel became peasants and learned to plant fruit trees. After they had become sedentary, they had to ward off fresh invasions of nomads from the desert.

VEGETATION AND WILDLIFE

The Holy Land's variety in surface forms and climate and its position at the juncture of three continents permitted a great number of plant species to enter the country and take root there. Three of the globe's major phytogeographic zones, the Mediterranean, the Irano-Turanian dry-steppe, and the totally arid Saharo-Arabian zone, meet in its narrow borders. Oases of the Sudanian wet-tropical vegetation in the Lower Jordan Valley, near the Dead Sea and in the Arabah, appear near sweet springs, while a few species originally from Europe appear on the higher reaches of the northern mountains.

Trees once grew around the Dead Sea when its level was lower. These remains are now encrusted with salt crystals.

The variety of species is thus exceptionally rich, but continual human activity has thinned out the plant cover. When the tribes of Ephraim and Manasseh complained that Joshua did not allocate them enough arable land, Joshua replied: "The mountain country shall be yours. Although it is wooded, you shall cut it down, and its farthest extent shall be yours" (Josh 17-18). Trees were also felled to harvest wood. Frequent wars, with fires laid to embarrass enemies, effected further ruin of vegetation. Where forests disappeared, erosion swept away fertile soil.

Animals invaded the land from different directions. Many species, among them large mammals such as elephants, rhinoceruses, and zebras, had disappeared at the end of the rain-rich periods which paralleled Europe's ice ages.

To this day, the country serves as a major traveling route for birds on their seasonal migrations. The biblical account of enormous flocks of quail which fed the Children of Israel in the Sinai desert is just one example (Num 11:31–32).

HUMANS IN PREHISTORY

Human presence in the Land of Israel dates back to the earliest phases of man's appearance on earth verified by research. Not periodically driven off by ice ages as they were further north, humans seem to have lived there almost without interruption, even if newcomers supplanted earlier inhabitants.

The earliest traces of human presence were discovered in the Jordan Valley. A subsequent type was called Paleanthropus palestinensis by the anthropologists who related him to the Neanderthal man. Alongside him, tribes belonging to Homo sapiens appeared. Remains of humans of mixed parentage, discovered in caves of Mount Carmel, offer proof that both races belonged to the species of humans and were thus able to procreate freely.

The country's climate was relatively mild for long periods, permitting primitive man to live in the open. Only when it cooled down did he have to take refuge in caves and the first nuclei of society, family, clan, and tribe, were formed. Cults of the dead and the hunt resulted in the early Paleolithic Age in crude artistic creations and mark the beginnings of spiritual activity.

THE REGIONS OF THE HOLY LAND

A. GALILEE

In the Old Testament the name "Galilee" applies only

The Judean Desert at En Geddi. Reeds and tamarisks appear close to the water. A step beyond the desert takes over.

Running water and forest trees are common in Galilee where fresh water springs are relatively abundant.

to a small area near the northern town of Kedesh, but in New Testament times Galilee comprised the entire hill country which Joshua had partitioned between the tribes of Asher, Zebulun, Issachar, and Naphtali. The areas settled by those tribes seem previously to have been uninhabited.

Mountainous Galilee is surrounded by lowlands on three sides: The Acre Plain and the Haifa Bay area in the west, the Esdraelon (Jezreel), Harod, and Beth Shean valleys in the south, and the Kinaroth and Huleh valleys of the Rift in the east. In the north the landscape of southern Lebanon resembles that of Upper Galilee and some geographers regard the stretch up to the Litani river as forming a topographic unit with Galilee.

Since the 1st century a distinction has been drawn between Lower Galilee, whose maximum altitudes are under 2,000 ft. (600 m), and Upper Galilee, where mountains exceed 3,000 ft. The Beth Hakerem Valley, running from west to east, forms a clear border between the two parts.

Both Lower and Upper Galilee are of considerable topographic variety. Lower Galilee has parallel hill chains running west-east and gorges or wider valleys between them. Southeastern Lower Galilee contains a few small plateaus, nearly flat, with a thin cover of *terra rossa* or basalt soil. Upper Galilee's relief is more irregular. Mountains are grouped in ridges and blocs. Some tops are isolated and present natural fortresses. Several stream courses are deeply incised. Most of these run west or east, but others go to the south.

Rainfall, sufficient in Lower and abundant in parts of Upper Galilee, gave the center of Upper Galilee a dense forest or macchia cover. In New Testament times and after, reliability of rainfall helped to make Galilee a fertile farming country with a dense population.

B. SAMARIA

The name Samaria was applied to the extensive hill region that Joshua allocated to the tribes of Manasseh and Ephraim (Josh 16; 17). In the partition after King Solomon's death, Samaria became the nucleus of the Northern Kingdom of Israel. Its delimitation includes the area bordered by the Sharon in the west, the Jordan Valley in the east, and the Jezreel (Esdraelon) and Harod valleys in the north. In the south, no natural features mark the transition to the domain of the tribe of Benjamin. From a geographical point of view, Mount Carmel and the Manasseh and Irron Hills in the northwest form part of Samaria, but in history they were not always within its boundaries.

Most of Samaria has medium height hills topped by Mount Ebal, 3,084 ft. (940 m) and Mount Gerizim, 2,890 ft. (881 m) in the center of Samaria, on both sides of the narrow valley of Shechem (Nablus). In the northeast, Mount Gilboa rises steeply above the valleys of Jezreel, Harod, and Beth Shean.

Broad interior valleys, particularly in the north, and

Landscape in Samaria.

narrower ones farther south, all covered with fertile soil, enabled variegated farming. The soil cover of the hillsides was suitable for olive groves, vineyards, and other crops.

C. JUDEA

This geographical term approximately conforms with the domain of the tribes of Judah and Benjamin as delineated in Joshua 15 and 18. It also largely coincides with the Kingdom of Judah after the secession of the Kingdom of Israel, as well as with the initial borders of the Hasmonean Kingdom.

Three regions are to be discerned in Judea: the hills proper, the Shephelah (foothills) in the west, and the Desert of Judah in the east. The hills comprise those of Bethel in the north, of Jerusalem in the center, and of Hebron in the south. The highest elevation of the north is Mount Baal Hazor, 3,332 ft. (1,016 m) above sea level, and that of the south Mount Halhul, 3,346 ft. (1,020 m). The Jerusalem hills present a somewhat lower saddle of the crest, with relatively less difficult ascents from west and east than further north and south. This fact made it a highway crossing point.

The main fold of the rock layers parallels Judea's watershed at a distance of 6-7 miles (10-12 km) farther west. The area between these two lines receives the amplest rains. Its porous rocks readily absorb the rain water and permit it to trickle eastward subterrane-

Among the hills of Judea.

ously. The groundwater reaches strong springs in the arid Rift and forms oases such as Jericho and En Gedi.

The Gibeon and Jerusalem region had broad fields where grain crops could be grown. Elsewhere, terraces on the slopes were planted with olive groves and vineyards. Farming constituted the principal economic base of all Judean towns, but crafts diversified and provided additional citizens with a livelihood. Towns near the border between the fruitland and the desert developed a barter trade between wares of the agriculturalists and those of the herdsmen.

The foothills zone has a relief of low hills and broad valleys. Its soil is easily arable and water sources are attainable. Valleys such as those of Aijalon or Elah, excelent for farming, served foreign armies as marching ground when trying to invade the hills in the east.

In the Desert of Judah, rain is scarce, and the impervious chalk of the surface lets the water run off quickly to the Rift, instead of absorbing it to benefit plant life. The collecting run-off has incised precipitous clefts and gorges, like those of Nahal Kidron or Nahal Zeelim. The Desert of Judah always lacked towns and sedentary villages, while in Christian times, hermits lived in its caves.

D. THE COASTAL PLAIN.

The lowland along the Mediterranean coast was in antiquity inhabited by only few Israelites and is there-

fore only rarely mentioned in the Bible. The Coastal Plain broadens from 2–3 miles (3–5 km) in the north to about 22 miles (35 km) in the south. The coast is poor in natural harbors which could aid invaders from overseas. The shore rises either gently from the sea or forms vertical cliffs of crumbly sandstone which are up to 120 ft. (40 m) high.

The westernmost strip of the Plain is covered by sand dunes, with low sandstone ridges running parallel to the coast. The first ridge separates the dune stretch from the Western Plain and was formerly largely covered by oak trees or brush. A second ridge divides the Western from the Eastern Plain that touches the foothills and hills. It has heavier soils, better suited for agriculture, and therefore was more inhabited than the west.

Annual rainfall diminishes from 24 in. (600 mm) in the extreme north to 14 in. (350 mm) in the Gaza neighborhood, but from there southward the climate rapidly becomes desert-like, with only 6 in. (150 mm) near the Sinai border. The Coastal Plain's summer is somewhat less hot than farther inland, but high humidity makes it harder to bear. Winter frost is practically absent from all parts of the Coastal Plain.

Sections distinguished from north to south are: the Tyre Valley, the Acre Plain, the Haifa Bay area ("Zebulun Valley"), the very narrow Carmel Coast, the Sharon, the section south of the Jarkon river, the South ("Darom"), which was sometimes referred to as the "Plain of the Philistines," and the Negeb Coast.

The Land promised to Israel reached, according to Exodus 23:31, "to the Sea of the Philistines," i.e., to the Mediterranean Sea. Joshua, when determining the territories of the tribes, included in them most parts of the Coastal Plain. In fact, these mostly belonged to land which the Israelites could not take from the Canaanites or Philistines. Only during the United Kingdom did Israelites settle there, principally in Jaffa, which served Jerusalem as a port. (In Jonah 1:3, Jaffa is the port from which the prophet fled by boat to Tarshish.) Ethnically it remained mostly foreign; the Roman general Pompey in the 1st century BC could separate the coast from Judea, and Gabinius restored to the port cities their Hellenistic character. Herod received Jaffa from Caesar and built Ascalon and Caesarea as great port cities, but left their non-Jewish character. The New Testament reports on Jaffa and other places and on converts won there for Christianity. In the Roman period, Caesarea was the country's most populous city.

E. THE NEGEB.

In modern Israel, the term "Negeb" comprises all the southern half of the State, its western and eastern limits identical with the political frontiers with Egypt and Jordan. The biblical extent of the Negeb, however, cannot be so precisely determined.

The word "Negeb" is derived from a Hebrew root

meaning "dry." It refers both to "dry areas" in general, e.g., "Watercourses in the Negeb" (Ps 126:4) and also to the direction of the south as, for example, "Look northward and southward" ("to the Negeb") (Gen 13:14). When adding the Hebrew article, "Ha-Negeb," or the attribute "Land of the Negeb," the Bible refers to a definite geographical region, mentioning, for instance, that "Abraham traveled to the Land of the Negeb" (Gen. 20:1), or that "Amalek lives in the Land of the Negeb" (Num 13:29).

The extent reached by the biblical Negeb is difficult to establish. Judah's borders certainly did not include what in modern terms is regarded as the central and southern Negeb Hills or the Arabah Valley. The present-day Negeb incorporates the regions of the Negeb Coast and the Beersheba Plain, the Negeb Hills, the Paran Plateau, the Elath Hills, and the Arabah Valley.

The **Beersheba Region** rises imperceptibly from the shore south of Gaza to approximately 800 ft. (250 m) above sea level around the city of Beersheba and 1,650 ft. (500 m) at its eastern extremity. Geologically, the Beersheba Region is a depression which was covered to a thickness of 100 ft. (30 m) by fine-grained loess soil, typical for desert outskirts. Sudden winter flash floods tear into its deep zigzagging gullies. Wadis like those of the stream of Besor and its tributaries indicate that in the recent geological past water erosion was stronger than at present. There are areas of rolling dunes, not only along the shore but also inland. In biblical and later times, grain could be grown on the loess soil in good rain years. Flocks of sheep, goats, and camels found their pasture in the area.

The **Negeb Hills** occupy more than half of the total Negeb area. Their highest elevations exceed 3,280 ft. (1,000 m). The deep canyon of Zin divides the Negeb Hills into a northern and a southern half. Basically the result of tectonic folding, erosion has scarcely changed the Hills' topography, although it created the three *cirques* (craters), the Ramon crater, and the Great and Small Craters. These are deeply incised into the highest fold crests, are surrounded by perpendicular walls, and expose rock strata that are elsewhere concealed in depth. Erosion has also cut spectacular, mostly dry wadi courses, e.g., the streams of Zin and Paran. The rather flat surface around the latter is sometimes called the Paran Plateau.

Hard limestones and dolomites or, on originally lower areas, softer chalk with hard flint intercalations characterize the Negeb Hills. Much of the ground bears a loose stone cover. With an annual rainfall of between 2-6 in. (50-150 mm), the Hills have an extremely sparse plant cover, only locally sufficing for pasture. The Negeb Hills must therefore have had only a thin nomad population in antiquity. Only where ancient Israelites, and later especially Nabateans, developed the art of stormwater collection and preservation, could their settlements grow crops on fields and serve as rest stations for caravans.

The **Elath Hills** form, west of the Great Rift, the northernmost extremity of the South Sinai Mountains

Hills in the central Negeb.

A view of the Elath Hills.

and therefore differ with their crystalline rocks (granites, porphyries, quartzites, gneisses, etc.) or their colorful Nubian sandstones from the rest of the Land of Israel's hills. The region was practically empty of population, although the Egyptians mined copper at Timna in the 2nd millennium BC, and others later repeated the operation for short periods.

The **Arabah Valley**, extending 103 miles (165 km) between the Dead Sea and the Elath Gulf of the Red Sea, is Israel's southern section of the Great Rift. Thickly covered by sand and gravel, it is hemmed in by rock walls on both sides. Its width varies between three and 20 miles (5 and 32 km). Its northern end is nearly 1,000 ft. (300 m) below sea level. Its center rises to 690 ft. (210 m) above sea level, to descend from there south to the sea shore. Rainfall may be absent for years on end, its annual average of 2-8 in. (50-75 mm) being the outcome of rare shortlived rainstorms. The climate is hot and dry at all seasons. Some springs and wells, on the eastern more than on the western side, receive subterraneous water from a distance. Playas (salt flats) appear in the south, with a salt-loving vegetation in their vicinity. The south has a surprisingly dense cover of thorny acacias, while desert grasses and bushes grow elsewhere. A number of stations of the Children of Israel on their desert wandering lay in the Arabah Valley.

F. SINAI.

The desert peninsula of Sinai is wedged in between the continents of Asia and Africa. Most geographers include it in Asia. Throughout history, Sinai had a negligible population, mostly nomads or semi-nomads. It had hardly any farming produce and its minerals were only rarely exploited, but the ways and roads which crossed it were always of prime importance.

The peninsula's size, 21,000 sq. miles (60,000 sq. km), is at least double that of the Holy Land proper. Distances are considerable: at least 130 miles (200 km) across and 260 miles (400 km) from north to south. On the map, Sinai appears as a triangle, with the Mediterranean coast as its base line and the apex protruding south into the Red Sea, where the two gulfs of Suez and of Elath (Akaba) meet.

Its southern mountain massif rises to over 6,850 ft. (2,000 m) above sea-level; some of its peaks are even higher, among them Mount Catherine, 8,050 ft. (2,637 m.) and Jebel Musa or Mount Moses, 7,503 ft. (2,285 m). The dark or reddish crystalline rocks rise with enormous perpendicular walls and columns over abysmal clefts.

Further north Jebel Ikma, a rim of sandstone and calcareous mountains in a semi-circle, surrounds the vast a-Tih Plateau that occupies 60% of Sinai's total area. It is mostly covered by rough gravel and sand, but is hardly flat. In the north, it merges imperceptibly with the Northern Plain that bears a thick cover of wandering quartz sand dunes, from which rise a number of steeply sloping mountains and elongated ridges. The western half of its Mediterranean coast is occupied by the shallow Bardawil Lagoon (its name derives from the Crusader king Baldwin who died nearby). The lagoon is assumed to have been created by an eastern arm of the river Nile that no longer exists. The northwestern corner of the peninsula forms an impassable salt swamp, home of unique flora and a rich fauna of fish and water fowl.

All of Sinai lies within an arid belt of high pressure and trade winds. On an annual average, 80% of its area receives less than 4 in. (100 mm) of rain that may result from one violent downpour of a few hours after several completely rainless years. Only the northeastern corner and the mountain tops of the south receive a somewhat higher amount of rain. Its desert character is emphasized by generally cloudless skies, a great diurnal temperature span, and high evaporation rates.

Practically all of Sinai belongs to the arid Saharo-Arabian vegetation zone. In the north, a sparse cover of grassy and bushy plants permits grazing, at least in the spring season. In gorges of the crystalline massif appear thorny acacias and, at some spots, the manna tamarisk believed to be the origin of the biblical manna; the sugar-rich manna is secreted by certain grubs living on these tamarisks. Equally sparse is Sinai's land fauna but the water of the two gulfs is rich in colorful fish and mollusks connected either to coral reefs or to mangrove plants near the coast.

An oasis by the Mediterranean shore of Sinai.

There are a few scattered oases, including the el-Arish region on the Mediterranean shore (the biblical Brook of Egypt), and Kadesh Barnea, where the Israelites camped during most of their period in the Sinai desert. The date palm is their predominant plant.

Minerals were exploited by Egyptian rulers in antiquity with a cheap labor force composed of slaves and prisoners of war. They extracted turquoise and perhaps also copper ore in southern Sinai.

The roads traversing Sinai, which linked Egypt with Mesopotamia and, to a degree, with Arabia, were highly important, at least from the early Bronze Age. Of greatest interest was the so-called Sea Road that kept close to the northern shore. It was paralleled in the south by the Way of Shur, running from the Nile Valley to the Negeb border and continuing through Beersheba to ascend to Jerusalem and northern Israel. The Patriarchs may have descended to Egypt along this highway. A thoroughfare from south to north served ancient merchants, such as the Nabateans, in transporting oriental luxury goods to the Mediterranean basin.

G. TRANSJORDAN.

Extending more than 250 miles (400 km) from south to north, most parts of Transjordan show a similar topography: they rise over the rift valley with sheer cliffs and slant from this high edge eastward; only the Bashan is an exception to this rule. Closer examination, however, reveals differences between the four provinces: Edom, Moab and Ammon, Gilead, and Golan-Bashan.

Edom, from the Zered (Wadi Hasi) watercourse to the Red Sea in the south, towers over the Arabah Valley. Most of its rocks are either dark to reddish crystalline granites, porphyries, etc., chiseled by abrasion into crenelated crests, or bulky table mounts, towers, or pyramids of flaming red, violet, or orange sandstone. Their red color, *adom* in Hebrew, gave the province its name. Southern Edom is highest, with peaks exceeding 5,000 ft. (1,500 m) above sea level. In central Edom faults multiply, creating gorges, rockwalls, etc. Here, at Petra, capital of the ancient Nabatean kingdom, artists hollowed out of the sheet walls sanctuaries of enormous size ornamented with sculptured columns, portals, statues, and inscriptions.

The northern section has a mosaic of rocks. Beside the granites there are also limestone, chalk, and patches of black basalt. One peak is over 5,180 ft. (1,600 m) high, but the average is lower. The climate is not as arid as farther south, with annual precipitation coming to 12–16 in. (300–400 mm), sometimes even in the form of snow. This made farming feasible in places and promoted the growth of natural forest, brush, or scrub. The vegetation was, however, progressively destroyed up to World War I when the Turks used wood instead of coal for the engines of the Hejaz railroad.

Moab and Ammon, east of the Dead Sea and the

The Jordan Valley with the mountains of Moab in the background.

lower Jordan Valley, between the Zered and Jabbok watercourses, constitute a flat plateau slanting eastward for about 19–25 miles (30–40 km). Highest is the southwest corner, up to 5,940 ft. (1,626 m) above the Dead Sea. Most of the rock is whitish chalk, but there are small patches of black basalt and some sandstone on the edges of deep gorges. Deep canyons like those of the Arnon cut southern Moab into easily defensible blocs, and the Romans built their *limes arabicus* to link these blocs.

The Moab plateau, higher than the Judean Hills to the west, receives a rather reliable precipitation enabling rain farming. The Book of Ruth describes Naomi and her family migrating from Bethlehem to Moab which was less hit by drought.

The town of Heshbon was in flatter, less-dissected northern Moab. It was later replaced by Medaba, northwest of which Mount Nebo juts out from the plateau, a credible background to the biblical tale of Moses viewing the Promised Land without being allowed to enter it (Deut 32:49–52).

No clear boundary is perceptible between Moab and Ammon, the latter lying farther northeast. Ammon is traversed by the wide arch of the Jabbok River (Wadi Zerqa) that carries water perennially in most of its length. It first moves eastward, then turns north and finally west where its deep gorge marks the province's northern border. On the upper Jabbok lies the center Rabbah or Rabbath Ammon (later known by the Greek name Philadelphia) which declined to a small village but in the 20th century grew anew as the capital of the Kingdom of Jordan.

Gilead. In landscape, climate, and settlement conditions, Gilead resembles the hill and foothill regions of Cisjordan more than any other part of Transjordan.

Today, the belt of permanent settlement attains a width of 28-43 miles (45-70 km) and it does not seem to have been narrower in biblical times. Southern Gilead has a mountainous topography, its highest elevation reaching 4,092 ft. (1,247 m), but its center and north flatten out and gently slope to the impressive escarpments which dominate the deep Jordan and Jarmuk valleys. Dolomites and chalks prevail and only the northwest and northeast corners have patches of basalt. Rainfall amounts to 24-32 in. (600-800 mm) annually in the south; farther north, the amount is smaller. The relatively ample precipitation provides for many perennial streams which flow west to the Jordan.

Gilead had towns of the tribe of Gad and the half-tribe of Manasseh interspersed among an Ammonite and Amorite population. Elijah came from Gilead, which was first taken from the Kingdom of Israel by the Arameans, then by the Assyrians. In the period of the Second Temple and under Roman rule, the upper Gilead had the important Hellenistic center Gerasa of which magnificent ruins have been admirably preserved. In the Hellenistic and Roman eras, Gerasa, Gadara, and Philadelphia formed, together with Beth Shean and six other cities of Gilead and the Golan, the Decapolis (Ten Cities) federation, nurturing Hellenistic civilization.

Bashan. Bashan has a thick continuous cover of basalt and fertile basalt soil, which made it the granary of the ancient Levant, as well as a pasture for "the fat cows of Bashan" (Ezek 39:18; Amos 4:1). It was covered with the "oaks of Bashan" (Ezek 27:6; Zech 11:2).

Three subregions of the Bashan were: the Golan (Gaulanitis) along the western edge, the Bashan Plateau beyond it, and the Hauran farthest east, bordered by the practically uninhabited region of Trachonitis. In lower Golan, a thick cover of fertile basalt soil adds to the flatness of the surface and made it a primary grain-growing region. Upper Golan has many silent volcanic cones with deep craters, other remnants of geologically recent volcanic activity, and basalt boulders which on many fields impeded farming. The Bashan Plateau gradually rises to 3,000 ft. (900 m) above sea level, with a rainfall of 12-24 in. (300-600 mm) per year. Generally it was adapted to grain farming, but the irregularity of the precipitation meant that bumper crops were often followed by severe drought. The Hauran is more mountainous, its highest peak rising to 5,900 ft. (1,820 m). Abundant rain or snow enabled its intermontane valleys to yield grain or fruit.

The Golan belonged to the territory of the half-tribe of Manasseh. One of its regions was called Argob. King Herod, with Roman aid, took all of the Bashan. He systematically settled there Jews who held fast to their national and religious identity until after the Muslim conquest of the 7th century. Herod's son Philip remained ruler of all the Bashan.

H. PHOENICIA.

This name may be applied to the northwestern section of the Fertile Crescent. In particular, it fits the northern half of the Mediterranean Sea's eastern shore, from Mount Carmel northward to Antiochia Bay.

Thanks to ample winter rains and the fertile soil of the small valleys, a relatively numerous population of independent farmers could maintain itself on farm produce. Without the need of irrigation, they tended grain fields, olive orchards, and vineyards. Pasture of sheep, goats, and cattle supplemented agriculture.

In the second part of the 2nd millennium BC, the Phoenicians commenced overseas trading. They became experts in shipbuilding, felling cedar and cypress trees on the near mountains for their boats.

The coast was indented with pocket beaches, each of which constructed its own port and set up independent realms or kingdoms. These included Ugarit and Arvad in the north, Gebal (Byblos), Berytos, Sidon, Zarephat, Tyre, Achziv, and Acre farther south. In the 1st millennium BC they founded colonies along Europe's and Africa's Mediterranean coasts, of which Carthage (Keret Hadasha, "New City") became the most famous. Repeatedly, they struggled with each other, especially the principal ports of Sidon and Tyre.

The Bible calls the Phoenicians either Sidonians or Tyrians or simply "Canaanites." Hiram, King of Tyre, sent building timber and experts to King David and had an agreement with King Solomon for the supply of building materials and experts for the Temple (I Kgs 5), perhaps also for naval construction on the Red Sea. Several kings of Judah and Israel took Phoenician wives. The name Phoenicia is derived from the Greek name for the murex shell from which the Phoenicians extracted the purple dye, one of their export monopolies. Another major industry was glass-manufacture.

THE MOUNTAINS OF THE HOLY LAND

Mountain of Abarim. God instructed Moses to climb this mountain and see the land he was giving to the Children of Israel (Num 27:12). The Israelites camped "on Mount Abarim close to Mount Nebo" on the Moab border (Num 33:47-48).

Hill of the Amalekites. Situated in the land of Ephraim, where the judge Abdon was buried (Judg 12:15).

Hill country of the Amorites. Mountainous region in Transjordan mentioned by Moses in his speech after the battle against the kings there (Deut 1:7).

Mount Baalah. Hill in the Judean foothills, mentioned in the description of the borders of the tribe of Judah (Josh 15:11).

Mountains of Bashan (Basan, Batanaea). See Transjordan, above.

Mount of Beatitudes. Hill north of the Sea of Galilee, where Jesus delivered the Sermon on the Mount (Matt

Mount Ebal.

Snow-capped Mount Hermon.

5:3–11; Luke 6:20–22). The hill is not named in the text.

Mount Carmel. See Transjordan, above.

Mount Ebal. Steep mountain north of the narrow Nablus valley, 3,048 ft. (940 m) high; Samaria's highest elevation. In the Bible it is "the mountain of the curse," as opposed to Mount Gerizim, "the mountain of the blessing," to its south (Deut 11:29; 27:12–13). Joshua read there Moses' law before the people (Josh 8:34).

Mountains of Ephraim. See Transjordan, above.

Mount Ephron. Hill west of Jerusalem, mentioned in the description of the borders of the tribe of Judah (Josh 15:9).

Mount Esau. See Edom Mountains, Transjordan, above.

Mountain of Gaash. Mountain in the territory of Ephraim in Samaria, north of which Joshua was buried (Josh 24:30; Judg 2:9).

Mount Gerizim. Steep mountain in Samaria, 2,890 ft. (881 m) above sea level, south of the narrow Nablus valley. Deuteronomy 11:29 makes Mount Gerizim the symbol of blessing as opposed to Mount Ebal, the symbol of curse. On the top of the mountain, Jotham related the parable of the trees (Judg 9:7). Later, the Samaritans built their sanctuary on the top of Mount Gerizim to compete with the Jerusalem Temple.

Mountains of Gilead. Mountains in Transjordan, mentioned only once in the Bible, which says that half of the Gilead mountains was allocated to the tribe of Reuben (Deut 3:12).

Mount Gilboa. The steep slopes of this mountain face the Jezreel Valley to the west, the Harod Valley to the north, and the Beth Shean Valley to the east. It is part of Samaria. On Mount Gilboa, King Saul lost his battle against the Philistines and he and his son Jonathan were killed there (I Sam 31:1; II Sam 1:6; I Chr 10:1–8). David cursed the mount in his lamentation: "O mountains of Gilboa, let there be no dew, nor let there be rain upon you" (II Sam 1:21).

Mount Halak (literally "smooth" or "slippery"). The Bible says that the land which Joshua took stretches "from Mount Halak that rises toward Seir, as far as Baal-gad in the Lebanon Valley" (Josh 11:17; 12:7). This hints that its position is in the central or southern Negeb, but not necessarily identical with the mountain now bearing the name.

Mount Heres. Judges 1:35 reports that the Amorites continued to live on Mount Heres, in Aijalon. It is not certain whether the site is identical with the ascent of Heres where Gideon was victorious over the Midianite kings (Judg 8:13).

Mount Hermon. Mountain range on the northern border of Palestine, marking the limit of the conquests of Moses and Joshua on the east of the Jordan, and of the Israelite expansion (Deut 3:8; 4:48; Josh 11:17, etc.; Judg 3:3). The Hermon rises above the valley of Lebanon (Josh 11:17) and above the land of Mizpeh (Josh 11:3–8). The Amorites called it Shenir, while to the Sidonians it was known as Sirion (Deut 3:9), the name by which it is mentioned in the Execration Texts and in the documents of Ugarit.

The name Hermon referred only to the southern part of the Anti-Lebanon. The highest peak rises to about 8,500 ft (2,800 m) above sea level. The mountain range is about 18 miles (29 km) long and is separated from the northern Anti-Lebanon by the deep gorge of the River Barada. It is known in Arabic as Jebel esh-Sheik or Jebel et-Talg ("mountain of snow") because it is snow-covered for most of the year.

Mount Hor. Mountain on the northern border of Edom, on which Aaron died (Num 20:22–29; 33:37–39; Deut 32:50).

Mount Horeb (literally "drought"). Mountain in Sinai. Deuteronomy identifies it with Mount Sinai (Deut 1:6, 4:10, 15; 18:16, etc.; see also I Kgs 8:9; Ps 106:19), while Exodus only calls it "The Mountain". On the various assumptions on the mountain's geographical location see section on Sinai.

Mount Jearim ("woodland mountain"). The name occurs in Joshua (15:10) in the description of the border of the tribe of Judah and refers to a mountain west of Jerusalem.

Lebanon Mountains. Range along the northern border of Palestine, 270 miles (430 km) long and 45 miles (72 km) wide, with peaks rising to a height of 10,000 ft (3,100 m). The tops of the mountains are covered with snow for most of the year (Jer 18:14), hence its name, which in Hebrew means "white."

Lebanon became famous for its cedars, cypresses, and other splendid trees (Judg 9:15). In early historic times its timber was already being exported, especially to Egypt, which had no timber of its own for roofing and ship-building. The cedars of Lebanon were used in the building of the First Temple, for Solomon's palace, and for the Second Temple in Jerusalem (I Kgs 5:6; 7:2, etc.). The Assyrian kings cut down trees in Lebanon for their buildings and palaces and used the tall cedars to make masts for their ships (Ezek 27:5). The area was also noted for its grapes and wine.

Mount Mashhit ("Mount of the Corruption"). A mountain top near Jerusalem where King Josiah destroyed heathen sanctuaries (II Kgs 23:13).

Mountains of Naphtali. All the tribal territory of Naphtali in eastern Galilee was mountainous. Kadesh, one of the cities of refuge, is described as being "in the mountains of Naphtali" (Josh 20:7).

Mount Nebo. Mountain protruding westward from the Land of Moab, facing Jericho. From Nebo God showed Moses the Land of Israel before Moses' death and burial on the mountain (Deut 34). The mountain's exact location is unknown.

Mount of Olives. Mountain east of Jerusalem rising to 2,500 ft. (800 m). Along its slopes lie Bethphage, Bethany, and Gethsemane, and on its west is the traditional site of the Ascension of Jesus. It is also known as Olivet.

Mount Paran. See Negeb.

Mountains of Samaria. See Transjordan.

Mount Seir. Generally an epithet of mountainous Edom, Genesis 14:6 says it was originally inhabited by the Horites. The name was also given to a mountain on the borders of Judah (Josh 15:10).

Mount Senir, Sion, Siryon. Alternative biblical names of Mount Hermon.

Mount Shepher. One of the camping sites of the Israelites on their desert wandering (Num 33:23).

Mount Tabor. One of Israel's most prominent mountains. Although only 1,929 ft. (588 m) above sea level, its rounded form, in southeastern Galilee, rises steeply above the Jezreel Valley and can be seen from a considerable distance. Today it is covered by brush and planted forests; it may have had richer woodlands in the biblical period. The border of the territory allocated to the tribe of Issachar "touched on the Tabor" (Josh 19:22).. Barak and Deborah assembled their troops on Mount Tabor prior to the great battle against Sisera's army (Judg 4). According to Hosea (5:1) it was a place of worship from ancient times. In Christian tradition, Mount Tabor is the site of Jesus' transfiguration (Matt 17:1-9, etc.).

Mount Tabor.

The Gilboa range overlooking the Valley of Jezreel.

Mountain of Temptation. Site where Jesus was tempted by the devil (Luke 4:1-5 and other gospels). Traditionally identified with the Mountain of Quarantal overlooking Jericho. The name Quarantal derives from the 40 days and nights that Jesus fasted in the desert.

Mount Zalmon. Name of two mountains, one in Samaria where Abimelech and his followers burned an enemy tower (Judg 9:48), and the second apparently in the Bashan on which snow falls (Ps 68:14-15).

Mount Zion. See Jerusalem.

THE RIVERS OF THE HOLY LAND

Jordan. The longest river in Palestine, flowing along the geological Syrian-African Rift. The river is formed by the confluence of four streams in the foothills of Mount Hermon. As it descends to the Huleh region it divides into several streams. On its passage southwards it receives numerous tributaries.

HEADSTREAMS

Hermon (Banias). Its spring is at the foot of Mount Hermon at Banias (the Hellenistic Paneas or Caesarea Philippi) northeast of the Huleh Valley. After gathering in a shallow pond it rushes over several waterfalls to its unison with the other headstreams. Its annual flow today averages 122 million cbm.

Dan. Its spring water, gathering in a pond near the ancient town of Dan, is ice-cold even in midsummer, because it is fed by melting snow from the top of Mount Hermon, absorbed in the permeable rock and subterraneously led to the spring. Its annual flow averages 252 million cbm.

Senir (Hazbani). The longest of the headstreams, its origin is on the northwest slope of Mount Hermon, over 30 miles (50 km) north of the Huleh Valley. It flows another 4 miles (6.5 km) to the point where it joins the other headstreams. In contrast with the Hermon and the Dan, most of its water is surface runoff and therefore subjected to sharp seasonal variations. There are also differences between wet and dry years: the annual flow average in the Huleh Valley is 117 million cbm, but a maximum of 252 million cbm has been measured in a rainy year.

Ijon (Ajun). This stream drains the Ijon (Ajun) Valley of Lebanon and descends to the Huleh Valley in a series of waterfalls. At present, much of its water is diverted for irrigation in the Ijun Valley, making its bed in the Huleh Valley frequently dry in summer.

WESTERN TRIBUTARIES

Ammud. This stream, perennial in its lower part, flows from eastern Galilee southwards into the Sea of Galilee.

Harod. From its spring at the northern foot of Mount Gilboa (En Harod) it flows eastwards through the Harod Valley, passes the city of Beth Shean, and reaches the Jordan farther east. The spring is famous as the site where Gideon examined his men for their readiness for battle (Judg 7:1).

Tirzah (Wadi Faria). This long perennial stream has its springs in the area of Tirzah, northeast of Nablus. It flows in a deep gorge southeastwards to enter the Jordan 18 miles (28 km) north of the Dead Sea.

EASTERN TRIBUTARIES

These tributaries of the jordan are much longer and

Two views of the Jordan River: a capricious stream between the Golan heights and Galilee, it broadens as it flows through the plain into a delta before entering the Sea of Galilee.

Nahal Ammud flows in a deep canyon, southwards into the Sea of Galilee.

richer in water than the streams coming from the west.

Jarmuk. This long perennial river comes from Syria and flows to the southwest and west, receiving strong tributaries from the Bashan and the Gilead. To the confluence with the Jordan south of the Sea of Galilee the two rivers bring similar quantities of water. In history, the Jarmuk was repeatedly the border of empires or their spheres of influence.

Jabesh Gilead. One of the perennial streams draining Gilead, this river is, in spite of its name (*jabesh* means "dry"), perennial in most of its length.

Jabbok. One of the country's longest rivers, the flow of its lower half is perennial and strong. Its course is oval, going first to the southeast, then northeast between Amman and Zerqa, then turning to the west, and finally to the southwest, to shed into the Jordan 25 miles (40 km) north of the Dead Sea. Its deeply incised gorge marked the border between the Land of Ammon and Gilead.

Nimrin, Abu Aruba. Perennial streams draining northern Moab.

Of the Jordan headstreams and tributaries, only the Jabbok is mentioned in the Bible (Gen 32:22; Num 21:24; Deut 2:37; 3:16; Josh 12:2, 13:22). The names "Hermon" and "Senir" refer only to the mountains of that name, and "Dan" and "Ijon" to towns.

STREAMS SHEDDING INTO THE DEAD SEA.

The numerous stream courses reaching the Dead Sea from the Wilderness of Judah in the west are all ephemeral and only rarely carry water, although their precipitously incised gorges, the impressive steps of former waterfalls, and the small deltas at their estuaries testify to an incomparably stronger flow in the recent geologic past. The streams descending from central and southern Moab and from Edom are much longer and also much richer in water.

Kidron. This mostly dry stream course separates Jerusalem's Temple Mount from Mount Scopus and the Mount of Olives. South of the city it turns eastwards and runs through a deep gorge. It reaches the Dead Sea 5 miles (8 km) south of Qumran. The Bible frequently mentions the Kidron, repeatedly relating that the remnants of demolished heathen sanctuaries were dumped into its bed (I Kgs 15:13; II Kgs 23:4). Jesus crossed it on his way to Gethsemane (John 18:1).

Nahal David, Nahal Arugot (*Nahal* means "brook" or "wadi"). Two streams reaching the Dead Sea at En Gedi. The brief course of the former, named after David who sought refuge at En Gedi from King Saul's persecutions (I Sam 24:1), originates in the strong spring of En David. The latter is longer and the lowest section of its bed has been turned into fruit plantations at En Gedi.

Nahal Hever. In the precipitous wall rising over its gorge the cave was discovered where Bar Kokhba, the 2nd century Jewish leader, and his fighters held out under Roman siege.

Nahal Ben Jair, Nahal Masada. Their gorges contribute to isolate the Masada rock, defended by the last

The Jarmuk flows from the north to the southwest and west receiving tributaries from the Bashan and the Gilead regions.

fighters holding out under Roman siege under Eleazar ben Jair until AD 73.

Arnon (Wadi Mujib). Largest of the streams shedding into the Dead Sea from the Moab plateau in the east. Near its mouth, 22 miles (35 km) south of the Dead Sea's northern end, it flows into a narrow gorge. The Israelites had to cross the Arnon when fighting their way through Moab (Num 21:13; Deut 2:24). The river marked borders between the Moabites and the tribe of Reuben (Josh 13:16).

Zered (Wadi Hasa). Long, perennial river reaching the southeast corner of the Dead Sea from the east. Its deep gorge marked the border between Edom and southern Moab. It was crossed by the Israelites fighting their way through Edom and Moab (Num 21; Deut 2). Since the southern basin of the Dead Sea has dried out in the second half of the 20th century, the Zered estuary is no longer recognizable.

STREAMS SHEDDING INTO THE MEDITER ·RANEAN .

Kishon. Coming from south of Mount Gilboa, this river flows northwestwards, draining the Jezreel (Esdraelon) Valley and entering the Haifa Bay area through a pass between Mount Carmel and the Tivon Hills of Lower Galilee. The Kishon is mentioned as the scene of the battle of Deborah and Barak against the Canaanites under Sisera (Judg 4), and of the killing of the Baal priests by the prophet Elijah (I Kgs 18:40).

Jarkon (the biblical Me-jarkon). This important stream, flowing perennially from the strong spring of Rosh ha-Ayin (Antipatris), is only once mentioned in the Bible, in the description of the borders of the tribe of Dan (Josh 19:46). Its own course is short and it sheds into the sea 6 miles (10 km) north of Jaffa Hill in today's Tel-Aviv, but its many, mostly ephemeral, tributaries drain a large part of southern Samaria and northern Judea.

Among them is **Nahal Kanah** (the brook Kanah), which marks parts of the border between the tribes of Ephraim and Manasseh (Josh 16:8; 17:9). Also well

The Kishon, a trickle in summer, swells with the winter rains.

known are **Nahal Aijalon** and **Nahal Shiloh**.

Of the numerous other streams flowing through the Coastal Plain to the Mediterranean Sea, none is mentioned as such in the Bible.

VALLEYS AND LOWLANDS OF THE HOLY LAND

Achor Valley. A desert side valley near Jericho where Joshua had Achan and his family punished by stoning after the latter had taken forbidden booty (Josh 7:24-26). The name means "Valley of Trouble." Hosea prophesies "I shall [make] the Valley of Achor into an opening of hope" (Hos 2:15).

Aijalon Valley. Large fertile valley in the Judean Foothills, mentioned in Joshua's prayer during his battle against the Amorite kings: "Sun stand still in Gibeon and Moon in the Valley of Aijalon" (Josh 10:12).

Valley of Baca. A symbolic name, "Valley of Weeping" (Ps 84:6), it cannot be identified geographically, but was near Jerusalem.

Valley of Beraca (i.e., "Valley of Benediction"). In the Tekoa Desert of southern Judea, where King Jehoshaphat was victorious over Moabites, Ammonites, and Edomites (II Chr 20:26).

Beth Shean Valley. The Bible does not expressly mention the valley as such in the Jordan Rift south of the Sea of Galilee, but does refer to "[the town of] Beth Shean and its daughters" which were allocated to the tribe of Manasseh (e.g., Josh 17:11; Judg 1:27; I Kgs 4:12; I Chr 7:29).

Dothan Valley. A fairly large fertile valley in northern Samaria. Joseph was sent there to his brothers pasturing flocks in the valley, who put him into a well-hole and later sold him to Ishmaelites (Gen 37). At a battle around the Dothan Valley between Aramites and Israelites, the prophet Elisha implored God to blind the enemy (II Kgs 6).

Valley of Elah ("The Terebinth Valley"). In the southern Judean foothills. The Bible describes it as the site of the battle between the Israelites and the Philistines, which was decided by young David killing Goliath (I Sam 17).

Valley of Harashim (i.e., craftsmen). Valley inhabited by a Kenazite family of artisans (I Chr 4:14). It may be in the northern Arabah.

Valley of Hinnom (Gehinnom or Gehenna). Valley of the son of Hinnom adjoining Jerusalem which was the center of Moloch worship (II Kgs 23:10). Jeremiah, condemning the barbarous rites practiced there, foretold that it would be the Valley of Slaughter (Jer 7:31; 19:5-6).

Valley of Jezreel (Esdraelon). Largest of the interior valleys of the Land of Israel, between Galilee in the north, Mount Carmel and the Hills of Samaria to the south, and Mount Gilboa to the southeast. It has mostly heavy, black, and fertile soil. Parts of it were swampy in

Beth Shean Valley.

The Valley of Jezreel (Esdraelon).

the past. The name Jezreel means "God will sow." The tribes of Manasseh and Ephraim complained to Joshua of the danger from the Canaanites "possessing iron chariots who live in the Valley of Jezreel" (Josh 17:16). Some of the valley was allocated to the tribe of Issachar (Josh 19:18), other parts to Zebulun and Manasseh. The valley was the scene of the great battle of Deborah and Barak against the Canaanites under Sisera (Judg 4). "All the Midianites and the Amalekites and the people of the East" camped there (Judg 6:33) and Gideon vanquished them. Hosea prophesies "On that day, I will break Israel's bow in the Valley of Jezreel" (Hos 1:5), but also speaks of the mercy of God who will give "corn and new wine and olive oil in Jezreel." In Christian tradition it is also "the Valley of Armageddon" (derived from the city of Megiddo), the site of mankind's last battle.

Valley of Rephaim ("Giants' Valley"). Valley which extends from Jerusalem to the southwest. The border fixed by Joshua for the tribe of Judah "went down over the Valley of the Son of Hinnom which is at the north end of the Rephaim valley" (Josh 18:16). The Philistines ascended to Jerusalm and David defeated them twice in the Rephaim Valley (II Sam 5:18; 22). The Philistines encamped in the lower Rephaim valley near Adullam (II Sam 23:13; I Chr 11:15) from where David sent men to bring him water from Bethlehem.

Sharon Valley. The name is used both for a region where families of the tribe of Gad lived east of the Jordan (I Chr 5:16), and for the section of the Coastal Plain between Mount Carmel and the Jarkon River. The cattle that grazed in the Sharon are mentioned in I Chronicles 27:29. Famous is the description of the woman's beauty: "I am the rose of Sharon" (Song 2:1).

Isaiah prophesied: "The beauty of the Sharon will be like the Arabah [dry steppe]" (33:9), and "The Sharon will be a pasture of sheep" (65:10).

Valley of Shaveh. Valley near the Dead Sea, where Abraham met the king of Sodom (Gen 14:17).

Valley of Siddim ("Valley of Lime") near the Dead Sea, where Abraham vanquished Chedarlaomer and other kings (Gen 14:3, 8).

Sorek Valley. Stream gorge in the Judean Hills, widening in the foothills and shedding into the Mediterranean Sea. The Bible mentions Sorek only once, as the place where Samson loved Delilah (Judg 16:4).

THE DESERTS OF THE HOLY LAND

Wilderness of Beersheba. Mentioned in Genesis 21:14 as a place where Hagar, banned from Abraham's home, wandered, apparently quite far to the south or southeast of the town, in southern Israel.

Wilderness of Edom. The kings Jehoram of Israel and Jehoshaphat of Judah planned their marching route against the Moabite king Mesha through this desert (II Kgs 3:8).

Wilderness of En Gedi. When Saul pursued David, he was told that David was in this desert (I Sam 24:1). The following passages make clear that David hid in one of the caves found in the wild ravines, west of the oasis, on the banks of the Dead Sea.

Wilderness of Etham. Summarizing Israel's exodus from Egypt, Numbers 33:8 reports that they "crossed the sea... and marched three days in the Etham Desert," which is presumably in northwestern Sinai.

Wilderness of Gibeon. Joab and Abishai pursued

View in the Judean Desert.

The Wilderness of Zin.

Abner, who had killed Asahel, "through the Gibeon Desert" (II Sam 2:24), north of Jerusalem.

Wilderness of Jeruel. Stretch of desert in the wilderness of Judah (II Chr 20:16).

Wilderness of Judah. In the two references (Judg 1:16; Ps 63:1) it is not clear whether the entire region called today the "Judean Desert" is meant or only a part of it. According to Judges it is in the Negeb near Arad.

Wilderness of Kadesh. According to Psalms 29:8, God's voice "shakes the Wilderness of Kadesh" in the Sinai desert.

Wilderness of Kedemoth. After the Israelites reached Transjordan in their journey from Egypt, God said: "I sent angels from the wilderness of Kedemoth to Sihon, the king of Heshbon, with words of peace..." (Deut 2:26).

Wilderness of the Land of Egypt. The prophet Ezekiel says that God judged Israel in this wilderness (Ezek 20:36).

Wilderness of Maon. When Saul pursued David he found him hiding "in the wilderness of Maon, in the Arabah on the south of Jeshimon" (I Sam 23:24–25), i.e., in southern Israel.

Wilderness of Moab. At the end of their desert wanderings, Moses said "We turned and went in the direction of the wilderness of Moab" (Deut 2:8), in Transjordan.

Wilderness of Paran. The biblical Paran Desert was not identical with the area now called the Paran Region of the southern Negeb (see Negeb), but must be sought deeper in the Sinai Peninsula. Hagar's son Ishmael lived "in the wilderness of Paran" (Gen 21:21). Numbers 10:12 reports that on their Sinai wanderings the Israelites followed the cloud which "settled down on the

wilderness of Paran." Afterwards, the people traveled "from Hazeroth and camped in the wilderness of Paran" (Num 12:16). Moses sent the spies from the Paran Desert (Num 13:3) and they returned there (Num 13:26).

Wilderness of Shur. After crossing the Red Sea, Moses led Israel into the Wilderness of Shur, which is presumably located in northwestern Sinai (Ex 15:22).

Wilderness of Sin. Desert in the western Sinai Peninsula. Six weeks after leaving Egypt, the Children of Israel reached the Wilderness of Sin which is between Elim and Sinai (Ex 16:1). Ezekiel's prophecy on Egypt mentions Sin which in his time must have been part of that country (Ezek 30:15–16).

Wilderness of Sinai. The biblical term "Wilderness of Sinai" does not seem to include the entire peninsula but apparently only a stretch close to Mount Sinai. According to Exodus 19:1–2, the Children of Israel reached Sinai "on the third new moon" after leaving Egypt. This desert is mentioned most frequently in the first chapter of Numbers, in connection with the Israelite wandering.

Wilderness of Tekoa. Stretch of the upper Wilderness of Judah where King Jehoshaphat battled against the armies of the Moabites and Ammonites (II Chr 20:20).

Wilderness of Zin. Desert near Kadesh Barnea, on the border of the Land of Israel (Num 34:3). The spies set out to explore the Promised Land from the Zin wilderness (Num 13:21), and it was the site of the death and burial of Miriam (Num 20:1).

Wilderness of Ziph. Mentioned in the story of David hiding from the pursuing Saul (I Sam 23:14–15; 26:2), the location is hard to identify, but it must be somewhere in the Judean Desert.

II. 5 Places in the Bible

Abdon. Town belonging to the Gershon family of Levites situated within the territory of the tribe of Asher (Josh 21:30). It was located some four miles (six km) east of Achzib.

Abel Beth Maachah (Abel of Beth Maachah, also called Abel Maim or Abel). The rebel Sheba, son of Bichri, fled to this fortified town in the territory of Naphtali, and Joab led David's men in a siege of the town (II Sam 20:1-2,7,13-15). Before the fall of the Kingdom of Israel, its citizens were deported to Assyria.

Abel Meholah. Town in the Jordan Valley, near Beth Shean (Beisan). It was the hometown of the husband of Saul's daughter, Merab (II Sam 21:8), and of the prophet Elisha (I Kgs 19:16,19).

Abronah ("passage" or "place opposite"). Site of one of the Israelite camps en route from Egypt to Canaan, between Jotbathah and Ezion Geber (Num 33:1,34-35).

Acco (Acre). Canaanite-Phoenician city mentioned by this name only once in the Bible in connection with the tribe of Asher (Judg 1:31-32). It appears in the Egyptian Execration Texts of the 19th century BC. Ancient Acco is one mile (1.6 km) east of the location of Acre in post-biblical times. Acco reached the peak of its development during the 9th-7th centuries BC when it was a center for the metal industry. In classical sources, it is mentioned in connection with the invention of glass-blowing. Known as Akku, it was conquered by King Sennacherib of Assyria in 701 BC. It seems to have been an autonomous Phoenician harbor in the Persian period. In the Hellenistic period, Acco was a cosmopolitan center called Ptolemais. By the time Paul landed there upon conclusion of his third missionary journey, it contained a Christian church (Acts 21:7).

Achor, Valley of ("Valley of Trouble"). Valley on the northern border of the tribe of Judah in the vicinity of Jericho (Josh 15:7). At this place Achan and the members of his household were executed by stoning for taking booty captured in Jericho from the treasury of the house of the Lord (Josh 7:1,24-26). Hosea (2:15) and Isaiah (65:10) cite it as a symbol of improved conditions in the future.

Achshaph. Seat of a Canaanite king who answered the call of Jabin, king of Hazor, to join a coalition to fight the Israelites (Josh 11:1-5). The king of Achshaph was killed in the battle and the city was captured by Joshua (Josh 11:1; 12:20), who allotted it to the tribe of Asher (Josh 19:24-25). Achshaph is believed to have been southeast of Acco.

Achzib.

1) Town located in the territory of the tribe of Judah (Josh 15:44). The prophet Micah foretold its destruction (1:13-15).

2) Canaanite city on the Mediterranean coast, along the borders of the tribe of Asher (Josh 19:29). Joshua did not conquer the town and the Asherites settled alongside the existing inhabitants (Judg 1:31-32).

Achzib is identified with ez-Zib, 11 miles (18 km) north of Acco (Acre). Archaeologists have discovered remains of the fortification of the town walls dating from as early as 2000 BC, and Phoenician tombs.

Adam. City on the Jordan "near Zaretan," identified

The modern harbor of Acco.

View of the Mediterranean coast at Achzib.

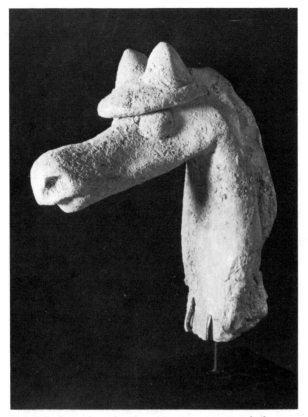

Head of a horse from the Phoenician cemetery at Achzib.

with Tell ed-Damiyeh today. Here in the invasion of Canaan the waters "failed and were cut off," allowing the Israelites to cross the river and reach Jericho (Josh 3:16).

Admah. One of five Canaanite "Cities of the Plain" in the Valley of Siddim (Gen 10:19). Its ruler, Shinab, in a coalition with the kings of Sodom, Gomorrah, Zeboiim, and Bela (or Zoar), was defeated by four kings from the east (Gen 14:8-11). Admah and its allies (except Bela) were later destroyed (Deut 29:23).

Adoraim. City in Judah, located in the modern village of Dura, southwest of Hebron. Rehoboam fortified the city and also used it to store food (II Chr 11:5-9,11).

Adramyttium (today Edremit). Port on the Aegean Sea on the northwest coast of Turkey, north of Pergamos. While a prisoner in the custody of the centurion Julius, Paul embarked at Caesarea on a ship from Adramyttium and sailed to Myra, on his way to Rome (Acts 27:1-2).

Adriatic Sea (known as the Sea of Adrias). An arm of the Mediterranean Sea between Italy and the Balkan Peninsula. Before being shipwrecked on the island of Malta, Paul spent several stormy days on the Adriatic Sea en route to Rome (Acts 27:27).

Adullam. Ancient city on the coastal plain; first mentioned as site of Judah's marriage to the daughter of Shua, a Canaanite (Gen 38:1-2). It was one of the 14 kingdoms conquered by Joshua (Josh 12:7,15) and was assigned to the tribe of Judah. When David fled from Saul he hid in one of the many caves in the region after escaping from Achish, the Philistine king of Gath (I Sam 22:1-5). After becoming king, David continued to use that cave as his headquarters to fight the Philistines. King Rehoboam fortified Adullam for the defense of Judah (II Chr 11:5-12). During the reign of Hezekiah, it was conquered by Sennacherib's army (II Kgs 18:13). The exiles returning from Babylon resettled the city (Neh 11:30).

Adummin, Ascent of. Steep pass between Jericho and Jerusalem connecting the Jordan Valley with the Judean mountains. It served as the boundary between the territories of the tribes of Judah and Benjamin (Josh 15:7; 18:17).

Aenon. Site near Salim where John baptized on the River Jordan (John 3:23). Its exact location is uncertain but Eusebius (4th century) reports that it was situated about 6 miles (10 km) south of Beth Shean in the Beth Shean valley. The Madeba map shows Aenon on the eastern bank of the Jordan, opposite Bethabara. Another theory places it close to Shechem (Nablus).

Ahlab. Canaanite city in the territory belonging to the tribe of Asher (II Sam 8:17). The tribe was unable to drive out its inhabitants at the time the Israelites were settling the land. It is identified with a site some 4 miles (6.5 km) northeast of Tyre.

Ai ("the ruin"). Canaanite town east of Bethel. Shortly after coming to Canaan, Abraham pitched his tent there; he revisited the place after his journey to Egypt (Gen 12:8; 13:3). Following the fall of Jericho during the conquest of Canaan, Joshua sent a small force to attack Ai, having been told by his spies that it was sparsely inhabited. The Israelites sustained a total, demoralizing defeat. When Joshua appealed to God, he was told that this was retribution for Achan's sin (Josh 7:1-12). As soon as the latter was brought to justice, Joshua attacked Ai again and reduced it to "a heap forever, a desolation to this day" (Josh 8:1-29). Men of Ai and Bethel were among the exiles returning from Babylon with Zerubbabel (Ezra 2:1-2,28; Neh 7:32). Most scholars identify Ai with et-Tell, 1 mile (1.6 km) southwest of Bethel, north of Jerusalem. Excavations have revealed a large settlement from the Early Bronze Age around 3000 BC. The place was destroyed by the 24th century BC and rebuilt in the 13th-12th centuries BC. Biblical Ai was probably an Iron Age village which was finally abandoned in the 11th century BC. See also II.9, Digging up the Bible: Ai.

Aijalon. An important valley and city of the same name. The valley ran from the coastal plain through the central mountain range to the northwest of Jerusalem. It was in the Aijalon valley that Joshua commanded the sun and the moon to stand still while he was fighting the confederation of five Amorite kings (Josh 10: 5-12). Later the city of Aijalon was assigned to the tribe of Dan and it eventually became a Levitical

The valley of Aijalon

town. The Danites were never able to control the valley
fully and they had to rely on help from the tribe of
Ephraim in order to defeat the Amorites (Judg 1:34–35).
When King Saul defeated the Philistines at Michmash,
his son Jonathan pursued them as far as Aijalon. Under
the rule of David Aijalon became a city of refuge and it
was later given to the tribe of Benjamin. During the
reign of Ahaz it was seized by the Philistines (II Chr
28:18). The minor judge Elon was buried in another
Aijalon (Judg 12:12), whose location is unknown but
may have been in the territory of Zebulun.

Ain. One of the southernmost cities given to the tribe
of Judah. However, the city was later assigned to
Simeonites because Judah could not cope with all the
territory it had received (Josh 19:7–9). Later Ain was
handed over to the Levites.

Akrabbim, Ascent of ("Scorpion Pass"). Pass between
the Dead Sea and the Wilderness of Zin that formed
one of the southern boundaries of Canaan (Num
34:1–4) as well as of the tribe of Judah.

Alexandria. The capital of Egypt during the Hellenistic and Roman periods. Situated on the Nile Delta, the
city was founded by Alexander the Great in 332 BC.
Alexandria soon grew wealthy on trade from India and
Arabia. A large Jewish community lived in Alexandria.
Their outstanding cultural achievement was the translation of the Hebrew Bible into Greek, known as the
Septuagint, in the 3rd century BC. A considerable
community of Alexandrian Jews lived in Jerusalem;
some of them argued with Stephen, accusing him of
blasphemy (Acts 6:9).

Allon Bachuth ("oak" or "terebinth of weeping").
Tree under which Rebekah's nurse, Deborah, was buried (Gen 35:8).

Amana. Mountain mentioned in the Song of Solomon
along with the peaks of Hermon and Senir; located in
the Anti-Lebanon Range (Song 4:8).

*Pillar erected at Alexandria on the highest spot of the city by the
Roman prefect Pompey, c.AD 300.*

Ammah ("cubit"). A hill in the territory of Benjamin.
Its exact location is not known but it is thought to lie
between Gibeon and the descent into the Jordan Val-
ley. Here Joab and Abishai halted their pursuit of
Abner and his forces, after Abner asked for a truce (II
Sam 2:24–30).

Ammon. See I, 4: Regions (Transjordan).

Amphipolis. Town in Macedonia near the Aegean Sea
where Paul and Silas stayed briefly on their way from
Philippi to Thessalonica (Acts 17:1).

Anab. A settlement south of Hebron inhabited by the
Anakim until they were expelled by Joshua. The town
was given to the tribe of Judah (Josh 11:21; 15:50).

Anathoth. A Levitical city belonging to Benjamin in
the Judean Hills northeast of Jerusalem. Anathoth was
the home of Abiezer and Jehu, two of David's "mighty
men." Solomon banished the chief priest Abiathar to
the town (I Kgs 2:26) and later it was devastated by the
Assyrian army on its way to Jerusalem. The town was
also the birthplace of Jeremiah and residents threatened his life once he began to prophesy. The prophet
responded by predicting an ill fate for Anathoth (Jer
11:21–23) although he kept some ties there (Jer
32:7–15). When Zerubbabel led the return of the Jews
from Babylon he was joined by 128 men from Ana-

Remains of a frieze of a Greek temple at Antioch of Pisidia.

A statue of Tyche, goddess of Antioch, with the river Orontes at her feet.

thoth. The town's name is preserved in the modern Arab village of Anata three miles (five km) north of Jerúsalem.

Antioch.

1) Antioch of Pisidia (so-called to distinguish it from other cities with the same name). A large city located in central Asia Minor near the village of Yalvac in modern Turkey. It lay on the important trade route between Ephesus and Cilicia. Later it became part of the Roman province of Galatia. Paul and Barnabas visited the city twice on their missionary journeys to preach to its large Jewish community. After Paul spoke in the synagogue his message aroused great interest throughout the whole city (Acts 13:14-44), awakening the anger of some Jewish leaders who expelled the apostles and even pursued them to Lystra. In the Second Epistle to Timothy, Paul refers to his persecution in Antioch (II Tim 3:11).

2) Important ancient city on the Orontes River, not far from the Mediterranean Sea; capital of the province of Syria. In the history of Christianity Antioch occupies a distinguished place. While its large Jewish community offered the early church an important mission field, it was also here that the growth of Gentile Christianity began. It is mentioned in connection with Nicolas, a convert to Judaism, who later became a follower of Jesus and was in Jerusalem at the time of Stephen's death (Acts 6:5). After the persecution that followed Stephen's martyrdom some of the disciples from Jerusalem came to Antioch where they con-

tinued to preach to their fellow Jews (Acts 11:19). They also began to spread their new faith among the "Hellenists" (Greeks interested in Judaism). When the church leadership in Jerusalem learnt that many people were becoming believers in Jesus they dispatched Barnabas to the city to teach the new converts. Later he brought Paul from Tarsus to help in the ministry. The believers at Antioch responded generously by helping their brethren in Jerusalem during a famine (Acts 11:27-30). Antioch was the starting point for all three of Paul's missionary journeys. It is also the place where the followers of Jesus were first called "Christians" (Acts 11:26).

Antipatris. See Aphek (1).

Aphek.

1) A royal Canaanite city located on the ancient Via Maris trade route in the plain of Sharon. The king of Aphek was one of the 31 rulers defeated by Joshua. When Herod the Great came to power he built a new city on the site, naming it Antipatris after his father; this became the center of a prosperous agricultural district. Paul spent the night there when he was being

Aerial view of Apollonia, in Macedonia; known as Apollonia Mygdonis.

Alabaster figurine from South Arabia.

escorted from Jerusalem to Caesarea (Acts 23:31).

2) City east of the Sea of Galilee where a small Israelite force under King Ahab killed 100,000 Arameans led by Ben-Hadad in a bloody one-day battle (I Kgs 20:26–30). The 27,000 surviving Arameans died when a wall in Aphek fell on them. Their king Ben-Hadad was taken prisoner after he was found hiding inside the city. Ahab spared his life and entered into a treaty with the Syrian monarch.

Apollonia. A city named after the Greek sun-god Apollo in the Mygdonia district of Macedonia; known as Apollonia Mygdonis to distinguish it from the many other cities named after Apollo. Paul and Silas passed through the town on their journey to Thessalonica, but do not have appeared to have stayed there (Acts 17:1).

Ar (Ar Moab). A region in northern Moab along the south banks of the Arnon river (Num 21:15,28). At times the name was used as a synonym for the entire land of Moab. The prophet Isaiah foretold its ruin (15:1).

Arabah. Narrow desert valley that extends from the Dead Sea to the Gulf of Elath at the Red Sea (Deut 3:17),

part of the Great Rift Valley stretching from Syria to East Africa. In the Bible the Arabah is sometimes called the "plain" (II Sam 2:29). The prophets used the word Arabah to refer to any "desert" or "steppe" (Jer 17:6) or to the entire Jordan Valley south of the Sea of Galilee (II Sam 4:7). The Sea of the Arabah or the Salt Sea is sometimes used by the Bible to indicate the Dead Sea (Deut 3:17; II Kgs 4:25).

Arabia. A large peninsular desert between Africa and Asia. Surrounded by the Indian Ocean and the Red Sea, Arabia is arid with scattered oases throughout the interior. The peninsula was once on the major trade routes of the ancient world. Its inhabitants, the Arabs, who were nomadic tent dwellers, are mentioned frequently in the Bible. The Israelite monarchy maintained close ties with the Arabs especially from the reign of Solomon. Arabia supplied Israel with gold and silver (II Chr 9:14) as well as spices and precious stones (Ezek 27:22). According to the New Testament, Jews from Arabia were in Jerusalem on Pentecost when Peter preached his first sermon (Acts 2:11). Paul also "went away" to Arabia after his conversion (Gal 1:17).

Arad. City in the northeast Negeb which controlled the roads to Edom and Elath. Arad joined in the attack on the Israelites as they approached Canaan. The Israelites responded by destroying the city and renaming it Hormah (Num 21:1–3). The site was later occupied by the Kenites and assigned to the tribe of Judah. During the period of the united monarchy Arad was conquered on several occasions.

Areopagus. The "hill of Ares" (Mars Hill), northwest of the Acropolis in Athens. The area was a meeting place of the ancient council of the city. The court concerned itself with political and educational affairs and at times it heard cases dealing with capital crime. On a visit to Athens Paul was taken to the Areopagus (Acts 17:16) where he urged Athenians to turn from idols and spoke of the resurrection of Jesus. The audience mocked him although a few in the crowd believed Paul's message.

Argob. Region of Bashan that was in the kingdom of Og. Conquered by the Israelites before they crossed the Jordan, it had 60 fortified cities (Deut.3:12-14). The area was conquered by Jair, son of Manasseh, who renamed it Havoth Jair (i.e., the "villages of Jair") after himself. Later King Solomon divided the area into two districts, with their governor residing at Ramoth Gilead (I Kgs 4:13).

Ariel ("lion of God"). Name given to Jerusalem by Isaiah (29:1).

Armageddon. Site in the Jezreel Valley where the final confrontation between good and evil will take place (Rev 16:14-16). In New Testament eschatology, demonic spirits will entice the "kings of the earth" into the valley where they will meet their destruction (Rev 16:14-16). The name is derived from the Hebrew Har (i.e., mount) Megiddon, which is another name for Megiddo (Zech 12:11). Strategically located on the trade route that ran from Egypt to Damascus, Megiddo was the scene of numerous battles.

Aroer.

1) An Amorite city on the edge of the valley of the Arnon (Deut 4:48). It was first conquered by the tribe of Reuben (Josh 13:16) but later fortified by the Gadites. Hazael king of Aram captured the city from the Kingdom of Israel (II Kgs 10:32-33), but by the time of Jeremiah, it was in the hands of the Moabites.

2) A settlement in Gilead near the Ammonite city of Rabbah (Josh 13:25). Assigned to the territory of Gad, it is possibly the city mentioned in Jephthah's conquest of the Ammonites which extended from "Aroer to Minnith" (Judg 11:33).

Arpad. A city in northern Syria, north of Aleppo, captured on several occasions by the Assyrians (Is 36:19; Jer 49:23). It is always mentioned together with the larger and more important city of Hammath.

Arvad, Arvadites. A Phoenician city on the island of Ruad off the coast of Syria. Its inhabitants, known for their skill as sailors and warriors, are listed in the genealogy of Noah as the sons of Canaan (Gen 10:1).

Ashan. A town in the southern foothills of Judah that was initially assigned to the tribe of Judah, later given to the Simeonites (Josh 19:1,7), and afterwards passed to a family of Levites (I Chr 6:54). In a corresponding list of Levitical cities (Josh 21:16) it is called Ain.

Ashdod. One of the five principal cities of the Philistines, located 3 miles (5 km) inland from the Mediter-

Aerial view of Megiddo (Armageddon).

ranean on the southern coastal plain. At the time of the Israelite conquest it was inhabited by the Anakim (Giants) who prevented it from being occupied by the tribe of Judah (Josh 15:20). After the Philistines defeated the Israelites at Ebenezer, they captured the Ark of the Covenant and carried it to Ashdod, where they placed it in a temple dedicated to their god Dagon. Shortly thereafter the stone image of the Philistine idol fell on its face and was smashed in the presence of the Ark. After a plague the terrified residents of Ashdod sent the Ark back to the Israelites (I Sam 5:1-12). Ashdod was finally subdued and dismantled by King Uzziah of Judah, but his grandson King Ahaz lost the city to the Philistines (II Chr 28:18). Soon afterwards Ashdod was seized by the Assyrians and became one of their provincial capitals. The prophet Amos predicted calamity for the city (Amos 1:8) while other prophets mention its desolate condition (Jer 25:20; Zech 9:6). Some of the Jews who returned from Babylon married women from Ashdod, much to the anger of Nehemiah (Neh 13:23). Known as Azotus during the Hellenistic period, it was sacked by the Maccabean leaders (I Macc 5:68). In New Testament times the city prospered and was given by Augustus to his sister Salome. At that time it had a mixed population of Jews and Gentiles. Philip the Evangelist passed through Ashdod (Azotus) while on a preaching journey (Acts 8:40).

Ashkelon (Ascalon). One of the five principal cities of the Philistines and one of the oldest inhabited settlements in the Holy Land. Situated along the southern coastal plain, Ashkelon was assigned to Judah. It was captured by the Israelites (Judg 1:18–19) but not long afterwards it was conquered by the Philistines and was raided by Samson. In the 8th century BC it came under Assyrian rule. During Nebuchadnezzar's campaigns many of the residents of Ashkelon were deported to Babylon. Tyre took control of the city as Babylon's power waned. Herod the Great was born in Ashkelon, and during the New Testament times the city flourished and became known as a center of scholarship.

Ashkenaz. Kingdom associated with Ararat and Minni (Jer 51:27).

Ashtaroth. Capital city of Og, king of Bashan (Deut 1:4). The name is derived from a plural form of "Ashtoreth," the Canaanite fertility goddess. After the Israelites took possession of the land it was given to Machir the son of Manasseh. It later became a Levitical city, when it was known as Be-Eshterah (Josh 21:27).

Asia. In the New Testament, a Roman province; later Asia Minor; at that time, one of the richest provinces of the Roman Empire. It was home to a large number of Jews, and the New Testament mentions that some of these Jews visited Jerusalem for Pentecost (Acts 2:9). There were also Asian Jews in Jerusalem's Synagogue of the Freedmen who disputed with Stephen (Acts 6:9). Asia was the scene of much of Paul's proselytizing although on his second missonary journey he and Timothy were prevented by the Holy Spirit from preaching the word in the province (Acts 16:6). Later Paul spent a short time at Ephesus, the capital of the province. During his third missionary journey Paul stayed in Ephesus and the surrounding area for two years preaching about Jesus to both Jews and Greeks (Acts 19:1). When writing to the church at Corinth Paul recounts his hardships and successes in Asia (II Cor 1:8). In the Book of Revelation John addresses his message to the Seven Churches in Asia (Rev 1:4).

Assos. City and seaport of Mysia in the Roman province of Asia. The city was separate from the port, half a mile (one km) inland, and was built on terraces of a volcanic rock formation. On his third missionary journey Paul met his companions at Assos to board the boat that took him to Mitylene (Acts 20:13).

Ataroth. Amorite town east of the Jordan River. Both the tribes of Gad and Reuben wanted the area because of its good pasture land (Num 32:1–5). Moses assigned the city to the Gadites who rebuilt it.

Athens. Greek city, center of Greek culture. On his second journey Paul preached daily in the city's market place and synagogue (Acts 17:15–17). He delivered one of his sermons at the Areopagus (Mars Hill), where his concept of the resurrection of the dead drew a mixed response from the audience (Acts 17:18–34).

Attalia. A seaport on the Asia Minor coast of Pamphylia, now known as Antalia. At the end of his second missionary journey, Paul, accompanied by Silas, set sail from Attalia to Antioch in Syria (Acts 14:25).

Azekah. A strategically located town in the territory of Judah. The Philistines assembled near here to fight Israel in the days of Saul (I Sam 17:1). It was fortified by Rehoboam for the defense of his kingdom. Azekah was one of the last towns to hold out against the armies of Nebuchadnezzer (Jer 34:7). After the Babylonian exile it was resettled by Jewish returnees.

Baalath. Town located in the wilderness of Judah, rebuilt by Solomon 20 years after he finished the Temple (I Kgs 9:17–18).

Baal Gad. The northernmost place conquered by Joshua in the Land of Canaan. Located in the "valley of Lebanon under Mount Hermon" (Josh 11:17), it may have been a holy site for the Canaanite god of good fortune, Gad.

Baal Meon. Moabite city also known as Beon (Num

Conquest of the city of Ashtaroth by the Assyrians, depicted on a relief from the palace of Tiglath-Pileser III.

32:3), Beth Meon (Jer 48:23), and Beth Baal Meon (Josh 13:17). Moses apportioned the town to the tribe of Reuben (Num. 32:3, 37-38), who lived there until Mesha, king of Moab, seized the entire area. In the time of Ezekiel it was ruled by the Moabites (Ezek 25:9).

Baal Perazim. Hill south of Jerusalem where David triumphed over the Philistines (II Sam 5:20).

Baal Shalisha. City from which, during a famine, a man brought barley and corn to the prophet Elisha (II Kgs 4:42).

Baal Tamar. City located near Gibeah, where the men of Israel prepared for their victorious battle against the men of Benjamin (Judg 20:30-34, 40, 43).

Baal Zephon. Place in northern Egypt near the site of the crossing of the Red Sea by the Children of Israel (Ex 14:2). Baal Zephon, "Lord of the North," is a Canaanite god associated with the sea and storms.

Babylon. See Shinhar, below, and Babylonians, I.2, People of the Ancient Near East.

Bahurim. Village near Jerusalem. As Michal, the daughter of Saul, was being returned to David her betrothed, her husband Paltiel turned back at this village (II Sam 3:16). Shimei, whose home was in Bahurim, cursed David when he was fleeing from Absalom (II Sam 16:5).

Bamoth Baal. High Place of Baal where Balaam blessed the Children of Israel instead of cursing them as Balak, King of Moab, had commanded him (Num 22:41, 23:5-11). Later Moses designated it as part of the territory of the tribe of Reuben (Josh 13:17).

Bashan. See II.4, Geography of the Holy Land: Regions.

Beer Lahai Roi. Oasis in the Negeb where God spoke to Hagar when she fled from Sarah. Hence the spring was literally called "well of the Living One who sees me" (Gen 16:14). It was here that Isaac first caught sight of the caravan of his bride, Rebekah (Gen 16:14), and where they lived after Abraham's death.

Beeroth ("wells"). One of four cities of the Gibeonites, who made a covenant with the Israelites (Josh 9:18). The town was later included in the portion of Benjamin (II Sam 4:2). Usually identified with the modern town El Bireh, 10 miles (16 km) north of Jerusalem.

Beeroth Bene Jakan ("wells of the sons of Jakan"). Desert camp of the Children of Israel near the border of Edom (Deut 10:6).

Beersheba. City in the Negeb. Here both Abraham and Isaac made a covenant with Abimelech, king of Gerar, and dug a well (Gen 21:22-32, 26:23-33); hence the etymology of the name Beersheba, meaning "well of the oath." Both Isaac and Jacob experienced theophanies there. It is listed as a town both of Judah and of Simeon. It played little part in Israelite history but is often mentioned as the southern limit of the country in the phrase "from Dan to Beersheba" (Judg 20:1, etc). Biblical Beersheba is thought to be 3 miles (5 km) east of the modern city of that name. See also II.9, Digging up the Bible: Beersheba.

The traditional site of Abraham's Well in Beersheba where the patriarch and Abimelech, the king of Gerar, made a covenant.

Churn from Beersheba of the Chalcolithic period.

Berea (Beroea). Macedonian city. The Christians of Thessalonica sent Paul and Silas there after the two clashed with the Jews of their city (Acts 17:10) and they preached in the synagogue, persuading many Jews, as well as Greek nobles, to believe in Jesus (Acts 17:11-12).

Besor. Brook in southern Judah where David left tired soldiers while he continued to chase the Amalekites who had raided Ziklag and carried off the wives and children of David's men (I Sam 30:9-10,21).

Bethabara. Place in Transjordan where John was baptizing when visited by Jesus (John 1:28-29).

Beth Acacia. Place to which the Midianites fled after Gideon defeated them; sometimes called by its Hebrew name, Beth Shittah. It is associated with modern Shatta, a few miles west of Beth Shean.

Bethany. Located on the Mount of Olives, about 2 miles (3 km) southeast of Jerusalem; home of Mary and Martha. Here Jesus raised their brother Lazarus from the dead (John 11). Later Mary anointed Jesus with costly perfume in Bethany, a few days before he was crucified (John 12:1-3). Jesus ascended into heaven from this vicinity (Luke 24:50).

Beth Arabah. City in the region allotted to Judah (Josh 15:1, 6), situated in the wilderness or in the Arabah desert (Josh 18:22).

A general view of Bethany, present-day al-Azarieh. On the right is the dome of the Church of St. Lazarus.

The Pool of Bethesda in Jerusalem where Jesus found a paralytic. Jesus commanded him to walk, and he was healed.

Beth Aven. Town on the border of Benjamin (Josh 18:12) where Saul fought the Philistines and God delivered Israel (I Sam 13:5, 14:23).

Bethel ("House of God"). Place where Abraham built an altar and called on the Lord (Gen 12:6-9). Originally called Luz, Jacob named it Bethel after he experienced a theophany there (Gen 28:11-15). On his return to Canaan, God spoke to Jacob again in Bethel and there renamed him Israel (Gen 35:1-15). After the return of the Israelites to Canaan, the tabernacle and the ark of the covenant rested in Bethel, which was a place of assembly for all the people (Judg 20). After the split in the kingdom it became associated with idol worship when Jeroboam built a golden calf there to compete with Jerusalem. Hosea condemned the idolatry in Bethel, calling it the "house of iniquity" (Hos 4:15; 10:5).

Bethel is associated with present-day Beitin, about 12 miles (19 km) north of Jerusalem. Excavations have shown that the area was inhabited continuously from 2000 BC to the Christian era.

Bethesda (Bethzatha in some manuscripts). Pool outside Jerusalem's Sheep Gate (John 5:2). In the time of Jesus the infirm waited there for an angel to "trouble the water." Jesus found a paralytic at the pool who had been sick for 38 years. He commanded the man to take up his bed and walk, and he was healed (John 5:3-9). Two pools next to the church of St. Anne in the Old City of Jerusalem are thought to be Bethesda.

Beth Horon. Two adjacent towns in the Valley of Aijalon distinguished by being called "upper" and "lower," in the territory of Ephraim along the boundary with Benjamin (Josh 16:5; 18:13-14). Joshua pursued five Amorite kings to upper Beth Horon and while the fugitives were coming down from the place God cast hailstones on them from heaven (Josh 10:10-11). Beth Horon was apportioned to the Levite family of Kohath

(Josh 21:22). It was the home of Nehemiah's enemy, Sanballat. Much later Judah Maccabee defeated the Syrian army there (I Macc 3:16).

The ascent to "upper" Beth Horon.

Beth Jeshimoth, Beth Jesimoth. A camping place of the Israelites, east of the Jordan River, on their way from Egypt to the Promised Land (Num 33:49). It was allotted to the tribe of Benjamin.

Bethlehem.

1) Judean town 5 miles (8 km) south of Jerusalem. Jacob's wife, Rachel, died and was buried on the way to Bethlehem (Gen 35:19). Elimelech and Naomi came from the town (Ruth 1:1) and later Naomi returned there, a widow, with her daughter-in-law Ruth the

Partial view of Bethlehem with the mountains of Moab in the background.

Moabitess (Ruth 1:19). Ruth married Boaz and became the great-grandmother of King David (Ruth 4:17). As the birthplace of David, Bethlehem was seen as the town from which his descendant, the Messiah of Israel, would come forth (Micah 5:2-5). That passage is quoted in Mattew 2:6 and John 7:42 as the fulfillment of prophecy in Jesus' birth. The account of Jesus' humble birth in a manger in Bethlehem has become the beloved Christmas story (Matt 2:1 ff; Luke 2:4 ff).

2) Town in the territory of Zebulun (Josh 19:15); home of the judge Ibzan (Judg 12:8-10). It is associated with Beit Lahm, 7 miles (11.5 km) northwest of Nazareth.

Beth Pelet. Town in southern Judah, near Beersheba (Josh 14:1, 15:20,27).

Beth Peor. Town, east of the Jordan, in the territory of the tribe of Reuben (Josh 13:20). The Israelites camped in the valley near Beth Peor before crossing into the Promised Land. There Moses set the law before them (Deut 3:29, 4:46). Moses was buried not far from the town, although the exact place of his grave is unknown (Deut. 34:6). Beth Peor is thought to be a few miles east of Mount Nebo.

Bethphage ("house of figs"). Village on the Mount of Olives. Jesus sent two of his disciples to Bethphage to fetch a colt to ride into Jerusalem (Matt 21:2-5, Mark 11:2; Luke 19:30).

Bethsaida. Fishing village on the northeast shore of the Sea of Galilee; home of the apostles Peter, Andrew, and Philip (John 1:44; 12:21). After feeding the five thousand in a desert place belonging to Bethsaida (Luke 9:10), Jesus sent his disciples across the Sea of Galilee to the village itself. At night he came to them walking on the water (Mark 6:45). Jesus healed a blind man from the village by placing mud on his eyes (Mark 8:22-26). Bethsaida was rebuked for its lack of repentance and warned of a terrible judgment (Matt 11:20-24; Luke 10:13-15).

Beth Shean, Beth Shan. City in the southeast corner of the plain of Esdraelon (Jezreel); strategic military point near the junction of the Jezreel and Jordan valleys. In biblical times it was one of the Canaanite towns that withstood the Israelites. After the Philistines defeated the Israelites they hung the bodies of Saul and his sons on the walls of Beth Shean (I Sam 31:10,12). David later conquered the city. In the Hellenistic period it became known as Scythopolis, i.e., city of the Scythians. After Pompey captured it in 63 BC, Beth Shean became the capital of the Greek cities of the Decapolis. The mound at Beth Shean has been extensively excavated, revealing 18 levels of civilization.

Beth Shemesh ("house of sun").

1) Located in the foothills of Jerusalem, 12 miles (20 km) west of the city, along the main highway from Philistia to Jerusalem. The name was probably derived from sun worship in the Canaanite city, which is called "Ir Shemesh" (City of Sun) in the book of Joshua. It

The Roman theater at Beth Shean.

Inscribed stele of Pharaoh Seti I found at Beth Shean.

was allotted to the tribe of Judah (Josh 15:10) and became a Levitical city (Josh 21:16; I Chr 6:59). When the Philistines returned the ark of the covenant they left it at Beth Shemesh (I Sam 6:12-21). The armies of Israel and Judah fought near Beth Shemesh and King Amaziah of Judah was taken captive there (II Kgs 14:11-13). The city probably was in existence until the Babylonian destruction of Judah in 586 BC.

2) Idolatrous city in lower Egypt. Located near Cairo, it was called Heliopolis ("city of the sun") and is the same as On (Jer 43:13).

Beth Zur. City in the inheritance given to Judah (Josh 15:58) in a key position along the road from Beersheba to Hebron. King Rehoboam strengthened it (II Chr 11:5,7). Later it played an important part in the Hasmonean wars.

Bezer. City in Transjordan belonging to the tribe of Reuben. Moses set it apart as a city of refuge (Deut 4:43).

Bithynia. Roman province (from 74 BC) in northwest Asia Minor which was combined with its neighbor Pontus. Paul attempted to go there but was prevented by the Holy Spirit (Acts 16:7). The first epistle of Peter is directed to believers in Bithynia, among other places (1:1), indicating that Christians lived there in the 1st century.

Bozrah. An important city in the kingdom of Edom. Amos predicted its destruction as a punishment (Amos 1:12) and similarly harsh destinies were foretold by Isaiah (Is 34:6) and Jeremiah (Jer 49:13).

Cabul. Name of a district and a city bordering Galilee. Solomon gave the territory to King Hiram of Tyre (I Kgs 9:11).

Caesarea. Mediterranean port city dating back to the 3rd century BC when the Phoenicians built a small fortified anchorage called the Tower of Straton. For a short period the city came under Jewish control when it was captured by the Hasmoneans in 96 BC. However, after the Roman general Pompey conquered the country a generation later, the port became a non-Jewish town once again. Herod the Great built an entirely new and magnificent city with an artificial harbor on the site, renaming it Caesarea in honor of the emperor Augustus. To distinguish it from Caesarea Philippi the city was sometimes called Caesarea Maritima (Caesarea near the sea) or Augusta. It became the Roman capital of Judea, the seat of the procurator, as well as the headquarters of the Roman legions that controlled the province. During this period it was the country's principal seaport and a mixed city of Syrian Greeks and Jews. Caesarea was the home of Philip the Evangelist (Acts 8:40). Peter was sent to the city to minister to the Roman centurion Cornelius (Acts 10). Paul passed through the city three times; he was imprisoned for two years there and tried before the Roman procurator (Acts 23:23 ff). See also II.9, Digging up the Bible: Caesarea.

Caesarea Philippi. Town on the southwestern slope of Mount Hermon. The region was called Panion or Panias (modern Banias) after the Greek god Pan. Herod erected there a temple to Augustus and the city was built by Herod's son Philip the Tetrarch. He called the city Caesarea in honor of the emperor but added his own name to distinguish it from the Mediterranean port of the same name. Jesus and his disciples were in the area of Caesarea Philippi when Peter declared Jesus to be the Messiah (Mark 8:27-30).

Calah. Assyrian city. See II.9, Digging up the Bible.

Calvary. See Golgotha.

Cana. Town in Galilee northeast of Nazareth, where Jesus turned water into wine at a wedding feast (John 2:1). It was here that Jesus healed a nobleman's son (John 4:46-54).

Capernaum. Important town on the northwestern shore of the Sea of Galilee, 23 miles (37 km) from Nazareth. Located on the highway between Egypt and Damascus, Capernaum had a customs station as well as a small port for fishermen. The town is often mentioned in the Gospels. When Jesus left Nazareth he went to live there (Matt 4:13) and made the city his base for a large part of his ministry. Here he taught in the synagogue (Luke 4:31) healed the sick (Mark 2:1-12) and cast out unclean spirits (Mark 1:23). At Capernaum Jesus gave his memorable discourse on the Bread of Life, while nearby he found his first disciples (Matt 4:18–22). However, Jesus condemned the town for its failure to heed his calls for repentance (Luke 10:15). See also II.9, Digging up the Bible.

Caphtor, Caphtorim. Original home of the Philistines (Amos 9:7). According to Genesis, the Caphtorim were descendants of Ham, the son of Noah. Most scholars believe they originated in the Mediterranean island of Crete.

Cappadocia. Large Roman province in what is now Eastern Turkey. Representatives of Cappadocia's Jewish community were present in Jerualem on Pentecost (Acts 2:9). The first epistle of Peter is addressed to the Christian communities of Cappadocia (I Peter 1:1) and the province was a center of early Christianity.

Carchemish. Major Hittite city on the banks of the Euphrates River in northern Syria, identified with modern Jarablus. Here Nebuchadnezzar, king of Babylon, defeated the Egyptians in 605 BC (Jer 46:2) in a historic battle that decided the fate of western Asia.

Carmel. Town in the southern hills of Judah near Hebron where Saul put up a monument after defeating the Amalekites (I Sam 15:12). Also the home of Nabal, the miserly landowner who refused to honor David's request for hospitality (I Sam 25:2 ff.)

Cenchreae. Port city of Corinth where Paul had his hair cut in observance of a Nazirite vow before he sailed for Syria (Acts 18:18). A local church must have been established here by Paul. Phoebe (Rom 16:1) was the deaconess of this church and was entrusted with the delivery of the Letter to the Romans.

Chebar, Chebar River. Canal of the Euphrates which ran through an area of Babylon inhabited by exiles from Judah (Ezek 1:1). It is also the place where Ezekiel had many visions (Ezek 3:15).

Chephirah (Hachephirah). One of the four cities of the Hivites spared by Joshua because they tricked the Israelites into making an alliance with them (Josh 9:11–12,15). The city, which was northwest of Jerusalem, was allotted to the tribe of Benjamin.

Cherith, Brook of. Place where Elijah hid and was miraculously fed by ravens after announcing the onset of a drought to King Ahab (I Kgs 17:3).

Chinnereth, Chinneroth.

1) Sea of Galilee. The name "Sea of Chinnereth" is mentioned twice in Scripture to designate the eastern border of the land of Canaan (Num 34:11; Deut 3:17). See Galilee, Sea of.

2) City located at the northwestern corner of the Sea of Galilee which was allotted to the tribe of Naphtali (Josh 14:1). In the period of the divided monarchy the city was attacked by Ben-Hadad, king of Syria (I Kgs 15:20).

Chios. Island in the Aegean Sea off the coast of Turkey where Paul's ship anchored overnight on his last voyage to Jerusalem (Acts 20:15).

Chorazin. Town north of Capernaum that was condemned by Jesus for its unbelief (Matt 11:20–24).

The Sea of Chinneret, better known as the Sea of Galilee.

Reconstructed synagogue at Chorazin.

Sculptured architraves from the synagogue at Chorazin.

Cilicia. Roman province in the southeast corner of what is now Turkey. During the New Testament period the area was divided into two districts (Tracheia in the west and Pedias in the east) and administered by other provinces. The capital and foremost city of Cilicia was Tarsus, hometown of the Apostle Paul (Acts 21:39). In his early ministry Paul spent some time working in Cilicia (Gal 1:21), which had early Christian communities (Acts 15:23). Jews from Cilicia disputed with Stephen in Jerusalem (Acts 6:9).

Clauda (Cauda). Small island near Crete where the ship carrying Paul to Rome was forced to take shelter from a violent storm (Acts 27:16).

Colosse (Colossae). City in Phrygia situated in the upper Lycus Valley. During the New Testament period it had declined in importance and was overshadowed by its more prosperous neighbors, Laodicea and Hierapolis. The city was largely destroyed in an earthquake during the reign of Nero and never fully recovered from the disaster. A Christian community was founded in the city by Epaphras (Col 1:7), himself a native of Colosse (Col 4:12).

Corinth. Greatest trading city of ancient Greece, strategically situated on the narrow isthmus that separates the Aegean and Adriatic Seas. The city was destroyed by the Romans but rebuilt by Julius Caesar in AD 44. Corinth was famous for its Isthmian Games (second only to the Olympics) which were celebrated there every two years. Paul uses an image of the games to encourage the followers of Jesus in Corinth to lead disciplined lives like the athletes who participated in those events (I Cor 9:24-27). Paul labored there for 18 months to build a Christian community (Acts 18:1-18). He paid two other visits to Corinth in order to correct abuses and theological errors that had crept into the church. His second visit was brief and unhappy for both the apostle and the community. He lived with

Decorated vase from Corinth; early 6th century BC.

Aquila and Priscilla but was rejected by the Jewish community (II Cor 2). The situation improved on his third visit (II Cor 13:1-2).

Cos. Island on the Aegean Sea, passed by Paul on his way to Rhodes (Acts 21:1).

Crete. Largest Greek island, thought to be the original home of the Philistines. A Jewish community existed there from before the time of Jesus. Jews from Crete heard Peter's sermon at Pentecost (Acts 2:10). Paul was shipwrecked along the southern coast of the island (Acts 27:7,12). Later Titus was in charge of a church on Crete. In a letter to Titus, Paul quoted with approval a saying that the Cretans were liars and lazy gluttons (Titus 1:12).

Cush. Land mentioned by Isaiah (11:11; 45:14) as a country from which the exiles of Judah would be gathered. See Ethiopia.

Cuth, Cuthah. Sumerian city, northeast of Babylon, dedicated to the god Nergal, lord of the underworld. When the Assyrians conquered Samaria they replaced the deported Israelites with Cuthites who brought the worship of Nergal to the new country (II Kgs 17:24).

Cyprus. Island in the Eastern Mediterranean, usually identified with Elishah and Kittim, mentioned in the Old Testament. By the New Testament period, it was home to a large Jewish community (Acts 4:36; 15:39). One of these was Barnabas, a Levite who accompanied Paul on his first missionary journey. They encountered opposition from Bar-Jesus who was described as a magician and false prophet. Christianity was first brought to Cyprus by Jewish Christians from Jerusalem fleeing persecution (Acts 11:19ff).

Cyrene. Town in Libya with a large Jewish population. One resident of the town, Simon, was forced by the authorities to help Jesus carry his cross to Calvary (Matt 27:32). People from Cyrene were also in Jerusalem on Pentecost (Acts 2:10); some later disputed with Stephen. Lucius, one of the prophets and teachers in

The temple of Apollo at Corinth.

Antioch, was also from Cyrene (Acts 13:1).

Daberath. Town in the territory of Issachar, allotted to the Gershonite Levites (Josh 21:28).

Dalmanutha. Town north of Tiberias on the west side of the Sea of Galilee. After feeding the four thousand, Jesus and his disciples went there by boat (Mark 8:10). The parallel passage in Matthew (15:39) reads Magadan, and many scholars identify it with Magdala.

Dalmatia. Part of the Roman province of Illyria on the east coast of the Adriatic Sea. Paul preached the gospel there (Rom 15:19). Titus left Paul when he departed for Dalmatia (II Tim 4:10).

Damascus, Damascenes. Capital city of the Arameans. It is first mentioned in the Bible as the hometown of Abraham's servant Eliezer (Gen 15:2). The city was captured by David (II Sam 8:5-6), and Aram-Damascus was in frequent conflict with Israel over the next centuries. Ben-Hadad I of Aram-Damascus broke his alliance with Baasha of Israel to make a league with Asa of Judah (I Kgs 15:18). Ben-Hadad II and his son Hadadezer fought against Ahab, who fell in battle at Ramoth Gilead in 853 BC (I Kgs 22). Ben-Hadad IV conquered almost all the northern kingdom of Israel, and his siege of Samaria was lifted only through the intervention of Elisha (II Kgs 6:24ff). The Assyrian king Shalmanezer IV weakened Damascus sufficiently to allow Jeroboam II, king of Israel, to impose his rule over it in 773 BC (II Kgs 14:28). During the Syro-Ephraimate war, Rezin of Damascus allied with Pekah of Israel against Ahaz of Judah, who in turn called upon Tiglath-pileser III, king of Assyria, who captured Damascus (732 BC), carried the inhabitants captive to Kir, and killed Rezin II (II Kgs 16:5-9; Is 7:1-8; Amos 1:3-5), thereby reducing the city to the status of an Assyrian provincial center. It later came under various foreign rules, eventually that of Rome. In the time of Paul it was ruled by Aretas, an Arabian prince who reigned under the authority of the Romans. It had a large and important Jewish community as well as a Christian population. Judas lived there on "the street called Straight." While on his way to persecute those who believed in Jesus in Damascus, Paul was blinded by a light from heaven (Acts 9:2-3,8-10; 22:6; 10-12; 26:12). After three days he received his sight in the city and was let down over the wall of Damascus (9:24-25; 26:20; Gal 1:17).

Dan. City, originally called Laish, which was conquered and settled by the Danites (Josh 19:47; Judg 18:7,27ff). From the time of the Judges, Dan was known as the northernmost border of the Land of Israel, whose boundaries were expressed in the phrase "from Dan to Beersheba" (Judg 20:1, etc). Jeroboam I built a temple in Dan devoted to calf-worship, which was roundly criticized by Amos (8:14). Extensive excavations have shown that the town was established in the Early Bronze Age II. It was destroyed in the 11th century BC but was soon rebuilt, and a century later became the

Iron and bronze utensils from Ekron; end 7th century BC.

religious and administrative center of the region.

Dead Sea. Salt lake in the southern Jordan valley, the lowest point on earth. As the Salt Sea, it is mentioned in the Bible several times as marking Israel's westward border (Num 34:3, 12; Deut 3:17; Josh 3:16).

Debir (also called Kirjath Sepher and Kirjath Sannah). Royal city of the Canaanites in the southern Judean hill country conquered by Caleb's nephew, Othniel (Judg 1:11-13), although the Book of Joshua attributes

Niche with horned altar from Ekron; end 7th century BC.

its capture to Joshua (10:38–39; 12:13). The city was given to the Levites (Josh 21:15; I Chr 6:58).

Decapolis. Federation of ten Hellenistic cities with a Jewish minority. It is first mentioned in the New Testament (Matt 4:25; Mark 5:20) and was part of the Roman general Pompey's settlement of the East.

Dibon (Dibon Gad). City 10 miles (16 km) east of the Dead Sea in the high plains of Moab. It was taken by the Israelites from Sihon king of the Amorites (Num 21:23–30; 32:3) and rebuilt by the tribe of Gad (Num 32:34). Later it was allotted to the Reubenites (Josh 13:17). However, by the time of Isaiah and Jeremiah it had reverted to Moabite control.

Dizahab. Place east of the Arabah, near to which Moses delivered his last address to the Children of Israel (Deut 1:1).

Dor (Dora). Coastal town 8 miles (13 km) north of Caesarea. It was one of the important Canaanite city-states in the confederation of Jabin, king of Hazor, defeated by Joshua (Josh 11:2). It was allotted to Manasseh and Ephraim but lay in the territory of Asher. However, it was retained by the Canaanites (Judg 1:27). Excavations have shown it was founded by the Canaanites in the 20th century BC.

Dothan. Town of central Palestine at the extreme southern end of the Jezreel Valley. It was here that Joseph's brothers sold him into slavery (Gen 37:17–28). The prophet Elisha dwelt in the walled city when the Arameans were trying to capture him (II Kgs 6:13ff.). Excavations have uncovered 11 layers of occupation between 3100 and 700 BC.

Ebal. See II.5, Geography of the Holy Land: Mountains; II.9, Digging up the Bible.

Ebenezer. Unidentified site, thought to be in the vicinity of Aphek, where the Philistines inflicted a major defeat on the Israelites in the time of Samuel. After their rout the Israelites sent for the ark of the Lord to save themselves, but the Philistines took possession of the ark when they defeated the Israelites again (I Sam 4). Later Samuel led the Israelites to victory over the Philistines at Ebenezer. To commemorate the victory Samuel set up a stone and called the place Ebenezer, i.e., "stone of help" (I Sam 7:12).

Edom. See I.2, Peoples of the Ancient Near East: Edomites.

Edrei. Town in Bashan where Og, the King of Bashan, was defeated by Moses (Num 21:31–35). Moses gave the city to the family of Machir from the half-tribe of Manasseh (Josh 13:31).

Eglon. Amorite city whose monarch allied himself with other Canaanite kings to fight the Israelites. Joshua defeated and killed the king of Eglon and later destroyed his city (Josh 10:35). The city was allocated to the tribe of Judah.

Egypt, Brook of. Southwestern boundary of Canaan (Num 34:5; Is 27:12), identified with Wadi el-Arish in northeastern Sinai.

Ekron. Northernmost of the five Philistine cities (Josh 3:3) and one of two located inland. The city was never conquered by Joshua although it was allotted to the tribe of Judah and later to Dan (Josh 19:34). Judah took possession of the city for a short period of time (Judg 1:18) but it appears to have reverted to the Philis-

Colonnaded street at Gerasa, one of the cities of the Decapolis.

tines soon afterwards. The ark of the covenant was brought to Ekron when it was captured by the Philistines but a plague struck the city and the terrified residents proposed returning the Ark to the Israelites (I Sam 5:10). After David killed Goliath, the Israelites pursued the Philistines as far as Ekron (I Sam 17:52). The Israelites reconquered the city during the reign of David (II Sam 8:1). When Ahaziah was sick he appealed to Baal-Zebub, the god of Ekron, to heal him (II Kgs 1:2-16). The city was denounced by the prophets (Jer 25:20; Amos 1:8; Zeph 2:4).

Elah, Valley of. Small valley southwest of Bethlehem where Saul and the men of Israel faced the Philistines (I Sam 17:2). There David went out to confront Goliath and slew him (I Sam 21:9).

Elath (Eloth). Seaport at the head of the Red Sea. It is mentioned together with Ezion Geber in the account of the Exodus (Deut 2:8). In the days of the united monarchy Elath was an important trading station. From here Solomon's merchant fleet carried on a rich trade with Arabia and Ophir (I Kgs 9:26-28). The Edomites reconquered the city during the reign of Joram. It passed back to the Kingdom of Judah but was finally taken out of Jewish hands by Rezin, king of Aram (II Kgs 16:6). See Ezion Geber.

Elealeh. Amorite town in Transjordan, conquered from the Amorite king Sihon and given to the tribes of Reuben and Gad. It later fell to the Moabites and Isaiah foretold its destruction (Is 16:9).

Emmaus. Town in Judah where the risen Jesus met two of his disciples after the crucifixion (Luke 24:31). In the encounter the disciples only recognized their teacher when they broke bread together. The exact location of Emmaus is unknown; it has been traditionally identified with Imwas, about 18 miles (29 km) northwest of Jerusalem. However, it has also been suggested that the site should be located near the modern village of Motza just outside Jerusalem.

En Gedi (Engeddi). Oasis-town in the Judean Desert on the western shores of the Dead Sea, also identified, perhaps incorrectly, as Hazezon Tamar (II Chr 20:1). Situated midway between the northern and the southern ends of the Dead Sea, the oasis was part of the territory of Judah. David hid from Saul in the "strongholds" of En Gedi (I Sam 23:29) and a battle between the men of Judah, Ammon, and Moab was fought near by. The settlements around En Gedi were apparently destroyed at the time of Nebuchadnezzar's siege of Jerusalem, but were rebuilt after the exile. In the time of Solomon, Ein Gedi was known for its aromatic plants (Song 1:14).

En Rogel. Spring outside Jerusalem that bordered the territories of Benjamin and Judah (Josh 15:7; 18:16). Located at the juncture of the Kidron and Hinnom Valleys, it was the site where Jonathan and Ahimaaz hid while waiting for the outcome of Absalom's rebellion against his father David (II Sam 17:17). Later Absa-

The spring of En Rogel, southeast of Jerusalem at the confluence of the Hinnom and Kidron Valleys.

lom's brother, Adonijah, sacrificed by the spring during his attempt to seize the throne (I Kgs 1:9).

En Shemesh. Spring between En Rogel and Gilgal (Josh 15:7).

En Tappuah. Town east of Shechem bordering Ephraim and Manasseh (Josh 15:7). Another name for Tappuah.

Ephesus. Major city in west Asia Minor. It enjoyed great wealth as the market center of Asia, with its harbor accessible to the largest ships and located on the East-West trade routes. Many different ethnic and religious groups lived there. Its religious life centered on a fertility goddess, identified by the Greeks as Artemis and by the Romans as Diana. She was worshiped in a temple that was known as one of the wonders of the ancient world (Acts 19:35). Ephesus had more than its share of exorcists and magicians, some of whom tried to cast out evil spirits by the "Jesus whom Paul preaches" (Acts 19:13-19). Preaching in synagogues, the market place, and private homes, Paul persuaded many to believe in Jesus and turn from idols (Acts 19:22), but as the Ephesians began renouncing their idolatry the silversmiths grew alarmed at their dwindling sales of statues of Artemis and organized a noisy protest at the city's massive theater (Acts 19:28-29) against Paul. During his two-year stay in Ephesus Paul wrote the first epistle to the Corinthians. Priscilla and Aquila also worked in Ephesus, as did Apollos. Ephesus is one of the seven churches of Asia addressed in the Book of Revelation (2:1-7). See also II.9, Digging up the Bible.

Ephrath. Another name for Bethlehem or the district in which Bethlehem is situated. Here Rachel died and was buried after giving birth to Benjamin (Gen 35:19).

Erech (Babylonian Uruk). City of Mesopotamia on the Euphrates founded by Nimrod (Gen 10:10).

Eshcol ("a cluster of grapes"). Valley near Hebron rich in vineyards, where the 12 Israelite spies cut a cluster of grapes, hence its name (Num 13:23–24).

Esdraelon. See Jezreel.

Eshtaol. Town in the Judean foothills northeast of Beth Shemesh that was allotted to the tribe of Judah at the time of the Israelite conquest and later to Dan. It was halfway between Eshtaol and Zorah where the Spirit of the Lord began to move Samson (Judg 13:25), who was later buried in Eshtaol after his death in Philistine captivity.

Eshtemoa. Levitical city south of Hebron in the Judean Hills (Josh 21:14). After David routed the Amalekites he sent spoils from the battle to his friends in the town (I Sam 30:28).

Etam, Rock of. Cleft of a rock where Samson lived after he avenged the death of his wife by the Philistines (Judg 15:7).

Ethiopia. Country south of Egypt. Called Cush in the Old Testament, the name Ethiopia was used in the Septuagint. The Egyptians employed an Ethiopian general to subdue King Asa of Judah (II Chr 14:9) but with no success. Ethiopian mercenaries were also to be found in the service of the kings of Israel and Judah. After gaining independence in the 9th century Ethiopia eventually conquered Egypt itself. One of the last great pharaohs of Ethiopia, Tirhakah, meddled in the affairs of Judah (II Kgs 19:9). Ethiopian rule began to decline with the Persian conquest. The Persians never attempted to subdue Ethiopia as it was too remote to be permanently ruled by a great power. Ethiopians are described as being proud of their nationality and war-like. Amos declares that God loves the children of Ethiopia as he loves Israel (Amos 9:7). In the New Testament Ethiopia is mentioned when a eunuch who was an official in the court of Queen Candace of Ethiopia was converted by Philip (Acts 8:27).

Euphrates. Longest and most important river in Western Asia, referred to as "the river" (Ex 23:31). Stretching almost 1800 miles (2700 km), the Euphrates joins the Tigris to form the Shatt al-Arab at the head of the Persian Gulf. In the Bible the Euphrates was one of the four rivers that flowed from the Garden of Eden (Gen 2:14). Along the banks of the river some of the most important cities of Mesopotamia flourished, notably Babylon. The river was the scene of some of the greatest battles in antiquity, notably Nebuchadnezzar II's victory over the Egyptians (Jer 46:2). The Euphrates is mentioned as the northeastern limit of the Promised Land (Gen 15:18).

Ezion Geber (Ezion Gaber). Port which, along with Elath, was located at the northern end of the Red Sea. Both cities were mentioned at the time of the Exodus (Num 33:35) but no archaeological evidence of either site has been uncovered. Ezion Geber is next mentioned when King Solomon used the port to trade with countries along the Red Sea (I Kgs 10:11,22). In a later period Jehoshaphat also built a fleet there but it was destroyed by a storm before it set sail.

Fair Havens. Harbor in southern Crete. Paul sailed through it with other prisoners on their voyage to Rome (Acts 27:8).

Gadara. City south of the River Jarmuk that was one of the towns of the Decapolis. The city is not mentioned

Jezirat Far'un, also known as Pharaoh's Island, in the Gulf of Elath. It has been identified by some with Ezion Geber.

as such but there are references to the Gadarenes from which it appears that Gadara was the place where Jesus healed two demoniacs and a herd of swine plunged into the lake. A church was later built on the traditional site.

Galatia. Region in Asia Minor, which included the cities of Antioch, Iconium, and Lystra. Paul wrote an epistle to the Galatians, speaking to the communities in the province. He visited there on his first (Acts 13:50–14:28), second (Acts 16:6), and third (Acts 18:23) journeys. From his epistle it appears that the community was made up primarily of Gentile Christians (Gal 4:8, 5:2). Peter also addressed his first epistle to the believers in Galatia as well as other places (I Pet 1:1).

Gath ("winepress").

1) Philistine city, originally, together with Gaza and Ashdod, a stronghold of the Anakim ("giants") (II Sam 21:18–22; I Chr 20:4–8). Goliath ("the Gittite") was from Gath (I Sam 17:4, 23). In the early years of Israel it was not conquered by the Israelites (Josh 13:1–6; Judg 3:1–3). In the battle of Ebenezer, the ark of the covenant fell into Philistine hands and subsequently reached Gath, bringing with it a plague (I Sam 5:8–9). Twice David sought refuge with Achish, king of Gath. The first time he was unsuccessful (I Sam 21:10–15) but later he was accepted as a mercenary (I Sam 27). Although he was commissioned to protect Achish's southeastern flank against Israelite invasion, David deceived the king and defended the Israelites by attacking their enemies and guarding their frontier (I Sam 27:10). In the mid-8th century BC, Uzziah, king of Judah, undertook a campaign against Philistia and conquered Gath (II Chr 26:6).

2) Another Gath (Gittaim) was in the northern Shephelah and commanded the strategic crossroads northwest of Gezer. Although it was allotted to the tribe of Benjamin, it was apparently populated by non-Israelites in the time of Saul.

Gath Rimmon.

1) Levitical city in the territory allotted to Dan (Josh 21:24; I Chr 6:54). The Kehath clan settled there and administered the land (cf I Chr 26:30–32).

2) Levitical city of the Kehath clan of the tribe of Manasseh, located near Taanach (Josh 21:25). However, the Septuagint version of this verse lists the city of Ibleam instead of Gath Rimmon, and some scholars detect here a scribal error in the Hebrew text.

Gaza. One of five Philistine cities, located in the southern coastal plain (I Sam 6:17); previously one of the cities of the Anakim (Josh 11:22). Situated along the route to Egypt, it was the last stop before entering the desert. From earliest times it was an important oasis and a military base, being constantly involved in wars. The Roman city extended to the Mediterranean Sea, but present-day Gaza is about 3 miles (5 km) from the coast. Gaza is mentioned as a Canaanite city in Genesis (10:19). The god Dagon was worshiped there

The "Good Shepherd"; figurine from Gaza; Byzantine period.

and Samson carried off the city gates (Judg 16). It is mentioned in the New Testament as being on the caravan route to Egypt (Acts 8:26).

Geba. Benjamite town (called Gaba in Josh 18:24), north of Jerusalem. It was a priestly city (Josh 21:17). Saul and Jonathan used Geba as a military base during the battle with the Philistines at Michmash (I Sam 13:16; 14:5). In the time of Nehemiah, the townspeople were counted among the inhabitants of Benjamin. Geba is sometimes confused with Gibeah, both lying in the territory of Benjamin; some scholars even maintain that they are the same place.

Gebal (commonly known as Byblos). City located north of Beirut in Lebanon. In the 3rd and 2nd millennia BC it was the most important port on the Phoenician coast, but by the time of the Israelite conquest of Canaan, its importance had declined. Gebalites were part of the labor force used in building Solomon's Temple (I Kgs 5:18). It was never conquered by the Israelites (Josh 13:5), and is mentioned in Psalms 83:7 as among those seeking to destroy Israel.

Gehenna. See Hinnom, Valley of.

Gerar. City district in the western Negeb near the southern frontier of Canaan. The patriarchs pastured their flocks in the land of Gerar, whose king was Abimelech. He desired Sarah, but sent her away when he discovered that she was Abraham's wife (Gen 20). A similar incident occurred when Isaac sought refuge in

Gerar in a time of famine. After a quarrel with the herdsmen of Gerar, Isaac made a covenant with the king of Gerar (Gen 26:28).

Gergesa. Place on the eastern shore of the Sea of Galilee, where some translations of Matthew say Jesus cast out devils and sent them into a herd of swine (Matt 8:28 ff). See Gadara; II, 9 Digging up the Bible: Kursi.

Gerizim. See II.4: Gerizim. Geography of the Holy Land; see also II.9, Digging up the Bible.

Geshur. Kingdom near Bashan (Deut 3:14) extending along the eastern shore of the Sea of Galilee to the northern bank of the Jarmuk River. Joshua did not conquer Geshur (Josh 13:13), and when the Kingdom of Judah was set up, a small Aramean state was founded at Geshur. David married the daughter of Talmai, its king (II Sam 3:3). Absalom, the child of this marriage, fled to his mother's family in Geshur after he murdered Amnon (II Sam 13:37).

Gezer. City of Canaan in the coastal plain, situated at a strategic crossroads from Egypt to Syria and from the sea coast to the mountains. King Horam of Gezer and all his people were killed by Joshua after they came to the help of Lachish (Josh 10:33). Despite this, the Canaanites of the city were not dispossessed and they lived within the territory of Ephraim (Josh 16:10). Later it was given to Solomon by Pharaoh as a dowry for his daughter and Solomon built there one of his royal cities (I Kgs 9:15,17). See also II.9, Digging up the Bible.

Gibbethon. Town on the border between Israel and Philistia, allotted to the tribe of Dan (Josh 19:44). It was given to the Kehathite Levites who settled there among the mostly non-Israelite population (Josh 21:23). It belonged to the Philistines at least until the 9th century.

Gibeah ("hill"). Benjamite city near Jerusalem lying along the watershed that linked the land of Judah to the hills of Ephraim (Judg 19:11-13). It was destroyed in a war between Benjamin and the other Israelite tribes after the concubine of a Levite was raped by the people of Gibeah (Judg 19:25 ff). King Saul came from Gibeah (I Sam 10:26). After he subdued the Philistines, Saul made Gibeah his capital and its name became Gibeah of Saul (I Sam 15:34). Another city of the same name lay in the Judean hills (Josh 15:57).

Gibeon. Canaanite city mentioned as one of the four cities of the Hivites (Josh 9:17). After deceiving Joshua, the Gibeonites were condemned to be eternal bondservants but under the protection of Joshua (Josh 9). It was at Gibeon that Joshua subdued the king of Jerusalem and his allies and on that occasion the sun stood still (Josh 10). It was allotted to the tribe of Benjamin (Josh 18:25) and was a Levitical city (Josh 21:19). It was at the great port of Gibeon (which can still be seen) that the men of Joab competed and then fought with the men of Abner (II Sam 2). The young King Solomon offered a sacrifice and prayed for wisdom at the noted high place at Gibeon (I Kgs 3:4ff; II

Rock-cut circular pool of the water-system at Gibeon; Iron Age.

Chr 1:3ff). Ishmael, murderer of Gedaliah, was defeated by the pool of Gibeon (Jer 41:12–16). Gibeon is identified with el-Jib, 8 miles (13 km) northwest of Jerusalem.

Gihon.

1) One of four rivers which had its source in the Garden of Eden and from there flowed to the entire land of Ethiopia (Gen 2:13).

2) A spring in the Kidron Valley. In biblical times it was the principal source of water for Jerusalem. It was the scene of Solomon's coronation (I Kgs 1:33). Later Hezekiah diverted the spring through a tunnel into the city of David (II Chr 32:30) and thus ensured the city a water supply during the Assyrian siege, at the same time preventing the use of the spring by the enemy (II Chr 32:3–4). "Hezekiah's tunnel" is still in existence. It is about 1600 feet (490m) long and terminates at the Pool of Siloam. The making of the tunnel is commemorated in an inscription discovered on its roof in the 19th century.

Gilead. See II.4, Geography of the Holy Land: Regions.

Gilgal. Place west of the Jordan, which was the last stopping point of the Exodus. There Joshua set up 12 stones, symbolic of the twelve tribes, to commemorate the crossover into the Promised Land (Josh 4:19-20). Here, in the plain of Jericho, the men of Israel were circumcised (Josh 5:3-9). After the conquest of Canaan, Gilgal remained a holy place, and there Samuel judged

A hillock outside the walls of Jerusalem, thought to resemble a human skull (Golgotha in Aramaic), is believed by many Protestants to be the site of Calvary. On the right, an altar in the Church of the Holy Sepulcher which traditionally marks the place of the Crucifixion.

Israel (I Sam 7:16) and crowned Saul king (I Sam 10:8; 11:14ff). Saul used it as his base for wars against the Philistines and Amalekites (I Sam 13:4ff; 15:12ff).

Golgotha. Also known as Calvary, it is the place of the Crucifixion (Matt 27:33; Mark 15:22; John 19:17). The name was derived from the Aramaic "golgolta," meaning "skull" or "place of the skull." According to early Christian tradition it is located west of Jerusalem.

Gomorrah. One of five Canaanite cities (Gen 10:19) in the Jordan Valley ("the Cities of the Plain"; Gen 13:10). It was destroyed with Sodom by fire and hail from heaven because of its wickedness.

Goren Atad ("the threshing floor of Atad"). Place near the Jordan River, where Jacob's funeral procession moving from Egypt to Canaan stopped to mourn for seven days. When the Canaanites saw the lamentation they called the name of the place "Abel Mizraim" ("Mourning of Egypt"; Gen 50:7-13).

Goshen. Area of rich pastureland in Egypt, allotted to the Children of Israel in the time of Joseph (Gen 46:34; 47:6, 11). It is also called "the land of Rameses" (Gen 47:11).

Gozan. Region in northwestern Mesopotamia to which, in 732 BC, Tiglath-pileser III, the ruler of Assyria, deported some of the inhabitants of northern Israel. The inhabitants of Samaria suffered the same fate after they were conquered in 721 BC.

Habor. Tributary of the Euphrates to which the ten tribes were deported after the Assyrian conquest of Israel (II Kings 17:6). Gozan and other important Mesopotamian cities were found along its banks. It is now identified with the Khabur river.

Hadrach. Name of a town and country in Aram mentioned only once in Scripture (Zech 9:1) with Damascus, Tyre and Sidon, apparently in reference to a revolt which it joined with Israel and Phoenician cities against Assyria.

Halah. Place in Mesopotamia to which the kings of Assyria exiled the Israelites who lived in northern Transjordan (I Chr 5:26). Some of the residents of Samaria were also taken there.

Hamath. Important city on the banks of the Orontes in northern Syria, now known as Hama. It had friendly relations with King David (II Sam 8:9) and Solomon built a store city in the vicinity. Later, Jeroboam II conquered the city and held it for a short time. In the 8th century the city was taken from the Hittites by the Assyrians, who deported its residents to Israel (II Kgs 17:24) while some people of Samaria were moved to Hamath. The "entrance to Hamath" is often designated as the northern border of the land of Canaan (Num 34:8).

Hammath. Fortified settlement of Naphtali, probably the same as Hammath Dor, a Levitical city (Josh 21:32). In New Testament times it was known as Hamtha and was famous for its hot springs. It lay south of Tiberias on the shores of the Sea of Galilee.

Haran. Town in northern Mesopotamia on the river Balih. Lying on the ancient caravan route from Syria to Mesopotamia, Haran was a trade and cultural center from the 2nd millennium onwards. Terah, the father of Abraham, settled there (Gen 11:31). Abraham's servant found there a wife for Isaac from Abraham's family, and Jacob later fled to Haran to escape from Esau's anger (Gen 28:10). Ezekiel (27:23) also speaks of the merchants of Haran as trading with Tyre.

Harod. Spring in the Jezreel Valley at the foot of Mount Gilboa, where Gideon and his men camped before their fight with the Midianites (Judg 7:1).

Harosheth Hagoyim. Place where Sisera assembled an army before his battle with Deborah and Barak (Judg 4:2). After their defeat Sisera's army fled back to the area. Some scholars suggest that the name, literally "woodland of the nations," is a description of the wooded hill country of Galilee and not a specific place.

Havilah. Country encircled by the Pishon River (Gen 2:12), legendary for its gold, onyx, and bdellium. Its exact location is unknown but some have identified it with Arabia or a district in Ethiopia. Ishmael lived in the area and later it was inhabited by the Amalekites.

Havoth Jair ("villages of Jair"). Group of small villages in Gilead along the banks of the Jarmuk River. Jair the son of Manasseh took the area from the Amorites (Deut 3:14).

Hazor. One of the most important cities in the Land of Israel, situated 9 miles (14 kms) north of the Sea of Galilee. Before the Israelite conquest Hazor was a center of Canaanite wealth and political power. Its king, Jabin, forged an ill-fated coalition of northern monarchs to fight Joshua (Josh 11:1–5). After the victory over Jabin, Joshua burned the city and assigned it to Naphtali. At a later time the Jabin dynasty appears to have regained the city (Judg 4:2) but Deborah and Barak restored Israelite rule. Solomon fortified Hazor and

Partial view of Hebron with the Cave of Machpelah in the center.

made it one of his royal cities, but, along with other towns in Galilee, it was seized by Ben-Hadad of Damascus (I Kgs 15:20). It was rebuilt by Omri but destroyed once again, this time by the Assyrians. It was still in ruins when Jonathan the Hasmonean re-established Jewish control over parts of Galilee (I Macc 11:67). See also II.9, Digging up the Bible.

Hebron. Ancient Judean city lying 20 miles (36 kms) south of Jerusalem and one of the oldest continuously inhabited sites in the world. It was a city of Levites as well as a city of refuge (Josh 21:13). In earliest antiquity it was called Kirjath Arba, named possibly after Arba, the father of Anak (Josh 15:13). When Abraham came to the city he pitched his tents by the the oaks of Mamre. It was from here he went to rescue Lot and his name was changed to Abraham. Later three angels appeared to the patriarch in the city with the promise of a son (Gen 18:1). Sarah died in Hebron and Isaac and Jacob spent much of their lives in the area. In Hebron's cave of Machpelah Abraham, Isaac, Jacob, and their wives (except Rachel) are buried. The king of Hebron was defeated by Joshua and his city was given to Caleb who had captured it. In the time of the judges one of Samson's exploits involved carrying the gate of Gaza to a mountain just outside Hebron. David went to live there after the death of Saul. He was anointed king and reigned from Hebron for seven and a half years (II Sam 5:5). Joab treacherously killed Saul's commander-in-chief, Abner, at the gate of the city. After the division of Israel, Rehoboam fortified Hebron. During the Babylonian exile it fell into the hands of Edom. Although it was resettled by Jews it did not return to their control until the time of the Maccabean revolt, when it was sacked by Judah the Maccabee.

Heshbon. Royal city of Sihon, king of the Amorites, in Transjordan. Moses occupied the city (Num 21:25) and gave it to the tribe of Reuben. Isaiah (15:4) and Jeremiah (48:2) foretold its destruction. In the Maccabean period it fell into Jewish hands again.

Hiddekel. The Tigris, one of the rivers of Eden (Gen 2:14) which is described in the Bible as running eastwards to Assyria.

Hierapolis ("sacred city"). City in southwest Asia Minor, mentioned by Paul in the Epistle to the Colossians (4:13) as the home of a Christian community.

Hinnom, Valley of (Heb. *Ge-Hinnom*). Valley that bordered Jerusalem and served as a boundary between Judah and Benjamin (Josh 15:8). A continuation of the Kidron Valley, it was also known as Ge-Henna and later identified as the site of Hell. In the days of Ahaz and Manasseh, children were sacrificed there to the fire-god Moloch (II Kgs 23:10). As part of his religious reforms, King Josiah of Judah defiled the valley. In the New Testament it is a place of unquenchable fire into which the wicked are cast. The Pharisees are destined for the destruction of Gehenna (Matt 23:33). See II.9, Digging up the Bible: Archaeology of Jerusalem.

Hor. Mountain bordering Edom and Canaan and one of the sites where the Israelites camped during the Exodus. Here the Children of Israel tried unsuccessfully to enter the Promised Land. Also the site of Aaron's death (Num 20:22–29).

Horeb. Another name for Mount Sinai. See Sinai.

Hormah. City in the Negeb first mentioned in connection with the Israelite defeat by the Amalekites and Canaanites (Num 14:45). It was eventually conquered and destroyed by Judah and Simeon (Judg 12:14). The city was occupied by the tribe of Judah and later by the tribe of Simeon. David sent presents to Hormah after his victory over the Amalekites.

Ibleam. City situated along the road from the Jezreel Valley to the Samarian Hills. It was located in the midst of the inheritance of Issachar, but, like other cities, was given to the tribe of Manasseh (Josh 17:11). Joshua could not expel the Canaanites from there (Josh 17:12–13; Judg 1:27–28) but it was conquered by David. It was probably a Levitical city.

Iconium. Roman city in the province of Galatia (present-day Turkey), which was a thriving center in New Testament times. Paul and Barnabas visited it on their first missionary journey (Acts 13:50–51) and spoke in its synagogue. Many believed, but others wanted to stone them and the apostles fled (Acts 14:5–6). Nevertheless Paul returned to Iconium to encourage the disciples in the faith (Acts 14:22).

Idumea (later name for Edom [q.v.]). Its inhabitants were forcibly converted to Judaism by John Hyrcanus and one of their descendants was Herod. Residents of Idumea heard of Jesus and his miracles and came to him in Galilee (Mark 3:7–8).

Ijon. Town in the Kingdom of Israel, belonging to the tribe of Naphtali. Ben-Hadad conquered Ijon during the reign of Baasha, king of Israel (I Kgs 15:20). In the time of Pekah, king of Israel, Tiglath-pileser III captured the town and sent the inhabitants to Assyria (II Kgs 15:29).

Ish-Tob ("man of Tob"). Aramean city and its vicinity, located north of Gilead. Jephthah fled there when his half-brothers drove him away (Judg 11:3–5). Later Tob sent 12,000 men to fight against David (II Sam 10:6,8).

Iturea. Region south of Mount Hermon. Herod's brother, Philip the tetrarch, ruled the area in New Testament times.

Jabesh Gilead. Town in Gilead, east of the Jordan River. During the Israelite war against the Gibeonites the men of Jabesh Gilead refused to take part. For this, all the inhabitants of the town were slain except 400 virgins who were given to the Benjamites as wives (Judg 21:6–14). In the time of Saul the town was again inhabited by Israelites, and Saul rallied his troops on its behalf when it was attacked by the Ammonites (I Sam 11:1–13). Later when Saul was killed and his body hung on the wall of Beth Shean, it was the men of Jabesh Gilead who removed it and buried it in their town (I

The Valley of Jehoshaphat, part of the Kidron Valley in Jerusalem, between the Mount of Olives and Mount Moriah.

Sam 31:11–13). David sent them a message of gratitude (II Sam 2:4).

Jahaz, Jahaza. Town in the territory of Reuben where the Israelites vanquished Sihon, king of the Amorites (Num 21:36). In the days of the Israelite kingdom it belonged to Moab (Is 15:4).

Jarmuth. Canaanite city-state located in the coastal plain (Josh 15:35); one of the five confederated cities defeated by Joshua (Josh 10:3–5). After the Babylonian exile the town was reconstructed (Neh 11:29).

Jattir. Town of Levites in southern Judah (Josh 15:48; 21:14). After his triumph over the Amalekites David sent gifts to Jattir (I Sam 30:27).

Jazer (Jaazer). Amorite town east of the Jordan River, which was captured by the Israelites (Num 21:32). The tribe of Gad settled there and built a city (Num 32:35), which was a city of refuge (I Chr 6:81). It was in the kingdom of David (II Sam 24:5). Later, Isaiah (16:8–9) and Jeremiah (48:32) mention it as a Moabite town. In the Second Temple period it was ruled by the Ammonites, but was afterwards conquered by the Hasmoneans (I Macc 5:8).

Jehoshaphat, Valley of (called "the valley of decision" in Joel 3:14). Scene of the apocalyptic Last Judgment (Joel 3:2). Early traditions identified it with the Kidron valley in Jerusalem, but it is probable that the name Jehoshaphat ("God has judged") is symbolic and does not refer to an actual place.

Jericho. Oasis town near the Jordan River in the southern Jordan Valley. Allotted to the tribe of Benjamin, it was also called the city of palm trees (Josh 4:13). Excavations have shown that it was one of the earliest known towns. For the invading Israelites, Jericho was a strategic strongpoint blocking the conquest of Canaan. While at Shittim, Joshua sent two scouts to spy out the land, including Jericho (Josh 2:1); they completed their mission with the help of Rahab the harlot (Josh 2:3-6). After they returned with their report, Joshua prepared his army for the battle on the plains of Jericho (Josh 4:13). Jericho was heavily fortified and seemed impregnable. The Children of Israel were instructed to march around the city once a day for six days without uttering a word. On the seventh day they encompassed the city seven times, and when the priests blew their rams' horns, the people shouted and the walls collapsed. The city was stormed and burned and only Rahab and her family were saved (Josh 6:15, 20, 24-25). Joshua cursed Jericho, proclaiming that whoever would rebuild it would do so at the cost of his firstborn and youngest sons (Josh 6:26). In the days of Ahab, Hiel of Bethel rebuilt Jericho at the expense of the lives of his firstborn and youngest sons (I Kgs 16:34).

The city existed in New Testament times. Here the blind Bartholomew was healed (Matt 20:29ff) and Zachaeus the publican hosted Jesus (Luke 19:1ff). See also II.9, Digging up the Bible.

Jerusalem. See II.6, Jerusalem in the Bible, and II.9, Digging up the Bible: Jerusalem.

Jeshimon ("a wasteland"). Plain north of the wilderness of Maon and opposite the land of Hachilah. David hid there from Saul (I Sam 23:19,24).

Jezreel (or Esdraelon).

1) Town at the foot of Mount Gilboa, among the cities of Issachar (Josh 19:18, etc). It was an important city in Ahab's kingdom (I Kgs 18:45) and the location of his palace and of Naboth's vineyard (I Kgs 21:1ff). Ahab's descendants were slain by Jehu at Jezreel (II Kgs 10:7, 11).

2) Name of a plain, called after the town. It is situated between Mount Carmel, Mount Gilboa, and the hills of Lower Galilee. It was an important communications

link between the coast and the countries to the north and east, and as a result fortified towns like Megiddo, Ibleam, and Beth Shean were built in order to guard the mountain passes. Because of its strategic importance, famous battles were fought in the plain, including those between Deborah and Jabin, king of Hazor; Thutmosis III of Egypt and the Caananites; Saul and the Philistines; Gideon and the Midianites; and Josiah and Pharaoh Necho. Sometimes the plain is called simply "the Valley."

Jokneam. Town near Megiddo, on the western edge of the Jezreel Valley, commanding a major junction on the coastal road leading from Egypt and Israel to Phoenicia. It was captured by Joshua (Josh 12:22) and allotted to the Levites (Josh 21:34).

Joppa (present-day Jaffa). Mediterranean port city allotted to Dan but conquered by the Philistines and not included in any Israelite inheritance. Solomon brought timber from Lebanon via Joppa to build his Temple (II Chr 2:16). The prophet Jonah sailed from Joppa to Tarshish (Jonah 1:3). Simon the Maccabee conquered the city in 144 BC and from then on it was de facto under Jewish rule. Joppa is mentioned several times in the New Testament. Here Tabitha, a disciple of Jesus, died and was revived by Peter (Acts 9:36ff). Peter also saw the vision of clean and unclean beasts on a rooftop while in Joppa (Acts 10:5ff).

Kadesh, Kadesh Barnea. Oasis in the Zin desert that served as headquarters of the Israelites for 38 years during their long journey to the Promised Land. From here 12 men were sent to spy out the land and upon their return Israel was condemned to remain in the desert until the generation that left Egypt had died (Num 13; Deut 1:46). Later Miriam died here and Moses brought judgment upon himself by striking the rock to bring forth water (Num 20:12). The location of the site has long been a source of controversy among scholars but is now generally identified with the oasis of Ain el-Kudeirat in the Sinai desert. See II.9, Digging up the Bible.

View of Jaffa (Joppa) from the sea. On the right, excavations showing remains of the Hellenistic period.

Left: the oasis of Ain el-Kudeirat, identified as Kadesh Barnea. Right: clay figurine from the same site, dated to the 8th-7th century BC.

Karnaim. City near Ashtaroth that became the capital of Bashan in the days of Assyrian and Aramean rule (Amos 6:3). It was properly known as Ashtaroth Karnaim although in the Maccabean period it was called Karnein (II Mac 12:21).

Kedemoth. Place in Transjordan allotted to the tribe of Reuben and assigned to the Levitical family of Merari. From the wilderness of Kedemoth Moses sent messengers to Sihon, king of Heshbon, seeking permission to pass through his territory (Deut 2:26).

Kedesh. City of refuge in Upper Galilee in the land of Naphtali (Josh 20:7). Its Canaanite ruler was one of the 31 kings subdued by Joshua. The city was given to the Levitical family of Gershon. It was the home of Barak and here he assembled an army to fight the Caananites under Sisera. When the Assyrians invaded Israel under Tiglath-pileser III in 734 BC, it was one of the first cities captured (II Kgs 21:32).

Keilah. Town in the Judean foothills that was rescued from the Philistines by David (I Sam 23:1-8), who had to abandon it in the face of an offensive by King Saul. In the time of Rehoboam it was conquered by the Egyptians.

Kibroth Hattaavah ("graves of lust"). One of the encampments of the Israelites in the wilderness between Sinai and Hazeroth. All those who gorged themselves on the quails provided by God died there; hence the name (Num 11:34).

Kidron. See II.4, Geography of the Holy Land: Rivers.

Kir Haraseth (Kir Heres). Moabite city dominating the road from Elath to Damascus. Situated on the top of a lofty mountain and surrounded by a strong wall, the kings of Judah and Israel together were unable to subdue the city (II Kgs 3;24-25). The site is identified with el-Kerak.

Kirjath Arba. Original name of Hebron (Gen 23:2), so called because of Arba, "the greatest man among the Anakim" (Josh 14:15). See Hebron.

Kirjath Jearim ("city of woods"). Town on the border of Benjamin and Judah. Initially a Canaanite high place and center of Baal worship, it was consequently known in ancient times as Baalah and Mount Baalah (Josh 15:9; II Sam 6:2). The city was held by the Gibeonites at the time of the Israelite conquest (Josh 9:17). It was the last place where the ark rested before it reached Jerusalem (II Sam 6:2). After the Babylonian exile, Kirjath Jearim was resettled. It is identified with Abu Ghosh, a village west of Jerusalem.

Kishon. See II.4, Geography of the Holy Land: Rivers.

Lachish. Ancient Amorite city in a strategic location in the Hebron foothills. Its ruler joined four other kings in chastising the Gibeonites for their alliance with Israel. Joshua came to the aid of the Gibeonites and defeated the coalition (Josh 10:3,5,26,32-33). The land of Lachish was given to the tribe of Judah (Josh 15:39). It was fortified by Rehoboam (II Chr 11:9). Amaziah, king of Judea, went to Lachish when he fled from conspirators in Jerusalem, and was later killed there (II Kgs 14:19; II Chr 25:27). In the time of Hezekiah, Sennacherib of Assyria captured the city as he conducted a campaign in Judah. It was one of his greatest victories and was depicted on reliefs discovered in his palace. A century later, when Nebuchadnezzar, king of Babylon, conquered the kingdom of Judah, Lachish and nearby Azekah were the last cities to fall (Jer 34:7). Letters written by its commander shortly before its surrender have been discovered. It was abandoned but resettled after the Babylonian exile (Neh 11:30). See also II.9, Digging up the Bible.

Laish. Canaanite town situated near the headwaters of the river Jordan. The tribe of Dan conquered the city and changed its name to Dan (Judg 18).

Laodicea. City in southwestern Phrygia in Asia Minor; an early seat of Christianity. Paul wrote a letter to Laodicea but this has not survived (Col 21). Laodicea is one of the seven churches addressed in Revelation 1-3.

Remains of a Roman aqueduct at Laodicea in Phrygia.

Pinpointing its areas of pride, it is rebuked for being lukewarm, like its water.

Lehi ("jawbone"). Place in Judah near the Philistine frontier where Samson killed thousands of Philistines with the jawbone of an ass, as a result of which he named the place Ramath Lehi (Judg 15:15–17).

Lo Debar. Town in Transjordan where Jonathan's son, Merib-baal (Mephibosheth), lived for a time in the house of Machor (II Sam 9:4–5; 17:27).

Luz. Canaanite city. At this site Jacob dreamed of a ladder rising up to heaven. He erected an altar there and renamed the place Bethel (Gen 28:19; 48:3). Luz and Bethel are mentioned as two separate cities in Josh 16:2, but in all other instances Luz is identified with Bethel (Gen 35:6; Josh 18:13; Judg 1:23). See Bethel.

Lycaonia. Region of central Asia Minor, a plateau bounded by Galatia and Cappadocia to the north and east, and by hills to the west and south. The Lycaonians worshiped Greek gods. A sizeable Jewish population lived there (Acts 14:11, 16:1). Paul visited its principal cities on two occasions (Acts 13–14, 16:1–5).

Lycia. Region in southwestern Asia Minor. Patara and Myra, Mediterranean ports, were two of its major cities. Paul journeyed through Patara and went on to Phoenicia (Acts 21:1–2). Later he set sail for Italy from Myra (Acts 27:5–6).

Lydda. Town belonging to the tribe of Benjamin (I Chr 8:12; Ezra 2:33). It is situated between Jerusalem and Joppa in the Sharon plain. In New Testament times the apostle Peter visited the believers in Lydda and healed Aeneas, who had been paralyzed for eight years (Acts 9:32–34).

Lystra. City in the province of Lycaonia in Asia Minor. Paul and Barnabas preached the gospel and Paul healed a cripple there. The pagan residents saluted the two men as gods, calling them Zeus and Hermes (Acts 14:11–12). However, some Jews from Antioch and Iconium, angered by Paul's preaching, stirred up the crowd and they stoned Paul (Acts 14:19). In spite of this Paul returned to Lystra to encourage the converts and there met Timothy (Acts 14:21; 16:1–2).

Machpelah. Cave and field near Hebron purchased by Abraham from Ephron the Hittite as burial place for Sarah (Gen 23:19). Abraham himself, and Isaac, Rebekah, Leah, and Jacob were also buried there. A cave in Hebron has been identified with the site since Second Temple times.

Magdala. Town on the western shore of the Sea of Galilee which was the birthplace of Mary Magdalene (Luke 8:2). Identified as Migdal, about 3 miles (5 kms) north of Tiberias.

Mahanaim. Levitical town in Gilead bordering Gad and Manasseh. Here Jacob had a vision of angels (Gen 32:1–2). Later it was the place where David sought refuge and organized resistance when Absalom revolted (II Sam 17:24). For a short time it was also the capital of Israel (II Sam 2:8).

Makkedah. Canaanite city-state in the Judean foothills soundly defeated by the Israelites (Josh 10:28). Nearby was the cave where five Canaanite kings were found hiding by Joshua (Josh 10:17). During the reign of Rehoboam it was taken by the Egyptians.

Malta (Melita). Island in the central Mediterranean, where Paul and Luke spent three months after being shipwrecked. They won the admiration of the local population, many of whom were healed by Paul (Acts 28:9). After the winter storms passed, Paul and Luke continued their journey to Rome.

Mamre. Grove of oaks named after Mamre the Amorite (Gen 14:13) who lived nearby in Hebron. Abraham pitched his tents there and built an altar to the Lord. Later God appeared to him in a vision at Mamre (Gen 15:1ff). Isaac also lived there.

Maon. Town in the Judean hills where David found refuge from Saul (I Sam 23:24). Also the home of Nabal and Abigail (I Sam 23:1–3).

Wall painting depicting a hunting scene, on a tomb of the Hellenistic period at Mareshah.

Marah ("bitter"). First camp of the Israelites after crossing the Red Sea, where they found only bitter water (Ex 15:23). When the people complained God told Moses to throw a tree in the water in order to make it sweet.

Mareshah. Fortified town in Judah where Asa defeated Zerah the Ethiopian (II Chr 14:8–15). It was conquered by the Assyrian king Sennacherib, as recorded by Micah (1:15). After 586 BC it fell again, this time to Idumea, from whom it was conquered by John Hyrcanus in the 2nd century BC.

Coin of Medeba depicting the chariot of the god Helios, AD 210.

Massah and Meribah. Two places in Rephidim where the Israelites in the desert tested the Lord and argued with Moses over the lack of water (Ex 17:7; in Hebrew both Massah and Meribah mean "quarrel"). It was there that the people asked "Is the Lord among us?" Moses struck the rock at Horeb and water flowed out for the thirsty people.

Medeba (Medaba). City in the pasturelands of Moab, seized by the Israelites from the Amorites (Num 21:30) and given to the tribe of Reuben. David's commander-in-chief Joab battled the Amorites and Ammonites there (I Chr 19:7ff.). The biblical record and the Moabite Stone show Medeba was constantly changing

Part of the Medeba Map showing Jerusalem.

hands. The town became famous in 1896 when a 6th-century mosaic map of the Holy Land was discovered in an ancient church. The map has proved to be an extremely useful source of information on the topography of Bible lands.

Megiddo. One of the most strategically important cities in the Land of Israel. It lay at the entrance to the Jezreel Valley and dominated the trade route between Egypt and Damascus. Since ancient times, numerous battles have been fought in and around the city. According to the New Testament the final battle between good and evil will occur here (Rev 16:12ff). Megiddo is first mentioned in Egyptian documents describing attempts by Pharaoh Thutmosis III (15th century BC) to subdue the kings of Canaan. The Egyptians took Megiddo after a long siege and converted it into a military base. The Israelites were less successful and were unable to conquer the city until the reign of David. Solomon fortified it and made it the administrative capital of a district and one of his chariot cities (I Kgs 9:15). Megiddo was seized and destroyed by the Egyptians again, this time during the days of Rehoboam. Rebuilt by Omri and Ahab, Megiddo regained its importance and became a prosperous city in the kingdom of Israel. King Josiah of Judah was killed at Megiddo fighting Pharaoh Necho in 609 BC (II Kgs 23:29). See Armageddon. See also II.9, Digging up the Bible.

Mephaath. Town in Moab, assigned to the territory of Reuben and given to the Levitical family of Merari (I Chr 6:63). Jeremiah also mentions the town in his prophecy against Moab (48:21).

Meribah. See Massah.

Merom (The Waters of Merom, Meron). Site of Joshua's victory over the rulers of northern Canaan (Josh 11:7) who assembled under the king of Hazor. In the New Testament period it was known as Meron, a name it retains today. Located northwest of Safed.

Meshech. Sixth son of Japheth (Gen 10:2) whose descendants settled in the area of Armenia. In Scripture they are often associated with Magog, Javan, and Tubal. Ezekiel mentions them as traders in copper and slaves (39:1). Meshech is sometimes used as a synonym for barbarians (Ps 120:5) and the remotest parts of the civilized world (Is 66:19).

Michmas, Michmash. Benjamite town near Bethel, where Saul's army mustered against the Philistines (I Sam 13:2) in a battle that was won by Jonathan's courage. It was resettled by the tribe of Benjamin after the return from Babylon (Ezra 2:27).

Midian. See Midianites in I.1, Peoples of the Ancient near East.

Migdol. Place on the route of the Exodus (Ex 14:2); possibly identical with the place where Jews lived after the fall of Jerusalem (Jer 44:1).

Miletus. Ionian coastal city in Asia Minor south of Ephesus. Here Paul met the elders of the Ephesian church (Acts 20:15) on his final voyage to Jerusalem, and Trophimus lived there during a sickness (II Tim 4:20).

Mitylene (Mytilene). Capital of Lesbos, an island off the coast of Asia Minor. Paul sailed to Chios from Mitylene on his last missionary journey (Acts 20:14).

Mizpah (Mizpeh). Name of several towns. One was a place in Gilead where Jacob and Laban set up a pile of stones and parted company (Gen 31:49). Later, this was the residence of Jephthah and an area where the Israelites fought the Amorites under his command (Judg 11:11). Another Mizpah was a town in Benjamin where the Israelites often assembled in the days of the Judges

and Samuel. Here they gathered (Judg 20:1) to hear the Levite's account of the death of his concubine. Samuel made Mizpah the center of his activities (I Sam 7:16). While praying at Mizpah the Israelites were attacked by the Philistines, and here Saul was elected king. The city became an important border town between Judah and Israel following the split in the united monarchy. After the destruction of the First Temple, Mizpah was the seat of Gedaliah son of Ahikam, who was appointed by the Babylonians to rule Judah (II Kgs 22:26). Jews resettled the town after their return from Babylon.

Mizraim. Son of Ham whose descendants are listed in the Table of Nations in Genesis 10:13 and are believed to have settled in Lower Egypt. The word "Mizraim" was used in Hebrew for Egypt.

Moab. See II.4, Geography of the Holy Land: Regions (Transjordan).

Moreh, Oak of. Place near Shechem where Abraham camped and erected an altar to the Lord (Gen.12:6). Moses mentions the site as a landmark near Mount Ebal (Deut 11:26).

Moresheth, Moresheth-Gath. Town in the Judean foothills where Micah was born.

Moriah. The area where Abraham was commanded to take his son Isaac for sacrifice (Gen 22:2). The Bible describes the location as a three-day journey from Beersheba. On Mount Moriah Solomon built the Temple (II Chr 3:1), but whether this is the same Moriah mentioned in Genesis is unclear. See II.6, Jerusalem in the Bible.

Moserah, Moseroth. Desert camp of the Israelites where Aaron died and was buried (Num 33:30-31). Here Eleazar succeeded his father as high priest.

Myra. Chief seaport of the province of Lycia in southwestern Asia Minor. On his voyage to Rome Paul stopped there briefly in order to transfer to another ship (Acts 27:5).

Nahor. City in Mesopotamia, located in the upper Balih River. Abraham sent his servant to his relatives who lived there to find a bride for his son Isaac (Gen 24:10).

Nain. A village in Galilee, about 6 miles (10 km) southeast of Nazareth. At its gate Jesus raised a widow's only son from the dead (Luke 7:11-14).

Naioth. Place "in Ramah" where Samuel and a company of prophets lived when David fled from Saul. Three times Saul sent messengers to bring David to him and each time the messengers joined in prophesying with the prophets. Finally Saul went to Naioth and he too prophesied and David escaped (I Sam 19:18-19, 22-23; 20:1).

Nazareth. Small town in the hills of Galilee, where Mary was told of Jesus' birth (Luke 1:26), and where Mary and Joseph lived after their betrothal. Here Jesus grew up; he left the town for his baptism by John (Mark 1:9), returning to Nazareth before beginning to preach (Matt 4:13). Later he was rejected by the people of the

Partial view of Nazareth in the hills of Galilee, where Jesus grew up.

town because they supposed him to be no more than a carpenter's son (Matt 13:54-58). He was associated with the town (Matt 21:11) and was called a "Nazarene," his followers being later called by the same name (Acts 24:5).

Neapolis (modern Kavalla). Port of Philippi in Macedonia. Paul traveled there from Troas in Asia (Acts 16:11). Later he began his second missionary journey in Greece from Neapolis.

Nebo.

1) Mountain in Moab on which Moses died (Deut 32:49; 34:1).

2) Town of Moab, in the territory of Reuben and Gad (Num 32:3, 34-38). It had reverted to a Moabite city by the time of Isaiah (15:2) and Jeremiah (48:1, 22).

One of the mountains of the Abarim range in Moab identified by some as Mount Nebo.

According to to Ezra 10:43, the "sons of Nebo" were among those who had married foreign wives.

Negeb. See II.4, Geography of the Holy Land Regions.

Nephtoah. Spring on the border between Judah and Benjamin (Josh 15:9; 18:15).

Netophah. Town of Judah close to Bethlehem. Two of David's "mighty men" were born there (II Sam 23:28-29). Levites settled in Netophah (I Chr 9:16). After the Babylonian exile, the "sons of singers" lived there (Neh 12:28).

Nineveh. Last capital of the Assyrian empire; located on the east bank of the Tigris river, opposite present-day Mosul. According to Genesis 10:10-12 it was founded by Ashur (eponymous ancestor of the Assyrians) in the days of Nimrod. It was the capital of the Assyrian kingdom during the reign of Sennacherib, who was murdered there by his two sons (II Kgs 19:36-37; Is 37:37-38). The prophet Jonah was sent to Nineveh to warn it of destruction (1:2), but its inhabitants repented and were spared (Jonah 3). The city was eventually destroyed in 612 BC by a coalition of the Babylonians and Medes. Its destruction is mentioned by Zephaniah (Zeph 2:13-15) and Nahum. See also II.9 Digging up the Bible.

No Amon. Capital of Upper Egypt and at certain times also the capital of the entire country. No Amon meant "city of the god Amun." It is in this context that most biblical references should be understood (cf Jer 46:25; Ezek 30:14; Nah 3:8). It is identified with Thebes, the center of the cult of the god Amun.

Nob. Town of Benjamin, home of Abimelech and the priests. After the priests gave David sanctuary there, Saul retaliated by massacring the priests of Nob (I Sam

Alabaster sphinx at Memphis (Noph), of Pharaoh Amenophis II.

21, 22). From there the Assyrians could see the city of Jerusalem for the first time on their march from the north (Is 10:32). After the Babylonian exile, Nob was again settled by Benjamites (Neh 11:32).

Noph (Memphis). Egyptian city at the head of the Nile. For the prophets the city was symbolic of evil (Hos 9:6; Is 19:13; Jer 2:16), and its destruction was foretold by Jeremiah (46:19) and Ezekiel (30:13,16). During the Babylonian wars against Judah many Jews fled to Noph, and Jeremiah prophesied against them (Jer 44:1ff).

On. Hebrew name for an Egyptian city known as Heliopolis to the Greeks (Gen 41:45,50). Ezekiel calls it Aven (30:17).

Ono. Town in the vicinity of Lydda built by the tribe of Benjamin. After the return from Babylon the town was resettled (Ezra 2:33).

Ophir. Land that provided Solomon with a source of gold (I Kgs 9:28). Jehoshaphat also sought to acquire the precious metal from Ophir, but his fleet of trading ships was destroyed in a storm at Ezion Geber (I Kgs 22:48). Gold from Ophir was known for its high quality (Is 13:12). The exact location of the country is uncertain but the Bible hints at southern Arabia (Gen 10:29).

Ophrah.

1) City in the northern territory of Benjamin that was a key site in one of Saul's first battles against the Philistines as king of Israel (I Sam 13:17).

2) Town in the Jezreel Valley where Gideon was born and received his commission from the angel of the Lord to lead the Israelites against the Midianites (Judg 6:11).

Padan, Padan Aram. Land in northwestern Mesopotamia, home of Nahor and his family (Gen 48:7). Both Isaac's and Jacob's brides, Rebekah, Leah, and Rachel, came from there (Gen 25:20, 28:2).

Paphos. Port at the southwest end of Cyprus. Paul and Barnabas visited there on their first journey (Acts 13:6, 13).

Paran. Region in the Sinai peninsula, located between Midian and Egypt (I Kgs 11:18), home of the Ishmaelites (Gen 21:21). The Israelites stopped at Paran on their way from Egypt to the Promised Land (Deut 33:2). From there Moses sent men to spy out the land (Num 13:3). Later, after the death of Samuel, David found refuge in the wilderness of Paran (I Sam 25:1).

Pathros. Name for Upper Egypt used in conjunction with Mizraim, which means Lower Egypt.

Patmos. Rocky, desolate island in the Aegean Sea, used in Roman times as a place of banishment. The apostle John was exiled to the island and there he wrote the Book of Revelation.

Pekod. Geographical name mentioned in connection with the destruction of Babylon (Jer 50:21).

Peor. Mountain in the land of Moab, from which Balak wanted Balaam to curse the children of Israel (Num 23:28ff).

Perazim (also Baal Perazim and Mount Perazim). Scene of David's defeat of the Philistines. It was near Jerusalem.

Perga. Religious center of the province of Pamphylia, along the southern coast of Asia Minor. It had a temple to Artemis. Paul traveled through the city twice on his first missionary journey, but only preached there on his return from the interior (Acts 13:13-14; 14:25).

Pergamos. City in the district of Mysia in western Asia Minor, one of the seven churches mentioned by the author of Revelation (1:11; 2:12), who characterizes the city as the place "where Satan's throne is" (Rev 2:13). See also II.9, Digging up the Bible: Pergamon.

Pethor. Place of origin of Balaam, near the Euphrates (Num 22:5). Also called Pethor of Mesopotamia in Deut 23:4 and in the Septuagint.

Philadelphia. One of the seven cities addressed by the author of Revelation (1:11; 3:17). It was located in the district of Lydia in the Roman province of Asia.

Philippi. Macedonian city on the Gulf of Neapolis. Philippi was visited by Paul and Silas on the second missionary journey as a result of a dream Paul experienced in Troas (Acts 16:12-19). This is the first Christian missionary visit to Europe. Paul stayed there a few days and founded the first church in the West (I Phil 4:15). While in Philippi Paul and Silas were imprisoned but Paul was released when he revealed his Roman citizenship (Acts 16:23). He visited Philippi again on his third journey (Acts 20:6).

Phoenix. Harbor on the island of Crete where the crew of the ship carrying Paul from Fair Havens, Cyprus, proposed to spend the winter, but were prevented from doing so by bad weather (Acts 27:8-12).

Phrygia. Region in northwestern Asia Minor. Jews from Phrygia traveled to Jerusalem for the feast of Pentecost (Acts 2:1, 10). Paul passed through the area on his second and third journeys but was forbidden to preach there (Acts 16:6-7).

Pirathon. Town in Ephraim, home of the judge Abdon (Judg 12:14-15), and of David's warrior, Benaiah (II Sam 23:30).

Pisgah. Heights of the mountains between the plains of Moab and the Dead Sea (Deut 3:27; 32:49; 34:1). Balak met Balaam at the top of Pisgah (Num 23:14). From the peak of Pisgah, called Nebo, Moses saw the Promised Land before his death (Deut 3:27; 34:1-4).

Pishon. One of the four rivers of Eden. It flowed around the entire land of Havilah (Gen 2:11).

Pisidia. Region of central Asia Minor, visited by Paul on his first journey (Acts 13:14; 14:24).

Pithom. Egyptian store city in the land of Goshen built by the Children of Israel when they were enslaved to Pharaoh (Ex 1:11).

Pontus. Region of northeastern Asia Minor located from the Black Sea to the Caucasus. Jews from Pontus journeyed to Jerusalem for Pentecost (Acts 2:9). Aquila, Paul's friend and co-worker, was born in Pontus (Acts 18:2). Peter addressed the church there (I Pet 1:1).

Puteoli (modern Puzzuoli). Seaport in the Bay of Naples. Paul arrived there on his journey to Rome aboard an Alexandrian grain freighter. He found a Christian community already established there (Acts 28:13-14).

Raamses, Rameses. An Egyptian city and region. In this rich area, Jacob and his family were settled by Joseph (Gen.47:11). It was one of the store cities built by the Israelites for Pharaoh (Ex 1:11) and was the place from which they began their long journey to the Promised Land (Ex 12:37).

Rabbah, Rabbath Ammon. Royal city of Ammon (modern Amman) in Transjordan, strategically located on a junction of trade routes. It was surrounded by many small villages known as the "daughters of Rabbah." The city was besieged by Joab, who summoned David to complete its conquest (II Sam 12:27-29). This campaign was the occasion of the planned death of

The Roman theater at Philadelphia (Rabbath Ammon).

Uriah, husband of Bathsheba. After the split in the United Monarchy the Ammonites gained their independence and established their capital in Rabbath Ammon, but early in the 6th century it was laid waste by "men from the east" (Ezek 25:4). Ptolemy II Philadelphus (285-246 BC) rebuilt the city and renamed it Philadelphia. During the New Testament period it was part of the Decapolis.

Ramah (Ramathaim Zophim). Town in Benjamin, headquarters of Deborah during the days of Sisera (Judg 4:5), the home of Elkanah and Hannah and the birthplace of Samuel (I Sam 1:19), when it was known as Ramathaim Zophim. Isaiah records how Ramah was terrified at the advance of Sennacherib's army on Jerusalem, while Jeremiah describes the town as the place where Rachel was weeping for her children (31:15). Ramah was resettled by some of its former residents after the return from Babylon. It is identified with er-Ram, 5 miles (9 kms) north of Jerusalem.

Ramath Lehi. See Lehi.

Ramoth Gilead. Town in Transjordan in the tribal allotment of Gad; given to the Merarite clan of Levites, it was a city of refuge. After the death of Solomon possession of the city was contested by the Arameans and Israelites. Here Ahab was killed in battle after attempting to recapture the city (I Kgs 22). His son Joram continued the war to retake the city but was wounded (II Kgs 8:28). In the reign of Jehoash, the Israelites finally conquered the city and re-established their rule over the area (II Kgs 14:25-28). However, their triumph was shortlived, and Ramoth Gilead eventually returned to Aramean hands, remaining so until it was finally overwhelmed by the Assyrians (II Kgs 15:29) and renamed Galada.

Rehoboth. Name given by Isaac to a site in the Negeb where he dug a well after having been driven from the land of the Philistines (Gen 26:9).

Rephaim. Productive agricultural valley south of Jerusalem highly prized by the Philistines, who were twice defeated here by David (I Chr 14:8-12; 14:16).

Rephidim. Site of an Israelite camp on the Exodus from Egypt. Here Moses struck a rock to provide the people with water (Ex 17:6) and Joshua fought the Amalekites (Ex 17:9).

Rhegium. Seaport in southern Italy where Paul spent one day on his journey to Rome (Acts 28:13).

Rhodes. Mediterranean island where Paul stayed in the course of his final voyage to Jerusalem (Acts 21:1).

Riblah. Syrian city near the Orontes river. It was held by Pharaoh Necho who imprisoned Jehoahaz there (II Kgs 23:33). Later Nebuchadnezzar used it as his base for attacking Judah and had Zedekiah and his sons executed there (II Kgs 25).

Rimmon. Name of two places. One was a town assigned to Judah but later given to Simeon (Josh 15:20; 19:1). The other was a Levitical city in the territory of Zebulun (Josh 19:13). Rimmon was also the name of a rock to which the men of Benjamin fled after their defeat by a coalition of the other tribes (Judg 20-21).

Salamis. Port on the southern coast of Cyprus, near present-day Famagusta. Paul, Barnabas and John preached in synagogues there during their first missionary journey (Acts 13:5). Of all the Greek cities which Paul visited, Salamis alone is recorded as having "synagogues" in the plural, indicating a large Jewish population.

Salcah. City in Transjordan. Conquered by Moses (Deut 3:10; Josh 12:5; 13:11), it was part of the inheritance of the half- tribe of Manasseh (Deut 3:13).

Salem. City of Melchizedek (Gen 14:18), later identified with Jerusalem.

Salt Sea. See Dead Sea.

Samaria. See II.4, Geography in the Holy Land, and II.9, Digging up the Bible.

Sardis. City in west Asia Minor, 50 miles (80 km) east of Smyrna. The church at Sardis is one of seven mentioned in the Book of Revelation (Rev 1:11). Mystery religions flourished in Sardis and many in the Christian community returned to their former religions. This is probably the reason for the exhortation to remember what they had "heard and received...and repent" (Rev 3:3).

The forecourt of the synagogue at Sardis, dating from the 2nd century AD.

Seir. Name of mountain and land substantially identical with Edom (see II.4, Geography of the Holy Land). It was the region of Esau. The Israelites coming from Egypt skirted Mount Seir to avoid Edomite territory (Deut 2:1-5).

Sela ("rock"). Town in northern Edom taken from the Edomites by Amaziah, who changed its name to Joktheel (II Kgs 14:7; II Chr 25:12ff).

Seleucia. City at the mouth of the Orontes river, which was the port of Antioch. Paul and Barnabas sailed from Seleucia when they set out on their first missionary expedition.

Sepharad. Place to which the Jews of Jerusalem were exiled (Obad 20).

Sepharvaim. City captured by the Assyrians. Its deportees were settled in Samaria by the king of Assyria to take the place of the exiled Israelites (II Kgs 17:24).

Sheba. Region in southwest Arabia identified with modern Yemen. According to biblical and other sources, the kingdom of Sheba throve for over 1500 years, from 1000 BC until c. AD 500, known for its fine spices, jewels and gold (Ezek 27:22). The queen of Sheba came to Jerusalem with gifts of gold, precious stones, and spices to visit Solomon and to test his wisdom (I Kgs 10:1-13). The Sabeans participated in the slave trade (Joel 3:8). They were responsible for the beginning of Job's woes, when they stole his oxen and killed his servants (Job 1:15).

Shebam (also Shibmah, Sibmah). Town on the east bank of the Jordan River, belonging to Sihon, king of the Amorites. The Children of Israel conquered the land, which became part of the inheritance of Reuben (Num 32:3, 38; Josh 13:19). It was renowned for its wine (Is 16:8-9; Jer 48:32).

Shechem. Town in the hill country of Ephraim. Abraham stopped there on his arrival in the country and experienced a theophany in which God promised him the land of Canaan. In response Abraham built an altar (Gen 12:5-7). Shechem was closely associated with Jacob who settled there, built an altar, and purchased land. It was assigned to the Levites as a city of refuge (Josh 21:21; I Chr 6:67). Joshua made a covenant with the people there and set up a stone marker (Josh 24:25-26). Gideon's family lived in Shechem. His son, Abimelech, was welcomed by the men of Shechem (Judg 9), and after his family was slain they made him king. However, his popularity was short-lived and three years later they rose up and cursed him (Judg 9:27). Abimelech defeated the Shechemites (Judg 9:45), but was then killed by a woman who dropped a stone on his head (Judg 9:53). Rehoboam was enthroned in Shechem (I Kgs 12:1). Immediately after the schism in the kingdom, Jeroboam fortified Shechem and made it his capital (I Kgs 12:25). The city was conquered and destroyed many times, leading to its decline. Eventually the Samaritans occupied it. The town was probably Sychar in John 4:5-7 ("Sychem" in the Syriac version), near Jacob's well, where Jesus met the woman of Samaria. See also II.9, Digging up the Bible: Shechem.

Sheshach A name used only in Jeremiah to describe Babylon (25:26; 51:41). It is a cypher based on reversing the letters of the Hebrew alphabet.

Shihor, Sihor. Stream east of Egypt, referred to as the southern frontier of the land of Canaan (Josh 13:3) and the outer boundary of David's kingdom (I Chr 13:5). Isaiah (23:3) parallels Sihor with "the River" (the Nile) and Jeremiah mentions the waters of Sihor to symbolize Egypt (Jer 2:18). Egyptian monuments apply the name Shihor to the eastern Delta and to Lake Fayum.

Shiloah (Siloah, Siloam). Water source for Jerusalem, probably connected with the spring of Gihon. It is mentioned in the Old Testament as the "waters of Shiloah" (Is 8:6) and "the Pool of Shelah" (Neh 3:15), and in the New Testament as "the Pool of Siloam" (John 9:7). Nehemiah (3:15) says that the wall of the pool was close to the king's garden, known to have been on the south side of the city. Hezekiah's cistern (II Kgs 20:20) is identified with the Pool of Shiloah.

Shiloh. An early religious center of the Israelites situated on Mount Ephraim, north of Bethel (Judg 21:19). Joshua set up the tabernacle of the congregation there (Josh 18:1). It was the place of the general assembly of the Israelites (displacing Shechem). Eli and his sons officiated at Shiloh, and there God appeared to Samuel (I Sam 1:9; 3:1ff). An annual vineyard harvest was celebrated there (Judg 21:19-21), and its girls were raped by the men of Benjamin after a war between the tribes. The priests of Shiloh continued to minister before the ark until Solomon deposed Abiathar (I Kgs 2:27).

The village of Silwan on the outskirts of which is the Siloam Tunnel.

Shinar. Name for Babylon. It is actually the Hebrew name for Sumer. It was the land ruled by Nimrod (Gen 10:10), site of the tower of Babel (Gen 11:2) and of the kingdom of Amraphel (Gen 14). It was a place where Isaiah foresaw a Diaspora community would be living (Is 11:11). According to the Book of Daniel, after Nebuchadnezzar, king of Babylon, destroyed Jerusalem, the Temple treasures were brought to Shinar (Dan 1:2).

Shittim. A town in Moab, east of Jordan and northeast of the Dead Sea. The Children of Israel camped there before crossing the Jordan (Josh 2:1; 3:1). In this area Balaam tried to curse the Israelites (Num 22-23) and here the Israelites went astray with Moabite women and worshiped idols (Num 25:1-9).

Shunem. One of the towns of the tribes of Issachar, site of the Philistine camp before the battle of Mount Gilboa (I Sam 28:4) and home of Abishag, David's companion, and of the woman whose son was revived from the dead by Elisha (II Kgs 4). It was situated in the Valley of Jezreel.

Shur. Desert near the Red Sea. Hagar fled to Shur (Gen 16:7), and the Ishmaelites lived in the vicinity (Gen 25:18). The Israelites crossed the desert of Shur on their way from the Red Sea (Ex 15:22).

Shushan. Capital of Elam, later royal city of the Persians. Shushan, the seat of King Ahasuerus, is the setting of the Book of Esther. Daniel was kept in Shushan during the reign of King Belshazzar (Dan 8:2).

Siddim, Valley of. Scene of battle between Canaanite and Mesopotamian kings (Gen 14). The Valley of Siddim is identified with the Salt Sea in Genesis 14:3, and according to biblical tradition it was flooded over when Sodom and Gomorrah were destroyed.

Sidon. Ancient Phoenician port city, situated between Tyre and modern Beirut on the coast of Lebanon, which in biblical times marked the border of Canaan (Gen 10:19). It was ruled by kings, who extended their reign over cities to the south. Laish (Dan) was built by the Sidonians, but later burned by the Danites (Judg 18:7, 27). After its destruction in the 12th century BC, the inhabitants fled to Tyre, but the city soon revived. It was in its satellite town of Zarephath that Elijah performed a miracle for a poor woman (I Kgs 17:9ff). Jezebel, the wife of King Ahab, was the daughter of Ethbaal, king of the Sidonians, and brought with her to Israel her pagan religious practices. Nebuchadnezzar triumphed over Sidon on his way to Judah, but subsequently Sidon revived once again and spread out to include the Plain of Sharon from Mount Carmel to Joppa. In the New Testament Jesus reached Sidon and healed the daughter of a Syro-Phoenician woman (Matt 15:21-28; Mark 7:24-30), and Jews from Tyre and Sidon came to listen to him (Mark 3:8). It was the first port visited by Paul on his way to Rome as a prisoner (Acts 27:1,3).

Siloam. See Shiloah.

Sin. Egyptian frontier city, which Ezekiel called the "stronghold of Egypt" (30:15-16).

Sin, Wilderness of. See Zin.

Sinai. Desert peninsula bounded on two sides by the Red Sea: the Gulf of Akaba (Elath) on the east and the Gulf of Suez on the west; and on its third side by the Mediterranean Sea. The northern area is a sandy belt with a rock plateau inland, while the southern part consists of a granite mountain chain. It is very arid, with a few oases, and was inhabited primarily by nom-

On the left, some three thousand steps leading up to the summit of Jebel Musa, the traditional Mount Sinai. On the right, the monastery of Santa Caterina at the foot of Mount Sinai.

ads. Trade routes traversed the peninsula, as it is the only land bridge connecting Egypt with areas to the east.

In the Bible Sinai is also the name of a specific mountain (Ps 68:8), scene of the great theophany, where Moses received the Law. It is sometimes called

Where Was Mount Sinai?

Bible research has long been concerned with the Israelite Exodus and the site of Mount Sinai on which the Tablets of the Law were given. The ancient tradition that this was venerable Mount Moses was found hard to accept, because the way to it from the Land of Goshen must have been too long and tiresome and because there is no vegetation at the mount's foot where the wanderers' herds could graze. Some scholars have proposed Gebel Hallal in northeastern Sinai. To its 2,690 ft. (892 m) high top, clouds cling on clear spring days and on the flat surrounding terrain flocks may have grazed while Moses climbed the mountain. This view was challenged by a geographer who claimed that the great distance from Egypt to Mt. Hallal does not tie in with the description of the route in the Book of Exodus. He instead proposed as a probable site Gebel Sinn Bishr, southeast of the present town of Suez.

Horeb (I Kgs 19:8), and Mount Horeb is also referred to as the "mountain of God" (Ex 3:1). The patriarchs crossed Sinai on their journeys from Egypt to the land of Canaan. It was the wilderness in which the Israelites lived for 40 years, and the stopping points along the way of the Exodus are listed in Numbers 33, although few can be identified today. Mount Sinai, too, is still not clearly identified. See also II.4 Geography of the Holy Land: Regions.

Smyrna. Port city in Asia Minor, on the Aegean Sea. Its church is one of seven mentioned in the Book of Revelation and one of two that were not rebuked (2:9–11). Smyrna is modern Izmir in Asiatic Turkey.

Socoh, Sochoh. Town in the Judean Hills; site of the Philistine camp when David fought Goliath (I Sam 17:1; AV: "Shochoh"). Rehoboam fortified it (II Chr 11:7). The Egyptian Pharaoh Sheshonk (biblical Shishak) captured the city and later restored it to Judah. In Ahaz's time, the Philistines raided it (II Chr 28:18) but it returned to Judah in the days of Hezekiah. Another town of that name in the Judean hill country (Josh 15:48) was home to a family of scribes (I Chr 2:55; AV: "Suchathites"), and a further Socoh was in Solomon's third district in northern Samaria (I Kgs 4:10).

Sodom See Gomorrah.

Sorek. Valley in the territory of Dan which was the home of Delilah (Judg 16:4).

Syracuse. City on the east coast of Sicily, where the ship carrying Paul docked for three days while on its way to Italy (Acts 28:12).

Syria, Syrians. In the New Testament the name refers to the Roman province which included Palestine, with a legate resident in Antioch. Paul visited there frequently (Acts 15:23, 41; 18:18) and it was while on the road to Damascus (one of Syria's main cities) to persecute those who believed in Jesus, that Paul himself came to believe (Acts 9). Syria later became a major center of the early Christian church.

Taanach. City in the territory of Manasseh at the southern entrance to the Jezreel Valley, first mentioned in ancient Egyptian documents. Taanach appears in the list of 31 Canaanite cities defeated by Joshua (Josh 12:21) but did not come under Israelite control until the days of Deborah (Judg 5:19). Under the Israelites it became a Levitical city. After the death of Solomon Taanach was destroyed by the Egyptians and never heard of again.

Cultic stand from Taanach; 10th century BC.

Tadmor. Oasis city northeast of Damascus on the caravan route between the Mediterranean and the Euphrates. Solomon constructed a fortress city nearby or rebuilt the old after his conquest of Hamath-zobah (II Chr 8:4). In the classical period it was a wealthy caravan center called Palmyra.

Tahpanhes, Tehaphnehes. Fortress city on the eastern edge of the Nile delta. It was renowned for its commercial activity and worship of Baal-Zephon, the god of seafarers. Here Jeremiah and other Jews took refuge after the murder of Gedaliah. Jeremiah buried stones there as a symbolic threat against Egypt (Jer

43:7–13). Ezekiel foretold its destruction (30:18) and by the Hellenistic period it was an insignificant village.

Tappuah. City in the Judean hills whose king was defeated by Joshua (Josh 12:17). Also the name of a Canaanite kingdom defeated by the Israelites and assigned to Ephraim.

Tarshish. A distant land (Is 23:6) known for its silver, iron, tin, and lead. Solomon sent his ships there (II Chr 9:21) and it was the destination to which Jonah set sail in order to flee the word of the Lord (Jonah 1:3). Some have identified Tarshish with Tartasus in Spain, while others relate it to Tarsus in Cilicia.

Tarsus. City of Asia Minor, birthplace of Paul ("Saul of Tarsus"). After coming to believe in Jesus he continued to live there, until Barnabas took him to Antioch (Acts 11:25). He called it "no mean city" (Acts 21:39).

Tekoa. Town bordering the Judean Desert near Bethlehem. It was the home of Ira, one of David's "mighty men" (II Sam 23:26) and of a wise woman who persuaded David to bring Absalom back to Jerusalem (II Sam 14). Rehoboam fortified it and after the return from Babylon the residents of Tekoa took part in rebuilding the walls of Jerusalem. The nobles of the city, however, did not do their share of the work. Amos was a herdsman from Tekoa (Amos 1:1).

Tel Abib ("hill of the storm flood"). Site in southern Babylon near the River Chebar visited by Ezekiel, where some Jewish exiles were settled (Ezek 3:15).

Tema. Place in the northern Arabian desert identified with the oasis of Teima. It was an important caravan stop on the way from southern Arabia to Babylon or the countries of the eastern Mediterranean. The Bible refers to luxury-laden camel trains as "caravans from Tema" (Job 6:19).

Teman. City and region in northeastern Edom whose residents were noted for their wisdom (Jer 49:7). It is frequently mentioned together with Edom (Jer 49:20; Ezek 25:13).

Thebez. Town near Shechem where Abimelech was slain by a millstone thrown down from the wall by a woman of the city (II Sam 11:21).

Thyatira. City in Asia Minor between Sardis and Pergamos famous for its weaving and dyeing. Paul's first convert in Europe, Lydia, was from Thyatira (Acts 16:14). Thyatira is one of the seven churches to which the Book of Revelation was addressed (Rev 1:11).

Tiberias. City built by Herod Antipas in AD 18 on the western shores of the Sea of Galilee and named in honor of the Emperor Tiberius. Built on a graveyard, it was considered unclean by Jewish law, and Orthodox Jews, including Jesus himself, did not set foot in Tiberias. The city is mentioned once in the New Testament (John 6:23). The Sea of Galilee is occasionally called the Sea of Tiberias (John 21:1).

Tigris. See Hiddekel.

Timnah. Town in the hill country of Judah, first men-

A view of Tiberias.

Roman columns at Tyre.

A silver shekel minted at Tyre, the most important coin in the Holy Land in the Roman period.

tioned in connection with Judah and Tamar (Gen 38:14). It was birthplace of Samson's Philistine wife and the scene of his fight with a lion (Judg 14:1–5). An Edomite town of the same name is mentioned in Gen 26:40. See also II.9, Digging up the Bible.

Timnat Heres, Timnat Serah. Town in Ephraim that Joshua requested as an inheritance (Josh 19:50). He rebuilt the town and was buried there (Josh 24:30).

Tirzah. Canaanite city conquered by Joshua. It was long the royal residence of kings of Israel until the capital was transferred to Samaria in the reign of Omri. It seems to have been a few miles north of Shechem.

Tob. Region northeast of Gilead where Jephthah lived as an outlaw (Judg 11:3). During the reign of King David, the Ammonites hired mercenaries from Tob (II Sam 10:6–8).

Togarmah. Country named as one of the future enemies of Israel (Ezek 38:6) along with Gog and Magog.

Tophet(h). High place in the Hinnom Valley in the vicinity of Jerusalem where child sacrifices were offered to the gods Molech and Baal (Jer 32:35). Jeremiah cursed Tophet and renamed it the "Valley of Slaughter" (7:32ff).

Troas. Region and port in northwestern Asia Minor where Paul had a vision of a man from Macedonia appealing for help. The apostle immediately left Troas and traveled to Macedonia (Acts 16:8–10). On his final missionary journey Paul returned to Troas. While he was teaching there, Eutychus fell from the third storey and was pronounced dead, but Paul restored him to life (Acts 20:9).

Tyre. Phoenician port and city-state on the southern coast of what is now Lebanon. The modern Lebanese city of the same name is built on the ancient site. When the Israelites entered the Promised Land, Tyre was assigned to the tribe of Asher but it proved too strong to be conquered (Josh 19:29) and is mentioned as the limit of David's kingdom (II Sam 24:7). David and Solomon had a friendly alliance with King Hiram of Tyre, who supplied cedar trees, carpenters, and masons to build David's palace (II Sam 5:11) and played an important part in providing craftsmen and materials to construct Solomon's Temple (I Kgs 5). In return Solomon gave Hiram 20 cities in western Galilee. During the days of King Ahab close relations existed between Israel and Tyre. The city was condemned for idolatry by many of the prophets, including Isaiah (23), Jeremiah (25:22), and Joel (3:4), who foretold its eventual destruction. The city features prominently in the prophecies of Ezekiel. When the Jews returned to their land from Babylon, the merchants of Tyre could be found selling their goods in Jerusalem on the Sabbath (Neh 13:16). In the New Testament period it was a flourishing commercial city and is usually mentioned together with Sidon. Jesus visited the region (Mark 7:2) and Paul stayed there for seven days.

Ur. Mesopotamian city ("Ur of the Chaldees") from

where Abraham's father, Terah, originated (Gen 11:28,31).

Uz. Region of uncertain identification where Job lived (Job 1:1). In Jeremiah (25:15,17,20), it is one of the places made to drink the wine of God's wrath. It is associated with both Edom (Lam 4:21) and Aram (Gen 10:23).

Zalmon. Mountain range with many peaks, also known as the "hill of God" and the "hill of Bashan" (Ps 68:14–15).

Zarephath. Phoenician harbor south of Sidon, where Elijah revived the widow's son (I Kgs 17). The episode is mentioned by Jesus (Luke 4:26).

Zeboim, Zeboiim. One of the five "Cities of the Plain" in the Dead Sea region. King Chedorlaomer of Elam and his cohorts fought King Shemeber of Zeboiim and the other cities of the Plain (Gen 14:2,8,10). According to Moses, it was annihilated along with Sodom and Gomorrah (Deut 29:23) and Hosea referred to it as an example of a place which received God's wrath (Hos 11:8).

Zered. Wadi (dry river bed except in the rainy season) delineating the border between the plains of Moab and the mountains of Edom. Moses led the Israelites across the brook (Num 21:12; Deut 2:13–14).

Ziklag. Town in southern Judah (Josh 15:31). It was apportioned to Simeon (Josh 19:5), but in Saul's time it still belonged to the Philistines. After David fled from Saul's wrath to the land of the Philistines, he was given Ziklag as his residence (I Sam 27:1–6). Ziklag was re-established after the Babylonian captivity.

Zin. Desert region south of Canaan (Josh 15:1–3). The Israelites journeyed through it on their way from Egypt to Canaan and it was from this wilderness that men were sent to spy out the land of Canaan (Num 13:21). Massah and Meribah, where water for the multitude came forth from the rock, were located in this wilderness (Ex 17:7; Num 20).

Zion. See II.6, Jerusalem in the Bible.

Ziph. Town of Judah whose residents betrayed David's hiding place to Saul (I Sam 23:19ff). Later fortified by Rehoboam for the defense of Judah.

Zoan. Ancient Egyptian city on the eastern Nile delta built seven years after Hebron (Num 13:22). It was mentioned by Isaiah (19:11–13; 30:4) as a seat of Pharaoh's counselors, and by Ezekiel (30:14). According to Psalms 78:12,43, Moses met Pharaoh there.

Zoar. City in the Dead Sea region where Lot fled after the destruction of Sodom and Gomorrah (Gen 19:20–23). Initially known as Bela (Gen 14:8), it was, at Lot's request, the only one of the Cities of the Plain that was not destroyed.

Zobah, Zoba. Aramean kingdom (Aram-Zobah) which was a persistent enemy of Israel. The kings of Zobah fought Saul (I Sam 14:7), and Zobah united all the Aramean kingdoms into an alliance to fight the Israelites (II Sam 10:19). They were defeated by David on three occasions, and in the last of those battles David's victory was overwhelming (I Chr 18:45).

Zorah. Town straddling the territory between Dan and Judah (Josh 19:41) which was the place of Samuel's birth (Judg 13:2) and burial. From here five men from Dan set out to find a more hospitable place for their tribe to live (Judg 18). It was fortified by Rehoboam at the breakup of the united monarchy and was resettled by Jews after the return from Babylon.

II.6 JERUSALEM IN THE BIBLE

Straddling a rocky hillside, Jerusalem was first populated in the Early Bronze Age (c.2500 BC). Egyptian clay texts of the 19th century BC refer to the Canaanite city-state of Urushamem or Rushalimum. Nearby, according to biblical tradition, lay Mount Moriah, where Abraham prepared to sacrifice Isaac in a test of faith (Gen 22:2) and on which Solomon's Temple would later arise (II Chr 3:1). In the patriarchal era, Jerusalem was already the center of a religious cult; its ruler, Melchizedek "king of Salem," is also entitled "Priest of God the Most High" (Gen 14:18–20). During the conquest of Canaan, another ruler of Jerusalem named Adoni-Zedek headed a warlike Amorite confederacy which Joshua's troops defeated in battle (Josh 10:1ff.) The Jebusites inhabiting the city (then known as Jebus) could not be dislodged at that time (Josh 15:63) and, for upward of 200 years, controlled a small enclave between the tribal lands of Judah and Benjamin.

King David's awareness of the need for a political center, independent of tribal rivalries and capable of withstanding Philistine incursions, motivated his northward march from Hebron to capture Jerusalem shortly before 1,000 BC. Around Zion, the old citadel, a new City of David was built, fortified, and populated; there, the Ark of the Covenant subsequently arrived and was installed in a temporary home amidst vast rejoicing (II Sam 6:12–15). As a man of war, however, David was not allowed to fulfill his cherished hope of building the Temple, God's House, in Jerusalem. That project was reserved for his son and successor, Solomon, whose hands had not been stained with blood (I Chr 22:6–10).

Favorable political circumstances enabled King Solomon to expand the realm which he inherited from

A view of Jerusalem with the Temple Mount in the center.

David into an extensive empire. This brought riches and prestige to Jerusalem, which almost tripled in size, extending north from the City of David to encompass the Ophel (a site identified with Mount Moriah), where the Temple and an adjoining royal palace eventually dominated the skyline. Renewing his late father's alliance with Hiram king of Tyre, Solomon imported Phoenician timber and craftsmen for these architectural schemes, in which nearly 200,000 laborers found employment.

With daily worship and the offering of sacrifices concentrated in the Temple, Jerusalem became a holy city and the focus of regular pilgrimages. Israel's priests, prophets, and psalmists all congregated there. Jerusalem was also Israel's administrative capital and commercial center, with a standing army to protect it, high officials in attendance at court, envoys speeding to and fro, and foreign dignitaries such as the Queen of Sheba (I Kgs 10) paying state visits. "Fair in situation, the joy of the whole earth," Jerusalem had indeed become "the city of the great King" (Ps 48:3). Yet there was evidence of a social and religious deterioration in the latter years of Solomon's reign: a costly harem, oppressive taxation, and idolatrous shrines erected beyond the city walls to cater for alien residents. Nor was Solomon's own fabled wisdom proof against the alluring heathenism of his many foreign wives. Jeroboam, a rebellious official, exploited popular grievances in Solomon's lifetime; after his death in 928 BC, the new king Rehoboam's tyrannical shortsightedness played into Jeroboam's hands, leading to the establishment of a breakaway Northern Kingdom in Samaria (I Kgs 11-12).

Although now less significant politically, Jerusalem, as capital of Judah, the Southern Kingdom ruled by the Davidic line, and guardian of the Temple, held fast to its religious importance. In the eyes of the biblical chronicler, Samaria and its rulers were almost invariably idolatrous, whereas at least seven kings of Judah, from Asa (908-867) to Josiah (639-609), followed a righteous path. Sometimes there was an alliance between the rival kingdoms, but more often they fought each other, as when Jehoash king of Israel defeated Amaziah in battle, smashed through the walls of Jerusalem, and then ransacked the Temple and the palace (c.785 BC; II Kgs 14:12-14). Prosperity was restored under Uzziah (769-733), who repaired the walls breached in his father's time, strengthening them with towers and catapults (II Chr 26). After the fall of the Northern Kingdom in 721, Judah and Jerusalem stood alone against the might of conquering Assyria.

Thanks to the zealous monotheism of Hezekiah (727-698), a campaign to stamp out idolatry was launched throughout Judah. Both the Temple and the priesthood were reconsecrated. Hezekiah also prepared for an Assyrian invasion, fortifying Jerusalem's defense system and cutting an underground tunnel through solid rock to divert water from the Gihon spring outside the eastern wall into a reservoir, the pool of Siloam, within. As foreseen, the heavily armed troops of Sennacherib overcame one Judean city after another, laying siege to the capital in 701 BC. With its massive walls and guaranteed water supply, however, Jerusalem stood firm. Unexpectedly, perhaps because of an epidemic or some other disastrous event, the Assyrians beat a hasty retreat and marched home. Jerusalem had been granted a miraculous deliverance (II Kgs 18-19; II Chr 29-32).

The fact that it had remained secure when a hundred other cities had fallen to the victorious Assyrians, that it had survived because of its proven devotion to God, now lent Jerusalem a near mystical sanctity. Later kings (apart from Josiah) may have flirted with pagan cults, religious and ethical transgressions may have angered the prophets, yet the ideal of Zion and God's house of prayer took hold. From every corner of the land, pilgrims arrived in their thousands; hostelries filled and trade flourished as they came to "give thanks to the Lord" and "pray for the peace of Jerusalem" (Ps 122). A century after Hezekiah's death, however, Judah was transformed into one of the Babylonian empire's vassal states. The Babylonian ruler, Nebuchadnezzar, conducted a year-long siege of Jerusalem (587-6), battering down its walls prior to the looting and destruction of Solomon's Temple. With the political and religious center of the nation a charred ruin, most of the population led away into exile, and the myth of inviolability exploded, it seemed that Jerusalem would share the fate of Samaria.

The exilic community in Babylon never forgot Jerusalem and the Temple. After vanquishing the Babylonians in 539 BC, Cyrus the Great of Persia issued a historic proclamation allowing the Judean exiles to return to their homeland, "go up to Jerusalem," and rebuild the "house of the Lord God of Israel" there. Armed with all the gold and silver vessels which had been taken from the Temple, Sheshbazzar (a prince of the Davidic line) headed the first group of exiles that chose to depart. They were reinforced by a second group, under the leadership of Zerubbabel, and as a result of their combined efforts the building of a new Temple was completed in 515 BC, despite an attempt by resentful Samaritans to obstruct this project (Ezra 1-6).

According to an early census (Ezra 2; Neh 7), the returning exiles numbered less than 50,000. During the reign of Artaxerxes I, a larger wave of immigrants came from Babylon with Ezra the Scribe (c.458 BC), whose effort to build protective walls around the sparsely populated capital met with renewed opposition, including acts of sabotage. Nehemiah, a high official at the Persian court, was given a detailed report of the situation in 445 and obtained leave of absence from Artaxerxes as temporary governor of Judah. Arriving in Jerusalem, he immediately breathed enthusiasm into the dispirited people: each contingent worked on its own section of the wall, one half standing guard to repel enemy attacks while the other half saw to the necessary repairs. Under Nehemiah's tireless and resolute lead-

The minaret of the citadel of Jerusalem, popularly known as the Tower of David.

ership, the task of reconstruction was completed in just 52 days.

After Nehemiah's return to Susa, an uneventful century elapsed before Alexander the Great conquered the Persian satrapy of which Judah formed part (332 BC). Jerusalem retained the nation's spiritual allegiance: Jews turned to it in prayer, sent contributions for the upkeep of the Temple, and went on pilgrimages to the city. Following the Seleucid conquest in 198, however, there was a gradual change for the worse. Jewish Hellenists and loyalists struggled for power as a Syrian form of "Greek culture" penetrated Jerusalem.

Under Antiochus IV Epiphanes, nude athletes thronged a gymnasium built next to the Temple, and the capital became a Greek *polis* renamed Antiochia. Having plundered the Temple, slaughtered his opponents, and garrisoned a newly-built fortress (the Akra) dominating the Temple Mount, Antiochus proceeded to make any observance of Judaism an offense incurring the death penalty (167). Within the Temple, his agents destroyed the sacred scrolls, erected and worshiped a statue of Zeus, and sacrificed pigs on the altar; throughout Judah, anyone found circumcising a boy, keeping the Sabbath, refusing to eat pork, or not bowing to an idol, was summarily executed. Passive resistance soon gave way to armed revolt when the Hasmonean clan adopted guerrilla tacts in a war of liberation (I Macc 1-2). Inspired by their leader, Judah the Maccabee, Hasmonean forces entered Jerusalem in 164 BC, and cleansed and rededicated the Temple.

As the capital of an independent Hasmonean kingdom, Jerusalem attained splendor and renown, but witnessed the growth of conflicting outlooks and ideologies. Alexander Janneus or Yannai (c.126-76 BC), whose empire came close to Solomonic proportions, favored the aristocratic Sadducean party and was involved in civil war because of his enmity toward the more liberal and popular Pharisees. When Yannai's sons, Hyrcanus II and Aristobulus, fought each other over the succession, the Roman general Pompey intervened on the former's behalf, stormed his way into the Temple, and reduced Judea to a Roman puppet state (63). The throne was finally usurped by a cunning and ruthless outsider, Herod "the Great." Herod embarked on a vast program of reconstruction that transformed his capital into one of the glories of the ancient world.

During Herod's reign (37–4 BC), the Temple was rebuilt on a magnificent scale, with colossal outer walls that partly survived its later destruction. The Temple's musical service and the convoys of pilgrims arriving to worship and offer sacrifice there, helped to focus attention on what Pliny the Elder called "the most famous among the great cities of the East." Jerusalem now had a population of some 250,000, but heavy taxation and the conduct of Roman procurators after Herod's time led to seething discontent. Apocalyptic and ultra-nationalist groups also won many converts. The standard Roman punishment for "dangerous agitators" was crucifixion. Jesus of Nazareth, who visited the Jerusalem Temple as a child, met his terrible death on Golgotha or Calvary, just outside the city's northwestern wall (c. AD 32).

An upsurge of Jewish zealotry, provoked by years of increasingly savage Roman oppression, led to a nationwide revolt in 66. The Roman general (and future emperor) Titus and his legions finally captured Jerusalem after a long siege and, having breached successive defenses, razed Herod's Temple to the ground. A last desperate revolt under Bar Kokhba (132–135) merely confirmed the triumph of paganism: Judea was renamed Syria Palaestina, Hadrian's Aelia Capitolina obliterated the Herodian Jerusalem, and Jews were forbidden to venture inside on pain of death. Condemned to exile, Judaism lost its territorial base, although Jerusalem remained the focus of its prayers. However, the Old Testament concept of "Jerusalem the holy city" (Isa 52:1; Neh 11:1) had a powerful impact on Judaism's two daughter religions. It reappeared in the New Testament (Matt 4:5; Rev 11:2), also inspiring Christianity's vision of a heavenly "New Jerusalem" (Rev 21:2,10) and no fewer than eight medieval Crusades. From the Bible Islam likewise drew its own reverence for the Temple Mount, identified as Mohammed's "Outer Mosque" in the Koran (17:1) and for El Kuds, its third holiest city. To this day, Jerusalem is a holy city for Jews, Christians, and Muslims.

For Archaeology of Jerusalem, see II.9, Digging up the Bible: Jerusalem.

MAJOR EVENTS IN THE BIBLICAL HISTORY OF JERUSALEM

	BC
Bronze Age Canaanite settlement	c.2500
Earliest reference to the city in Egyptian documents	c.1850
Letter by local ruler in Tel el-Amarna documents	14th cent.
Jebusite fortress, captured by David, becomes his religious and political capital	c.1003
Temple of Solomon built	c.962/954
Hezekiah, king of Judah, withstands attack by Assyrian forces under Sennacherib	701
Nebuchadnezzar conquers Jerusalem and destroys the First Temple	587–586
Proclamation of Cyrus the Great in favor of the Return to Zion	538
Second Temple completed by Zerubbabel	520–515
Nehemiah rebuilds the city walls	445
Alexander the Great confirms Jewish privileges	332
Seleucid conquerors grant Jews the right to maintain their "ancestral laws"	198
Antiochus IV Epiphanes plunders the Temple and converts it into a pagan (Greek) shrine	169–167
Maccabean war of liberation	167–141
Judah the Maccabee recaptures Jerusalem, cleanses and rededicates the Temple	164
Hasmonean civil war leads to Roman conquest under Pompey	63
Herod the Great adds a splendid reconstruction of the Temple to his building program	20
	AD
Jesus of Nazareth crucified	c.32
Third city wall constructed by Herod's grandson, Agrippa I	41–44
Zealots wage war against Rome (the Great Revolt)	66–73
Titus conquers Jerusalem and destroys the Second Temple; surviving Jews provide a Roman triumph	70
Outbreak of the Bar Kokhba Revolt	132
Hadrian quells the uprising, builds Aelia Capitolina on the ruins of Jerusalem, and forbids any Jewish presence there	135

NAMES, SYNONYMS, AND DESCRIPTIONS OF JERUSALEM

Aholibah	Name given to Jerusalem by the prophet Ezekiel (23:4).
Ariel ("Lion of God")	Name used by the prophet Isaiah to refer to both the city and the Temple (Is 22:1).
Beautiful of Elevation	Name used in Psalms to describe the city (48:2).
Beulah ("married")	Future name for Jerusalem according to the prophet Isaiah (Is 62:4).
Burdenstone of the Peoples	Name used by the prophet Zechariah, referring to the city's future status among the nations (12:3).
City of David	Appears 34 times in the Old Testament. The name refers to David's conquest of the city.
City of God	Poetic name appearing in the Book of Psalms (46:4).
City of the Lord	Name used by the prophet Isaiah to describe the city (60:14).
City of Joy	Synonym used by the prophet Jeremiah (49:25).
City of Judah	Name reflecting Jerusalem's status as the capital of the kingdom of Judah (II Chr 14:20).
City of our Solemnities	Synonym used by the prophet Isaiah (33:20).
City of Praise	Synonym used by the prophet Jeremiah (49:25).
City of Righteousness	Name foretold for the city by the prophet Isaiah (1:26).
City of the Great King	Name for the city reflecting its status as the royal city (Ps 48:2).
City of Truth	Name foretold for the city by the prophet Zechariah (8:3).
City that is Compact Together	Description of the city given in the Book of Psalms (122:3).
City where David Encamped	Synonym used by the prophet Isaiah (29:1).
Cup of Staggering	Name used by the prophet Zechariah, referring to the city's future status among the nations (12:2).
Faithful City	Name foretold by the prophet Isaiah (1:26).
Full of People	Description found in Lamentations (1:1).
Gates of the Peoples	Name used by the prophet Ezekiel (26:2).
Great among the Nations	Description found in Lamentations (1:1).
Hephzibah	Future name according to the prophet Isaiah (62:4).
Holy City	Synonym used by the prophet Isaiah (52:1).
Holy Mountain	Name used by the author of Psalms and by the prophets Joel and Zechariah (Ps 48:1; Joel 3:17; Zech 8:3).
Holy Mountains	Name used by the author of Psalms (87:1). Rabbinic tradition explains the name by declaring that the sanctity of Jerusalem stems from two sacred mountains, Moriah and Sinai.

One of Israel	Name foretold for the city by the prophet Isaiah (60:14).
Inhabitant of the Valley	Name used by the prophet Jeremiah (21:13)
Jebus	Name of the city prior to its conquest by David (I Chr 11:4–5). The name stems from the inhabitants of the city, the Jebusites.
Jerusalem	Most common name for the city, it appears 656 times in the Old Testament. The name may originally have meant "city of the god Shalem," but a popular folk explanation derives it from the Hebrew for "City of Peace."
Joy of all the Earth	Name found in Psalms (48:2) and Lamentations (2:15).
Joyous City	Synonym used by the prophet Isaiah (22:2).
Lofty City	Synonym used by the prophet Isaiah (26:5).
The Lord is our Righteousness	Name foretold by the prophet Jeremiah (33:16).
The Lord is There	Name foretold for the city by the prophet Ezekiel (48:35).
The Lord will Appear	Name given to Mount Moriah by Abraham following the binding of Isaac (Gen. 22:14).
Mount of the Congregation	Synonym used by the prophet Isaiah (14:13).
Oppressing City	Name used by the prophet Zephaniah (3:1)
Paragon of Beauty	Name used in both Lamentations (2:15) and Psalms (50:2).
Perpetual Desolations	Name used in Psalms (74:3).
Princess among the Provinces	Description found in Lamentations (1:1).
Quiet Habitation	Name used by the prophet Isaiah (33:20).
Rock of the Plain	Name used by the prophet Jeremiah (21:13). The source of the name is probably the view encountered by the prophet from Mount Scopus, as he ascended to Jerusalem.
Salem	First name given to Jerusalem in the Bible. The king of Salem was Melchizedek, a contemporary of Abraham (Gen 14:18).
Sanctuary	Name appearing in Psalms (20:2). The Hebrew equivalent, *kodesh*, is preserved in the present-day Arabic name for the city, "Al Kuds."
Sought Out	Future name for Jerusalem according to the prophet Isaiah (62:12).
Summit of the North	Name found in Psalms 48:2.
Throne of God	Name foretold by the prophet Jeremiah (3:17).
Tumultuous City	Synonym for Jerusalem used by the prophet Isaiah (22:2).
Zela Ha-Eleph	Name of Jerusalem before the Israelite conquest (Josh 18:28).
Zion	Name of the mountain upon which the original city was built. The name appears 150 times in the Old Testament.

II. 7 Chronology of Bible Times

BC	EGYPT	MESOPOTAMIA AND PERSIA	PALESTINE		GREECE AND ROME	CULTURAL EVENTS
1800	Hyksos Hebrews in Egypt	Hammurabi 1728-1686	Patriarchs			Code of Hammurabi
1500	Akhenaton 1370-1353 Tutankhamon 1353-1344					
1300	Rameses II 1290-1224 Exodus					Sinai — The Ten Commandments
1200			Conquest of Canaan by Joshua Philistine invasions Judges Saul — Monarchy established		Trojan War	
1000		ARAM DAMASCUS	David — Empire established Solomon Kingdom divided ISRAEL Jeroboam Nadab	JUDAH Rehoboam Abijah		First Temple built
900		Ben Hadad I	Baasha Elah Zimri Omri Samaria founded	Asa Abijah	Latins settle Italy	
	Shishak 935-914	Ben Hadad II	Ahab	Jehoshaphat		Elijah
		Battle of Karkur 853	Ahaziah			
850			Jehoram Jehu	Jehoram Ahaziah		
800		Ben Hadad III	Jehoahaz Jehoash	Athaliah Jehoash Amaziah		Amos
		Rezin	Jeroboam Zechariah	Uzziah Jotham (regent)	First Olympics 776	Hosea
			Shallum Menahem Pekahiah (regent) Pekah	Ahaziah	Rome founded 753	Isaiah Micah
		ASSYRIAN EMPIRE Shalmanezzyr V Sargon II	Hoshea Fall of Northern Kingdom 722	Ahaz Exile of the Ten Tribes		
700		Sennacherib		Hezekiah Siege of Jerusalem by Assyrians 701 Manasseh Amon Josiah. Battle of Megiddo	Homer	Religious reformation
		Fall of Nineveh 612 BABYLONIAN EMPIRE		Jehoahaz	First Athenian Constitution	Jeremiah
		Battle of Carchemish 605		Jehoiakim Jehoiachin		
600	Necho 610-595	Nebuchadnezzar	War with Babylonia 597 Jehoiachin exiled			

BC	EGYPT	MESOPOTAMIA AND PERSIA	PALESTINE	GREECE AND ROME	CULTURAL EVENTS
			Zedekiah	Solon	
		Judeans exiled to Babylonia	Destruction of Jerusalem 586; Temple destroyed; Exile to Babylonia		Ezekiel Deutero-Isaiah
			Governor Gedaliah assassinated		Canonizatio of Pentateuch
		PERSIAN EMPIRE Cyrus conquers Babylonia 539			
		Cyrus' Edict 538	Exiles Return with Sheshbazzar		
		Cambyses	Zerubbabel 522		
		Darius I			Construction of the Second Temple
				Roman Republic Founded 509	
500				Persian Wars 499-497	
		Xerkes	Ezra; Nehemiah rebuilds walls of Jerusalem	Thermopylae 480	
		Artaxerxes I		Pericles	
		Darius II		Herodotus	
400				Death of Socrates	
				Sack of Rome	
				Alexander the Great 334-323	Hellenism enters Middle East
300	Ptolemaic Empire	Seleucid Empire	Ptolemaic rule		
			Seleucid rule		Canonization of Prophets
		Antiochus I			
		Seleucus II			First Greek translation of Pentateuch (Septuagint)
		Antiochus II		Hannibal in Italy 218	
200		Antiochus III			
		Antiochus IV Epiphanes	Antiochus IV bans practice of Judaism; Hasmonean revolt 167	Spain annexed by Rome	
			Rededication of Temple; Beginning of Hasmonean Rule 164		
			Jonathan 160-142	ROMAN EMPIRE Cartgage destrited 146	Ecclesiasticus
			Simon 142-134		
			John Hyrcanus 134-104		
100			Alexander Jannai 103-76	Gallic Wars	
			Pompey captures Jerusalem 63		
			Antipater	Julius Caesar assassinated 44	
			Herod the Great 37 BC-AD 4	Augustus Caesar 27 BC-AD 14	Herod rebuilds the Temple
			Birth of Jesus c. 4 BC		
AD 1			Herod Philip 4 BC-AD 34	Tiberius	
			Herod Antipas 4 BC-AD 39	Gaius Caligula	
			Baptism of Jesus c. 26		
			Pontius Pilate 26-36		
			Crucifixion of Jesus c. 30		
			Martyrdom of Stephen 31		
			Conversion of Paul 35		Philo Judaeus in Alezandria
			Paul's 1st Missionary Journey 47-48		
			Jerusalem Council 48		
	Cleopatra		Paul's 2nd Missionary Journey 49-52		Pauline Epistles
			Paul's 3rd Missionary Journey 52-56	Nero	
			Jewish Revolt against Rome 66	Vespasian	Josephus Flavius
			Destruction of Qumran Community c. 70		
			Fall of Jerusalem and Destruction of Second Temple 70	Titus	Gospels written
			Fall of Masada 73		
				Domitian persecutes Christians 93-96	

II.8 CALENDAR

The ancient Israelites, along with most peoples of the ancient world, observed a lunar calendar based on the observable cycles of the moon. Only the Egyptians used a solar calendar. The lunar calendar consists of 354 days, which were divided into months of 29 or 30 days. In a lunar system, the new day begins at nightfall, when the moon is first visible. In Genesis it is stated, "And the evening and the morning were the first day" (Gen 1:5). Seven days formed a week, approximating the stages of the moon's orbit. The importance of the week was significant in view of the biblical account of creation lasting seven days (Gen 1:1–2:3).

The Israelites did not have a standardized division of the day. Various terms appear in the Bible to denote particular times of day, based on observable natural phenomena. Among these are: "rising of the morning" (Neh 4:21), "dawning of the day" (Job 3:9), "day break" (Song 2:17), "light of the morning" (II Sam 23:4), "morning" (Ps 55:17), "noon" (Ps 55:17), "heat of the day" (Gen 18:1), "noonday" (Job 5:14), "long shadows" (Jer 6:4), "twilight" (Prov 7:9), "evening" (Prov 7:9), and "dark night" (Gen 1:5; Prov 7:9). The time of day was also reckoned by the tasks performed then. Evening is once referred to as "the time that women go out to draw water" (Gen 24:11). King Ahaz is noted for having a sundial (II Kgs 20:11; Is 38:8), although this innovation was probably borrowed from the Assyrians. The night was divided into three watches, called: "the beginning of the watches" (Lam 2:19), "the middle watch" (Judg 7:19), and "the morning watch" (I Sam 11:11).

Zodiac wheel with the four seasons in the corners; 6th-century mosaic.

The Hebrew year began in the fall. Since the lunar year, however, is somewhat shorter than the solar year, difficulties arose in both religious and economic spheres, as over time, the beginning of the year was eventually celebrated at different seasons. The feast of Tabernacles was intended as a harvest festival (Ex 23:16) and Passover was originally a spring festival (Ex 23:15). The Bible cautioned the Israelites to observe Passover "in its appointed season" (Num 9:2). It became necessary, therefore to add days or possibly a month to the year to coordinate the solar and lunar years, thereby ensuring the celebration of the festivals in their proper seasons. In the 6th century BC, the Babylonians introduced a system by which they added a month three times in an eight-year cycle. The

THE MONTHS OF THE HEBREW CALENDAR

MONTH	CANAANITE NAME	BABYLONIAN NAME	FESTIVALS
1	Abib (Ex 13:4)	Nisan (Neh 2:1; Est 3:7)	Passover
2	Ziv (I Kgs 6:37)	Iyar	
3		Sivan (Est 8:9)	Pentecost
4		Tammuz	
5		Ab	Tradition dates the destruction of the Temple on 9th of A
6		Elul (Neh 6:15)	
7	Ethanim (I Kgs 8:2)	Tishrei	New Year, Day of Atonement, Tabernacles
8	Bul (I Kgs 6:38)	Marheshvan	
9		Kislev (Neh 1:1)	Hanukkah
10		Tebeth (Est 2:16)	
11		Shebat (Zech 1:7)	
12		Adar (Ezra 6:15; Est 3:7, 13; 8:12; 9:1, 15, 17, 19, 21)	Purim
13		II Adar	Month added in lea years.

Babylonian calendar was later adopted by the Jews of Palestine and Egypt.

In the Second Temple period, the new month was determined by the priests of Jerusalem. It was announced to the populace by a series of beacons lit on mountaintops throughout the country. Following the destruction of the Second Temple, Rabbi Gamaliel instituted a standardized calendar of 12 months, with a 13th month added at regular intervals. The number of days in the month, (29 or 30) was also standardized.

A solar calendar, known as the Julian calendar, was instituted by Julius Caesar in 47 BC. This calendar of 365 1/4 days, beginning on January 1, was used by the Jews simultaneously with the traditional calendar.

The Bible contains three systems for naming the months. The first system simply refers to the months by numbers. The first month was the one in which Passover fell, and the New Year was celebrated on the first day of the seventh month. In the First Temple period, months were also referred to by their Canaanite names, of which four are mentioned in the Bible. During the Babylonian exile, the Babylonian names of the months were adopted. Seven are mentioned in the Bible.

II.9 DIGGING UP THE BIBLE:
SOME OUTSTANDING ARCHAOLOGICAL FINDS

Ai. The second city (after Jericho) destroyed by the Israelites (Josh 7-8), its exact location being described in the Bible: "Ai, which is beside Bethel, on the east side of Bethel" (Josh 7:2). Ai has been identified with the prominent mound known as e-Tell, 18 miles (25 km) north of Jerusalem. Appropriately, it lies close to the village of Beitin, identified with biblical Bethel. The Arabic name E-Tell means "the ruin," as does the Hebrew Ai, and indeed "Joshua burnt Ai, and made it a heap for ever, even a desolation until this day" (Josh 8:28).

Excavations of the mound have shown that the site was initially occupied during the first half of the 3rd millennium BC, when the settlement grew from a center for nomads into a well-fortified city with a series of walls, a temple, and a palace, the last demonstrating Egyptian influence. The city was destroyed in c.2500 BC, and the site lay in ruins for about 1,300 years, until a small village was built there by the Israelites in the 12th century BC. The village existed for about 200 years, after which the site was abandoned for good. As the early city preceded the Israelite conquest by over a thousand years, while the Israelite village clearly succeeded the conquest, the location of the biblical Ai of Joshua's time remains in doubt. Two archaeological teams have wrestled with this problem, one in 1933-1935 and the other in 1964-1968, and neither found a solution. Assuming that the identification of Ai with e-Tell may be wrong, several teams have since surveyed and excavated adjacent hills, but a definitive placing for biblical Ai has not yet been found.

(El) Amarna. New capital built by Pharaoh Amenophis IV (1379-1362 BC), near the modern-day village of El-Amarna in Middle Egypt. This Pharaoh, better known as Akhenaton, started his rule in the traditional capital of Thebes, some 300 miles further up the Nile, but he underwent a profound religious change, denying all Egyptian gods except Aton, the sun god, whom he declared supreme god of Egypt. His revolutionary ideas caused an open conflict with the religious establishment of the temple of Amon, so Amenophis IV, now Akhenaton, left the capital and chose a new site on which to build his city, Akhetaton. This new city, known today as El-Amarna, was abandoned soon after its founder died. All findings on the site, therefore, date to a limited, well-defined period in the 14th century BC, which, known as the El-Amarna period, forms a cornerstone in Near Eastern chronology. Excavations have unearthed substantial sections of the city, with a palace, temples to Aton, and residential quarters, as well as many tombs of noblemen who followed Akhenaton to his new capital. The most sensational of the findings are the El-Amarna Letters (see box) discovered by chance in 1887 by a peasant woman in her field. It was this discovery that led to the identification of the site of Akhetaton.

Pharaoh Akhenaton of Egypt and Queen Nefertiti; a sculptor's limestone model from Tell el-Amarna.

El-Amarna Letters

The collection of 540 letters discovered at El-Amarna was part of the royal archives of Pharaoh Akhenaton, as well as that of his father Amenophis III, which were transfered to the new capital. This is the royal correspondence between the Egyptian court and the kings of Babylonia, Assyria, the Hittite kingdom, Mittani, and Cyprus, as well as with the rulers of many Canaanite towns. The Canaanite letters shed a clear light on life in the El-Amarna period, complete with animosity and quarrels among the Canaanite rulers, who kept complaining against each other to the Egyptian monarch in an attempt to win his favor. Especially interesting is the frequent mention of the "Habiru," a group of nomadic people who contributed to the unrest in this period of slackened Egyptian power. It has been suggested that these "Habiru" were somehow connected to the biblical "Hebrews." The letters are written in Akkadian, the diplomatic *lingua franca* of the period.

Two ivory figurines of the Chalcolithic period from Bir-es-Safadi, south of Beersheba.

Beersheba. Although the place was intimately connected with stories of the Patriarchs, almost no remnants from the 2nd millennium BC have been found either on the mound of Beersheba or in the very early settlements that dot both banks of the Beersheba stream. The biblical period settlement was located at Tell Beersheba, 2.5 miles (4 km) east of the modern town. Intensive excavations carried out between 1969 and 1979 have revealed that the site was first occupied in the times of the Judges (12th century BC), and continued to exist without interruption down to the destruction of the kingdom of Judah in the 6th century BC. From the 10th century BC, Beersheba, which the Bible always describes as the southern border town of Israel, was a small town with strong defenses, a granary, and private residences. It provides a good example of town planning in a small provincial Judean town, having been built as a circle with private residences on the periphery, in fact as an integral part of the city wall, and public buildings close to the gate and perhaps also in the center.

The earliest sites in the Beersheba area date to the 4th millennium BC, when a series of small villages were built along both banks of the Beersheba stream, as part of an intensive occupation of the northern Negeb. These early villages demonstrate a surprisingly high standard of living. Their inhabitants were mainly shepherds, but some were master-craftsmen working in copper and ivory, their artistic products being among the most sophisticated in the entire Near East.

Calah (Nimrud). According to Genesis 10:12, the "great city" of Calah was built by Nimrod. Known in Assyrian as Kalhu, it was one of the great cities of Assyria, situated at the junction of the Tigris and the Great Zab river. The city, already in existence from the 18th century BC, was rebuilt in the 13th century by Shalmaneser I who made it one of his capitals. Its main importance dates from the reign of Ashurnasirpal II (c.883-c.859), under whom it was Assyria's military

Ivory carving from Nimrod (Calah).

capital. Calah remained an important center for two centuries but then declined and was sacked in c.614 BC.

It was first excavated in 1845–51 by the British archaeologist Sir Austen Henry Layard, and many of his discoveries, including winged lions and bulls with human heads, are still on display in the British Museum. A systematic excavation was carried out between 1949 and 1958 by Sir Max Mallowan (whose wife, Agatha Christie, used her experiences at the site for one of her mystery stories, *Murder in Mesopotamia*, and who commented that an archaeologist was an ideal husband because the older his wife became, the more interested he was in her). The archaeologists uncovered the palaces of the Assyrian kings, decorated with reliefs and paintings. The rooms contained many finds taken as spoil from Judah and Israel, including a rich collection of ivories. Among the monuments found was the Black Obelisk of Shalmaneser III with a representation of the Israelite king Jehu submitting to the Assyrian monarch.

In 1988–1989 an Iraqi archaeological expedition found one of the richest gold caches since that of Tutankhamun. It started below a small paved room which had been cleared by Mallowan. Digging down, a gold treasure was discovered of crowns, necklaces, and bracelets. An inscription identified it as the tomb of the queen of Tiglath-pileser III who ruled from 744 BC and expanded the empire in a series of military campaigns. A further tomb in the vicinity contained 90 necklaces, 80 gold earrings, and a golden diadem. In a third tomb were 440 golden objects, weighing over 50 lbs, including a magnificent crown. They may have belonged to the queen of Ashurnasirpal II. The collection is now housed in the Iraq Museum, Baghdad.

Caesarea. The coastal city of Caesarea has been the site of many digs, in recent decades by Italian, US, Canadian, and Israeli archaeologists. Before Herod built there, it had been known as Strato's Tower, of which excavators have uncovered remains of the town and its harbors. Its city plan included defensive walls, two harbors, and the offshore tower guarding the harbors after which the place was named. Caesarea itself was a magnificent Roman city of which many impressive aspects have been uncovered. An Italian expedition excavated the Roman theater with stone bench seats providing accommodation for 3,500 spectators. The theater was again brought into use in the early 1960s and at the inaugural concert the playing of the great cellist Pablo Casals proved its remarkable acoustical quality. An amphitheater was also identified by aerial photography, but little remains.

Josephus gives a detailed description of the city, much of which has been identified, although the central marketplace has not yet been located. Large numbers of vaults were found, the lower parts of warehouses for goods passing in and out of this international entrepot. These were close to the harbor, site of some of the most exciting discoveries. Underwater archaeologists surveyed and mapped the remains of the ancient harbor, and they have confirmed Josephus' description of its impressive dimensions (even his comment that it surpassed in size Piraeus, the harbor of ancient Athens, may not be so farfetched). Much evidence of shipwrecks also survives, usually as concentrations of pottery from cargo and in one case, the hull of a merchant ship.

On land, many fine Roman constructions have been excavated including the twin high-level aqueducts, impressive statues, and one inscription in Latin from a small temple, reading "Pontius Pilate, the prefect of Judea, gave and dedicated the temple of Tiberius" — a rare direct connection with a New Testament personality.

Capernaum. The first archaeological excavations here were conducted only in 1866, although the site was

The Roman aqueduct at Caesarea.

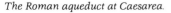

The holy ark on wheels; carving in stone from the synagogue of Capernaum.

identified as early as 1838. In 1905, after the entire area had been purchased by the Franciscan order, work was carried out on a larger scale, and an impressive synagogue was found and cleared. Excavations in and near it were continued until recently. Explorations made in 1977–1982 established that settlement on the site began in the 2nd century BC, and that it was a small, unfortified town, that did not take part in the wars against the Romans, remaining peaceful and unscathed. It continued to exist until the 11th century.

The most conspicuous structure in the excavated town was the synagogue, built around AD 300, of white limestone brought from a distant quarry to this region of black basalt. The rich carvings which adorned the synagogue testify to the wealth of the local Jewish community. Among the carvings are figures of an eagle and of cupids holding wreaths, and other ornamental motifs more in keeping with Jewish norms, as well as objects of ritual significance, such as the portable Ark of the Covenant. It is possible that the earlier synagogue in which Jesus preached lies below this building. Several dwellings dating from the 1st century BC have been excavated around the synagogue. Of special significance is the so-called House of Peter. Between the 1st century BC and the beginning of the 4th century AD this was a common residence with several rooms grouped around an irregular courtyard. One of the rooms was distinguished by a floor of crushed limestone and a painted plaster coating on the walls. In the second stage, in the first half of the 4th century, this room became a center of a building surrounded by a wall and secluded from the town, and may have been a church. In the middle of the 5th or the early 6th century, this building was leveled, and an octagonal church built on the site.

Mount Ebal. This "Mountain of the Curse" stands on the northern side of the narrow valley where Shechem is situated. On the summit of the mountain a unique structure, most likely an altar, was unearthed in excavations carried out in the 1980s. This is a large, square structure built of unhewn stones and ascended by a sloping ramp. It has been dated to the 12th century BC, and has been suggested as identifying with the altar built by Joshua and the Israelites immediately after the conquest of Canaan (Josh 8:30–31). The numerous animal bones found scattered around the structure confirm that it was indeed an altar. This sacred enclosure stood isolated on the mountain, with no settlement around.

Ebla. Ancient Ebla is the most recent addition to the short list of sites whose fame stems mainly from the discovery of their ancient archives. Situated in northern Syria, not far from Aleppo, Ebla was excavated in the 1960s and 1970s, with sensational results. In one of the rooms of a palace on the mound's acropolis, a small archive of some 2,000 clay tablets was discovered in 1974, followed by the main archive with 15,000 further tablets. It is possible that other archives have still to be discovered, as the palace has not yet been completely excavated.

While the other famous Syro-Mesopotamian archives of Mari, Nuzi, and Ugarit all date from the 2nd millennium BC, the Ebla tablets are earlier, dating from the second half of the 3rd millennium BC. Most tablets are in the Sumerian language, but others, quite easily read (they are all written in cuneiform script), may introduce a new language, perhaps Paleo-Canaanite or an ancient dialect of Akkadian. Although only very few of the tablets have as yet been published, it is already known that the archives include bi-lingual Sumerian-Eblian dictionaries, lexicons, and grammatical texts for the use of scribal schools, administrative, historical, and legal texts, and literary texts on mythological subjects and collections of proverbs and incantations. Soon after their discovery, it was disclosed that the tablets mention place names as well as personal names known from the Bible. This initially created much excitement, especially when their early date is taken into account, but nothing concrete has yet been published to establish any direct connection whatsoever between these tablets and the Bible.

The city of Ebla was very large, and well protected by huge earth ramparts. A monumental gate and a fortress were excavated on the slopes of the mound, while on its acropolis two large palaces and two temples with very thick walls have been unearthed. The temples are particularly important for Canaanite archaeology, as they may have been the source of inspiration for very similar temples discovered at Hazor, Meggido, and Shechem.

Elephantine (Yeb). This town, on an island in the

upper Nile river near the town of Aswan, has yielded an important collection of papyri written in the Aramaic language. The papyri revealed the astonishing fact that in the 5th century BC there existed on the island a military Jewish colony founded by soldiers in the army of the Assyrian ruler, Ashurbanipal. The documents, mainly legal in nature, reflect the everyday life of this colony, established already in the 6th century BC, perhaps by refugees from Judah, and destroyed in 411 BC. Most intriguing are the documents that tell something about the religious life of these Jewish soldiers. They established a large temple with an altar. They even appealed to the high priest in Jerusalem to help rebuild their temple after it had been destroyed, and were surprised when they received no reply from him.

Ephesus. An important and prosperous ancient city on the Aegean coast of Turkey, Ephesus extended over the slopes of two hills and the intervening valley, where the ancient harbor, once the scene of bustling trade, is now silted up. The site was first occupied in the 2nd millennium BC by a population which worshiped the great mother goddess Cybele, later identified with the Greek-Roman goddess Artemis-Diana. The succession of temples built to these goddesses, now completely destroyed, added to the reputation of the city, which continued its existence without a break down to the 14th century AD. For Bible readers Ephesus is connected with the visits of Paul between AD 55 and 58, and with the fierce opposition he met from the priests of the temple of Diana.

Archaeological excavations at Ephesus began as early as 1866, and have continued since, with many interruptions. Substantial sections of the Hellenistic, Roman, and Byzantine cities have been unearthed, including both sides of one of the main paved and colonnaded avenues, temples, a library, a public bathhouse and toilet, a market place, a theater, a stadium, and a complete residential section. The excavations were followed by extensive restoration works that have made Ephesus one of the best preserved ancient sites in the world.

Mount Gerizim. Also known as the "Mountain of Blessing," Mount Gerizim is on the southern side of the valley where the town of Shechem is located. It is connected with the Samaritans, who believe that events associated by Jews with the Temple Mount in Jerusalem, such as the Foundation of the World and the Binding of Isaac, occurred on Mount Gerizim. In the 4th century BC, after they seceded from the main body of Judaism, the Samaritans built their central temple here, following the plan of the Temple in Jerusalem. This temple, a huge edifice uncovered in excavations carried out in the 1980s, was destroyed in 128 BC, rebuilt, and functioned until the 4th century AD, when it was replaced by an octagonal church.

Gezer. Gezer was excavated twice, in the first decade of the 20th century and again in the 1960s. Large sections of various city walls from different periods were found,

The Gezer Calendar

Ancient Israel is not very rich in epigraphic material. The majority of inscriptions found are short, bearing names or cryptic notes, while lengthy insriptions with a meaningful content are very rare. To this last category belongs the Gezer Calendar, a 10th-century BC seven-line inscription incised on a piece of soft limestone, the only known inscription from the time of Solomon. The inscription is a monthly and bi-monthly list of agricultural tasks such as sowing, reaping, and tending to the flax, and also mentions the months of vintage and olive harvest, spring pasture, wheat harvest, and pruning. Its rhythmic style has suggested to some that it may have been a poem. It is difficult to know what it was used for: was it kept in the home of a farmer as a calendar, or was it a pupil's exercise? The three letters AVI carved at the bottom left-hand side of the stone may perhaps be the name of its owner.

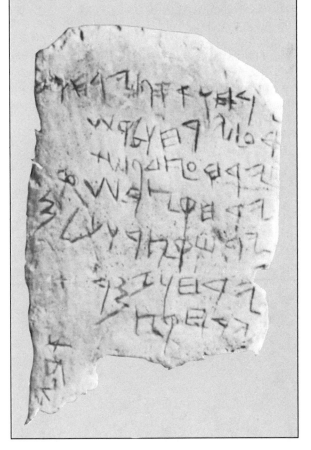

the earliest dating to the 3rd millennium BC. The second earliest, a 30 ft (10 m) wide brick wall with a monumental gate, is one of the finest remnants of Middle Bronze Age fortifications. The date of the third wall, the so-called Outer Wall which encircles the largest area of the site, may be either of the Late Bronze or of the First Temple period. A huge water tunnel joining the city to a spring was discovered, which may date from the First Temple period. Another interesting find is a Canaanite high place with ten standing limestones. These seem to be the "pillars" often mentioned in the Bible, such as that anointed with oil by Jacob at Bethel (Gen 28:18). The massive system of an inner and an outer gate joined to a double wall was built by Solomon. Both gates and wall are almost identical to the Solomonic fortification of Megiddo and Hazor, in accordance with the biblical verse that mentions them together (I Kgs 9:15). To the same period belongs the unique Gezer Calendar written in ancient Hebrew script, listing the months of of the year by the agricultural work performed in them (see box). Many private houses, protected by restored earlier walls, were discovered, dating from the Second Temple period. The inhabitants were buried in typical Jewish burial caves with niches and ossuaries. To this last phase of habitation belong six inscriptions in square Hebrew script cut into the rocks south of the mound, mentioning Gezer by name. This is one of the very few instances in which an identification of a site is verified by an ancient inscription.

Hazor. This largest archaeological mound (tell) in Israel (210 acres), situated in the upper Jordan Valley nine miles (14 km) north of the Sea of Galilee, is best known to Bible readers as the city of Jabin, head of the coalition of the kings of the north against Joshua (Josh 11). After his victory over these kings in the Battle of the Waters of Meron, "Joshua ... took Hazor ... for Hazor beforetimes was the head of all those kingdoms ... And he burnt Hazor with fire" (Josh 11:10–13). Hazor is mentioned again in the Bible only twice: once for being rebuilt by Solomon (I Kgs 9:15), once for being destroyed by Tiglath-pileser III of Assyria (II Kgs 15:29). Its days of glory were indeed prior to the Israelite conquest. Hazor is the only Canaanite city mentioned in the Mari texts of the 18th century BC, where it figures as an important distribution center for tin, a metal vital in the bronze industry. In the El-Amarna Letters of the 14th century BC, Abdi-Tirshi of Hazor is the only Canaanite ruler who dares call himself king.

Hazor was excavated in 1955–1958 and again in 1968 and 1990. Numerous small segments of the mound, both in the very distinctive upper city and in the enormous lower city, have been dug. Pottery sherds collected in the upper city proved that this part of the site was inhabited as early as the Early Bronze Age (3rd millennium BC). The lower city, however, was first occupied only in the 18th century BC. The entire site was then continuously inhabited until the end of the 13th century BC, when a violent fire destroyed it. The new settlement, established in the 12th-11th century BC on the upper level, never spread to the lower. After the Assyrian destruction of 732 BC, occupation was confined to the western point of the upper city, and it ceased to exist altogether in the 2nd century BC.

The hopes of finding the palace of the kings of Hazor of the 2nd millennium BC and its archives, aroused by the sheer size and documented importance of this metropolis, have not yet been realized. However, other important finds of that period have come to light,

Clay mask from Hazor.

Bronze plaque of a Canaanite, from Hazor; late Bronze Age.

Left: Excavations showing fortifications at ancient Jericho, from the Early and Middle Bronze Age. Right: Clay anthropomorphic jar from Jericho, Middle Bronze Age.

including a few clay cuneiform tablets. Most noteworthy are five series of monumental temples with rich collections of ritual and art objects, which have made Hazor a key site for the study of Canaanite temple architecture. The enormous earth rampart that surrounds the lower city and the gateway on its eastern side are spectacular examples of the type of fortifications that prevailed in the Levant in the first half of the 2nd millennium BC.

In the upper city the most interesting find is Solomon's wall and gate, discovered in an unexpected place in the center of the site, an area with no topographic advantages. Solomon's Hazor occupied only the western half of the upper city. It expanded in the days of Ahab, king of Israel in the 9th century BC, to include the entire upper city. Ahab reinforced the city by encircling it with a wall, by constructing a fortress on its western tip, and by digging a large and sophisticated water-supply system that catches subterranean waters in the bedrock under the city. These fortifications, however, did not withstand the Assyrian siege.

Of the many puzzles that still await answers, perhaps the most intriguing is the absence of cemeteries of all periods on, near, or even far from Hazor. The new excavation efforts are aimed at locating them.

Jericho. Jericho is a site that has captured the imagination of many generations of Bible readers, and consequently aroused the interest of several teams of archaeologists, who directed their excavations to uncovering the walls that came "tumbling down" at the sound of the trumpets of the Israelites (Josh 6). It was not difficult to identify Tel-e-Sultan, a 650-ft (215

m) high mound situated in the largest oasis in the Judean Desert whose modern Arabic name, e-Riha, preserves the ancient name of Jericho. The mound is situated close to one of the most important shallows of the Jordan River, a place fit for the dramatic crossing of the Israelites.

However, despite the many excavations, Joshua's walls have not yet been securely identified. The first excavator of the mound, in 1880, declared it devoid of any ancient remains. A second attempt was made in 1907–1909, and long sections of a city wall and various buildings were found. These excavations attributed the wall to the time of Joshua, but the dating was mistaken, as later excavations established that the wall was built in the 3rd millennium BC. The 1930–1939 large-scale excavation did not further the mystery of the missing wall, as it too erred in dating the finds. It was left to the British archaeologist, Kathleen Kenyon, who headed yet another attempt at excavating Jericho in 1952–1958, to put some chronological order into the jumble of findings. She also discovered a massive tower and defense wall of the Neolithic period, around 8000 BC. Because of this sensational discovery, Jericho is considered the oldest city in the world. The many occupation layers of the Mesolithic (10th–9th millennia BC) and Neolithic (8th–6th millennia BC) periods at Jericho have shed new light on crucial developments of human society, such as the domestication of plants and animals, the transition from temporary to permanent settlements to cities, and the discovery of pottery. Particularly interesting finds of the Neolithic period are plastered and modeled human skulls, without the lower jaw, buried under floors of dwellings.

During the 3rd and the first half of the 2nd millennia BC, Jericho was one of many fortified cities that existed throughout the country. Burial caves of these periods have been discovered, some yielding rich burial equipment, including wooden furniture, well preserved in the dry desert climate. After having been destroyed violently at the end of the Middle Bronze Age, and then again in about 1400 BC, Jericho was rebuilt only in the 7th century BC. Not only was Jericho of the 15th century BC a small town (probably not even fortified and so there are no tumbled walls), but its destruction came about 200 years earlier than the commonly agreed date of the Israelite conquest. Lately, the question of the date of the Israelite conquest has been the subject of renewed investigation, and it has been suggested by some that it may have occurred in the 15th rather than in the 13th century BC. If so, Jericho may still have been destroyed by the Israelites. A fierce debate is still going on in archaeological circles concerning the walls of Jericho.

Jerusalem. Jerusalem was one of the first sites in the world in which archaeological excavations were undertaken, aiming at discovering the background of biblical events. For the last 130 years, numerous teams have dug in various areas, unearthing a wealth of material: public and private structures, vast quantities of pottery

Pottery from the Hinnom Valley burial caves in Jerusalem; 7th century BC.

vessels, inscriptions, and numerous small finds of all kinds.

First Temple Period. Excavations undertaken in the City of David since the 1960s, and in the Jewish Quarter of the Old City, have confirmed that habitation in Jerusalem began in the City of David (a small and narrow hill that juts out from the Temple Mount southwards and is now outside the Old City) near the only perennial water-source in the area, the Siloam Spring. For centuries, starting around 3000 BC, people lived on the eastern slopes of what was later known as the City of David. Around 1850 BC, they surrounded their settlement with a wall, large sections of which have been unearthed. This wall served Jerusalem for about 1,000 years, and was replaced in the 8th century BC by a new wall built along the line of the old one. Substantial sections of the new wall have come to light, with an impressive section with towers and a gateway farther up the slope, towards the Temple Mount.

Another section, 200 ft. (60 meters) long and 21 ft. (60 meters) wide, was recently unearthed in the Jewish Quarter, and near it a somewhat later massive tower, preserved to the height of 45 ft. (13.5 meters). This discovery has changed our views on the size of Jerusalem in the last 150 years of the First Temple period. For years the extent of the city has been hotly debated. Not having found any architectural remains on the western hill, several archaeologists insisted that the city was small in size, confined to the City of David and the Temple Mount. Others held a maximalist view and believed that Jerusalem was a city of much more substantial dimensions. The latter have now been proved right, and it is clear that Jerusalem spread from the City of David, first northwards to incorporate the Temple Mount, then westwards to include the entire western hill, today occupied by the Jewish and Armenian Quarters, as well as Mount Zion. The walls of Jerusalem at that time encircled an area of about 150 acres (75.5 ha.), and with its outlying suburbs was one of the largest cities in the region.

Small areas of residential neighborhoods have been unearthed in the City of David. A complete house of the four-room type has come to light, alongside rooms of several other houses. These houses were built against a massive stone retaining wall, a remnant of earlier times, perhaps from the days of King Solomon. This retaining wall, preserved in sections to a height of over 100 ft. (30 meters), probably was meant to widen the narrow summit of the hill and make room for a large public building, which has not been preserved. In today's Jewish Quarter only very badly preserved fragments of houses came to light, having been damaged by later, Herodian, construction.

Among the finds was a collection of 51 *bullae* (clay pieces used to seal letters and documents). These carried names of officials, some, such as Gemariahu son of Shaphan, mentioned in the Bible (Jer 36:10). The

Aerial view of excavations along the southern side of the Temple area, looking west.

house where the *bullae* were found was probably a public archive.

The city's water supply was ensured by a succession of three systems, two cut under the City of David, one cut and built along its eastern slope. The earliest conveyed the water of the Gihon Spring to an underground pool reached by shafts and tunnels. Hezekiah's Tunnel conveyed the water to an open pool on the western side of the City of David.

Archaeological excavations have revealed numerous rock-cut burial caves in a wide circle around the city walls. These were family sepulchers, the dead being first placed on rock-cut benches, and then their bones heaped together in repositories. Some sepulchers were quite elaborate, demonstrating the wealth of at least some of the citizens of Jerusalem. One such cemetery, on the western slopes of the Hinnom Valley, was found intact, and yielded numerous objects that were put in the caves to accompany the deceased. Unique were two small rolled silver plaques, inscribed with the biblical verses of the Priestly Benediction (Num 6:24–26). Dating from the 7th century BC, these are the oldest biblical texts as yet discovered.

Second Temple Period. After the destruction of Jerusalem by Nebuchadnezzar, King of Babylonia (587/586 BC), the city diminished in size and was again confined to the City of David and the Temple Mount. The main finds of the first 300 years of this period are stamped jar handles and a few coins.

Jerusalem started to flourish again in the Hasmonean period, when it spread again to the western hill.

Sections of the old wall were re-used and incorporated in what is known as the First Wall, surrounding an area of the same size and layout as that of the city of the First Temple period. Sections of this wall have been excavated in several locations. Jerusalem continued to grow, and two new walls were built during the Second Temple period, to defend northern suburbs. Fragments of the Second Wall of the time of Herod were excavated in the Christian Quarter of the Old City, while sections of the Third Wall, started by King Agrippa and hastily completed on the eve of the Roman siege, were found at a distance north of the northern wall of today's Old City.

The reign of King Herod was a period of major construction in Jerusalem. Herod rebuilt the Temple and doubled the size of its retaining wall, making it one of the most splendid structures of the day. Nothing, however, remains of the Second Temple itself, except for an inscription that was inserted in a fence around the Temple on the eastern slopes of the hill. Another fragmentary inscription was discovered at the place where the "ram's horn was blown" on the Temple Mount. The entire length of the western wall of the Temple Mount retaining wall is now known; one part of it has always been a sacred area to the Jewish people, the "Western Wall." Substantial sections have also survived of the southern and eastern retaining walls. The southern wall, which is a huge retaining wall that holds up the Temple Mount plaza, and the area in front of it, have been dug extensively since 1967. Wide flights of steps which once led into the Temple Mount through gates ("Huldah Gates") now blocked, were cleared, as was a stepped street that ran along the wall. Further digging at the Western Wall has uncovered foundations of arches that once carried steps leading to an entrance to the Temple Mount on that side.

To the north of the Temple Mount stood the Antonia fortress, where a Roman garrison was stationed. It is believed that Jesus was detained and judged here, and the Lithostrotos, the stone pavement of this fortress on which his trial took place, has been excavated under the monastery of the Sisters of Zion.

Herod chose for his palace an area near the western gate to the city, next to Jaffa Gate. Nothing remains of this palace, but the lower part of a massive tower, one of three, that guarded both the palace and the city gate, is still standing in the Citadel.

The residential section situated under the Jewish Quarter has been extensively excavated. Here several three- to four-storey houses of the upper classes have come to light, with spacious rooms and patios, mosaic floors, painted walls, and a wealth of pottery and small finds. A unique feature was the ritual baths in their basements. One house, known as the "Burnt House," still bears very visible signs of the conflagration that destroyed Jerusalem in the summer of AD 70, after a long siege by the Romans.

To the Second Temple period belong numerous, often decorated, burial caves that dot the hills surrounding Jerusalem. As in the First Temple period, these were family sepulchers. The deceased were first placed there intact, and after a year their bones were collected and placed in stone ossuaries that often carry decorations and short inscriptions. Some bodies were placed in large sarcophagi and were not moved again. Perhaps the best known tombs of this period are the group of monuments in the Kidron Valley: Absalom's Tomb, the Tomb of Zechariah, and the tomb of the Hezir family, as well as the Tombs of the Kings situated to the north of the Old City. The tomb of Herod's family is located near the King David Hotel. Herod himself was buried on Mount Herodion, some 12 miles (8 km) south-east of Jerusalem, but extensive digging has not discovered his tomb.

The tombs of the Hezir family (left) and the tomb of Zechariah (right) in the Kidron Valley; Second Temple period.

The sites connected with the death and burial of Jesus present a special problem. They must have been outside the city walls at the time of the events, as executions and burials were not allowed inside the city, but tradition places them in the Church of the Holy Sepulcher, in the heart of the Old City of today. The "Second Wall," that defended the city at that time, must therefore have run east of the church. Although there are several typical burial caves of the period behind the Church of the Holy Sepulcher, archaeology cannot prove or disprove the authenticity of the tradition. A contender to the traditional tomb of Jesus is the Garden Tomb north of the Old City, but it has lately been shown that this was originally a burial cave of the First Temple period.

Kadesh Barnea. This desert site was the base of the

Israelites for 38 of the 40 years of the Exodus. The site in western Sinai was first identified in 1914, and excavations were made there in 1956 and again between 1976 and 1982. Despite its importance in the days of the Patriarchs and the Exodus, these periods remain archaeologically elusive, as the earliest remains on the site date to the 10th century BC, when the first of a series of three fortresses was built. The second fortress, built in the 8th century BC after the destruction of the first, is most impressive. It covers an area of about 120 x 180 ft (40 x 60 m), and its 12 ft (4 m) thick wall with eight towers was preserved to almost six feet (1.80 m). The third fortress occupied the same area as the second, but had rooms in place of the thick wall. It was destroyed by fire in 586 BC. Remains on the debris of this fortress indicate that the site was occupied in the 5th-4th centuries BC.

Kursi (Country of the Gadarenes). Located on the eastern shore of the Sea of Galilee next to the road that leads up to the Golan Heights, Kursi is identified as the country of the Gergesenes (Matt 8:28) or the country of the Gadarenes (Luke 8:26). A monastery commemorates the traditional site where Jesus performed the miracle of the swine (Matt 8:28–32; Luke 8:26–33). The identification of the place of the miracle with the village of Kursi was made by early Christian writers and pilgrims.

Excavations carried out in 1970–1972 established

Part of the 5th-century church at Kursi, on the eastern shore of the Sea of Galilee.

that the church and monastery were built in the middle of the 5th century. The compound was surrounded by a wall with a gate, flanked by a tower. In front of the church was a paved courtyard surrounded by columns. The church was built as a basilica, with stone benches around the apse. South of the apse was a baptistry. The floor of the church was covered with colorful mosaics. Under the chapel, on the southern side of the main hall, was a crypt in which 30 skeletons, presumably of monks, were buried.

Lachish. Ancient Lachish is identified with a mound in the foothills of the Hebron mountains. Lachish features in the Bible, and also in Egyptian and Assyrian sources, the most important of which is the series of stone reliefs depicting the siege of Lachish by the Assyrian king Sennacherib, found on the walls of his palace in Nineveh and now in the British Museum. The mound, one of the largest and most prominent in the country, was excavated in the 1930s and again from 1972. The site, occupied almost without interruption from the 4th millennium BC to the Hellenistic period, proved rich in finds, with impressive public and private architectural remains, burials, and inscriptions in several languages and scripts.

As archaeological work starts from the top of a mound, the latest layers are the best known, and thus extensive sections have been unearthed of the Israelite cities. The first of these was destroyed by Sennacherib in 701 BC, following the siege depicted in the above-mentioned reliefs. Assyrian weapons and a piece of a bronze helmet from that time were found in the excavations. Also found was the massive stone-and-earth rampart built by the Assyrian army for its battering rams. This is the only site in which such a rampart, often depicted on Assyrian siege reliefs, has indeed been excavated. The second city was built shortly thereafter, and destroyed by Nebuchadnezzar in 586-5 BC. Both cities were fortified by a massive wall and had a strong main gate-house. In one of the rooms near the gate a unique collection of 21 letters written with ink on potsherds was found (see box).

During the First Temple period a large palace stood in the center of the city, the only one of its kind discovered as yet. It was built in part over a Late Bronze Age temple with many Egyptian architectural elements, and in part over the ruins of a Middle Bronze Age palace. A series of three Late Bronze Age temples was excavated in the protective ditch in front of the massive fortification. These temples yielded important collections of objects, as did the extensive series of burials of all periods.

Mari. One of the largest archives ever found in an archaeological excavation is that of ancient Mari. Situated on the Euphrates River in Syria, Mari was one of the most important political and commercial centers

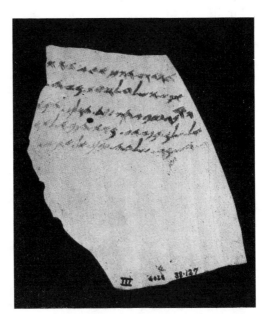

One of the 21 Lachish Letters inscribed on pottery sherds in ancient Hebrew script; beginning 6th century BC.

The Lachish Letters

Discovered in 1935, the Lachish Letters are among the most important epigraphic finds of the First Temple period. The 21 letters are *ostraca*, that is, inscribed pottery sherds. They are written in ink in the ancient Hebrew script, and their language is fluent biblical Hebrew.

The letters were found in debris in a room in the outer gate of the city, and are dated from the last days before the fall of Lachish to the Babylonian army of Nebuchadnezzar. Most of the letters are addressed to Yaush, apparently the military commander of the city, from an officer stationed in a nearby town. In one of the letters the officer remarks that he is watching for fire signals from Lachish and Azekah, indicating that, because of the siege, communication was already poor if not impossible. The date given in one of the letters, "Year Nine," is most probably the ninth year of King Zedekiah, the year in which the Babylonians started their siege of Jerusalem.

of the ancient Near East, especially during the first centuries of the 2nd millennium BC. To this period preceding the capture of Mari by Hammurabi king of Babylonia in the 18th century BC, belong the 20,000 documents from the royal archives of the spacious and luxurious palace of the local kings. The palace is a marvel in its own right. The walls of many of its 300 rooms and courtyards, covering an area of over eight acres, have been preserved almost intact, displaying extraordinary multi-colored wall frescoes, many statues, and numerous household installations and vessels. Next to the palace were two temples and a huge ziggurat (an artifical mound of unbaked bricks).

Goddess carrying a pot of water, from Mari; 2nd millennium BC.

The documents, which will take many years to publish in their entirety, mostly belong to a short period of about 60 years just preceding the Babylonian conquest. They are mostly of a historical nature, and shed light on the administration, the internal and external politics, the economy, and the cultural and religious life of Mesopotamia and neighboring countries from the island of Crete in the west to the island of Dilmun in the Persian Gulf, from Canaanite Hazor to Hittite Hatushash. They are also invaluable for the study of the early history of Israel and for biblical studies in general. Mari was not far from Haran, where Abraham's family was living about the time that the archives were being written. Rebecca's home town of Nahor (Gen 24:10) is one of the places mentioned in the tablets. References to census-taking show striking parallels with the methods used by Moses and David (Num 1-4, 26; II Sam 24). Another interesting phenomenon prominent in the Mari documents are the so-called prophetic texts, which exhibit ideological and literary features similar to those found in the commissioning and mission of the pre-classical Former Prophets. The documents are written in the Akkadian language, inscribed in cuneiform script on clay tablets.

Megiddo. This prominent mound, in which are buried the remains of one of the most important cities on the main Egypt-Syria highway (the Via Maris, as it was called in Roman times), is strategically situated where the narrow Irron Valley opens up to the wide Jezreel Valley. Megiddo's history can serve as an excellent illustration for the benefits and troubles experienced by a city on a major highway. Excavations carried out between 1903 and 1905, again between 1925 and 1939, and yet again in 1960, showed that it was built and destroyed 25 times over a period of 3,000 years, and was still one of the most affluent cities in the country. Two famous battles were fought in ancient times in the Jezreel Valley close to Meggido: the battle of the Egyptian king Thutmosis III against a coalition of Canaanite kings in 1482 BC, and the battle of Josiah, king of Judah, against an Egyptian army in 609 BC (II Chr 25:22). In both, the Egyptians were victorious. A modern parallel occurred in 1918 when the British General Allenby surprised the Turkish army under General Von Sanders, using similar tactics to those employed by Thutmosis III. Von Sanders escaped in his pajamas, and for his victory the British commander became Viscount Allenby of Megiddo.

The earliest structures on the site date to around 3,300 BC, but there are signs of much earlier occupation. From the start the settlement centered around a temple, which had grown by the 3rd millennium BC into a sacred compound with three temples and a unique large stone altar, with numerous charred animal bones found scattered around it. In the 2nd millennium BC a monumental temple with very thick walls was built on the same spot. The Israelite occupa-

Model of the city of Megiddo showing mainly the five levels of the Iron Age.

Cherub, ivory carving from Megiddo; Iron Age.

tion in the 10th century BC put an end to 2,000 years of sacred history at Megiddo.

In the days of Solomon, Megiddo was again surrounded by a wall, this time a double wall with well-built monumental outer and inner gates, of the same type and measurement as those of the same period at Hazor and Gezer. Indeed, these three towns are mentioned in a verse that lists the building activities of Solomon (I Kgs 9:15). Two palaces, one in the north of the city, the other in the south, also belong to this period. What were first known as Solomon's Stables

have been re-dated to the 9th century BC, the days of Ahab, who kept a strong army in preparation for the growing Assyrian menace. To his days belong also a new wall and gate, and the long water tunnel that connects the city with its water springs. Having been destroyed by the Assyrians in 733 BC, Megiddo was rebuilt, this time with strong Assyrian influences. It continued to exist until about 350 BC, when it was deserted for ever.

Nag Hammadi. Town in Upper Egypt, in the vicinity of which 13 volumes of 4th-century Gnostic writings were discovered in 1945. The 45 documents, written in the Coptic language on papyrus, have shed light on a rather obscure Gnostic sect and on its doctrines, developed out of a mixture of Jewish, Christian, and pagan sources, which attracted a widespread following in the first centuries AD and posed a serious challenge, especially to Christianity, at that time a new religion still struggling to win adherents. The Christian church conducted a bitter and, in the end, successful combat with Gnosticism. The Nag Hammadi writings aided in the understanding of this vital period in Christian history. They include the "Gospel of Thomas," which throws light on early traditions of the sayings of Jesus.

Nineveh. The kingdom of Assyria, which flourished in the 9th-7th centuries BC, did not have one official capital city. Each king chose his own capital where he built his major palace, while having palaces also in other cities. Nineveh, on the Tigris river near Mosul in northern Iraq, was one of the important Assyrian capitals. Ashurnasirpal II (883–859 BC) and Sargon II

Details of a relief from Nineveh, depicting the besieged city of Lachish, with defenders on its walls, resisting the Assyrians equipped with siege engines.

(722-705 BC) built palaces there, but it was Sennacherib (705-681 BC) who extensively rebuilt the city, and added walls, gates, and a water supply system. The palace he built in the city is renowned for its wall reliefs depicting his victories, including the famous Siege of Lachish Relief, now in the British Museum, to where it was transferred by Sir Austen Henry Layard, excavator of Nineveh in the middle of the 19th century. Clay prisms inscribed with descriptions of Sennacherib's attack on Jerusalem in the days of King Hezekiah, were placed in the foundations of buildings in the city.

Another king who made Nineveh his chief capital was Ashurbanipal (669-627 BC). His palace is especially famous for the lion-hunting reliefs that decorated its walls, now too at the British Museum. The palace had an extensive library of about 25,000 clay tablets, among which were many literary works, including the Babylonian account of the Flood.

In the days of Sennacherib and Ashurbanipal, Nineveh was a great world metropolis. Its 8-mile (12 km) long wall encircled an area that could house 175,000 people. This was the city visited by the prophet Jonah. Its excavations, one of the pioneering archaeological efforts of the mid-19th century, continued with many gaps throughout the 19th and 20th centuries, greatly enriching knowledge of the history, art, religion, and everyday life of the kingdom of Assyria.

Nuzi. The fame of ancient Nuzi among modern archaeologists, historians, and Bible scholars is due to a rich collection of more than 4,000 inscribed clay tablets unearthed in its ruins in 1925. The documents date to the 15th-14th centuries BC, the second period of importance in the life of the city, the first being in the 3rd millennium BC. Nuzi is situated ten miles (15 km) southwest of oil-rich Kirkuk in northern Iraq. The documents were discovered when a poor patient gave a doctor in Kirkuk in payment a torn sack in which he said were valuable tablets. The doctor gave them to the famous archaeologist, Gertrude Bell, and this led to the excavation of Nuzi.

In the 15th-14th centuries BC, Nuzi was an important city in the kingdom of Mitanni, established by the Hurrians, a mixed Semitic/Indo-European warlike people. The documents are inscribed on clay cuneiform tablets written in the Akkadian language.

The tablets were found in groups, both in royal archives such as the thousand-tablet archive of a wealthy Nuzian noble called Tehiptilla, and in private homes, such as the illuminating letters and documents of the successful businesswoman, Tulpunnaya. The information gathered from the archives relates to various topics such as family law concerning adoption, wills, and marriage, the status of women and slaves, and property laws concerning land and goods. The Nuzi tablets provide an unusually detailed illustration of everyday life in a Mesopotamian city.

Several topics that come up in the Nuzi archives have a bearing on the social customs of ancient Israel, especially in the age of the Patriarchs. One example, of special interest is the behavior in cases of childlessness. In Nuzi a man could adopt his slave, as Abraham did Eliezer, or take a concubine, or his wife could provide him with her own slave-girl, as did Sarah, Leah, and Rachel. The children of such a union were under the authority of the primary wife, as indeed were the children of Hagar, Bilhah, and Zilpah. Another biblical parallel, to the story of Jacob and Esau, is the case of a Nuzian who was in trouble and sold his inheritance to his younger brother in exchange for three sheep. Light is thrown on the story of Rachel stealing her father's household gods (Gen 31:19ff) by the Nuzi document which shows that these idols were the symbols of family property. Once Jacob and Rachel had these gods, they possessed inheritance rights to Laban's property.

Pergamon. An important ancient city in western Turkey, located inland, on the upper slopes of a high hill. Pergamon rose to prominence despite its unfavorable, yet spectacular, location, due to the efforts of its king Attalus in the 2nd century BC. It continued to flourish under the Romans and in the period of Seven Churches mentioned in the Book of Revelation (1:11; 2:12) but lost its importance with the decline of the Roman empire. Excavations in Pergamon have cleared many important sections of the city, including its walls, its temples, and its theater, as well as the famous Aesclapeion (temple to Esclapius, the god of healing), which attracted numerous seekers after medical help in antiquity. Best known is the Zeus Altar of Pergamon, a Hellenistic period artistic creation, with many expressive reliefs and sculptures of gods and heroes, now housed in the archaeological museum in Berlin.

The Zeus Altar of Pergamon; Hellenistic period creation with sculptures of gods and heroes.

Samaria. Former capital of the kingdom of Israel, Samaria is one of the largest archaeological sites in the Holy Land.

Unlike the case in many other ancient sites, the history of Samaria is well documented, from its foundation by King Omri on a barren hill in the 9th century BC, to its destruction by the Assyrians in 721 BC. Archaeological excavations carried out between 1909–1910 and again in 1931–1935 have concentrated on the city's royal section only, and revealed there a complicated series of building and rebuilding, the exact dating of which has been much debated.

Omri seems to have built the inner wall of the royal compound, known for its fine ashlar masonry, and perhaps also the palace, later enlarged by his son Ahab, an ambitious builder, whose influence can be traced in every Israelite town. This palace may be the biblical "Ivory House" (I Kgs 22:37), where many pieces of ivory carvings have come to light (see box: Samaria Ivories). Ahab also enlarged the area of the royal compound with huge amounts of fill, and surrounded this enlarged area with a new strong double wall that withstood an Aramean siege. The later Israelite kings mainly repaired the existing structures, making the exact dating of each rather difficult. In one of the buildings in the royal compound was found a group of 63 inscribed potsherds, mostly lists of agricultural products.

A second period of glory in Samaria was the time of King Herod in the 1st century BC. Herod built Samaria as a Roman city and changed its name to Sebaste ("the illustrious") in honor of the Roman emperor Augustus. The city was embellished with several temples, a stadium, a theater, and a forum, and was protected by a wall with gates. Later in the Roman period, a magnificent colonnaded road was added.

Carved ivory inlay found at Samaria, dated to the time of King Ahab.

Samaria Ivories

The collection of hundreds of small ivory pieces that once decorated wooden furniture, is the most important group of art work ever found in a First Temple period site. The ivories were discovered in various places in the royal palace that were destroyed and rebuilt several times, and therefore it is difficult to date them accurately. However, many seem to have belonged to King Ahab's "Ivory House" (I Kgs 22:39). The ivory pieces are all engraved, and display two main styles. One group is made in high relief, with an indented background, in Syrian style. The motifs are also mainly Syrian, with some Egyptian influence: animals, sphinxes, and other hybrid animals, and human figures, the best known of which is the "woman in the window" motif. The second group is made in a shallow relief in Egyptian style, with inlays of glass, semiprecious stones, and gold foil. The motifs are all Egyptian, taken from the rich Egyptian mythology, such as the goddesses Isis and Nepthis, the child Horus on a lotus flower, and the god Ra.

The Samaria ivories are similar in style and motif to other collections of ivories found in palaces of Assyrian kings where, so it seems, they were brought as booty of war from captured Phoenician towns. As the Samaria ivories display the typical Phoenician eclectic style, and as the kingdom of Israel had very close relations with Phoenicia, Ahab having married Jezebel, daughter of the king of Sidon, it is reasonable to assume that the Samaria ivories are a Phoenician product. Inscriptions in the Phoenician script on the back of some of the ivories lend credence to this suggestion.

Shechem. In the center of the Samaria Mountains, Shechem is one of the oldest and most important cities in the Holy Land. Excavations carried out in 1913–1914, in 1926–1927, and again between 1956 and 1964, revealed that ancient Shechem, located at Tell Balata east of present-day Nablus, was inhabited continuously from the beginning of the 2nd millennium BC to the 1st century AD. Important remnants of fortifications and temples uncovered in excavations testify to the fact that Shechem was the most prosperous and active Canaanite city in the mountain region of Canaan. Here the Patriarchs roamed, sometimes conducting peaceful business transactions with its inhab-

Remains of the Roman theater at Shechem.

itants (Gen 33:19), sometimes entering into violent conflicts (Gen 34). In the times of the Judges there was still in Shechem a Canaanite temple, the "House of Baal-brith" (Judg 9:4, 46). Substantial remains of this massive temple have been unearthed on the tell, including a large sanctified standing stone of the type common in Canaanite places of worship.

A stone chair with a sculptured dolphin was found in the Roman theater at Shechem.

Timnah. The copper of Timnah Valley was already known and used in antiquity. The ancient mines in this valley, situated in the extreme south of the country, some 15 miles (22 km) north of Elath, were first attributed to Solomon and named King Solomon's Mines. However, extensive explorations and excavations carried out between 1959 and 1969 along the Timnah Valley, ascertained that while copper was indeed mined in several periods in antiquity, it was disappointingly not in the days of Solomon.

First to utilize the copper were people of the Chalcolithic period (4th millennium BC), whose stone-built copper smelting furnace is the oldest known anywhere so far. After a very long gap, the mines were open again in the 12th century BC. The finds from this period, including a working camp, three copper smelting furnaces, many working tools, and copper tools in various degrees of completion, allowed the specialists to make a complete reconstruction of ancient copper production methods and processes. The miners were Egyptians, as shown by a temple to Hathor, Egyptian goddess of mining, found and excavated in the very center of the Timnah copper region. The temple, spectacularly located at the foot of "Solomon's Pillars," was built and destroyed four times during its short period of existence. A large tent in the middle of a courtyard rather than a building, the temple yielded many interesting finds, among them sandstone pillars with the face of Hathor carved on their sides. Alongside the numerous local objects, a large collection of Egyptian-made small objects was found, including hieroglyphic inscriptions and royal scarabs carrying names of Pharaohs of the 19th and 20th Dynasties. A long period of inactivity followed, and mining was resumed only in the 2nd and 3rd centuries AD, again to be followed by total desertion of the site until the 1950s.

Group of pottery of the 7th century BC found at Timnah.

Ugarit. Anyone who wishes to study the culture of the biblical Canaanites should look at the excavations and finds of Ras Shamra, a large mound situated on the northern coast of Syria and identified with ancient Ugarit, the largest and richest Canaanite city as yet discovered. Like many epoch-making archaeological discoveries, Ugarit was found accidentally, when a farmer plowed his field and stumbled upon a tomb in what proved to be Ugarit's harbor.

Excavations, which began in 1929, unearthed large sections of a flourishing city from the 14th-13th centuries BC with a huge palace, monumental temples, and fine residential quarters with well-built tombs under the floors of many houses. Ugarit was a commercial center of great importance in those days, trading with Cyprus, Crete, and Mycenean Greece, and was a major distribution point for the products of these countries to the entire Levantine coast and inland Syria. The influence of these occidental cultures was shown in the art-work found at Ugarit, especially in the many ivory plaques that once decorated wooden furniture and boxes. But the sensational finds made at Ugarit were collections of hundreds of documents unearthed in several rooms of the palace, and in a house now identified as a library and school for scribes. While the palace archives were of an administrative and legal nature, the library yielded an invaluable collection of Canaanite mythological texts and epics of heroes. Documents of all sorts were written on clay tablets in cuneiform script, which contained only some 30 characters and was deciphered as a Semitic alphabet. Thanks to the Ugarit texts, light has been thrown on the figures of the great Canaanite gods El,

Baal, Anath, and others, formerly known only from the Bible. The Ugarit language, which is a form of early Canaanite, has contributed to the understanding of many biblical words, expressions, images, and literary devices.

Bronze statuette of a Phoenician god from Ugarit.

II.10 WAR AND WARFARE

War was a constant feature in the history of the ancient Near East. Paintings and drawings found in Egypt and Mesopotamia depict battles in open terrain and attacks on fortified towns. Monuments from Mesopotamia show close formations of infantry organized in a deep phalanx, as well as chariots. Much light is also shed on methods of warfare by innumerable Egyptian and Mesopotamian documents. An account of the Egyptian battle against the Hittite-Canaanite coalition at Kadesh-on-the-Orontes in 1286 BC relates that Rameses II of Egypt received false information from two Beduins concerning the location of the Hittites and as a result divided his forces. This account describes the tactical employment of infantry and chariots, the use of the surprise attack, and the role played by intelligence reports. The Bible also is a very important written source for the study of warfare. Biblical accounts of battles that took place between the ancient Israelites

and their various enemies provide information about systems of recruiting, the structure and organization of the army, and military tactics.

Methods of warfare were dependent upon technical advances of the time, such as the development of the metallurgical industry, and upon the supply of raw materials, such as stone, metal, and wood and, of course, upon the actual needs of the battlefield.

The methods of pressing siege in the ancient Near East were varied. They included scaling walls by ladders, breaching walls with battering rams, breaking down gates with axes and fire, and undermining walls. At times several of these methods were employed simultaneously. If the city managed to resist all these measures, inhabitants were cut off from all supplies and repeated attacks were made upon the weak spots of the city.

Excavations in the land of Israel reveal much about

The horrors of war depicted on the bronze doors of the palace of the Assyrian king Shalmaneser III; 9th century BC.

the Canaanite fortifications but little about their Israelite conquerors. The nature of Israelite war and warfare differed according to political and military conditions. They included wars of conquest and settlement, defensive tribal wars, wars of consolidation on the borders, and military struggles for the actual existence of the kingdoms of Israel and Judah.

The first wars fought by the Israelites were in connection with the conquest of the promised land (Num 21:21-35, 31:1-12; Josh 1-9). During the period of the Judges and the reign of Saul, they conducted defensive wars, first against the Canaanites and later against the invasions of the Philistines. Later, David engaged in wars of expansion and conquest. Subsequently, the two kingdoms, Israel and Judah, occasionally battled against each other and, at the same time, fought against neighboring nations and empires.

Only by maintaining a strong army could a nation keep potential enemies at bay, and the only alternative to war was to accept all of the enemy's demands. In the early period of the conquest of Canaan, Israelite military inferiority often forced the various tribes to rely on deception in order to defeat the Canaanites, since they usually found it too difficult to penetrate fortified cities by force. They resorted to various means: They sent spies into the city of Jericho (Josh 2) and lured the enemy out of the city by a ruse, as they did at Ai (Josh 8). David captured Jerusalem by secretly penetrating an underground water conduit (II Sam 5:7-8). They also launched night and dawn attacks, as well as other forms of surprise actions (Josh 10:9; I Sam 11:11).

Some of the laws of war which were followed in Israel are described in Deuteronomy 20-21. The priests assured the troops of the support of the Lord (Deut 20:1-4). In some of the early battles, the priests, along with the Holy Ark, accompanied the army to the battlefield (I Sam 4:4; 30:7; II Sam 11:11). The laws in Deuteronomy also list the persons who could be exempt from military services, such as those who had recently built a house or planted a vineyard (Deut 20:5-6), those who were newly married (Deut 20:7), and those who were seized with fear (Deut 20:8). Other laws deal with the vanquished peoples (e.g., the detailed law concerning the beautiful woman taken captive: Deut 21:10-14), with spoil, prisoners, and the prohibition of cutting down fruit trees when waging siege warfare (Deut 20:19-20). All adults "aged twenty years and over, all who were able to bear arms" (Num 1:3), carried their own arms and were expected, in time of danger, to defend the life, property, and rights of family or clan.

The idea that God himself initiates war (Ex 15:3) and leads Israel in its military campaigns is prevalent throughout the Bible (I Sam 18:17; 25:28). The deity declares war (Ex 17:16; Num 31:2), and any enemy of Israel is, by definition, the Lord's enemy (Judg 5:31). God selects charismatic military leaders to lead his people in warfare (Judg 6:34). He is consulted by various cultic means prior to the battle in order to secure his support, and sacrifices are offered (Judg 6:20,26; 20:26; I Sam 28:6; 30:7-8; II Sam 5:19,23; I Kgs 22:5-7). Since the Lord is the strength of Israel, any attempt on the part of secular rulers to rely solely on their own means and resources is doomed to failure (Is 30:1-5; 31:1,3; Jer 9:23; Amos 2:13-16). The booty was consecrated to God and men were forbidden to touch it (Deut 7:25; Josh 8:2; I Sam 15:3). The Lord of Israel also conducted warfare against foreign nations, who are punished either for oppressing Israel (Jer 46:10; Obad vs. 10-14), or for their own pride and major infractions of human conduct (Is 16:6-7; 18:1-5; Jer 49:16; Amos

Egyptian soldiers arranged in four colomns of ten each, armed with lance and shield; model from Siut, Egypt; Middle Kingdom.

1:3–2:3). The prophets, however, foresaw the day when all warfare would eventually cease and in its stead there would reign universal peace (Is 2:2–4; 11:1–9; Mic 4:3–4).

Army. The military institutions and hierarchies underwent changes depending upon the political and economic conditions, the nature of the rival enemies, the topographical circumstances, and the available arms. Fighting was generally limited to the agricultural off-seasons, from just after harvest until the first rains.

During the period of Joshua's conquest and shortly thereafter, the Israelites inhabited cities and villages which they had to defend against their Canaanite neighbors whose military systems and organization were superior to theirs. The Israelites faced new and unfamiliar military problems and were obliged to develop an elaborate system of logistics. Although the tribes, led by their own charismatic leaders, the so-called Judges, rallied for special missions against a common enemy (Josh 24; Judg 6:35, 7:24, 8:1, ch. 20, etc.), they were still divided and each tribe functioned as an autonomous unit. The size of a military unit was completely dependent on the size of the clan or tribe from which it was taken. The largest unit or "division" mentioned in the Bible is "ten thousand," which was derived from a coalition of a few tribes. There were also smaller units of a thousand (Heb. *elef*) and a hundred (Heb. *me'ah*).

The urgent need for a central and permanent rule and a steady and organized military leadership was felt by the people. The rule of Saul marked the transition from the judges to the kings. After being appointed king, Saul began to build a standing army corps to face the threat of the Philistines and their chariots, thus fulfilling the Israelites' demand for a king who "may govern us and fight our battles" (I Sam 8:20). Under the leadership of David, this army was turned into a well-organized and efficient tool, and successfully defeated its neighboring enemies, expanding the borders of the country.

David's army was composed of the regular army and the militia. The core of the army consisted of 400 (I Sam 22:2), later 600, men (I Sam 25:13; 27:2), who had gathered around him as early as his wanderings in the Judean border lands. They were headed by a small group numbering no more than 30 "mighty men" — the military elite (drawn mainly from the tribe of Judah: II Sam 23:24–39). Later, when he became king, they were appointed to the highest posts in the regular army as well as the militia (I Chr 11:10–12). David also hired non-Israelite mercenaries (Cherethites, Pelethites: II Sam 15:18; 20:7, etc., and Gittites: II Sam 15:18). They served as the king's bodyguard and were employed mainly in time of internal crises, as the king could always rely on their loyalty (II Sam 15:18).

The other section of David's army was the militia (I Chr 27). Each unit, composed of 24,000 men, served one month a year. In an emergency, it was relatively easy to mobilize them, as their staff officers were regular army men. This structure was probably maintained during the days of the United Kingdom.

Weapons. Much information is available concerning weapons used in the countries neighboring Israel from the first appearance of metal weapons in the 4th millennium BC. Pictorial images, such as reliefs, monumental steles, and sculptures, provide information about weapons and the way they were used in battle. Many documents discovered in mounds of the ancient Near East, spell out the names of the various weapons. Finally, an impressive number of weapons has been found in archaeological excavations.

The weapons used in biblical times in Israel would not have differed from those in use in the neighboring countries, especially Egypt to the south and Mesopotamia to the north. During the period of the Patriarchs, bows, spears, and javelins, sickle swords, dagger-swords, and axes were used in the Near East. Other weapons in Egypt at that time are known from pictorial images, such as the famous wall-painting from the tomb of Bani Hasan which depicts a group of men holding a duck-bill ax, a double convex bow, spears, and slings. The sling is mentioned in the battle of Israel against the Benjaminites, among whom were "seven hundred selected men who were left-handed; every one could sling a stone at a hair's breadth and not miss" (Judg 20:16). Stones and staffs were the weapons of shepherds. When David fought his duel with Goliath, he declined Saul's offer of a coat of mail and sword because he was not used to them and found them cumbersome (I Sam 17:39-40).

Documents from the archives of Mari provide the earliest evidence that duels were fought. These were contests between two heroes and the outcome determined the issue between two opposing forces. In the well known biblical example, David used the simple but effective sling, while Goliath wielded an array of offensive and defensive weapons, introducing for the first time personal weapons made of iron (I Sam 17:5-7).

Of the many Egyptian pictorial images and documents depicting warfare, the most noteworthy are the ivories found at Megiddo. They show that the weapon used by Syrian and Palestinian warriors during the late Bronze Age was the composite bow, which was capable of penetrating the coat of mail widely used by archers and charioteers.

The chariot appeared in Egypt for the first time in the Late Bronze Age, probably via Canaan, to where it was presumably brought by the Hyksos. Like the Canaanite chariot, it had at first four-spoked wheels, but from the end of the 15th century, the Egyptian chariot had six-spoked wheels, which made it more stable and maneuverable. As time went on, the chariots became heavier, and in the 8th century BC, the wheels had eight spokes and were larger than ever before. They were drawn by four horses and could carry four warriors. The introduction of the chariot into the Israelite army occurred in the time of Solomon (I Kgs 10:22).

Javelins and spears of the Late Bronze Age were not very different from those of earlier days. From the few available examples, it appears that spears of both the socket and the tong type were used; they were leaf-shaped, with a prominent spine, and were used along with lances and pikes by the infantry of all armies. As

can be seen from the reliefs portraying the battle of Kadesh, spears and javelins were the main weapons of

Detail of the siege of Lachish reliefs at Nineveh, showing Assyrian warriors, a chariot and camels carrying equipment.

the Hittites, while the Egyptian charioteers used the bow. Swords and daggers were introduced towards the end of the Bronze Age and continued to be used in the Iron Age. Swords and daggers were not usually double-edged; when they were, a special mention was made of the fact, as in the case of the weapon used by Ehud the son of Gera to kill King Eglon (Judg 3:16).

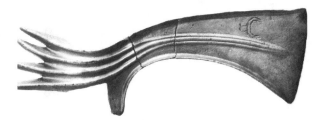

Bronze socketed piercing axe in the form of a hand with out-stretched fingers, from Beth Shean, 13th century BC.

Warriors wore a number of protective devices. The shield came in many shapes. Initially it was rectangular and was made of reeds or wood covered with leather. From the 13th century BC onwards, round shields also appeared, introduced under the influence of the Sea Peoples. A smaller shield was carried on the arm (II Chr 23:9). Helmets were rounded and cap-shaped, designed to protect the forehead and the back of the neck. They were usually of bronze, but sometimes of wood or leather, or of wood covered with leather. The shape of metal helmets varied from pointed and conical, elongated at the sides to protect the wearer's ears, like those worn by the warriors of Judah, to feather-crested. Coats of mail were also in widespread use and many scales have been found in excavations in Palestine. The coat of armor was shaped like a sack with an opening for the head, and short sleeves. It was full length in the 9th century BC but was shortened into a shirt in the 8th century BC. Usually it was made of leather or some woven fabric with metal scales sewn on and was articulated. A special scarf of scales used by archers connected the helmet to the armor. The joints seem to have been especially vulnerable: King Ahab was killed when struck by an arrow "between the joints of his armor" (I Kgs 22:34). A warrior could also wear protective armor on his legs (I Sam 17:6). Hebrew warriors, e.g., Abimelech (Judg 9:54), often used the service of an armorbearer. David was Saul's armorbearer (I Sam 16:21).

Fortifications. The oldest known fortified city in Palestine is Jericho, which was first built c.7000 BC. Several fortified towns, such as Megiddo, Gezer, Ai, and Arad, which were destroyed and rebuilt several times, are known from the 3rd millennium. The fortifications were built of the materials available in the region, primarily stone. The Hyksos invasion of Palestine (c.1750) marks a turning point in the whole concept of planning towns and fortifications. The use of a chariot and the need to accommodate numbers of warriors with their chariots produced a change in the character of the towns and their gates. The battering ram, one of the most important inventions in the history of warfare, was first introduced in the Middle Bronze Age. This caused the addition of two important features to the town wall: a bank sloping down from the fort (i.e., a glacis), and a ditch. On top of the glacis, at the perimeter of the town, the walls were erected. The glacis of Hazor, Lachish, and Dan consisted of separated layers of beaten earth, clay, gravel, and stones, the outer surface being covered with plaster and smoothed. Those of Jericho and Shechem were of a battered stone glacis covering the foot of the hill. The main feature of the town gates of this period was a direct approach, with a passageway 50-60 feet (15-18 m) long and 10 feet (3 m) wide. The gate was built against the inner face of the city wall. Three pairs of pilasters to which three doors could be fixed flanked the passageway. In the excavations in Hazor, Gezer, Beth Shemesh, and Shechem, the gates were protected by two multistoried rectangular towers, usually not protruding from the outer face of the wall.

One of the main problems in preparing a fortified city to withstand a siege was to provide for an adequate source of water. This was achieved either by digging vast cisterns for storing quantities of rain water, or by diverting water sources beneath the ground to within the fortified area, concealing any original opening outside.

The first known Israelite fortifications are attributed to Saul or David. During the reign of Solomon a more elaborate system of fortification was developed (I Kgs 9:15). Excavations in the towns of Hazor, Megiddo, and Gezer have shown that all were built according to the same specifications, comprising a casemate wall, an inner gate with six chambers, and an outer gate. Between these two gates, a passageway led into the town. The development of warfare techniques in Assyria, especially the use of the battering ram, encouraged radical improvements in fortification methods during the divided Monarchy. Old casemate walls were replaced by massive walls of salients and recesses. Battlements and balconies were built on top of the walls. The depth of the entrance of the inner gate was reduced. A description of preparations for an imminent siege is given in II Chronicles 32:3-5, 30.

From the 10th century onward, chains of citadels, such as those of Kadesh-Barnea and Arad (8th-7th cent. BC), were built along the main roads and frontiers (II Chr 26:9-10). More than 20 citadels have been discovered in the Negev; the six found in Arad cover a period from the 10th to the early 6th century BC.

Few settlements of the Persian period have been excavated, so that detailed knowledge of its fortifications is limited.

II.11 MUSICAL INSTRUMENTS

The invention of musical instruments is attributed in the Bible to Jubal who "was the ancestor of those who play the harp and pipe" (Gen 4:21). Sources concerning musical instruments are of two kinds: written documents, including the Bible and its translations, and archaeological findings. Numerous musical instruments are mentioned in the Bible but the usage, sources, and character of some of them cannot be satisfactorily identified. They were employed for sacred, as well as for secular purposes. Because of the uncertainty of many identifications, they are listed by their Hebrew names.

times; a metal instrument with a mouthpiece narrower than the body, which produced a sharp sound. The silver trumpets which Moses was ordered to make had two functions: one was military (their sound was a signal for moving camp in battle); and the other liturgical, during new moon festivities and holy days (Num 10:10). They were used to assemble the congregation (Num 10:2), and also functioned in the coronation of kings (II Kgs 11:14). Trumpets were mainly sounded by the priests (Num 10:8; 31:6; Ezra 3:10; I Chr 15:24, etc.) and are listed among the Temple instruments (II Chr 5:12–13; 12–14).

From left to right: Three figures playing the double pipe, the cymbals and the flute; 7th century, 1st and 2nd millennium BC.

Alamoth (Ps 46:1). Identification unknown; probably an instrument that produced high soprano sounds.

Al Gittith (Ps 8:1; 81:1; 84:1). Identification not certain; perhaps the name of a group of instruments.

Halil ("flute," AV: "pipe"). This was the most popular of woodwinds in the Near East, made of cane, hollowed wood, or bone. It served in diverse occasions from feasts and joy (Is 5:12) to deep mourning (Jer 48:36). It is mentioned as a popular instrument in the descriptions of the coronation of Solomon (I Kgs 1:40) and the pilgrimage to Jerusalem (Is 30:29). It is not mentioned as a liturgical instrument and never functioned in the Temple service.

Hatzotzra ("trumpet"). Mentioned in the Bible 30

Keren ("horn," AV: "cornet"). A wind instrument made of horn. It is mentioned twice in the Hebrew (Josh 6:5; I Chr 25:5) and a few times in Aramaic (*karna*, Dan 3:5, 7, 10, 15).

Kinnor ("lyre"). A stringed instrument used on secular occasions (Gen 31:27), at festivities and banquets (Is 5:12, etc.), as well as on sacred occasions, mainly in the Temple. According to I Chr 15:17, the use of the *kinnor* in the Temple is attributed to David. It was the instrument of the Levites (II Chr 5:12; 9:11). Prophecies were made to the sound of its strings (I Chr 25:1) and it was one of the instruments in the hands of the prophets whom Saul encountered after being anointed by Samuel (I Sam 10:5). In the Psalms, the *kinnor* is mentioned in connection with joy and thanksgiving (Ps 33:2; 43:4; 57:9, etc.). It was played either solo, or together with string, wind, or percussion instruments. The number of its strings is unknown.

Kitaros ("harp"). A stringed instrument mentioned only in Daniel 3:5, 7, 10, 15. The name is derived from the Greek *kitharis* (lyre).

Mahol. Mentioned only in Psalms (150:4), among the many instruments that formed the orchestra of praise.

Menaaneim ("sistrums"). A percussion instrument, probably made of metal plates, mentioned only in II Samuel 6:5.

Metziltaim ("cymbals"). A percussion instrument made of copper, probably identified with *tzaltzalim* (II Sam 6:5; Ps 100:5), which stands for the plural, while *metziltaim* implies a pair of instruments. Mentioned in the Bible mainly in connection with the Levites in the Temple service (I Chr 15:16; II Chr 29:25; Ezra 3:10; etc.). The cymbals may have been been employed as a signal for the singers and instruments and perhaps as a sign for the congregation, to mark the beginnings, endings, and pauses in the chapters sung.

Minnim ("stringed instrument," Ps 150:4). Its identification is not known. It may be derived from the Akkadian word *mananu*, "sinews."

Nebel ("lute," AV: "psaltery"). A stringed instrument, its identification not clear. With the exception of Ps 33:2 and 144:9, it is always mentioned with the *kinnor*. It was used in sacred life and appears in the description of the Temple service; it is also mentioned in secular contexts, as an entertainment instrument at banquets (Is 5:12). In Psalms, it is linked with *asor*, "ten" (33:2; 144:9; 92:3) and some scholars believe that this refers to a special kind of ten-string psaltery.

Neginoth ("stringed instrument"). A name that occurs in the opening lines of six of the Psalms (4, 6, 54, 67, 76). Identification not known.

Psanterin ("psaltery"). One of the instruments in the orchestra which marked the beginning of the worship of the golden image set up by King Nebuchadnezzar (Dan 3:5ff). The name derived from the Greek *psalterion*. Its form is unknown.

Sabbah ("lyre"). A stringed instrument mentioned in Dan 3:5ff), probably of Syriac origin.

Shalishim. Appears only once in I Samuel 18:6; thought by some scholars to be a three-stringed instrument or a triangular percussion instrument.

Sheminit. Appears only once in the Bible (Ps 6:1). Some believe that it was an eight-stringed instrument. Others suggest that it was an instrument pitched one octave higher than usual.

Shofar ("trumpet"). A wind instrument made of ram's horn, used along with stringed instruments (Ps 150:3), wind instruments (Ps 98:6), or both (I Chr 15:28). Because of its role at Mount Sinai (Ex 19:13–19; 20:18) and at the fall of the walls of Jericho, it was common to attribute magical properties to the *shofar*. The *shofar*

had military usages (Ex 19:13–19; 20:18), it was employed to alert the people (Judg 3:27; 6:34; Neh 4:12–14), to alarm the enemy (Judg 7:8, 16–22); as blast of triumph (I Sam 13:3), as a warning (Jer 4:21), etc. The *shofar* was used at the coronation of kings (II Sam 15:10, II Kgs 9:13) and to proclaim the Jubilee year (Lev 25:9). The *shofar* was, and still is, used in Jewish ritual during the penitential period around the New Year and the Day of Atonement. In the State of Israel, it is also sounded at the inauguration of new presidents of the State.

Sumphonia. Word of Greek origin, meaning "accompanying sound." Some scholars believe that it was a bagpipe. Others think that it refers to the sound of some instruments playing together or a whole orchestra, and not a specific instrument.

Tof ("timbrel/tambourine"). A percussion instrument with a membrane or timbrel, mentioned frequently in the Bible (Is 5:12; Ps 81:2, etc.), always with other instruments. It was used on sacred as well as secular occasions, but never in the Temple service. It is mentioned in connection with joy (Jer 31:4; Ps 149:3; etc.) and dances, and was usually played by women (Ex 15:20–21; Judg 11:34; I Sam 18:6–7). Timbrels varied in size and were played with the bare hand or with sticks. Larger ones were played by two people.

Ugab ("flute"). The nature of this instrument is

Horn and drum players on a basalt relief from Carchemish.

unknown, but it is commonly thought to be a flute. It is mentioned in the Bible four times (Gen 4:21; Job 21:12, 30:31; Ps 150:4).

In the Second Temple, the rituals were accompanied by cymbals, harps, lyres, and trumpets. An orchestra in the Temple consisted of six psalteries, an unlimited number of harps, one pair of cymbals, and two trumpets. Music is seldom mentioned in the New Testament (but cf. Luke 7:32; 15:25; Matt 9:23). Paul referred to the Corinthians' knowledge of music (I Cor 14:7ff). The author of Revelation speaks of harpists and singers (Rev 14:2–3) but, predicting the end of Babylon (i.e., Rome), foretells that music "shall be heard in you no more" (Rev 18:22).

II.12 WEIGHTS AND MEASURES

The most ancient standards of weights and measures are those of Egypt and Babylon. The Babylonian six-decimal system is based on a linear unit derived from astronomical calculations. The capacity unit is the basic linear unit cubed, and the weight of water that such a cube can contain gave the basic unit of weight. The Babylonian system of measures was accepted by all the peoples of the ancient Near East.

In Palestine both the Babylonian system and the Egyptian decimal system were in use. The Hebrews, who had used the Babylonian system, introduced changes into it, as a result of Egyptian influence. Further changes were introduced by the Phoenicians and the Persians, who added some units of their own to the Babylonian system and dropped others.

The units of weights and measures referred to in the Bible belong to both these systems, according to the degree of contact with the different cultures at the particular time on question.

Linear Measures. Among primitive peoples the limbs of the human body served as units of length. Thus in the Bible the finger was the smallest unit (Jer 52:21); 4 fingers made one hand (I Kgs 7:26); 3 hands made one span (Ex 28:16); and 2 spans made 1 cubit. There were at least two kinds of cubit, the long cubit that was used for sacred matters (Ezek 40:5), and the ordinary cubit, which was 1 hand shorter than the sacred cubit.

Measures of Volume. Israelite measures of volume were based on the Babylonian six-decimal system. The smallest unit was the *log* (Lev 14:10, etc.) which was used both for dry goods and for liquids; 4 *logs* make 1 *kab* (II Kgs 6:25); 1 4/5 *kab* make 1 *omer* (Ex 16:16, etc.); 5 *ephah* make 1 *leteck*; 2 *leteck* make 1 homer (or *kor*) (Is 5:10; Ezek 45:10–14).

Liquid Measures. *Log* (Lev 14:10, etc.); *kab* (II Kgs 6:25); *hin* (Ex 29:4); *bath* (I Kgs 7:26,38), equal in capacity to the *ephah*; *kor* (I Kgs 4:22; 5:11), equal to the *homer*. The *mesurah* is not a specific measure, but denotes a small quantity of liquid (Lev 19:35, etc.).

Weights. The Israelite weight system was based on the Babylonian standard, although the values of some of the weights were not always identical. The Babylonian values were as follows:

60 shekels = 1 *maneh*
60 *manehs* = 3,600 shekels — 1 *kikar*

There were two weight systems, the values of one being double the other. This double standard of weights which included a light *maneh* (weighing about 15 3/4 oz [450 g]) spread over all the ancient Near East.

Shekel stone weights inscribed with their values, found at En Geddi; 7th century BC.

In addition to the Babylonian system, the Phoenicians and the Greeks developed another system with a heavy shekel weighing 218–224 grains and a light one of 112 grains. In this system the *maneh* contained 50 instead of 60 shekels, and there were 3,000 instead of 3,600 shekels to the *kikar*. The division into fifties probably originated in the Egyptian decimal system. This system, which was used by the Phoenician merchants, was accepted by the Israelites, the Persians, the Greeks, and later also by the Romans, who all made some modifications arising from their specific needs. Alongside these systems others were also used at different times and in different places.

In excavations in Palestine, especially in the strata of the 7th-6th centuries BC, small stone weights with symbols on them have been found. Some of these symbols represent metrological values, while others are the actual names of the weights. Hundreds of weights have been measured and the results have shown that the same unit could vary considerably. It seems in fact that different values of the same basic units were used for different commodities, as is still done in some places today.

In the Hebrew Bible a weight is called a stone, indicating the material from which it was made. The Scriptures warn against cheating by using small weights for selling and heavy ones for buying (Deut 25:13:16; Amos 8:5, etc.). The merchant would carry the weights on his person (Deut 25:13, etc.). A weight that had been approved by the authorities was known as the "king's standard" (II Sam 14:26). Commodities were weighed

One mina (or maneh) weight of the time of Nebuchadnezzar II, (605–562 BC).

on scales consisting of two bowls, equal in size and weight, suspended on three or four strings at the ends of a horizontal cane, which was held by a short rope. Another method involved placing the cane on a fixed base standing on the ground. Many such balances of all periods have been found in excavations.

Israelite Weights. The smallest unit is the *gerah*, or 1/20 shekel (Ex 30:13). There was also a 1/4 shekel (I Sam 9:8: "fourth part"); a 1/3 shekel and a *beka*, or 1/2 shekel (Ex 38:26). These are all small units. The unit most frequently mentioned in the Bible is the shekel (Ex 30:23ff etc.) and it is not always easy to decide which standard it was related to in any particular passage. It is possible that the shekel referred to in Exodus, Leviticus, and I Kings was equal to the shekel of Aegina, which weighed about 177 grains. The *maneh* ("mina") (Neh 7:71, etc.) belongs to the Phoenician standard and was therefore equal to 50 shekels. The *maneh* of the earlier books (I Kgs 10:17) was probably the Babylonian one of 50 heavy shekels. The *kikar* ("talent") is mentioned frequently in terms of a quantity of silver and sometimes as a weighing unit (Ex 37:24). The *kikar* of the later books of the Bible is the Phoenician *kikar* of 3,000 shekels, while in the early writings the Babylonian or Syrian unit is referred to.

During the time of the Second Temple the Jews developed a system of weights based on a combination of the Phoenician with the Greek (Attic) and Roman systems. The values of the weights according to this system are:

6 *maoth* (*maah* = obolos)	= 1 *zuz*	
2 *zuzim*	= 1 shekel (light)	
4 *zuzim*	= 1 shekel (heavy)	
50 *zuzim*	= 1/2 *maneh*	
100 *zuzim*	= 1 *maneh*	
6,000 *zuzim*	= 1 *kikar*	

II.13 COINS AND CURRENCY

Money, in terms of a standardized system of currency, appeared only towards the end of the Old Testament period. Until the advent of coinage, wealth was measured by the amount of moveable property a person owned, including slaves, livestock, precious metals, and agricultural produce. Most trade was carried out using the barter system. The most frequently bartered items were livestock (Gen 12:14–16; 29–30; II Kgs 3:4), but often other items were bartered as well. Solomon purchased the materials and craftsmen for the construction of the Temple from Hiram, king of Tyre, by paying him with grain and oil (I Kgs 5:11), and even land, in the form of twenty northern cities (I Kgs 9:11).

Precious metals, particularly gold and silver, were also weighed out and used in barter. The most common weight of precious metals was the shekel. Abraham bought the Cave of the Machpelah from Ephron

Collection of Jewish and Tyrian shekels found in Jerusalem.

From left to right: Tetradrachm of Alexander the Great minted in Acco, 4th century BC; double shekel of Sidon, 4th century BC; coin of Herod Archelaus, depicting a galley, struck in Jerusalem, 4 BC.

the Hittite for 400 silver shekels (Gen 23:16), and David purchased the threshing floor of Araunah the Jebusite for 50 silver shekels (II Sam 24:24). The silver shekel was such a popular unit of weight that it was often simply called silver. It was divisible into a *bekah* worth 1/2 shekel (Ex 38:26), a third (Neh 10:32), a *rebah*, worth 1/4 shekel (I Sam 9:8) and a *gerah*, worth 1/20 shekel (Lev 27:25). Another measure of silver was the *kesitah*, with which Jacob bought land in Shechem (Gen 33:19). A talent of silver was sufficient to keep servants until the return of their master from a distant land (Matt 25:15); a talent of gold was the value of a royal crown (II Sam 12:30). King Hezekiah paid tribute to Sennacherib of 300 talents of silver and 30 talents of gold (II Kgs 18:14).

The minting of coins was begun in Lydia, around the time of the destruction of the First Temple. The practice spread rapidly throughout the ancient world, and was adopted by the Jews in the Persian period. Archaeologists have found numerous coins of the Hasmonean period, inscribed with the king's name and engraved with various religious and agricultural symbols such as palm branches and pomegranates. The Jewish prohibition against casting graven images forbade the introduction of engraved royal portraits.

Coins mentioned in the New Testament were apparently those minted by Herod in Caesarea. Herod's coins were based on Roman currency and included the *denarius*, equivalent to a day's wages (Matt 20:9), the *aureus*, equivalent to 25 *denarii*, the *assarion*, worth 1/16th of a *denarius*, or the value of two sparrows (Matt 10:29) and the *quadrans*, worth a quarter of an *assarion* (Matt 5:26).

Herod expressed his sensitivity to the Jewish inhabitants of Judea by not minting coins bearing human figures. Only Philip, his son (4 BC-AD 34), who reigned in the northeastern part of the kingdom in Transjordan, where the majority of the population was non-Jewish, minted coins bearing his portrait and that of the Roman emperor.

Greek coins were also popular in Judea. The *drachma*, equivalent to the Roman *denarius*, was the standard of Greek currency. Jews paid their taxes to the Temple with *didrachmas* worth two *drachmas* (Matt 17:24-17), or with *staters*, worth four *drachmas* (Matt 17:27). The most valued Greek coin was the *mina*, worth 100 *drachmas* (Luke 19:11-27).

The only native Judean coin mentioned in the New Testament is the *lepton*, or mite, of little value. Jesus praised the widow who placed a mite in the Temple coffers, noting that for the poor woman it was "her whole livelihood" (Mark 12:44).

Coins were minted in ancient Israel until the end of the Bar-Kokhba revolt (AD 132-135).

II.14 METALS, MINERALS AND PRECIOUS STONES

METALS

A variety of metals are mentioned in biblical sources. The advent of metallurgy was a major scientific leap in the ancient world, and the peoples who were first able to smelt and shape metals had great technological advantages over those who had not yet acquired the skill. Certain metals, notably gold and silver and to a lesser extent copper, were so highly regarded that they were used as an early form of currency. Other metals and alloys, particularly iron and bronze, were utilized in tools and weaponry, giving their users unprecedented capabilities in both peace and war.

Many of the metals mentioned in the Bible are not indigenous to the land of Israel and its surrounding territories. Some iron was found in Israel; the most abundant metal was copper, which was mined in the Arabah and in the Sinai. Copper was also found in Asia Minor, Northern Syria and Cyprus. The Hittite territory in Asia Minor was rich in iron. Gold, the most important of the ornamental metals, was imported from Ophir (I Chr 29:4) and from Havilah (Gen 2:11).

Little is known about the means employed to extract metals. Whereas it is certain that surface veins were exploited, a reference in Job 28:1-7 seems to indicate that tunnels were sometimes dug to reach subterranean deposits. After extraction, the metal was placed in a furnace (Deut 4:20; Is 48:10) to separate impurities, and finally smelted. The liquid metal was placed in molds, many of which have been found by archaeologists. A description of the metalworker's activities, which included beating, soldering, and engraving, is found in Isaiah 41:6-7.

Copper. Copper was the most exploited metal mentioned in the Bible. Its use as the predominant metal extended from the early 3rd millennium until the 13th century BC, when it was replaced by iron. "Copper" in the Bible generally refers to bronze, an alloy of copper and tin. Copper was found at Timnah and at Punon in the Arabah, as well as in the Sinai Peninsula. After being ground in stone mortars, the ore was then smelted. Slag heaps from the copper refining process are still found in abundance along the southern coast of the Sinai and in the Arabah. According to the biblical account, Solomon apparently cast the copper vessels for the Temple in the area between Succoth and

Ram's head on a copper stand found in a cave in the Judean Desert; Chalcolithic period.

Zaretan (I Kgs 7:46). Copper was used in making weapons, agricultural and household tools, and ornaments. The pillars of the Tabernacle were supported by copper sockets (Ex 27:11) and the laver was made entirely of copper (Ex 30:17-21). In the Temple, there was also a Molten Sea made of copper (I Kgs 7:23-26; II Chr 4:2-5).

Gold. The most highly valued metal of biblical times. Gold is not known in the soil of Palestine, but can be found in Egypt, where the Israelites apparently learned

Goldsmith weighing gold. Egyptian wall painting; 15th century BC.

the art of gold-smithing. Gold was later imported from Ophir (I Chr 29:4), Havilah, Tarshish, Arabia, and India. The importance of gold in the biblical world is indicated by the many terms used to define various states of the metal: pure gold (Ex 25:36,38, I Kgs 6:20-21), refined gold (I Chr 28:18), and hammered gold (I Kgs 10:17). Apart from its ornamental and decorative use, gold was a form of payment before the minting of coins (Josh 7:21). It was widely used in the ornamentation of both the Tabernacle (Ex 26) and the Temple (II Chr 2), and was often given as a gift, being listed among the gifts brought by the three wise men to the infant Jesus (Matt 2:11).

Iron. Although iron was known to the ancient Egyptians, the relatively difficult process of extracting the metal from its oxides was only mastered by the Hittites of Asia Minor in the 13th century BC. Iron implements such as weapons, tools, and jewelry were imported by the Phoenicians and the Philistines into Israel, where the Philistines monopolized production (I Sam 13:19-20). It is possible that iron ores found in Sinai were later exploited (Deut 4:20; I Kgs 8:51). Iron was later imported from Tarshish (Ezek 27:12) and from Javan (Ezek 27:19). Biblical references state that the metal was used in making weapons (Num 35:16; I Sam 17:7), chariots (Josh 17:16), agricultural tools (I Sam 13:20-21), weights, bolts for gates (Is 45:2), chains (Ps 105:18), and nails (I Chr 22:3).

Lead. A metal relatively unused in the early biblical period, although it was imported by the Phoenicians from Tarshish (Ezek 27:12). In the Second Temple period, its use became more widespread. It was used to make weights and weapons, as well as in binding building stones together. Lead was sometimes added to bronze coins.

Silver. Metal known and utilized in the earliest biblical times. The metal rarely appears in its natural state and must therefore be obtained by a process of smelting, in which the lighter silver, in liquid form, floats atop its alloys (Jer 6:28–30; Ezek 22:17–21). Silver was relatively rare. It was used in the manufacture of household utensils (Ex 3:22; 11:2) and jewelry, as well as in barter (Gen 20:16). Although silver can be found in Israel, it was also imported from Tarshish (II Chr 9:21; Jer 10:9), and from Arabia (II Chr 9:14). Job speaks of silver mines (28:1) and the refining of silver is mentioned in Proverbs (17:3) and Zechariah (13:9). Silver was widely used in the ornamentation of the Tabernacle (Ex 26) and the Temple (II Chr 2).

Tin. A metal combined with copper to form the alloy bronze. Since tin is not indigenous to Palestine, it had to be imported, apparently from Tarshish (Ezek 22:18–20).

MINERALS

Alabaster. Soft white mineral used in carvings in ancient times. Alabaster was first used by the Egyptians as early as the Third Dynasty in making small household utensils and scent bottles. In Esther (1:6) reference is made both to alabaster columns and alabaster stones used to pave the palace of Ahasuerus in Shushan. In the New Testament, a woman broke a scent bottle of alabaster and poured the contents over Jesus' head (Mark 14:3). Although high grade alabaster is found in Egypt, a lesser grade of the mineral can be found in Palestine.

Asphalt, Bitumen, Lime, Mortar, Pitch. Material used by the Israelites in stonework and in making

Alabaster head of a bull from Mesopotamia; 4th-3rd millennium BC.

bricks. The material is found in abundance in the tar pits surrounding the Dead Sea (Gen 14:10). Asphalt was used in bonding building stones and in waterproofing both Noah's ark and that of Moses (Gen 6:14; Ex 2:3). In one instance, the Moabites burnt the bones of the Edomite king in lime (Amos 2:1). Lime was often mixed with other materials, notably sand and sea

shells, to make bricks and mortar, such as that used by the Israelites in Egypt (Ex 1:14).

Glass. The use of glass goes as far back as the Neolithic and Chalcolithic periods, when natural, volcanic glass (obsidian) was occasionally imported into Palestine from Anatolia. Man-made glass was first manufactured in Egypt and Mesopotamia towards the end of the 3rd millennium BC. The first glass objects manufactured were small beads used as ornaments. In the middle of the 2nd millennium, the process of molding glass was learnt. Glass objects were exceedingly rare, and have been discovered primarily in temples and tombs.

Glass bottle in the shape of a fish from el-Amarna, Egypt; late 18th Dynasty.

Although these objects were sometimes imported into Palestine, and have been found in Beth Shean, Megiddo, and Lachish, there is no evidence that they were produced locally. With the fall of the New Kingdom in Egypt and the Middle Assyrian period in Mesopotamia, glass-making went into a decline. In the 8th and 7th centuries BC, glass served as an inlay in the ivory works used to decorate the royal palaces of Samaria. The rareness of glass is indicated by the meager mention of the material in the Bible. In the Old Testament, glass is only mentioned in the Book of Job (28:17). In the New Testament period, glass was apparently more abundant, with Alexandria serving as a major center of glass-making. Nevertheless, mention of glass in the New Testament is confined to the Book of Revelation (4:6; 15:2; 21:18,21).

Sulphur. Sulphur (brimstone) was known to the ancient world as an inflammable material and is mentioned in the Bible in descriptions of destruction, as a divine retribution against sinners in general. Thus "the Lord rained brimstone and fire against Sodom and Gomorrah" (Gen 19:24; cf also Is 30:33; Ezek 38:22; Job 18:15; Rev 14:10, etc.). There are deposits of sulphur in the lands bordering the Mediterranean Sea. There are sulphur deposits south of Gaza and in smaller quantities around the Dead Sea where there are some sulphurous springs; the sulphur content adds to their medicinal qualities.

PRECIOUS STONES

The ancient Hebrews were fascinated by precious stones, their shapes and their colors. They valued them not only as ornaments but as possessing magic qualities as well, and went to great efforts to obtain gems. Since most of the gems mentioned in the Bible were not native to the land of Israel, they were imported, often from afar. The Bible records gems being brought from Havilah in Arabia (Gen 2:11-12), Ophir (I Kgs 10:11), Sheba and Raamah (Ezek 27:22), and Ethiopia (Job 28:19).

Lists of precious stones exist in three separate sections in the Bible. Twelve gems adorned the breastplate of the High Priest (Ex 28:17-20), and with variations, these stones reappear in Ezekiel's description of the Garden of Eden (Ezek 28:13) and in John's description of the walls of the New Jerusalem (Rev 21:18-21).

Scholars find it difficult to identify many of the stones mentioned in the Bible. The modern system of mineral classification was unknown to the Israelites, who grouped stones according to shape and color. Translations of the Bible offer little help, since the translators often mentioned stones with which they themselves were familiar, but which were unknown in the ancient world. The Hebrew word *yahalom*, for example, is commonly translated as diamond, but this mineral was unknown before the medieval period. Thus stones that are listed in the Bible as belonging to different groups sometimes form a single mineralogical family. The following list includes precious stones mentioned in the Bible with tentative identifications.

Ahlamah ("amethyst" Ex 28:19; 39:12). The identification of this stone is not certain. In the Septuagint it is rendered as "amethyst," one of the quartzes which is purple or violet in color. Some scholars agree with this identification of the stone.

Bareket ("emerald") Ex 28:17). This stone has the same name in Akkadian. The Septuagint calls it *smaragdos*, and the identification with *smaragd*, emerald, is generally accepted. During the Hellenistic period this name was applied to a different stone, the "false emerald" or malachite, whose greenish shade is close to that of the true emerald. Real emeralds were extremely rare in the ancient world and could not be easily worked. Some scholars hold that *bareket* should be identified with jasper.

Dar. The court of the garden of the Persian king was paved with *dar* ("alabaster, turquoise, white and black marble" Est 1:6). In Arabic *dar* means pearl, and some scholars believe that it should be identified with mother-of-pearl. Others believe that it was an orange-colored stone.

Ekdah ("crystal" Is 54:12). The Septuagint refers to this as *lithus crystallou*, which would be the equivalent of rock crystal. Some maintain that it should be identified with *carbunculus*, the garnet, a red stone.

Kadkod ("ruby"). Listed among the precious stones which the Aramean merchants brought to Tyre (Ezek 27:16). According to Isaiah (54:12) God will make the windows of the house of Jerusalem of *kadkod*. The Arabs give the name *karkund* to a red stone resembling the ruby, identified today with the pinel. Scholars are of the view that *kadkod* should be identified with hyacinth, the medieval name for a yellow stone with sorts of lilac and purple. It may possibly be one of the quartzes that the Greeks and Romans used for jewelry. Pliny says that it was blue and that it came from Gaul. Today, under the name of hyacinth, it is classified among the zircons, stones that range from a colorless quality to green, blue, red, and golden yellow.

Leshem ("jacinth" Ex 28:19). The Septuagint has *ligurion*, a corruption of the *lyncurium* of the classical sources, which is a shining yellow color; probably the opal, which is multicolored or a glimmering orange. Some identify it with aventurine, a quartz containing very fine crystals of hematite, limonite, or mica, which sparkle when the light catches them. Still others identify it with amber.

Nopheh ("turquoise" Ex 28:18; Ezek 28:13). The Septuagint has *anthrax*. Ancient Greek sources refer to it as a hard red stone. Pliny calls the same stone *carbunculus*. Some scholars identify it with turquoise; a sulfate of aluminium, the small percentage of copper it contains gives it a distinctive red color. It was very much used in jewelry.

Odem ("sardius" Ex 28:17; Ezek 28:13). Some identify it with the Akkadian *samtu*, a red stone, but it is more likely the carnelian. Others believe it was red jasper, an opaque stone found abundantly in Palestine and Egypt. The identification of the *odem* with the ruby cannot be sustained, because this was not known before the 3rd century AD.

Pitdah ("topaz" Ex 28:17; Ezek 28:13). Most Biblical commentators understand this to be a greenish stone. Pliny uses the name *topazion* for a stone known as chyrsolithos or as olivine, but *pitdah* is now identified with plasma, a greenish semi-translucent stone, one of the chalcedonies. The *pitdah* of Ethiopia symbolizes the value of wisdom in Job 28:19.

Ramoth ("coral" Ezek 27:16; Job 28:18). The identification of this stone is not certain. Some suggest that it is not a stone at all, but a shell.

Sapir ("sapphire" Ex 28:18). In the OT this is referred to among the most precious stones (Job 28:16). Ezekiel sees the firmament as resembling the sapphire and his vision of the Garden of Eden includes the *sapir* (Ezek 28:13). It is also a symbol of beauty (Song 5:14). This is not to be mistaken for the sapphire of our day, which is the corundum, a stone that was not known in ancient times. Theophrastos, a Greek scholar, in his book on stones, refers to it as blue with gold-white specks, like lapis lazuli.

Shebo ("agate" Ex 28:19). The identification with

agate is accepted by all scholars. It is believed that the agate of the OT was not the white stone, but a mixed black and white stone. White-grey agates were found in Egypt.

Shoham ("onyx" Ex 28:20; Ezek 28:13; Job 28:16). One of the stones brought from Havilah (Gen 2:11-12). It seems that onyx is the most appropriate identification. It comes from the East and has three colors arranged in three stripes: red, blue or brown and black or dark brown. To Job (28:16) it was a symbol of wealth.

Soheret ("black marble" Est 1:6). The identification is not known. Some scholars think that it was a black stone used for paving floors.

Tarshish ("beryl" Ex 28:20). Believed to have been identical with mother-of-pearl. To Ezekiel the wheels of his vision resemble tarshish (Ezek 10:9).

Yahalom ("diamond" Ex 28:18; Ezek 28:13). According to the Midrash this stone is white. Some identify it with anthrax or carbuncle, which is red, and others with onyx, which has different colors arranged in layers, or even with chalcedony, which was much used for beads and seals. However, its identification with the diamond should be rejected, as this stone was not known before the Middle Ages. Ezekiel (28:13) sees it as one of the precious stones in the Garden of Eden.

Yaspeh ("jasper" Ex 28:20; 39:13). A translucent green stone; but may refer to opaque red quartz. *Yaspeh* is mentioned in the El Amarna Letters as a royal stone.

Ivory

Ivory was first used in Egypt in the Neolithic period, when it was utilized in the manufacture of harpoons. The material was later used in making trinkets and figurines. As tusked mammals retreated from the region, ivory became increasingly valuable. Solomon imported ivory from Tarshish (I Kgs 10:22; II Chr 9:21) and used it for his throne (I Kgs 10:18; II Chr 9:17). It was common practice for the wealthy to inlay their beds with ivory, and even to decorate their houses with ivory panels (Amos 3:15; 6:4). Such a house was built by King Ahab of the Northern Kingdom of Israel (I Kgs 22:39). A poetic reference to an ivory tower also serves as part of the description of the beloved Shulamith in the Song of Songs (7:4). Ivory carvings have been found throughout Palestine; similar carvings found in Nineveh attest to the value attributed to ivory as a spoil of war.

Cherub ivory carving from Samaria; Iron Age.

II.15 JEWELRY AND ORNAMENTS

Ornaments and jewelry figure prominently in the Bible, both in the literal and in the figurative sense. They were worn by men and women, rulers and warriors. They were part of the ceremonial dress of the high priest and also served as an indication of social standing. The prophetic books of the Old Testament as well as the New Testament employ the imagery of jewels and ornaments as symbols to convey their message.

Jewels were part of the daily life of the ancient Hebrews. They could be used as a betrothal present, as when the servant sent by Abraham to find a bride for his son, Isaac, gave Rebekah "a golden nose ring weighing half a shekel, and two bracelets for her wrists weighing ten shekels of god" (Gen 24:22). When the father of the girl agreed to the match, "he brought out jewelry of silver, jewelry of gold...and gave them to Rebekah" (Gen 24:53). Jewels were also used as a pledge: Tamar received from her father-in-law Judah a signet ring as a pledge (Gen 38:18). Since they were

A jewelry hoard from BethShemesh; early Israelite period.

easily movable assets, before leaving Egypt the Children of Israel took the jewels of their Egyptian neighbors (Ex 3:22; 11:2; 12:35). In the desert, when the Children of Israel demanded that Aaron make them an image (since Moses was on Mount Sinai receiving the Ten Commandments), he instructed them to "break off the golden earrings which are in the ears of your wives, your sons, and your daughters and bring them to me" (Ex 32:2) and with the gold that they brought he molded a calf (Ex 32:4).

Although there are about 25 different names of jewels in the Bible, not all have been identified. Some occur only once and still puzzle scholars; others are translated merely as "ornaments" for want of a more precise word (e.g., II Sam 1:24; Jer 2:32). In the long tirade condemning the luxury of the women of Israel, Isaiah lists their finery along with many jewels (3:18-23). A similar condemnation of costly jewels is to be found in the first epistle of Paul to Timothy (I Tim 2:9).

Among ornaments ordinarily worn by men were "ornaments of gold, armlets and bracelets and signet rings and earrings and necklaces" (Num 31:50). Isaiah writes approvingly of "a bride adorning herself with

Hawk-shaped gold pendant; Gaza, late Bronze Age.

her jewels" while her bridegroom "decks himself with ornaments" (61:10).

The exact difference between armlet and bracelet is not clear. Scholars are also not sure of the exact difference between the various headdresses (headbands, crescents, diadems, etc.) mentioned in the Scriptures, which could be a single ribbon or veil embroidered with pearls or a gold ornament studded with precious stones.

Kings were fond of jewels and ornaments. They wore ornate crowns of gold set with precious stones (II Sam 12:30) and surrounded themselves with priceless objects (I Kgs 10:14-23). Solomon "made silver as common in Jerusalem as stones" (I Kgs 10:27).

One of the ornaments on the breastplate of judgment worn by the high priest on or over the ephod, is described in great detail (Ex 28:15-29). Both the ephod and the breastplate were made of rich material and lavishly covered with gold and precious stones.

Ezekiel compared Jerusalem to a beautiful woman "adorned with gold and silver" (16:13), who later was stripped of her "beautiful jewelry" (16:39) as punishment because "you have taken your beautiful jewelry from my gold and my silver which I had given you, and made for yourself male images" (16:17).

In the book of Revelation Babylon is depicted as "arraying in purple and scarlet, and adorned with gold and precious stones and pearls" (17:4). The city of New Jerusalem in Revelation is made of gold, pearls, and precious stones (21:9-21).

The predilection shown by biblical figures for jewels and jewelry is confirmed by extensive archaeological discoveries. The finds of the Late Bronze Age in tombs and in public and private buildings in the Land of Israel are especially rich, reflecting the prosperity of the area at the time. A rich collection of gold jewelry was found in pottery vessels at Tell el-Ajjul in southern Israel. Outstanding are plaques worn as pendants depicting the Canaanite goddess of fertility, a pendant in the form of an eight-pointed star, crescent-shaped earrings with rich granular decoration, gold pendants (used as amulets) in the form of animals, faience beads depicting animals and flowers, and a headdress belonging to one of the wives of Pharaoh Thutmosis III. Bracelets of gold and silver are numerous, as are pairs of golden earrings and finger rings decorated with scarabs. In the Middle and Late Bronze Ages, Egyptian influence is illustrated by numerous jewelry finds. A jewelry cache of some 200 pieces found in a pottery vessel in Beth Shemesh is dated to the early period of the Israelite settlement, and a hoard from Canaanite Megiddo is dated to the second half of the 11th century BC. From the Persian period onwards the jewelry belongs to types developed in many cultures, including Greece, Asia Minor, Phoenicia, and Persia. Gold jewelry is common, much of it connected with religious belief and cult images such as gods, snakes, and dolphins.

II.16 EVERYDAY LIFE IN BIBLE TIMES

GENERAL BACKGROUND

During the biblical period in the Land of Israel, many things threatened life and made it fragile. Survival was a major effort and it occupied a great deal of time and attention. The threat that prevailed was on two levels: individual (will I myself live until tomorrow or next year?); and communal (will my group — family, clan, village, town, city, tribe, nation — survive?). The survival of the nation or community was often more important than the survival of the individual, as it was not a question of whether an invading army was coming, but when.

Threats were of two kinds, natural and human. Consider life with no doctors, no medicine, no public health, no hospitals, no surgery. Many things that are not considered dangerous at all today were lethal then.

- Mortality rates for mothers and infants were high.
- Illnesses were lethal, and people were helpless to prevent death.
- Injury made everyone vulnerable. To break a limb could mean maiming for life and the inability to keep up with one's group on the move, or defend oneself or one's family from other dangers. An injury could get infected and, without medication and stitches, result in death by loss of blood, gangrene, or tetanus. Nothing could be done.
- Plagues often threatened the community as a whole.
- Starvation was always a possibility with an agricultural economy and subsistence farming. In a land of marginal rainfall, slight variations in rainfall result in poor crops or none. Crops and stores were also subject to pestilence, locust plagues, and invading armies. Also food storage capabilities were limited to grain, preserving by salting, and drying processes, as no refrigeration was available. Even if grain or other foodstuffs were available in a neighboring region or nation, how much could be carried home in two sacks on a donkey? The result of crop failure, drought, or spoilage meant famine, sickness, malnutrition, and death. Or one had to pack up and move in an effort to find water and food, a difficult task without knowing where to go, or how to get there in the quick, comfortable mode we enjoy today.

Human threats came from people who had the power to hurt, which included an enemy army, those in authority, or even neighbors. For this reason, one had to consider how to defend oneself from these perils.

The primary human threats derived from war. Geographically, the Land of Israel is located between various great powers, forming a land bridge between empires. The Bible is full of accounts of war or impending wars between these powers with the Land of Israel caught in the middle. Major roads passed through the land used by outside armies on the march; Israel found itself as a buffer zone between warring nations. At times Israel itself was the target of direct attack, not to mention civil war between the Northern and Southern Kingdoms during the period of the divided monarchy.

Armies marched through constantly, taking what they pleased: slaves, treasures, provisions. Those they did not take as slaves were killed or abused and left for dead. War did not affect only the able-bodied men who were killed in battle, but also women and children. Those who survived rapes and beatings starved because the earth was scorched.

Narmer, king of Egypt, smashing the head of enemies with a mace.

Another human threat came from kings and rulers, one's own as well as those of an occupying power, on both regional and national levels. Displeasing them could be fatal in a time when rulers had absolute power over life and death.

What were the responses to the natural and human threats to one's life?

- Avoid trouble. Do one's job, farm well, and make as few enemies as possible. The Bible, like other ancient Near Eastern writings, is full of advice for conducting one's life so as to stay out of trouble. It provides guidance for conforming to the principles which underlie society in general and also the universe as a whole, thus avoiding alienating the people and powers which could be harmful. The Book of Proverbs is a virtual survival manual for many aspects of life and its potential dangers, as are the bodies of law in Leviticus and Deuteronomy.

- Complain to God. More than 50 psalms of lament are a cry to God in time of deep trouble, often mentioning the threat of death. When they do so, they are not in mere figurative language. The psalmists were in real danger of their lives in a world that was fragile (cf. Ps 13:4; 17:11-14; 18:4-6; 22:19-21; 30:1-3; 39:10).

- People helped each other, or at least they should have. The prophets frequently make such failure the target of their criticism.

- People looked for help and security on a national level. The big question for the rulers was: "Where shall we place our trust?" Internally, some answers were in large grain and water storage facilities, large armies, many chariots, major fortifications. Externally, they worked to secure treaties and strategic alliances with other nations, particularly alignments with the superpower of the day.

Finally, people found help or hope in the divine sphere. Biblically, the correct response was to trust in the God of Israel who would provide divine protection and help. To receive divine protection from the God of Israel was guaranteed. However, there were ethical strings attached to this expectation (cf. Lev 26:3-10; Deut 30:15-20; I Kgs 8:33-40, 46-53). On the one hand, in a world of pagan deities that were seen as whimsical and capricious, the God of Israel was forthright with what was required to receive his blessing. This was seen as a comfort. On the other hand, following his law took discipline and faith, which many lacked. The average person in the biblical period often neglected this option, or worse, looked to pagan deities.

This was a time when all deities were considered to be most effective in their own realm. The Canaanite god Baal was the god of rain, fertility, and national security. Furthermore, there were no ethical requirements in Baal worship. For this reason, the Bible is full of accounts of Israelites looking for the easy path of following the example of the world around them and straying from God's law and his worship to adopt the deities of the nations around them, including Baal. The common man wanted rain and offspring, while the kings wanted national security.

GOVERNMENT AND SOCIETY

As with all ancient peoples, the social structures of the Israelites developed over a long period, from a semi-nomadic tribal society based on family units to a fully developed national government under kings, with national boundaries subject to invasion and foreign occupation.

During the biblical period, there were four phases of societal and governmental development and response: patriarchal, settlement-judges, national-monarchy, and occupation, each imposing different challenges on the everyday life of the people.

Patriarchal. The patriarchal society was semi-nomadic, a tribal society based on family units. Inter-family relationships were largely governed by blood ties with the head of the clan or tribe directing its social order.

Being called out from Ur of the Chaldees to "go to the land I will show you" (Gen 12:1), Abraham and his immediate descendants became immigrants to another land possessing a people, culture, religion, and language that were foreign to them. They moved from their urban setting to a semi-nomadic lifestyle, having to depend on their skills as herdsmen, seeking water and food for themselves and their flocks and herds.

The internal group laws were not written, but formed a tradition passed along by the elders, and encompassed elements to ensure the group's security, integrity, hospitality, progeny, property, family solidarity, and the worship of the one God.

Even in Egypt, though subject to the laws of the Pharaoh, an internal societal order continued to exist among the Hebrews, and their ability to maintain group integrity and not assimilate among the Egyptians is what was ultimately seen as a threat to the Pharaoh who "knew not Joseph" (Ex 1:8-10).

This patriarchal governance existed through the period of the Exodus when it became more organized and directed under Moses and the elders, until the Children of Israel settled in the Land of Israel.

Settlement-Judges. Once the Children of Israel were settled in the Land of Israel, they lacked real political cohesion. "In those days there was no king in Israel: every man did what was right in his own eyes" (Judg 17:6). They were settled in tribal areas, as allocated by Joshua (Josh 13-22). Yet there was no capital, no central government, no army, no taxation, and no international trade.

Of the 354 cities mentioned in the Bible, 75 percent were small, unwalled villages found in the hill-country, not the lush coastal plains. The local economy was based on farming or herding. Some of the towns more strategically located became centers for marketing, administration, and refuge. The Children of Israel were now out of the close-knit, introverted unit of the Exodus. They lived among the Canaanites who had not been expelled from the land. The local Canaanite customs, laws, and even religious practices, began to influence them, particularly as individual submission to the authority of the tribal patriarchs declined. The tribal areas became a loose confederation, existing independently of one another, although they came to each other's assistance in times of need.

The unit of internal social authority continued to be based on the authority of the head of the household over his family.

Local government authority was based on the council of elders. Since the time of the Exodus, the elders were the heads of the leading families in the clans. Once the people began to settle in villages, the elders became a more central authority on the local scene, with community-wide influence. During the settlement period, it was the elders who represented the collective wisdom of the community. They supervised legal procedures and were arbiters of disputes. They formulated legal policy based on the traditions and customs of the group, and the law given to them in Sinai (Deut 16:18-20).

In the unwalled villages, their "courtroom" was probably the threshing floor, which was a central meeting place. Later, as the villages acquired walls, the elders could be found at the city gates, where they heard and arbitrated disputes, e.g., when Ruth confronted Boaz at the threshing floor, he went to the city gate and sat with the elders to decide her case (Ruth 4:1-2).

During the period of the Judges, a wider level of authority was given to judges raised up by God. These judges were charismatic leaders whose primary role was as deliverers to evict foreign invaders. While they could advise on areas of public life, they were not primarily judicial or religious leaders. However, they probably did hear cases that could not be decided by the heads of households or the council of elders.

With the exception of Samuel, none of the judges was national in scope, and most functioned in regions with their authority extending to one or more tribal units only. Judges could call upon other tribal groups to assist in a military campaign, but it was up to the tribal leaders to decide whether or not to join. For example, when Deborah called upon the Israelites to join her in a campaign against Jabin, king of Hazor, the tribes of Reuben, Gilead, Dan, and Asher chose not to respond (Judg 5:16,17).

While the military function of the judges was taken over by the kings of Israel, their functional legal role continued, as magistrates (II Chr 19:5), also known as governors (II Chr 18:25) were placed in cities to implement the king's laws.

National-Monarchy. Even though the Israelites' demand for a king was immediately answered with the anointing of Saul, the move from a confederation of tribal areas to a centralized national government was not immediate. The rudiments of a centralized government did not exist. There was no seat of central government, no civil service, and no national army.

Tribal autonomy persisted and only the threat of invasion from other nations motivated the tribes to begin to unite. With David came the beginnings of true centralization, when he established Jerusalem as his capital, where he built his palace to establish a seat of government, and to where he moved the Ark of the Covenant, in an effort to make Jerusalem the religious and political center of national Israel. He established officials over a standing army, a centralized priesthood, record keepers, civil servants, and conscription. Nevertheless, David was still only a war chief of a tribal confederation.

Solomon took steps to further strengthen the religious and political centralization of the nation. Religiously, he built the First Temple (I Kgs 5:7-12) to "house" the presence of God, in an effort to further develop Jerusalem as the religious center of the nation. This, too, was important to the priests, who saw the Israelites worshiping pagan gods in high places throughout the land. With the definitive place for the worship of God in his Temple in Jerusalem, separate places of worship would no longer be necessary or tolerated. The great pilgrimage feasts requiring the people to come up to Jerusalem three times each year further strengthened the centrality of Jerusalem as the religious center of the nation.

Politically, Solomon worked to strengthen his rule both externally and internally. Externally, he developed international trade and also expanded and fortified his borders, increasing the wealth and influence of the nation, and consequently improving the material lifestyle of the people. Internally, to weaken tribal loyalties and reduce the threat of revolt, he strengthened the central government by setting up 12 administrative districts and hiring more civil servants to administer them (I Kgs 4:1-21). He even instituted a form of taxation by requiring each district to provide foodstuffs for the royal household for one month each year (I Kgs 4:7), and he conscripted workers from the Israelites (I Kgs 9:20-21) for building projects, including the Temple and his magnificent palace. Taxation and conscription bred dissension among the people, which split the kingdom after Solomon's death. Then, the people had to live in a divided nation and suffer the consequences of being caught in the middle of the conflict that developed between the two rival kings, including two capitals and conflicting laws and armies.

Even though the king exercised almost full authority over the political functions of the state, a total dictatorship could not evolve. Religious faith and practice, which was still a strong unifying factor for the nation, was administered by the priests, prophets, and elders in their respective roles. This served to counterbalance totalitarian rule by a political leader. Nevertheless, by the time of the division of the kingdom after Solomon's death, Rehoboam refused to listen to the counsel of the elders (I Kgs 12:8,13), and the whole nation suffered the consequences.

Occupation. When Nebuchadnezzar destroyed Jerusa-

Bearing tribute (of cloth, vessels and furniture) to Shalmaneser, the king of Assyria; detail from the "Black Obelisk"

lem in 586 BC, this signaled the end of an independent nation, and Israel lived under occupation from then on, first under the Babylonians, followed by the Persians, Greeks, and then the Romans. Life would never be the same. There would be no Israelite king, no central Israelite government, and no national army to preserve a distinct Israelite nation and enforce national institutions and inspirations.

Nebuchadnezzar carried much of the nation off into captivity, further rupturing family and community institutions. Even though the Israelites were allowed to return to the land in 538 BC, they found their former capital in ruins and the countryside neglected. Much of their land had been occupied by neighboring groups and those who had been transferred there by the Babylonians, many of whom remained.

Returning and living among foreigners with different customs and religious beliefs created conflict in the social and religious practices of the Israelites, who were not accustomed to pluralism. Further, the occupying governments added new pressures and burdens. Life was now controlled by local and foreign dignitaries, court officials, and governors. The occupiers set up military camps at strategic centers so that they could maintain control. Laws were imposed which contradicted the biblical law, faith, and practice of the Jewish people. Heavy taxation, including tribute paid to the king by his subjects; customs, a tax on consumption; and tolls, a road tax, or tax on land (Ezra 4:13), was another burden on the local population.

The consequence of non-compliance with the occupying power was persecution, punishment, and even death. Nevertheless, the Jews possessed too many distinctive cultural and spiritual values and customs to be fully assimilated.

As the Jews were more religiously than politically motivated, a council of religious leaders, that ultimately evolved into the Sanhedrin, became a central authority between the foreign rulers and the people. Even as early as the return from exile, there were civil leaders among the Jews who were given authority as local governors for the foreign powers, e.g., Nehemiah. Jewish authorities had some latitude to enforce some of their own laws, except the death penalty, although the foreign authority could intervene or overrule. This system of using Jews in the enforcement of law and order was so effective that during some intervals under Hellenistic and Roman rule, Israel was practically under home rule.

Nevertheless, when occupation became too severe, revolt by the Jews was definitely an option. An outstanding instance was the revolt against Antiochus IV in 164 BC which resulted in a period of Jewish independence under the Hasmonean dynasty. This independent Jewish state flourished under this dynasty of priest-kings until the Roman occupation under Pompey in 63 BC. Other examples of revolt are those against the Romans, the First Jewish Revolt in AD 66 and the Second Jewish Revolt in AD 132.

Citizenship involves receiving the rights and privileges of a native or adopted citizen as distinguished from a foreigner. In Old Testament Israel, citizenship was not political, i.e., based upon a relationship to a city or state, as elsewhere in the ancient world. Rather, it was based on Israel as a religious organization. As a covenant people, the idea of the commonwealth was merged into that of the congregation, according to the Mosaic constitution. Within this system, non-Israelites were accorded the same protection by the law as Israelites, and they were required not to perform acts to hurt or offend the religious feelings of the people.

From 586 BC onwards, when Israel was under occupation, the Israelite concept of citizenship was still functional, since it was based on a covenantal-religious rather than a national-political relationship to the community.

In the New Testament, the Apostle Paul illustrates this dichotomy, as he was of pure Jewish descent, of the tribe of Benjamin (Phil 3:5). He was born in Tarsus, a city of Cilicia (Acts 21:39), and was a Pharisee, "zealous towards God" (Acts 22:3). Nevertheless, he was also a Roman citizen (Acts 22:38), and was therefore considered a free man in the Roman empire, receiving all the benefits of this status, including his right to appeal before the Roman emperor himself (Acts 28:32).

If there could be a positive side to occupation, it was economic. Being part of a larger economic system brought commerce, transportation, military security, education, and other opportunities. However, what was lost was freedom, both political and religious. Foreign occupation always brought trauma to Israelite society as it violated the purity of Jewish life under God's laws. For this reason, no matter what benefits it might bring, occupation was seen as a reminder of failure before God (Deut 28:15–48).

LIFE IN THE CITIES AND VILLAGES

In ancient times, cities and villages developed out of the semi-nomadic lifestyle of the people. Before the settlement into villages, the semi-nomads lived in tents and traveled in search of water and pasture. Their needs were very basic and fulfilled by making tents by weaving goat's hair and clothing from wool; making pottery vessels, simple jewelry, and tools including weapons for protection; collecting wood for their cooking fires; and preparing their diet of bread from wheat they grew themselves or bought from villages along their way, milk and curds from their flocks, dried fruits (figs and dates) and nuts gathered along the way or purchased from villagers, olive oil, and rarely meat, eaten on special occasions as it depleted their herds.

The characters in Genesis fit into this category. Although they lived the life of semi-nomads, they came from a world that was already well-civilized. In Mesopotamia there is evidence of cities dating back to 3000 BC or earlier, e.g., Ur, Nineveh, Kish, etc. The city of Jericho in the Jordan Valley was founded as early as 10000–7500 BC. Nevertheless, most of the population of the ancient world lived as nomads and semi-nomads.

Location. As tribal groups became more sedentary and began to cultivate the soil, they often found their flocks and herds, as well as their crops, endangered by nomadic tribes. To protect themselves from these enemies, they grouped their tents or houses together and these became the first settlements or villages.

Cities and villages were always located with survival in mind. Therefore water supplies, arable land, and pasture, defensibility, building materials, and access to trade were crucial. To sustain the inhabitants, water and agricultural considerations were important; for safety, a defensible location was a necessity; for easier building of the structures, building material nearby was required, as importing these heavy materials was impossible; and for commerce, trade provided needed items not locally produced while providing an external market for locally produced goods. As the nation-state developed, other considerations for the location of new cities were strategic, commercial, or administrative. Many of the Israelite cities were founded on the ruins of earlier Canaanite cities, as these sites were already located with the aforementioned requirements met.

The names of cities often indicated one of these functional characteristics which determine location of the settlement. For example, the Hebrew *Beer* and *Ein* mean "well" and "spring" respectively: thus the biblical sites Beersheba and Ein Gedi. Names like Mizpah, Gibeah, Ramah, are from Hebrew root words meaning "height"; these three cities were located in the mountains of Benjamin. Other cities bore names which began with "Beth," meaning "house of," cf. Bethel, meaning House of God (Gen 35:7).

Cities, "daughters," and villages. The apportionment of the land to the tribes of Israel (Josh 13:23,28; 15:32,36,44; 19) refers to "cities and villages" or "cities and their daughters." During the Monarchy period, with a growing national infrastructure and increasing population, villages developed into walled cities with "daughters" (i.e., suburbs) which were dependent upon the city for protection, while providing food and labor to the city and men for the army. The main distinction between a city and a village was the presence of a wall around an assemblage of houses and buildings (Lev 25:29–31). Villages were simply described as "unwalled cities" which housed extended family groups of 100–150 people in clusters of 15–20 homes. Cities became distinguished by a larger number of houses, the size, strength, and grandeur of their buildings, including public buildings, surplus storage, and a religious center; a higher level of social order;

availability of goods and services; trade; and the presence of a defense wall encircling the compound. Nevertheless, even by the standards of the day, Israelite cities were no more than villages in size as compared with Egyptian and Mesopotamian cities. It has been estimated that even large administrative cities, like Megiddo, Dan, and Gezer, had populations of no more than 7,500 people.

Village and "daughter" houses were made of stone or sun-dried mud brick, and covered no more than five acres. Life in the village centered around agriculture: preparing and storing food for later use, including dried fruits and nuts, grain storage, and making olive oil and wine; maintaining small flocks and herds; and the production of pottery, clothing, tools, and weapons. Life was easier than that of the semi-nomadic, since the sedentary lifestyle allowed them more time to concentrate on a better quality of life, including more secure and comfortable housing, and more and better food, household implements, clothing, and tools.

Throughout the ancient world, the largest cities were the seats of powerful rulers who required a centralized administrative, military, commercial, and religious center, where each function required a large number of people living in close proximity. In the larger realms, other fortified cities were established, which were regional administrative and military centers to defend the realm and to oversee the life of the regional populations, e.g., Solomon's fortified cities (I Kgs 10:26; II Chr 8:1,4-6).

The walled city housed between 1,000–3,000 inhabitants, some 10–15 percent of the population, including the aristocracy and officials; the priestly class and wealthy businessmen; on an area of between 5–12 acres. An additional 85 percent of the population associated with the walled city lived in the unwalled "daughter" settlements outside the city walls.

Important features of the city.

Walls. The city wall was the most prominent feature as viewed from the outside. It has been estimated that the walls and towers occupied about 15 percent of the available space of the city. The city was usually built on a natural hill, or on top of the ruins of a previous settlement on the same site which provided the ability

---

The City and its Daughters

The relationship between the city and its daughters is a key to understanding everyday life in Bible times. The city provided protection, administration, justice, a religious center, a marketplace, and storage facilities. The daughters produced the food and supplies that were stored in the city, and provided essential services. They were also the population who helped to sustain the economy of the city through their buying and selling of goods and services. Nevertheless, there was a class distinction between those living within and without the city walls. For example, in Megiddo there is a large graded chariot ramp up to the main gate for the wealthy, but steps through a small gate for the inhabitants of the "poor daughters."

As long as there was peace in the region, the relationship worked well. However, in time of war, the daughters were at the mercy of those living within the city walls. The grain was stored in silos inside the city walls. The water tunnels, engineered to protect the city water source and provide water for the inhabitants within the wall in time of siege, was inaccessible to those left on the outside, who were completely at the mercy of enemy armies. They could be killed, their children made slaves, and their wives made prostitutes. Their only protection was to get inside the walls. But did those living within the walls let them in? After all, the more they let in, the more quickly the stored provisions were used up, if the enemy laid siege to the city. A good king or governor would send his army out to protect the entire region, keeping the enemy at bay, and not just think of protecting himself and the inhabitants of his walled city.

The cities and villages of the Land of Israel were relatively small in size, yet large in number; 354 are mentioned in the Bible. About 50 of these were in the coastal plains, which comprise most of the larger, walled cities, while the remainder were mostly smaller, unwalled cities and a few walled cities in the mountains.

After the exile of Israel, the returning Jews reinhabited former dwellings, rebuilding those that had fallen into disrepair. The relationship between rural and urban centers did not change much. Under the Greeks, colonies were established along the coastal plain, which eventually became towns and trading centers in the region. Along with this came a more developed infrastructure. This was accelerated under the Romans.

Fortifications from the time of King Solomon at Megiddo.

Model of a gate at Megiddo from the time of Ahab.

to see from afar the approach of an enemy and thus prepare a better defense in the event of an attack.

Early walls were made from earth or mud brick reinforced with straw. By the Late Bronze Age, walls were made from quarried stone, some having towers placed at their corners and at the gates for defense (II Chr 26:9). Walls generally followed the circumference of the hill on which the city was built. Since this was typically irregular, by the time of the Divided Monarchy, a method of building walls with an offset-inset pattern provided for greater defense. This pattern gave the enemy less frontage to breach, and provided better angles of defensive fire as side firing was possible where an offset section joined an inset section.

The larger the city, the higher and thicker was the wall. For example, the largest walls around Babylon were 12 meters (36 ft) wide where one or two chariots of four horses abreast could race side-by-side on top of the walls. In the Land of Israel, some walls were found that were 10 meters (30 ft) thick and 16 meters (50 ft) high. In some cities, such as Megiddo and Beersheba, "casemate" walls were built, consisting of two parallel defense walls about one and a half meters (five ft) apart, divided by perpendicular cross-walls creating a series of rooms or chambers. These were used for soldiers, or living quarters for some of the very poor, as they were the first victims in the event of an enemy breach.

Around the outside of the wall could be found ramparts, or glacis, covered with a thick layer of chalk to make them slippery. Also, a ditch was dug in particularly vulnerable places at the base of the glacis to keep armies and their battering rams from breaching the wall. Where the exterior terrain was higher than the wall, a deep quarry was dug, which also kept enemy armies at bay. Such a quarry existed along the northwest wall of Second Temple Jerusalem.

City Gates. The city gate was the busiest place in the city. Near or immediately inside the gates, there were courtyards or a broadening of the street where much of the city's social, business, and legal interaction took place. Here, the law was read and proclamations announced (I Chr 32:6; Neh 8:1-3); justice was administered as the elders judged legal cases and business transactions were made (Deut 16:18; II Sam 15:2; Amos 5:10-15); news (Gen 19:1) and local gossip (Ps 69:12) were exchanged. It was where markets flourished, e.g., the Fish Gate (Neh 3:3) or Sheep Gate (Neh 3:1) in Jerusalem. Prophets and priests delivered admonitions and pronouncements at the gate (Is 29:21; Amos 5:10; Jer 17:19; etc.) and criminals were punished outside the gates (I Kgs 21:10; Acts 7:58). It was even the place where one could attract the attention of the sovereign or dignitary (Est 2:19, 21; 3:2).

The main gate of each city was large enough for the entry of chariots and carts, and was built in a carefully planned design to deter the entrance of enemy soldiers. Some were built in a zigzag design, others with multiple chambers in the passageway from which soldiers could attack intruders as a first line of defense, e.g., David awaited Absalom's army in one of these chambers (II Sam 18:24). Most gates had vertical and horizontal openings to atack enemy soldiers from within with boiling liquids, spears, rocks, and other sharp objects.

Streets. Smaller cities, particularly those in mountainous areas, did not have an organized street plan, while larger cities and those on more level ground displayed two different plans. One had a belt of houses along the interior of the wall, and in front of these houses was a circular road around the interior circumference. However, the other streets were haphazard alleys winding between buildings. The other, dating from the later 6th century BC, was like a grid of criss-crossing streets at right angles to each other, enclosing blocks of buildings. In general, though, buildings were built before streets were planned, and thus they were narrow, winding, and unpaved, e.g., the streets of Jerusalem were not paved until Herod Agrippa II (AD 53). They were rarely cleaned and not lighted. Often streets took the name of the business to be found there, e.g., bakers (Jer 37:21).

The Citadel. This was the administrative center where were located the public buildings, the palace of the king or governor, and an inner stronghold, which was an inner fort protected by soldiers, to which the inhabitants could flee in the event that the outer wall was breached. It was also the site of the religious center, or high place, where religious ceremonies were conducted including the offering of sacrifices and celebrations of feasts. The high place was very important in the Canaanite cities, and it was retained in Israelite cities (I Sam 9:12ff) until the centralization of the Israelite cult in the Temple in Jerusalem (I Kgs 3:2). Whether or not the high place was actually an elevated area or not, the term was applied to any sanctuary area.

Public buildings, Markets, and Industry. One of the features that distinguished a city was the presence of public buildings, markets for the buying and selling of goods, and local industry which produced goods. Public buildings were administrative and included storage facilities. The markets, originally open trading near the city gates or open courtyard area, eventually developed into shops along market streets. Industry was known in the cities, and even in the biblical cities there was zoning due to the offensiveness of the odors produced by certain industries, e.g., dyeing and tanning. Other industries were metalworking, pottery-making,

The Cardo in Jerusalem, a street built in the Byzantine period.

perfume-making, woodworking, basket and mat weaving, glass-blowing in later periods, and the crafts, e.g., jewelry-making, silversmiths, goldsmiths, ivory carvers, and lapidaries.

Residential Areas. The style and size of private dwellings depended on the building materials at hand, available space, and the importance and wealth of the individual living there. In the Israelite cities that were

Model of the residential quarter in Jerusalem in Roman times.

reinhabited Canaanite sites, archaeologists have found humble four-room houses with a central courtyard next to larger and more elaborate structures. In the newer cities, the larger and more palatial homes were on the western side of the city, as in Samaria, or on the higher elevations, e.g., Jerusalem, to take advantage of the prevailing western breezes which kept them cool and upwind of any offensive odors. Conversely, the poorer classes were located on the eastern side or lower portions of the city. In all cases, as the city grew and the competition for space between public and private building increased, the wealthy and most influential remained within the walls, and the poor and nonessential were forced into unwalled communities outside the walls.

Water Sources. The ability to transport water over long distances via aqueduct was not available until Roman times, and then only in major urban or administrative centers. Therefore, cities and villages had to be located at or near a water source, such as wells, springs, rivers, or lakes, or in a region of reasonable rainfall to take advantage of storing winter rains in cisterns. However, even with cisterns, water was often retrieved from a freshwater source in order to save the stored water for the long hot rainless months from May to October. Indoor plumbing was also unavailable, and therefore the retrieval of water was a daily event. Water was carried by the women in large clay jars, drawn at the cool times of the day, early and late. Bathing was limited as most water was restricted and needed for cooking and drinking.

A well was an artificial shaft by means of which an underground spring or underground water table could be tapped. Of special importance in Israel were the wells dug in the desert, where hardly any other natural sources of water exist (Gen 21:17–18).

In the mountains, where wells could not be dug to reach the water table, cisterns were excavated. Their interior walls were lined with stones, or hewn out of solid rock. In the early Iron Age, the sides of cisterns began to be covered with watertight plaster, which

Left: Aerial view of the entrance to the water supply system at Hazor, showing steps leading to a pool. Right: The Beduin in the desert zones rely on wells for their supply of water.

prolonged the length of time water could be stored. Early cisterns were for use by a clan or small village community. Later, however, individual homes had their own cisterns, utilizing the rain run-off from their flat-topped roofs.

Another method of collecting water was a pool hewn in the rock or formed by building a wall across a dry river bed. The Bible contains references to famous pools of Hebron (II Sam 4:12), Gibeon (II Sam 2:13), Samaria (I Kgs 22:38), and several references to pools in Jerusalem (Is 7:3; 22:9,11; 36:2).

The most elaborate engineering feature was the water tunnel designed to allow access to the city's nearby water source from inside the city walls, while concealing it from the outside. This was to ensure water in the event of an enemy siege. These tunnels either brought the water to an inner city collection area by means of gravity, e.g., Hezekiah's tunnel in Jerusalem (II Kgs 20:20), or provided a safe approach to the source, e.g., Megiddo and Hazor. In either case, a steep descent to the level of the water was required.

In the Roman period, aqueducts carried on bridges and arches or covered channels provided water to large cities, where clay pipes distributed it to public fountains within the city, e.g., Caesarea and Samaria.

Prisons. The punitive system of the Bible is similar to that of the ancient Near East, i.e., the task of the legal authorities was confined to the assessment of guilt, and if a man was found guilty, the penalty was automatic. For the Israelites, the code of law outlining the penalty for different types of offenses or crimes was found in the Laws of Moses, which are detailed and extensive (cf. Ex chaps 21-23, etc.) The penalties were usually material reimbursement or in severe cases according to Exodus 21:23-25, "If there is a serious injury, you are to take life for life, eye for eye, tooth for tooth, hand for hand, foot for foot, burn for burn,

wound for wound, bruise for bruise." At a certain period, this was taken to mean monetary compensation.

Imprisonment as a punishment for criminal behavior is never referred to in the Bible or in other ancient legal codes. Nevertheless, there are numerous terms in the Bible denoting places of imprisonment. Not until the time of the return from exile is imprisonment mentioned as a punishment (see Ezra 7:26). On the other hand, it seems that detention before trial sometimes occurred (Num 15:32-35). Detention on political grounds is frequently mentioned (cf.I Kgs 22:26-27; II Kgs 17:4; Jer 32:11, 37:15-21). In the New Testament, for example, John the Baptist was imprisoned for criticizing a king's marriage (Matt 412; 11:2; 14:3,10); Peter and John for preaching about Jesus (Acts 4:3; 5:18-25); Paul led Christians to prison (Acts 8:3; 22:4; 26:10); and was himself in prison (II Cor 11:23; Acts 16:23-40; 23:18; 25:27; 27:1,42, etc.). Jesus speaks of imprisonment on civil process, as for debt (Matt 5:25; 18:30; Luke 12:58), visiting those in prison (Matt 25:36,39,43-44), and predicts that his followers will be put in prison during persecution (Luke 21:12).

It seems that no special place was set aside as a prison, the need being met as it arose. It was often a chamber in a house, e.g., Joseph was detained in a prison in the house of the captain of the guard (Gen 39:20-23); Jeremiah was placed in prison in the house of Jonathan the scribe (Jer 37:21). In larger houses of the wealthy, prison chambers have been found, which were used for detention of slaves. Palaces had prison chambers, as did the Temple where wrongdoers were held in custody of the priests.

The conditions in prison seem to have been pitiable (cf. Ps 79:11; Is 14:17; 42:22; Lam 3:34; Zech 9:11). A prisoner would be bound in chains (Jer 40:1; Is 45:4) of brass (Judg 16:21) or of iron (Ps 105:18). Sometimes his feet would be placed in stocks (Job 13:27; Jer 20:2; Acts 16:24).

Cities of Refuge

Unique to Israel was the concept of the City of Refuge. Six cities were assigned by Moses to serve as havens for accidental homicide (Num 35:13; Deut 19:9), called "Cities of Refuge." Moses established those east of the Jordan, namely Bezer in Reuben, Ramoth-Gilead in Gad, and Golan in Manasseh (Deut 4:41-43). Joshua established those west of the Jordan at Hebron in Judah, Shechem in Ephraim, and Kedesh in Naphtali (Josh 20:7,8). These were all Levitical cities, and later 42 additional Levitical cities functioned in much the same way (Josh 21; I Chr 6:54-81).

In the Near East, if a man was slain, it was the duty of his nearest relative to avenge his death by slaying the assailant. No distinction was made between premeditated and unpremeditated killing. The purpose of the Cities of Refuge was to intercede between the man-slayer and the next-of-kin avenger of his blood, and thus bring under control the custom of blood vengeance. In order to assist the killer, it was prescribed that all roads to these cities be kept open. Since each of these cities was within 30 miles (50 km) of some part of the Land of Israel, it was assumed that they could be reached in one day's time.

After a homicide, the killer fled to the nearest city of refuge where he presented himself to the elders at the city gate, to be assigned accommodation (Josh 20:4). The concept of the city of refuge allowed for an asylum for the killer until a fair trial could be arranged. The killer was then taken under protective custody to the location of the slaying, where his trial would determine the circumstances of the death. If he was found guilty of premeditated murder, he was put to death at once. If the killing was proved unpremeditated, the man-slayer was brought back to the city of refuge where he had to stay until the death of the then officiating high priest. Only then was he released to go wherever he chose. If, however, he strayed out of the limits of the city of refuge before his time, the avenging relative could lawfully slay him. However, after the death of the high priest when he was released, if the avenger killed him, then the avenger would be guilty of murder.

Life in the refuge city was made as normal as possible for the killer, who was allowed to earn his livelihood and even permitted to hold positions of honor. There were different procedures between the original six cities and the other 42 Levitical cities. In the former, asylum was automatic and housing was given as a right. In the latter, asylum had to be requested and rent had to be paid for housing.

In the ancient world (e.g, Phoenicia, Syria, Greece, Rome), certain shrines or sacred places were regarded as providing absolute security to fugitives. In Israel, the altars also served as places of asylum (I Kgs 1:50-53; 2:28-34), including the Temple in Jerusalem. But, like the cities of refuge, this was for the innocent. The deliberate murderer was to be taken from his asylum at the altar to be executed (Ex 21:14). The altar provided temporary refuge for the innocent manslayer, and from there he was to be taken to a city of refuge.

AGRICULTURE

General characteristics. Throughout the biblical period farming was not a choice, but a requirement for communities to exist. Even the cities were built in close proximity to the arable land needed to provide food for their inhabitants, as the importing of food supplies from great distances was not possible. The agricultural tasks were performed by the inhabitants from the unwalled villages. The farmers cultivated the land and raised livestock, and brought their surplus to the city to sell in the central markets, trade for other items needed, or to store in central storage houses.

When the Israelites settled in the land, they consolidated their hold in the central mountain areas that required cisterns for water storage and terrace farming.

With improved security in the monarchy period, more land could be safely cultivated without fear of destruction or theft by invaders. However, under the monarchy, larger estates were held by the king and his notables at the expense of the small peasant and a royal tenantry emerged, much to the vexation of the prophets.

After the return from exile, the enslavement of peasants for debt, as well as land-grabbing by the aristocracy, are reported, although the process was curbed by Nehemiah. Judah remained a country largely of peasant holdings. In southwest Samaria, four-roomed farmhouses from the early Israelite period were inhabited into the Hellenistic period (late 4th century BC).

The Hellenistic and Roman periods saw the growth of the isolated farms as opposed to farming focused on village centers. Fields were customarily open in the lowlands and enclosed in the hills. Small square fields (possibly small market gardens) have been uncovered near Ashkelon and in the northern Negeb. Hellenization accelerated technical progress. Ptolemaic control led to the expansion of state-owned lands worked by tied peasants.

In general, Israelite farming products and methods did not differ greatly from those of other nations in the region. What distinguished them were the regulations contained in the Mosaic laws governing use of land, such as planting of mixed species, tithing, and leaving harvest produce for the poor, the strangers, the widows, and the orphans. These injunctions also regulated the preparation and storage of food.

Water. Water came in the form of the early rains in October and latter rains in May, with a more predictable rainy season from December to February. No rain fell from May to October. The early rains helped the seeds to germinate, and the latter rains provided the needed moisture for crops to finish ripening. Rainfall varied dramatically, the rule of thumb being: the farther east and south, the drier; the farther north and west and higher, the wetter it will be. Dew was extremely important for agriculture and in some years could be the deciding factor in the maturing of the fall crops. The Jerusalem region, for example, receives about 5 ins. (12.5 cm) of dew each year. Limited irrigation was known, utilizing waste water and water from nearby rivers, lakes, wells, or springs. During the Greek and Roman period, irrigation methods improved, resulting in greatly increased grain yields.

Terrain. The greater part of the biblical stories and prophecies are set in an area 50 miles (80 km) wide by 150 miles (240 km) in length. There is probably more variety of land and climate in this tiny region than in any other location of similar size in the world, and the changes are often rapid and extreme. Here one finds everything from swamps to parched desert, lush coastal plains, high altitudes with acceptable rain, to the lowest place on earth, the Dead Sea, with extremely high salinity and very little rain. Therefore, the land and climate were a blessing or a curse on agriculture, depending on where one lived in the land.

Natural disasters. Natural disasters literally plagued the Israelite farmer. Hot desert winds from the east came in late spring and early fall. Their effects could be devastating. Insects were another problem, and there were no insecticides for pest control, which included beetles, caterpillars, worms, weevils, and the most damaging of all, the locusts (I Kgs 8:37). Too much dampness caused mildew (I Kgs 8:37) and too little rain brought the inevitable drought which resulted in famine, e.g., in the time of Joseph (Gen 41:53–42:2). Animals, particularly goats, could also destroy crops, and

thus fences of stone were built around fields, often with briars laid on the top (Is 5:5). Stone watchtowers were often built in the vineyards for the farmer to watch and protect his crop from predators, including humans, birds, and foxes (Is 5:4).

Biblical injunctions. Additionally, the Israelite farmer had to abide by biblical injunctions on when he could cultivate crops, i.e., every seventh year fields had to lie fallow (Ex 23:10–11); on when he could harvest fruit, i.e., the fruits of new orchards could only be gathered after the fourth year of production as an offering to the Lord, and eaten only after the fifth year (Lev 19:23–25); and on what he could consume or sell, i.e., a tithe of all production, including livestock, was offered to the Lord (Deut 14:22–27).

Taxes. Taxes had to be paid, and were instituted even as early as the time of King Saul. For the farmer, taxation was on his production, consuming an ever greater proportion of his produce. Archaeological evidence has shown numerous jar handles stamped "to the king," indicating that payment in kind, usually wine and olive oil, was well established. It seems that this was the method used by villagers, while city-dwellers paid in silver. Taxes increased in the monarchy period (9th-6th centuries BC) and grew even more grueling under occupation (late 6th century BC onwards).

Produce. The biblical farm was based on the small family unit, and was responsible for producing as much variety as the land and climate would allow. This included the cultivation of grain (wheat and barley); flax; vegetables (leeks, onions, garlic, cucumbers, red and green peppers, eggplant, and melons); fruit trees (pomegranates, dates, figs); olive and nut trees; vines for grapes; legumes such as lentils; and herbs (hyssop, myrtle, camphor, crocus, rose, etc.). Deuteronomy 8:8 describes the Land of Israel as a "land with wheat and barley, vines and fig trees, pomegranates, olive oil and honey; a land where bread will not be scarce and you will lack nothing."

There was little change in the mix of farm production until the Hellenistic period (4th century BC) when some new products were introduced: Egyptian beans, lentils, and gourds. Apricots, peaches, cherries, oranges, and lemons ultimately reached the area from Asia via Italy. Cotton and rice also entered the country in this period. Mishnaic and Talmudic sources list numerous plants first imported in the Hellenistic and Roman periods, including lupins, asparagus, marrows, and turnips.

Farmers maintained small herds of goats and flocks of sheep. They also had beasts of burden to help them with plowing, threshing, grinding, and transportation. Such animals included donkeys, oxen, mules, and even camels. Geese and ducks were known to exist, but

The wooden plow, still used today by some Arab peasants, has not changed for centuries.

chickens did not appear before the 6th century BC. Poultry production not only provided meat, but eggs, known to be part of the diet from the patriarchal period onwards (Deut 22:6–7; Luke 11:12).

Farming techniques. Through archaeology and biblical description, some of the agricultural tools described and discovered show the techniques used by the biblical farmer.

Tools. Agricultural tools mentioned in the Bible are plowshares, coulters, forks, axes, mattocks, and goads (I Sam 13:20–21), sickles (Jer 50:16; Joel 3:13), scythes (Deut 16:9), threshing instruments (II Sam 24:22; Is 41:15, etc.), sieves (Is 30:28; Amos 9:9), fans (I Kgs 30:24; Jer 15:7), and pruning hooks (Is 18:5).

The earliest plows were made of hard wood, with two handles to which a flint blade was sometimes attached. Metal blades were used from the second half of the 2nd millennium BC, but as they were made of bronze, they broke easily. By the end of the 11th century BC iron had been introduced, and it was only after this that metal blades were used for plows. The blades had to be sharpened frequently. The Israelites had to take their tools to the Philistines and pay for this service (I Sam 13:20–21).

Model of an Egyptian plowman.

Coulters were not the same as plows, but were an implement used for turning the soil by hand. They were made of iron and were about 3–4 ins. (7.5–10 cm) wide. Sickles and scythes were used for mowing. The early version had blades of flint and handles of bone or wood; later, iron blades were found on Iron Age sites. Pruning hooks were used to prune the grape vines after the flowers had germinated into fruit. The pruning hook was a small, sharp, curved blade. In addition to these tools, knives of various shapes and sizes, shaving blades, and hoes for weeding have been found in archaeological excavations.

Terracing. Since most of Israel's population lived in the central mountain regions, terrace farming was required. Fortunately, the geology is cenomanian limestone which fractures in large flat slabs, leaving natural terraces behind. The terrace was formed by building a low stone wall along the downhill side of the hill, and leveling the area with soil. Plenty of small stones were available for the wall. Approximately 60 percent of the hills west of Jerusalem are terraced, some with ancient terraces going back to the settlement period.

Planting. The first step was removing large stones and breaking up the fallow ground by means of a plow pulled by an animal. Ancient plows could only turn one furrow at a time and the work was time-consuming and difficult, particularly in the rocky soil. Each furrow needed to be straight and parallel to the next one. To accomplish this, the plowman had to concentrate and hold onto and guide the plow when it hit a stone or clump of grass. Any distraction would cause him to wander off course. Jesus used this image when he said, "No one, having put his hand to the plow, and looking back, is fit for the kingdom of God" (Luke 9:62). The plow was pulled by a donkey, mule, or ox, or two of each. However, it was forbidden under Mosaic law to use two different animals in the pair (Deut 22:10). Jesus also used this image when he told believers not to yoke themselves with unbelievers (II Cor 6:14). Farmers with no plows used coulters, hoes, or mattocks. Plowing was the work of men, usually done by each family or clan.

After the field was prepared, the farmer would sow his seed by hand, scattering the seed across the turned soil. The parable of the sower reflects this method, and describes the fate of seed scattered on terraces, i.e., some of the seed would naturally fall on rocky ground at the outer perimeter, some in the border edge of briars, some on the pathway, and some on the good soil (Matt 13:3-8; Mark 4:3-8; Luke 8:5-8).

According to Mosaic law, the sowing of mixed seed was forbidden (Lev 19:19; Deut 22:9). The field had to be protected from birds that would eat the seed, and animals that might eat the crop. Isaiah gives a picture of sowing seed: "Does the plowman keep plowing all day to sow? Does he keep turning his soil and breaking the clods? When he has leveled its surface, does he not sow the black cummin and scatter the cummin, plant the wheat in rows, the barley in its appointed place, and the spelt in its place?" (Is 28:24-26).

Harvest. The harvest season began in March-April with flax, followed by barley in April-May, wheat in September-October. Grain was harvested with a sickle, high up so as to leave most of the stalk in the field. It was bundled into sheaves to be removed for storage (Gen 37:7). The Israelite farmer was not to be too careful about getting in everything, including sheaves that were forgotten in the field, as these were left for the poor. This was true also when gathering grapes and olives (Deut 24:19-21).

Threshing and winnowing. After the grain was harvested, it was taken to a threshing floor so that the grain kernels could be separated from the stalks. Rich landowners had their own threshing floors, but most communities had a communal threshing floor. It was a hard flat surface of exposed bedrock. The earliest method was beating the grain with a long wooden stick (Judg 6:11). Using a large animal to trample the wheat was another method. A third was to use a sledge made of wood, with sharp stones or pieces of iron embedded in its underside (Is 28:27). An animal pulled the sledge over the grain, and the owner was not allowed to stop the animal from eating of the grain (Deut 25:4).

Once the grain was separated, it was winnowed to remove the chaff. Since grain is heavier than chaff, one simply had to toss it into the air and let the wind carry the chaff away. A six-pronged fork or a scoop like a shovel was used for this purpose. In this region, even on days without wind, there is always a breeze near dusk. The final process was to use the sieve or fan to purify the grain of small bits of chaff before making flour or storing in clay jars for personal use, or silos for community use (Is 41:15-16; Amos 9:9).

Grain Storage. Grain had to be stored in carefully prepared silos to prevent rot, mildew, internal combustion, and infestation by insects or rodents. Grain was usually stored as whole kernels (I Sam 17:17), as flour was likely to spoil more quickly than the kernels. However, there is scriptural evidence that for personal use grain was milled into flour and sealed into jars (I Kgs 17:12,14,16).

Royal and communal buildings for storing grain were common to most cities. The four Hebrew names by which they were called have been rendered "storehouses" and "barns" (Deut 28:8; Jer 50:26; Joel 1:17). Granaries were usually circular, with openings below the almost flat roof so that air could circulate. In free-standing structures, stairs on the outside formed a kind of ramp upon which grain was carried before being poured in at the top. In those hewn in rock into the ground, the stairs spiraled down the interior wall, used to retrieve the grain as the level declined.

Milling. To use the grain, it had to be ground into flour. Both individual and commercial mills have been found, and both involved coarse rocks, often of basalt from Galilee, riddled with small holes to catch the grain kernels, facilitating the grinding. A home version was a rectangular slab of stone 1.5-3 ft. (1-2 m.) long

Winnowing; detail of a series of agricultural scenes depicted on an Egyptian wall painting; c.1400 BC.

with a concave surface, into which a loaf-shaped, hand-held stone was slid forward and backward over the grains. Grinding was generally women's work, except at the commercial mill where men were the millers.

A second method, probably introduced in the late Israelite period, consisted of a large rectangular upper stone which was rocked back and forth with the aid of a lever placed in notches in the stone. A third, larger type, probably introduced during the Monarchy period, consisted of two large round flat stones that were turned against one another. Grain was introduced through a hole in the center, and the resulting flour came out of the sides. Some were so large that an animal or a strong man was needed to turn them (Judg 16:21).

The Mosaic Law appreciated just how important the milling of flour was to the livelihood of each family. For this reason, Deuteronomy 24:6 states: "No man shall take the lower or upper millstone in pledge, for he takes one's living in pledge."

In the Roman/New Testament period, another type was used. It consisted of a cone-shaped stone over which fit a tall stone device in the shape of a hollow hourglass. The grain was poured into the top chamber and was crushed between the lower chamber and the cone. The hourglass device was turned by animal power, and the resulting flour came out from the bottom.

Olive oil production. Olive trees were plentiful and olives and olive oil played an important role in the daily life of Israel. The trees are capable of growing in almost any conditions, terraced hills or valleys, rocky or fertile soil, and can thrive in great heat with a minimum of water. The olive tree is known for its tenacity and long life; even if it is cut down or burned, new shoots will come up from the roots and a new tree will grow. Some trees in Jerusalem have been estimated to be 2,000 years old. While the trees last for generations, the olive producer has to wait 15 years for his first harvest. Olive oil was so plentiful in Israel that it was one of the products regularly exported. Solomon sent the king of Tyre 100,000 gallons (40,000 liters) (I Kgs 5:11).

Vegetable oil was already known in early periods, but the most common oil in use was olive oil. Olives intended for oil were left on the tree until they were fully ripened and black (in late October). The trees are not very tall, so the fruit could be shaken from the branches with long wooden sticks onto mats where they could be easily collected into baskets. They were then taken to the olive press and spread on the floor where they could ferment, which facilitated the extraction of oil.

The harvesting process was usually a family enterprise. However, the pressing process was either done at home or at centralized or commercial presses. The family brought its harvested olives to a commercial press along with storage jars to collect the oil. Often, the pressman was paid with a percentage of the oil produced.

The first phase of the process involved treading the olives or crushing them in a stone bowl to aid the release of the oil from the pulp. In biblical times, the crushed olives were put on a mat or goatskin, tied into a bundle, and placed in a deep, narrow rock-hewn channel. Over this was placed a heavy stone; then a heavy beam was placed across the stone with one end in a hole in the wall as an anchor. The beam was used as a lever to press out the oil. On this lever was placed a series of four large stone weights. A hole in the stone with a rope through it allowed the weight to be slid onto the lever, one at a time. The oil that was produced after the first weight was applied was of high quality for religious use; the second stone produced oil for cooking; the third stone, oil for lamps; and the fourth stone, oil that was full of lye and was used for making soap. The oil was conveyed through small channels to a collecting vat, where any water and impurities settled in the bottom, and the oil was collected and stored in clay jars. The Hebrew term for "press" is *gat* and the term for "oil" is *shemen*. Therefore, Gat Shemen (Gethsemane), the garden where Jesus retreated to pray after the Last Supper (Matt 26:36), was a place of olive trees and an olive press, which has been located in the area.

From the Roman period onwards, other methods were used. For crushing the olives, a large millstone was placed upright in a circular receptacle where it was driven around by an animal. The crushed olives were placed in rope bags and pressed.

Olive oil was a staple food, but it was also used in medicine, for lamps to light the home, and in cult practices. Other oils were not as widespread in Israel.

Wine making. According to biblical tradition, Noah was the first man to plant a vineyard (Gen 9:20). From the Bible, Egyptian wall paintings and reliefs, and the remains of winepresses in Israel, it is possible to

An oil press from the 15th century.

Gathering grapes, treading and storage of wine in jars; Egyptian wall painting; c.1400 BC.

determine methods of wine-making in the biblical period.

The grape vine required little soil and no rain in the growing season, making it well-suited to the climate of Israel. The soil was loosened and choice vines planted. Maintenance required pruning, hoeing, removal of weeds, and some watering.

After being cut back severely in the fall, the new growth appeared early in the spring. Once it flowered and germinated, it was time to prune the vines with a pruning hook. Isaiah 18:5 describes this procedure: "For before the harvest, when the bud is perfect and the sour grape is ripening in the flower, he will both cut off the sprigs with pruning hooks and take away and cut down the branches." The intention was to channel all the growing energy of the plant into the fruit. The grapes grew throughout the summer season, watered simply by the nightly dew.

In August-September, the grapes were harvested, being brought in baskets from the vineyard to the winepress, which was either a naturally or an artificially flattened rock or a slight angle (Is 5:2; 16:10; Jer 48:33). The grapes were spread out on the rock and trodden, so that the juice flowed through shallow channels to a vat, hewn at the lower end of the pressing ground. The pulps and skins of the grapes left over after the first pressing, were pressed again to extract the remaining juice. The natural yeast on the skins of the grapes resulted in fermentation, the only method of preservation. The wine was quickly put into clay jars sealed with clay stoppers, and taken to cool wine cellars for storage. The cellar might be a natural cave or a hewn cistern, in which the correct temperature for fermentation would be maintained. Once fermentation was completed, the origin and quality of the wine, plus the name of its owner, would be marked on the seal. For the average farmer, this procedure was usually a family project. However, as with olive pressing, there were centralized or commercial winepresses.

The Bible records several names and types of wines, e.g., "blood of grapes" (Gen 49:11), "wines on the lees" (Is 25:6), "wine of Helbon" (Ezek 27:18), "wine of Lebanon" (Hos 14:7). Additional names have been found inscribed on jars found in archaeological excavation in Israel.

Wine was also made from pomegranates, dates, and other fruit, and from grain. From the New Testament, we know that wine was sometimes mixed with other substances such as gall (Matt 27:34), myrrh (Mark 15:23), or oil for medicinal purposes (Luke 10:34).

Alongside the local wines, foreign wines were imported into Israel. However, only locally produced wine, processed according to Jewish law, which included tithing a portion of the wine to God, was considered ritually fit.

Livestock raising. Livestock raising required continuous care and the daily provision of water and food. Often, the men of the family had to go great distances to find pasture or water for their flocks, taking them away from their family for significant periods of time (Gen 37:12-17).

Animals provided wool for making clothing, tents, and rugs; hides for making clothing and shoes; food (meat and milk); intestines for stringed instruments, bone for utensils, and the means of religious sacrifices.

Sheep. The shepherd's life was hard as he had to care for the sheep, including finding them food and water, braving the elements, and defending them. Sheep were also subject to sickness, injury, theft, or loss. Their natural predators were wolves, lions, bears (I Sam 17:34-35), and panthers, which still roamed the countryside until the end of the Monarchy period.

A vivid description of the shepherd's life emerges from Jacob's words to Laban in Genesis 31:38-40: "These twenty years I have been with you; your ewes and your female goats have not miscarried their young, and I have not eaten the rams of your flock. That which was torn by beasts I did not bring to you; I bore the loss of it. You required it from my hand, whether stolen by day or stolen by night. There I was! In the day the drought consumed me, and the frost by night, and my sleep departed from my eyes."

Sheep have to be defended. The most often used weapon was the sling, a pouch held by two strings, which allowed the shepherd to hurl a rock at high speed with great accuracy (I Sam 17:49); a wooden club, often made more lethal by studding it with metal or rocks; and a staff curved at one end (Ps 23:4). For protection at night, sheep were kept in a sheepfold, an area surrounded by a stone wall and topped with briars to keep out predators. Often the sheepfold had a protected area, such as a cave, for protection from the elements. The gate was guarded by the shepherd (cf. John 10:7-9).

Shearing was hard and dirty work, done twice a year at the sheepfold. The first shearing was at the end of summer grazing, and the second near the end of winter. Small owners sheared their own, and those with larger flocks, including the king, used hired shearers (I Sam 25:2). The sheep were washed before shearing, and the fleece was washed again to remove dirt and natural oils, and combed to remove matting. It was then spun into cloth. Like all other produce, the first wool sheared each spring was presented as an offering to God (Deut 18:4).

Besides wool, sheep were used for sacrifices (Lev 4:23) and food.

Goats. Goats played an equally important role in the life of Israel. They were a good source of food as they provided meat, milk, cheese (I Sam 17:18), and butter.

Their hair was used for weaving. Black goat hair was used for tents. Goatskins were sewn together and used as containers (Matt 9:17).

Sheep and goats could utilize land for grazing that was not well-suited for agriculture. They could also survive an arid climate quite well. Females predominated the flock in a ratio of ten to one (Gen 32:14-16), and the surplus males were eaten or sold.

Beasts of burden. Other animals used in the everyday life of the Israelites were the ox, often called cattle in the Bible, the donkey, mule, and camel. The ox, donkey, and mule were work animals used to pull a plow (Is 30:24), drag threshing sleds, turn a waterwheel, and pull carts or wagons. The average farmer could only afford a donkey or a mule. Oxen could be eaten, but it was an expensive meal only for the wealthy (I Sam 14:31-34); and they could be used for sacrifices (Lev 3:1). Donkeys were the most prevalent animals as they were able workers and affordable. The mule was a good worker and very strong. The camel was ideal for desert living, and also supplied milk, dung for fuel, and leather. It was forbidden for Jews to eat camel-meat (Lev 11:4). The donkey, mule, and camel were also used for transportation over longer distances.

Butchering. Although individual farmers probably butchered their own animals, there were butchers by trade in the larger cities. The Bible says nothing about how an animal must be butchered, but it does give regulations on not eating the blood of any animal or the fat of cattle, sheep, or goats (Lev 3:17; 7:22-27). Apparently, gazelle, deer, and certain other animals were exempt from the fat restriction, but not the blood

Sheep tended by Arab shepherds in the Shepherds' Field near Bethlehem.

restriction (Deut 12:15–16). These restrictions require certain methods of slaughtering an animal so as to render it bloodless and fatless, with some parts not being edible at all because this was physically impossible to achieve. "All the fat is the Lord's" (Lev 3:16) and was to be burned on the altar, not eaten. Likewise, the "life of the creature is in the blood" (Lev 17:11; Deut 12:16), and it too was given for a sacrifice for atonement of sin, not to be eaten. Also, based on Genesis 32:33, the thighs of domesticated or wild animals could not be eaten unless the ischiatic nerve was removed, and in order to avoid accidentally eating this nerve, the thigh was often not eaten at all. The Jews were forbidden to eat an animal that had died a natural death (Lev 7:24; 17:15–16).

FOOD

In the Bible, good food and drink were considered one of the great joys of life. While some of the religious, e.g., Nazirites and Essenes, practiced an austere lifestyle, they were in the minority. Even Jesus appreciated a good meal, a feast or a party, which drew some criticism (Matt 11:19; Luke 7:34).

The diet of the ancient Israelite was closely connected to his agriculture, which was in most cases, locally produced, processed, and stored. Since Palestine was along the great north-south trade routes, certain imports could be acquired from the caravans that traveled through the land. Later, in the Roman/New Testament period, foods were available from all over the Roman Empire.

Bread. In the Bible, the general term for food is "bread" (Gen 3:19; Ex 2:20), probably because this was the staple element in the diet. Bread was made from wheat or barley and sometimes from a mixture of other ingredients when grain was scarce. Wheat was preferred to barley, but was twice as expensive. Grain was eaten dried (I Sam 17:17), green (II Sam 17:28), or roasted (Lev 23:14). However, it was most often made into flour which was used both for baking bread and for fried dishes (Lev 7:12), cakes (II Sam 13:8), and wafers mixed with honey. Bread was dipped in sour wine (vinegar) (Ruth 2:14), olive oil (Num 6:15), eaten alone, or with other foods.

Bread was also used in religious practices (Ex 29:2), the showbread being a bread offering placed in the sanctuary of the Lord (Ex 25:30; Lev 24:5–9). It was taken on long journeys (Mark 6:8; Luke 9:3), and was eaten at the Last Supper (Matt 26:26). On eating bread, a special blessing was said, thanking God for his provision of the bread (Matt 14:19).

The method of preparing and baking bread has not changed much through the ages. First, the flour was mixed with oil and water to make dough, which could be baked immediately after kneading to produce

unleavened bread (which was mandatory during Passover), or left for some time to rise with the addition of yeast (I Kgs 17:12–13).

In biblical times, there were several methods of baking bread. The easiest and oldest method was to use flat stones, previously heated on an open fire (I Kgs 19:6). Cakes were cooked in a pan (Lev 2:7). A third method was to use a flat bowl which was heated in an open fire. The flat loaves were placed on the outer, convex side, which had small projections and cavities to facilitate the removal of the bread when ready.

A fourth method of baking was to use clay ovens that took the shape of truncated open-topped cones about 2.5 ft. (0.75 m.) high, with an opening at the bottom for stoking the fire. The prepared dough was stuck to the insides of the heated walls. In Roman times, the clay ovens developed into a closed cone-shape, with a place for a fire underneath an interior clay shelf on which the bread was baked. Any of these methods resulted in flat loaves, not more than an inch (2.5 cm) thick, frequently referred to in the Bible as cakes. In New Testament times, as in earlier periods, bread was generally prepared by each housewife in the courtyard of her house.

Clay figurine of a woman kneading dough, found in the Phoenician cemetery at Achzib; Iron Age.

Fuel for the fire was of wood, dried animal dung cakes, the dried pulp residue from olive oil press, and chaff (I Kgs 17:10,12; Is 44:15).

Dairy. Milk and milk products were widely consumed. The milk came from cows, sheep, and goats (Deut 32:14) and was kept in skins (Judg 4:19). Butter (Prov 30:33), cheese (Job 10:10; I Sam 17:18), and curds (Ezek 34:3) were from milk.

A bowl with dry pomegranates, olive and date stones, found in one of the caves in the Judean Desert, almost two thousand years old.

Vegetables. Vegetables were also eaten, mainly beans, pulses (II Sam 17:28), and lentils, from which a soup was made (Gen 25:34). Vegetables were eaten raw, cooked, and in soups or in stew. See also II.18, Plants.

Fruit. Fruit was abundant. Grapes, figs, dates, pomegranates, and olives were among the characteristic fruits of the land (Deut 8:8). Grapes were eaten fresh or pressed into clusters and dried as raisins (I Sam 25:18). Figs were also eaten fresh or dried (I Sam 30:12), as were dates. Raisins, figs, and dates keep for years, and were therefore the kind of food taken on long journeys or stored for emergencies. Pomegranates were eaten raw, and the juice of pomegranate and date was probably used for making wine. Pits of these fruits have been found in caves in several locations in the Judean and Negeb deserts, some dating to the Early Bronze Age. Of the wild fruits, that of the sycamore was eaten (Amos 7:14). By the Roman/New Testament period, apricots, peaches, and cherries had reached the area. Olives were abundant. Nuts were important in the diet, including almonds, walnuts, and pistachio.

Condiments. Sugar was not known at the time, so honey was the main sweetener. Although apiculture was known in Egypt and Mesopotamia, it is not mentioned in the Bible. All the evidence indicates that honey came from a natural source. Wild bees produced honey on the ground (I Sam 14:25–27), in rock crevices (Deut 32:13), and even in the carcasses of animals (Judg 14:8). However, some scholars believe the honey mentioned in the Bible was a kind of syrup made from fruit, particularly carob and dates.

Herbs and spices were usually imported or grown for perfumes, flavorings in cooking, and preservatives, and included cumin, black cumin, mustard, capers, hyssop, aloe, bay, myrtle, camphor, crocus, rose, etc. In the New Testament, herbs were mentioned as part of the tithe of the Pharisees, e.g., mint, dill, and cumin (Matt 23:23).

Other than herbs, the most widely used seasoning in the biblical period was salt (Job 6:6), which was obtained in an endless supply from sodium chloride (table salt) hills near the Dead Sea (Zeph 2:9). Most of the Dead Sea salts are of inedible and unpalatable varieties. Sodium chloride was also found in evaporated pools along the Mediterranean Sea. Salt was not refined as known today. Instead, a lump of salt, including the surrounding dirt, was placed on the table. The white crystals could be picked out of the lump, and when they were gone, the lump, having lost its savor, was tossed outside to be trodden underfoot (Matt 5:13). In the Hellenistic and Roman/New Testament period, spices now associated with the Near East were brought from Arabia, India, and eastern Africa.

Meat. Meat was restricted by dietary laws. "You may eat any animal that has a split hoof completely divided and that chews the cud" (Lev 11:3). The key word is "and," for Leviticus 11 continues to describe the animals which have one or the other attribute, but not both at the same time, e.g., the camel, coney, rabbit, and pig. Of them, it says: "You must not eat their meat or touch their carcasses" (Lev 11:4–8). This leaves the sheep, goat, ox, steer, and wild game, e.g., gazelle, deer, roebuck, wild goat, wild ox, and chamois. Even ritually fit animals, however, were subject to certain regulations and methods of preparation.

Meat was usually boiled (Ex 12:9; Deut 14:21), but was also roasted as prescribed for the paschal lamb at Passover (Ex 12:8–9), or cooked in a stew. The soup mentioned at the Last Supper (John 13:26) may well have been a lamb stew prepared on Passover so that everyone could enjoy part of the lamb. At no time could a kid be boiled in its mother's milk (Ex 23:19; 34:26; Deut 14:21). This regulation was later extended to include the prohibition against even eating meat and milk products together at the same meal. Archaeology has proved it to have been a ban on a pagan practice. Findings at Ugarit have shown that it was the custom there to boil a kid in its mother's milk as a lucky charm.

Meat would have been eaten only on special occasions, e.g., wedding feasts or religious feasts such as Passover. For the average person, his flocks were also a source of milk, cheese, and wool, and therefore killing

A family meal with servants in attendance, on the left; detail from a relief on a Roman funerary monument of the 3rd century.

them for food would deplete his numbers and his daily basic provisions. The wealthy and royalty ate meat more frequently.

Fowl. Certain kinds of fowl were forbidden, including birds of prey (eagle, osprey, hawk, falcon, owl); those that feed on carrion (vulture, buzzard, raven); certain water birds (pelican, stork, heron, swan, sea gull); and other birds (ostrich, bat, lapwing). Poultry (goose, chicken, duck), pigeon and doves, and wild birds not on the above list were permitted (Lev 11:13-19:; Deut 14:12-18). Only the eggs of clean fowl could be eaten.

Fish. Fish could be eaten if it had fins and scales. This excluded all shellfish and fish that had fins but no scales, e.g., shark, catfish, and eels (Lev 11:9-12; Deut 14:9-10). Only fishermen and those living in close proximity to their catch could eat fresh fish, as it spoiled quickly. Most of the fish that was eaten was salted. Fish were plentiful in Israel, as there were several major sources, the Sea of Galilee, the Jordan River, and the Mediterranean and Red Seas. One of Jerusalem's gates was called the Fish Gate. One method of preparing fresh fish was to roast it over an open fire (John 21:9). Salted fish was soaked in water to desalt it, and then it was cooked.

Insects and creeping things. Certain insects were acceptable as food, including the locust, katydid, cricket, and grasshopper. "All other flying insects which have four feet shall be an abomination to you" (Lev 11:20-24). Creeping things which crawl upon the earth are considered unclean, including worms, caterpillars, snakes, snails, lizards, chameleon, and moles (Lev 11:30,41-43).

According to Mosaic law, if any of the unclean creeping things dies and falls into a clay water pot, the water is to be considered unclean, and a source of contamination. The clay pot must be broken and if the carcass of a creeping thing touches the oven, it must be broken as well (Lev 11:33-35).

DRINK

Water. Water was the staple beverage, both in the home and, carried in skins, in the fields and on journeys. Fresh water from a spring was especially enjoyed, followed by well water and finally water from cisterns. An ample supply of water was a major consideration in site location.

Milk. Milk was also a regular part of the diet. It was offered to important personages, often instead of water (Gen 18:8; Judg 4:19). While milk was drunk fresh, it was most likely drunk in a fermented state, as it spoils quickly. Milk was kept in skins which were moistened to keep it cool for as long as possible. Nevertheless, it ultimately separated into curds and whey (Judg 5:25).

Wine and Vinegar. Wine was a staple drink as it could be preserved for later use. It also played an important role in the religious rituals of the ancient Near East. It was used in the daily (Ex 29:40) and monthly (Num 28:14) sacrifices and holy days (Num 15:5ff). The law of the Nazirites forbade the consumption of wine (Num 6:3; Judg 13:4). John the Baptist was destined to be a Nazirite and therefore avoided strong drink (Luke 1:15). The Rechabites willingly refrained from wine (Jer 35:2ff).

Wine was also used as vinegar, which was drunk when diluted with water and used as a cheap drink to refresh field workers. On the cross, Jesus was offered a sponge soaked in vinegar (John 19:29). Wine is recommended for medicinal purposes in I Timothy 5:23.

The vine was a symbol of prosperity and fertility (I Kgs 4:25; II Kgs 18:31) and grapes were one of the seven "fruits" of which the Holy Land boasted (Deut 7:13). Important personages would be greeted with bread and wine (Gen 14:18). The Bible does not favor intoxication (Prov 23:29-35; Is 22:12-14, 28:1, etc.), but on the other hand, abstention was a sign of mourning (Dan 10:3). People on a journey would drink wine (Josh 9:13; Judg

19:19), as would the weary and those who had lost thei way (II Sam 16:2; Prov 31:6-7). As well as being used in medicine, it was an everyday beverage for kings and special ministers were appointed to supply it (Gen 40:2; Neh 2:1). The kings of Israel and Judah owned large vineyards and the wine was stored in the royal stores (I Chr 12:40, 27:27; II Chr 11:11).

Beer. Beer made from fermented barley was a common drink in Egypt and Philistia. Many beer jugs have been found with strainer spouts in Philistine sites. The Hebrew word *shekhar* is often translated as "ale," but it can also mean a fermented date mead.

Philistine "beer jug" with a strainer in the spout; 12th century BC.

HUNTING AND FISHING

Hunting. Hunting was not practiced to a great extent in the biblical period, but it was known. Nimrod was famed as a hunter (Gen 10:9), and so was Esau (Gen 27:5). Ishmael, when cast away from Abraham, lived in the desert around Beersheba and became an archer (Gen 21:20). In hundreds of rock drawings on Har Karkom in the Negeb south of Beersheba, hunters are depicted as archers pursuing ibex for food.

Hunting with bow and arrow or spear, as was the custom in other nations, does not allow the ritual killing of an animal, whih ensures that the blood is drained properly, and that the animal does not die in pain. The dietary laws forbidding the consumption of blood may have had an effect on hunting. Some scholars feel that hunting was practiced solely for self-protection or to prevent damage to fields and other property by wild animals.

The trapper's methods are portrayed in Job: "For he is cast into a net by his own feet, and he walks into a snare. The net takes him by the heel, and a snare lays

hold of him. A noose is hidden for him on the ground, and a trap for him on the road" (Job 18:8-10). The implication is that one kind of trap was a net. A bigger and stronger net would be used for larger game, with a smaller mesh net for birds (cf. Ezek 12:13, 17:20; Ecc 9:12; Amos 3:5). There is also the image of a noose snaring the leg of an unsuspecting animal. Larger game could also be caught in an older method of digging a pit and covering it with branches to conceal it. With all of these methods, the animal was captured alive and well, and therefore could later be slaughtered properly, so as to be ritually clean.

Fishing. There is little evidence in the Bible of fishing in the Old Testament period, or at least until the Jews had more access to the coast. Fish is mentioned as one

Netting wild geese; Egyptian tomb wall painting. 15th century BC.

of the foods eaten by the Children of Israel in Egypt (Num 11:5; Is 19:8). In the New Testament there is much evidence of fishing in the Sea of Galilee (Matt 4:18-22).

Because there was no way of keeping fish fresh, it had to be salted and dried immediately if it was to be preserved for storage or transport. One of the major salting centers on the Sea of Galilee was at Taricheae (Magdala), a Greek name which means "fish-salting." An earlier Aramaic name for the town was Migdal Nunayah, "Tower of the Fishermen". In the Negeb, many fish bones have been found in the kitchen refuse, indicating the eating of fish, possibly brought from the Red Sea.

The method of fishing was with a hook and line, and nets (Is 19:8). Fishing from boats with gill nets was also known (Hab 1:15; Ezek 26:5; Luke 5:4). Clay or stone weights were used to sink the lower edge of the nets, quantities of which were found in Caesarea and other port towns. Floats of cork or wood were found along the opposite edge to give maximum vertical use of net area.

The dragnet or seine is the oldest method of net fishing, and is still found on the Sea of Galilee. The seine is a 250-300 yd.-long (270 m) piece of netting, 3-4 yds. (2.7-3.5 m) high on the ends, and 8 yds. (6.5 m) high at the center. It was spread from a boat 100 yds. (27 m) or more from the shore and parallel to it. Once in place, two teams of as many as eight men each began to haul in the net with towing lines attached to each end. Once the hauling began, the motion had to be continuous to keep the fish from escaping through the net. After the process was complete and the catch was on shore, the fish could be sorted, putting the good fish in baskets and casting the rest back into the sea. The fish were then taken to be processed for storage or trading. Jesus compared the Kingdom of Heaven to a seine (Matt 13:47-48). On the Sea of Galilee, most fishing was done at night, and just before the dawn.

A second method of fishing with a net on the Sea of Galilee, still employed today, was with the use of gill nets. These nets, with weights on the bottom and floats on the top, were lowered in a snake-like pattern behind the boat not far from shore. Then the fisherman passed between the shore and his net while beating on the bottom of his boat, the noise causing any nearby fish to be scared into the net. After about ten minutes of beating, the nets were drawn, the fish boated, and then the fisherman moved to another location to start the process over again.

Assyrian stone relief showing a man fishing with a line.

A third method involved a round casting, which was thrown with a broad spinning motion over shallow water. The net fell in a ring as the weights on the perimeter of the find mesh dragged it down, and as the net sank, it took the shape of a dome which enclosed the fish. The fisherman drew it closed with a line attached to the center and collected the catch entangled in it.

Hooks were also used in the New Testament period, as indicated by the miracle of Peter catching the fish and finding the coin for his and Jesus' taxes in its mouth, just as Jesus had predicted (Matt 17:27).

It is possible that seven of Jesus' disciples were fishermen: Peter, Andrew, Philip, James, John, Thomas, and Nathanael. For this reason, and probably because much of his ministry was around the Sea of Galilee, Jesus spoke often of fish and fishing in his teachings. Several of Jesus' miracles involved fish, e.g., feeding multitudes with fish (Matt 14:15-21, 15:29-39) and the miraculous catches of fish (Luke 5:1-7; John 21:1-14).

TRANSPORTATION

The most prevalent mode of transportation in the biblical period was by foot. Vehicles drawn by animals were not very common. The few mentioned were usually in the service of kings and warriors, notably the chariot, and should be classified as military (Ex 14:6-7) or government vehicles (Acts 8:26-29), and not an everyday means of transport. Short journeys were made by foot, but for longer distances, or where the transport of goods was necessary, an animal was used.

Roads. The road system was not well developed, and most of the connecting roads between villages were winding paths used by pedestrians, sometimes accompanied by beasts of burden. For many thousands of years, preparing roadways consisted solely of clearing the path of boulders, placing them at the side of the road, and filling in the larger holes. Road building with wide roadbeds and paving stones was not known in the full sense of the word until later periods. If crossing a river was necessary, a ford was usually identified, and not until the Roman period were large flat stones laid in the river. Therefore, the use of wagons and other vehicles, while perhaps desirable, was not always possible, particularly in the mountain regions.

Only on the main international trade routes and a few secondary roads was travel easily accomplished, as they were built on the most natural and easy course. In Palestine, there were three main north-south routes; the King's Highway (Num 20), running from Damascus to the Gulf of Akaba; the Sinai route from the coastal towns of Sidon and Tyre to Acre, Shechem, Bethel, Jerusalem, Hebron, Beersheba, through the Negeb to Egypt; and the Via Maris ("Maritime Road"), stretching from Damascus along the lower Mediterranean coast passing through Hazor, Megiddo, and Gaza to Egypt. Main east-west routes were from Arabia to Gaza via Beersheba; from across the Jordan through Jericho and Bethel to Joppa, and also via Shechem to Joppa; and from Ramoth-Gilead via Beth Shean to the Via Maris.

Modes of Transportation. Animals for transportation were vital for access to the outside world and commerce. The most common animal used was the ass or

Caravans of camels are still used by the Beduin in the Negeb to transport whole households from camp to camp.

donkey for both riding and carrying goods. Asses were probably domesticated as early as the 4th millennium BC. On their return from the Babylonian Exile, the Jews utilized 6,720 asses (Neh 7:69). Both men and women rode asses, and Jesus rode an ass into Jerusalem (Matt 21:2-11).

The horse was most probably introduced into Israel in the 19th century BC by the Hyksos, but it is likely that it was only used for war. Horses were seldom found in everyday life, even in the post-biblical period.

The camel (or dromedary) was known in early times. Its special characteristics enable it to survive the most difficult desert conditions, and a good camel can travel up to 100 miles (160 km) a day, carrying loads weighing up to 500 lbs (250 kg). Hence, they were much used by caravans that had to make long journeys. Camels are frequently mentioned in the Bible (perhaps anachronistically) already from the time of the Patriarchs (Gen 12:16, 24:10, 31:17, 32:7). On their way back to the Land of Israel from the Babylonian Exile, the Jews employed 435 camels (Neh 7:69). Camels were used for riding in peace and war (I Sam 30:17; Is 21:7), for carrying valuable merchandise (Gen 37:25), and food (I Chr 12:40). During the reign of David a special overseer was appointed for the camels, and another official was placed in charge of the donkeys (I Chr 27:30).

The mule was a very strong and hardy animal used for tasks that in other countries were allotted to the horse. It was a fast animal (II Sam 13:29), a beast of burden (II Kgs 5:17; I Chr 12:40), and a mount for a king (I Kgs 1:44).

In the Bible, the wagon is distinguished as a vehicle used for transporting men and goods in peacetime. The lighter chariot was used mainly in time of war (Ex 14:6-9), although in peacetime it was often used by the king and his retinue. Chariots were first used in Syria and Egypt in the Middle Bronze Age. Wagons drawn by asses or camels were not uncommon in Babylonia and Egypt for transporting loads. In the Persian Empire, lighter, horse-drawn chariots were used by the royal mail. Normally, men did not ride on a loaded wagon

but walked beside it. A Hittite relief shows a wagon with four wheels. Similar wagons were used by the Philistines in their wanderings. The Bible makes a distinction between a covered wagon, probably for conveying goods, and a simpler wagon or cart (Num 7:3; I Sam 6:7). The latter was used mainly in the plains, where the Israelites may have adopted the idea from their neighbors the Philistines (I Sam 6:7ff; I Sam 6:3ff). An Assyrian relief depicting the retreat of the Jews from Lachish shows a cart with two wheels, drawn by oxen. It is loaded with bundles on which two women and children are sitting, while the men walk alongside.

TRAVEL

In ancient times, the traveler faced numerous dangers. He was at the mercy of robbers and the none-too-friendly attitude of the people of the towns and villages through which he passed. The account of Judges 19 with its story of the rape and murder of the Levite's concubine illustrates the perils that could befall a traveler. The inhabitants of Shechem would lie in ambush on the high mountains and rob passers-by of their belongings (Judg 9:25; John 10:24-37); anyone who wandered through deserted parts of the country sometimes had to face wild beasts (Is 30:6); while those who journeyed by sea were restricted by the seasons and the danger of sto ms (Jonah 1:4; Ps 107:23-30; Mark 4:35-41; Acts 27:9-44).

People did not travel much, unless they had to. Nowhere in the Bible is there an account of anyone undertaking a journey purely for pleasure. There was always a grave or important reason for any long expedition, e.g., the wanderings of Jacob and his sons to Egypt because of the great famine in the land of Canaan (Gen 43ff.), or the flight of Mary and Joseph to Egypt with Jesus to escape the wrath of King Herod (Matt 2:13-18).

The main reasons for making a journey were:
Cultic requirements. Already in early times, the Israelites were in the habit of traveling considerable distances to central cult places (Ex 5:3). Later, God com-

The Flight to Egypt of the Holy Family, depicted on a column of the Church of the Nativity, Bethlehem.

manded them, "Three times a year all your men are to appear before the Sovereign Lord, the God of Israel" (Ex 34:23). Both men and women were in the habit of making a pilgrimage to a place where an altar was set up in order to sacrifice to God (I Sam 1:3,21), and later, when Temple worship was established, to Jerusalem, for the three pilgrimage feasts: Passover, Pentecost, and Tabernacles (Luke 2:41).

Commercial transactions. Objects of foreign origin found in sites in Palestine as early as the Chalcolithic period indicate that goods were bartered, and people traveled great distances to acquire these goods. Solomon brought the Israelites into the orbit of international trade (I Kgs 10:28-29). His merchant fleet sailed to ports on the Arabian and African coasts. Israelite merchants were also frequent visitors to Damascus and even had "streets," i.e., bazaars, there (I Kgs 20:34).

Political and diplomatic missions. These were quite common reasons for making a journey. Ehud went up to Eglon, king of Moab, to take him a present (Judg 3:15ff.). Later, Israelite and Judean kings had to go to foreign countries to visit the kings to whom they were subject (II Kgs 16:10). Messengers from foreign countries would also visit Jerusalem (Jer 27:3).

Family. In general, extended families lived in close proximity. However, families periodically visited members who had moved away, e.g., Mary's visit to Elizabeth (Luke 1:39-40). At times, those who had moved went to their place of birth for a census, e.g., Mary and Joseph traveled from Nazareth to Bethlehem (Luke 2:1-5).

Preparations for travel. Traveling required careful preparation, including letters of recommendation (Neh 2:7ff.), locating and traveling with a caravan for safety and survival; and the means to pay a heavy road tax to

ensure safe passage (I Kgs 10:15). The traveler in the desert had to carry provisions with him (Gen 21:14), sometimes even in populated areas. Travelers who came to a strange city in Israel, however, would enjoy the hospitality of the citizens (II Sam 17:27-29; Is 21:14-15). The Bible provides no specific rules concerning hospitality, but Genesis 18:1-8; 24:31, and Exodus 2:18 show how important hospitality was considered, and Job says "I opened my doors to the traveler" (Job 31:32).

In the Hellenistic and Roman periods, many new roads were constructed and more caravanseries were built. Here travelers could find lodging and obtain stabling for their beasts and storage for their merchandise. Inns for Jews coming from the Diaspora or elsewhere could sometimes be found next to the local synagogue, not only in Israel, but later in the Diaspora, thus relieving the Jewish traveler from the potential danger of staying in a local inn or tavern.

TRADE

Palestine, situated at the geographical crossroads between Africa, Asia, and Europe, was in a position to play an important role in international trade. Some of the most important trade routes crossed the country. Except by sea, Palestine offered the only approach to Egypt from the north, and the trade routes were thronged with merchant traffic (Gen 37:25; I Kgs 10:15).

Exports. The chief exports from Israel in the biblical period were grain, oil, and wine. Other products known to have been exported were balm, honey, spices, myrrh, pistachio nuts, and almonds (Gen 43:11). The tolls collected were an important source of revenue during all periods.

Land trade. In time of peace, land merchants would make their way singly or in small groups, with few beasts of burden, traveling from village to village buying local products (Prov 31:24). Larger groups of traders used camels (Gen 37:25), donkeys (Gen 42:46), mules (I Chr 12:40), and servants (II Kgs 5:23). During the Persian period, armed guards accompanied the caravans (Ezra 8:22).

Shipping. As the Israelites did not possess good natural ports, nor a Mediterranean fleet, Phoenicia was the intermediary in maritime trade between western Asia and the cities on the Mediterranean coast. According to the Bible, the tribe of Zebulun was connected with seafaring activities (Gen 49:13). In Deborah's Song, Dan and Asher were also seafarers (Judg 5:17). The close commercial relations between Israel and Tyre, which developed in the time of David and expanded

A Canaanite merchant ship, reconstructed according to a drawing on an Egyptian tomb of 1400 BC.

under Solomon, led to advances in Israelite shipping. Solomon established a merchant navy at Ezion-Geber (I Kgs 9:26). These ships were jointly operated by Israelite and Tyrian sailors (II Chr 9:21). King Jehoshaphat of Judah constructed Tarshish ships to sail to Ophir for gold (I Kgs 22:48), but this effort failed when they were wrecked at Ezion-Geber port. After this, the Bible says nothing further about Israelite naval enterprise.

Under Solomon, international trade was on a large scale. Tyre bought the products of Israel to resell them to markets along the Mediterranean coast (Ezek 27:17), e.g., oil was shipped to Egypt (Hos 12:1). Tyre bought firs and cedars from Hermon for the masts of its ships, and the oaks of the Bashan for its oars (Ezek 27:5-6), while the Israelites imported cedars and pines from Lebanon (I Kgs 5:6,9).

After the return from the Babylonian Exile, trade was in the hands of foreigners, including Tyre, Sidon, and later Greece. During the 5th and 4th centuries BC, Greeks set up trading posts along the Mediterranean coast, which they colonized and used as distribution centers. Under Hellenistic rulers, Jews were allowed to settle in Alexandria, Egypt, as well as the newly founded Antioch-on-the-Orontes which did much for trade from Judah under the Ptolemaic and Seleucid kingdoms. In the 3rd century BC, the country was exporting summer wheat, olive oil, wine, meat, and cheese, with Judah's prime exports being dates and incense. After 165 BC, the conquest of Joppa by the Hasmoneans provided the Judean kingdom with access to the sea, opening this port to Greek merchants and turning it into an international center of commerce.

Throughout the Roman period, trade was firmly in the hands of the Romans and was the backbone of the empire. Any threat to their trade monopoly was looked upon very seriously. Traders were licensed and received a mark on their forehead and right hand, a practice that John extended into the end of time (Rev 13:16-17). The Romans had built 50,000 miles (80,000 km) of main roads and an additional 250,000 miles (400,000 km) of secondary roads throughout the empire. Judah became part of the huge Roman commercial complex with its extensive and well-kept road system, and its great prosperity in the early centuries AD is due to this connection. Herod the Great established the artificial

Remains of the rock-hewn Roman road which ran through the Elah Valley connecting Jerusalem and Gaza.

harbor at Caesarea which became the maritime distribution center of the region. Also, Nabatean traders brought countless camel trains from the Far East and southern Arabia laden with perfumes, herbs, precious wood, spices, and gems to ports in Gaza, adding to the importance of Judah in world commerce.

Buying and Selling. All trade was negotiated, and any sale was preceded by bargaining. Most transactions were not recorded, but when they were, some were on parchment (Jer 21:1-15), while most were on a piece of broken pottery.

As with most other areas of Jewish life, Mosaic law ruled: "You shall do no injustice in judgment, in measurement of length, weight, or value. You shall have just balances, just weights, a just ephah, and a just hin" (Lev 19:35-36).

Coins and Currency. See II.13

INDUSTRY

Early periods found extended family units living in concert, providing for their own group needs, with outside requirements being acquired by trading with neighboring groups. With the semi-nomadic lifestyle, trade was transacted with the villages the nomads passed on their migrations.

As communities settled down, the individual components were still relatively self-sufficient. Families, clans, or small villages made every effort to provide their own raw materials, tools, food, and household and personal needs.

As the walled cities developed with their market centers, so did specialization of labor. Walled cities also had a more complex infrastructure allowing more trade by individuals. Since barter was the most common medium of exchange, it was the availability of surplus production on the family level that provided the means for acquiring other needed items in the marketplace. As society developed and more specialization became economically possible, divisions of labor developed, which included the trades, artisans and craftsmen, and the professions.

Eventually, the various trades and professions were grouped into guilds, or "families," each specializing in its trade. Often streets or city gates took on the name of the type of business to be found there, e.g., bakers, silversmiths, cheesemakers, etc. Jewish boys would be apprenticed to their fathers. By the New Testament period, craftsmen wore a symbol of their trade, e.g., a carpenter wore a shaving of wood behind his ear, a tailor a needle on his garment, and a dyer, a colored rag. The wearing of these symbols was forbidden on the Sabbath, as was work. By the 6th century BC, Jeremiah implies that potters and bakers in Jerusalem had their own quarters in the city (Jer 19:1-2; 37:21). Nehemiah

(11:35) refers to the Valley of Craftsmen. I Chronicles 4:21-23 lists the clans of Judah and refers to "the clans of the linen workers of the house of Ashbea," and "the potters who lived at Netaim and Gederah" who worked for the king.

Throughout the entire biblical period, the villages continued to function, for the most part, on a self sufficiency basis. Individual families and small communities grew and processed their own food, raised their own livestock, made their own clothes, and built their own houses.

Trades, Artisans and Craftsmen

Stone working. Stone was used extensively in the biblical period for building material and, together with clay, for tools and utensils. Stone artifacts found have included: altars, weights made to conform with national standards (Deut 25:13), flint blades, ax heads, scrapers, bowls, three-legged mortars and pestles, querns and millstones for grinding flour, olive presses, potters' wheels, cosmetic bowls, beads, scarabs, jewelry molds, and seals.

Stone was difficult to work because of its hardness. Stoneworkers shaped their objects roughly with a metal chisel, bored the interior with bow drills, and finished them by polishing the outside and inside with polishing stones.

There was specialization among those who carved large stone objects for construction; those who made bowls, querns and millstones; and those who made more delicate objects. Included in this trade were also the brickmakers and masons.

Metalsmiths. Metal working was introduced to the Land of Israel during the Chalcolithic period (4th millennium BC), and revolutionized the culture as the technology developed. It enabled the cutting of stone, better farming, stronger weapons, and more durable tools and utensils. Metal objects were expensive. Metal was also used for making idols, which were forbidden for the Jews. In the New Testament period, metalsmiths in Ephesus prospered by making statues of Diana, and rioted when the preaching of the Gospel threatened their business (Acts 19:24).

During the biblical period, the metals worked in Israel were copper (bronze), iron, gold, silver, and to some extent, lead. Other than copper, none of these metals is found in Israel. Metals were brought to Palestine by Tyrian merchants from Tarshish (Ezek 27:12), probably transporting it in bars. The Phoenicians, merchants from Arabia (II Chr 9:14) and Egypt were also sources of metals for Palestine.

The Bible mentions the tunneling method for mining (Job 28:1-7), and where possible, extracting ore from surface veins was most desirable. Scripture also refers to smelting metal in the furnace (Deut 4:20; Is 48:10; cf. Dan 3:19-20). Solomon set up foundries in the Jordan Valley (I Kgs 7:46). The imported metal had to

Metal workers (top row) and carpenters at work. Detail from an Egyptian tomb wall painting; c.2400 BC.

be purified by reheating in a crucible, covered with charcoal, or placed over a charcoal fire and blown with bellows in order to remove any impurities. The molten metal was poured into a stone or clay mold, or onto a flat surface and hammered into shape.

The tools of the smith mentioned in the Bible are the tongs, hammer (Is 44:12), and nails (Jer 10:4). While no anvils have yet been found, they certainly existed. Bellows were also used to provide a steady draft of air to heat the coal to its maximum for forging. Clay crucibles and bellows for copper and iron work have been found in several sites in the region, as have molds for forming the molten metal into various objects.

The earliest objects made were spearheads, arrowheads, swords, daggers, crowns and other objects of authority for both religious and temporal purposes. The first metal worked was copper and later bronze, which is a mixture of copper and arsenic or tin. However, it was relatively brittle, and the introduction of iron, about the 11th century BC, allowed further advances in metal technology.

In later periods, skilled metalworkers banded together into guilds, known as "families." These included those making military and agricultural objects, and also the goldsmiths and silversmiths. See also II.14, Metals.

Goldsmiths and Silversmiths. Gold and silver were smelted on hot charcoal in closed crucibles so as not to lose any of the precious metals. For gold, the smith blew on the molten liquid through a blow pipe to oxidize out the impurities into slag. Silver, found in the same ore as lead, was more difficult to purify. The metals were then worked into jewelry and religious objects by pouring into molds, beating, soldering, engraving and using filigree. A vivid picture of a metal worker can be found in Isaiah (41:7). These metals were also used for barter (e.g., Gen 20:16), and for paying taxes or tribute (I Kgs 15:19). Silver was used for money, and to fashion cups, bowls, plates, jewelry (Ex 3:22; 11:2), and idols (Ex 20:23). Together with gold, silver was much used in the tabernacle (Ex 26) and in the Temple (II Chr 2, etc.). Gold- and silversmiths eventually developed their own guilds.

Woodworkers. The carpenter's craft was known in biblical times. Isaiah's description of a carpenter gives a good picture of the woodworker's job: "The craftsman stretches out his rule; he marks one out with chalk; he fashions it with a plane; he marks it out with the compass, and makes it like the figure of a man, according to the beauty of a man, that it may remain in the house" (Is 44:13). Jeremiah gives a similar description: "For the customs of the peoples are futile; For one cuts a tree from the forest, the work of the hands of the workman, with the ax. They decorate it with silver and gold; they fasten it with nails and hammers so that it will not topple" (Jer 10:3-4).

Few wooden remains have been found in Israel, due to the relatively wet climate. However, it can be assumed that the techniques used in Israel were similar to those of Egypt, where many examples have been found. From Egypt, we learn that the carpenter made boards by tying a log vertically to an upright post and sawing the board downwards from the top, holding the

A goldsmith at his furnace. Detail from an Egyptian tomb wall painting; c.1470 BC.

saw with two hands. To join wooden pieces together, several methods were used: lashing with thongs of leather, linen string, or copper bands; dovetailing; and dowels.

The carpenter's tools mentioned in the Bible or found in archaeological excavations in Israel and nearby Egypt, include an ax for cutting trees (Deut 19:5) the saw and adze, the carpenter's plane for smoothing wood, a marking tool, compass or dividers, square, a wooden mallet (Judg 5:26), the chisel, bow drill, hammer and nails (Jer 10:3–4), and the awl (Ex 21:6).

Carpentry reached a very high level in the biblical period, indicated by the elaborate furniture found in Egypt, depicted on Mesopotamian reliefs, and from the Greeks and Romans, as well as the fact that shipbuilding existed, e.g., the Phoenicians, Greeks and Romans.

The carpenter made roofs, doors, window shutters, latticework; paneling for temples, palaces and villas; furniture (beds, chairs, stools, tables, and divan frames); boxes; handles; bowls; wheels; wagons and carts; some boat building on the coast; plows; yokes and wooden parts of tools and weapons.

In the New Testament, Joseph, husband of Mary, was a carpenter (Matt 13:55), as was Jesus (Mark 6:3).

Wood was in sufficient supply in biblical Israel, although it was not of a good quality. Fine wood had to be imported. See also II.18, Plants.

Potters. Pottery making is one of the earliest known industries. It went through many transformations of

---

Pottery

Pottery was made of clay which was almost universally available. However, some special clays were imported. Pottery was made by molding wet clay into almost any desired shape. When fired, the shape given was retained and the resulting vessel could be used over and over again.

The potter first prepared the clay to remove impurities, including sand and stones. The clay or clay soil was immersed in a water bath to aid in the separation. The rocks and sand fell to the bottom, and before the liquid clay settled, it was channeled into another settling vat. Once settled, the water was poured off and the clay was removed and cut into chunks to be stored until needed.

When the potter was ready to make a vessel, he would take some of his clay, add water and knead it by hand or by foot (Is 41:25) to the required consistency. The prepared clay was then formed on the potter's wheel. The pot was removed from the wheel and set on the ground to dry, then dipped into a thin clay solution to seal any open pores.

At this stage, the decoration was added, although in the days of the kings of Judah and Israel, decoration was rare. In other periods the decoration on the vessels changed. Some had decorations burnished on them before firing (achieved by rubbing with burnishing stones). This resulted in red, black, yellow, or brown burnishing, sometimes separately and sometimes together. Designs were also painted. Most of them were stripes, but sometimes geometric and criss-cross patterns appeared; even birds, palm trees, gazelles, and crabs can be seen on excavated pottery. Decoration also took the form of single lines scored into the wet clay, or parallel lines scored in straight, wavy, or criss-cross designs, made by means of a comb.

Pottery was fired in kilns so that it would harden and retain its shape and decoration, making it durable enough for use. The kiln consisted of an underground firing chamber and an above-ground, dome-shaped chamber in which the pots were stacked for firing. The firing took two to three days, as raising and lowering the temperature too quickly could crack the pots.

The tools of the potter were the wheel, pottery templates used to smooth the surface of the object on the wheel, a bone point for cutting surplus clay from the rim, combs for scoring designs in the finished vessel, pebbles for burnishing, stone mortars and pestles for grinding the pigments used for coloring the vessel, and the kiln. Several people worked together in the potter's shop which was usually located outside the city walls. There were two reasons for this: one was the smoke billowing from the kilns, and the other was to prevent the possibility of fire from the kiln destroying the city.

Large chunks of broken pottery, called sherds, had some use. Isaiah speaks of them being used as braziers to take fire from the hearth or as ladles to scoop water from a puddle (Is 30:14). They were also used to scrape oil or dirt off the skin (Job 2:8), to line ovens for baking, to press into plaster walls lining cisterns, and to write upon when little else was available, the characters being etched on the hardened clay.

production and style, depending on the technology of the day and uses for the container. In many cases pottery was preferred over leather or baskets because it lasted longer, held liquids better, could be used for cooking, and offered protection from animals and insects.

In the earliest periods, pots were coarse. They were formed by hand on grass mats, which left an impression on the bottoms of the vessel. The Chalcolithic period saw the introduction of a simple, slow stone potter's wheel which greatly facilitated a more uniform design although only part of the pot was produced on the wheel and part by hand. By the end of the 3rd millennium BC, the potter's skill developed into the

Wooden model of a pottter's workshop; Egypt, 21st century BC.

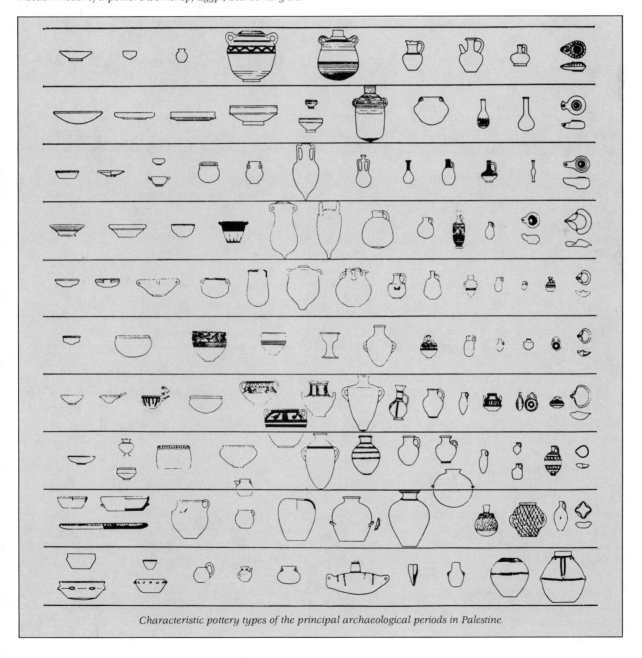

Characteristic pottery types of the principal archaeological periods in Palestine.

making of the entire pot on the fast potter's wheel, allowing more refined designs.

The transition from bronze to iron in the mid-2nd millennium BC marks a sharp change in shape and decoration of the pottery. The rounded shapes of the Bronze Age gave way to more angular shapes in the Iron Age. Imports in the later Iron Age and after added to the variety of designs.

Later in the Hellenistic period, a more advanced type of wheel was developed as described in Ecclesiasticus 38:29-30: "So it is with the potter, sitting at his work, turning the wheel with his feet, always engrossed in the task of making up his tally; he molds the clay with his arm, crouching forward to apply his strength." Similar to the wheel used today in the Near East, this wheel consisted of a throwing surface on the upper wheel connected with a shaft to a heavy lower kickwheel that was turned by foot, leaving both hands free for molding the vessel. Ecclesiasticus further describes the work of the potter: "He concentrates on finishing the glazing, and stays awake to clean out the furnace" (38:30).

In the Hellenistic period pottery in Palestine took on the more uniform style found all over the Greek empire. The Hellenistic style continued into the Roman/New Testament period with only minor variations.

Over time, many types of vessels were developed. Some were used for storage (I Kgs 17:12), including grain, flour, oil, wine, dates, and water (John 2:6); some for food preparation and consumption, e.g., cooking pots (II Kgs 4:38), colanders, bowls for eating (Matt 26:23) and drinking (II Sam 12:3); and some specialty vessels, e.g. chalices, jar stands, rattles, incense burners, oil lamps (Ps 119:105; Matt 25:1-8), braziers for holding fire or coals for heat (Jer 36:22-23), and ceremonial objects.

Tanners. Raw hides and skins were since early times used for clothing and protection for the feet; as containers of liquids, grain, seed, and valuables; for tents; for military purposes as shields, armor, and helmets; and for parchment.

In order for leather to be used and prevent its decay, the skins had to be prepared from the hides of slaughtered animals. The earliest tanning process was by washing the hides, scraping them to remove any dirt, hair, and flesh still adhering, and salting and drying them in the sun. The leather was softened by soaking in oil, spread out in the street for passers-by to walk upon, or beaten and treated with dog's dung. It was washed and dried again and beaten with a hammer to make it thin before being cut for making the various leather products. It could also be dyed. Hides for making parchment were salted and treated with flour.

The Bible mentions skins (Lev 11:2; 15:17), shoes (Amos 2:6), and the oiling of leather. The New Testament records that Peter stayed with Simon the tanner in Joppa (Acts 9:43; 10:6,32).

A shoemaker, depicted on a Gallo-Roman tombstone.

A tanner was not accepted in society because of the stench of the materials that he had to handle and the carcasses that he was forced to touch. As he never had time to purify himself before he had to be back at work, he remained an outcast. The fact that he had to collect dung with his own hands was, according to Jewish law, enough grounds for his wife to divorce him, if she so chose. Jewish law also required that a tannery had to be built away from town, on the east side, away from the prevailing wind so that the stench would not be blown into the town.

Dyers. Most of the earliest dyes were natural products, mainly obtained from colored earth, plants or animals. Dyes were used for linen and wool, for leather, on pottery, and in cosmetics.

The dyer prepared a solution of water, potash, and lime in vessels of earthenware or of a stone basis, many of which have been found in archaeological excavations. After two days, he added the pigments. The item being dyed was placed in a pot or basin containing a weak solution of the dyeing pigment, then transferred to another pot, in which the final stage of dyeing took place in a more concentrated solution. Once the color set, the finished product was rinsed in clean water and dried. Wool and linen were dyed before they were woven.

The dyeing process is not mentioned in the Bible, but there are references to colored cloth. Blue was used for the curtains of the tabernacle, for precious cloth (Est 8:15), and for the fringes of garments (Num 15:38); and purple for the tabernacle altar cloth (Num 4:13) and precious cloth. Both blue and purple were extracted from the murex snail found on the Phoenician coast in a very laborious process, which explains the high cost of this particular dye. Lydia, an early convert to Chris-

Dyeing and spinning plant; from an Egyptian wall painting.

tianity at Philippi (Acts 16:11-15), was a seller of purple. Among the skilled workers Solomon requested from Hiram, king of Tyre, for work on the Temple, was "...a man skilled to work...in purple, crimson and blue yarn" (II Chr 2:7,14).

Scarlet (Ex 25:4) or crimson (Is 1:18) was extracted from the eggs of certain lice, which were dried and crushed into a red powder for use. Vermilion was used for staining wood (Jer 22:14; Ezek 23:14), and was probably made from red and yellow ocher, the natural iron oxide found in Palestine and used as early as the Chalcolithic period. From the Roman/New Testament period onwards, red oxide of lead was used in addition to the ochers to produce the red color.

By analyzing dye pigments from paint on archaeological artifacts in Egypt, it has been possible to determine from which substances they were made. Red and yellow pigments were extracted from the safflower, and in the Roman/New Testament period, yellow was also obtained from the crocus. Blue pigment was also made from isatis leaves, and in the Roman/New Testament period, indigo was used. Black was obtained by painting red on blue, or by using powdered charcoal. Green was produced from powdered malachite, a hydrous carbonate of copper; white was made from chalk. For painting pottery, other earth pigments were mostly used.

Only in the Roman/New Testament period were lead oxide and other metallic oxides used on pottery and then to a limited extent.

Weavers The art of weaving was known in the Near East from early times. Most of our knowledge of weaving comes from Egypt where archaeologists have uncovered samples of cloth, mostly linen. Examples have also been found in caves in the Judean and Negeb

deserts. Cloth was produced from two main sources, animal (wool) and vegetable (linen). The weaver had to prepare his own raw material, spinning his wool or linen thread.

In Palestine, wool came mostly from sheep, rams, or goats. The wool of white sheep was used and thus wool became synonymous with purity (Is 1:18). Black goat hair was utilized for tent fabric (Ex 26:7). When the wool was sheared, it went to the fuller or washerman who washed, bleached, shrank, and beat it. The fibers contain natural oils which had to be removed before the wool could be spun, dyed, and woven.

The spinning of wool was usually, but not exclusively, the work of women (Ex 35:25-26). The spindle consisted of a rod about three feet (90 cm) long, at the end of which were one or two weights. These weights, hundreds of which have been found on sites from the Iron Age and later, were made of wood, bone, or stone. The method of spinning was quite simple and did not differ essentially from the one used today by Bedouin women in the Near East. The fibers of wool were placed in a ball on the distaff, which was held under the left arm, and the spindle was held in the left hand. The wool was plucked from the distaff with the right hand and drawn on to the spindle which was turned at great speed, twisting and producing the yarn. Proverbs 31:19 gives a picture of this process. Yarn spun in this manner was washed and cleaned with niter and soap (Jer 2:22) and was then ready for dyeing. Once dyed, it was ready for weaving.

Flax was the source of linen. After it was harvested, it was dried in the sun, then soaked in water for several days to loosen the fibers; drawn over the edge of a stone or board to separate the fibers; beaten with a wooden mallet, and finally combed. The linen thread was woven in the same manner as wool. At this stage, the fibers could be dyed, although they were usually kept white.

Weaving was done on a horizontal hand loom placed on the ground. It consisted of two parallel rows of pegs driven into the ground, to which the vertical threads (warp threads) on which the actual weaving was done, were attached. The process is referred to in Judges 16:14.

Another type of loom was vertical. It consisted of two long posts driven into the ground, with a third placed horizontally on top of them. This crossbeam is the "weaver's beam" referred to in I Samuel 17:7. The warp threads were tied to the crossbeam, each thread being suspended by a weight. Loom weights made of stone and clay have been found in many sites in Israel. The weaving started at the upper part of the loom, and the woven fabric was rolled on top of the crossbeam.

On either of these looms, either monochrome or polychrome fabrics were produced. Joseph's "tunic of many colors" (Gen 37:3) or Aaron's "skillfully woven tunic" (Ex 28:4) may have been of the latter kind. It was not until late in the Roman/New Testament period that more advanced methods of weaving were introduced. Clothing was woven in two or three pieces that were joined together.

Perfumers and apothecaries. Perfumers who processed spices, herbs and flowers into perfumes, also mixed compounds as ointments and creams for medical use and cosmetics, and were therefore the apothecaries of their day. The perfumers' stock included fragrances in spirit, oil or fat; loose and compressed powders; seeds, leaves and bark; medicines; and incense, sweet spices and anointing oil, and confectionery.

Perfumes were used in connection with religious ritual, e.g., the holy oil and incense of the tabernacle (Ex 30:25, 35; 37:29; Neh 3:8), and in pagan rituals, such as those to the god Baal (Is 57:9). Perfumes, ointments and spices were used for therapeutic purposes and for cosmetics, e.g., for make-up and deodorant. They were also used in the embalming of the dead and rites of burial (Gen 1:12; II Chr 16:14; Luke 23:56). Incense was also used in the home to help cover strong odors, including the smell of livestock which lived in close proximity, and keep flies, fleas and mosquitoes at bay.

In Exodus, Moses is given instructions on how to make anointing oil: "Take quality spices: 500 shekels of liquid myrrh, half as much sweet-smelling cinnamon

Woman holding a spindle and wool, with an attendant holding a fan; stone relief from Susa.

(250 shekels), 250 shekels of sweet-smelling cane, 500 shekels of cassia, according to the shekel of the sanctuary, and a hin of olive oil. Make from these a holy anointing oil, an ointment compounded according to the art of the perfumer" (Ex 30:23-25).

In the ancient world, perfumes and spices were precious commodities and sometimes even exceeded silver and gold in value. Their high price stemmed from the relatively small quantities that could be extracted from plants, their complicated processing, and the difficulty in getting the raw plant materials. They were, therefore, a luxury item used in Temple worship and in the homes of the wealthy. The Judean kings kept perfumes in their treasure houses (I Kgs 20:13) with their gold and silver. The queen of Sheba included spices in her gifts to Solomon (I Kgs 10:2,10-11).

The preparation of perfumes requires great skill, and has therefore always been the work of specialists. It requires a highly developed sense of smell, a good memory for fragrances, and the ability to combine and reconstitute various ingredients to achieve consistent results. Guilds were formed and formulas became closely guarded secrets. In the Temple where large quantities of perfume were used, some of the priestly families were skilled in perfume making (I Chr 9:30).

The Bible mentions various plants from whose flowers, fruits, leaves, bark or resin perfumes and ointments were produced (see II.18, Plants). Some grew in the Land of Israel, others were brought in by traders from as far away as India and South Arabia. The imported spices and other raw materials for making perfume were the mainstay of the traders, as relatively small quantities could be sold for high prices, making their trading effort profitable.

The tools of the perfumer were basins and pots for steeping, heating, and mixing; large jars for storing the

Gathering flowers for perfume. Detail from a stone relief on an Egyptian sarcophagus; 17th century BC.

oil; mortars and pestles for crushing the aromatic substances; wooden or bone spoons for stirring; strainers and funnels; and small vessels of pottery, alabaster, metal, ivory, and in the Roman/New Testament times, glass for storing the finished product. Ostrich eggs, used as containers for liquids in the 3rd and 2nd centuries BC, were also used to hold perfumed oils because of the impermeability of the shell. Pottery was least effective since it was porous, while stone alabaster was the most effective since it was non-porous and kept its contents cool. Perfume bottles that have been found feature only one narrow spout or opening that could be stoppered, so that the contents could not spill or evaporate easily.

Cosmetics were also made by the perfumer and consisted of body ointments, often applied after the bath or used to soften and protect the skin, preserve its freshness, and rejuvenate its appearance. The ointments were prepared from vegetable oils and sometimes from animal fat, often with aromatic resin or perfumed beeswax added. Make-up consisted of rouge powders and paint for the eyelids (Ezek 28:40) called kohl. Kohl was made from powdered minerals or vegetable products. Green eyeliner was produced from malachite, a carbonate of copper; or black, from ground sunflower soot, charred almondshells, and frankincense, and later in the Roman/New Testament period, galena.

Luxury trades. Jewelry was fashioned from gold, silver, precious stones, and ivory. Ezekiel said: "I adorned you with ornaments, put bracelets on your wrists, and a chain on your neck. And I put a jewel in your nose, earrings in your ears, and a beautiful crown on your head. Thus you were adorned with gold and silver..." (Ezek 16:11–13).

Some of the gold and silversmiths were specialists in jewelry-making, fashioning the metal and using precious stones to make intricate ornaments. Samples of their work have been found in graves, as well as hidden under floors in excavations. It seems that the people of the Bible hid their jewelry to avoid theft. When disaster struck, the precious items remained hidden until the excavator's trowel uncovered them, millennia later. Much was lost, however, as jewelry, if not hidden, would be a prime target for plunderers and looters at time of war and conquest.

As gold, silver, and precious stones were not found in Palestine, they had to be imported. For the precious and semi-precious stones mentioned in the Bible, see II.14, Metals, Minerals and Precious Stones.

Jewelers worked with abrasive stones for filing, fine quartz sand for smoothing, and wool or fiber pad for polishing. They probably used bronze or iron chisels, and engraving tools for cutting patterns in the stones. Jeremiah speaks of an iron tool with a flint point turned for engraving (Jer 17:1). Holes were drilled in beads with the use of a bow drill, an instrument with two parts, a bow and a drill. The bow string was wound

around the drill and when it was pushed and pulled, it caused the drill to spin at relatively high speeds. The drill was turned on abrasive sand that eventually made a hole in the stone. The techniques did not change much between the Old and New Testament periods. See II.15, Jewelry and Ornaments.

Ivory carvers. Much of ivory carving was learned from the Egyptians and Phoenicians, who were known for their skill. While ivory was used for jewelry, it was also carved into figurines of humans and animals, perfume bottles (two found in the shape of a woman), kohl spoons, combs, decorative boxes, game boards, jars, bas-relief pictures to hang on the wall, and as an overlay or inlay on furniture, such as beds (Amos 6:4), tables, chairs, thrones (I Kgs 10:18), and even the walls of King Ahab's palace in Samaria (I Kgs 22:39). Ivory itself was often inlaid with precious stones or gold foil. Ivory pieces have been found carved with female figures, ibex and dogs, sphinxes, a lion and trees, and a cherub. Carved overlay for furniture has been found with letters inscribed on the back to indicate where the parts fit together when pieced together. See also II.14, Metals, Minerals and Precious Stones.

Glassmaking. The first use of glass dates back to the 5th millennium BC, when glazed pottery was first

Glass Phoenician amphora and necklace of "eye beads."

made in the Near East. The first examples of man-made glass date to the last quarter of the 3rd millennium BC when glass beads were made in Egypt and Mesopotamia. By the middle of the 2nd millennium BC, the first glass vessels appear there as well. Glassblowing was unknown at this time, so melted glass was simply molded around a core that could be removed when cool. The surface was decorated with threads of colored glass, combed into ornamental patterns, rolled on a flat surface, and then a handle and base were added.

Egyptian glassmaking flourished in the 14th century BC, but in Israel and Syria it was rare, and only princes and the very rich could afford it. In Israel, glass objects still had to be imported in this period.

By the monarchy period, the glassmaking industry had shifted to Phoenicia (Lebanon), where monochrome and mosaic-glass inlays were produced. These were used as inlays in making exquisite furniture (mainly banquet beds), stone cosmetic palettes, or inlaid in ivories. Remains of ivory inlaid with glass were found in the palaces of the kings of Israel at Samaria. Small juglets were imported into Israel in the 6th to 4th centuries BC, and glass drinking bowls became popular in the 2nd to 1st centuries BC.

In the 1st century BC, the Phoenicians discovered the technique of glassblowing. These techniques were immediately learned by local glassmakers in Israel, and the remains of a dump of a glassmaking workshop from about the mid-1st century BC have been found in the Old City of Jerusalem. Glassblowing was introduced to the Roman world from the region of Israel and Phoenicia. The objects blown were perfume bottles, cosmetic jars, containers for various liquids, bowls, beads, juglets, and pitchers.

Food production occupations. These were usually the prerogative of individual families or clans. Nevertheless, as communities grew into cities or became associated with a nearby city, some of these agricultural tasks became centralized, as it was more efficient to have one olive or wine press in the community, than one for every family.

THE PROFESSIONS

Kings and Governors. Governors were appointed by the king to help him rule his realm. Before the monarchy, the judges were governors, but under the monarchy, the military function of the judges was taken over by the kings of Israel, although the functional legal role of a judge continued with judicial judges (II Chr 19:5), also known as governors (II Chr 18:25), who were placed in cities to implement the king's laws.

During the occupations, governors were placed strategically in the region to govern for foreign kings.

Sometimes these governor were Jewish, e.g., Ezra, but most often they were not. The administration of the gentile rulers was often at odds with the people and religious leaders who were trying to maintain adherence to biblical laws. See also III.27, The Kings of Judah and Israel.

Occupations of the court. Kings and governors had courts and administrative centers to maintain. These functions required professional practitioners and supervisors, including:

The **cupbearer,** whose job was to taste the foods and beverages before serving them to be sure they were not poisoned. A cupbearer (Gen 40:1; Neh 1:11) enjoyed the esteem and confidence of his masters.

The **chamberlain** or **steward,** who was employed to look after the personal affairs of the king (Gen. 39:1), introduced into the court of Israel by Solomon, and employed by later kings (I Kgs 4:6; 16:9; 18:3). He seems to have been a superintendent of the palace and to have attended to royal etiquette. He had great influence in court, including the right of introduction to the king.

The **secretary** and **recorder** worked together, the former maintaining a written chronicle of the affairs of state and the latter keeping a record of the transactions of government (Is 36:3,22; II Sam 8:16; 20:24; I Kgs 4:3; II Kgs 18:18).

The **taskmaster** was responsible for assigning tasks to workers and for supervising forced labor. He was answerable directly to the king (Ex 5:6), and Solomon named one of his chief officials to this position (I Kgs 4:6).

Lesser duties in court were carried out by doorkeepers, cooks, servers, cleaners, guards, etc.

Occupations of religion.

The **priests** were of the Tribe of Levi, appointed to special service (Ex 28), and maintained the administration of all the functions and necessities of religion, both sacred and temporal, particularly when centralized Temple worship existed. Not only overseeing the religion of the people of Israel, the priest was the only one who was consecrated to offer sacrifices to the Lord for the people (II Chr 26:18). All the posterity of Aaron were priests except those disqualified by the special qualifications set forth in the Mosaic Law.

There were other individuals related to the religion of the people.

The **prophet** was a person raised up by God to communicate his message to men, from peasant to king, especially in regard to the consequences for failure to uphold God's laws, and future events. (See Chapter II.26, Prophets and Prophecy)

The **scribe** was appointed to handle correspondence and keep accounts, particularly associated with the priesthood. He was given a position alongside the high priest. Hezekiah gave the scribes the charge of trans-

Statue in painted limestone of an Egyptian scribe, holding a partly opened roll of papyrus; c.2500 BC.

cribing old records and writing what had been handed down orally (Prov 25:1). In the course of time, the scribe came to be an interpreter of the law. In the New Testament, the scribes attained a class of their own, and were regarded with great respect. They were given the best places at feasts and the chief seats in the synagogues.

The *porter,* also known as a doorman or gatekeeper (II Sam 18:26; I Chr 9:22). The Levites who had charge of the various entrances to the Temple were called porters (I Chr 9:17; 15:18; II Chr 23:19). In David's time, porters at the Temple were in fact guards and numbered 4,000 (I Chr 23:5). Porters were also stationed at the city gates, not for religious purposes, but for security.

Rabbi is a term given to teachers of the law in the latter Second Temple period, and literally means "master" (John 1:38; 20:16). It became an official title for ordained members of the Sanhedrin. This title was applied to Jesus by his disciples and others (Matt 23:7,8; John 1:38,49; 3:2,26; 6:25), but more out of respect than as an official designation.

Occupations of religious/civil law.

The *elder* was an early judge who could be found at the city gates. Local government authority was based in the council of elders. From the time of the Exodus, elders were established who were heads of families, ruling clans. The internal group laws were not written, but formed a tradition passed along by the elders and encompassed elements to ensure the group's security,

integrity, hospitality, progeny, property, family solidarity, and the worship of the one God. Once the people began to settle in villages, the elders became a more central authority on the local scene, with community-wide influence. From the settlement period, it was the elders who represented the collective wisdom of the community (Prov 31:23). They supervised legal procedures and were arbiters of local disputes, formulated legal policy based on the legal traditions and customs of the group, and the law of Moses (Deut 16:18–20).

Later, the interpreters of the law were teachers or experts in the law and acted as court lawyers and synagogue lawyers (Matt 22:35; Luke 7:30; 10:25; 11:45,46,52; 14:3; Titus 3:13). The scribe acted in the function of a lawyer in his pronouncements on legal decisions.

Occupations of the arts.

Music played an important role in the life of the Israelites, particularly related to worship and festivals, requiring the skills of a musician to play musical instruments, and singing hymns and psalms. (See II.11, Musical Instruments.)

Dancing often accompanied music, as part of worship (Ps 150:4), during festivities (Luke 15:25), and at court (Matt 14:4).

Sculpture in antiquity was related to depicting real-life forms and pagan gods, and therefore sculpture as a profession was not known among the Jews. "You shall not make for yourself an idol in the form of anything in heaven above or on the earth beneath or in the waters below" (Ex 20:4). Nevertheless, some relief is found on stone and earthenware, although this was the work of the stonecutter and potter, not a professional sculptor.

Painting in the ancient world also depicted real-life forms, and so while there could be no possibility of creating an idol, even accidentally, painting was limited. The painting of geometric designs on earthenware was the work of the potter. Frescoes have been found in Second Temple period structures, e.g., Herod's palace at Massada.

Mosaic floors depicting geometric patterns and life forms have been found in Second Temple period dwellings, and even in 1st-century synagogues. Such designs took the skills of a trained artisan.

Occupations of medicine.

The medical profession included, by the New Testament period, professional physicians, e.g. Luke (Col 4:14), as well as magicians and charlatans. Interestingly, in the Roman/New Testament period, physicians were classed with laborers, and in rabbinic texts, in the professions that were associated with the "craft of robbers," mainly because they were seen as overcharging the rich and neglecting the poor.

Physicians understood the practice of medicine and the art of healing. Priests and prophets were expected to have some knowledge of medicine. In the days of Moses, there were midwives and regular physicians who attended the Israelites (Ex 21:19). They doubtless brought some knowledge of medicine from Egypt, where medicine was quite advanced for its day. The Edwin Smith Surgical Papyrus gives some insight into the medical knowledge and practices of the Egyptians. This document lists 48 cases of injury, including 10 possible cases of injury to the brain. Broken bones were set with an adhesive plaster cast. Skeletons show evidence of well-healed fractures. Castor oil was prescribed as a laxative and many herbs were recommended to cure ailments. Medicines were prepared by perfumers and were based mostly on herbal compounds.

Nurse. A nurse in the biblical period was more of a governess or tutor who helped raise children (II Sam 4:4; II Kgs 11:2). However, her duties would have also included helping in time of sickness, a role more closely associated with the modern use of the word. Wetnurses for infants were also known, particularly when mothers could not nurse their own children, usually for reasons of illness or even death during childbirth (Ex 2:9). Most patriarchal families had a nurse or nurses. Rebekah's nurse went with her to Canaan, and was buried with great mourning (Gen 24:59; 35:8).

Occupations of the military/security. During the patriarchal period, security was carried out by clan members for the defense of the group. This included defense of the homestead, and their possessions, flocks and fields. By the exodus/settlement period, it was necessary to organize to defend the larger group (Num 31), and actually conquer and possess the Promised Land (Num 33:50-54). Nevertheless, the "army" of Israel was a volunteer, people's army, into the period of the Judges when men and arms were called into action when needed. In the early period, it was expected that every man over the age of 20 and able to fight would participate in the mutual security of the group (Num 1:3).

In the monarchy period, the military of Israel was at its apex, as an organized, centralized army. Later, under occupation, Israel did not have an army. However, during the independent Hasmonean period, a Jewish army was raised and later assisted the Roman conquest of Egypt. However, once Israel was fully integrated into the Pax Romana, the security and military presence in the nation was entirely under the authority of Rome. See II.10, War and Warfare.

Watchmen. Another occupation for the security of the people involved the role of a watchman whose duty was to stand in the tower on the walls or at the gates of the city to observe and report any unusual activity. Watchmen also patrolled the streets and besides protecting the city and its inhabitants from violence, were required to call out the hours of the night (II Sam 18:24-27; Song 5:7; Is 21:11-12). The watchmen on the

Man watching from a tower. Detail of an Assyrian bas-relief, 8th century BC.

walls used a trumpet to warn of an invading army, not only to those living in the city, but especially those living and working outside the walls who were most vulnerable.

Occupations of money. One of the professions associated with money was that of the *tax collector*, known as the publican in the New Testament/Roman world. As in any society, the tax collector was one of the most unwelcomed people, particularly when he was the tax collector of an occupying power.

In Israel, taxation was introduced in the monarchy period when Solomon instituted a form of taxation by requiring each district to provide foodstuffs for the royal household for one month each year (I Kgs 4:7), and conscripting workers from the Israelites (I Kgs 5:13-17) and from his conquered peoples (I Kgs 9:20-21), for building projects, including the Temple and his magnificent palace. Taxation and conscription bred dissension among the people.

Later, under occupation, heavy taxation was enforced, including tribute paid to the king by his subjects; customs; a tax on consumption; and tolls, a road tax or tax on land (Ezra 4:13). The consequences of non-compliance to the occupying power was persecution, punishment, and even death.

In the Roman period, tax collectors worked for a commercial company which guaranteed to the government a fixed sum for a certain tax or monopoly. They then overcharged or even extorted illegal taxes. This led to a feeling of hostility towards anything connected with the government, particularly the tax collector himself. In the case of Jews who were tax collectors, they were even more despised and considered traitors and apostates for working for non-Jews and being willing tools of the oppressor (Matt 9:11; 18:17: 21:31; Luke 19:1-9).

Money-changers. By the Roman/New Testament period, the occupation of money changer came into being in the area of the Temple. Roman money was legal tender and was used for ordinary purposes. But the priests taught the people that only Jewish currency was fit for worship and the paying of the temple tax, so the changers made a very profitable business. They were situated in the Court of Gentiles and also sold animals for sacrifice in the Temple (John 2:14). Jesus, incensed at this activity in the Temple, overturned the tables of the money-changers, saying "Is it not written: My house will be called a house of prayer for all nations?; But you have made it 'a den of thieves'" (Mark 11:15-17).

Merchants. Trade was small-scale, with most of the trade of goods done directly with the tradesmen who produced the goods themselves, or by the farmer who brought his produce into the village or city. Barter was practiced widely, even involving second party transactions, so that a tailor could buy a procurement of

A money-changer, or tax-collector, with a pile of coins in front of him, depicted on a Roman relief.

pepper from a caravan for resale to a colleague in the trade.

Some enterprising wholesalers made journeys to procure goods not available to bring back for resale. Merchants with goods to sell would ply their wares to anyone who would buy along the way.

Servants and Slavery. The term "servant" in the Bible did not always refer to one engaged in menial tasks, as would the term "domestic" or "slave." In some passages, the term properly means "young man" or "minister" (e.g., Gen 15:2; 24:2).

There were also domestic servants who served the households of the wealthy or royalty. Slaves, too, were common. The slave was held in bondage, having no freedom of action, his person and service being wholly under the control of his master or owner.

Slavery was practiced widely in the ancient Near East and was an important part of the economy. Therefore, ancient law codes which regulated society also regulated the lives of these bonded individuals. There were five sources for slaves:

(1) Slaves were usually captives of war. The earliest word for "slave," in Sumerian, means "male of a foreign country." These could be captured soldiers or members of the defeated population.

(2) Another source was people kidnaped and sold in the foreign slave market, e.g., Joseph (Gen 37:27-28). In Mesopotamia this was a big business and people were kidnaped and sold through an international slave broker. This was strictly forbidden in the Mosaic law on pain of death (Ex 21: Deut 24). Exodus 23 goes further in forbidding the Israelites to give back foreign slaves who have come to them for protection.

(3) A third source was the sale of minors because parents needed the money and could not afford to feed their children (Ex 21:7-11; Neh 5:1-13). These would be household slaves, and not found in the slave camps. This was a common solution to poverty.

(4) Hunger and debt also caused individuals to sell themselves into slavery as an act of survival (Ex 21:5-6; Lev 29:39-55; Deut 15:15-17).

(5) Some who took out loans and found themselves unable to pay were taken as slaves and sold on the lucrative slave market to repay the debt. In Deuteronomy 15, there are laws limiting the slavery of the insolvent to six years.

In the ancient world, the status of slaves was that of chattel or livestock. They were worked hard, often to death. Egyptian slaves were branded with the cartouche of the current Pharaoh on their forehead or marked with a tag or iron collar. Receiving or harboring a runaway slave was treated by the ancient laws as receiving stolen goods. By contrast, the Bible instructs the Israelites to break with this practice (Deut 23:15,16): "You shall not give back to his master the slave who has escaped from his master to you. He may dwell with you in your midst, in the place which he chooses." In the ancient world, if a third party abused or harmed a slave, the owner received compensation from the third party for damaging his property. Again, in contrast to this, the Bible considers the owner of a slave a murderer if he beats his slave to death: the first law in history to view the slave as a person and not chattel (Ex 21:20-21).

If an owner wounds a slave, the slave is to be set free, implying that the owner is not worthy of having the responsibility of another human being (Ex 21:26–27).

In biblical terms, there were more ways to acquire freedom from slavery than in any other Near Eastern law code. Without money to buy this freedom, there were five different ways to acquire it: (1) Release after six years (Deut 15:12); (2) release in the Year of Jubilee (Lev 25); (3) the example of the Hebrew maid (Ex 21:7–11); (4) release as a result of being wounded by his/her master (Ex 21:26–27); and (5) the right of asylum, the fugitive slave being sheltered and given a home (Deut 23:15,16).

In the New Testament period, slavery was still an accepted practice. The New Testament gives servants and slaves instructions on how to treat their masters, and likewise, masters their slaves, with an eye towards their basic relationship in an effort to change the system from within (e.g., Eph 6:5–9; Col 3:22–23).

Prisoners of war depicted on the so-called Cosmetic Palette of the Does from Abydos, Upper Egypt.

The Unseemly Professions.

Thieves and robbers. Theft was strictly forbidden by Mosaic law. But there were robbers (Matt 6:19), and highwaymen who preyed upon travelers. The New Testament story of the good Samaritan tells of highway robbers who were particularly ruthless: not only did they rob the traveler of his possessions and clothing, but also beat him and left him half dead (Luke 10:30–37).

Prostitutes/harlots. Prostitution was widely practiced in the ancient world in connection with cult worship, but was forbidden in the Bible and associated with wickedness (Lev 19:29). Priests were not allowed to marry women who had been defiled by prostitution (Lev 21:7). The most famous harlot in the Bible was Rahab, who harbored Joshua's spies in Jericho (Josh 2). In the New Testament, male prostitutes, whore-mongers, fornicators, and those engaged in immoral sexual practices, are subject to the wrath of God (e.g., Eph 5:3–6).

Beggars. Most of these unfortunates were victims of circumstances, e.g., poor, maimed, lame, or blind (Luke 14:13). Beggars lived from the alms of others, soliciting them publicly or from door to door. They could often be found sitting in places where they were assured of foot traffic, e.g., the side of a busy road (Mark 10:46; Luke 18:35), the city gates, or the gate of the Temple (Acts 3:1–10). It was customary to give alms, and in the New Testament, one example of a God-fearer was one who gave alms generously (Acts 10:2).

Magicians, diviners, sorcerers, and witches. Occult practices were part of pagan religious rites in the effort to discern the future and the supernatural world. In the Bible, God required all who believed in him to seek him through prophets and not through divination or sorcerers (Deut 18:14–16). Deuteronomy 18:9–11 makes this quite clear: "When you come into the land which the Lord your God is giving you, you shall not learn to follow the abominations of those nations. There shall not be found among you anyone who makes his son or his daughter pass through the fire, or one who practices witchcraft, or a soothsayer, or one who interprets omens, or a sorcerer, or one who conjures spells, or a medium or a spiritist, or one who calls up the dead." Nevertheless, such practices were found in Israel. One of the more striking examples was King Saul, who had "cut off mediums and spiritists from the land," yet visited the witch of Endor to have her consult the deceased Samuel for him (I Sam 28:1–24). The practice of the occult was usually associated with idolatry (Gal 5:20).

HOUSING AND FURNISHINGS

Building Materials. The earliest human dwellings were made of simple materials, i.e., uncut stone, rubble, and mud brick serving as low walls around a depression in the ground, with reeds or branches for a roof.

Wood. Palestine was a fairly heavily forested region, particularly in the biblical period (cf.Josh 17:15; II Kgs 19:23, etc.). Nevertheless, wood for construction was relatively rarely used. When it was utilized, the ordinary people used inexpensive local sycamore (I Kgs 10:27; Is 9:10), while palaces and the houses of the wealthy were built of timber from Lebanon and Syria, areas rich in cedar and fir (I Kgs 5:8), or almug (a type of sandalwood) brought from Ophir (I Kgs 10:11).

Stone. Much of Israel consists of rocky hills, and thus stone was the natural and most easily cared for raw material. In Galilee, black basalt predominates, while on the Coastal Plain, sandstone was much in use even though it is an inferior stone. Even the great seaport of Caesarea built by Herod the Great utilized sandstone.

In the hill country, hard limestone was available of a quality which permitted blocks to be cut and smoothed. Quarries that provided the stone for the large cities of Hazor, Megiddo, Gezer, and Jerusalem have been found near these sites. Often stone quarries were located near a particularly indefensible wall of a city, and the deep pit provided needed protection from the enemy. Such a quarry is located in the area of the Church of the Holy Sepulcher in Jerusalem, which, from the 7th century BC to the 1st century AD, was outside the indefensible northwest wall of the city. It was later filled by the Romans.

Before Solomon, city walls, houses, even temples and palaces, were mostly built of rubble or roughly dressed stone. However, with the introduction of iron stone-cutting tools, larger and more impressive structures were made possible. Even though ordinary homes continued to be built of roughly hewn stones, rubble or mud brick, the homes of royalty, the wealthy, and public buildings, temples, and aqueducts required ashlar masonry and precision-cut stone. Solomon conscripted tens of thousands of stonecutters to provide blocks for his building projects (I Kgs 5:15).

Ashlar masonry utilizes large rectangular stone blocks that must fit together exactly, without mortar, for the structure to stand. At first, ashlar stones were used for foundations or the corners or walls to reinforce these potential weak points. Rougher stones could be used for the rest of the building. This technique is seen in Israelite Megiddo, where ashlar pillars were incorporated in intervals in a rubble wall to reinforce it.

Ashlar stones were smoothed on the sides that inter-

The Western Wall in Jerusalem showing some of the large ashlars of the Herodian period.

faced or showed. An early example of ashlar foundation can be seen in Samaria, where the citadel dating from Omri and Ahab still bears the marks of the chisels and adzes used by the masons. In the Hellenistic period and earlier, smaller stones were used. In the Roman and Herodian period, large blocks were used. The hallmark of the Herodian construction was beautifully beveled edges on the face of the stone blocks with a low smoothed boss. Herod did not use these stones only at potential weak points, but for entire structures. The Western Wall in Jerusalem, the retaining wall for the Second Temple built by Herod the Great, is one of the largest remaining vestiges of these Herodian stones. The largest block found is 30 ft (9 m) long by 13 ft (4 m) wide. Remains of Herod's city also reveal stairways, arches, pavements, and beautiful friezes and moldings, all of dressed stone, which took time and great skill to produce. With the invention of the arch in the early Roman period, stone was also used for roofing.

The tools of the stone-dresser who faced these stones were: hammers (Jer 23:9) made of stone prior to the Roman period, and iron thereafter; the ax (I Kgs 6:7; Is 10:15), which was not unlike the chisel used for dressing stone today; a saw (Is 10:15) for cutting stone, and an iron pick (II Sam 12:31). In the quarry, five of the six sides of the block were cut with a chisel. Into these grooves, wooden beams were inserted and soaked with water. As the wood expanded, the pressure broke off the sixth side. Once free, the block could be dressed.

Brick The most common and cheapest building material, in the valleys and plains, was brick. Bricks were produced by a simple method. A hole was dug in the ground and filled with water. The resulting mud was mixed with straw and trodden until it became thick and workable. The straw also prevented the bricks from cracking easily. In early periods, bricks were formed by hand, but later a wooden square without a top or bottom gave greater uniformity. The newly made bricks were sun-dried. This is the method used

Making bricks and building. Egyptian tomb wall painting.

by the Children of Israel in Goshen before their departure from Egypt (Ex 1:14). After Moses revealed his plans to leave with the Hebrews, their punishment from Pharaoh was to make them find their own straw while maintaining their quotas (Ex 4:6-9).

This primitive method was used until the Roman period. With the need for speedier methods of production to fill building requirements, fired brick was introduced from Rome, though this may also have been known in the Iron Age. Certainly, fired brick was used very early in Mesopotamia. The Roman brick was considerably thinner than the earlier version, and was square, rectangular, round, or polygonal. Roof tiles were produced in the same manner, which made roofing cheaper. A factory used by the Roman Tenth Legion for the production of fired brick and roof tiles has been found near Jerusalem. The product was stamped with their seal.

Mortar. A mixture of readily available lime, sand, ashes, and water was known in the Israelite period, and used for plastering cisterns and reservoirs to make them waterproof. In the Roman period, the quality of mortar was greatly improved and it was then used as a binding material in construction, much as cement is used today. Plaster was made more durable, and indeed, reservoirs built in the Roman period can still hold water today.

Renovations. Most structures needed continual renovation, due to the nature of the building materials and the ravages of the elements. Since the walls of most houses were made of mud brick or small stones with mortar, they needed to be repaired after the long dry summer, before the rains, and after the rainy season when water damage would be evident.

Biblical prohibition of the presence of mildew in dwelling places would have caused the Israelites to take extra care in home repairs, particularly in the winter when the cold and damp would be a prime breeding ground for mildew. Leviticus (14:33-57) gives a detailed account of what to do if mildew was found.

Palaces. The earliest palaces unearthed in Palestine are the "palace of Ai," dated to the Early Bronze Age, and others from the period of Hyksos domination in the mid-2nd millennium BC. The general plan is typical of oriental dwellings, with rooms arranged around a central court. The building had at least two storeys, the lower one being used for domestic purposes and the accommodation of servants, while the upper storey served as the family's living quarters. Excavators often classify a dwelling structure as a palace simply by its size. But the quality of the architecture or a significant find, e.g., large numbers of scarabs, inscribed material, a hoard of ivory plaques, or gold jewelry, would point to the inhabitants having belonged to a privileged class.

Most palaces were made of stone, some serving as fortress palaces, such as the one uncovered in Gezer.

Columns of the lower-level structure of Herod's impressive palace, built on three levels, on the summit of Masada.

The most famous palace constructed in Israel was Solomon's royal palace in Jerusalem. Its description can be found in I Kings (7:1-12): it took 13 years to construct, using the finest local and imported materials and craftsmanship. Solomon's palace and the adjoining Temple were built under the influence of architecture which originated in Syria in the 2nd millennium BC. The complex was entered through a portico with a single pillar opening into an entrance hall or "porch of pillars" (I Kgs 7:6) that led into the throne room or "porch for the throne" (I Kgs 7:7). Then came the living quarters, rooms surrounding "another court" (I Kgs 7:8). The "great court" (I Kgs 7:12) was apparently a huge court in front of the entrance.

Another outstanding palace from the Iron Age is that of Omri and Ahab at Samaria, which followed the usual plan of rooms grouped around a central court. Its fame derives from the decoration of its furniture with ivory plaques on low or high relief or open-work: hence the reference to "the palace he [Ahab] built and inlaid with ivory" in I Kgs 22:39. A palace of the later Iron Age, the first to be discovered in Judah, was found at Ramat Rachel near Jerusalem, and identified with the palace built by Jehoiakim (609-597 BC), referrred to by Jeremiah (22:13-14).

Residences. Less information is available on the everyday living conditions of the masses in the early periods, because excavations of mounds usually reveal only the foundation stones of buildings, and excavators tend to concentrate on public buildings. Also, most of the people associated with a city lived outside the walls in mud brick or rough stone dwellings, the only identifiable remnants of which today are some broken pottery. In later periods, where houses are still standing to the level of the first floor or higher, more can be determined about living conditions.

Tents. The simplest dwelling was not a permanent structure, but a tent. Most often, each extended family within a clan or tribe possessed a tent. Tents were pitched in close proximity to one another for communal living, and were made from goatskins or goat hair. A tent made from goatskins would have been dark and stuffy, but it would also have been warm and dry in winter and relatively cool in summer. Tents were placed on hilltops in summer to capture the breeze, and in winter on the leeward side of valleys, just above the base where flash floods could occur, to keep out of the wind and rains. Tent fabric was woven as long panels on looms about one yard (90 cm) wide, the panels being stitched together to the width needed to accommodate the family. Tents were tied down by ropes and tent pegs. The center of the roof would have been raised slightly to help rainwater run off. Channels were dug around the tent to allow water flowing downhill to run around the tent rather than through it. Briars were also placed around the base of the tent to keep small animals and creatures such as snakes from crawling inside. Tents were portable, and the covering and poles could be bundled up and taken to a new site with relative ease.

Up to and including the period of the Judges, even people who were not necessarily nomadic lived in tents. Later, when most people dwelt in permanent housing, nomadic peoples continued to live in tent dwellings and travel with their herds for food and water.

Permanent Homes. The earliest permanent homes in the region date from the Neolithic and Chalcolithic periods. Neolithic homes consisted of one round room with its interior floor cut into the ground and walls made of hand-molded brick. Several homes were often clustered around a small court, and had adjoining storage chambers. In the Chalcolithic period, there was a variety of shapes, the most prevalent being rectangular one-room structures with one rounded end. Their foundations were stone with hand-molded brick walls. They were of moderate size, and were often built close together.

By the Early Bronze Age, sun-dried brick was still used, but there were almost always one or two courses of foundation stones, with dressed stone beginning to be used. The bricks were bonded with fresh clay. The houses had one or more rectangular rooms and floors were of beaten earth, often below the outside ground level. Flat roofs were supported by wooden poles.

From the Middle Bronze Age, when Abraham entered Canaan, houses built entirely of stone have been

A Beduin camp in Galilee. These nomadic tribes pitch their tents where they find a patch for their flocks to graze.

found. While Abraham and his family pitched their tents, some others already in the land were living in more permanent housing. Indeed, Abraham too would have lived in a mud brick house in Ur of the Chaldees before starting his trek to Canaan. The houses in Canaan at that time were built with flat roofs supported by stone pillars made of several cylindrical drums. The floors were bedrock, leveled down or filled with flat stones. Sometimes there were benches along the walls. The majority of the homes were simple and modest, with small rooms, about 10 x 7 ft (3 x 2 m), and a courtyard, and were built closely together. Most of them probably had two storeys, the ground floor being used for storage and workrooms, and the upper floor providing living accommodation. Food was prepared and cooked in the courtyard. Some larger homes have also been found from this period, belonging to the more prosperous members of society. However, the average home of this period was very small.

In the Late Bronze Age, about the time of the Exodus and the conquest of Joshua and the Judges, little had changed, though there is found an increasing number of larger homes belonging to nobles or important citizens. The average house of the period had an inner courtyard with several rooms arranged around it.

At the time of the early Israelite kings, a new type of Iron Age house developed, known as the four-room house. The plan is nearly square, and the inner partition consists of three oblong rooms parallel to each other and a fourth room running along the width of the building at one end. This style of home, with several variations, has been found in numerous locations, both north and south. The middle of the three oblong rooms was usually an unroofed courtyard containing the fireplace. In some cases, this court was shut off from the adjoining rooms by a solid wall; in others, one of the rooms was separated from it only by a row of pillars or upright stones just over three feet (90 cm) high, either free-standing or incorporated in low rubble walls. These stone pillars provided a base for wooden pillars to hold the roof. Typically, the two oblong rooms on either side of the court were used for storing supplies and family industry, e.g., weaving, basketry, mending, food preparation, washing, etc. The perpendicular room running the width of the house at one end was for socializing with guests, eating, and sleeping.

In the Hellenistic and Roman/New Testament periods, the courtyard style continued to be utilized. However, craftsmanship had developed to the point of offering distinctive differences in interior decoration, depending on the ability to pay for it. In the cities, which had grown larger by this time, there were more larger homes of the wealthy than in previous periods. The courtyards of the more expensive houses were surrounded by colonnades. The walls were built of finely cut stones arranged in neat rows. Much decora-

tion was added in the form of carved lintels, attached capitals, and doorpost bases. Many houses had their walls covered with white plaster; some had frescoes. The second floor was always carried by arches spanning the room below. On these arches (two, three, four, or more placed parallel to one another) were placed stone slabs to form the floor of the storey above. The homes had their own water reservoirs in the courtyard or in cisterns. Winter rainwater channeled from the roof would replenish cistern supplies. Sometimes in the hilly regions homes were built against a cliff, particularly if the rock face contained a small cave, which was used for cool storage.

Model of St. Peter's house at Capernaum.

Roofs. In all periods, the flat roofs, reached by means of a stairway or ladder on the outside of the structure, provided a good lookout (Is 22:1; Matt 10:27) and an area for working (including washing and weaving, cleaning grain, drying flax and fruit such as dates and figs, playing, sleeping in the summer when it was hot, and praying (Zeph 1:5; Acts 10:9-16). Most of these roofs were constructed of wooden beams resting on the lower walls. Over the larger beams was laid a combination of smaller branches, brush, reeds, grass, chopped straw, clay, and mud. This was leveled with a roller, a process that had to be repeated after each rain. By the end of the rainy season in the spring, grass and weeds would be growing on the roof, making it green (II Kgs 19:26; Ps 129:6; Is 37:27).

Jewish law required that a short wall or parapet be constructed around the roof "so that you may not bring bloodguiltiness on your house if anyone falls from it" (Deut 22:8). By the New Testament period, the Romans had introduced terra cotta tiles which strengthened the roof, but this was only affordable by the wealthy.

Courtyards. The interior, unroofed courtyard was the center of activity, as all rooms opened into it. Given the better light and open space, it would be the logical place to perform many household chores, particularly when it was hot, since the roof was not the most comfortable place to work.

Windows. To provide protection from the heat, cold, and intruders, buildings were constructed with as few outside windows and doors as possible. Windows were usually just holes in the wall, small and very high up. They let some light in and smoke out. Sometimes they were big enough to crawl through: e.g., Michal let her husband David out through a window when he had to flee from King Saul (I Sam 19:12). Queen Jezebel was looking out of a window when Jehu arrived in Jezreel (II Kgs 9:30–33), and he ordered her servants to throw her out of it. Clear glass did not appear until Roman times, and the only protection over the window, if any, would have been some form of latticework. As windows also functioned as chimneys, they were probably blackened from soot.

Doors. Doorways were small, and where doors were utilized (usually in the cities) they were made of wood. As hinges had not yet been invented, doors were fixed to a wooden pole on one long side. The pole was tipped with stone on the lower end and it rotated on a hollow stone below the threshold. The upper end of the pole was held between the beams of the lintel. There is evidence that houses were locked in some way in biblical times (Song 5:5; Neh 3:3), but nowhere in the Land of Israel have keys or locks of this earlier period been found. On the other hand, there are numerous examples from the Hellenistic and Roman periods. A very simple lock existed in ancient Greece: a wooden bar set behind the door, which slid into a hole in the doorpost. A more elaborate arrangement involved the bar being pulled across by a strap from the outside; the door could be opened by a key that passed through a hole in the door and lifted the pegs that held the bar in place. By Roman times, the locks were more complicated: an iron bolt was forced through the end link of a chain and secured by pins which fitted into perforations in the bolt. They were kept down by means of a spring. The bolt was released by a key with teeth corresponding to the perforations.

In every doorway of a Jewish home would be found a small tubular wooden or metal box called a *mezuzah*, fixed to the doorpost. Inside the *mezuzah* was a parchment, handwritten by specially trained scribes, bearing the words of Deuteronomy 6:4–9.

Floors. Floors were usually hardpacked brushed earth or clay, although the wealthier homes and palaces used limestone slabs for flooring, which was easy to care for and keep clean. In the later periods mosaic floors could be found. The floor of the upper storey would be stone, which spanned beams that rested on the first-floor walls.

Walls. Interior walls were usually stark with little decoration. By the Roman period, plastered walls could be found in homes, with frescoes painted on those of the wealthy. Small niches were cut into the interior walls, about 4–5 ft (1.5 m) high for oil lamps. Walls were often made of mud brick which took considerable upkeep, especially just before and after the rain season.

Heating. Heating in the winter, and cooking year-round, were done by fire, using natural combustible fuel, i.e., sticks, dried grass, straw (Matt 6:30), dried animal manure (Ezek 4:15), briars (II Sam 23:7; Is 10:17), or charcoal (John 18:18, 21:9). The fire was built in the open in a shallow pit or earthenware container, usually in the courtyard, creating a great deal of smoke in the house. The fire was kindled by flint or friction. One of the most important fuels was the wood of the white broom plant, because its embers stay hot for a long time, and seemingly cold ashes can be fanned into a flame quite easily. Heating was most important in the hilly regions, where winters are cold and damp, with occasional snowfall.

Lighting. As doors and windows were small and let in very little light, artificial light was necessary. In the dark corners of the house during the day, and everywhere at night, oil lamps would have provided dim light.

The earliest lamp was probably a piece of broken pottery jar filled with oil and containing a wick. The first simple lamps, made for this purpose, came in the form of a small clay bowl in which oil was burned. This was the most common form of domestic lighting from very early times. As olive oil was plentiful, this was the fuel normally used in lamps (Ex 27:20; Lev 24:2), and the wick was usually made of flax (Is 42:3). A great variety of oil was used during the Roman/New Testament period, e.g., oils extracted from sesame seeds, nuts, horseradish, and vegetable resins; and naphta, an inflammable oil obtained by dry distillation of coal, shale, etc.

To ensure that the rather dim lighting from the oil lamp illuminated as large an area as possible, it was placed in a niche in the wall about 4–5 ft (1.5 m) above the floor, which reflected some of the light and also protected the lamp from being accidentally knocked over. Lamps had to be refilled often. Jesus' parable of the ten virgins used their filling of their lamps as an illustration of preparedness (Matt 25:1–13).

Street lighting was minimal, with torches or oil lamps being found only at the city gates and at main intersections in the cities. Therefore it was important to carry a lamp at night to find one's way.

Clay lamps are among the most common pottery vessels found in excavations, both in dwellings and in tombs. During different periods, distinct shapes were developed for common use, which is an aid in dating excavation levels. The earliest identifiable lamps are those of the Early Bronze Age. These take the form of simple round bowls. By the Middle Bronze Age I, the rims were pinched together on four sides to form four spouts into which wicks were inserted. These were replaced by bowls with a slightly inward curving rim and only one spout. The basic design remained relatively unchanged into the Iron Age, when lamps had a broad flat rim with a pronounced wick spout and a flat base that gradually developed into a high stand, which was sometimes attached to the lamp. In the Persian period (586-332 BC), lamps on high stands disappeared, and there was a return to the Iron Age style of low lamps with broad rims. During this period, bronze lamps, similar in shape to their clay prototypes, made their first appearance. From the Hellenistic period onwards, particularly in the Roman/New Testament period, it was the bronze lamps that ultimately influenced the design of the clay vessels.

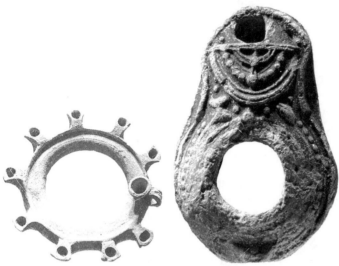

Left: Lamp with ten wicks from the Herodian period.
Right: Lamp from the Roman period.

In the 5th century BC, as closer contact with the western world was established, Greek lamps began to appear. Greek potters had succeeded in producing a closed lamp with a small opening for adding oil, thus preventing the oil from spilling. It was round with a nozzle that was produced separately and attached to the body. Handles were used on these lamps, which made them easier to carry from place to place. The clay of the Greek lamp was of higher quality than locally made lamps, and had a lustrous black glaze. The clay lamps were usually made on the potter's wheel, to get the round shape. However, in the early Hellenistic period, the mold made its debut. This speeded up production and provided a means to produce decoration on the surface of the lamps.

Furniture. Well-preserved wooden furniture found in the wealthy Middle Bronze Age tombs of Jericho shows that the design and construction of furniture has changed little down through the millennia. Their construction showed the skill of the carpenter, with accurately cut mortised and mitered joints.

The furniture of the average home in the biblical period was quite austere, consisting of a bed, table, and chairs. For example, when Elijah went to stay in the house of the Shunammite woman, she provided him with a table, chair, bed, and lamp in her upper room (II Kgs 4:10). Even into the Roman/New Testament period, austerity remained the norm. Again, furniture consisted of beds, dining couches in the richer homes, tables and chairs of wood in the poorer homes and of marble or bronze in the richer.

Beds. Most people slept on the floor or on a mud brick bench, using a mat, made of animal skins or reeds, or their garments both as a mattress and a blanket (I Sam 28:23). Only the upper classes could afford real beds. Many beds have been found in Egypt, consisting of four metal legs attached to a flat wooden surface on which a sheet of linen was spread. They were piled high with cushions and sometimes steps were needed to mount them. In Israel, beds were used by kings and wealthy people (I Sam 19:15-16; II Sam 4:7), and could also be utilized as a dining couch. The prophet Amos in the 8th century BC criticized the idle rich, "who lie on beds of ivory, stretch out on your couches" (Amos 6:4). Jesus told an invalid, "Rise, take up your bed, and walk" (John 5:8), which probably referred to a simple mat. On the other hand, in Mark 4:21, Jesus asks, "Is a lamp brought to be put under a basket or under a bed?" indicating the prevalence of beds on legs.

Tables. Although tables were a normal item of furniture, dining tables were found only in the homes of the rich. Normally, Israelites would sit on an animal skin, wooden board, or a cloth or straw mat on the floor. If they were eating, it was from a common tray or platter, around which the family and guests sat or reclined. Some scholars believe that the table mentioned in the Bible was not a table as we know it but some kind of plate which served both as a table and as a dish for food, which may or may not have had legs.

The New Testament use of the word table (*trapeza*) literally means an object with four feet. In the story of the rich man and Lazarus, Jesus speaks of crumbs falling from the rich man's table, suggesting a table with legs (Luke 16:21). In wealthier homes, one custom borrowed from the Romans was to recline around the outer side of a three-sided table or triclinium (shaped like three sides of a square) on which the food was served from the interior. It was probably at a triclinium that Jesus ate the Last Supper with his disciples.

Chairs. Three types of seating have been found in the Near East. The simplest was a stool without back supports, which was used to sit on or rest one's legs on (Ps 110:1) while sitting on a higher stool (Lam 2:1). To this class belongs a similar folding stool. Both originated in Syria and spread into Egypt. Some stools had holes bored into the frame so that woven cords could be threaded across the top to make a surface like the

diseases, as well as for purely ritualistic purposes; the washing of clothes should they be found infested with mildew (Lev 13:47-59) or the rebuilding of walls and houses if so infested (Lev. 14:33-57).

Bathing. Washing, bathing, and immersion were primarily a means of ritual purification (Lev 14:18, John 1:28). Various degrees of ritual impurity were removed by bathing in water, which involved immersion of the entire body. It later developed into a special ceremonial bath, called a *mikve*. All Israelites were required to perform this ritual bath when they had become impure, e.g., when a person had eaten carrion (Lev 17:15-16) or had come into contact with a corpse (Num 19:19), or had touched a menstruating woman.

Bathing for purely non-ritualistic reasons was not very common due to the primitive conditions of life in the biblical period. However, when it was done, it would have taken place in a natural source of water, such as a river (Ex 2:5; II Kgs 5:9-14). Bathing for pleasure was probably limited to special occasions, such as when Ruth washed herself before dressing for her meeting with Boaz (Ruth 3:3), or when an individual was particularly dirty (implied in Is 4:4; Prov 30:12). It is recorded that David bathed himself at the end of a period of mourning (II Sam 12:20). However, there is no biblical or extra-biblical evidence for regular bathing. Nevertheless, weekly bathing of at least the hands, face and feet in anticipation of the onset of the Sabbath is confirmed in the later Rabbinic period (Babylonian

Clay models of furniture of the Israelite period from Lachish.

modern cane-bottom stool. The second type was a chair with a back support, sometimes provided with a footstool. This category included folding chairs with back supports. Chairs of the third type have support for the back and arm rests on the sides. These chairs had elaborate decoration and were used by kings and princes.

THE INDIVIDUAL

Personal Hygiene. References to hygiene, cleanliness, and bathing in the writings or pictorial remains of the ancient world are not readily found. Nevertheless, it was a part of daily life and we know from reading the laws in the Pentateuch that sanitation and hygiene were important in the life of the Israelite. There were regulations for bathing for a variety of hygienic and ritual reasons including the touching of carrion, a corpse, or dung, uncleanness due to childbirth, menstruation, sexual relations, skin infections, or other

Figurine of a woman bathing, found in the Phoenician cemetery at Achzib.

Talmud, Tractate Sabbath 25b), as well as the washing of one's hands every morning and evening and before prayer (Babylonian Talmud, Tractate Sabbath, 109a).

The washing of the hands was a practice common to all ancient peoples, and it was customary to wash the hands on rising in the morning, before meals, and after meals. In the New Testament, we read that "the Pharisees, and all the Jews, do not eat unless they wash their hands" (Mark 7:3).

The average dwelling rarely had bathing facilities, and only in the richer houses could a special chamber with a tub, or even the use of a tub, be found. A 7th-century BC figurine of a woman bathing was found in Achziv. Presumably an attendant poured a small quantity of water over her, thus conserving water. Bathsheba may have bathed in such a tub (I Sam 11:2).

Bronze mirror in a wooden case found in a cave in the Judean Desert; Roman period.

Various vegetal and mineral substances were added to the bathwater in antiquity. Solid bar soap did not exist until the Middle Ages in Europe. Jeremiah (2:22) speaks of washing with niter and vegetable alkali, both containing potassium, which dissolved dirt. However, it also irritated the skin, which may account for one of the reasons the body was rubbed with oils or perfumed oil, if available, after the bath (II Sam 12:20; Ruth 3:3; Ezek 16:9). This was also done as protection for the skin against the hot, dry climate, and as a deodorant against body odors. The Romans were particularly known for this practice, even perfuming the soles of their feet. The use of perfumes was not only associated with a bath, but also as a deodorant when a bath was not possible.

Oiling the body was considered a necessity and not a luxury, and this was done by a majority of the population. One of the gestures of hospitality in the New Testament home was to anoint the visitor with oil,

along with washing his feet, giving him a cup of cold water, and/or burning incense in the home to freshen the air. The wealthy used unguents and creams composed on a base of vegetable oils, such as olive oil, almond oil, sesame oil, or of the fat of geese, sheep, goats, or cattle. Added to these were minerals, salts, milk, and/or honey. Fragrant resins or aromatic flowers were added to give them a sweet scent. The common man used oils of inferior quality, like castor oil. So customary was anointing oneself with oil, that it was a sign of mourning to refrain from it: "...be a mourner, and put on mourning apparel; do not anoint yourself with oil" (II Sam 14:2). Anointing with oil was also part of religious practice, including the anointing of kings by a prophet or priest; "Then Zadok the priest took a horn of oil from the tabernacle and anointed Solomon" (I Kgs 1:39).

As it was hard work to collect water and store it in jars in the home, water was primarily used for cooking, drinking, and only limited bathing, e.g., the Jewish custom was to wash the hands before meals, and visitors arriving after a long journey were furnished with water to bathe their feet. Abraham observed this custom when the three angels came to visit him: "Let a little water be brought and wash your feet" (Gen 18:4), as did Lot (Gen 19:2). Numerous clay basins for this purpose have been found in dwellings, particularly those of the Iron Age. The oval bowl had perpendicular sides several inches high with a raised foot pad in its middle. When a person entered the home, water was poured over his feet and collected in the basin.

As nothing was ever wasted, water from wash basins was probably poured onto the floor, if it were stone or mosaic, and swept away to cleanse it of dust and dirt. In Byzantine homes with mosaic floors, shallow, bowl-like depressions were found in the floors in the corners of rooms to collect the water and dirt when the floors were washed.

Public baths were not built until the late Hellenistic and Roman periods. The earliest public baths were only built in the New Testament period by Herod the Great at two of his fortress palaces, Masada and Herodium, which were constructed on the regular Roman plan. The public bath eventually became a social institution, and baths built in the Roman plan have been found throughout Palestine, even in regions where water was precious, such as Mampsis and Avdat. It was customary to go to the public bath in the morning before the main meal at midday.

In the Bible, there are miracles associated with bathing. Naaman was instructed to bathe seven times in the Jordan as a symbol of his purification from leprosy (II Kgs 5:9-14), and Jesus told the blind man to bathe in the Pool of Siloam, where his sight was restored (John 9:11). Throughout the Bible, washing the body, when used as a metaphor, is symbolic of spiritual cleansing from sin, which every person is said to

The floor of the caldarium in the bathhouse at Masada.

require. For example, David, in a psalm which is related to the affair he had with Bathsheba and the subsequent murder of her husband, says to God, "Purge me with hyssop, and I shall be clean; wash me, and I shall be whiter than snow" (Ps 51:7). When Jesus washed the feet of his disciples at the Last Supper, he used it as a spiritual illustration of forgiveness, saying, "If I do not wash you, you have no part with me" (John 13:8).

The Roman Bath

The Roman bath was constructed on the following plan: 1) the apodyterium, a room in which discarded clothes were kept in built-in cupboards; 2) a frigidarium, a cold bath in which the bather was expected to cleanse himself before passing into the other parts of the bath, and which took the form of a pool or basin with benches to sit on; 3) the tepidarium, a tepid bath, usually in the form of a shallow pool faced with water-resistant plaster where the bather would warm himself before proceeding; 4) the caldarium, a hot bath, which sometimes consisted of more than one room, one which contained tubs for bathing built of bricks and faced with plaster or marble, and another which was a steam-bath. The caldarium was heated by a hypocaust, which consisted of a furnace built of bricks outside the house. The heat was conveyed to the rooms via a brick tunnel or clay pipes.

COSMETICS AND MAKE-UP

Cosmetics originated in the ancient East and spread westward, first to Greece and afterwards to Rome. In the ancient world perfumes, oils, and ointments were widely used in association with bathing and skin care (See above: Industry — Perfumers), as was make-up for therapeutic purposes and ornamentation. During the First Temple period, make-up was used, but apparently less so than in the Second Temple period, where there is widespread evidence of facial care and use of make-up. Until the advent of Christianity, cosmetics were widely used, at times to excess. The Christian emphasis on the life of the spirit, rejecting the pleasures of the body, caused a decline in the demand for cosmetics and perfumes.

The toiletries of the wealthy household in biblical times would have included perfume, ointments and creams, and fragrant oils in containers with lids. Women also had polished bronze mirrors, eye-paint ingredients and implements, spoons, a curling rod and metal coils; an ivory, bone, or wooden comb; assorted hair pins of ivory, bone, wood, or metal; and tweezers (in the Roman period). Henna oil was used to dye nails and to darken hair. In the common home, little of this could be afforded, yet most women would have eye-paint accessories and a wooden comb and mirror, perhaps some scented oil, and certainly a desire to obtain more accessories as they could be afforded.

Little is known of the use of make-up among Israelite women, as compared with Egyptian women, due to the lack of pictorial representation or statuary left behind. Nevertheless, implements used in the production of make-up and accessories for its application have been found which give an idea of the practice. The objects found were the ever popular stone cosmetic palettes for mixing make-up, common in the First Temple period, and a luxury ivory kohl spoon found in Hazor from the 8th century BC, both used in the preparation of the black and green eyeliner called kohl used by women of the ancient world. The eyeliner was applied with a "kohl stick," which was a small pointed implement, like a toothpick, often made of bronze or ivory, and thickened at one end.

The use of kohl eyeliner first began in Egypt about 4,000 BC, for medical purposes as protection against eye diseases. The eye-paint repelled the little flies that transmitted eye inflammations, prevented the delicate skin around the eyes from drying, and sheltered the eyes from the glare of the desert sun. When Egyptian women realized that kohl also made their eyes look larger, the use of eyeliner became a beauty-enhancing practice.

In the Bible, the use of kohl eyeliner is mentioned three times, always with disapprobation, and mostly in imagery associated with prostitutes. When Jezebel, the wife of Ahab, heard of the arrival of Jehu, "she painted her eyes" (II Kgs 9:30). Jeremiah, comparing Jerusalem to a harlot embellishing herself, uses the expression, "you enlarge your eyes with paint" (Jer 4:30), and Ezekiel uses a similar figure of speech (Ezek 23:40). In contrast, Job named one of his daughters "Keren Happukh," or "horn of eye-paint" (Job 42:14). Nevertheless, eye make-up was used for both therapeutic purposes and embellishment. Rabbi Shema ben Elazar recommended: "If for healing, to kohl one eye, and if for ornament, to kohl both" (Tosefta Shabbath, 8:33). However, as applying make-up was considered work, it was forbidden on the Sabbath.

Applying rouge to the cheeks is also mentioned in rabbinic sources. It was customary to put light red or mauve make-up on the cheeks, and it is possible that a white powder was used as well. Tattoos were forbidden by Jewish law (Lev 19:28), so make-up, clothing, hairdos, and jewelry were all that was permitted.

Hairstyles. Great importance was attached to the care of the hair in the biblical period. Long hair was a mark of beauty, and kings, noblemen, and the wealthy grew their hair long and kept it well-groomed. However, ordinary people and slaves usually kept their hair short, mainly for hygienic reasons, since they could not afford to invest in the kind of care that long hair required.

Again, due to the lack of pictorial artifacts or statuary, it is difficult to determine how the biblical characters wore their hair. Figurines of fertility goddesses found in the region show them with hair arranged in an elaborate style, which was apparently the style of the wealthier women. The Lachish reliefs of King Sennacherib of Assyria show the Israelite inhabitants being led away into exile. It appears that the women generally grew their hair long and let it fall down to their shoulders, but some wore it gathered, or in braids. Isaiah describes the hairstyles of the women of Jerusalem as "well-set hair" (Is 3:24), meaning hair gathered and rolled into a knot at the back of the head, or a rolled up braid held by a pin. A description of a beautiful woman with long hair is given in the Song of Songs: "You are fair, my love... your hair is like a flock of goats, coming down from Mount Gilead" (Song 4:1).

Hair was also important for male beauty: "His locks are wavy and black as a raven" (Song 5:11); Samson wore his hair in "seven locks" (Judg 16:13). In Israel, a long and well-groomed beard was distinctive: "It is like the precious oil upon the head, running down on the beard, on the beard of Aaron, running down on the edge of his garments" (Ps 133:2). Unlike the Egyptians, who shaved off their hair and wore wigs, the custom of shaving the beard and the hair of the head was not practiced by the Israelites.

Egyptian priests shaved their bodies every three days. In contrast, Israelite priests were forbidden to shave the hair of their heads and the edges of their

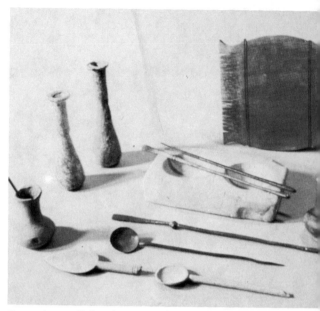

Cosmetic utensils found in one of the rooms at Masada, including a kohl jar and stick, a comb, make-up bowls and other accessories; Roman period.

beards (Lev 21:5), and all Israelites were forbidden to cut their hair to an equal length, in a round shape, and also to shave the edges of their beards (Lev 19:27). In Israel, a shaved head was a sign of disgrace (II Sam 10:4), and mourning (Jer 41:5). In rabbinical times, the custom of cutting hair and shaving as a sign of mourning was prohibited.

In the later Hellenistic period much attention was devoted to hair care among men and women. Women wore their hair long, sometimes to the ground. It was not allowed to flow free, but was braided and wound around the head, or gathered and fastened with ribbons, nets, clips or pins. It was often scented with perfume. Wealthy women had their own hairdressers. Because these hairstyles were intricate, it was forbidden to unravel or arrange them on the Sabbath, as this was considered work. Men, too, took regular care of their hair. The higher a man's standing in the community, the more often he visited the barber. The Talmud sets fixed times for hairdressing: the king will cut his hair every day, the High Priest every Sabbath eve, ordinary priests once every 30 days (Babylonian Talmud, Sanhedrin, 22b). Josephus had a rather low opinion of men who sprinkled gold dust in their hair. It can be assumed that women of means followed this practice as well.

Hair Treatment. Hair treatment included washing, combing, dyeing, and oiling. The practice of oiling the hair is also mentioned in the New Testament when it tells of a woman anointing the head of Jesus with oil: "A woman came up to him having an alabaster flask of very costly fragrant oil, and she poured it on his head" (Matt 26:7). Jesus advised that when fasting, "anoint your head and wash your face, so that you do not appear to men to be fasting" (Matt 6:17).

Washing and combing regularly was for cosmetic purposes and a way of getting rid of lice, which certainly bothered most of the population. Microscopic examination of ancient combs found in archaeological sites in Israel reveal lice and louse eggs. Curlers of two types were used, one a curling rod that curled the hair, and the other a metal coil used as a curl-like ornament. Razors were used for limited shaving, and later in the Roman/New Testament period, scissors and tweezers were introduced.

Hand mirrors of polished copper or bronze, with handles of alabaster, wood, ivory, bone, or faience, were an absolute must. They were not highly reflective as the mirrors we have today, and grew dull with tarnish. Paul makes reference to this when discussing man's ability to see spiritual things clearly in this world: "Now we see in a mirror dimly" (I Cor 13:12). Nevertheless, mirrors were an essential household item. Mirrors were found from the time of the Bar Kokhba revolt (AD 133) in the Cave of Letters in the Judean Desert.

Gray hair was considered a sign of old age and honor (Prov 20:29), although not all relished it. Plucking out white hairs and dyeing the hair were common practices. Josephus relates that when King Herod grew old and wanted to hide his age, he started dyeing his hair black (Ant. 16:233). Even the dyeing of beards was known among the Jews. Wigs and hair pieces made

A woman having her hair dressed while she looks in a mirror held by an attendant, Roman period.

from both human and animal hair were available.

Dental Hygiene. There is no indication of the brushing of teeth. Honey, figs, dates, and other sweets caused tooth decay in the biblical period. Cavities and false teeth were frequent, and dentists were busy trying to cure toothaches. Garlic and pellitory root were used to relieve pain. Salt and yeast were rubbed into the gums to fight aches of both the teeth and gums. False teeth were fashioned out of wood, gold or silver, the latter two only affordable to the wealthy.

Laundering. There is no evidence as to the frequency with which clothes were washed. The Greeks are said to have washed their clothes only twice a year. From Talmudic sources, it is known that the Israelites would have washed their clothes at least before festivals and entering the temple area. Certainly, with the injunction to wash one's clothes should they be infested with mildew (Lev 13:47-59), it is likely that they washed clothes at other times when they became dirty. Washing of clothes would have taken place in a stream, or a basin if running water was unavailable. The clothes would be dried by laying them on the ground, or hanging them over a bush, on a tree, or a peg. Isaiah indicates the existence of professional fullers (Is 7:3); however, most people washed their own clothes, using lye as a detergent (Mal 3:2). It is also likely that the clothes were simply worn into a lake or stream, accomplishing the washing of both the clothes and the body at the same time.

Waste Disposal. With the exception of a lavatory found in the City of David excavations in Jerusalem, there is no evidence for the existence of an indoor toilet in biblical homes. There was likely a corner in the courtyard away from food and food storage, where a chamber pot was located, which was dumped frequently outside the home. In excavations, there are often found small rooms on either side of courtyards that may have been used for this purpose. The tendency to relieve onself in a concealed area is reflected in the story of the death of Eglon, king of Moab, at the hands of Ehud, in Judges 3:24-25).

HEALTH AND MEDICINE

Israelites were promised health if they obeyed God (Ex 15:26; Deut 28:60-61). In the pagan world, the cause of disease was looked upon as the work of evil spirits, and doctors were called upon to counteract this. However, medical practice in other lands was not just magic; there were developments in surgery, such as brain and eye surgery and extraction of teeth in Egypt and in Mesopotamia. This belief that evil spirits caused illness may have rubbed off on the Israelites. Nevertheless, we do find in scripture some medical practices, such as Hezekiah making a poultice to treat his boil (II Kgs 20:7) and the use of a crutch (Ex 21:9). Isaiah knew that Judah's condition needed cleansing, bandaging, and ointment (Is 1:6); wine mixed with myrrh was used as a painkiller (Matt 27:34); and midwifery was practiced throughout the Bible (Ex 1:15; Est 16:4). Ecclesiastes indicated that God gives gifts of healing to men, and Luke was called the beloved physician (Col 4:14).

Many diseases are mentioned in the Bible, including leprosy, diseases of diet and pollution (dysentery, cholera, typhoid, parasites), blindness, deafness, and crippling diseases.

All throughout scripture, doctors were not looked on too favorably (Mark 5:26; Luke 4:23). In the Second Temple period, they were classed with the lowest of professions, as many were actually charlatans or magicians. If a person wanted to avoid a doctor altogether, he could go to a pharmacist or apothecary, where he could get herbal medications.

CLOTHING

Very few fragments of actual clothing exist from the biblical period, so one has to rely on written descriptions, pictorial examples from wall paintings, reliefs, and statues to determine how the ancient Israelites may have covered themselves. Clothing was simple and functional, and without a great deal of variety. The basic style of dress for both men and women was a tunic which went from the neck to the knee or ankle. The tunic style was easy to produce, and kept one warm in winter and cool in summer.

Because all clothing had to be hand-made and was not easy to come by, it was a valuable commodity and worn by most until threadbare. The poor usually had one garment, while the rich had a larger wardrobe. What distinguished the clothing of the rich from that of the poor was quality of weave, embroidery, and color. Clothing was usually made of linen, wool, or leather. The very poor, or those in mourning, wore sackcloth. The very rich had clothing of silk or cotton, adorned with rich embroidery, jewelry, and ornamentation.

The oldest pictorial example of clothing is found on Egyptian tomb paintings (c.1900 BC) of travelers from the east, showing men and women in long tunics, of knee-length for the men and reaching the ankle for the women. Some men and one child wear kilt-like skirts from the waist to the knee. Some garments are white or off-white, and others are of brightly colored stripes, reminiscent of Joseph's coat (Gen 37:3).

In New Testament times men still wore tunics. Familiar passages show John the Baptist telling people who had two tunics to give one to someone who had none (Luke 3:11), and Jesus telling his twelve apostles to take only one tunic with them when they went out (Luke 9:3). The everyday dress of the common man was the "inner garment," a short tunic made of two panels, front and back, that were sewn together with holes for the head and arms. Occasionally, it was woven as one piece without seams for the shoulders, making it a treasured garment. At the crucifixion of Jesus, the soldiers "took his garments and made four parts, to each soldier a part, and also the tunic. Now the tunic was without seam, woven from the top in one piece. They said therefore among themselves, 'Let us not tear it, but cast lots for it, whose it shall be'" (John 19:23–24).

A belt, or girdle, was essential to keep the tunic from billowing. "Girding up the loins" meant pulling the skirt from back to front between the legs and tucking it into the belt in front which made heavy work or strenuous activity possible. A full-length tunic with sleeves was also worn without a belt, and was usually limited to indoors or familiar outdoor surroundings. Over the inner garment an outer tunic with full sleeves was worn, which could be a plain cloak that doubled as a blanket at night, or a highly decorated robe reflecting the wearer's status. This was the garment brought to the returning prodigal by his father (Luke 15:22). Jesus warned of the dangers of caring for fancy outer garments while neglecting inner qualities (Mark 12:38–40). A person with financial difficulties could surrender his cloak as collateral on a loan, but it had to be returned to him by nightfall (Ex 22:25–27).

Egyptian tomb painting showing travelers wearing tunics: ankle-length for the women, knee-length for the men. The garments are all white or in bright colored stripes.

For special occasions or in inclement weather, a mantle would be worn as a top layer under one arm and over the opposite shoulder. Such a garment was often worn by scribes, although it could not be worn to do manual tasks.

Head coverings were important to both men and women. Women usually wore scarves over their heads which could be pulled up over their faces, for modesty and protection against the elements. The head covering worn by most men was a long strip of cloth folded into a turban, or a square of cloth held on the head with a rope or cord.

The clothing of the Israelites was similar in style to that worn in the region, but was subject to Mosaic law, e.g., wool and linen could not be worn together (Deut 22:11), and Jewish men had to wear tassels on the four corners of their garments (Num 15:37ff.). In later periods, the Greek and Roman cultures influenced the apparel of the more Hellenized Jews.

Footwear. Soft leather shoes were worn mainly by the upper class and probably indoors. Most, however, wore open hard-sole sandals. Leather sandals found in the excavations of Masada look remarkably modern in style. Moses took off his sandals to approach the burning bush (Ex 3:5). The refusal of Ruth's kinsman to marry her and redeem her dead husband's property was symbolized by his taking off his sandal, as was the custom at that time (Ruth 4:7-8). John the Baptist considered himself too unworthy even to tie the straps on Jesus' sandals (John 1:27).

Ornaments and accessories. There are references in the Bible to girdles, or belts, which must have been needed to keep tunics from billowing when the wearer was walking or working. They could also hold a scabbard for a sword or dagger. Wealthy men also wore

Sandal found at Masada; Roman period.

signet rings on their finger (Luke 15:22) or on a string around their neck (Gen 38:18,25). Such a ring served as their "credit card" or legal signature, as it could be pressed into wax or clay as a form of credit payment, or on a legal document. Since garments had no pockets, a purse (Luke 12:32) was also carried, usually a small leather bag that could be tucked under the belt.

Isaiah's denunciation of the finery of the rich women of Jerusalem in his day gives us a description of the clothing, jewelry, and ornaments that women wore: "the jingling anklets, the scarves, and the crescents; the pendants, the bracelets, and the veils; the headdresses, the leg ornaments, and the headbands; the perfume boxes, the charms, and the rings; the nose jewels, the festal apparel, and the mantles; the outer garments, the purses, and the mirrors; the fine linen, the turbans, and the robes" (Is 3:18-23).

In the New Testament, Peter and Paul taught that too much concern with style and trends could be detrimental to one's spiritual life. While Peter did not oppose the wish of women to be fashionable, he emphasized that external appearance was not an indication of the inner, spiritual self: "Do not let your beauty be that outward adorning of arranging the hair, of wearing gold, or of putting on fine apparel; but let it be the hidden person of the heart, with the incorruptible ornament of a gentle and quiet spirit, which is very precious in the sight of God" (I Pet 3:3). Paul concurred that women should "adorn themselves in modest apparel, with propriety and moderation, not with braided hair or gold or pearls or costly clothing, but, which is proper for women professing godliness, with good works" (I Tim 2:9-10).

EDUCATION

The primary motivation for knowledge was the strong desire of the Israelites to know and follow God. It was also important to be able to read, so that this knowledge could be passed from generation to generation. There was little interest in general knowledge, and the philosophy of other nations, as it was pagan in its orientation, was also a subject to avoid. By the New Testament period, Jews did receive a more widespread education, due to the influence of Greece and Rome.

There is little evidence of formal education in early periods, as fathers passed down to their sons whatever knowledge of faith and skills they possessed. By the end of the Babylonian Exile, Ezra trained scribes to be teachers (Ezra 7:6) so that the laws of God could be explained to the people (Neh 8:2-8).

Writing. The earliest writing systems were complicated and only a skilled elite was capable of mastering them. Even when the systems were simplified, writing remained in the realm of a limited class of people.

Both the Bible and archaeology indicate that many different materials were used for writing. The earliest documents were written on stone, the inscriptions being engraved on large rocks with a hammer and chisel, a stylus (a pointed metal engraving tool), or an iron pen. Stones were also plastered with lime and the writing applied with a brush or a pen, dipped into ink (Deut 27:2-3). Stone could also be chiseled and smoothed, as with the tablets on which the Ten Commandments were written.

Tablets were common writing surfaces and clay tablets were the most frequently found. A medium-soft lump of clay was shaped into a flat tablet or a prism, on which the writing was engraved by means of a fine stylus. To preserve the document, the clay was baked by being left in the sun, or sometimes in an oven. Many such tablets have come down to us from ancient societies. Wooden tablets, sometimes coated with plaster or wax, were also used in Egypt and Israel (Ex 37:16). They were written on with a stylus or pen and ink.

Sherds of broken jars, called ostraca, with the writing mostly executed by means of ink and a fine brush, or by means of a pointed tool, were also very common.

The most common writing material in Egypt was papyrus, a tall reed found in the Nile river. Its stalks were cut lengthwise and the thin sheets glued together to produce writing paper. Writing was done with pen and ink.

Parchment, made from animal skins, mostly sheep, was also used in Palestine. The skins were tanned and cut into sheets and sewn into scrolls, if needed. Writing was with pen and ink.

Pens were made of cane, sharpened to a fine point, or

hard metal (Jer 17:1; Job 19:24). Black ink was made from soot, resin, olive oil and water. Rust was utilized for brown ink in place of soot, and a red pigment for red ink. The ink was thick, so that a scribe could readily carry it in an inkpot attached to his belt (Ezek 9:2). Water was added to produce the desired consistency. Pens, a penknife to sharpen the point, and an inkpot were kept by the scribe in an inkhorn. The most common task of the scribe was to transcribe books (Gen 5:1), legal documents (Ex 24:7; Deut 24:1-3), chronicles (I Kgs 14:19), and official letters (II Kgs 5:5).

RELIGION

There is no doubt that the strongest force that directed the everyday life of Israel was religion. It was the call of God on Abraham that started the process out of which the House of Israel, or the Jewish people, emerged. Every aspect of their lives was motivated by their faith and guidance from God. Their faith and practice became more codified under Moses, who presented them with five books, or the Torah, containing God's rules for daily life. These rules were not seen as God's demands, but as a blessing.

The Torah was a combination of affirmations and prohibitions, codified into 613 laws: 365 affirmations and 248 prohibitions. In later periods, oral traditions grew up around the laws, because circumstances dictated inquiry as to how to apply the law, and the response of learned sages of the Torah became as important to daily life as the original laws themselves.

ROLES

Husband/Father. The father was the undisputed head of the household, and respect was due him. He was responsible for overseeing religious observance for the family, for educating the children, teaching the sons a trade, administering the business, buying and selling, and negotiating the marriage of his children. He was accorded more rights over his wife than she over him, e.g., he could choose to divorce, an option not accorded the wife (Deut 24:1).

The New Testament teaches that wives are to submit to their husbands (Eph 5:22). On the other hand, it tells husbands to love their wives as Christ has loved his Church (Eph 5:25), and fathers to avoid "provoking their children to wrath" (Eph 6:4). Jesus refers to God as Abba, our equivalent of Daddy or Papa, a term indicating a close and loving relationship. The husband/father was the provider, and Timothy taught that a neglectful father was worse than a pagan (I Tim 5:8).

Wife/Mother. Girls were trained to be wives and mothers, learning from the example of their own mothers. The mother raised the children in their early

Equipment of an Egyptian scribe: rush pen, palette and water jar.

years. She held the household together by performing a wide variety of tasks. Proverbs 31:10-31 gives us an elaborate description of her duties and the honor accorded her: "Her worth is far above rubies. The heart of her husband safely trusts her... [She] willingly works with her hands... She also rises while it is yet night, and provides food for her household... She considers a field and buys it; from her profits she plants a vineyard... She perceives that her merchandise is good... She stretches out her hands to the distaff... She extends her hand to the poor... She opens her mouth with wisdom... and does not eat the bread of idleness. Her children rise up and call her blessed; her husband also, and he praises her."

Regarding the role of women in Israelite society, there is a paradox of scriptural precepts that protect the rights of women and emphasize their equality and worth, while others emphasize the strong male dominance of the society.

Some of the positive attitudes of Israelite society towards women can be seen throughout scripture. Men and women were both created in the image of God (Gen 1:26-27). Without Eve, Adam was not complete. Scripture commands one to honor and revere both mother and father (Ex 20:12, Lev 19:3). Throughout the Gospels, we see women involved with the ministry of Jesus, e.g., the four Marys and Martha, and in the Acts and Epistles, women took an active role in early Christianity, e.g., Dorcas, Lydia, etc.

Throughout Israelite history, women played key roles, from Jochebed who devised a plan to save her son Moses (Ex 2), to Miriam. There even was a female prophet, Hulda, who prophesied during the reign of Josiah (II Kgs 22:14-20).

On the other hand, Israel was definitely a patriarchal society. Under the law, only men could own property, and a daughter could only receive an inheritance if there were no sons (Num 27:8). If a man died, his wife would not inherit his estate. If a woman failed to have a child, it was assumed that her barrenness was a judgment of God (Gen 30:1-2,22). If a wife committed adultery, her husband could bring charges against her (Num 5:12), but the reverse was not the case. Likewise, if the husband chose to divorce his wife, he could do so (Deut 24:1), and again the reverse was not possible. A wife could keep a promise or vow only if her husband approved (Num ch.30). A woman's life was considered to have half the monetary value of a man's (Lev 27:1-8). However, though barred from the priesthood, women could become queens and rule the nation, e.g., Athaliah (II Kgs 8:18,26; 11:1-3,13-14,20).

The Poor. Care for the poor is a constant theme of the prophets and the New Testament (Is 61:1-2; Matt 11:5; Luke 4:18). Every third year, the tithe of produce was to be distributed to the poor (Deut 14:28-29). Every seven years, the Sabbatical year, all debts were to be canceled so all people could start afresh (Deut 15:1,4). The poor were allowed to glean the fields for food and farmers were not allowed to harvest the edges of their fields or to go over them a second time (Lev 19:9-10). Any Israelite who became a slave, presumably for debts, was to be released after six years (Deut 15:12-18). There were also laws against usury and abuse of a debtor, in order to try to prevent borrowing from being an ultimate cause of imprisonment, enslavement, and poverty (Deut 24:6,10-11).

Orphans and Widows. An orphan was any minor whose father had died, not necessarily a child who lost both parents. For this reason, widows and orphans are often mentioned in the same scripture. When a father died, the mother and children lost their means of livelihood. If the father owned property, it went to the eldest son, leaving the mother and daughters to the mercy of a benevolent son and brother. There was very little for a single woman to do to earn a living for herself alone, much less with a family. Therefore, care for widows and orphans is a theme throughout scripture, in both the Old and the New Testaments (Job 24:3,9; Ps 94:6; Is 10:2; James 2:27).

FAMILY CUSTOMS

Marriage. Marriage was seen as the norm. It was necessary to fulfill many of the commandments of God, e.g., to be fruitful and multiply (Gen 1:22,28) and also provided companionship for the couple and a secure environment for raising children. In the New Testament, celibacy is recommended for those who have that gift, in order to attend fully to the things of the Lord (I Cor 7:8-9, 32-35). But it was not the expected norm.

The marriage age was quite young. By the Second Temple period, the rabbis fixed the minimum ages at 12 for a girl and 13 for a boy.

In biblical times, marriages were arranged by the parents without consulting the children. Abraham sent his servant to choose a wife for Isaac; he drew up the contract with Rebekah's brother Laban, and she was consulted only afterwards (Gen 24:34-58). On the other hand, Samson's father was grieved that his son did not choose a wife from his own people, which indicated that some children did make their own choice (Judg 14:3). These stories also show how important it was to choose a spouse from one's own kin or group. Abraham's servant traveled 1,000 miles (1,600 km) to choose a wife for Isaac. Mixed marriages were not encouraged, and there was strict biblical teaching against marrying members of other religions, as this would dilute the faith and bring pagan practices into Israel (Ex 34:15-16; Ezra 9:1-2). When the kings of Israel married foreign women for political reasons, it usually presaged disaster, as they brought pagan influences with them (I Kgs 11:3-5).

Sons stayed with their families and brought their wives to the paternal household, and subsequent offspring into the clan. On the other hand, a daughter left her family and joined the family of her husband. To lose or gain a daughter was to lose or gain a worker. Therefore, marriage contracts were negotiated and a dowry was paid to a father for his "loss." This price depended on the wealth of the would-be husband and his family. In the case of Jacob, he worked for his future wives' father for an agreed period (Gen 29:18).

Once accepted, the groom would give presents to the bride's family. Some fathers gave their children gifts, e.g., Caleb gave his daughter a piece of land (Josh 15:18), and Pharaoh gave the city of Gezer to his daughter (I Kgs 9:16).

The couple were now engaged, or betrothed, which was a more binding legal relationship than engagement is today. This period lasted for about one year. In the early days of Israel, a betrothed man was exempt from military service so he would not be killed before he could marry (Deut 20:7). If the wedding was called off, a financial penalty was imposed on the offending party. The couple were not to have sexual relations during the betrothal.

The wedding ceremony itself was surrounded by much celebration, sometimes lasting for a week or more. The groom selected a friend to be his "best man" (Judg 14:20). At the appointed time for the marriage ceremony the bride and her party would walk in procession from her house to the groom's father's house. The procession was festive, with singing, dancing, and music along the way. The bride was usually carried on a litter, and she wore beautiful clothing and jewelry. The guests also came in special attire (Matt 22:11).

The couple was then left alone to consummate the marriage in a tent or room arranged as a bridal chamber, while the guests continued to celebrate outside until the couple emerged from their wedding chamber with the evidence of the bride's virginity and their union. They joined the festivities which continued for a week.

Sexual Conduct. Marriage was the time for sexual relations, as premarital and extramarital relations were biblically forbidden. Both adultery and fornication were forbidden by biblical law. A girl found not to be a virgin on her wedding night was liable to be stoned to death for disgracing her father's house (Deut 22:20-21). Likewise, in the cases of a man found to be sleeping with another man's wife, or with a woman in a city who is betrothed to be married, both the man and the woman were stoned to death.

The biblical code is also full of regulations about unnatural sexual acts practiced by the pagan world and deemed ungodly and defiling for the Israelite (Lev 18). In the New Testament, there are many verses on the Church's view of sexual conduct (I Cor 5:1-2; 6:12-20; Gal 5:19; Eph 5:3; Col 3:5, etc.), including within mar-

riage (I Cor 7:3-7). Since the sexual standards of the non-Jewish, non-Christian world were very low, and Christianity attracted many social outcasts and prostitutes, the rules of sexual conduct needed to be clearly understood.

Polygamy and concubines. Genesis makes it clear that God's intention is for each person to have only one partner in life (Gen 1:28; 2:18,24). Nevertheless, polygamy did find acceptance among the early patriarchs through the period of David and Solomon. It was mostly the kings of Israel who were engaged in polygamy in an effort to reinforce their thrones with political marriages and large families. For the most part, biblical society seems to have been basically monogamous, partly because more than one wife was an economic burden.

Where it was required for a man to marry his brother's widow to continue the blood line and afford protection for the widow, no mention is made of the man's marital status, only that he should marry his brother's widow (Deut 25:5-10). This is also the motivation in an ancient custom which allowed a wife, if she was barren, to choose a surrogate so that the family line could continue. This was the case when Sarah chose Hagar to be the mother of Abraham's first child (Gen 16:1-4).

Jealousy could not help entering the family (Gen 16:5-6) and ultimately affect relationships adversely. Various laws are prescribed in the Bible to prevent family feuds over property between children of rival mothers (Deut 21:15-17).

The practice of polygamy was still found in the New Testament period, as King Herod the Great had many wives. Conservative leaders seemed to protest the practice, although it was continued.

Concubines are mentioned often in scripture from the patriarchal period through the kings. Jacob, Gideon, Saul, David, and Solomon all had concubines. In fact, Solomon possessed 700 wives and 300 concubines.

Divorce. Divorce was possible for Israelites, but it was available for men to initiate only; women had no right to petition for divorce. The main ground for a divorce was unfaithfulness by the wife, although the biblical injunction seems to give wide latitude: "When a man takes a wife and marries her, and it happens that she finds no favor in his eyes because he has found some uncleanness in her..." (Deut 24:1). A man who falsely accused his wife of not being a virgin when he married her was fined 100 shekels of silver by the elders and not allowed to divorce her (Deut 22:13-19). Nor could a man divorce a woman he had had to marry after raping her (Deut 22:28-29). Where divorce was permitted, a writ of divorce was written and the woman was put out of the man's house without rights (Deut 24:1-4).

In the New Testament, Jesus stresses God's original intention for strict monogamy, but does allow divorce for unfaithfulness (Matt 19:3-12). Jesus' teaching on divorce was designed to protect the woman from being put out of her home, without legal rights (Matt 5:27-32; Mark 10:2-12; Luke 16:18). In I Corinthians 7:11, Paul teaches that a man should not divorce his wife, nor should a man or woman divorce an unbelieving spouse. It seems that divorce was fairly rare among the Israelites, since the ties to the extended family were very close, which provided emotional support and encouragement.

BIRTH

The Jewish community was family-oriented, and births were cause for celebration. A new birth was looked upon with hope, anticipation, and happiness in an era when delivery complications were usually fatal. Children were considered a blessing (Ps 127:3-5), and an opportunity for parents to "train a child in the way he should go" (Prov 22:6).

There were high motivations to have children in the ancient world, the most prominent being economic and for posterity. A large family, particularly of sons, insured one's well-being when in need of care due to age, injury, or inability to work. Without the support of a family, the future of the aged could be bleak. To die

The Nativity, depicted on a mosaic on the dome of the monastery church at Delphi; 11th century.

without children meant the annihilation of the family name and property. For this reason, the levirate practice of a widow marrying her husband's next of kin to pass on the family name became prevalent among the Israelites (Deut 25:5-6; Ruth 3:12).

Since childbirth was considered normal, childlessness was seen as a curse or judgment from God. Barren women were seen as deficient and open to ridicule (I Sam 1:1-8). God's punishment for certain acts of unlawful sexual relations was to render the person childless (Lev 20:20-21).

Birthright. The birthright went to the first-born son, and he received rights and privileges not given to the other male children, or to daughters. His inheritance was also double what each of the others received. The eldest son was expected to carry on the family business and be the administrator for the family and property.

There is no direct mention of birthright in the New Testament except in Hebrews 12:16, and this is in connection with an Old Testament passage. However, the parallel concept of the first-born is mentioned, in reference to Jesus being the literal first-born of Mary (Matt 1:25; Luke 2:7), and on a spiritual level, of the supremacy of Messiah (Col 1:15; 11:18). In the story of the prodigal son, the insult felt by the elder brother when his younger brother was doubly blessed, can be traced to the concept of birthright privileges (Luke 15:11-32).

Natural childbirth was the only type of delivery in ancient times, and pain in labor was seen as a consequence of sin in the Garden of Eden (Gen 3:16). It is not known if there were efforts to reduce this pain, but certain sedative potions did exist. Jesus noted that women soon forgot the pain once their child was safely born (John 16:21). If there were any complications or difficulty in delivery for the mother or baby, death or birth defects would surely result. For this reason, there was a relatively high mortality rate. There were restrictions on children born with deformities from joining the priesthood (Lev 21:16-23).

Doctors were not used for delivery, but midwives occasionally were. The Bible mentions midwives in several instances, e.g., Rachel was told by the midwife that she was the mother of another son just before she died (Gen 35:17); when Tamar gave birth to twins, a midwife was in attendance (Gen 38:28). Pharaoh told two midwives, Shiphrah and Puah, to kill the first-born male babies of the Israelites, which they did not do (Ex 1:15-21).

Women gave birth in a sitting or squatting position, not lying down. The birthstool may have been little more than two stones on which the woman could sit (Ex 1:16).

When the baby was born, there were four important acts done to ensure a healthy start (Ezek. 16:4): (1) The umbilical cord was tied and cut; (2) The baby was washed with water; (3) It was then rubbed with salt, possibly a salt water solution; (4) Finally, the baby was wrapped in swaddling clothes. These were tightly bound strips of cloth wrapped around the body, arms, and legs like a mummy. Jesus was similarly wrapped (Luke 2:12).

After the Delivery.

Circumcision. On the eighth day after birth, boys were circumcised. This practice was also required for those in an Israelite household, e.g., servants and resident aliens, as well as those who wanted to become part of the house of Israel (Gen 17:1-14). Throughout the Old Testament, the term "uncircumcised" was used to indicate one who was cursed because he was a heathen outside God's covenant (Ezek 32:28; 44:7), and as a pejorative term, e.g., David mocking Goliath by calling him an "uncircumcised Philistine" (I Sam 17:26).

What's in a name? The naming of a child carried great importance in the Israelite household. The ancients were interested in the meaning of names, which expressed a character hoped for the child. Often parents named their children as a praise to God or a statement of faith, e.g., Isaiah, "God is salvation," or Jonathan, "God has given." By the time of the New Testament people were adding appendages to help identify a person, e.g., Joseph of Arimathea, Paul of Tarsus, Jesus of Nazareth; who was their father, e.g., Jesus bar (son of) Jonah; by their profession, e.g., Simon the Tanner; or ideology, e.g., Simon the Zealot.

Consecration of first-born. After 30 days, a first-born male was taken to the Temple in Jerusalem to be consecrated before God. This instruction was given to Moses to commemorate the saving of the first-born in Egypt by the blood of the Passover lamb. This consecration of the first-born was for all first-born male offspring, including animals, as all first-born belonged to God (Ex 13:11-16). The procedure involved presenting the child to the priest and paying five shekels to buy him back or redeem him (Num 18:16).

Purification of the mother. The new mother was considered ritually "unclean" after the birth, and was required to make an offering for her purification. The sacrifice was a yearling lamb and a pigeon or a dove. If she could not afford a lamb, then two doves or pigeons alone would suffice (Lev 12:8). Mary, the mother of Jesus, must have had little money, since she offered the two pigeons (Luke 2:24).

Growing up. In most cases, the baby was breastfed by his mother. However, if she was unable to do so, a wet nurse was hired to nourish the child, e.g., Moses (Ex 2:9). Nursing lasted for two to three years before weaning. Abraham celebrated with a feast when his son Isaac was weaned (Gen 21:8).

Discipline was part of childrearing, in an effort to help children know right from wrong (Prov 22:6,15), and the New Testament reminds fathers not to exasperate children, but rather "bring them up in the train-

The Presentation of Christ at the Temple, depicted on a stone relief at the Church of Moissac, France; 12th century.

ing and instruction of the Lord" (Eph 6:1-4). It is for the sake of the children that the Passover meal is eaten to remember and pass along the story of the Exodus to succeeding generations (Deut 6:20-25)

Education was passed on to the children by their parents, whom they were to honor and revere (Ex 20:12; Lev 19:3). Schools did not come into being until about the 2nd-3rd century BC, when the rabbis took on the role of teachers. Their teaching was religious and moral in orientation, based on the Torah and the oral law. Education started at about age six for boys; girls did not receive formal education. The children sat at the feet of their teachers and learned primarily by repetition. From the New Testament, we can see that Jesus demonstrated knowledge of the law (Luke 2:41-51) and an ability to read Hebrew, even though he was only the son of a carpenter (Luke 4:16-17).

LEISURE TIME

Games. Game boards from about 2000 BC are the oldest games found in Israel. Pieces were moved around the board, determined by the spinning of a teetotum, a type of four-sided top with letters or numbers on the sides. If a teetotum were not available, then discs could be spun, or dice or knucklebones tossed. These games originated in Mesopotamia and spread throughout the East, apparently reaching Palestine under Egyptian influence. The game board was a stone slab marked with three rows of four squares at top and bottom, and 12 squares in the center. It had 10 playing pieces made of blue faience. The teetotum was made of ivory and was pierced on four sides and numbered from one to four. This game continued to be favored for well over 1,000 years.

In excavations under the Convent of Notre Dame de Sion in Jerusalem, traces of board games popular with Roman soldiers were found on the limestone slabs of the courtyard of the Antonia Fortress. Christian tradition associates these games with the mocking of Jesus by the Roman soldiers in the courtyard of the Praetorium (Matt 27:27-31; Mark 15:16-20).

Among the ancient Israelites, no form of gambling is ever mentioned, but in the Second Temple period, a game played with dice was adopted by the Jews. Since gambling was popular among the Greeks and Romans, the rabbis strongly condemned it, and a gambler was disqualified from testifying before a court of justice.

Children's Games and Toys. One of the prophecies of the restoration of Israel to Jerusalem is that "the streets of the city shall be full of boys and girls playing" (Zech 8:5). Children sang and danced, played chase and tug-of-war, imitated adults and play-acted funerals, weddings and other ceremonies (Matt 11:16-17). There was not a plentiful variety of children's toys, but considerable numbers of rattles and whistles have been found, indicating that these were probably toys owned by most children. The pottery rattles were usually box shaped, closed on all sides, sometimes with perforations, and filled with small stones or pieces of pottery which made a noise when shaken. Others are in the shape of dolls or birds. Also found have been clay figures of animals, chariots, and household furniture and pots; small wooden pull toys on wheels; balls; dolls, some with movable parts; all presumably children's toys.

Sports. References to sports are rare in the Bible. However, other ancient peoples enjoyed wrestling, running, throwing, and archery. The servants of Joab and David arranged a wrestling or boxing match to settle a dispute, which ended in bloodshed (II Sam 2:14-16). Jonathan used a pre-arranged archery sign to signal David (I Sam 20:20). When Greek athletic games were introduced into Israel under the Seleucids, they caused concern among the Jews, because these games were associated with pagan religious festivals, they were conducted in the nude, and winners received gold and silver statuettes and a wreath of olive, pine, parsley or laurel leaves to wear as a crown of victory.
Nevertheless, Hellenized Jews participated as competitors or spectators. These games included chariot races, archery, javelin and discus throwing, wrestling and boxing.

In the New Testament, Paul used the images of an athlete's strict training and disciplined life to illustrate to Christians how they should live a disciplined Christian life. He said runners and boxers had to race and fight with purpose and not aimlessly beat the air (I Cor 9:24-27).

Music. Music was popular in the daily life of the Israelites, as well as other ancient societies in the Near East. What they played and heard ranged from a shepherd's flute in the hills of Judea, to the orchestra for worship in the Temple. Any occasion was an excuse to enjoy or be comforted by music. When Jacob left his father-in-law Laban without warning, the old man finally caught up with him and said: "Why did you flee away secretly, and steal away from me, and not tell me; for I might have sent you away with joy and songs, with timbrel and harp?" (Gen 31:27). People sang and danced at military victories (II Chr 20:27ff.); banquets, feasts and festivals (Is 5:12); there were working songs to encourage the laborers (Ps 67); songs of love, e.g., the Song of Songs; and songs of mourning (II Sam 1:17-27). Not

Left: Game board carved by Roman soldiers at the Antonia Fortress, Jerusalem; Right: Game board and playing pieces from Ur.

only were there musical instruments, but much singing in solo or in choruses (I Sam 18:6-7), and dancing, simply for pleasure, or as part of worship (II Sam 6:5,14-15).

In the New Testament, there are numerous references to music and musical instruments. Jesus compared the contrariness of the people of the day with children who called out, "we played for you and you did not dance; we sang a dirge, and you did not cry" (Luke 7:32); and Paul likened Christians without love to the hollow and empty sound of "a resounding gong or a clanging cymbal"(I Cor 13:1).

What were ancient instruments like? Some are known from excavations, while others are seen on wall paintings from Assyria and Egypt. Numerous musical instruments are mentioned in the Bible, which may indicate that music was important both in religion and in private life (Ps 150:3-6), although many of these instruments cannot be satisfactorily identified. (See II.11, Musical Instruments)

Drama. The Greeks and Romans enjoyed live entertainment, including dramatic plays and reading. These pastimes found their way to Israel, and numerous Roman amphitheaters have been uncovered in all areas of the country. Paul even quotes from some Greek plays, indicating just how familiar the people of the 1st century were with them, e.g., I Corinthians 15:33: "Bad company ruins good morals" (a phrase from Menander); and Titus 1:12: "Cretans are always liars, evil beasts, lazy gluttons" (quoted from Epimenides).

OLD AGE

People put a great deal of faith in those who had survived the years and thereby were believed to have acquired great wisdom. It was built into Israelite society to respect one's parents and elders (Ex 20:12): a society that no longer respects its elders is on its way to ruin (Is 3:4-5). Gray hair was seen as a crown of splendor (Prov 20:29; Job 15:10). Old age of course brought with it infirmities, a crooked back, lost teeth, failing eyesight, and hearing loss (Ecc 12:1-7; II Sam 19:35).

As there were no retirement homes, it was expected that the elderly would be supported by their children. This is one of the motivations for a large family and many sons; to provide protection and refuge when one is no longer able to work and care for oneself.

DEATH

Respect for the dead was of great importance to Jewish families, who nevertheless avoided the extremes of other peoples of the region, from the near worship of the dead by the Egyptians to the contempt for the body shown by the Greeks. There was no set of laws concerning the burial of a body, and many burial practices were borrowed from precedent and customs of the day, unless specifically forbidden in biblical law, e.g., some mourning practices of the Canaanites.

The only biblical references to death and burial are the indirect references about someone hung on a tree, that "his body shall not remain all night upon the tree, but you shall surely bury him the same day" (Deut 21:23), and "for dust you are, and unto dust shall you return" (Gen 3:19). Also, there were some laws concerning contact with the dead (Num 5:1-4; 19:16; Deut 21:22-23), which certainly influenced how and where a body was prepared for burial and entombed.

In Jewish belief, death did not mean annihilation. The body returned to the dust from which it was taken (Ecc 3:20), and the soul descended to Sheol (Gen 37:35), the realm of the dead where it lived an ethereal, shadowy existence (Num 16:33; Ps 6:6; Is 38:18). Not until the time of Daniel was there belief in a resurrection, of some to eternal life and others to eternal punishment (Dan 12:2). In the Second Temple period, there was a divergence of views between the sects of the Sadducees and Pharisees on the concept of resurrection.

In the New Testament, the concept of eternal life was well developed throughout the Gospels and Epistles. The basic Christian premise is that man is born in sin, and through repentance, forgiveness, and belief in the atoning death of Jesus, will spend eternity in heaven with God. Without this conscious act of faith, the alternative is an eternity in hell, separated from God. The concept of a bodily resurrection at the end of days when Jesus returns to earth, is also well developed in the New Testament (John 3:16,36; Rom 5:12; 6:23; I Cor 15:12-23).

Burial practices. The belief in an afterlife is as old as man. This is validated by the ample evidence of the care taken, from the very earliest times, for the burial of a dead person. It can be seen from the position in which he was placed in the grave, to the offerings with which he was supplied and to the marking of the site of the tomb. Burial was very important to the ancients. Not to be buried was feared by all in the ancient world, and considered a punishment (Deut 28:26; I Kgs 14:11; Jer 22:19). Most biblical accounts of a man's life end with the statement that the man died and that he was buried. Jacob and Joseph give a glimpse of how important was burial with the family to the early Jews. Jacob, who died in Egypt, requested that he be buried in the family burial cave of Machpelah (Gen 49:30; 50:5). Joseph too, on his deathbed, prophesied that his own bones were to be buried in Israel (Gen 50:25; Josh 24:32).

The general rule was to bury a person as soon as possible after death (Deut 21:22-23), although never on the Sabbath or a holy day (John 11:39; 19:31). Since the body was to return to dust, there was no need for embalming, the example of Jacob being embalmed being Egyptian custom, not Israelite. Also, laws concerning contact with a dead body (Lev 21:1; Num 5:1-4) may have discouraged the practice. Such contact made a person ceremonially unclean, requiring him to go outside the camp or community, and later requiring a ritual immersion to restore ritual purification. In the Roman/New Testament period, Jewish tombs were whitewashed as a warning to the living that the dead were there (Matt 23:27).

After the body was washed, generous amounts of spices and perfumes were used, not to preserve the body, but to allow it to decompose as easily as possible. Since visits to the tomb were customary, this would also help control odors. The spices were placed inside the linen cloth, or strips of cloth, which were wrapped around the body for burial (II Chr 16:14; John 19:39-40). A second cloth was wrapped around the head and the jaw was held closed with a strip of cloth under the chin. The preparation of the body was usually done by the family (Lev 21:1), or very close friends, if family were not available.

The account of the burial of Jesus gives a glimpse of burial practices in the Second Temple period: "After this, Joseph of Arimathea... asked Pilate that he might take away the body of Jesus, and Pilate gave him permission. So he came and took the body of Jesus. And Nicodemus... also came, bringing a mixture of myrrh and aloes, about 100 pounds. Then they took the body of Jesus, and bound it in strips of linen with the spices, as the custom of the Jews is to bury. Now in the place where he was crucified there was a garden, and in the garden a new tomb in which no one had yet been laid... On the first day of the week Mary Magdalene came to the tomb early, while it was still dark, and saw that the stone had been taken away from the tomb... Then Simon Peter... went into the tomb; and he saw the linen cloths lying there, and the handkerchief that had been around his head" (John 19:38-41; 20:1,6-7).

Coffins as we know them were uncommon. Rather, the body was wrapped in linen and allowed to decompose. The bones were later collected and placed in ossuaries, and stored in a cave in another area of the same tomb. Ossuaries were decorated boxes about 2 ft (60 cm) in length, 18 in (45 cm) wide, and a little over 1 ft (30 cm) deep.

Cremation is not specifically mentioned in the Bible. In the biblical period, it was clearly considered to be a humiliation inflicted on criminals (Josh 7:15; Is 30:33), and burning was one of the four death penalties imposed by the biblical code for a number of offenses (Lev 20:14; 21:9). It could also be associated with pagan practices.

Mourning. When a parent, close relative or even a child died, there was not only the sense of emotional loss, but potential hardship for the group that could not

be easily rectified. A woman who survived her husband was in a very difficult position. She could not inherit from her husband, but could remain in her husband's family if the next of kin would take her in marriage (Deut 25:5-6; Ruth 3:12). More often, the widow was without any financial support. The law, therefore, said that widows were to be protected and cared for (Deut 10:18; 14:29; 24:17-21).

In the early Church, money was set aside to care for widows (Acts 6:1), and Christians are instructed to care for widows and orphans, James equating this care with true religion (I Tim 5:3-4, 8-11; James 1:27).

On the death of an important personage (II Sam 3:31), when a calamity befell an individual (II Sam 12:15-16), or the whole congregation, or on hearing bad tidings (Num 14:1-6), the news was received with a loud wail and the rending of one's clothing (Gen 37:29,34; II Sam 1:11; 3:31)

Mourning normally lasted for seven days (Gen 50:10). During this period, people would bring food and drink, and come to console the mourners (II Sam 3:35; Job 2:11-12). To enhance the atmosphere of grief, professional mourners, who were almost always women, would be invited (Jer 9:17ff.).

Mourning also involved beating one's breast (Luke 23:48), walking barefoot, and covering one's head (II

Clay figurine of a mourner, from the Philistine cemetery at Azor.

What were tombs like in different periods?

The very earliest tombs to be found in the Land of Israel date to prehistory. Here, the dead person was placed on his side in a shallow pit in a contracted position, with his knees drawn up and his hands near the breast. Sometimes, funerary objects were placed near the body, and the same grave might be used over and over.

By the 4th millennium BC, new burial customs emerged which included the use of clay ossuaries containing detached bones. The ossuaries were stored in artificial caves carved out for this purpose, and were shaped like houses, believed to represent the actual dwellings of the deceased, while others were in the shape of animals.

By the Early Bronze Age, burials were either single or collective in shaft tombs. These tombs had a deep shaft, horizontal or slanting, leading into a square or oval burial chamber which was provided with a large number of pottery vessels, some containing food. These tombs were sealed with rocks or a large stone over the opening.

By the Middle Bronze Age, several types of burial took place. In some cases, tombs were in town, sometimes near to the houses. The tombs were stone and were reopened whenever a new burial took place. Where collective burial was practiced, a vertical shaft was used which opened into a chamber. The body was placed on a mat on its back, sometimes with the knees raised. Each corpse was supplied with food and toilet articles, e.g., an oil juglet, combs, and a basket with carved boxes in it. With each new burial, the previous corpse and offerings were pushed to the side, creating a pile on the sides of the chamber. The number of internments generally did not exceed 40.

The Early Bronze Age burial method was in use into the Late Bronze Age, although other cultures occupying the territory brought different burial customs. In the Negeb desert, tumuli are found, which are above-ground tombs consisting of a chamber for the body which was piled high with stones. The Philistines put the deceased into a large clay anthropoid coffin, about the size of an adult. Part of the top was removable so that the body could be inserted. The coffin was painted to look human, with the face in high relief.

In the Iron Age, with the coming of the Israelites into the Land of Israel, burial chambers of previous periods were still used with some variation. An entirely new form of burial was the catacomb, a multiple-chamber tomb cut into the rock. This had an open court from which high steps led into an underground antechamber which had a high ledge along the wall. From this ledge, openings led to additional chambers with benches along the walls on which the dead were placed. Offerings were still common, and many tombs had repositories at the back of the chambers in which the offerings were placed. Some walls had cavities instead of benches for the placement of the body. This style became very common in the Second Temple period.

The Roman-style tombs found in Israel have an open anteroom from which there was a corridor into a chamber or series of chambers where cavities are found along the walls. Family tombs were rock-cut and had an anteroom with one burial chamber containing one or more benches on which a body was laid. This is the type of tomb in which Jesus was buried. When space was needed, the bones of the previous corpse were collected and placed in decorated ossuaries made of wood, clay, metal, or stone (mostly the latter). The entrances of these tombs were blocked with a large slab of stone, but the more elaborate ones had a large rolling stone which moved in a narrow slot and could be opened mechanically.

Some very elaborate tombs from the Second Temple period found in Jerusalem have monuments, e.g., the pyramid found over the tomb of Jason. In a class all their own are the large funerary monuments in the Kidron Valley which are free-standing cubes, decorated with columns and pyramids, cut out of living rock.

In any case, because of the Mosaic prohibition against contact with a corpse, Jewish graves were located outside towns.

Sam 15:30; 19:4), putting on sackcloth (Gen 37:34; II Sam 13:19; Jer 6:26), or putting ashes on one's head, face, or clothing as a demonstration of deep humiliation before God and man (Josh 7:6; I Sam 4:12; II Sam 13:19). The mourner would abstain from washing his feet, trimming his beard, washing his clothes (II Sam

19:24) and from anointing himself with perfume or oil (II Sam 14:2). He might abstain altogether from meat and wine (Dan 10:3). Mourners would sit on the ground, in dust or ashes (Ezek 26:16), shave their heads, and cut their flesh (Jer 16:6). Some of these mourning signs, such as shaving one's head, shaving a corner of one's beard, and cutting the flesh, all of which were very common among the Canaanites, were forbidden for the Israelites (Lev 19:27–28; 21:5; Deut 14:1), but it seems that habit was stronger than law (Jer 16:6).

According to Jewish custom, in the funeral procession, the wrapped body was carried on a wooden bier, often consisting of little more than flat boards, although wealthier families had more elaborate ones. This custom is known to date back at least to the days of King David (II Sam 3:31), and was practiced into the Roman/New Testament period (Luke 7:12).

A funeral procession was anything but quiet. There

Right. Top: Part of the necropolis at Beth Shearim, with tombs and sarcophagi, from the 2nd to 4th centuries, along a tunnel dug in the soft chalk rock. Bottom: Rock-cut tomb with burial chamber; on the side is a rolling stone in a slot to close the tomb. Below: Clay ossuary from Azor, dating to the Chalcolithic period.

was a great deal of weeping and rending of clothing as the procession progressed. Mourners, both genuine and paid, gave themselves over to unbridled grief. Dirges were sung, and instruments were played. On the death of a particularly important person, special memorial laments were written in his honor (II Chr 35:25). In the New Testament period, the rabbis taught that every funeral procession should have at least two flutes and one weeping woman to mourn the dead.

In excavations from the Second Temple Period, a variety of tear cups have been found. The custom of the day was not to hold back your tears of grief and "keep a stiff upper lip," but to cry openly and to keep your tears of grief in a bottle made especially for this purpose. It was believed that it was not only grief that brought tears, but tears brought grief.

A wide range of animals, both domestic and wild, is mentioned in the Bible. Early translators were unfamiliar with the fauna of Palestine in biblical times, and therefore tended to identify animals mentioned in the Bible with species with which they were familiar. The advent of critical study of biblical texts in the 19th century created a need for scientific identification of biblical species. It became apparent that not only were translators often inaccurate in their identifications, but that the biblical text as a whole was generally vague. Animals which would today be classed as separate species were often lumped together because of outward similarities, e.g., the bat, which today is regarded as a mammal, is listed amongst the unclean birds in Leviticus and Deuteronomy (Lev 11:19; Deut 14:18). Conversely, domestic animals with which the Israelites were in daily contact often received more than one name, reflecting age, sex, and breed. There are 12 Hebrew words for sheep in the Bible. The present day identification of animals is based on the context in which the animal appears and archaeological evidence of the fauna prevalent in Israel at the time of the text's composition. The more common animals are easier to identify than those appearing rarely or only in lists. Often linguistic clues aid scholars in difficult identifications, but this is not always dependable. Although many of the animals mentioned in the Bible have been positively identified, it appears that many more will always provide difficulties to scholars.

The identification of animals marked with an asterisk is doubtful.

BIRDS

Bat. Mammal mentioned in the lists of unclean birds (Lev 11:19; Deut 14:18). Although not technically a bird, the animal's ability to fly was considered by the Israelites as a characteristic peculiar to birds. Isaiah refers to bats as dwelling in caves (Is 2:20–21).

*Bittern. Small marsh bird sometimes identified with a bird mentioned by Zephaniah as dwelling in desolate places (Zeph 2:14).

*Buzzard. Bird of prey mentioned in the lists of unclean birds (Lev 11:13; Deut 14:13).

*Cormorant. Bird of prey mentioned in the lists of unclean birds (Lev 11:17; Deut 14:16).

*Crane. Long-legged, migratory bird to which King Hezekiah compared himself (Is 38:14).

*Crow. A possible translation for the Hebrew *oreb*, another being "raven."

Dove, Turtledove, Pigeon. Migratory bird whose appearance in Israel symbolizes the start of spring (Song 2:11–12). Doves and pigeons were offered as sacrifices by the poor of Israel who could not afford a larger animal (Lev 1:14; 5:7–11). They were also used in purification rites for women after childbirth (Lev 12:6), by lepers (Lev 14:22), and by impure Nazirites (Num 6:10). Mary offered a pigeon in the Temple following the birth of Jesus (Luke 2:22–24), and the New Testament states that pigeons and doves were sold at the entrance to the Temple compound (Matt 21:12; Mark 11:15; John 2:14). Israel is compared to doves (Ps 74:19). The species mentioned in the Bible were apparently the rock and Barbary dove.

Eagle. Bird of prey mentioned in the lists of unclean birds (Lev 11:13; Deut 14:12). The eagle was noted by the biblical authors for its strength and speed. God is said to have taken Israel out of Egypt "on eagle's wings" (Ex 19:4), and to protect Israel as an eagle "broods over her young" (Deut 32:11). The enemies of Israel are compared to eagles for their swiftness in attacking Israel (Jer 4:13; 48:40). Eagles are also depicted in descriptions of God's attending creatures (Ezek 1:10; Rev 4:7). It is suggested that "eagle" is a comprehensive term denoting many different large birds of prey. The description of the eagle as bald (Mic 1:16) more accurately describes the griffin vulture.

Falcon. Bird of prey mentioned in the lists of unclean birds (Lev 11:14; Deut 14:13). The falcon's vision is noted in the Book of Job (Job 28:7).

Fowl, Chick, Hen. Domestic birds possibly referred to as a source of food. The "fatted fowl" provided for Solomon (I Kgs 4:23) and Nehemiah (Neh 5:18) could, however, refer to a type of wild fowl as well. "A hen protecting her chicks" was used as a simile denoting protection (Matt 23:37).

Hawk. Bird of prey mentioned in the lists of unclean birds (Lev 11:16; Deut 14:15).

Heron. Water bird mentioned in the lists of unclean birds (Lev 11:19; Deut 14:18).

Hoopoe. Bird of prey mentioned in the lists of unclean birds (Lev 11:19; Deut 14:18).

Jackdaw. Crow-like bird mentioned in the lists of unclean birds (Lev 11:18; Deut 14:17).

Kite. Bird of prey mentioned in the lists of unclean birds (Lev 11:14; Deut 14:13).

Martin. Another possible identification for the Hebrew *dror*, commonly translated as "swallow."

Night-hawk. Bird of prey mentioned in the lists of unclean birds (Lev 11:16; Deut 14:15).

*Osprey. Bird of prey mentioned in the lists of unclean birds (Lev 11:13; Deut 14:12).

*Ossifrage. Bird of prey mentioned in the lists of unclean birds (Lev 11:13; Deut 14:12).

Ostrich. Bird mentioned in the lists of unclean birds (Lev 11:16; Deut 14:15). The ostrich is mentioned by Job as a stupid bird who treats her chicks harshly (Job 39:13-18). In Lamentations, the bird is compared to the jackal for its cruelty (Lam 4:3).

Owl. Generic term for four birds of prey mentioned in the lists of unclean birds (Lev 11:17-18; Deut 14:15-16). Owls are associated with desolation in the Bible; Isaiah prophesies that owls will inhabit the ruins of Babylonia and Edom (Is 13:21; 34:11).

Partridge. Game bird to which David was compared when pursued by Saul (I Sam 26:20). Jeremiah's reference to a bird "that broods but does not hatch" (Jer 17:11) may be a reference to the mistaken notion that the partridge raids the nests of other birds to brood their eggs.

Rock partridge and its chicks; detail from the mosaic pavement of the 6th-century synagogue of Beth Alpha.

Peacock. Bird mentioned as being brought to Solomon's court from Tarsus every three years (I Kgs 10:22). Since the peacock is a native of India, the text shows the great extent of Solomon's trade.

*Pelican. Possible translation for a bird associated with the wilderness (Ps 102:6). The translation is based on the questionable assumption that "wilderness" refers to a swamp.

Quail. Small game bird that, on its migration from Africa in the spring, alights in exhaustion on the Mediterranean coast. Quails served as a source of meat for the Israelites in the wilderness (Ex 16:13; Num 11:31-32).

Raven. Bird mentioned in the lists of unclean birds (Lev 11:15; Deut 14:14). A raven was the first bird sent by Noah from the ark (Gen 8:7). Ravens later provided the prophet Elijah with food while he hid from Ahab (I Kgs 17:4-6). Young ravens are depicted as helpless creatures to whom God provides sustenance (Ps 147:9; Luke 12:24).

Rooster, Cock. Bird appearing only in the New Testament. Its crow is said to usher in the morning (Matt 26:75; Mark 13:35, 14:30; Luke 22:61; John 13:38).

Seagull. Sea bird mentioned in the lists of unclean birds (Lev 11:16; Deut 14:15).

Sparrow. Small bird which inhabited the Temple compound (Ps 84:3). Jesus regarded his disciples as being of "more value than many sparrows" (Matt 10:31).

Stork. Large bird mentioned in the lists of unclean birds (Lev 11:19; Deut 14:18). Zechariah describes two women who had the large "wings of a stork" (Zech 5:7-9).

Swallow. Long-winged bird which inhabited the Temple compound (Ps 84:3). A causeless curse is compared to the flight of the swallow (Prov 26:2).

*Swift. Another possible identification for the Hebrew *dror*, commonly translated as "swallow."

Vulture. Bird of prey mentioned in the lists of unclean birds (Lev 11:13; Deut 14:12). It is suggested that several of the references to eagles are, in fact, intended for vultures.

*Water Hen. Bird of prey mentioned in the lists of unclean birds (Lev 11:16; Deut 14:18).

DOMESTICATED ANIMALS

Bull. Male cattle, used both as a beast of burden (Deut 22:10) and in the sacrificial rite. Because of its size and importance, the bull was only sacrificed on the most solemn occasions such as the Day of Atonement (Lev 16:6), or as a sin offering for the High Priest or the entire community of Israel (Lev 4:3,13-14). The bull is also mentioned as a symbol of strength and virility (Deut 33:17; Is 34:7; Jer 50:27). In the Temple, the molten sea was supported on the backs of 12 bronze bulls (I Kgs 7:25).

Camel, Dromedary. Beast of burden, used by the Israelites as a means of transportation (Neh 7:69). The camel was not fit to eat since, although it chews its cud, it does not have split hooves (Lev 11:4; Deut 14:7). Camel hair was used as a source of fabric (Matt 3:4). Camels were also used in warfare (I Chr 5:19-22), and this may be the reason why David appointed a special "keeper of the camels" (I Chr 27:30). The first references to camels in the Bible (which may be anachronistic) date from the Patriarchal period (Gen 24:10; 32:15). The camel's immense size figured in the parables of Jesus. "It is easier to get a camel through the eye of a needle than for a rich man to enter the kingdom of God" (Matt 19:24).

Colt. Young of the donkey, horse, or camel (Gen 32:15; Matt 21:1-10).

Cow, Heifer, Calf. Domestic cattle used by the Israelites as a beast of burden, a source of food, and a sacrificial animal. The most prominent of the sacrificial uses of the beast was in the offering of the red heifer, whose ashes were a prerequisite for regaining ritual purity after contact with a corpse (Num 19). Calves played a significant role in the surrounding Egyptian and Canaanite cultures. When Moses ascended Mount Sinai to receive the Decalogue, the Israelites forced Aaron to build a golden calf which they believed either represented the deity or was the animal upon which the unseen deity stood (Ex 32). Following the secession of the Northern Kingdom of Israel, King Jeroboam set up golden calves in the cultic centers of Dan and Bethel (I Kgs 12:28-30). Cows appear figuratively in Pharaoh's dream of seven fat cows, representing seven years of plenty, being devoured by seven lean cows, representing seven years of famine (Gen 41). Compare, too, the "cows of Bashan" which describe the plump women of Samaria (Amos 4:1).

Dog. Animal held in disdain by the ancient Israelites. Dogs in the Bible were not domestic animals but scavengers. They occasionally ate human flesh, as is described following the deaths of Ahab and Jezebel, when dogs licked Ahab's blood and ate Jezebel's flesh (I Kgs 22:38; II Kgs 9:35-36). The term "dog" was used as an insult; Goliath asked David, "Am I a dog, that you come to me with sticks?" (I Sam 17:43; cf. Phil 3:2); and as a figure for excessive abasement and humility (II Kgs 8:13; so, too, in the literature of the ancient Near East). The term also referred to male prostitutes (Deut 23:17-18). In one instance, however, the greyhound is described as a comely animal (Prov 30:29-31).

Donkey, Foal, Ass. Horse-like animal used in biblical times as a beast of burden. Donkeys were valued as a sign of wealth, and were used as transportation by all members of society. The prophet Zechariah declared that the Messiah would enter Jerusalem "riding upon an ass, and upon a colt, the foal of an ass" (Zech 9:9). Jesus enacted this prophecy by entering the city on an ass (Matt 21:2-10; John 12:14-16). In one instance a donkey was enabled to speak, warning its rider Balaam that an angel was blocking his way (Num 22:28).

Goat, Kid. Domesticated animal herded by the Israelites. Both the meal and the milk of the goat served as a source of food for the Israelites (Deut 14:4; 32:14); however, it was forbidden to cook the meat of a kid in its mother's milk (Deut 14:21). This prohibition later formed the basis of the Jewish prohibition of eating meat and milk together. The hair and hides of goats were used to make garments and other household articles (I Sam 19:13; Heb 11:37), and goat's hair was used to make a covering of the Tabernacle (Ex 26:7). Goats figured prominently in the sacrificial ritual. On the Day of Atonement, a goat was chosen as a "scapegoat" for the sins of the nation and sent into the wilderness (Lev 16:21-22). Its death signified God's forgiveness of the people.

Horse. Domestic animal used as a means of transportation. Horses often symbolized great wealth and royalty, and the chariots which they pulled were consi-

Man playing the flute to his dog; detail from the mosaic pavement of a monastery of the end of the 6th century at Beth Shean.

Man leading a donkey; detail from the mosaic pavement at the 6th-century synagogue of Beth Alpha.

A goat, representing the zodiac sign of the month of Tebeth (Capricorn) on the mosaic pavement of the Beth Alpha synagogue.

A ram, representing the zodiac sign of the month of Nisan (Aries) on the mosaic pavement of the Beth Alpha synagogue.

dered a symbol of great military strength (Judg 5:22). Kings amassed horses as a sign of wealth and might, and it was considered a great honor to mount the king's horse (Est 6:7-11). Israelite kings were forbidden to "multiply horses" (Deut 17:16), but Solomon ignored this law and accumulated horses to fill 40,000 stalls. He imported them from Egypt at the price of 150 silver shekels per horse (I Kgs 4:26, 10:29). Horses were perceived as being beautiful animals (Song 1:9; Job 39:19.25). In the Apocalypse described in the Book of Revelations, earthly judgments are represented by different colored horses (Rev 6:2-8; see also Zech ch. 6). Jesus himself rides a white horse (Rev 19:11).

Mule. Hybrid result of mating a horse with a donkey. Since crossbreeding is forbidden in the Bible (Lev 19:19), it is assumed that the animal was imported by the Israelites from the neighboring states. Mules were generally ridden by the aristocracy (I Kgs 1:33) and employed as burden-bearers (II Kgs 5:17).

Ox. Domesticated bovine animal used as food (Deut 14:4), for work (I Kgs 19:19) and in the sacrificial rites (Num 7:88). Specific laws were enacted concerning the treatment of oxen (e.g., they were forbidden to work on the Sabbath; Ex 23:12), and concerning injuries caused to humans, as well as injuries to themselves as property (Ex 21:28-22:13).

Ram. Adult male sheep, domesticated as a source of meat and as a sacrificial animal. Rams' hides dyed red were used as the uppermost covering of the Tabernacle (Ex 26:14). Rams' horns were used in biblical times as trumpets (Josh 6:4), and are still blown on the Jewish New Year. Abraham, after being forbidden to sacrifice Isaac, saw a ram entangled by its horns in the bushes, and sacrificed it in Isaac's stead (Gen 22:13). In the apocalyptic visions of Daniel, the horns of the ram represented Persia and Media (Dan 8).

Sheep, Lamb, Ewe. The most commonly mentioned animal in the Bible. Sheep are given 12 different Hebrew names according to gender, maturity, and breed. Sheep were a source of both meat and milk, wool and leather. The Patriarchs tended sheep in Canaan (Gen 46:32) where the size of one's flocks was a measure of wealth (I Sam 25:2). After Jacob went to Egypt, his family was given their own territory, evidently because the practice of tending flocks was loathsome to the Egyptians (Gen 46:34). Sheep were sacrificed in the earliest times. Abel's sacrifice of a sheep was acceptable to God, whereas his brother Cain's sacrifice of produce was not (Gen 4). Sheep later became the main sacrificial animal in the Temple. On Passover, every Israelite family was commanded to sacrifice a sheep (Ex 12:21-28). Because of the care needed to tend and protect sheep, they were regarded as symbols of meekness, protected by an all-powerful shepherd. This formed one of the most common metaphors in the Old Testament concerning the relationship between man and God. The Psalmist sings, "The Lord is my shepherd, I shall not want" (Ps 23:1). In the New Testament, Jesus is said to be the shepherd (Heb 13:20). Many of the great biblical leaders such as Moses (Ex 3:1), David (I Sam 17:15), and the prophet Amos (Amos 1:1; 7:14) were shepherds.

Swine, Sow, Pig. Animal considered unclean since, although it has split hooves, it does not chew the cud (Lev 11:7; Deut 14:8). Swine represented filth and repulsion to Jews throughout the ages. This was already figuratively expressed in Proverbs: "As a ring of gold in a swine's snout, so is a lovely woman who lacks discretion" (11:22). Jesus warned his followers not to cast pearls before swine (Matt 7:6). In the New Testament the pig is also used as a symbol of heresy (II Pet 2:22). A swineherd was a symbol of extreme poverty

(Luke 15:15). In one instance, Jesus exorcised demons into a herd of swine; the beasts then rushed into the sea and were drowned (Matt 8:30–32; Mark 5:11–13; Luke 8:32–33).

INSECTS

Ant. Small insect noted by the author of the Book of Proverbs for its industriousness. Man is advised to "Go to the ant, you sluggard, consider her ways and be wise" (Prov 6:6).

Bee. Small insect to which the enemies of Israel were compared (Deut 1:44; Ps 118:12; Is 7:18). In only one instance was the bee noted for its honey (Judg 14:8); most honey mentioned in the Bible was produced from dates.

Caterpillar. Larval stage of moths and butterflies. Caterpillars were noted for their destructiveness to crops (Ps 78:46).

Cricket. Insect permissible to the Israelites for consumption (Lev 11:22).

Flea. Small insect to which David, stressing his insignificance, compared himself when speaking with Saul (I Sam 24:14; 26:20).

Fly. Term for two insects mentioned in the Bible. The first was a stinging insect, traveling in swarms, that invaded Egypt in the fourth plague (Ex 8:21–31). The second was probably the common housefly to which Isaiah compared the invading Egyptian armies (Is 7:18). The Philistine god, Baal Zebub was worshiped in Ekron. His name, in the form "Beelzebub," was later used to represent Satan (Matt 12:24).

Gnat. Small insect mentioned in a parable of Jesus, who depicted the Pharisees as people who "strain out a gnat and swallow a camel" (Matt 23:24), meaning that they attach importance to minor issues while neglecting major ones.

Grasshopper. Insect permitted to the Israelites for consumption (Lev 11:22). Grasshoppers were harmful to crops (Ecc 12:5). The spies sent by Moses to Canaan described themselves as grasshoppers in the eyes of the natives, emphasizing their insignificance (Num 13:33). A swarm of grasshoppers was used as a metaphor for large multitudes of people (Jer 46:23).

Hornet. Small stinging insect which God sent to attack the Hivites, Canaanites, and Hittites, as a harbinger of the Israelite conquest of Canaan (Ex 23:28; Josh 24:12).

Locust. Grasshopper-like insect permitted to the Israelites as food (Lev 11:22). John the Baptist lived on locusts and honey (Matt 3:4). Swarms of locusts did great damage to crops and were considered a plague (Joel 1), and the eighth plague on Egypt was a plague of locusts (Ex 10:12–20). The Israelites had special ceremonies to prevent such plagues (Joel 2:12–17).

Louse. Small insect that breeds on animals and humans. Lice constituted the third plague on Egypt (Ex 8:16–19).

Moth. Butterfly-like insect noted for the damage it causes to clothing (Is 50:9; 51:8; Job 31:28; James 5:2). It is cited in the Bible as a metaphor of man's frailty (Job 4:19).

REPTILES AND AMPHIBIANS

*Adder. A stinging snake mentioned in the Book of Proverbs. The reference may be to the asp or the basilisk (Prov 23:32).

Asp. Venomous snake to which evil men were compared (Ps 140:2–3; Rom. 3:13).

Chameleon. Lizard forbidden to the Israelites as food. Any contact with a dead chameleon would render a person unclean (Lev 11:30–31).

Cobra. Poisonous snake to which the wicked were compared (Ps 58:4–5). The prophet Isaiah foretells that in the End of Days, "the nursing child shall paly by the cobra's hole" (Is 11:8).

Crocodile. Reptile. Biblical references are to the Nile crocodile and to mythological monsters (Is 51:9; Ps 74:13–14; Job 7:12).

Frog. Amphibian. The second plague to befall Egypt was one of frogs (Ex 7:26–8:11). In the New Testament, evil spirits are compared to frogs (Rev 16:13).

Gecko. Lizard forbidden to the Israelites as food (Lev 11:30).

Lizard. Reptile forbidden to the Israelites as food (Lev 11:30).

Monitor. Lizard forbidden to the Israelites as food (Lev 11:30).

Serpent, Snake. Generic term for a variety of reptiles, some poisonous. A serpent tempted Adam and Eve into sin (Gen 3), causing snakes to be later associated with Satan (Rev 12:9; 20:2). The serpent of Genesis was cursed, forced to crawl on its belly, and declared the enemy of humanity (Gen 3:14–15). Moses exhibited his power before Pharaoh by casting Aaron's rod before him; the rod was miraculously transformed into a serpent. When Pharaoh's soothsayers rivaled this miracle, the serpent formed from Aaron's rod swallowed the serpents formed from the soothsayers' rods (Ex 7:8–12). While in the wilderness, the Israelites were plagued by serpents. God instructed Moses to make a bronze serpent, and the Israelites who looked at it would be cured (Num 21:6–9). It was eventually destroyed by King Hezekiah as part of his reforms (II Kgs 18:4). The serpent was used to represent the enemies of Israel (Deut 32:33; Ps 58:4; Is 14:29; Jer 8:17. The disciples of Jesus had power over serpents (Luke 10:19). Isaiah foretold that in the End of Days, the serpent will revert to eating dust (Is 65:25).

Skink, Snail. Animal, commonly translated as snail, listed as forbidden food (Lev 11:29). The wicked are compared to a snail which leaves a slimy trail (Ps 58:8).

Tortoise. Amphibious creature forbidden to the Israelites as food (Lev 11:29).

Viper. Poisonous snake whose bite often meant death (Acts 28:3-6). Jacob's son Dan was compared to a viper because of his prowess as a warrior (Gen 49:17). In the New Testament Pharisees, Sadducees, and the scribes were compared to a "brood of vipers" (Matt 3:7; 12:34; 23:33; Luke 3:7). In Proverbs, the effects of wine are compared to a viper's bite (Prov 23:31-32).

WILD BEASTS

*Antelope, Oryx. Animal which both chews the cud and has cloven hooves, making it permissible for consumption (Deut 14:5). This identification is based primarily on a verse in Isaiah stating that the beast is caught in a net (Is 51:20).

*Badger. Mammal whose skin has been suggested as the material from which the upper curtain covering the Tabernacle was made (Ex 26:14; 36:19). Modern scholars reject this hypothesis, stating that the badger's pelt would be unsuitable for such a purpose.

Bear. Large furry mammal indigenous to Palestine until recent times. The bear mentioned in the Bible is the Syrian brown bear. Bears are generally herbivorous, but are known to attack flocks (I Sam 17:34), and to maul humans when their cubs are threatened (Prov 17:12). Two bears attacked a group of children who were mocking the prophet Elisha (II Kgs 2:24). Daniel represented Media as a bear (Dan 7:5).

Boar. Wild pig to whom Israel was compared (Ps 80:13). The same term also refers to domestic swine.

Deer, Doe, Fawn, Roe, Roebuck. Animal which both chews the cud and has cloven hooves, making it permissible for consumption (Deut 14:5). Jacob, in his final testament, compared Naphtali to a hind (Gen 49:21).

*Dolphin. Marine mammal whose skin has been suggested as the material from which the upper curtain covering the Tabernacle was made (Ex 26:14; 36:19).

*Dugong. Marine mammal whose skin has been suggested as the material from which the upper curtain covering the Tabernacle was made (Ex 26:14; 36:19).

Elephant. Large mammal not mentioned by name in the Bible. Ivory produced from the tusks of the elephant was mentioned in several instances; it was imported into Israel (I Kgs 10:22).

Fox. Dog-like animal. Samson used foxes to attack the Philistines. He tied lit torches to the tails of 300 foxes, and set the animals loose in the Philistines' fields (Judg 15:4-5). Foxes are described as prowling the ruins of destroyed Jerusalem (Lam 5:18). In the New Testament, foxes represent cunning (Luke 13:31-32).

Gazelle. Animal which both chews the cud and has cloven hooves, making it permissible for consumption (Deut 14:5). The gazelle was included in the list of animals that Solomon served at his table (I Kgs 4:23). The gazelle appears in similes denoting swiftness (II Sam 2:18).

Hare. Small rabbit-like mammal which, although it appeared to chew the cud, did not have split hooves, and was therefore considered unfit for consumption (Lev 11:6; Deut 14:7).

*Hartebeest. Animal which both chews the cud and has cloven hooves, making it permissible for consumption (Deut 14:5). The hartebeest was also included in the list of animals that Solomon served at his table (I Kgs 4:23).

*Hippopotamus. Suggested translation for the Hebrew word *behemoth* appearing in Job (Job 40:15).

Hyena. Carrion-eating beast noted in the Bible for inhabiting desolate places and for its howl (Is 13:22).

Jackal. Carrion-eating beast noted in the Bible for inhabiting desolate places (Jer 9:11) and for its howl (Is 13:22). It is prophesied that Babylonia (Jer 51:37), Edom (Is 34:13), and Jerusalem (Jer 9:11) will become the haunts of jackals.

Leopard, Cheetah. Cat-like animal noted for its spots (Jer 13:23) and speed (Hab 1:8). Although it is a predator (Jer 5:6), Isaiah foretold that in the future it will dwell in peace with the lamb (Is 11:6). In one of Daniel's apocalyptic visions, Persia is represented by a four-headed, winged leopard (Dan 7:6), whereas the leopard that comes from the sea in the Book of Revelations represents the Roman Empire (Rev 13:2).

Lion. Large cat-like animal noted for its strength (Prov 30:30) and its roar (Amos 3:8). The lion represented courage (Prov 28:1) and majesty (Ezek 1:10). The tribe of Judah was compared to a lion (Gen 49:9), as were Jesus (Rev 5:5) and God (Hos 5:14). Figures of lions were used as ornaments on Solomon's throne (I Kgs

A leopard; detail from the mosaic pavement of the 6th-century synagogue of Maon.

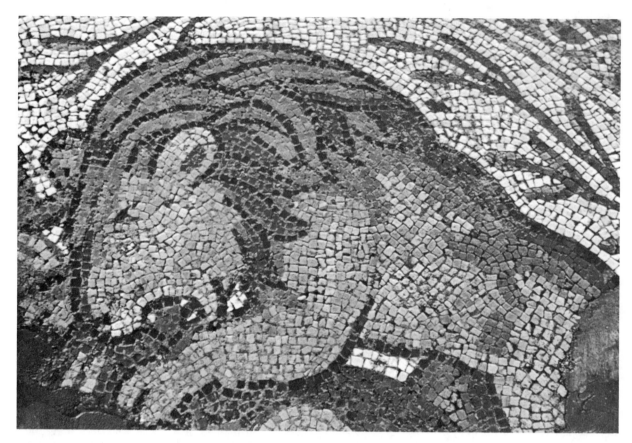

A lion; detail from the mosaic pavement at the 6th-century synagogue of Beth Guvrin.

10:19). Because of their fierceness, lions were sometimes used to administer the death penalty. In one famous incident, Daniel and his companions were cast into a den of lions and emerged unscathed (Dan 6:16). The prophet Isaiah foretold that in the future the lion will be tamed and will lie down with the lamb (Is 11:6). Lions commonly inhabited the deserts of ancient Israel (Is 30:6), and sometimes attacked shepherds (I Sam 17:34–35).

Mole. Small mammal similar to a rat which was considered by the Israelites as unclean and therefore inedible (Lev 11:29).

Monkey, Ape, Langur. Primate brought to Solomon's court from Tarsus (I Kgs 10:22).

Mouse, Rat. Rodents prohibited to the Israelites as food (Lev 11:29). After the Philistines captured the Ark of the Covenant, they were plagued with rats (I Sam 6:5). They therefore returned the Ark with a trespass offering of five golden rats (I Sam 6:17-18).

*Porcupine, Hedgehog. Animal foretold by Isaiah to inhabit the desolate places of Edom (Is 34:11).

Rock Badger, Hyrax, Coney. Small rodent which, although it appeared to chew its cud, did not have split hooves, and was therefore considered unfit for consumption (Lev 11:5; Deut 14:7).

*Weasel. Animal mentioned in the list of forbidden foods (Lev 11:29).

Whale. Jonah was swallowed by a "great fish" which is unidentified, but it became traditional to regard it as a whale (Jonah 1:17).

Wild Ass, Onager. Wild variety of the donkey, noted for inhabiting the wilderness (Job 39:5).

Wolf. Large canine to which Jacob's son Benjamin was compared (Gen 49:27). Although it was noted for its ferocity, Isaiah foretold that in the End of Days the wolf will lie down with the lamb (Is 11:6). In the New Testament, the wolf represents false teachers (Matt 7:15; Acts 20:29).

OTHERS

Leech. Blood-sucking, wormlike creature used in Proverbs to represent greed (Prov 30:15).

Scorpion. Poisonous arachnid which inhabits desert regions (Deut 8:15). The sting of the scorpion is extremely painful (I Kgs 12:11; Rev 9:5,10).

Spider. Arachnid noted for the frail web it spins (Job 8:14:15). The sins of the wicked are compared to spiders' webs which cannot adequately cover the sinner (Is 59:6).

Worm, Maggot. Crawling animal noted for feeding on plants (Jonah 4:7) and corpses (Job 21:26). Worms appear in the Bible as a symbol of insignificance (Ps 22:6).

Plants are often mentioned in the Bible. The society in which the biblical authors lived was primarily agricultural, and they came into daily contact with a wide variety of plants, both cultivated and wild. Plants were the major source of food, light (olive oil), cosmetics, and clothing. They also figured widely in art, and much of the description of biblical art is of plants. A wide variety of plants appear in the Bible, both in their natural settings and in metaphors and similes. The rich poetry of the Song of Songs draws abundantly from the flora with which the author was familiar. Scholars today are uncertain as to the precise identity of many of the plants appearing in the Bible. Whereas numerous studies have been made to attempt to identify even the most common biblical species, it seems that the identity of many of the plants can only be guessed at.

FLOWERS

Lily. Most commonly mentioned flower in the Bible. It is thought that the term "lily" may refer to any beautiful flower indigenous to the area, including the anemone, crocus, narcissus, and wild tulip. The lily appears often in the descriptive love poetry of the Song of Songs ("lily of the valley," Song 2:1). It was prominent in art; the capitals of the two pillars, Jachin and Boaz, at the entrance of Solomon's Temple and the rim of the molten sea were shaped like lilies (I Kgs 7:19, 22). Jesus mentioned the lily as a symbol of beauty, stating that not even Solomon had garments as beautiful as the lily (Matt 6:28-19).

Lotus. Possible translation of a plant under which the *behemoth* is said to find shade (Job 40:21-22).

Rose. Possible translation of a flower mentioned by Isaiah in his prophecy "and the desert shall blossom like the rose" (Is 35:1). The lover in Song of Songs compared himself to the "rose of Sharon" (Song 2:1).

FRUITS

Almond. The almond tree is common to the Mediterranean basin. It blossoms as early as January or the beginning of February, producing a fruit which has long been considered a delicacy. Jacob sent almonds as a gift to the Egyptian chief minister who, unbeknown to him, was actually his son Joseph (Gen 43:11). When Aaron's authority was challenged during Korah's uprising, his rod, an almond branch, miraculously blossomed (Num 17:8). Almond blossoms were frequently used to represent beauty. The head of the elderly is compared to the white blossoms of the almond (Ecc 12:5). As a symbol of beauty, almond blossoms figured in art; the branches of the candelabrum in the Taber-

nacle were shaped like almond blossoms (Ex 25:33-34; 37:19-20).

Apple. The apple tree was often mentioned in the Bible as a metaphor for beauty and fragrance (Song 2:3,5; 7:8, 8:5). Although tradition and art generally depict the forbidden Tree of Knowledge as an apple tree, the Bible makes no mention of the actual type of fruit from which Adam and Eve ate.

Carob, Pod. Fruit common to ancient Israel, mentioned as fodder for pigs in the story of the prodigal son (Luke 15:16).

Citron. Identified as the "goodly fruit" used in the rituals of the Feast of Tabernacles (Lev 23:40).

Dates see Palm

Fig. Tree known for the sweetness of its fruit (Judg 9:11). Adam and Eve sewed their first garments from fig leaves (Gen 3:7). Figs were one of the seven species with which the Land of Israel was blessed (Deut 8:8). The fruit was used as food, both raw and pressed into cakes (I Sam 25:18), and also as a medicine (Is 38:21). Although fig trees were a symbol of peace (Mic 4:4), in one instance Jesus cursed a fig tree for not providing him with fruit (Matt 21:18-22; Mark 11:12-14).

Grape, Raisin, Vine. Plant used as a source of food, and in making wine. The grapevine was among the seven species with which the Land of Israel was blessed (Deut 8:8). Grapes were eaten both fresh and dried. Since raisins keep for a long time, they were suitable food for long journeys (II Sam 6:19) and military expe-

Cluster of grapes on a coin of Bar-Kokhba; AD 134.

ditions (II Sam 16:1). Grape wine was a common drink among the Israelites but was forbidden to those who took the oath of the Nazirite (Num 6:3). Vineyards were common in biblical Israel, dotting the hills of Judah (Jer 31:5). The spies brought back a cluster of grapes to Moses, as representative of the produce of Canaan (Num 13:23). Isaiah gives a description of the planting of vineyards (Is 5:1-2), which were often surrounded by a hedge to protect them from wild animals (Ps 80:13; Song 2:15) and thieves (Jer 49:9). A well-cultivated vineyard represented great wealth, and King Ahab's jealousy of Naboth's vineyard led him to engineer Naboth's death (I Kgs 21). Vineyards figured prominently in prophetic symbolism. A flourishing vineyard represented stability; the image of each man dwelling under his vine and under his fig tree was often used to portray a period of peace (I Kgs 4:25; Mic 4:4; Zech 3:10). Israel was compared to a vine (Is 5:2; Ps 80:8-9), and Jesus declared, "I am the vine, you are the branches" (John 15:5).

Mulberry. Tall tree producing sweet fruit, sometimes used to produce a drink. David ambushed the Philistines from a grove of mulberry trees (II Sam 5:23-24). Jesus later noted the size of the mulberry tree in a parable on faith (Luke 17:6).

Nuts. Fruit regarded as a delicacy in biblical times. Jacob sent nuts with his sons as a gift to the Egyptian chief minister (Gen 43:11). A "garden of nuts" is mentioned in the Song of Songs (Song 6:11). In the Bible they are generally thought to have been pistachios or walnuts.

Olive. Evergreen tree producing small fruit used as food and made into a fine oil. The olive was one of the seven species with which the Land of Israel was blessed (Deut 8:8). Olive oil was used for lighting (Lev 24:2) and anointing (Ex 30:24-25) as well as in various sacrifices (Ex 29:40; Lev 2:1-7; Num 28:5). The finest oil was often exported (I Kgs 5:11). An olive branch was brought by the dove to Noah, symbolizing that the flood had receded (Gen 8:11). Jeremiah compared Israel to an olive branch (Jer 11:16), and Paul later compared Gentile Christianity to a branch of wild olive grafted to a cultivated tree (Judaism) (Rom 11:17).

Palm. The date palm is a tall tree producing fruit from which a honey was made. The honey which was counted among the seven species with which the Land of Israel was blessed (Deut 8:8), is considered to have been date honey. A branch of palm was among the four species for the Feast of Tabernacles ritual (Lev 23:40). Palm trees were often quoted as a symbol of beauty, and several women in the Bible were named Tamar, the Hebrew word for palm. In the Song of Songs, the lover compared his love to a palm (Song 7:7), while the Book of Psalms, noting the stature and height of the palm, used it as a simile for the righteous (Ps 92:12). Palm trees were carved on the walls of the interior chamber of the Temple (I Kgs 6:29-35).

Palm tree on a coin of Bar-Kokhba; AD 134.

Pomegranate. Fruit mentioned as one of the seven species with which the Land of Israel was blessed (Deut 8:8). The seeds of the pomegranate were eaten and also made into a wine (Song 8:2). Pomegranates figured in biblical art. The hem of the High Priest's robe was decorated with the likeness of golden pomegranates (Ex 28:33-34), as were the capitals of the two pillars at the Temple portico (I Kgs 7:18, 20). The pomegranate, with its many seeds, symbolized fertility, both agricultural and human.

Pomegranate on a Jewish shekel, c.AD 68.

GRAINS

Barley. Used as food for both man and animals, barley was one of the seven species with which the Land of Israel was blessed (Deut 8:8), and figured prominently among the country's exports (II Chr 2:15). Since barley was the earliest grain to ripen (Ex 9:31), its first harvest was considered a mark of the beginning of the harvest season. A special offering of the first barley, the "omer," was brought to the Temple on the first day after Passover (Lev 23:9-10). Barley flour was not considered as fine as wheat flour, and was therefore sold for half the price (II Kgs 7:1).

Millet. Grain traded by Judah with Tyre (Ezek 27:17). Bread made from millet was not as rich as bread made from wheat. Ezekiel ate a loaf of millet bread to symbolize the siege of Jerusalem (Ezek 4:9).

Rye. Grain noted for the poor quality of its flour in comparison to wheat. Ezekiel combined rye flour with other flours to bake paupers' bread (Ezek 4:9).

Wheat. Staple of ancient Israel and one of the seven species with which the Land of Israel was blessed (Deut 8:8). It was exported to neighboring countries, particularly Tyre (I Kgs 5:11). The Feast of Pentecost symbolized the start of the wheat harvest. The centrality of wheat in ancient Israel is indicated by the biblical descriptions of all stages in the cultivation of the grain. Ruth met Boaz during the wheat harvest (Ruth 2); Gideon was summoned by the angel while threshing (Judg 6:11), and Ishbosheth was assassinated while cleaning wheat (II Sam 4:6). John the Baptist compared God's treatment of the sinners to the winnowing of wheat (Matt 3:12). Wheat was used allegorically to represent beauty (Song 7:2), and appears throughout the Bible in various images (Ps 81:16; Matt 13:24-30).

HERBS AND SPICES

Aloes. Perfume (Prov 7:17) made from the resin of a tree native to Northern India. Aloes was found in the garden to which the lover compared his bride in Song of Songs (Song 4:14). It was later listed among the spices used to prepare Jesus for burial (John 19:39).

Anise (also translated as dill). Plant bearing small licorice-like seeds. Jesus complained that the Pharisees, while taking tithes even from anise and other small shrubs, were not careful about observing the moral laws (Matt 23:23).

Balm. Spice native to the Gilead region of ancient Israel (Gen 37:25), sometimes used in preparing medicine (Jer 46:11). Balm was among the gifts brought by Jacob's sons as a gift to the Egyptian minister who proved to be their brother, Joseph (Gen 43:11). This spice was also exported to Tyre (Ezek 27:17).

Bitter Herbs. A mixture of various herbs eaten by the Israelites with the Passover offering prior to the Exodus from Egypt. Later it was interpreted as a reminder of the bitterness of slavery (Ex 12:8; Num 9:11).

Calamus. Type of fragrant reed found in the garden to which the lover compared his bride in Song of Songs (Song 4:14).

Cane. Sweet substance extracted from a reed, used in the preparation of the anointing oil (Ex 30:23).

Cassia. Plant used in the preparation of the anointing oil (Ex 30:24) and as a perfume (Ps 45:8).

Cinnamon. Bark of a tree native to Ceylon. Oil extracted from the bark was used in the preparation of the anointing oil (Ex 30:24) and as a perfume (Song 4:14).

Coriander. Small aromatic seed to which the taste of manna was compared (Ex 16:31).

Wheat on a bronze coin of King Herod Agrippa I.

Arabia holding cinammon sticks, on a coin; AD 106.

Cumin. Seed used as a condiment and in the preparation of medicines. The wisdom of the Lord is compared by Isaiah to the careful knowledge needed in cultivating and threshing cumin (Is 28:25–27). Jesus complained that the Pharisees, while taking tithes even from cumin and other small shrubs, were not careful about observing the moral laws (Matt 23:23).

Dill. Plant bearing small seeds, often translated as anise (Matt 23:23).

Frankincense. Expensive substance imported from Sheba (Jer 6:20), used as an ingredient in the Temple incense (Ex 30:34). Because of its great value, a special storeroom in the Temple was set aside for storing frankincense (Neh 13:9).

Galbanum. Ingredient of the Temple incense (Ex 30:34), it was also utilized as a condiment and in medicines.

Gall. Poisonous herb which symbolized misfortune. Moses declared of the wicked, "Their grapes are grapes of gall" (Deut 32:32).

Henna. Small tree with fragrant flowers, used for perfume and cosmetics. Henna was one of the plants mentioned in the lover's garden in the Song of Songs (Song 4:13).

Hyssop. Small plant used in various purification rites, including those of the red heifer (Num 19:6, 8) and the leper (Lev 14:4,49). Branches of hyssop were taken to daub the doorpost of the Israelite houses in Egypt with the blood of the paschal lamb (Ex 12:22). Hyssop mixed in sour wine was sprinkled over Jesus on the cross (John 19:29).

Mallow. Shrub growing on the banks of the Dead Sea. It was used by desert dwellers as food and a source of fuel (Job 30:4).

Mandrake. Fragrant herb (Song 7:13) used as an aphrodisiac. Reuben collected mandrakes for his mother Leah, and she traded them with Rachel for the privilege of lying with Jacob (Gen 30:14–16).

Mint. Sweet-smelling herb used as a seasoning and in making medicines. Jesus complained that the Pharisees, while taking tithes even from mint and other small shrubs, were not careful about observing the moral laws (Matt 23:23).

Mustard. Large plant whose tiny seeds were used as a condiment. Jesus compared the Kingdom of God to a mustard plant, noting the size of the plant sown from so small a seed (Mark 4:31–32).

Myrrh. Perfume made from the sap of a small tropical tree. Myrrh was a favorite perfume of women (Est 2:12). It was used in the preparation of the anointing oil (Ex 30:23–24), and in preparing Jesus' body for burial (John 19:39).

Onycha. Ingredient in the Temple incense (Ex 30:34). Some scholars suggest that onycha was not made from a plant but rather from mollusks.

Rue. Small shrub used as a condiment. Jesus complained that the Pharisees, while taking tithes even from rue and other small shrubs, were not careful about observing the moral laws (Matt 23:23).

Saffron. Flower used as a condiment and in making medicines. The lover in Song of Songs compared his love to a garden containing saffron and other fragrant plants (Song 4:14).

Stacte. Ingredient in the Temple incense (Ex 30:34). Scholars suppose that it was made of resin extracted from the bark of the storax tree.

Spikenard. Fragrant plant mentioned in the lover's garden in the Song of Songs (4:14). Oil from the spikenard was used in anointing Jesus (Mark 14:3).

Wormwood. Plant whose bitter juice was often employed in the preparation of medicines. Wormwood appears in several similes as a symbol of bitterness. In Lamentations, the destruction of Jerusalem is described as being as bitter as wormwood (Lam 3:15). In Proverbs, an immoral woman is compared to wormwood (Prov 5:4).

A lush garden, watered by irrigation channels; detail from an Egyptian wall painting; 13th century BC.

VEGETABLES AND LEGUMES

Beans. Leguminous pod eaten particularly in times of want. Beans were brought to David at his encampment in Mahanaim (II Sam 17:28). They were sometimes ground into a flour and mixed with wheat flour to make a poor bread (Ezek 4:9).

Cucumber. Vegetable eaten by the Israelites in Egypt. While sojourning in the wilderness, the Israelites longed for cucumbers (Num 11:5). Isaiah likened Jerusalem to "a lodge in a garden of cucumbers" (Is 1:8), signifying the city's desolation.

Garlic. Bulbous vegetable eaten by the Israelites in Egypt. While sojourning in the wilderness, the Israelites longed for garlic (Num 11:5).

Gourd. Two Hebrew words are translated as "gourd" in the Bible. The first was a highly poisonous wild gourd which was consumed by the disciples of the prophet Elisha (II Kgs 4:38–41). Another was the fruit of a plant which offered shade to Jonah outside Nineveh (Jonah 4:6–10). This plant, however, is generally understood to be the castor-oil plant.

Leek. Onion-like vegetable eaten by the Israelites in Egypt. While sojourning in the wilderness, the Israelites longed for leeks (Num 11:5).

Lentil. Orange-red legume eaten in a stew for which Esau traded his birthright with his brother Jacob (Gen 25:29–35). It was also mixed with grains to make a poor bread (Ezek 4:9).

Melon. Fruit eaten by the Israelites in Egypt. While sojourning in the wilderness, the Israelites longed for melons (Num 11:5).

Onion. Vegetable eaten by the Israelites in Egypt. While sojourning in the wilderness, the Israelites longed for onions (Num 11:5).

WOOD

Acacia. Acacia trees were common in ancient Israel, particularly in desert regions, and were the source of several place names such as Abel Shittim and Beth Shittah. From this tree came the wood used in the construction of the Tabernacle, the Ark of the Covenant, and the altar (Ex 25–27; 30:1–10; 36–38).

Almug. Wood imported by Solomon from Hiram of Tyre and used for the construction of the Temple and in making musical instruments (I Kgs 10:11–12). Almug is sometimes identified as sandalwood.

Bay. Suggested translation of a wide-branched tree to which the spread of the wicked was compared in Psalms (37:35).

Cedar. Large pine tree native to Lebanon, mentioned as a symbol of great strength and beauty (Ps 29:5; Ezek 31:13). King Solomon imported cedarwood to build the Temple. Another of Solomon's buildings was known as the House of the Forest of Lebanon since it was supported by 45 pillars of cedar (I Kgs 7:2–5). Carved cedars were also used as ornamental paneling (I Kgs 6:9, 15, 18). A twig of cedar with a bunch of hyssop and scarlet was employed in various cleansing rituals, including that of lepers (Lev 14:4,6,49, 51–52; Num 19:6).

Chestnut. Jacob set rods from chestnut and almond trees before his flocks so that they would conceive streaked and speckled flocks (Gen 30:37). The greatness of Assyria was compared to the chestnut tree (Ezek 31:3–8). Some scholars believe that in both instances, the correct translation is the plane tree.

Citron Wood. An expensive wood listed among the products which the merchants of the End of Days will be unable to sell (Rev 18:12).

Cypress. Possible translation for several species of trees mentioned in the Bible. Its wood was used in making ship's decks (Ezek 27:5) and musical instruments (II Sam 6:5). Solomon imported cypress trees from Lebanon for the construction of the Temple (I Kgs 5:6–8). Lebanon was often conquered for its cypress trees. Isaiah prophesied that God would cut down the cypress to punish the Assyrians (II Kgs 19:23) and Babylonians (Is 14:8). Isaiah foretold that in the End of Days, the cypress will blossom in the desert (Is 41:19).

Ebony. Wood mentioned by Ezekiel as being exported by the Arabian traders of Dedan (Ezek 27:15).

Gopher Wood. Wood named as the material of which Noah constructed the ark (Gen 6:14).

Juniper. Desert tree. According to one translation, Jeremiah warned the Moabites to "Flee, save your lives, and be like the juniper tree in the wilderness" (Jer 48:6).

Myrtle. Tree mentioned as one of the four species used

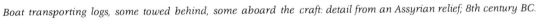

Boat transporting logs, some towed behind, some aboard the craft: detail from an Assyrian relief; 8th century BC.

in the ceremonial of the Feast of Tabernacles (Lev 23:40). The myrtle was considered a tree of great beauty. Esther was originally named Hadassah, meaning myrtle (Est 2:7). The prophet Isaiah foretold that in the End of Days, the myrtle will flourish in the wilderness (Is 41:19).

Oak. Tree noted for its great strength. The Amorites were compared to oaks (Amos 2:9). Because of the size and strength of the tree, pagan rituals were frequently conducted under oak trees (Hos 4:13).

Pine. Generic term for a variety of coniferous trees indigenous to Palestine. The pine trees mentioned in Isaiah (Is 41:19; 44:14; 60:13) have also been translated as firs, planes, and junipers.

Plane. Suggested translation for the tree commonly translated as chestnut (Gen 30:37; Ezek 31:3–8) and also for that translated as pine in Isaiah 41:19, etc.

Poplar. Tree which grew in the hilly regions of ancient Israel, with the oak and the terebinth (Hos 4:13). Jacob set rods of poplar along with almond and plane before his flocks so that they would conceive striped and speckled flocks (Gen 30:37).

Sycamore. Fig-like tree common to the coastal and desert regions of ancient Israel. The prophet Amos described himself as a "dresser of sycamore trees" (Amos 7:14). Zacchaeus climbed a sycamore tree to see Jesus (Luke 19:4).

Tamarisk. Tree common in ancient Israel. Abraham planted a tamarisk in Beersheba (Gen 21:33), and Saul was later buried under a tamarisk (I Sam 31:13).

Terebinth. Large tree often used as a landmark in ancient Israel. God appeared to Abraham by the terebinth of Mamre (Gen 18:1) and to Gideon by the terebinth of Ophrah (Judg 6:11). Rebekah's nurse Deborah was buried under a terebinth (Gen 35:4–8), and Gideon's son Abimelech was crowned under one (Judg 9:6). David's son Absalom was caught by his hair on the hanging branch of a terebinth (II Sam 18:9). Terebinths figured prominently in pagan rituals (Hos 4:13).

Willow. Tree noted for growing on the banks of rivers. A willow branch was one of the four species of plants used on the Feast of Tabernacles, the others being a palm branch, a myrtle branch, and a citron (Lev 23:40). The exiles in Babylonia are said to have hung their harps on willow branches and mourned Jerusalem (Ps 137:1–2).

OTHERS

Briar, Bramble, Thorn, Thistle. Generic term for a number of prickly plants. God cursed Adam that the earth would bring forth thorns and thistles in the fields to hinder agriculture (Gen 3:18). Thorns came to symbolize all that is evil (Mic 7:4), particularly the enemies of Israel (Ezek 28:24) and false prophets. Thorns were sometimes used to scourge enemies captured in war (Judg 8:7).

Broom. Desert shrub used as a source of food (Job 30:4) and of fuel (Ps 120:4). While hiding in the wilderness from Ahab and Jezebel, Elijah sheltered in the shade of a broom (I Kgs 19:4).

Bulrush. Common translation for the plant growing on the banks of the Nile, amid which the infant Moses was hidden (Ex 2:3).

Castor-oil plant. Possible translation of the plant under which Jonah shaded himself (Jonah 4:6–10).

Fine Linen. Possible translation for a Hebrew term generally translated as cotton, which mainly appears in lists of royal garments (Gen 41:42).

Flax. Plant whose fibers were used to make linen (Jer 13:1), candle wicks (Is 42:3), and rope (Ezek 40:3). Flax was often dried on rooftops, and in one instance provided a cover for Joshua's two spies in Jericho (Josh 2:6). Whereas a harlot would receive flax from her lovers (Hos 2:5), the faithful wife seeks out flax and works it willingly (Prov 31:13).

Grass. Common plant used to symbolize man's brief lifespan (Ps 90:5; 103:15–16).

Hemlock. Highly poisonous plant common to Palestine. Judgment is said to spring up "like hemlock in the furrows of the field" (Hos 10:4).

Nettle. Translation commonly given for two plants in the Bible. The nettle appears in visions of desolation (Is 34:13).

Papyrus. Reed common along the banks of the Nile. Papyrus was used in making boats (Is 18:2) and paper (II John 1:12). Scholars believe that the bulrushes in which the infant Moses was hidden were actually papyrus (Ex 2:3).

Reed. Grass-like plant growing on the banks of rivers. Some scholars suggest that the infant Moses was hidden in reeds (Ex 2:3). Reeds figure in the Bible as a metaphor for weakness. Sennacherib compared Egypt to a broken reed (II Kgs 18:21). Reeds were used as measuring rods (Rev 11:1; 21:15–16). Jesus was given a reed before being crucified to represent the scepter of the King of the Jews (Matt 27:29).

Armenian mosaic with motifs of fruit and birds; 7th century.

II.19 MIRACLES

A miracle is any extraordinary event outside the realm of natural phenomena, brought about by divine intervention. Miracles play an important role in the Bible by displaying the power of God beyond nature.

In the Old Testament, miracles served various purposes, among them: proving the divine nature of an individual's mission (Aaron's staff blossoming in Num 17:6–8); proving the eventual fulfillment of a particular prophecy (Hezekiah's sundial turning back in II Kgs 20:9–11); as signs of God's power and authority (the parting of the Red Sea in Ex 14:15–31); and as a means of showing God's ability to preserve human life (Elisha's resurrection of the Shunammite's son in II Kgs 4:32–37). Miracles often occurred at important junctures in Israelite history such as the exodus from Egypt, and various figures are most often attributed with the performance of miracles, among them Moses, Elijah, and Elisha.

Miracles play an important role in the ministry of Jesus, with more miracles attributed to him than to any other biblical personality. Jesus' miracles can be divided into four types: healing, resurrection, feeding multitudes, and signs of his divine authority. The miracles are viewed by the Gospels as a basic part of Jesus' mission in establishing the Kingdom of God on earth. "But if I cast out demons by the spirit of God, surely the Kingdom of God has come upon you" (Matt 12:28). Many of his miracles of healing indicated the universal nature of his mission; by healing a leper (Matt 8:2) and a Gentile child (Matt 15:21) his mission extended to the ritually unclean and the foreigner. In the Gospel according to John, the miracles of Jesus are regarded as signs intended to underscore Jesus' identity as "the resurrection and the life" (John 11:25). Miracles were later performed by the apostles; the power to heal was revered as a gift of the Spirit (I Cor 12:28).

MIRACLES IN THE OLD TESTAMENT			
A SELECTION			
BOOK	MIRACLE	AGENT	SOURCE
GENESIS	The birth of Isaac		Gen 21:1-3
EXODUS	The burning bush		Ex 3:1
	Moses' rod becomes a serpent	Moses	Ex 4:3
	Moses' hand becomes leprous	Moses	Ex 4:6
	Aaron's rod becomes a serpent	Aaron	Ex 7:10-12
	The Plagues		
	1) The waters turn to blood	Aaron	Ex 7:20-25
	2) Frogs	Aaron	Ex 8:1-11
	3) Lice	Aaron	Ex 8:12-15
	4) Flies		Ex 8:20-28
	5) Pestilence		Ex 9:1-7
	6) Boils	Moses	Ex 9:8-12
	7) Hail	Moses	Ex 9:22-26
	8) Locusts	Moses	Ex 10:12-20
	9) Darkness	Moses	Ex 10:21-29
	10) Death of the first born		Ex 12:29
	The Red Sea divided	Moses	Ex 14:15-31
	Sweetening of the waters at Marah	Moses	Ex 15:23-25
	Manna		Ex 16:14-35
	Water drawn from a rock at Rephidim	Moses	Ex 17:5-7
NUMBERS	The earth swallows Korah and his followrs		Num 16:31-35
	Aaron's rod blossoms		Num 17:6-8
	Water drawn from a rock at Meribah	Moses	Num 20:7-11
	The brass serpent heals the sick	Moses	Num 21:8-9
	Balaam's ass speaks	Num 22:28	

BOOK	MIRACLE	AGENT	SOURCE
JOSHUA	Jordan river stops	Joshua	Josh 3:11-17
	The walls of Jericho fall	Joshua	Josh 6:6-20
	Sun and moon stand still	Joshua	osh 10:12-14
I SAMUEL	Philistines and their gods smitten		I Sam 5
I KINGS	Jeroboam's hand withers and altar destroyed		I Kgs 13:4-6
	Widow's food increased	Elijah	I Kgs 17:14-16
	Widow's son resurrected	Elijah	I Kgs 17:17-24
	Elijah's sacrifice consumed by fire	Elijah	I Kgs 18:30-38
	Elijah brings rain	Elijah	I Kgs 18:41
II KINGS	Ahaziah's troops consumed by fire	Elijah	II Kgs 1:10-12
	Jordan River divided	Elijah	II Kgs 2:7-8
	Elijah taken to heaven	Elijah	II Kgs 2:11
	Jordan River divided	Elijah	II Kgs2:14
	Waters of Jericho sweetened	Elijah	II Kgs 2:21-22
	Children who mocked Elisha mauled by bears	Elijah	II Kgs 2:24
	Water given to Jehoshapat and his army	Elijah	II Kgs 3:14-20
	Widow's oil increased	Elijah	II Kgs 4:2-7
	Shunammite's son resurrected	Elijah	II Kgs 4:32-37
	Poisonous pottage corrected	Elijah	II Kgs 4:38-41
	100 men fed with 20 loaves	Elijah	II Kgs 4:42-44
	Naaman's leprosy healed and transfered to Gehazi	Elijah	II Kgs 5:10-27
	The exehead rises to the surface of the water	Elijah	II Kgs 6:5-7
	Syrian army blinded and cured	Elijah	II Kgs 6:18-20
	Dead man resurrected by Elisha's bones	Elijah	II Kgs 13:21
	Sennacherib's army destroyed	Angel of the Lord	II Kgs 19:35
	Shadow on Hezekiah's sundial turns backward	Isaiah	II Kgs 20:9-11
II CHRONICLES	Uzziah smitten with leprosy		II Chr 26:16-21
DANIEL	Shadrach, Meshach and Abed-Nego unharmed by the furnace		Dan 3:19-27
	Daniel unhurt in lions den		Dan 6:16-23
JONAH	Jonah survives the belly of the whale		Jonah 2:1-10

DICK CODOR © 80

JONAH

MIRACLES OF JESUS

MIRACLE	LOCATION	MATTHEW	MARK	LUKE	JOHN
Water turned water into wine	Cana			2:1	
Healing the nobleman's son	Cana			4:46	
Healing the demoniac in the synagogue	Capernaum		1:23	4:33	
Healing the impotent man					5:1
Passing unseen through the multitude	Nazareth			4:30	
Catching the fish	Lower Galilee			5:1	
Healing Peter's mother-in-law	Capernaum	8:14	1:30	4:38	
Healing a leper	Capernaum	8:2	1:40	5:12	
Healing the palsy	Jeruslam	9:2	2:3	5:18	
Healing the man with the withered hand	Galilee	12:10	3:1	6:6	
Healing the centurion's servant	Capernaum	8:5		7:1	
Raising the widow's son	Nain			7:11	
Healing the dumb demoniac	Capernaum	9:32			
Stilling the storm	Lower Galilee	8:26	4:37	8:22	
Legion of devils in the swine	Gadara	8:28	5:1	8:27	
Raising Jairus' daughter from the dead	Capernaum	9:23	5:38	8:49	
Healing the woman with the issue of blood	Capernaum	9:20	5:25	8:43	
Healing Bartimaeus of his blindness	Jericho	20:30 (two blind men)	10:46	18:35	
Feeding 5000	Lower Galilee	14:19	6:35	9:12	6:5
Walking on water	Lower Galilee	14:25	6:48		6:19
Healing the girl possessed by demons	Tyre	15:28	7:24		
Healing the deaf and dumb man	Lower Galilee		7:31		
Feeding the 4000	Lower Galilee	15:32	8:1		
Healing the blind man	Bethsaida		8:22		
Healing the demoniac child	Caesarea	17:14	9:17	9:38	
Finding the coin in the mouth of the fish	Capernaum	17:27			
Passing unseen through crowd	Temple				8:59
Healing a blind man	Jeruslam				9:1
Healing the blind and dumb demoniac	Galilee	12:22		11:14	
Healing the crooked woman	Peraea			13:11	
Healing the man with dropsy	Peraea			14:1	
Raising Lazarus from the dead	Bethany				11:43
Healing 10 lepers	Sammaria			17:11	
Healing two blind men	Capernaum	9:27			
Cursing the fig tree	Mt. of Olives	21:18	11:12		
Healing Malchus of his deafness	Gethsemane			22:50	
Catch of fish	Lower Galilee				21:6

MIRACLES OF THE APOSTLES (THE BOOK OF ACTS)		
MIRACLES	**AGENT**	**SOURCE**
The Holy Spirit fills a gathering at Pentecost		2:1-4
Cripple at the Beautiful Gate healed	Peter	3:1-10
Ananias ans Saphira die	Peter	5:1-11
Many miracles and wonders	Apostles	5:12
Apostles freed from prison	Apostles	5:21-26
Miracles and wonders	Stephen	6:8
Miracles and wonders	Philip	8:13
Conversion of Paul		9:1-9
Paul's blindness cured	Ananias	9:17-19
Aeneas cured of palsy	Peter	9:33-35
Dorcas raised to life	Peter	9:36-41
Peter freed from prison	Angel	12:6-11
Elymas the sorceror blinded	Paul	13:6-11
Miracles and wonders	Paul and Barnabas	14:3
Healing of a cripple	Paul	14:8-10
Healing of a maid possessed by an evil spirit	Paul	16:16-18
Paul and Silas freed from prison by an earthquake		16:26
Miracles and wonders	Paul	19:11-12
Raising of Eutychus	Paul	20:9-11
Paul uninjured from a viper's bite	Paul	28:3-6
Publius' father and others healed	Paul	28:7-10

The miracle of the multiplication of the loaves and the fishes, commemorated in a mosaic at the 5th-century church of Heptapegon on the shore of the Sea of Galilee.

ANGELS

The Bible assumes the existence of heavenly beings, superior to man but subservient to God. They serve various functions in the Bible, in both the Old and the New Testaments, as messengers of God (the Hebrew word for angel originally meant "messenger"), saviors of the righteous, imposers of divine judgment, harbingers of special events, and as a celestial chorus praising God.

The patriarch Abraham gives hospitality to the three angels; detail from an Italian manuscript of the 15th century.

The Bible mentions various types of angel, forming a hierarchy in heaven. They are led by seven archangels (Rev 1:4, 4:5): Uriel, Michael, Jermiel, Gabriel, Raphael, Raguel, and Sariel, who "go in and out before the glory of the Holy One" (Tob 12:15). They are wise (II Sam 14:20) and often assume human form (Gen 18:2; Josh 5:13-14). The Bible does not always distinguish clearly between the angel and God. Thus, the angel of God calls to Moses from the Burning Bush but the following conversation is with God (Ex 3). In many instances angels foretell the birth of a prominent biblical personality, e.g., Isaac (Gen 18), Samson (Judg 13), John the Baptist (Luke 1:11), and Jesus (Luke 1:26). Angels sometimes intervene in moments of crisis, as with Abraham about to sacrifice Isaac (Gen 22:11), warning Joseph to take his family to Egypt (Matt 2:13), or releasing Peter from prison (Acts 12:7-10).

Special names are given to the angels connected with the divine throne, especially the cherubs (*cherubim*) and seraphs (*seraphim*). Cherubs guarded the entrance of the Garden of Eden (Gen 3:24), while "God rode upon a cherub and flew" (II Sam 22:11; Ps 18:10). Two gold-plated wooden cherub images above the Ark of the Covenant served as the throne of God both in the tabernacle (Ex 25:18-30; 37:7-9), and in the Temple (I Kgs 6:23). Cherubs were conceived as winged creatures (Ex 25:20; I Kgs 6:24) with calves' feet and human hands at the ends of their wings (Ezek 1:7-8). They had one (Ex 25:20), two (Ezek 41:18-19), and even four (Ezek 1:6-10: a man, a lion, an ox, and an eagle) faces.

The seraphs, also winged creatures, surrounded God's heavenly throne (Is 6:1-6; Luke 2:13). They were considered to be similar to winged serpents (cf. Num 21:8; Is 14:29, 30:6).

The only two angels bearing personal names in the Old Testament are Gabriel and Michael (Dan 8:16, 9:21, 10:13,21, 12:1).

One angel, Satan, is particularly noted for his malevolence toward man. It is he who causes God to test Job (although it is not certain whether "Satan" at this time was the name of the angel or just the Hebrew word for the "accuser") and who accuses the High Priest Joshua (Zech 3:1-2). In the Old Testament he is subservient to God, whereas in the New Testament he is portrayed as a rebel angel cast down from heaven (Rev 12:9), and responsible for man's iniquities (Mark 4:15), physical affliction, and pain (Luke 13:16). He is known by several names, including: Lucifer (Is 14:12), Ruler of the Demons (Matt 9:34), Wicked One (Matt 13:19), Father of Lies (John 8:44), Lord of Death (Heb 2:14), and the Great Dragon (Rev 12:9). Despite his independence from God, Satan is destined to be subdued in the End of Days (Rev 20:10).

During the Second Temple period, the belief in angels became highly complex, as reflected especially in the apocalyptic literature of the time and the Dead Sea Scrolls. The most intense belief was among the Essenes who kept secret lists of the names of angels. The Sadducees denied their existence altogether (Acts 23:6-8).]

DICK CODOR ©80

JACOB'S DREAM

III. THE OLD TESTAMENT

III.20 CANON

OLD TESTAMENT		
HEBREW CANON	**STANDARD CANON**	**DOUAY VERSION**
Genesis	Genesis	Genesis
Exodus	Exodus	Exodus
Leviticus	Leviticus	Leviticus
Numbers	Numbers	Numbers
Deuteronomy	Deuteronomy	Deuteronomy
Joshua	Joshua	Joshua
Judges	Judges	Judges
Samuel (I, II)	Ruth	Ruth
Kings (I, II)	Samuel (I, II)	Kings (I-IV)
Isaiah	Kings (I, II)	(incl. Samuel)
Jeremiah	Chronicles (I, II)	Chronicles
Ezekiel	Ezra-Nehemiah (I,II)	
Hosea	Esther	Ezra-Nehemiah
Joel	Job	Tobias
Amos	Psalms	Judith
Obadiah	Proverbs	Esther
Jonah	Ecclesiastes	Job
Micah	Song of Songs	Psalms
Nahum	Isaiah	Proverbs
Habakkuk	Jeremiah	Ecclesiastes
Zephaniah	Lamentations	Song of Songs
Haggai	Ezekiel	Wisdom of Solomon
Zechariah	Daniel	Ecclesiasticus
Malachi	Hosea	Isaiah
	Joel	Jeremiah
Psalms	Amos	Lamentations
Proverbs	Obadiah	Baruch
Job	Jonah	Ezekiel
Ruth	Micah	Daniel
Song of Songs	Nahum	Hosea
Ecclesiastes	Habakkuk	Joel
Lamentations	Zephaniah	Amos
Esther	Haggai	Obadiah
Daniel	Zechariah	Jonah
Ezra-Nehemiah	Malachi	Micah
Chronicles (I, II)		Nahum
		Habakkuk
		Zephaniah
		Haggai
		Zechariah
		Malachi
		Maccabees (I, II)

The term "canon" denotes the sacred writings of a particular religious community. Both Judaism and Christianity have an accepted canon serving as the authoritative text of the religion. The Jewish Old Testament canon evolved over a lengthy period of time. The first section of the Hebrew Bible to be canonized was the Pentateuch in approximately 444 BC, although it appears that the Book of Deuteronomy was canonized already during the reign of Josiah (621 BC). The canonization of the second section, that of the Prophets, came a little later, sometime during the late Persian /early Hellenistic period. The final section of the Bible, the Hagiographa (Writings), was canonized only in the Greco-Roman period; however, it is probable that some of the books, including much of Psalms, were already accorded full status as authoritative texts as early as the Babylonian Exile. Jewish tradition attributes the bulk of biblical compilation and edition to the Great Assembly under the guidance of Ezra (c.500 BC). Modern scholars reject this date as being far too early; several of the books could only have been written in the Greek period, e.g., Ecclesiastes and the second part of Daniel (from chapter 7 on). It is generally assumed, but not verified, that the Hebrew Bible achieved its present form at the Council of Jamnia (c.AD 90).

The Pentateuch, comprising the first five books, has its logical continuation in the so-called Former Prophets section, which completes the historical narrative of the early Israelites. To the Former Prophets were added the Latter Prophets, mainly a collection of prophetic utterances dating from the time preceding the fall of the Kingdom of Israel until the restoration under Ezra. To this was later added the Hagiographa containing poetic and philosophical works and the history of the restoration.

Canonization of Old Testament texts was dependent upon their being attributed to a prophetic figure. To Moses, therefore, was attributed the composition of the entire Pentateuch; to David, authorship of Psalms, and to Solomon, Proverbs, Song of Songs, and Ecclesiastes. The Latter Prophets were credited with the composition of the books bearing their names and, according to tradition, with some of the later historical works (Jeremiah with Kings and Lamentations, Ezra with Chronicles).

PENTATEUCH

The Pentateuch (known in Hebrew as the Torah) is the name given to the Five Books of Moses: Genesis, Exodus, Leviticus, Numbers, and Deuteronomy. The books record the Israelite version of history from the Creation until the death of Moses immediately preceding the conquest of Canaan. Also preserved are several collections of laws reported to have been given to Moses on Mount Sinai. The Pentateuch forms the central part of the Old Testament, with the remaining sections, Prophets and Writings, subordinate to it. Since the story related in the Pentateuch ends before the conquest of Canaan, it has been suggested that the Book of Joshua was originally incorporated as part of a larger Hexateuch ("six books"), whose history also covered the conquest of the Land of Canaan. An alternative suggestion has been to consider Deuteronomy as part of the historical narrative comprising the books of Joshua, Judges, Samuel, and Kings. The Pentateuch would then have originally been a four- volume Tetrateuch.

The authenticity of the claim of Mosaic authorship of the Pentateuch, a basic belief in traditional Judaism, has been questioned since medieval times. The Spanish Jewish biblical commentator Abraham Ibn Ezra (1092–1167) pointed to various textual anachronisms (such as the account of the death of Moses) indicating a composition of at least part of the text later than previously accepted. Jean Astruc, an 18th-century French physician, argued that JHWH and Elohim, the two names used in the text to denote the deity, indicate that Moses based his composition upon earlier literary sources. The founder of the modern school of biblical criticism was Julius Wellhausen (1844–1918), whose theories on the composite origin of the text served as the basis of most schools of modern critical thought, although many of his conclusions are now challenged.

The "documentary theory" propounded by Wellhausen suggested that the present text is the combination of four distinct sources called J, E, P, and D. According to this theory, Deuteronomy (D) is a separate work to be identified with the scroll found during the reign of King Josiah (7th century BC), which provided the impetus for the religious reforms undertaken by the king (II Kgs 23). This scroll was added to the earlier J source, so called for its use of the name JHWH to denote the God of Israel. The J or Jahwist document is considered the earliest of the sources and is dated to the 10th-9th centuries BC. According to this theory, it originated in the tribe of Judah, and tends to highlight the supremacy of this tribe over the others. The second document is the E or Elohist (using Elohim as the name of God), written some hundred years after the J document. E is said to have been composed in the Northern Kingdom and tends to reject the supremacy of Judah in favor of the sons of Joseph. These two sources were redacted about 750 BC following the fall of the Northern Kingdom. King Josiah ordered the composition of the D document, that is, the book of Deuteronomy, as a means of gaining authority for his reforms. The last source, the P or Priestly source, deals almost entirely with cultic law and is considered the latest of the sources, added after the period of the Babylonian Exile.

The 20th century saw many modifications in the documentary theory, although many scholars continue to accept its basic propositions. In Jerusalem, Moshe David (Umberto) Cassuto rejected the theory altogether, while other scholars, such as Yehezkel Kaufmann, challenged the late dating of the Priestly document, holding that it preceded Deuteronomy.

Modern scholars also attempt to discover parallels between the Pentateuch and other sources which have recently come to light, notably Canaanite and Mesopotamian documents. Three segments have received considerable attention: the Creation narrative, the patriarchal history, and the Sinai legislation. Important advances have been made in understanding the Bible based on this comparative study. A further method of comprehending the biblical narrative is the use of literary criticism in analyzing the stories of the Pentateuch. Not only has this enhanced appreciation for the biblical narrative but it has also clarified many formerly obscure points in the texts. Contemporary scholarship tends to be more conservative than the theories suggested in the later 19th and early 20th centuries and uses the study of comparative history, religion, linguistics, etc., to discard many of the ideas of the earlier critics, often authenticating the biblical text and context.

PROPHETS AND WRITINGS

The Prophets constitute the second part of the Hebrew canon. The section contains two distinct parts: Former Prophets, consisting of the books of Joshua, Judges, Samuel, and Kings, and the Latter Prophets, consisting of Isaiah, Jeremiah, Ezekiel, and the Twelve Minor Prophets (Hosea, Joel, Amos, Obadiah, Jonah, Micah, Nahum, Habakkuk, Zephaniah, Haggai, Zechariah, and Malachi). The Former Prophets section continues the narrative of the Pentateuch, relating the history of the Israelites from the conquest of Canaan until the fall of the Kingdom of Judah in 586 BC. The Latter Prophets generally contain prophetic visions concerning the fate of Judah and Israel from the period preceding the fall of the Northern Kingdom until well into the period of the restoration. Often interspersed among the prophecies are historical notes about the prophet and the circumstances in which the prophecies were given. One exception to the theme of the Latter Prophets is the short Book of Jonah, containing a story concerning the prophet's mission to Nineveh; the message of the book that repentance is open to anyone probably merited its inclusion amongst the prophetic texts. Scholars suggest that the Former Prophets were once an integral part of the Pentateuch, forming a Primary History of the early Israelites.

The Latter Prophets contain works composed over several hundred years, and were canonized at a later date. The sequence of the books does not testify to the historical order in which the prophecies were given, and it is now widely maintained that a single book may contain the work of more than one prophet, some-times from different periods (e.g., Isaiah and Deutero-Isaiah, starting with chapter 40). Amos is the earliest of the prophetic books, composed c.750 BC, and Haggai, Zechariah, and Malachi the latest, composed after the return of the Jews from the Babylonian Exile.

Although secondary in importance to the Pentateuch, the books of the Prophets have endeared themselves to Jews and Christians alike. Often poetic, they have served as a source of inspiration and hope, particularly in times of despair. Jewish tradition has added a reading from the Prophets to the weekly Sabbath readings from the Pentateuch.

The Hagiographa section concludes the Hebrew canon. It contains 11 books which can be divided into three sections: 1) poetic works (Psalms, Proverbs, Job); 2) the Five Scrolls (Ruth, Song of Songs, Ecclesiastes, Lamentations, Esther), and 3) historic works (Daniel, Ezra-Nehemiah, Chronicles). The Hagiographa section was the last included in the Hebrew canon. The inclusion of a number of books in the canon inspired much debate, and their final status was only determined around the end of the first and beginning of the 2nd century AD.

Ruth

The Book of Ruth is the second of the Five Scrolls of the Hagiographa. In the Christian canon, Ruth is placed immediately after the Book of Judges, reflecting the story's historical setting (Ruth 1:1). In the Babylonian Talmud, the book opens the Hagiographa, immediately preceding Psalms (Bava Bathra 14b). This, too, is probably based on the historical nature of the text which relates the story of Ruth, an ancestress of David, the assumed author of Psalms.

Modern scholarship is uncertain as to the period in which Ruth was composed. Certain linguistic characteristics of the text indicate a period as early as that of the Judges, while the text has also been regarded as an appeal against the post-exilic decrees of Ezra, compelling the Jews to divorce their foreign wives. It tells the story of Ruth the Moabitess who insists on sharing the fate of her mother-in-law, Naomi, and becoming part of the Jewish people.

Samuel

The Book of Samuel is a historical work describing the establishment of the early Israelite monarchy. Although present editions of the Bible divide the text of Samuel into two distinct books, I and II Samuel, this division is fairly recent, first appearing in the earliest printed edition of the Hebrew Bible of 1516–1517.

The Book of Samuel receives its name from the prophet Samuel, whose biography is recorded in the first section of the text. The book goes on to relate the history of the early monarchy under Saul and David.

Although the death of Samuel is recorded at the end of the first book, the entire text maintains his name because of the role he played in the establishment of the monarchy. Some translations, however, notably the Douay Bible, refer to the two books of Samuel as I and II Kings, with the remaining books of Kings numbered as III and IV.

Kings

The books of Kings, I and II, were originally a single text, known as the "Book of Kings," which was later divided for reasons of convenience. The text records the history of the Israelite nation from the time of the United Kingdom under David and Solomon, to the fall of the kingdoms of Israel and Judah. The book is a compilation of several earlier sources, some of which are mentioned by name in the text, such as: "The Book of the Acts of Solomon" and "The Books of the Chronicles of Judah and Israel." The text stresses the various tragedies which befell the nation as fitting punishment for the neglect of religious centralization. Whereas the book gives a parallel history of the conflicting monarchies of Judah and Israel, it is overtly pro-Judah in tone, viewing the Kingdom of Israel as a historical aberration; no king of Israel is depicted positively in the book of Kings.

Chronicles

The books of Chronicles contain a summary of the history of Israel from the time of the Creation to the destruction of the First Temple and the fall of the Kingdom of Judah. The text originally consisted of a single book which was divided into two by the translators of the Septuagint for reasons of convenience. Whereas in the Hebrew Bible, the book, which was completed in the Persian era, after the canonization of the biblical section of Prophets, appears in the Hagiographa, the Septuagint and most later translations place Chronicles immediately after Kings, whose account they parallel. The Book of Chronicles in many instances fills in the historical gaps left by the Book of Kings. It is highlighted by its emphatic pro-Davidic outlook and its concern for the Temple in Jerusalem.

Ezra-Nehemiah

The Books of Ezra and Nehemiah along with the Books of Chronicles are the last books of the Bible. Although the events mentioned in Ezra and Nehemiah are a continuation of the events narrated in Chronicles, the Jewish canon places them first, since Chronicles, which presents an overview of most of the events of biblical history, is regarded as a final summary of the entire Bible. The books of Ezra and Nehemiah were originally regarded as a single book, and the division into two books first appears in Origen (3rd century AD). Many scholars regarded Ezra, Nehemiah, and Chronicles as one continuous work, but recent linguistic criticism has supported the view that they are independent compositions. The events covered in Ezra-Nehemiah cover the century from Cyrus' decree permitting the exiles in Babylon to return to Judah (538 BC) to the beginning of the reign of Darius II (420 BC). Much of the internal chronology remains problematic. The Book of Ezra contains sections in Aramaic.

Esther

The Book of Esther, last of the Five Scrolls of the Hagiographa, records the events leading to the establishment of the Feast of Purim. It tells the story of how the Jew Mordecai and his relation, Esther, foiled the plans of Haman, vizier to the Persian king, Ahasuerus, to destroy all the Jews in the Persian Empire. There exists no outside corroboration of the events recorded, leading scholars to debate whether it is a historical account (in all or part) or fiction. The debate surrounding the book has ancient roots; the rabbis were uncertain whether to include the scroll in the canon, especially as the name of God is nowhere mentioned. Both Ecclesiasticus and Josephus do not list the Book of Esther, indicating that they did not consider it sacred. The scroll is the only biblical work not found among the Dead Sea Scrolls, further indicating the controversy surrounding the text.

Despite its canonization in the Hebrew Bible, the Church, particularly the Eastern Orthodox rite, was late in accepting the text. Martin Luther is said to have declared that he would have preferred that the Book of Esther had never been written. It was only when Esther was interpreted as an allegorical representation of the Virgin Mary, or the book as a whole was explained as an allegorical representation of the Church, that it was accepted as part of the Christian canon.

Job

The Book of Job is categorized with the Wisdom Literature of the Hagiographa and is a poetic dialogue on the theme of the suffering of the righteous. It tells the story of the affliction of Job by Satan, his fidelity to his belief in God, and his ultimate vindication and restoration of his fortunes. The narrative forms the framework for discussions between Job and his friends and eventually with God on the cause of his sufferings. It is difficult to place Job in a historical context, since little information is given as to the chronological setting of the story. The Rabbis of the Talmud debated the identity of Job and variously described him as a righteous convert, a Jew, or a Gentile prophet. Also debated was the period in which Job lived, and the possibilities extend from the Patriarchal era to the Persian period. One opinion even states that the character is entirely fictional, created for the embellishment of the subject matter of the text.

Psalms

The Book of Psalms consists of 150 poetic chapters on a variety of subjects (the division in the Greek Septuagint differs somewhat from the Hebrew Bible), and expresses the spectrum of religious ideas prevalent in biblical times. The diversity of subjects indicates not only multiple authorship of the text, but also the lengthy period of the book's composition. Some of the Psalms are anonymous, but others are ascribed to various individuals, among them: the family of Korah, Ethan, Heman, Asaph (apparently all prominent Temple musicians), Moses, and Solomon. The most prom-

inent contributor, however, is clearly David, who is credited with 74 Psalms, all written in the first person singular.

In Jewish tradition the entire book is ascribed to David ("The Psalms of David"). Nevertheless, the intention of the introductory phrase "to David" which appears at the beginning of so many of the psalms may indicate the royal patronage of David and his dynasty, rather than his actual authorship of the material. Some Psalms start with a superscription which may indicate the melody to which they were sung. Psalms 120-134 are called "Songs of Ascent" and may have been chanted by the priests as they ascended the steps to the Temple.

Psalms is generally divided into five sections (beginning Ps 1, 42, 78, 90, 107), paralleling the five books of the Pentateuch, and each ending with a blessing of thanksgiving.

III.21 THE BOOKS OF THE OLD TESTAMENT

THE BOOKS OF THE BIBLE

PENTATEUCH	CHAPTERS	PROPHETS & WRITINGS	CHAPTERS
Genesis	50	Jonah	4
Exodus	40	Micah	7
Leviticus	27	Nahum	3
Numbers	36	Habakkuk	3
Deuteronomy	34	Zephaniah	3
		Haggai	2
PROPHETS & WRITINGS		Zechariah	14
		Malachi	3
Psalms	150	Joshua	24
Proverbs	31	Judges	21
Ecclesiastes	11	Ruth	4
Song of Songs	8	I Samuel	31
Isaiah	66	II Samuel	24
Jeremiah	52	I Kings	22
Lamentations	5	II Kings	25
Ezekiel	48	I Chronicles	29
Daniel	12	II Chronicles	36
Hosea	14	Ezra	10
Joel	4	Nehemiah	13
Amos	9	Esther	10
Obadiah	1	Job	42

Genesis

The Book of Genesis (Heb. *Bereshit*, "In the Beginning") starts by recording the earliest history of the

world, from creation, and then focuses on the family of Abraham down to the descent of Jacob and his sons into Egypt. The book is so named because of its opening theme, the creation epic (Gen 1-11). It opens with an account of the creation of the world (1:1-31). God labored six days in creating the world, each day dedicated to different acts of creation. God rested on the seventh day, which became the source of the Sabbath.

Man (Hebrew: *Adam*) was created to watch over the Garden of Eden (2:15), and that he have a companion, God created woman from man's own body to serve as his mate (2:20-23); although those who see Genesis 1 and 2 as differing accounts, point to Genesis 1:27 to show an alternative version according to which male and female were created at the same time. God placed the the Garden of Eden at their disposal, but commanded them not to eat of the Tree of the Knowledge of Good and Evil (2:16-17). A serpent seduced the woman, Eve, into eating of the forbidden fruit, and she in turn persuaded the man, Adam, to eat of it. As a result of their sin, they were cursed and expelled from the Garden (ch.3).

Following the expulsion from Eden, Eve bore Adam two sons, Cain and Abel. Cain was a farmer and Abel a shepherd. Both brothers sacrificed to God in thanksgiving for their abundant produce, but whereas Abel's sacrifice was accepted, Cain's was rejected. Cain slew Abel in a fit of jealousy, and was cursed by God for this and condemned to lead a nomadic lifestyle (ch.4). Eve bore Adam a third son, Seth, and the text records the genealogy of Seth to Noah (ch.5).

As humankind developed, it rejected God and became corrupted. God planned to destroy the world, deeming only Noah and his family worthy of survival, and commanded Noah to build an ark wherein he would gather his immediate family along with pairs of the different species of animals. When Noah had completed this task, God sent a flood to destroy the world. Only the inhabitants of the ark survived, making Noah the new forefather of all humanity (6-9). Even after the deluge, humankind persisted in its evil ways, and planned to build a tower mounting to the heavens in order to rebel against God. Rather than destroy the world again, God divided man by creating different languages to make communication difficult and thus ensure man's dispersion throughout the world (11:1-9). From this juncture, the text lists the continuing genealogy of the branch of the family leading to Abraham (11:10-32).

The second section of Genesis opens with God's command to Abraham to migrate from his ancestral homeland in Mesopotamia to the Land of Canaan. In return for Abraham's obedience, God promised to bless him and make him the father of a great nation (12:1-4). The text depicts Abraham's various tribulations, including famine (12:10), the abduction of his

Noah's Ark; Noah planting the vine; the drunkeness of Noah. Panel from the doors of the Baptistery of San Giovanni, Florence.

wife Sarah by the pharaoh of Egypt (12:11-20), the disagreement between Abraham and his nephew, Lot (ch.13), the carrying-off of Lot by an invading coalition and his ensuing rescue (ch.14), and Sarah's barrenness, leading to Abraham's taking of the maidservant, Hagar, as concubine, who produced an heir, Ishmael (ch.16). God renewed his covenant with Abraham (ch.15).

At an advanced age Sarah gave birth to Isaac, who replaced Hagar's son Ishmael as heir (ch. 21). God tested Abraham by commanding him to offer Isaac as a sacrifice. Abraham obeyed God, but at the last moment Isaac was spared and a ram offered in his stead (ch.22). Abraham sent his servant to find a wife for Isaac. He traveled to Abraham's family in Aram and selected Rebekah as Isaac's bride (ch.24). Upon Abraham's death at the age of 175 (25:1-10), Isaac continued the patriarchal legacy.

Rebekah bore Isaac twin sons, Esau and Jacob. Isaac preferred Esau, the hunter, while Rebekah favored the younger Jacob. Jacob acquired by a ruse the rights of the first-born from Esau, and by another ruse the paternal blessings designed for the elder son.

To escape Esau's wrath, Jacob fled to Aram. During this journey, God appeared to Jacob and made a covenant with him as the true heir of Abraham and Isaac (28:10-22). Jacob spent 14 years with his uncle, Laban, and married Laban's two daughters, Leah and Rachel, accepting their maidservants as concubines and fathering twelve sons (eponymous ancestors of the Twelve Tribes) and one daughter by these four women. After accumulating considerable wealth, he left Laban and returned to Canaan (29-30). Despite fears to the contrary, Jacob's reunion with Esau ended amicably, and he subsequently settled in Shechem (32-33).

The final theme of Genesis, the Joseph saga, opens with an account of the open preference over his other sons shown Joseph by Jacob. This, coupled with Joseph's dreams of superiority to his brothers, prompted the latter to sell him into slavery (ch.37). Following a series of events culminating in his imprisonment in

Jacob dreaming of a ladder with angels ascending and descending. Detail from an Austrian manuscript of the 18th century.

Egypt, Joseph came to Pharaoh's attention for his ability to interpret dreams (39-40). His interpretation of Pharaoh's recurring dream as representing seven years of plenty for Egypt to be followed by seven years of famine, resulted in his appointment as vizier for all Egypt, in charge of preparations for the impending famine (ch.41). When it struck, the famine also devastated the Land of Canaan, forcing Jacob to send his sons to Egypt to purchase grain. Although Joseph recognized his brothers, they did not recognize him. After testing their remorse for selling him into slavery, Joseph revealed himself to his brothers in a tearful reunion (42-45). He then sent for his father, Jacob, who led the entire clan into Egypt and settled there in the Land of Goshen (46:1-47:4). Jacob lived out the remainder of his days in Egypt. The Book of Genesis concludes with the death of Joseph at the age of 110 (50:26), by which time the Israelites were a well established minority in Egypt.

Exodus

The Book of Exodus (Heb. *Shemot*, "names"), the second of the biblical books, deals with the formation of both the Israelite nation and the Jewish religion. The book is named after its first theme, the exodus of the Israelites from Egypt. It begins with a description of the changing conditions in Egypt following the death of Joseph. The Israelites became powerful, much to the chagrin of the native inhabitants, and they were feared by a new regime which used various means, culminating in enslavement, to suppress them, but they continued to proliferate. Attempts were made to control the population by the murder of all newborn Israelite males.

To save her baby, one Israelite mother set him afloat in a basket in the Nile, where he was discovered by Pharaoh's daughter. The princess adopted the child, named him Moses, and raised him as a prince of the Egyptian court (2:1-10). Despite his position, Moses was eventually forced to flee the country for slaying an Egyptian taskmaster he saw beating an Israelite. He made his way to Midian where he married the daughter of Jethro, the high priest, and became a shepherd (2:11-22).

God appeared to Moses in a burning bush in the wilderness and appointed him redeemer of the Israelites (3:1-4:17). Moses returned to Egypt, and with his brother, Aaron, demanded that Pharaoh release the Israelites from bondage. Pharaoh's response was to increase the labors of the Israelites (4:18-5:11).

The Egyptians were afflicted with ten plagues culminating in the slaying of the first-born, after which Pharaoh released the Israelites (7:14-12:36).

In preparation for leaving Egypt, Moses commanded the Israelite families to slaughter a lamb and smear their doorposts with its blood. On the night of the slaying of the first-born, the Israelites gathered in their homes and celebrated their impending redemption, dining on the lamb. This feast was later repeated yearly at the Passover festival celebrating the exodus from Egypt.

Regretting his decision to release the Israelites, Pharaoh pursued them. His armies cornered them on the shores of the Red Sea, which miraculously split, enabling the Israelites to cross to safety. When the following Egyptian armies entered the sea, the waters closed in and drowned them (ch.14). The people celebrated their escape by reciting the "Song of the Sea," one of the earliest examples of biblical poetry (ch.15).

The Israelites were preserved miraculously throughout their wanderings in the desert, guided by a pillar of cloud during the day and a pillar of fire by night (14:19-20). God provided them with food, sending them manna (16:4-36) and fresh water (15:24-26; 17:4-7).

After three months of wandering in the desert, Moses brought the people to Mount Sinai, where they entered into a covenant with God (ch.19). As the people stood at the foot of the mountain, Moses ascended to its peak where God proclaimed the Ten Commandments as the basis of his covenant with the people

The dividing of the Red Sea at the time of the Exodus from Egypt. Illustration from an Italian manuscript, Trieste, 1864.

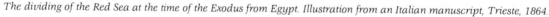

(20:1-17). Moses also received from God a compilation of laws known as the "Book of the Covenant," concerning primarily civil and criminal legislations along with several laws pertaining to ritual (20:22-23:33).

Moses' prolonged absence of 40 days caused the people to fear that God had rejected them, and they pleaded with Aaron to make them a golden calf. Aaron did as the people willed, and as a celebration was being held in honor of the idol, Moses appeared and shattered the tablets of the law in his wrath. After destroying the idol and punishing the offenders, he reascended the mountain, where he begged God to forgive the sins of the people, and re-established the covenant between God and the Israelites (31:18-34:27).

Moses then ordered the people to erect the tabernacle, a kind of mobile temple, to serve as a dwelling-place for God in the midst of the nation. With the construction of the tabernacle, Aaron and his descendants were consecrated as priests, and vestments were made for them (25-28). The establishment of the tabernacle saw the return of the divine presence to the people as "the glory of the Lord filled the tabernacle" (Ex 40:34).

Leviticus

The Book of Leviticus, sometimes referred to as the "Priests' Manual," is the third book of the Pentateuch. As its names imply, it is primarily a guide to the rituals performed by the priests in the tabernacle and later in the Temple. Modern scholarship views the text as a compilation of two sources, an older P (Priestly) source and a later H (Holiness) source, the latter comprised in chapters 17-27.

The book opens with an account of the various sacrifices offered by the individual on different occasions (1-7). Chapters 8-10 describe the consecration of the sanctuary and the anointment of Aaron and his sons as priests. Moses conducted the inauguration ceremony, initiating Aaron into the priesthood. Two of Aaron's sons, Nadab and Abihu, entered the sanctuary during the ceremony but "offered strange fire before the Lord." In response to this transgression, a fire descended from heaven and consumed them (10:1-2).

Chapters 11-15 give the laws of impurity. They start by listing the animals permissible for human consumption, all other species being considered unfit. Biblical impurity is embodied in all substances which can be considered as representing the conflict between life and death. Among the symbols of impurity are blood and semen, perceived as life-giving forces. Their unnatural emission is considered an impurity and calls for ritual purification. The service prescribed for the Day of Atonement (ch.16) is the culminating ritual in which the Temple and the entire people are purified.

The text next lists various moral and ritual laws

A priest inspecting possible cases of leprosy for ritual impurity. Hebrew-Latin edition of the Mishnah. Amsterdam, 1700.

intended to dissociate the Israelites from the practices of the pagan peoples surrounding them. Among these laws are prohibitions intended to guard against idolatry and forbidden sexual relationships. Various social commandments are also given, culminating in the famous axiom, "You shall love your neighbor as yourself" (19:18).

Among the rituals are listed the defects which exclude a priest from participating in the Temple ritual (21-22), the rites for the festivals (ch.23), and the laws of the sabbatical and jubilee years (ch.25). These are followed by a description of the punishments that will befall the nation should its members reject the code (ch.26). The Book of Leviticus ends with a description of the method of redeeming gifts offered to the sanctuary.

Numbers

The Book of Numbers receives its name from its opening chapter which contains a census of the tribes as they began their trek towards Canaan. The text comprises three central themes: 1) the 19 days spent at Sinai (1:1-10:10); 2) the 40-year trek towards the Plains of Moab (10:11-22:1); and 3) the five-month stay at the Plains of Moab (22:2-36:13).

Details of the census are followed by ritual laws pertaining to a woman suspected by her husband of adultery (5:11-29), and the regulations pertaining to a Nazirite (a person who, for a limited period, takes additional ritualistic regulations upon himself; ch.6).

Beginning with chapter 7, the book records the dedication of the tabernacle and the priesthood, and the preparations for the journey to Canaan (7:1-10:10). Following the arrangement of the tribes in their traveling order and the consecration of the tabernacle, the

Israelites left Sinai two years after their departure from Egypt (10:11).

The 40 years of wandering in the desert proved to be a difficult time for the Israelites, who were plagued with rebellion and dissent. Although Moses was a charismatic leader, his authority was sometimes challenged (11-12).

As the nation neared the borders of Canaan, Moses sent 12 men to "spy out the land of Canaan" (13:2). The unfavorable report of the majority upon their return dissuaded the tribes from invading the territory from the south. Since this was seen as a loss of faith in the ability of God to protect the nation, the entire generation was condemned to end its days in the desert without reaching the Promised Land (13-14).

Another rebellion was led by the Levite, Korah, who charged Moses with nepotism in his appointment of Aaron as high priest. The revolt was crushed when the earth opened and swallowed its leaders. God's choice of Aaron and his descendants was also challenged but miraculously vindicated (16-17). The text then lists the rights of the priesthood (ch.18) and details the priestly ritual of the red heifer, by which one could be cleansed of ritual impurity (Num 19).

When the people were left without water in the desert, God commanded Moses to speak to a rock, from which water would then gush forth, but Moses struck the rock instead. God rebuked Moses for disregarding the details of his command, and punished him by decreeing that he would not lead the people into Canaan (ch.20). Nevertheless, he successfully led the people in battle against Sihon and Og, kings of the Transjordanian frontier (21:21-35). The territory of these kings, along with territory later conquered from Midian, was allotted to the tribes of Reuben and Gad, and to half of the tribe of Manasseh (ch.32).

As the Israelites approached Canaan, Balak, king of Moab, hired the sorcerer, Balaam, to curse the Israelites. However, every curse he attempted to pronounce was altered into a blessing. The Midianites then sent their women to the Israelite encampment to seduce the men to idolatry. The leader of the tribe of Simeon indulged in sexual relations publicly with a Midianite woman, and as a result was slain by the zealous Phinehas, who is praised for this act and rewarded with the hereditary priesthood (22-24).

A second census was held in preparation for the conquest of the land. The total, somewhat lower than that of the original census, reflects the Israelite losses as a result of the experiences in the desert (ch.26). Moses selected Joshua as his successor and led the people in an attack against Midian, his final act of military leadership. The text interrupts these two episodes by describing the laws regarding the festival sacrifices (28-29), and the laws of vows made by a woman (ch. 30). With the desert sojourn nearing its close, a list is given of the sites of Israelite encampments (ch.33). The Book of Numbers closes with a series of laws regarding Israelite settlement in the land: 1) laws of the conquest and allocation of the land (ch.34); 2) laws of the levitical cities and the cities of refuge (ch.35); and 3) laws regarding inter-tribal marriage (ch.36).

Deuteronomy

The name of the Book of Deuteronomy, last of the books of the Pentateuch, stems from the Greek translation of a Hebrew phrase meaning "second law" or "repeated law" (Deut 17:18), reflecting the text's reiteration of the laws of the preceding books. There are, however, important differences between the laws of Deuteronomy and the law-codes of Exodus, Leviticus, and Numbers. In addition, Deuteronomy often refers to itself as a separate code of law (1:5; 27:3,8,26; 31:26). The text forms an organic whole, the last testimonies of Moses, in which he summarized the law in an exhortation to the Israelites to remain faithful to God.

The book represents the final speeches of Moses before his death, delivered in the first person. His first speech, emphasizing the lessons of the Exodus (1:6-3:29), is followed by an exposition of the uniqueness of God (ch.4). He then reviews the Ten Commandments as the basis of the entire law and expands on the reasons for their observance (5-11); this is followed by the Deuteronomic Code (12-26). The obligations of the code are reinforced with blessings and curses to be recited to the people upon entering Canaan (ch.27), and extended with a further list of blessings and curses emphasizing the need for upright behavior (ch.28).

Before his death, Moses renewed the covenant between God and the people, demanding continued loyalty to God. He informed the people that Joshua would lead them into the land of Canaan (29:1-31:13). As the day of Moses' death arrived, he recited what became known as the "Song of Moses," in which he

The Red Heifer. Illustration from a prayer-book. Italy, 1441.

called upon the heavens and the earth to testify to the covenant between God and the Israelites (32:1-43). He then addressed the tribes, predicting each one's fate (ch.33).

Finally, Moses ascended Mount Nebo in Transjordan, from where God showed him the land he was forbidden to enter. Moses died on Mount Nebo at the age of 120, and "no man knows his grave to this day" (34:6). The Book of Deuteronomy ends with a description of the mourning for Moses, and a brief eulogy, in which he is described as a prophet "whom the Lord knew face to face" (34:10).

Joshua

The Book of Joshua recounts the conquest of Canaan under the Israelite general Joshua. It opens with an account of the two earliest victories of the Israelites in Canaan, at Jericho and at Ai (1-8). Although the local nations were meant to be either expelled or destroyed, the Gibeonites succeeded in tricking Joshua into forging a treaty with them. Despite his vow not to harm the Gibeonites, they were punished for their deceit and made subservient to the Israelites (ch.9). Having

The Fall of Jericho. Miniature, France, 15th Century.

created an Israelite base in the center of the country, Joshua extended his conquests to the south and north (10-11).

There follows a summary of the conquests of Joshua. Having conquered the bulk of the territory allotted by God, Joshua divided it among the tribes; he then set aside 48 cities for the Levites and six cities of refuge (13-22). The book ends with the people performing the Deuteronomic ceremony (Deut 27), reaffirming their commitment to God. After reciting his own final testament to the people, demanding that they complete the conquest that he began, while continuing to observe the commandments, Joshua died at the age of 110 years.

Judges

The Book of Judges begins with a brief historical account of the Israelite conquest of Canaan. This differs in many ways from that appearing in the Book of Joshua. Whereas in Joshua the conquest is portrayed as a unified effort of the tribes under a strong central authority, in Judges the conquest appears to be a lengthy process undertaken individually by the various tribes and clans. The book continues by describing the leadership of the judges, local military heroes, immediately following the conquest, and ends with a portrayal of the internal anarchy rampant among the autonomous tribes.

The opening chapters recount the final battles in the conquest of Canaan that followed the death of Joshua, emphasizing the clans of Othniel and Caleb of the tribe of Judah, as well as several of the northern Canaanite strongholds including the cultic center of Bethel (1:1-2:5). This is followed by a short introduction to the period of the judges, in which local leaders assumed authority in times of need. The nation was harassed and frequently dominated by its neighbors, and this is seen as divine punishment for the inroads of idolatry among the people (2:6-3:6). The book continues with a listing of 13 of these judges (for details see III.26, The Judges).

The book closes with an account of the historical events preceding the monarchy. Chapters 17-18 describe the northerly migration of the tribe of Dan, against the background of the northern sanctuary established by Micah. An account is also given of the civil war between the tribe of Benjamin and the other tribes.

Ruth

The Book of Ruth is placed immediately after the Book of Judges in the Christian canon, reflecting the story's historical setting (Ruth 1:1). Modern scholarship is uncertain as to the period in which the Book of Ruth was composed. Certain linguistic characteristics of the

Ruth gleaning after the reapers (upper register), and Ruth in Boaz's tent. Illustration from the Admont Bible, c.1130–1150.

text indicate a period as early as that of the later judges, while others have assigned it to the time of Ezra.

The Book of Ruth is a love story taking place in the period of the judges. Because of a famine in Judah, Elimelech of Bethlehem and his wife Naomi were forced to move their family to Moab, where their two sons married Moabite women. However, not only Elimelech but also his two sons died soon after, leaving their widows childless. Upon hearing that the famine was over, Naomi decided to return to Judah, and one of the daughters-in-law, Ruth, insisted on accompanying her back to Bethlehem. Ruth's loyalty to Naomi is expressed in the famous statement, "Your people shall be my people, and your God my God" (1:16).

After their arrival in Judah, Ruth set out to the field of Boaz, a kinsman of Elimelech, to glean after the harvesters. There she encountered Boaz (ch.2) and told Naomi of the meeting. Naomi encouraged her to approach him and suggest that he fulfill his duty of levirate marriage with her (ch.3). Boaz accepted his responsibility and married Ruth, after a closer relative agreed to renounce rights to her (4:1–12). The genealogy at the end of the book shows Obed, child of Ruth and Boaz, to be the grandfather of David (4:13–22), and thus progenitor of Jesus (Matt 1:5).

Samuel

The Book of Samuel is essential for an understanding of the establishment of the early Israelite monarchy. Present editions of the Bible divide the text of Samuel into two distinct books, I and II Samuel. This division derives from the early Greek and Latin translations; it first appears in a Hebrew Bible in 1516–1517.

The Book of Samuel receives its name from the prophet Samuel, whose biography is recorded in its first section. The book goes on to relate the history of the early monarchy under Saul and David. Although Samuel dies at the end of the first book, the entire text maintains his name because of the role he played in the establishment of the monarchy. Some translations, however, notably the Douay Bible, refer to the two books of Samuel as I and II Kings, with the remaining books of Kings numbered III and IV.

The book opens with the birth of Samuel and his childhood in the tabernacle of Shiloh. Even as a child, he was subject to mantic visions, one of which foretold the downfall of the House of Eli, the high priest (I Sam 1:3). This prophecy was fulfilled when Eli's two sons were killed in battle against the Philistines and the Ark of the Covenant was captured. Eli died upon hearing of the disaster. However, the Ark did not remain long in the possession of the Philistines. A series of calamities befalling the Philistines was attributed to the power of the Ark, and it was duly returned to the Israelites (I Sam 4–6). Samuel assumed the leadership of the nation upon the death of Eli (I Sam 7).

Although Samuel proved to be a successful national leader whose authority was respected by all the tribes, the people recognized that his rule was only a temporary answer to the nation's temporal and religious problems. Samuel's sons were considered unworthy of continuing the legacy of their father (I Sam 8:1–3), and while a large segment of the population began clamoring for a king, Samuel himself expressed his initial opposition. The text gives two accounts of the establishment of the monarchy, one pro-monarchist (I Sam 10:17–25), and one anti-monarchist (I Sam 8:4–21). The debate was ended with the anointment of Saul as king (I Sam 10:1).

Saul proved to be a successful monarch in his rallying of the tribes against the Philistines (I Sam 13–14). Nonetheless, he aroused Samuel's wrath by performing cultic rituals without awaiting the arrival of the prophet. As a result, Saul lost his favored status as king, with Samuel prophesying that his descendants would not inherit his throne (I Sam 13). Saul once again proved his inadequacy as monarch when he failed to execute the Amalekite king, Agag, as commanded (I Sam 15). As a result, Samuel secretly anointed David as Saul's successor (I Sam 16).

David's slaying of the Philistine giant Goliath won him the love of the people, but this aroused Saul's jealousy, and David was banished from the court. David, now an outlaw, served as a mercenary for the Philistine garrison at Ziklag (I Sam 27); however, he continued to display loyalty to Saul, and on two occasions refrained from killing him (I Sam 23, 26). Only

Kirjath Jearim, where the ark of the covenant rested before reaching Jerusalem (I Sam 6:21).

General view of Bethlehem, where David was born and Mary gave birth to Jesus.

The Punishment of Korah, Dathan and Abiram (Num 16). Fresco by Botticelli in the Sistine Chapel.

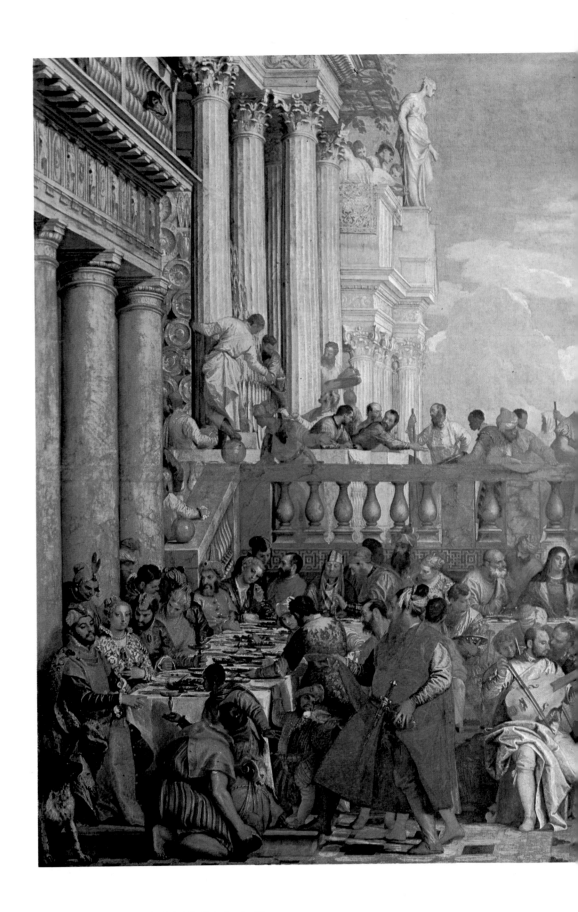

The Marriage at Cana (Jn 2:1–11). Painting by Veronese.

Left (top) Reconstruction of a lyre in the shape of a bull's head from Ur of the Chaldees.
(bottom) Horn made from elephant's tusk. Megiddo, late Bronze Age.

Right (top) Agricultural scene, from a wall painting in an Egyptian tomb, c.1420 BC.
(bottom) Back panel of the throne of the Egyptian Pharaoh Tut-ankhamon.

St. Peter's Church, on the shore of the Sea of Galilee, where Jesus appeared to his disciples (Jn. 21:1–25).

The Garden of Gethsemane, on the Mount of Olives, where Jesus spent the night before his arrest.

after the deaths of Saul and his son Jonathan at the battle of Gilboa (I Sam 31), did David assume the role of monarch, and initially his authority was limited to his own tribe of Judah (II Sam 1-2). Saul's son, Ishbosheth, was appointed king of the Northern Tribes but was soon assassinated by followers of David (II Sam 4). David utilized this opportunity to consolidate his rule over all the tribes, creating a centralized kingdom with its capital at Jerusalem, which he had conquered (II Sam 5). He then brought the Ark of the Covenant to Jerusalem and planned the construction of a central Temple to house it. He was denied this right, however, by the prophet Nathan, who nevertheless foretold that the Davidic dynasty would be established for ever, and that David's son would build the Temple (II Sam 6-7).

The Book of Samuel continues with an account of court life under David and the various threats to his reign. Chapter 9 records the entry of Mephibosheth, sole remaining scion of the house of Saul, into the court of David, and chapter 10 describes the battles of David against the Ammonites. The court of David was filled with intrigues, such as his seduction of and subsequent marriage to Bathsheba, and the ensuing condemnation of his actions by the prophet Nathan (II Sam 11-12); the rape by David's son Amnon of his half-sister Tamar; and the revenge and disgrace of his son Absalom stemming from this (II Sam 12-14). The greatest threat to David was Absalom's revolt (II Sam 15-18), which was crushed, as was the revolt of the Northern Tribes under the leadership of Sheba from the tribe of Benjamin (II Sam 20).

Chapters 22 and 23 are poetic works attributed to David; the first poem (II Sam 22) is almost identical to Psalm 18, whereas the second poem (II Sam 23:1-7) is an account of David's final testament.

The book ends with an account of the census conducted by David towards the end of his reign. The census was followed by a plague, which caused David to dedicate the threshing floor of Araunah the Jebusite as the future site of the Temple.

Kings

The two Books of Kings were originally a single text, known as the Book of Kings, which was later divided for reasons of convenience. It records the history of the Israelite nation from the time of the United Kingdom under David and Solomon, to the fall of the kingdoms of Judah and Israel. The book is a compilation of several earlier sources, some of which are mentioned by name in the text, such as "The Book of the Acts of Solomon" and "The Books of the Chronicles of Judah and Israel." The text leans heavily on the reforms of King Josiah, and describes the various tragedies which befell the nation as fitting punishment for its neglect of religious centralization in Jerusalem. Whereas the book gives a parallel history of the conflicting monar-

chies of Judah and Israel, the text is overtly pro-Judah in tone, viewing the Kingdom of Israel as a historical aberration; no king of Israel is depicted positively in the Book of Kings.

The book opens with an account of the final days of King David. Despite an attempt by his son, Adonijah, to usurp the throne, the enfeebled David, upon the instigation of the prophet Nathan and David's wife, Bathsheba, named Solomon his heir and abdicated in his favor (I Kgs 1-2). Solomon reorganized the kingdom and extended its limits through a series of treaties (I Kgs 4). With his power consolidated, he began building the Temple, a monumental task that lasted 13 years (I Kgs 5-8).

Although Solomon is depicted as a wise monarch, whose fame reached even the distant shores of Sheba (I Kgs 10), his later years saw a diminishing of his grandeur, depicted as religious lapses. Solomon was a polygamist whose 700 wives (and 300 concubines) eventually led him to apostasy, thereby incurring the wrath of the people and of God. Although a rebellion against Solomon led by Jeroboam was ultimately crushed, this was to have dire results during the reign of Solomon's heir, Rehoboam (I Kgs 11:26-40).

When he succeeded to the throne, Rehoboam was asked by the elders of the Northern tribes whether he would continue the harsh taxation policies of his father. When he responded that he intended even to increase the burden of taxation, the Northern tribes seceded from the kingdom and proclaimed Jeroboam monarch. Jeroboam consolidated his authority by initiating a religious reform that widened the gap between the two kingdoms. Among his innovations were the establishment of new cultic centers at Dan and Bethel, where golden calves were worshiped, and the adjustment of the calendar so that the Feast of Tabernacles would fall on a different date than in Judah.

The Kingdom of Judah was invaded by Egypt, but the Davidic dynasty remained intact. Rehoboam's grandson Asa restored Israelite ritual to its former pre-eminence. He waged war against Baasha of the Northern kingdom, but did not succeed in reuniting the kingdoms (I Kgs 14:25-15:24).

One of the outstanding rulers of the Northern kingdom was Omri. who ruled for 12 years, forging it into a local power. He erected a new capital, Samaria, and formed alliances with the neighboring states, notably Sidon. His son, Ahab, married the Sidonian princess, Jezebel. Upon his accession to the throne, Ahab was greatly influenced by the religious customs of Jezebel, and permitted a temple to Baal to be built in the capital (I Kgs 16).

Ahab found his nemesis in Elijah, a zealous prophet who confronted him over his excesses, both religious and political. Foremost among the successes of Elijah was his confrontation with the prophets of Baal on

The Queen of Sheba meeting Solomon. Fresco by Piero della Francesca (1452–1466). Basilica of San Francesco; Arezzo, Italy.

Mount Carmel. Following the death of Ahab at the battle of Ramoth Gilead, Elijah continued to confront Ahab's heir, Ahaziah.

Although Ahaziah, king of Israel, attempted to capture Elijah, he was unsuccessful (II Kgs 1), and Elijah ended his prophetic mission by miraculously ascending to heaven in a whirlwind. He was succeeded by his disciple, Elisha (II Kgs 2). Ahaziah was succeeded by his brother Jehoram. The kingdom of Moab utilized the period of transition to attack Israel. Jehoram made a pact with Jehoshaphat of Judah, and the two nations, under the prophetic guidance of Elisha, were able to crush the Moabites (II Kgs 3).

Chapters 5–8 record the miracles attributed to Elisha, including the increasing of the widow's oil and the curing of the Aramean general, Naaman, of his leprosy. Unlike his mentor, Elijah, Elisha's prophecies concerned the surrounding nations as well as the Israelites. He predicted the demise of Ben-Hadad of Aram and the succession of Hazael to the throne.

The reigns of Jehoram and Ahaziah of Judah (II Kgs 8:16–29) are briefly summarized, and this is followed by an account of the overthrow of the dynasty of Omri in the Northern kingdom of Israel by the general, Jehu. Ahaziah of Judah came to the aid of his beleaguered cousin, Jehoram, and was killed in battle against Jehu (II Kgs 9–10).

Jehu proceeded to eradicate Baal-worship in the Northern kingdom, while in Judah the queen-mother, Athaliah, daughter of Ahab, assumed the throne and strengthened the entrenchment of the pagan ritual. The high priest, Jehoiada, initiated a coup against her, replacing her with her grandson Joash who, upon his assassination, was succeeded by Amaziah (II Kgs 11–12).

Jehu of Israel was followed by Jehoahaz who was, in turn, succeeded by Joash. Elisha offered his last prophecy to Joash: Joash would smite Aram three times before succumbing (II Kgs 13). Joash was attacked by Judah but managed to defeat the Judean king, Amaziah, in battle. In 722 BC, the Northern kingdom finally collapsed in face of the Assyrian armies. The nation was exiled, and the territory was populated by other conquered peoples (II Kgs 14–17). The account of the fall of the Northern kingdom of Israel includes the description of the visit of Ahaz of Judah to Damascus, where he was influenced by the Aramean ritual. Upon his return to Jerusalem, he erected a new altar on the Aramean model to compete with the Temple ritual (II Kgs 16).

Under the reign of Hezekiah, Judah was spared defeat by the advancing Assyrian armies. Influenced by the prophet Isaiah, the king instituted a religious reform accredited with the miraculous lifting of the

Assyrian siege of Jerusalem. Hezekiah, however, incurred the wrath of Isaiah by receiving a diplomatic mission from Babylonia. Isaiah warned the king that as a result of his lack of faith in God, Babylonia would eventually destroy Judah and carry the descendants of Hezekiah into captivity (II Kgs 18-20). Hezekiah was succeeded by his son and grandson, Manasseh and Amon, both of whom rejected his religious reforms and restored idolatry to the nation (II Kgs 21).

However, Amon's son Josiah instituted the final great religious reform of the period. During the cleansing of the Temple, a scroll, apparently the Book of Deuteronomy, was found. The innovations made on the basis of this scroll include the total centralization of religious worship in Jerusalem. While still in the midst of his reforms, Josiah was killed in the battle of Megiddo (II Kgs 22:1-24:6).

It was in the reign of Jehoiachin that Nebuchadnezzar of Babylonia first captured Jerusalem (597 BC). Jehoiachin was led into exile and replaced by the puppet-king, Zedekiah, who was persuaded to revolt against the Babylonians, and it was this revolt that brought about the final destruction of the kingdom of Judah. Zedekiah was blinded and led into exile along with the kingdom's elite, and the Temple was destroyed (586 BC). Following the destruction of the Temple, the Babylonian-appointed governor, Gedaliah, was assassinated, causing much of the remaining population to flee the wrath of the Babylonians (II Kgs 24:7-25:26). For fuller information on the kings of the period, see III.27, Kingship and the Kings of Judah and Israel.

Chronicles

The Books of Chronicles contain a summary of the history of Israel from the time of the Creation to the destruction of the First Temple and the fall of the Kingdom of Judah. The text originally consisted of a single book which was divided into two by the translators of the Sepatuagint. Whereas in the Hebrew Bible, the book, which was completed in the Persian era, after the canonization of the biblical section of Prophets, appears in the Hagiographa, the Septuagint and most later translations place Chronicles immediately after Kings, whose account they parallel. The Book of Chronicles is important to scholars for filling in the historical gaps left by the Book of Kings.

The text was written as an account of the Davidic dynasty of the Kingdom of Judah, and all earlier history recorded in the book, primarily a list of genealogical tables, centers on the tribes inhabiting that kingdom (Judah, Benjamin, and Levi) (I Chr 1-9). The historical account opens with the death of Saul and David's accession to the throne (I Chr 10). The first book continues with an account of the monarchy under David (I Chr 11-29), stressing only the positive

aspects of his reign. Although the Chronicler drew heavily on the Book of Samuel for information, all negative aspects of David's and Solomon's reigns are omitted in an attempt to glorify the first two rulers of the dynasty. As opposed to the Samuel account, David was also credited with the initial planning of the Temple edifice (I Chr 22-29), and his heir, Solomon, is portrayed as merely the executor of those plans. Nonetheless, six out of the nine chapters devoted to Solomon (II Chr 1-9) are concerned with the Temple's actual construction.

The remainder of the book (II Chr 10-36) narrates the history of the Kingdom of Judah. The attitude adopted by the author is decidedly pro-Judah, and the Northern secessionists are referred to merely as "worthless rogues" (II Chr 13:7). In addition, the religious practices of the Northern kingdom are condemned as false, as only in Jerusalem could cultic practices be properly and legitimately conducted. Despite the scathing condemnations leveled at the Northern kingdom, the Chronicler still considers its inhabitants members of the people of Israel and calls on them to reunite with Judah.

The author adds much information about the kings of Judah that is omitted from the Book of Kings, and describes the wars and construction projects undertaken by the Judean monarchs. Emphasis is also placed on the religious reforms carried out in Judah, and four kings, Asa, Jehoshaphat, Hezekiah, and Josiah, are given special attention as the proponents of those reforms.

Apart from the Book of Kings, other sources of Chronicles are mentioned by the author; however, this is generally the only knowledge of the lost Book of Nathan and Annals of the Prophet Iddo. Despite his dependence on the Book of Kings as a primary source for his own work, the Chronicler is at variance with the author of Kings in his philosophy of history. Chronicles is primarily concerned with divine justice in history, and regards historical events as influenced by the actions of individuals. The pious King Josiah was killed in the battle of Megiddo in punishment for ignoring a divine warning given through Pharaoh Necho, while the wicked King Manasseh is recorded as having repented, thereby explaining his lengthy reign of 55 years.

Ezra-Nehemiah

The Books of Ezra and Nehemiah are a continuation of the events narrated in Chronicles. In the Jewish canon, Chronicles comes first as it presents an overview of most of the events of biblical history and is regarded as a final summary of the entire Bible. Although scholars have regarded the three books as one continuous work, linguistic comparison and the different ideological outlooks of the texts seem to point to Ezra and Nehemiah, on the one hand, and Chronicles on the other, as independent compositions. The books of Ezra and Nehemiah were originally regarded as a single book and the division into two books first appears in Origen (3rd century AD).

The historical events related in Ezra and Nehemiah span one hundred years and contain information on the early Second Temple period. This can be divided into three historical eras: 1) the return of Jewish exiles from Babylonia and the initial restoration under the authority of Sheshbazzar and Zerubbabel (corresponding to the period of the prophets Haggai, Zechariah, and Malachi); 2) the return and reforms of Ezra the Scribe; and 3) the governorship of Nehemiah.

The historical record of the books opens with the journey of Sheshbazzar and Zerubbabel from Babylonia to Jerusalem at the head of a wave of exiles. Upon arrival in Jerusalem, work was begun on the reconstruction of the Temple. Although the two figures are depicted as contemporaries, they apparently arrived in Israel separately at the heads of two waves of immigration (Ezra 1-3). Despite Sheshbazzar's leading the first group of exiles in their return to the land, it appears that his nephew Zerubbabel was the more prominent of the two; he was even referred to by Haggai as the chosen one (Hag 2:23). Zerubbabel did not complete the task he had begun, and is not recorded as having been present at the dedication of the new Temple (Ezra 6:14-18).

The text records that Ezra arrived in Jerusalem in the seventh regnal year of the Persian king Artaxerxes (probably 458 BC) and that Nehemiah joined him there 13 years later. Though some scholars assert that Nehemiah actually preceded Ezra in returning to Jerusalem, an abundance of new archaeological evidence seems to support the former view.

The text itself, a combination of Hebrew and Aramaic, is mostly a compilation of various documents and censuses from the restoration era. These include: a Hebrew and Aramaic document from Cyrus the Great, granting Jews the right to return to their land (Ezra 1:2-4; 6:3-12), correspondence between Jewish officials and the Persian court (Ezra 4:8-22; 5:7-17; Neh 6:2-9), lists of Temple vessels (Ezra 1:9-11; 8:26-27), and various censuses regarding the repatriates (Ezra 2:1-70; 10:18-44; Neh 3:1-32; 7:7-72; ch. 10; 11:3-36; 12:1-36). Also included are two prayers by the leaders (Ezra 9:6-15; Neh 1:5-11). Despite a lacuna of approximately 70 years from the period of Zerubbabel to the arrival of Ezra, the books give a clear indication of the early years of the Second Temple period.

Esther

The Book of Esther purports to record events leading to the establishment of the Feast of Purim (Lots). There exists no historical corroboration of the events recorded.

Some scholars believe it to be pure fiction, others that it is based on true events. The debate surrounding the book has ancient roots; the early Rabbis were uncertain whether to include it in the canon. Neither Ben Sira nor Josephus list the Book of Esther, indicating that they did not consider it sacred, and it is the only biblical work not found among the Dead Sea scrolls.

According to the narrative, a Persian emperor, Ahasuerus (Xerxes I?), celebrated his accession to the throne with a six-month-long feast. Enraged at the refusal of his consort, Vashti, to appear before him at the end of the feast, he deposed her and selected a new queen, Esther, a Jewish orphan raised by her cousin Mordecai. Mordecai cautioned her not to reveal her nation of origin.

Illuminated Scroll of Esther, Ferrara, 1616.

Shortly after Esther's selection, the king elevated Haman to the position of grand vizier. The power-hungry Haman decreed that all the Jews of the empire be slaughtered, and a date was chosen by lot. Upon hearing of Haman's plan, Mordecai persuaded Esther to intercede with the king. At a banquet, she asked Ahasuerus to spare her and her people. When asked who threatened her, she pointed to Haman, declaring that he was the cause of her misfortune. Ahasuerus decreed that Haman be hanged on the gallows intended for Mordecai. The king issued a new decree granting the Jews the right to defend themselves against their enemies, and Mordecai was appointed grand vizier in Haman's stead.

The book lacks the characteristics of a religious text. No mention is made of God, and the entire event occurs under natural circumstances. Despite its canonization in the Hebrew Bible, the Church, particularly the Eastern Orthodox rite, was late in accepting the text. Martin Luther is said to have declared that he would have preferred that the Book of Esther had never been written. Only when Esther was interpreted as an allegorical representation of the Virgin Mary, or the book as a whole was explained as an allegorical representation of the Church, was it accepted as part of the Christian canon.

Job

The Book of Job is categorized with the Wisdom Literature of the Hagiographa and is a poetic dialogue on the theme of the suffering of the righteous. Its principal characters and speakers are Job and the three friends who come to console him: Eliphaz, Bildad, and Zophar. The text opens with a prose prologue introducing Job and giving an account of the events leading to his misfortune (1-2), and concludes with a parallel epilogue (42:7-17) in which Job is restored to his fortunes.

At the beginning of the book, the reader is introduced to Job, a wealthy resident of the Land of Uz. When God holds Job up to Satan as an example of a righteous man, Satan responds that Job is righteous only because of the great favor shown him by God. Should God cause Job to suffer, Satan claims, Job will curse God. God responds to Satan's challenge by attempting to prove Job's righteousness. In a series of calamities, Job's children are killed and his wealth is lost. Despite the disasters, Job remains faithful to God, upon which God, still challenged by Satan, causes Job to contract various afflictions. It is under these circumstances that Job's three friends come to visit and the debate between them and Job develops (1-2).

The dialogue itself is a debate between Job and his friends on the nature of his suffering, with an underlying question, "Why do righteous people suffer in this world?" In a series of three debates (4-14; 15-21; 22-27) Job's friends attempt to convince him that his misfortunes are the result of either his natural sinfulness, or an attempt by God to exhort him to improve his character. Job will be spared future suffering if only he commits himself further to God. Job rejects the contentions of his comrades, and repeatedly declares his own innocence, thereby implying the unjust nature of God. A fourth friend, Elihu, then enters the conversation and attempts, in a series of long speeches, to rebut Job and his friends (32-37). Despite the variety of opinions expressed, only the appearance of God himself can quell Job's growing dissatisfaction.

The very appearance of God is a consolation to Job. Whereas previously he felt that God had neglected him, it now becomes apparent that although he cannot comprehend the workings of the Creator, he must nonetheless submit to the divine will. Job is reminded of his insignificance within the totality of creation, and of his resulting inability to understand the manner in which God controls the world. He finally accepts the divine will (38:1-42:6).

It is difficult to place Job in a historical context, since little information is given as to the chronological setting of the story. The rabbis of the Talmud variously described him as a righteous convert, a Jew, or a Gentile prophet. It has also been suggested that the author may have been an Edomite. Also debated was the period in which Job lived, and the possibilities extend from the Patriarchal era to the Persian period. One opinion even states that the character is entirely a parable, created for the embellishment of a philosophic text.

Psalms

The first book of the Hagiographa section of the Bible (the division in the Greek Septuagint differs somewhat from the Hebrew Bible) contains 150 Psalms, expressing the spectrum of religious ideas. According to Jewish tradition, King David was the author of the Book of Psalms. However, scholars suggest that the diversity of subjects treated indicates not only multiple authorship but also the lengthy period of the book's composition. Various individuals are credited with composition of some of the psalms, among them the family of Korah, Ethan, Heman, Asaph (apparently all prominent Temple musicians), Moses, and Solomon. The most prominent contributor, however, is clearly David. The introductory phrase "to David" which appears at the beginning of so many of the psalms may indicate the royal patronage of David and his dynasty, rather than his actual authorship of the material. Obscure words at the beginning of some psalms (e.g., "According to lilies" [Ps 45]; "According to Alamoth" [Ps 46]; "According to the Gittith" [Ps 84]) may be musical instructions.

The Book of Psalms is commonly divided into five collections (1-41; 42-72; 73:89; 90-106; 107-150), apparently paralleling the five books of the Pentateuch. The two opening psalms serve as an introduction, and the final psalm is a conclusion. Psalm 72:20 states, "The prayers of David son of Jesse are ended," indicating that the preceding psalms are of an earlier period than the succeeding ones. Despite the great differences between the styles of various psalms, only one can be dated, Psalm 137, which apparently belongs to the time of the Babylonian exile. Scholars have debated the date of Psalms, but no certainty can be reached. Most recent scholarship rejects earlier theories that posited a postexilic date for most Psalms, and maintain that many were composed in the First Temple period.

Four distinct types of Psalms exist: 1) hymns, in which God is praised as Creator and Redeemer; 2) laments, personal and communal, in which the psalmist bemoans disasters both natural, such as famine, and social, such as war and oppression which result from God's neglect of Israel; 3) songs of trust in God's ever-watchfulness; and 4) didactic poems, in which Israel's history and religious philosophy are examined. Several of the Psalms had a distinct role in the Temple ritual. Among these are the 15 "Songs of Ascent" (Ps 120-134) which were sung on the 15 steps of the Temple courtyard. Several words in the Psalms which apparently had musical connotations (*Selah, hallelujah*), also indicate use in the Temple ritual.

The so-called Map of Psalms, c.1250, depicting the world with Jerusalem at its center. It has an inscription: "...God... working Salvation in the midst of the world..." (taken from Ps.74:12).

Additional psalms are scattered through the rest of the Bible (Gen 49; Ex 15:1-18; Deut 32-33; Judg 5; I Sam 2:1-10; II Sam 22; Jonah 2:3-10; Hab 3), and more have been found at the Qumran excavations, suggesting that the recitation of psalms was an important part of early Israelite culture.

The Book of Psalms has served as an inspirational text and source for much of the liturgy of both Judaism and Christianity.

Proverbs

The Book of Proverbs is the second book of the Hagiographa and one of the works of biblical Wisdom Literature. Its 31 chapters contain aphorisms attributed to various wise individuals of the biblical period, primarily Solomon and the court of King Hezekiah, although two apparently foreign contributors, Agur son of Jakeh (ch.30), and the mother of King Lemuel (ch.31), are also mentioned. Modern scholars interpret the book to be an anthology of sayings whose composition evolved over several centuries. Close parallels to many of the statements in Proverbs exist in Egyptian, Sumerian, Babylonian, and Aramaic literature. It is possible that the traditional identification of Solomon as the author of many of the proverbs is a reflection of the great intellectual strides made in his court, which were later attributed directly to the king himself; the Bible records that Solomon recited 3,000 proverbs and 1,005 psalms (I Kgs 4:32).

The text was intended as a handbook of the wisdom current in its time and can be divided into nine thematic collections of sayings (1-9, 10:1-22:16, 22:7-24:22, 24:23-34, 25-29, 30:1-14; 30:15-33, 31:1-9, and 31:10-31). Numerous literary devices, such as allegory (5:15-19), anecdotes (7:6-23), statements of preference (beginning with the term "better") (15:16-17), numerical proverbs (30:15-19), and alphabetic acrostic (31:10-31), are utilized in the text. The sentences often contain a parallel structure, with the second half of the verse being either synonymous with or in contradiction to the first statement.

Among the main themes of the book is the search for wisdom, and the wise man is often contrasted with the fool. Other themes appearing in the text are the importance of discipline and eloquence, and the dangers of such slothful behavior as drunkenness, laziness, and gossip. While the dangers of seductive foreign women are emphasized, the text holds the virtuous wife in high esteem, and praises her in a celebrated acrostic poem (31:10-31). Wisdom, too, is highly acclaimed (8-9).

Little is known about the actual origin of the text. However, it appears to have evolved in three distinct settings, and contains advice pertaining to each: the immediate family (much importance is placed on the mutual responsibilities of parents and children); the royal court, where advice is given to courtiers and kings on how to govern properly; and the scribal schools, where some of the sayings received their religious character.

Ecclesiastes

The name Ecclesiastes, Latin for preacher, is based on a mistranslation of the name of the attributed author of the book, Koheleth son of David. The term Koheleth, traditionally accepted as a reference to Solomon, may refer to one responsible for the gathering of people or proverbs, and is a fitting description of the text.

Although authorship is traditionally attributed to Solomon, modern scholars regard the book as one of the latest of the biblical texts. Many opinions date the book to the Second Temple period, with its final editing in the 3rd century BC. It appears that the introductory verse (1:1) and the two closing statements (12:9-14) were added at a later date to bring the radical philosophy of the text into conformity with established religious opinions of the day.

The book is a poetic work, whose central theme is the apparent vanity of human existence. "Vanity of vanities, says the Preacher, all is vanity" serves as both opening and closing of the book (1:2; 12:8). Throughout the text, the author surveys various outlooks, such as the quest for wisdom, wealth, luxurious living, which are thought to give meaning to life, and rejects them all as inconsequential. By assuming the role of a monarch who has become acquainted with all sundry experiences and the rewards of existence, the author claims authority in his rejection of those endeavors, and declares that all of human achievement is rendered meaningless by death. This being the case, the author suggests that men live their brief lives to the greatest possible extent in the pursuit of enjoyment, if they are so capable. The book also is unique in espousing the principle of determinism (ch.3) and declaring that there "is nothing new under the sun" (1:9).

The Book of Ecclesiastes belongs to a series of wisdom manuals current in the ancient Near East and was apparently influenced by Egyptian and Babylonian works of the time. Although the radical opinions expressed in Ecclesiastes raised questions among the rabbis regarding its worthiness for canonization, the later addition of the prologue and epilogue resolved the problem of its acceptabilty.

Song of Songs (Song of Solomon)

The Song of Songs, also known as Canticles, appears after Ecclesiastes in the Christian canon. The book, apparently a love song between Solomon and a Shunammite woman, was long the subject of debate. The rabbis of the Talmud questioned whether the secular poetry of the text, in which the name of God is not mentioned, merited canonization; only the interpretation of the poem as an allegory of the love between God and Israel ensured the scroll's canonization. This interpretation was later adapted by the early Church fathers, who reinterpreted the figures of Solomon and the maiden as representing Christ and the Church. Medieval scholars interpreted the poem as a philosophical allegory of the love of Christ for man, or as a dialogue between personified Wisdom and Solomon.

Modern scholarship doubts if Solomon was the author of the text. The Persian word *pardes* ("orchard")

which appears in the text (4:13) indicates an authorship later than the First Temple period. In addition, elements of the syntax and some of the vocabulary point to Aramaic influence, leading scholars to believe that the poem was composed in the late Persian or early Greek period.

Modern interpretations of the poem are numerous and varied. One approach is to regard the poem as the story of a love triangle: a king becomes enamored of a shepherdess who was herself in love with a shepherd. Despite the seductions of the court, the shepherdess remains faithful to her true love. Most scholars, however, argue that the book is an anthology of unrelated love songs and pastoral poems which were collected into a single text. It is also possible that several of the poems were recited as part of ancient wedding rites. The poems are rich with vivid imagery praising the physical features of the lovers and reminiscent of love poetry in Mesopotamian and Egyptian literature. Both geographical locations and the flora and fauna of ancient Israel are employed in colorful metaphors.

Isaiah

Isaiah is the first of the Latter Prophets. There is a sharp contrast between the first section of the book (1-39) and the second (40-66). Historically the first section clearly contains the prophecies of the prophet Isaiah (II Kgs 19-20) who prophesied during the reign of four kings in the latter part of the 8th century BC. The second part refers to the period of the Babylonian Exile and the Return to Zion in the 6th century BC. The mood of the first part is one of impending doom about to befall the kingdom of Judah; the mood of the second is one of consolation after the catastrophe and of hope for the returning exiles. Traditionally, the book is regarded as a unity, written by the prophet Isaiah, with the positive nature of the second part carefully balancing the gloom of the first, and the second part, including specific references to King Cyrus of Persia, ascribed to Isaiah's prophetic powers. Modern scholars, however, ascribe the work to two authors: the prophet Isaiah, who wrote chapters 1-39, and an anonymous prophet of the Babylonian Exile (dubbed Deutero [i.e., Second] Isaiah), author of chapters 40-66. Some scholars have even identified a third author (Trito-Isaiah) to whom they attribute chapters 56-66.

The first section of the book (1-39) contains, apart from historical background (36-39), visions of disaster and destruction (28-35) and prophecies of the fate of Judah (2-12) and the surrounding nations (13-23). Isaiah blames the people for the problems they face, declaring that only by returning to God can they be saved. He also castigates the Northern kingdom, blaming its downfall on its treachery towards Judah. His prophecies of the end of days are directed not only to the Israelites but all the nations of the earth, and

Part of a page from the Dead Sea Scroll of Isaiah, found at Qumran; 1st century BC.

redemption is depicted as an era of universal peace and harmony (ch.2, 11).

The second section, chapters 40-55, centers on the anticipated miraculous return of Israel from the Babylonian captivity (ch.40). There are also several extended diatribes against the making of idols and their worship (40:17ff; 41:6-7; 47:9ff). One of the highlights of this prophet's message is his emphatic announcement of universal monotheism which will include all nations of the world (e.g., 45:21-25). The most enigmatic prophecies are those concerning the "servant of the Lord" (42:1ff; 49:1ff; 52:13-15; 53). Several hypotheses have been advanced concerning the identity of this servant of God. Among the figures suggested in Jewish tradition are Moses, Hezekiah, Isaiah, and the people of Israel, while to Christians, the "suffering servant" is Jesus Christ.

The final chapters (56-66) address the problems of Judah after the reconstruction of the Temple. The final redemption is at hand, and only the corrupt behavior of the people delays its coming.

Jeremiah

Jeremiah is the second of the three Major Prophets. The Book of Jeremiah recounts the history and prophecies of the prophet as delivered before and after the Babylonian conquest of 586 BC. It is unclear whether it is the work of Jeremiah himself, Baruch his scribe, or later editors collating earlier material. Much of the book is biographical (ch.26-29; 32-44; 52), but its main theme is the prophetic response of Jeremiah to the events of his time. His words are poetic and, after denouncing the sinfulness of the people and warning of the doom to come prior to the fall of Jerusalem, he speaks words of comfort to the people (ch.30-31).

Apart from the biographical material, the book contains three distinct types of prophecy. The opening chapters (1-25) are mostly poetic visions of the judgment about to befall the nation. Within these chapters are scattered sermons by the prophet exhorting the people to mend their ways and accept Babylonian domination (7; 11; 18; 21; 25). The book closes with oracles against various nations (45-51).

The prophecies of Jeremiah were concerned primarily with the political upheavals of his day. Throughout the text, the prophet warns of the imminence of disaster due to the wickedness of the people. He cautions against entering foreign alliances, particularly with Egypt, as salvation, conditioned on the true repentance of the people, could come only from within. Jeremiah, the "prophet of doom" who announced the 70-year captivity and exile of Israel, was also the "prophet of consolation" who encouraged his people to withstand their fate and who foresaw, in comforting terms, their eventual return to Israel. Jeremiah was a master of metaphor, both in his writings and in the symbolic acts he performed in order to dramatize his message of repentance to the people.

Jeremiah mourning the destruction of Jerusalem. Miniature from the Book of Lamentations; Germany, 12th century.

Lamentations

The Book of Lamentations is a poetic work mourning the Babylonian destruction of Jerusalem. Although tradition generally attributes authorship to Jeremiah, which corresponds to the period of its composition, modern scholars tend to view the text as the work of an anonymous witness to the destruction of the First Temple (586 BC).

The text consists of five chapters, each on a different theme of the destruction. Chapters 1, 2, and 4 contain an account of the desolation of the city, while chapter 3 is a personal account of the suffering of an individual. Chapter 5 recounts the confessions of the nation whose members regard their sinful behavior as the cause of the calamity and repent their past ways.

All the chapters are constructed as a poetic dirge, with each verse containing two sections, the second shorter than the first. In addition, the first four chapters are alphabetic acrostics.

The destruction of Jerusalem is attributed to the sinful behavior of its inhabitants, and although no particular sin is mentioned as being the cause of the destruction, it is viewed as the culmination of several generations of wantonness, and not merely the result of the excesses of that particular time (5:7). Not only is the general populace to blame, but also the leaders, both political and religious. The kings are guilty for their excesses and the prophets for not adequately rebuking the nation. Only total repentance and a complete mending of its ways will return the nation to its former glory (3:22-41).

Ezekiel

The Book of Ezekiel is the third book of the Latter Prophets, and most of its prophecies were first delivered to the exiles in Babylonia (the first part of the 6th century BC). The first section, chapters 1-24, comprises a denunciation of the sins of the inhabitants of Judah and Jerusalem. Ezekiel reviews the history of the people from the period of the Exodus to his own time, and categorizes this as a succession of sinful rebellions against God who, once provoked, will bring unspeakable calamity on the people (ch.20). Ezekiel dramatized his message in order to strengthen its effect by publicly eating a scroll of lamentations and woe (2:9-3:3) and baking a barley cake over human dung and eating it, to symbolize the unclean food eaten by the exiles (4:12-13). He engraved a picture of Jerusalem on a clay tablet and laid siege to it (4:1-8), implying the impending siege and destruction of Jerusalem. The book records that the words and deeds of the prophet attracted large crowds; however, many related to Ezekiel as mere entertainment (33:30-32).

The second section of the text, chapters 25-32, is a diatribe against the nations surrounding Judah. Ammon, Moab, Edom, the Philistines, Sidon, and particularly Tyre and Egypt, have betrayed Judah and will be severely punished. God will magnify his power by destroying the nations, and in their destruction their peoples will come to recognize the glory of God.

The third theme, chapters 33-48, consists of consolation for the people in exile. Despite their sufferings, Ezekiel predicts a glorious future. In a mantic vision, the prophet is transported to the rebuilt Land of Israel. After describing its new borders, Ezekiel goes into great detail concerning the reconstructed Temple, and suggests that a new law will be given to Israel. The famous "vision of the dry bones" (ch.37) represents the revival of Israel in its land. With this, however, Ezekiel also describes the horrors of the enemies of Israel sweeping down from the north (ch.38-39). In spite of the great upheaval, the aftermath of the battle will usher in a new world order under the dominion of God.

Daniel

Although the Book of Daniel is the last of the prophetic texts, due to its late composition (about the time of the Maccabean revolt, approx. 168 BC), the Jewish Bible places it in the Hagiographa rather than with the Prophets. The various Christian canons, on the other hand, place Daniel among the Prophets. Since one half of the book (ch.2-7) is written in Aramaic, the prevalent Jewish language at the time of its composition, several scholars have even speculated that the whole text might have been originally composed in that language, and that only upon canonization were several of the chapters (1; 8-12) translated into Hebrew.

Daniel comprises two sections. The first (1-6) consists of six stories about Daniel and his three friends at the Babylonian and Persian courts. The second section (7-12) contains a series of four apocalyptic visions, in the interpretation of which, Daniel, speaking in the first person, receives the aid of an angel. The first section is dated by scholars to about the mid-3rd century BC, while the second reflects the time of the persecutions of Antiochus IV Epiphanes, some 100 years later.

The book opens with an account of the position of Daniel and his three friends, Hananiah, Mishael, and Azariah (Shadrach, Meshach, and Abed-Nego), in the court of Nebuchadnezzar. Despite the allurements of the court, the Jewish youths remained faithful to God and maintained observance of the religious laws, particularly the dietary code.

Daniel further enhanced his position in court by accurately interpreting a dream of Nebuchadnezzar. Awed by the interpretation, Nebuchadnezzar renounced paganism and elevated Daniel and his companions in the royal court. Nevertheless, Daniel's three friends refused to worship a golden statue set up by the king, and were cast into a furnace. The three miraculously

Daniel's three companions in the fiery furnace. Miniature from an Armenian Manuscript on Rituals; 1266.

survived, causing Nebuchadnezzar to acknowledge the supremacy of the Jewish God once again (ch.3).

Daniel later interpreted another of Nebuchadnezzar's dreams as an allusion to the insanity the king would suffer in retribution for his arrogance. Because of his repentance, however, Nebuchadnezzar's insanity would be only temporary, and he would be restored to his senses (ch.4).

A dramatic chapter (5) describes the feast of the emperor Belshazzar, in which mysterious handwriting containing the message *Mene, Mene, Tekel u-Parsin* appeared on the wall. Daniel interpreted the statement as meaning that Belshazzar would soon be toppled from his throne and his kingdom divided. That same evening, Darius the Mede killed Belshazzar and assumed power. Upon his accession, it was decreed that no one, save the king, was to offer prayers throughout the month. Despite the prohibition, Daniel continued to pray to God; the royal ministers reported him, and he was cast into a den of lions. Daniel remained untouched in the lions' den, causing Darius to release him and grant national recognition to his God throughout the empire (ch.6).

The second section of the text, concerned with the visions of Daniel, opens with a mantic depiction of four beasts. A lion, a bear, a leopard, and a monster with ten horns emerge from the sea. An angel appears to Daniel and explains that the four beasts represent the four empires, Babylonian, Median, Persian, and Seleucid Greek, who will rule the earth. The monster is

eventually overcome by God, referred to as the "Ancient of Days." The angel explains to Daniel that the final empire will be an everlasting Jewish dominion under the authority of God (ch.7).

In a second vision, a two-horned ram, representing the empires of the Persians and the Medes, succumbs to a goat, representing the Greeks. The third vision of Daniel (ch.9) reinterprets the earlier prophecy of Jeremiah (Jer 25:11-12) of 70 years of devastation for Judah as actually meaning 70 weeks of years (490 years). His final prophecy (10-12) offers an overview of history from the rise of Cyrus the Great (538 BC) to the death of Antiochus IV (164 BC). This is followed by a brief attempt to calculate the end of history, and contains the only mention in the Old Testament of resurrection of the dead.

Medieval scholars had great regard for the book and used its historical content as a means of calculating the date of the Final Redemption.

Hosea

The Book of Hosea is the first book of the so-called twelve Minor Prophets. It is assigned in its first verse to the period of kings who ruled from the middle to the latter part of the 8th century BC. In the book's opening chapters, the prophet is commanded to marry a woman who turns to harlotry, her behavior with her lovers symbolizing the flirtations of the people of Israel with foreign gods, particularly Baal (ch. 1). The metaphor of the relationship of God and Israel as that of husband and wife originated with Hosea and was later adopted by other prophets, notably Jeremiah and Ezekiel. Despite the sinful behavior of the nation, which would be punished both by drought and by the cessation of the festivals, Hosea foresaw a time when Israel and Judah would return to God and enjoy a spiritual and economic revival, marked by the reunification of the two kingdoms (ch.2).

The later prophecies attack the excesses of the Northern kingdom. The prophet condemns the forging of alliances with foreign powers (5:13; 7:11; 12:1; 14:3), since only God can protect Israel from devastation. Hosea emphasizes the moral nature of the Law, declaring that cultic rituals do not release a man from his moral obligations.

Some scholars have suggested that the book contains the work of two separate prophets, Hosea (1-3), and a second, anonymous prophet (4-14) who lived at a later date, and whose writings were appended to the original text.

Joel

Scholars attribute the composition of the Book of Joel, the second of the Minor Prophets, to the time of the (1:8-18), and the prophet composes two prayers, one

Persian domination during the Second Temple period. The actual dating of the events described in the text, however, remains uncertain.

The Book of Joel begins by depicting a plague of locusts, described as punishment for the sins of the people (1:2-3). They are instructed to fast and repent

First page of the Book of Joel; from the Winchester Bible, England; 12th century.

for himself (1:19-20) and one for the priests (2:17), to avert further tragedy. Repentance will lead to the nation's redemption, which Joel later describes (2:18-27). Though all the nations will benefit from the redemption if they are worthy, God promises harsh judgment for those nations which have persecuted Israel, listing Tyre, Sidon, Philistia, Egypt, and Edom as particularly meriting punishment (ch.3). Joel refers to the final judgment of nations as the "Day of the Lord." He ends his prophecies with a description of the final redemption of Israel and the restoration of Jerusalem as its eternal capital (3:16-21).

Amos

The Book of Amos may be divided into five themes, each developed in a particular literary style, written just prior to the westerly expansion of the Assyrian king, Tiglath-pileser. The first two chapters recount the sins of the neighboring nations as well as those of Judah and Israel. Amos declares that God will no longer tolerate their recalcitrant behavior and will punish them according to their sins. Each oracle begins with the phrase "For three sins... and four I shall not turn away." The first six nations mentioned (Arameans, Philistines, Phoenicians, Edomites, Ammonites, and Moabites) are to be judged for their brutality and cruelty, whereas Judah and Israel are to be condemned for their abandonment of religious law and oppression of the weak. God views the sins of Judah

and Israel in the harshest light since "Only you have I known of all the families of the earth" (3:2).

The second section (3:1-5:17), commencing with a series of rhetorical questions, asserts the inevitable connection between the sins of the people and their impending doom, by pointing out the same law of cause and result in nature: "Will a lion roar in the forest when he has no prey?" (3:4). The punishment about to befall Israel is the consequence of its sins.

In the third section (5:18-6:14) Amos castigates the people for their sins. The "Day of the Lord" is indeed approaching, but contrary to common misconception, it is a day of judgment rather than redemption. Amos describes the indulgences of the rich which blind them to their sealed fate.

The fourth section (7:1-9:6) contains five visions symbolic of the fate of Israel. These begin with plagues of natural catastrophe and culminate with the final destruction of the Northern kingdom. The first two catastrophes, locusts and fire, were averted by the prayers of Amos. The following two visions of a plummet and a basket of summer fruits represent God's intention to carry out his judgment, symbolized in the final vision by the destruction of the sanctuary in Bethel.

Amos' final prophecy (9:7-16) is one of consolation; the nation shall be reunited under the restored House of David, never again to be exiled from its land.

Obadiah

The Book of Obadiah is the shortest book of the Old Testament. Its 21 verses contain a prediction of the eventual downfall of Edom (1:1-16) and a description of the redemption of Israel (1:17-21). Scholars are divided as to whether this book is an integral whole or a collation of several prophecies concerning Edom (1:1-10; 11-14; 15) and a "Day of the Lord" prophecy as an addendum. According to the second approach, the first verses would have been composed during the reign of King Amaziah of Judah, since they contain no reference to the destruction of the Temple in 586 BC. The remaining prophecy concerning Edom would be from the end of the 6th century BC and refers to the defeat of Edom by a coalition of Arab tribes. The prophet describes the downfall of Edom as a nation, abandoned by its allies, being hauled down from its rocky fortress. The punishment inflicted by God upon Edom is the result of its collaboration with the Babylonians in the destruction of Jerusalem.

Jonah

The Book of Jonah is the fifth book of the Minor Prophets. Jonah is unique as the only text of the Latter Prophets to narrate a story rather than prophetic visions and oracles. The key figure is the prophet

Jonah swallowed by the whale; from a 15th-century translation of the Bible.

Jonah, son of Amittai, who lived in the 8th century BC (II Kgs 14:25). However, the text was probably composed several centuries after the events related are presumed to have occurred: the linguistic style indicates Second Temple authorship.

It relates how Jonah was called by God to journey to Nineveh in the east and exhort the inhabitants of the city to repent. Unwilling to perform his mission, the prophet attempted to flee to Tarshish, in the west. However, the boat in which he was sailing was caught in a storm and threatened with destruction. At Jonah's insistence, the sailors saved the ship by casting him into the sea (1:1-17). He survived the ordeal by being swallowed by a great fish; after praying to God to deliver him, the prophet was vomited up onto dry land, from where he set out to perform his mission (1:17-2:10).

Upon arriving in Nineveh, Jonah met with success. The people repented, and the city was spared (ch.3). Jonah, however, was angered that God had abandoned his original plan to destroy the city, since Nineveh truly deserved punishment (4:1-5). The book closes with God's explanation to Jonah of his reasons for abandoning his original intentions. Using the example of the castor plant which shaded Jonah in the desert until it died, God declared, "You are concerned about the castor plant, for which you have not labored, and which you did not rear, which came up in a night, and perished in a night: and should I not be concerned for Nineveh, that great city?" (4:10-11).

The book has had great appeal over the ages because of its story and its universalistic message of the value of repentance. Christian tradition regards the sojourn of Jonah in the belly of the fish as an allegory of the three days between the death and resurrection of Jesus (Matt 12:39-41).

Micah

The Book of Micah, the sixth book of the Twelve Minor Prophets, consists of four distinct sections. The prophet begins with a tirade against Israel and Judah (1:2-3:12). The inhabitants of the Northern kingdom are guilty of idolatry, the idols purchased with the income of prostitutes. Judah is guilty of deceitful business practices. Although the proceeds of their dishonesty have gone to the aggrandizement of Jerusalem, the people of Judah are to be admonished for their ways. God takes offense at a city built upon corruption, and as a result the city will be destroyed. Micah describes the decay as having reached all sections of society; even the prophets accept money in return for their prophecies.

The second section (ch.4-5) is famous for its prophecy of an era of universal peace, in which Jerusalem will be reconstituted as the center of a new world order under the guidance of God. This prophecy, borrowed directly from Isaiah 2:2-4, ends, however, on a different note. Micah expounds a doctrine of religious tolerance which encompasses polytheism as well (4:1-14). Micah 5:1-5 announces that Israel shall be ruled by a descendant of David (cf Is 11; Hos 3:5; Amos 9:11) and delivered by him from the Assyrians. Micah 5:9-15 declares that when the glory of Zion and Jacob is restored, the Lord will force the Gentiles to abandon idolatry.

The third section of Micah (ch.6) attacks the corruption prevalent in the Northern kingdom and threatens Samaria with destruction. According to the prophet, all that the Lord requires of man is "to do justice, love mercy, and walk humbly with your God" (6:8). The final chapter contains Israel's confession of guilt (7:1-6). The enemies of the Northern kingdom are informed that Israel will appeal to God for forgiveness and God, in turn, will deliver her (7:19). Micah concludes with Israel's prayer for forgiveness (7:19).

Nahum

Nahum is the seventh of the Minor Prophets. The Book of Nahum is similar to the Book of Jonah in that its prophecies are directed to Nineveh rather than to Israel. Stylistically, however, the text is reminiscent of Isaiah, leading scholars to believe that Nahum was influenced by the earlier prophet.

Nahum begins his book with a declaration of faith in the just nature of God (1:1-10). God will be quick to reward the righteous and punish the wicked. The succeeding prophecy reveals God's promise to spare "the city," i.e, Jerusalem, and punish "the offenders," the Assyrians. The prophet then consoles Judah with the destruction of Nineveh (2:4-14), affirming the Greek tradition (quoted by Xenophon) that flooding of the Tigris was the primary cause of the city's downfall. Nahum then justifies the destruction of the city as the result of its overwhelming sinfulness (ch.3). Ultimately, divine justice must prevail.

Habakkuk

The background of the Book of Habakkuk, eighth of the Minor Prophets, is the Kingdom of Judah at the time of the Assyrian rise to power. The book's three chapters can be divided into two sections, the first being a narrative of five prophetic statements, and the second a psalm in praise of God. Habakkuk's mention of an "end of days" (2:3) influenced the later book of Daniel.

The book begins with the plea "How long, O Lord?" (1:2). Although the first prophecy is a condemnation of the cruelty and immoral behavior of the people of Judah, it remains unclear to what the plea actually refers: the iniquities of the people or the growing threat of the Chaldeans, whom Habakkuk describes as the tool of God in combating the sins of Judah (1:5-11). Habakkuk next questions God himself as to the justice of punishing the Judeans by a people more wicked than they (1:12-17) and responds that although the wicked may execute the will of God, they will in the end be punished (2:1-5). Habbakuk recounts the sins of the Chaldeans, which will lead to their destruction (2:6-20).

The third chapter, a song praising the greatness of God, from his miracles at the time of the Exodus to his constant struggle with "confusion and disorder," appears incongruent with the rest of the text. Since the Habakkuk fragment found in the Dead Sea Scrolls does not contain the final chapter, some scholars have speculated that it is a later addition. On the other hand, it is possible that "confusion and disorder" described as the enemy of God may, in fact, refer to the Chaldeans, in which case the chapter would be part of the original work.

Zephaniah

The Book of Zephaniah, the ninth of the Minor Prophets, was composed by a Judean prophet prior to the reforms of King Josiah. The first of the three prophecies recorded in the book is a condemnation of the people of Judah for their assimilation to foreign practices. Apart from an exhortation to the nation to reject idolatry, the prophet condemns the adoption of foreign dress and the Philistine practice of skipping over the threshold (1:8-9). Because of these sins, the nation is bound for catastrophe. Zephaniah describes the impending disaster in his "Day of the Lord" oracle, similar to other prophecies in Isaiah (Is ch.2) and Amos (Amos 5:18-20). The vivid detail, unique to Zephaniah, inspired later religious hymns including the Catholic "Dies Irae" (ch.1).

The second prophecy of Zephaniah is an exhortation to the nation to repent. Should the people return to God, disaster would be averted and the enemies of Judah would be eradicated (ch.2). In his final prophecy, Zephaniah blames the political and religious leaders for the nation's wayward behavior. God intends to crush them with an army composed of the righteous, who will usher in a new order characterized by justice and humility (ch.3).

Haggai

The Book of Haggai, the tenth of the Minor Prophets, contains the oracles of an otherwise unknown prophet of the period of the Return to Zion from the Babylonian exile. Four prophecies are contained in this short book, and on each occasion the actual date of the vision is given; all in the second year of the reign of Darius I (520 BC). The prophecies of Haggai are recorded in the third person, leading scholars to suggest that the text is an account of the prophecies rather than the actual work of the prophet himself.

The first prophecy (1:1-8) is an exhortation to the nation to complete the construction of the Temple which had previously been neglected. Haggai held the negligence of the Israelites to be the cause of the work stoppage and the prophet castigated the nation for seeking its own material benefit while the Temple remained unbuilt. He rejected the excuse of the elders that they were waiting for God to instruct them to carry on the construction, and responded that because of their negligence, the country would be plagued with drought (1:1-11). Three weeks after Haggai's initial exhortations, the people recommenced the construction of the Temple (1:12-15). Haggai's second prophecy was intended to console the people that the Temple they were building, although less imposing than the original structure of Solomon, was destined to be more magnificent (2:1-9).

In his third prophecy, Haggai reminded the people that despite the importance of the Temple, moral and upright behavior is the focus of Israelite religion. Should the returning nation act righteously, God promises them unparalleled prosperity (2:10-19).

The final prophecy of Haggai was probably influenced by the revolts shaking the Persian empire following the death of Cambyses (522 BC). Haggai predicts the imminent downfall of the Empire, to be replaced by a new world order under God and his regent, Zerubbabel.

Zechariah

The Book of Zechariah, the eleventh of the Minor Prophets, relates the prophecies of Zechariah active at the time of the Return to Zion from the Babylonian exile. Scholars have divided the book into two parts: the first, chapters 1-8, refers to the period of the restoration and is accepted as the authentic work of the prophet. In the remainder of the text, referring to the end of days, no mention is made of the prophet, leading to the theory that chapters 9-14 are a later addition.

In 520-519 BC, Zechariah had eight visions, described in chapters 1-6, foretelling the redemption. The first vision (1:7-17) consists of an angel "riding upon a red horse, and he stood among the myrtle bushes that were in the glen, and behind, there were three horses, red, sorrel, and white" (1:8). The horses and their rider were sent by God to discover the present situation of the world. Upon reporting that the world was at rest, the angel asked God if he would continue to ignore Jerusalem. God responds that he has returned to Jerusalem and will rebuild the Temple.

In the second vision, the prophet sees four horns, representing the four nations who participated in the destruction of Jerusalem, cast down by four craftsmen. This symbolizes the rebuilding of the city (1:18-21).

In the third vision (2:1-9), a man holding a measuring rod and planning the fortification of the rebuilt city, is chased away by two angels. From now on, God himself will defend the city. Zechariah then exhorts the people remaining in exile to return to Zion and escape the wrath of God, which will bring destruction to the nations that have persecuted Israel.

The fourth prophecy (ch.3) depicts the Heavenly Tribunal. Joshua the high priest is acquitted, and his soiled clothes, representing Israel's sins, are replaced with clean, new garments. Should he continue to follow the commandments of God, he will be counted among the angels.

The fifth prophecy (4:1-7), though the symbolism is obscure, is most poignant in its proclamation, "Not by might, nor by power, but by my spirit, says the Lord of Hosts" (4:6).

The sixth and seventh prophecies (ch.5) are concerned with the spiritual and moral level reached by the inhabitants of Judah. In the first vision, the prophet sees a flying scroll containing a curse against the thief and slanderer (5:1-4). In the second vision, a woman, representing wickedness, is carried by two winged women and set down in Shinar, as evil is exiled from the land. The eighth and final vision consists of two chariots running between two copper mountains, symbolizing peace in the land (6:1-8). The remainder of chapter 6 to the end of chapter 8 contains prophecies exhorting the people to act justly and morally. God is no longer interested in their fasts but rather that they "execute true judgment, and show loyal love and mercy, every man to his brother" (7:9).

In 9:9 the prophet foretells the coming of the king who is described as "humble, and riding on an ass." The enemies of Israel will be punished, and a period of peace will ensue. The final prophecies are apocalyptic, containing the imaginative perceptions of the prophet concerning the future of Israel.

The Candlestick of Gold in Zechariah's vision. Miniature from the Cervera Bible, Spain; c.1300.

Malachi

The Book of Malachi, the twelfth and last of the works of the Minor Prophets, was written by a religious reformer at the time of the return from the Babylonian exile. The name "Malachi" means "my messenger" and it is unclear whether it is a proper name or an epithet. The book is universal in its statement that all the nations of the world will recognize the glory of God (1:11). Nonetheless, it emphasizes the unique relationship between God and the people of Israel.

The Messiah entering Jerusalem, preceded by the prophet Elijah, as described in the Book of Malachi. Miniature from a Hebrew manuscript from Venice; 18th century.

The Book of Malachi contains seven themes relating both to the problems of the day and to the days of the Messiah. The prophet begins with a reminder of God's eternal love for the people of Israel (1:1-5). In order to merit God's love, however, the people must mend their ways. Malachi rebukes the priests for disgracing the Temple (1:6-2:9) and the commoners for abandoning their wives for foreign women (2:10-16). The people must take heed of their ways to prepare for the redemption (2:17-3:6). Malachi urges the people neither to be lax in their tithing (3:7-3:12) nor to deny God and reject the law (3:13-21). Keep the commandments, he concludes, in order that Elijah may herald the redemption (4:4-5).

III.22 THE TRIBES

A tribe is a collection of families connected by blood ties. The ancient Israelites constituted a loose confederation of tribes that, over the course of biblical times, sought to achieve national unity. The Israelites believed that their tribes shared a common ancestor, Jacob, and that each tribe was descended from one of his sons or, in the case of Ephraim and Manasseh, his grandsons. The twelve tribes later formed the administrative divisions of Israel. The term first appears in Jacob's blessings to his sons, which conclude with the statement, "All these are the twelve tribes of Israel, and this is what their father spoke to them" (Gen 49:28), indicating that the tribes, descendants of twelve brothers from a common father, Jacob, were regarded as subdivisions of a larger family unit. The tribes descended from Jacob's wife Leah were: Reuben, Simeon, Levi, Judah, Issachar and Zebulun; from Rachel: Joseph (which later split into the tribes of Ephraim and Manasseh) and Benjamin; from Bilhah: Dan and Naphtali, and from Zilpah: Gad and Asher. The biblical number of twelve does not always refer to the same tribes. In some instances Joseph is considered the forebear of a tribe; the tribe of Levi is then numbered among the tribes. In other instances, Joseph is divided into the tribes of Ephraim and Manasseh, and Levi is not counted.

The tribal divisions first achieved prominence during the Israelite wanderings in the wilderness. Each tribe was divided into subdivisions of families. A tribal leader was appointed, responsible for the tribal census taken by Moses in the wilderness (Num 1). It was he who led his tribe through the Sinai desert (Num 2), and presented his tribal offering at the dedication of the Tabernacle (Num 7). Another representative of each tribe was chosen by Moses to spy out the Land of Canaan prior to its conquest (Num 13:1-15).

Following Joshua's conquest of the land, territory was allotted to the people according to their tribes. The Book of Joshua describes in detail the territory assigned to each tribe (Josh 13-20). In the account of the conquest given in the Book of Judges, the conquest is described as not having been a unified effort of the Children of Israel but rather the result of the efforts of each individual tribe (Judg 1-2).

The tribe of Levi was not given a territory of its own, indicating its unique status as a clan of priests and teachers. The separate nature of the tribe of Levi is

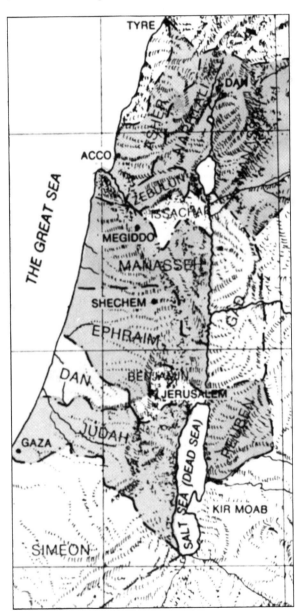

The territories of the tribes.

apparent in the census taken in the wilderness. Whereas in other tribes, only males suitable for military service (20 years and older) were counted, the Levite census included all males from the age of 30 days. It is also noted that in the wilderness, only the tribe of Levi camped according to their clans in the center of the larger encampment surrounding the Tabernacle.

Despite the original autonomy each tribe possessed, various tribes began losing their individual identity shortly after the conquest of Canaan. The tribe of Simeon is omitted from the blessing of Moses (Deut 33), leading scholars to believe that the tribe was absorbed into its bigger neighbor, Judah. Constant rivalry existed between the tribe of Judah and the tribes of Ephraim and Manasseh for primacy over the remaining tribes. Judah regarded itself as best fit to

Reuben ("Behold a son!"). Tribe descended from the firstborn son of Jacob and Leah. Reuben's mother, Leah, was scorned by Jacob, who preferred his other wife, Rachel. In one instance, Reuben brought his mother mandrakes, regarded as an aphrodisiac, to rekindle Jacob's affection towards her. Leah became pregnant and bore Jacob a fifth son, Issachar (Gen 30:14-18). Despite his loyalty to his mother, Reuben did not express the same commitment to his father, and even lay with Jacob's concubine, Bilhah, an act for which he forfeited his rights as firstborn (Gen 35:22). Reuben later proved his integrity by attempting to save Joseph from his brothers (Gen 37:21-30), and by offering his own children to Jacob as a security for Benjamin's safe return from Egypt (Gen 42:37). In his final will, Jacob castigated Reuben for sleeping with Bilhah,

Reuben.　　Simeon.　　Levi.　　Judah.　　Issachar.　　Zebulun.

Benjamin.　　Dan.　　Naphtali.　　Gad.　　Asher.　　Joseph (Manasseh and Ephraim)
Israel stamps of the Twelve Tribes.

lead the nation since it was descended from the oldest son of Jacob not disqualified for the role, as were Reuben, Simeon, and Levi (Gen 49:3-12). The descendants of Joseph, however, regarded themselves as being descended from the firstborn of the favored son of Jacob. This rivalry exploded with the secession of the ten Northern Tribes following the death of Solomon. They were eventually conquered by Assyria in 722 BC and their members were exiled. Only the tribe of Benjamin remained loyal to Judah (I Kgs 12).

The concept of the twelve tribes survived throughout the New Testament period. Jesus prophesied that his disciples would one day judge the twelve tribes (Matt 19:28), and James addressed an epistle to the twelve tribes in the diaspora (James 1:1). They are also mentioned by Paul (Acts 2:6-7) and John (Rev 7).

remarking that he is "unstable as water" and predicting that he "shall not excel" (Gen 49:4).

The tribes of Reuben and Gad requested that their inheritance be given to them in the fertile pastures of TransJordan. Moses agreed, provided that these two tribes first assist the other tribes to conquer their inheritances (Num 32). In time, the importance of Reuben diminished, and the tribe was all but absorbed into its stronger neighbor, Gad.

Simeon ("[God] has heard"). Tribe descended from the second son of Jacob and Leah. Simeon proved his unruliness following the rape of his sister Dinah by Hamor prince of Shechem. Although a covenant had been agreed upon between Jacob and the Shechemites whereby the inhabitants of the town would be circum-

TRIBES	SYMBOL	TERRITORY	KINGDOM AFTER SPLIT	ENCAMPMENT IN WILDERNESS	FIRST CENSUS	SECOND CENSUS
REUBEN	mandrakes	Trans-Jordan south of Gad	Israel	south	46,500	43,730
SIMEON	fortress	Negeb; south of Judah	Judah	south	59,300	22,200
LEVI	breast-plate	48 cities amongst tribes	no territory	center	22,200	23,000
JUDAH	lion	south, incl. coast, mountains, desert and Negeb	Judah	east	74,600	76,500
ISSACHAR	sun and moon	Mount Tabor; eastern Jezreel Valley	Israel	east	54,400	64,300
ZEBULUN	ship	southern Galilee	Israel	east	57,400	60,500
DAN	serpent	coastal plain; later migrated north	Israel	north	62,700	64,400
NAPHTALI	deer	northern Galilee	Israel	north	53,400	45,400
GAD	tent	Gilead in central Trans-Jordan	Israel	south	45,650	40,500
ASHER	olive tree	northern coast incl. Upper Galilee	Israel	north	41,500	53,400
EPHRAIM	bullock	central hills of Samaria	Israel	west	40,500	32,500
MANASSEH	wild bull	northern hills of Samaria	Israel	west	32,200	52,700
BENJAMIN	wolf	central hills between Judah and Ephraim	Judah	west	35,400	45,600

Embroidery of a sheath of wheat symbokixing Joseph from whom derived the tribes of Ephraim and Manasseh.

cised and Hamor would marry Dinah, Simeon and Levi took advantage of the recuperating Shechemites by entering the town and massacring its inhabitants (Gen 34). Jacob castigated his two sons for their treachery, and in his final testimony declared that "instruments of cruelty are their swords" (Gen 49:5). They lost the rights of the firstborn, as the tribe of Reuben had done. Simeon proved his faithfulness to the family by agreeing to be held captive by Joseph to ensure that the brothers would bring Benjamin to Egypt (Gen 42:24).

Simeon's territory was located south of Judah, and its main town was Beersheba. However, since Simeon is not mentioned among the tribes blessed by Moses (Deut 33), nor in the Song of Deborah (Judg 6), scholars believe that shortly after the conquest of Canaan, it was absorbed by its larger neighbor Judah.

Levi. Tribe descended from the third son of Jacob and Leah. Levi was a partner with Simeon in the massacre of the inhabitants of Shechem (Gen 34). In Jacob's last testament, he is paired with Simeon and likewise rebuked (Gen 49:5-7).

The tribe of Levi served as the priestly caste among the tribes. As such, it did not receive a contiguous tribal territory, but rather 48 cities of cultic significance scattered among the other tribes. The Levites are often omitted from the list of tribes; the number of twelve is obtained by counting the sons of Joseph as two distinct tribes. The Levite census in the wilderness also reveals the distinction of the Levites from the remaining tribes. Whereas the members of all other tribes were counted from the age of twenty and upwards (Num 1:3), indicating their ability to wage war, the Levites were counted from the age of one month (Num 3:15), indicating their potential eligibility for Temple service.

In time, the duties of the Levites diminished as the priesthood was assumed by the family of Aaron, himself a Levite. The Levites were made responsible for the transport of the Tabernacle in the wilderness (Deut 10:8), and served as musicians and gatekeepers for both the Tabernacle and the Temple (I Chr 9:18-19; 23:1-6). In certain instances, Levites did assume priestly roles, such as in the sanctuary at Dan, whose officiating priest was a descendant of Moses rather than of Aaron (Judg 17:7-13). Upon Solomon's centralization of the cult in Jerusalem the conflict between the various factions of the Levites reached a head. The official priesthood was granted to the Zadokite branch of the family (I Kgs 2:26-27), and the remaining Levites were relegated to duties as Temple servants (II Kgs 23:8-9). The Levites retained their rights to tithes, but are referred to as aliens (Judg 17:7) and listed with the widow and the orphan (Deut 14:28-29).

The most prominent figures among the Levites were Moses and Aaron. Throughout the First Temple period the Levites served as scribes and teachers.

Judah. Eponymous ancestor of the tribe of Judah; fourth son of Jacob and Leah. Judah emerged early as a leading tribe. In the Joseph epic he is often portrayed as the spokesman for his brothers (Gen 37:26; 43:3-8; 44:14-18; 46:28). In his testament, Jacob blessed Judah with primacy over the other tribes, declaring: "Your father's children shall bow down to you" (Gen 49:8). In both censuses taken in the wilderness, Judah is listed as the largest of the tribes (Num 1:27; 26:22).

Judah's eldest son, Er, died childless. His brother Onan refused to perform a levirate marriage with Er's widow Tamar and also died. Although Judah had promised to marry Tamar to his youngest son, Shela, he later forgot his promise. Tamar therefore disguised herself as a whore and lay with Judah. When Judah discovered that Tamar had become pregnant he sentenced her to death by burning. Only then did she reveal to Judah that he was the father of the child. Tamar gave birth to twins, Perez and Zerah, ancestors of two prominent clans of Judah (Gen 38).

The tribe of Judah became the dominant southern tribe. Their territory included the coastal plain, the lowlands, mountains and desert bearing their name, and a portion of the Negeb. Philistine expansion cost Judah its control over the coast and lowlands, and caused the tribe to look elsewhere for territory. The tribe absorbed its smaller neighbors, Simeon and the Danites remaining in the coastal plain. Still hungry for territory, Judah attempted to overcome its northern neighbor, Benjamin, in a war which brought about the near-eradication of that tribe.

Following the fall of Saul's short-lived dynasty, David, a member of the tribe of Judah, achieved hegemony over all the tribes. Most tribes accepted Judahite rule grudgingly. During the reign of his grandson, Rehoboam, the ten Northern Tribes seceded from Judah and established their own kingdom. With the fall of the Northern Kingdom in 722 BC, Judah absorbed refugees from the other tribes. Judah existed as an independent state until the Babylonian conquest of Jerusalem in 586 BC. The word "Jew" is derived from Judah.

As, according to Jewish belief, the messiah will be descended from David, he will come from the tribe of Judah. In the New Testament, the tribe appears at the head of the list of the sealed (Rev 7:5).

Issachar ("there is reward," or "man of wages"). Tribe descended from the ninth son of Jacob and fifth son of Leah. Its territory lay between Mount Gilboa and Lower Galilee, including Mount Tabor at the eastern end of the Valley of Jezreel. This territory adjoined Zebulun, and the tribes are always mentioned together. In Solomon's time, the territory of Issachar formed a separate province (I Kgs 4:17). The city of Jezreel, a royal residence of the Kingdom of Israel, was located in Issachar (I Kgs 18:45).

Moses touches a well with his rod and streams flow out to twelve tents, in each of which stands a figure. Fresco from the synagogue of Dura-Europos; 3rd century.

Despite its reputation for wise men (I Chr 12:32), only two minor historical figures came from Issachar: 1) the judge, Tola son of Puah (Judg 10:1), and 2) Baasha, king of Israel (I Kgs 15:27). The tribe is last mentioned participating in a Passover pilgrimage to Jerusalem during the reign of Hezekiah (II Chr 30:18).

Zebulun. Tribe descended from the tenth son of Jacob, the last son born to Leah. Its territory was located in southern Galilee, bordering the tribe of Issachar, to whom Zebulun had strong ties. Jacob's blessing to Zebulun states that he "shall dwell at the shore of the sea" (Gen 49:13). Zebulunites are identified with seafaring (Deut 33:18), though their territory had no access to the sea. It was one of the tribes exiled to Assyria after the fall of the Northern Kingdom.

Prominent members of the tribe of Zebulun include the minor judge, Eilon (Judg 12:11-12) and the prophet Jonah (I Kgs 14:15).

Dan ("judged"). Tribe comprised of descendants of Jacob's fifth son, the firstborn of Bilhah. Jacob, in his final blessings to the tribes, compared Dan to a serpent (Gen 49:17), indicating the tribe's military capacities which were also praised in the blessing of Moses (Deut 33:22). The original territory of Dan lay between Judah and the Mediterranean Sea (Josh 19:40-48). This region was densely populated by Canaanites and Philistines and the tribe was never able to fully conquer it. Desperate for land, the tribe migrated northwards (around the end of the 12th century), and inhabited the town of Laish, which they renamed Dan (Josh 19:47). Samson the judge was from the tribe of Dan

(Judg 13:2). Dan was one of the tribes of the Northern Kingdom of Israel.

Naphtali. Eponymous ancestor of the tribe of Naphtali; sixth son of Jacob and second son of Bilhah. The tribe of Naphtali inhabited the northernmost territory of the tribes. Jacob, in his final testament to the tribes, refers to Naphtali as "a deer let loose" (Gen 49:21), leading some to conjecture that the metaphor reflects the wanderings of the tribe before occupying its territory. Despite its remoteness, Naphtali was the major tribe of the far north. Its territory contained Kadesh, a city of refuge (Josh 20:7), as well as several of the Levitical cities (Josh 21:6). The territory later formed one of the regional divisions created by Solomon (I Kgs 4:15).

Because of its strategic position on the northern border of Israel, several important military leaders stemmed from Naphtali, among them Deborah's general Barak. Prior to the fall of the Northern Kingdom, the tribe's location made it easy prey for invading armies. Both the Arameans and the Assyrians conquered Naphtali and exiled many of the inhabitants (I Kgs 15:20; II Kgs 15:29). Isaiah attempted to console Naphtali, promising that it will one day return to its former glory (Is 8:19-9:7). Isaiah's prophecy regarding Northern Israel was regarded in the New Testament as a reference to the beginnings of Jesus' ministry in the North (Matt 4:13-22).

Gad ("good fortune"). Eponymous ancestor of the tribe of Gad; seventh son of Jacob, and firstborn son of Zilpah, Leah's maidservant. As the Israelites prepared to enter Canaan, the Gadites and Reubenites, being wealthy shepherds, requested that territory be allotted to them in the TransJordanian regions of Jazer and Gilead, regarded as good pastureland (Num 32:1). They were granted the land on the condition that they first assist the remaining tribes to conquer Canaan (Num 32). Gad became the major tribe of TransJordan, all but absorbing its weaker neighbor, Reuben.

The Gadites won renown for being fierce warriors, and are described as "men trained for battle" (I Chr 12:8). Gad was eventually overrun by the Arameans (II Kgs 10:33) and later conquered by Assyrians, who resettled the Gadites in Assyria. The land was then inhabited by Ammonites (II Kgs 15:29; Jer 49:1).

Asher ("happy"). Tribe descended from the eighth son of Jacob and the second son of Zilpah. In Jacob's last blessing, he foretold, "Bread from Asher shall be rich, and he shall yield royal dainties" (Gen 49:20). Moses' last blessing repeated the promise of fertility (Deut 33:24-25). The territory of Asher, stretching from Acco to Tyre, and including parts of Western Galilee and the Valley of Jezreel, is described as fertile (Deut 24-25), and contains some of the richest soil in Canaan.

Asher did not manage to conquer all its territory

(Judg 1:27). Its territory was further reduced when Solomon ceded 20 of its cities to Hiram, king of Tyre, in payment for materials he supplied for the construction of the Temple (I Kgs 9:11-13). Asher was one of the tribes constituting the Northern Kingdom of Israel.

Ephraim ("fruitful"). Tribe tracing its descent to the younger son of Joseph and Asenath, daughter of the Egyptian high priest of On. Jacob adopted Ephraim and his brother Manasseh, granting them equal status to his own sons (Gen 48:5). Although Ephraim was the younger of Joseph's sons, Jacob accorded him preference over Manasseh (Gen 48), and this precedence persists throughout the Bible. Ephraim precedes Manasseh in the march through the wilderness (Num 2:18-20), the order of consecration of gifts for the Tabernacle (Num 7:48-59), and the division of territory (Josh 16:5).

The territory of Ephraim was situated in the Samarian hills, between Benjamin and Manasseh. Its location in central Canaan protected it from most attacks, allowing the tribe to flourish in otherwise difficult periods. A strong sense of local identity developed, and the tribe grew aggressive towards its weaker neighbors (Josh 17:8-9).

Their sense of superiority was confirmed by the leadership of Joshua, who was a member of that tribe and by the fact that the religious shrine of Shilo was located in its territory. Their self-esteem contributed to the split of the United Kingdom of Israel. The leader of the Northern revolt, Jeroboam son of Nebat, was an Ephraimite (I Kgs 11:26), and the Northern Kingdom was often referred to simply as Ephraim (e.g. Is 7:17). Its members were exiled to Assyria after the fall of the Northern Kingdom.

Manasseh. Tribe descended from the elder son of Joseph. Manasseh and his brother Ephraim were adopted by Jacob and regarded as his sons. Genesis describes Jacob's favoring of Ephraim over his elder brother Manasseh (Gen 48). Scholars suggest that this story was composed to justify the emergence of Ephraim as the prominent tribe of the North. Several Manassite clans petitioned Moses to grant them territory in TransJordan, along with the tribes of Reuben and Gad. Moses agreed, granting them the northernmost territories of TransJordan, bordering on the Sea of Galilee (Num 32). Joshua allotted to the remaining Manassites the hilly region of Samaria, north of Ephraim (Josh 13-14).

Two judges, Gideon and Jephthah, were members of the tribe of Manasseh. Gideon's son Abimelech declared himself king, the first Israelite attempt at monarchy (Judg 9). Manasseh was one of the tribes exiled by the Assyrians (I Chr 5:23-26).

Benjamin ("son of my right hand"). Tribe tracing its descent to the younger son of Jacob and Rachel. Rachel, who died while giving birth to Benjamin, called him Ben-Oni, meaning "son of my sorrow" (Gen 35:16-20). Jacob favored Benjamin, his youngest son, and did not allow him to go to Egypt to buy grain. Joseph, his full brother, later demanded that Benjamin be brought to him in Egypt, and despite Jacob's protests his brothers brought him there. Joseph pretended to frame Benjamin with the theft of a goblet and threatened to execute him in order to test his brothers' reaction. The brothers' defense of Benjamin persuaded Joseph that they had repented selling him into exile, and led Joseph to reveal himself to them (Gen 42-45).

Although small, the territory allotted to Benjamin was of great political and strategic value. The land formed a buffer between the rival tribes of Judah and Ephraim, and two important roads, north-south and east-west, traversed its territory. Its strategic location attracted countless attacks against Benjamin, by Moabites (Judg 3:12), Philistines (I Sam 10:5; 13:3), and others.

With the division of the Kingdom, the territory of Benjamin served as the border between the two kingdoms and often changed hands. Perhaps it was because of its unique location that Benjaminites were often at the forefront of the quest for a united kingdom.

The judge, Ehud (Judg 3:15), and Saul, the first king (I Sam 9:16-17) were both from the tribe of Benjamin. During David's reign, the tribe, led by Shimi son of Gera, disassociated itself from its stronger neighbor, Judah, in protest against David, whom they regarded as a usurper of Saul's throne (II Sam 16:5-13). Despite this early attempt to divide the country, Benjamin remained loyal to Judah during Jeroboam's revolt against Solomon.

Benjamin was the only tribe that faced near eradication at the hands of the other tribes. Following the incident of the concubine in Gibeah, the tribes declared war on Benjamin, and massacred most of the tribe. The tribes then vowed never to intermarry with Benjamin, leaving the tribe on the brink of extinction. Only by kidnapping 600 women was the tribe able to ensure its survival (Judg 19-21).

Other important biblical figures who came from Benjamin included: the prophet Jeremiah from the town of Anathoth (Jer 1:1), Mordecai, uncle of Esther (Est 2:5), and Paul (Rom 11:1).

III.23 THE PATRIARCHS

The term "Patriarchs" refers to Abraham, Isaac, and Jacob, the founding fathers of the Israelite nation. Their religion was monotheistic, and was characterized by several covenants, which included the promise of descendants as numerous as the sand and the stars, and the eventual possession by their descendants of the Land of Canaan (Gen 12:7; 13:12-17; 15:4-5; 18; 22:16-18). The Patriarchs, Abraham in particular, were also subjected to tests of faith.

The Patriarchs traveled throughout the Land of Canaan, planting trees (Gen 15:6; 21:33; 35:4) and erecting altars (Gen 12:7; 13:4; 22:9; 31:54; 33:20; 46:1) in their worship of God. They entered into treaties with the local rulers, and regarded any infringement of these treaties, even by their own children, as crimes (Gen 26:28-30).

Abraham and Isaac each passed their traditions to only one son, rejecting a second son as being unworthy to carry on the legacy; Abraham preferred Isaac, rejecting the claim of Ishmael (Gen 21:9-42), and Isaac, in turn, made Jacob his heir and not Esau (Gen 27:22-29). Only Jacob felt that all twelve of his children were fit to become his spiritual heirs, and they became the founders of the Twelve Tribes (Gen 49:1ff).

Abraham. First patriarch of Israel, son of Terah. Known originally as Abram ("the father is exalted"), his name was changed to Abraham, explained as "father of a multitude of nations" (Gen 17). He was born in Ur of the Chaldees but his father moved the

The edifice over the Cave of Machpelah in Hebron where the Patriarchs and the Matriarchs (except Rachel) were buried.

family to Haran in northwest Mesopotamia, where Terah died. God then commanded Abraham to go to a land yet to be disclosed to him, where he would become a great people and a blessing to all the families of the earth (Gen 12). Accompanied by his wife, Sarah, and his nephew, Lot, Abraham made his way to the land of Canaan and settled in the Negeb. When a famine forced Abraham to move to Egypt for a time, he passed Sarah off as his sister, fearing that he would be killed on account of her beauty. Pharaoh took her to his court, but on being punished by God, returned her to her husband, showering Abraham with gifts in recompense (Gen 12:10-20).

Returning to Canaan, Abraham and Lot chose separate grazing lands for their flocks, Abraham leading a quiet pastoral life at Mamre, near Hebron (Gen 13), and Lot moving to the Dead Sea area. Later, Abraham rescued Lot from the captivity of four invading kings and upon his return was blessed by Melchizedek, king of Salem (usually identified with Jerusalem), whose offer of gifts Abraham declined. In a solemn covenant ceremony, God promised Abraham countless offspring and possession of the land of Canaan (Gen 15:7-20). As a sign of this covenant, Abraham circumcised himself and all his male household. As the archetypal man of faith, Abraham's trust in God remained steadfast even in the face of the apparent contradiction between the divine promise and his and Sarah's childlessness (Gen 17).

At the age of 86, Abraham became the father of Ishmael, son of Hagar, Sarah's servant, whom Sarah gave Abraham as another wife. The fulfillment of God's promise that Sarah would bear a son was announced by three angelic visitors, whose warm welcome made Abraham a symbol of hospitality in Jewish tradition. They also informed him of God's intention to destroy Sodom and Gomorrah because of their wickedness. Abraham's outraged reaction to the divine decree to destroy the righteous with the wicked convinced God to spare the cities if only ten righteous men could be found there. Abraham's failure to produce these resulted in the destruction of Sodom and Gomorrah, with only Lot and his daughters surviving (Gen 18:16-29).

Sarah gave birth to a son, Isaac, and fearing that his right of inheritance might be challenged, she persuaded Abraham to exile Hagar and Ishmael to the desert, where they were eventually redeemed by an angel.

Subsequently, God tested Abraham's faith by ordering him to sacrifice Isaac. He directed him to Mount Moriah where only at the last minute, after Isaac had been bound and Abraham had raised his knife, did an angel intervene to stop the sacrifice of Isaac. Abraham

Abraham about to sacrifice Isaac; detail of a bas-relief from a 4th-century sarcophagus, now in the Grotto vaticane, Rome.

sacrificed a ram in his stead. Because of his trusting action, Abraham was rewarded by a renewed promise of God's blessings.

The last years of Abraham's life witnessed the death of Sarah and her burial in Hebron in the Cave of Machpelah which Abraham purchased as a family burial place; the marriage of Isaac to Abraham's own great-niece, Rebekah, brought from Haran by Abraham's servant; and his own marriage to Keturah, who bore him six children (Gen 24:61–67). After Abraham's death, aged 175, Isaac and Ishmael buried him next to Sarah (Gen 25). Abraham's monotheistic vision became the foundation of Jewish faith and election. According to tradition, the altar on Mount Moriah upon which Isaac was to be offered, was destined to be the site of the Jerusalem Temple (II Chr 3:1).

The apostolic writings portray Abraham as the father of the truly faithful whose righteousness is received through Jesus and whose reward is ultimately to repose in the bosom of Abraham (Acts 7, Rom 4, and Luke 16). "The sacrifice of Isaac" in Christian tradition foreshadows the ultimate death of Jesus as the lamb of God.

Isaac. Isaac, the second of the Patriarchs, is one of the most enigmatic figures in the Bible. The account of his life is often tragic, and he is constantly faced with obstacles which must be overcome.

Isaac was born to Abraham and his wife, Sarah, after many years of barrenness. When they were both advanced in years, God promised that by the year's end, Sarah would give birth (Gen 17:17–19; 18:10–14; 21:1–3).

Abraham laughed at the promise, mentioning his and Sarah's advanced age (100 and 90 respectively) as being beyond the normal age for conception. Sarah, too, laughed at the prophecy. After his birth, Isaac was named for this laughter (the name in Hebrew, "Yitzhak," comes from the word for laughter).

As Isaac matured, Sarah's jealousy of Ishmael, Abraham's son by her handmaid Hagar, led her to persuade Abraham to expel Ishmael and his mother from the household, thereby making Isaac sole heir to the legacy of Abraham (Gen 21:10–12).

The "Binding of Isaac," in which Abraham nearly sacrificed his son on the altar, is an incident unique in the entire Bible. In order to test Abraham's devotion, God ordered him to offer Isaac as a burnt offering. Taking two servants and Isaac, Abraham journeyed to the designated site of the sacrifice, and as they neared the place, Abraham and Isaac continued alone carrying the wood and slaughtering knife for the offering. Isaac's innocent question, "Behold the fire and the wood, but where is the lamb for a burnt offering?" (Gen 22:7) provoked Abraham's reply, "My son, God will provide himself a lamb for a burnt offering" (Gen 22:8), after which, the Bible records, father and son continued walking together as before. As Abraham lifted the knife to slaughter his son, an angel appeared instructing Abraham to spare Isaac and declaring that

Isaac blessing Jacob and Esau. Relief from the candelabrum by Benno Elkan that stands in front of the Knesset in Jerusalem.

Abraham had clearly proved his devotion to God and that Isaac would be blessed with the covenant promised to Abraham. In celebration, Abraham offered a ram in Isaac's stead (Gen 22).

After the death of Sarah, Abraham decided that Isaac, now 40 years old, should wed and, therefore, sent his servant to his kin in Aram-Naharaim (Mesopotamia), in order to find a suitable bride for Isaac. Rebekah was selected and was brought to Canaan to wed Isaac. She remained barren for ten years, after which, following Isaac's and her own prayers, she gave birth to twins, Esau and Jacob (Gen 24:1-25:26).

The birth of the twins was followed by a period of famine in the land, and Isaac moved with his family to the Philistine city of Gerar (Gen 26:1-7). While there, Isaac suspected that, as had happened with his father Abraham, he would be persecuted on account of his wife's beauty and therefore declared that she was his sister (Gen 26:6). When the truth became known, Abimelech, king of Gerar, castigated Isaac for his deceit, and warned his countrymen to respect Rebekah as a married woman (Gen 26:8-11). Isaac prospered in Gerar, but this newfound wealth became a source of enmity between him and the local shepherds, and Isaac found it necessary to return to Beersheba (Gen 26:12-32).

Isaac felt a preference for his elder son Esau. Sensing the imminence of his own death, a blind and aging Isaac prepared to bless his sons and make Esau his primary heir. Rebekah, however, favoring Jacob, prepared a ruse to insure that he and not Esau would receive Isaac's final blessing. As Esau went out to hunt food for his father, Rebekah disguised Jacob in his brother's clothing and placed goatskins over his hands and neck so that Isaac would believe he was blessing the hirsute Esau and not Jacob. Jacob entered his father's tent with a feast prepared by Rebekah and received the blessing intended for Esau. Upon his return from the hunt, Esau was forced to receive a lesser blessing (Gen 27).

Isaac died at the age of 180 and was buried by his sons in the Cave of Machpelah at Hebron (Gen 35:28-29).

In the NT, Paul uses Isaac as a type for the Gentile Church for what he calls the "children of the Promise" (Rom 9:6; Gal 4:28-31).

Jacob (Israel) last of the Patriarchs, was the son of Isaac and Rebekah, and the younger twin of Esau. His early years were marked by conflict with his brother. The text describes the brothers in conflict while still in Rebekah's womb: "and they struggled within her" (Gen 25:22), foreshadowing the struggle which would continue throughout much of their lives. This rivalry apparently had sociological overtones, Esau representing the hunter and Jacob the husbandman who tends flocks and farms. Prior to their birth, Rebekah prophes-

ied that the younger of her two sons would be the favored of the two. Although Esau was born first, the younger brother came out from his mother's womb clutching his brother's heel and accordingly was named Jacob, a verbal form of the Hebrew root which means "heel" (Gen 25:26).

Already at an early age the differences between the brothers were distinct; Esau is described as "a cunning hunter, a man of the fields," and Jacob is portrayed as "a plain man, dwelling in tents" (Gen 25:27). It was these traits that caused Isaac to prefer Esau to Jacob, while Rebekah's loyalties remained with Jacob. Nonetheless, Jacob proved his cunning on an occasion when Esau returned famished from the hunt and begged Jacob to give him some lentil stew he was preparing. Jacob agreed to feed Esau only after the latter had promised to transfer to him his inheritance as first-born son in compensation. His conditions accepted, Jacob fed Esau, and attained the legal status of Isaac's first-born with rights to the main share of the inheritance (Gen 25:29-34).

When Isaac prepared to recite his will in the form of blessings to the sons, his preference was that Esau receive the major blessing and larger inheritance. Rebekah, however, disguised Jacob so that he would receive the blessings in Esau's stead. Although Isaac was at first suspicious that the son before him was not Esau, he could not, being blind, ascertain which of his two sons in fact stood before him, and granted the blessing to Jacob (Gen 27). Infuriated at the loss of his birthright, Esau swore to kill Jacob who, aided by his mother, fled from his brother's wrath and made his way to Padan-Aram, to Rebekah's brother, Laban (Gen 27:41-45). At the outset of his journey, Jacob spent the night in Bethel, where he dreamt of a ladder reaching to the heavens with angels ascending and descending. God then appeared and renewed the covenant made with Jacob's forefathers, promising to protect Jacob in his journeys. Upon arising, Jacob sanctified the rock upon which he had lain. This rock later became the foundation of the cultic center at Bethel (Gen 28).

Jacob was accepted into the household of Laban, where he was employed as a shepherd. Enamored with Laban's younger daughter, Rachel, Jacob agreed to work seven years for Laban in return for her hand in marriage. On the night of the wedding, however, Laban substituted the elder daughter, Leah, for Rachel, claiming that the elder should be the first to wed. Jacob then agreed to work an additional seven years for Rachel (Gen 29:10-29). Leah bore Jacob four sons, Reuben, Simeon, Levi, and Judah (Gen 29:30-35), while Rachel remained barren. As Sarah before her had done for her husband, Abraham, Rachel gave Jacob her maidservant, Bilhah, so that Jacob might father children, who would then be considered the progeny of Rachel (an ancient Near Eastern arrangement known also from the Nuzi documents). Bilhah bore Jacob two sons, Dan

Jacob Wrestling with the Angel; painting by Rembrandt van Rijn (1505–1669).

and Naphtali (Gen 30:1–8). When Leah ceased to give birth, she followed Rachel's example and gave Jacob her maidservant, Zilpah, who also gave birth to two sons, Gad and Asher (Gen 30:9–12). Leah then gave birth to two sons, Issachar and Zebulun, and to a daughter, Dinah (Gen 30:9–12, 21). After Rachel had finally given birth to a son, Joseph (Gen 30:22–24), Jacob decided to return to Canaan. Laban was, at first, unwilling that Jacob should leave him, not wishing to forgo both his daughters and his flocks. After a period of negotiations, however, he was able to come to an accord with Jacob, and Jacob set out for Canaan (Gen 31:43–45).

Jacob recognized that his earlier dispute with Esau over the birthright might cause him difficulty on his return to Canaan. He therefore sent messengers bearing gifts and informing his brother of his return. The messengers returned empty-handed, and warned Jacob that his brother was coming to meet him at the head of an army of 400 men (Gen 32: 1–23). Fearful but resolute, Jacob led his family across the Jabbok River, and entered Canaan. That evening an angel confronted Jacob and struggled with him until dawn. Although the angel managed to injure Jacob's leg, he was unable to overcome him. As the battle ended, the angel blessed Jacob and changed his name to Israel, derived from the phrase "for you have contended with God and with men, and have prevailed" (Gen 32:24–29). Contrary to expectations, the meeting with Esau ended amicably. When the brothers parted, Jacob continued to Shechem (Gen 33:1–20).

In Shechem, Dinah, Jacob's daughter, was captured and raped by the local ruler. Although Jacob tried to gloss over the incident by making a treaty with the local inhabitants and granting Dinah to the prince as wife, Simeon and Levi avenged their sister's disgrace and slaughtered the male inhabitants of Shechem (Gen 34). Unable to remain in the area, Jacob travelled southwards, where Rachel died giving birth to Jacob's youngest child, Benjamin (Gen 35:15–22).

Jacob's excessive favoritism of Rachel's elder son, Joseph, led to jealousy among the brothers who eventually sold the haughty Joseph into bondage, hinting to Jacob that some tragedy had befallen his favorite child (Gen 37). Joseph rose to great prominence in Egypt, and as famine struck Canaan, the brothers journeyed to Egypt to purchase grain. Joseph eventually revealed himself to his brothers, granting them fertile land in Egypt where they might be spared the famine plaguing Canaan. Jacob led his family to Egypt where he was reunited with Joseph (Gen 46:1). As he neared death, Jacob blessed his and Joseph's sons (Gen 48:9–49:28).

Jacob died in Egypt at the age of 147 (Gen 47:28). In keeping with his wishes, his sons carried his body back to Canaan where it was buried in the Cave of Machpelah (Gen 49:29; 50:13).

Throughout the Bible, the name Jacob often functions as an epithet for the Israelite nation (e.g., Num 23:7,10; 24:5; Deut 33:4, 28). Hosea (12) contains several references to Jacob's relations with Esau and the former's struggle with the angel, and in Isaiah (41:21), God appears as the King of Jacob.

Jacob also appears frequently as a synonym for Israel in the New Testament (e.g., Luke 1:33; Acts 7:46).

III.24 THE MATRIARCHS

The term "Matriarchs" denotes the "mothers of the Hebrew people," the four main wives of the Patriarchs, Sarah, Rebekah, Rachel, and Leah. The four Matriarchs were all blood relatives of their husbands and took an active role in their husbands' activities.

Although the Matriarchs gave birth to progeny which was to develop into the People of Israel, each of them was barren for a period. Some gave birth only in their later years, Sarah at the age of 90. The two sisters, Rachel and Leah, gave their respective maidservants,

Bilhah and Zilpah, to Jacob that they might bear children through them (a Middle Eastern practice), as did Sarah before them.

Sarah (Sarai). Sarah, the first of the Matriarchs, was the wife of the Patriarch Abraham. Originally named Sarai, she was a relation of Abraham (Gen 11:29-32), and participated in most of the major events in her husband's life. Just as God changed Abram's name to Abraham, symbolic of the covenant between them, so was Sarai's name changed to Sarah (Gen 17:15). "And I will bless her and also give you a son by her; then I will bless her, and she shall be a mother of nations; kings of peoples shall be from her" (Gen 17:16).

Sarah was well known for her beauty, and two foreign rulers, Pharaoh of Egypt (Gen 12:6-20) and Abimelech of Gerar (Gen 20), attempted to take possession of her when Abraham passed her off as his sister out of fear of being killed on her account. Although Sarah was universally recognized as the unopposed matriarch of the clan of Abraham, her barrenness brought into question the continuation of the line and the realization of the covenant between God and Abraham. Sarah attempted to have children by proxy through her maidservant, Hagar, who bore Abraham his first son, Ishmael (Gen 16:15). Sarah, nonetheless, was unable to consider Ishmael her own son, and mourned the fact that Abraham would father no children through her. When Sarah had reached the age of 90, angels appeared to Abraham, informing him that Sarah would bear him a child by the year's end. Sarah, listening at the doorpost, began to laugh, saying, "After I am grown old shall I have pleasure, my lord being old, also?" (Gen 18:12). The child was nevertheless duly conceived and born, being named Isaac, after the laughter of Sarah (the root of the name meaning laughter in Hebrew; Gen 21:3). Sarah then expelled Hagar and her son from the household, fearing Ishmael's influence on Isaac (Gen 21:9-13). Sarah died at the age of 127 in Hebron (Gen 23:1-2). Abraham purchased the cave of Machpelah on the outskirts of the town as a burial place for her (Gen 23), and the site later became the burial crypt for all the Patriarchs and Matriarchs (except Rachel).

The Beauty of Sarah

How splendid and beautiful the form of her face, and how soft the hair of her head; how lovely are her eyes and how pleasant is her nose and all the radiance of her face; how lovely is her breast and how beautiful is all her whiteness! Her arms, how beautiful! And her hands, how perfect! And how attractive all the appearance of her hands! How lovely are her palms, and how long and dainty all the fingers of her hands. Her feet, how beautiful! How perfect are her legs! There are no virgins or brides who enter a bridal chamber more beautiful than she. Indeed, her beauty surpasses that of all women; her beauty is high above all of them. Yet with all this beauty there is much wisdom in her; and whatever she has is lovely. (From the Dead Sea Scroll: The Genesis Apocryphon)

Rebekah (Rebecca) Daughter of Bethuel, and a relative of Abraham. When Abraham decided that the time was ripe for him to choose a wife for Isaac, he sent his senior servant to his relations in Aram-Naharaim in order to choose a wife from among his kin (Gen 24). Having selected Rebekah, his servant returned with her to Canaan, where she wed Isaac. After years of barrenness, she bore Isaac twins, Esau and Jacob (Gen 25:21-24). Although Isaac favored his elder son Esau, Rebekah disapproved of his marriages to Hittite women, and showed a preference for Jacob (Gen 26:34-35).

In the wake of a severe famine in Canaan, Isaac led his family to the Philistine city of Gerar. Fearing that the inhabitants might murder him in order to take Rebekah for themselves, Isaac declared that she was his sister. Abimelech, king of Gerar, discovered Rebekah's true identity, however, and remonstrated with Isaac over the deception. Abimelech subsequently forged a covenant between his people and the clan of Isaac (Gen 26).

When the time arrived for Isaac to bless his sons, Rebekah planned the ruse by which Jacob received the preferential blessing intended for the older son, Esau, in keeping with the prophecy she had received in her pregnancy, declaring the ascendancy of the younger son over the older (Gen 25:23; 27:6-10). Hearing Esau plot to kill his brother for stealing his blessing, Rebekah sent Jacob to her family in Aram to find a wife (Gen

The four matriarchs, Sarah, Rebekah, Rachel and Leah. Miniature from a Hebrew manuscript; Amsterdam, 1743.

27:42–46). Jacob eventually married Rebekah's nieces, daughters of her brother Laban. Upon her death, Rebekah was buried in the Cave of Machpelah (Gen 49:31).

Rachel. Rachel, daughter of Laban, was the favorite wife of the Patriarch, Jacob. Jacob, who met Rachel upon his arrival in Aram, fell in love with her and sought to marry her. Laban agreed to Jacob's proposal to work seven years to earn Rebekah's hand in marriage. On the night of the wedding, however, Laban replaced Rachel with her older sister, Leah, claiming that as first-born, Leah must be first to marry. Jacob then agreed to work a further seven years for the right to marry Rachel (Gen 29:1–30).

Although Rachel was the favored wife, it was through Leah that Jacob fathered children (Gen 29:30–35). Rachel, seeing that she was barren, gave Jacob her maidservant, Bilhah, so that Jacob might father children through her, children who would then be considered Rachel's. Bilhah bore Jacob two sons, Dan and Naphtali (Gen 30:3–8). Rachel eventually gave birth to a son, Joseph, while still in Aram (Gen 30:22–24).

As Jacob was about to return with his family to Canaan, Rachel stole the idols from her father's house, for the one in possession of the household gods also became the chief heir, as is known from cuneiform sources of that period. It was also commonly believed that the idols served as protection for the family. When Laban searched the possessions of Jacob, Rachel hid the idols under her seat, and refused to stand up for the search, pleading menstruation (Gen 31:34). Jacob showed his preference for Rachel and concern for her

safety by placing her and Joseph last as the camp prepared to greet Esau (Gen 33:2).

Rachel bore a further son to Jacob while the family was camped near Bethlehem, and Jacob named him Benjamin. Rachel died in childbirth and was buried at Bethlehem (Gen 35:16–20). She was the only one of the Matriarchs and Patriarchs not buried in the Cave of Machpelah. Already in biblical times Rachel became the symbol of Mother Israel mourning her exiled children. God promised Rachel that the exile was only temporary, and that the children of Israel would, one day, return to their land (Jer 31:14–16).

Leah. Leah, older daughter of Laban, was a wife of the Patriarch, Jacob. The only personal detail mentioned is that she was weak-eyed (Gen 29:17). Although Jacob loved her younger sister, Rachel, Laban tricked Jacob into marrying Leah first, claiming that "it must not be done so in our country, to give the younger before the first-born" (Gen 29:26). Although Jacob showed a preference for Rachel, it was through Leah that he fathered most of his children. Leah bore Jacob: Reuben, Simeon, Levi, and Judah (Gen 29:32–35). Then, seeing that she was no longer able to bear children, Leah gave Jacob her maidservant, Zilpah, so that Jacob might have children through her, and Zilpah bore Jacob two sons, Gad and Asher (Gen 30:9–13). Subsequently, Leah gave Rachel mandrakes (a fertility charm) in return for the right to sleep with Jacob and she then gave birth to two more sons, Issachar and Zebulun, as well as Jacob's only daughter, Dinah (Gen 30:17–21). She accompanied Jacob back to his homeland and on her death was buried in the Cave of Machpelah.

III.25 MOSES

Moses is the single most important figure in the formation of the people and religion of Israel. The Bible refers to him as the greatest of the prophets (Deut 34:10), but commends him in many other capacities as well. He was the political and religious leader who handed down both ritual and law. As military leader, he defeated Amalek and began the conquest of Canaan. Moses interceded before God on his people's behalf and succeeded in preventing numerous calamities. Not least, Moses was a poet; the Song of the Sea (Ex 15:1–18) and the Song of Moses (Deut 32:1–43), as well as Psalm 90, are attributed to him.

Moses was born in Egypt, the third child of Amram and Jochebed of the tribe of Levi. The couple's elder children, Miriam and Aaron, figured prominently in Moses' life. At the time of the birth of Moses, the Hebrews, slaves to Pharaoh, were suffering under new

decrees designed to keep them under Egyptian subjugation. Pharaoh had commanded that all male children be drowned in the Nile (Ex 1). At first Jochebed was able to hide the infant Moses, but as he grew, it became increasingly difficult to conceal his birth from the Egyptian authorities. Jochebed finally hid the newborn on a small raft in the Nile, where he could be watched by his sister Miriam. After a time, the baby was discovered by Pharaoh's daughter as she bathed in the river. Recognizing the child as a Hebrew, the princess decided to adopt him, naming him Moses (Ex 2:1–10). The biblical text (Ex 2:10) derives the name Moses from the verb meaning to draw water; however, it is probably related to an Egyptian root meaning "son of" as in the Pharaonic names Ramses and Thutmose.

Although he was raised as an Egyptian prince, Moses was forced to flee Egypt after killing an Egyptian over-

Moses taken from his floating ark. Fresco from the synagogue of Duro-Europos.

seer for beating an Israelite slave. Moses made his way to the Sinai desert where he rescued a group of shepherdesses harassed by a rival band of shepherds. The girls brought Moses to their father, Jethro, priest of Midian, who in turn betrothed him to Zipporah, his eldest daughter. Moses settled with his father-in-law and assisted him with his flocks. Two sons, Eliezer and Gershom, were born (Ex 2:11-25).

It was while tending his flocks that Moses first experienced a revelation from God. Wandering in the wilderness, Moses saw a "bush that burned but was not consumed" (Ex 3:1-6). A voice from the bush identified itself as the God of the Patriarchs and ordered Moses to return to Egypt and free his brethren from slavery. Moses protested that he was unfit for the task. He lacked the necessary eloquence to present the demands of the people before Pharaoh, and, moreover, the people would not accept a stranger. God gave Moses signs to prove his divine sanction to the people and appointed Aaron as his spokesman (Ex 4:28-30; 7:1-2).

The Hebrews, anxious for an end to their misery, quickly accepted Moses as their leader, and with their backing, Moses set off to meet Pharaoh. Pharaoh laughed off Moses' demands, rejecting him as a charlatan, and increased the Israelite slaves' workload. Moses responded by turning the Nile to blood, the first in a series of ten plagues culminating in the death of the first-born of all Egypt. Broken, Pharaoh expelled the Israelites (Ex 7:14-25; 8:1-32; 9:1-35; 10:1-29; chaps. 11-12).

As Moses led the people across the desert, Pharaoh had a change of heart. Quickly mobilizing his armies, he chased the escaped slaves and cornered them on the banks of the Red Sea. With no place to escape, Moses raised his rod over the sea and it divided. Although the Israelites crossed safely, when the armies of Pharaoh chased after them, the waters returned, drowning Pharaoh and his men (Ex 14:1-29).

Two months later, the people reached Mount Sinai, where Moses assembled them at the foot of the mountain while he ascended in order to receive the divine Law (Ex 19:3-6). When God revealed himself to the people, they were overwhelmed by the divine voice, and begged Moses to act as their intermediary. Moses then returned to the mountain top to receive the Ten Commandments (Ex 19:9-24:11).

Due to Moses' extended stay on the mountain top for 40 days, the people commissioned Aaron to fashion a representation of God. Moses descended the mountain only to be met by the sight of the people he had freed from Egyptian bondage worshiping the golden calf. In fury, he smashed the tablets, destroyed the golden calf, and forced the worshipers to consume its dust. God angrily decided to put an end to the people and only the intercession of Moses soothed the divine anger. Moses returned to the mountain, descending with a new set of tablets, representing a restored Covenant (Ex 32:1-29; 34:1-28).

Upon his return, Moses immediately began to erect a Tabernacle to serve as a focus for worship, anointing Aaron and his sons as priests (Ex 25:1-31:17). He also

Moses. Sculpture by Michelangelo in S. Pietro in Vincoli, Rome.

had conducted a Tent of Meeting where Moses spoke with God "face to face" (Ex 33:7–11).

After a lengthy encampment at Mount Sinai, Moses led the people on a 40-year trek towards Canaan. The Bible highlights the difficulty of this period, during which Moses' authority was challenged several times. When the people complained of their hunger, Moses intervened with God, who responded by sending the manna (Ex 16:11–36). Not satisfied with the manna, the people demanded meat. Once again Moses intervened with God and the people caught a flock of quail (Num 11:31–34).

Moses' frustration with the people was evidenced at the waters of Meribah (Num 20:1–13) when they complained to him of thirst. Although instructed by God to speak to a rock to coax forth water, Moses struck the rock. Displeased, God punished Moses, denying him entry into Canaan. Other challenges to Moses' authority were made by those who perceived themselves suitable to fulfill a greater role in the leadership of the people. Aaron and Miriam, regarding themselves as Moses' equals, murmured against his arrogation of all authority to himself. In punishment, Miriam was stricken with leprosy and Aaron was forced to beg Moses to intervene with God on her behalf (Num 12:1–15).

Perhaps the greatest threat to Moses' leadership was the rebellion of Korah and his followers. Korah charged Moses with usurping power for himself and his family. In a confrontation with Moses, the earth opened, devouring Korah and his entire congregation. The remaining rebels were smitten with plague and only Aaron's offering of incense at Moses' behest spared them. The people's discontent continued, however, provoking God to send a swarm of snakes to infest the camp. Moses stopped the plague by constructing a brass serpent (Num 21:4–9).

After forty years of wandering in the desert, Moses led the people to Canaan, conquering the eastern bank of the Jordan. God informed Moses that he was soon to die, and Moses gave the people a resume of the laws they had received (Deuteronomy = Second Law) and recited his last testament, which is known as the Song of Moses (Deut 32–33). Moses described the character of each tribe and implored the people to remain a united nation, faithful to God. Thereupon Moses ascended Mount Pisgah where he looked across the land he was forbidden to enter. He died in the Plain of Moab. To prevent its becoming a cultic center, the site of Moses' burial remained unknown.

Other than his marriage to the Cushite woman Zipporah and the birth and naming of his two sons, the Bible furnishes little information about Moses' personal life. In Deuteronomy, he is eulogized, "And there has not arisen a prophet since, in Israel, like unto Moses, whom the Lord knew face to face" (Deut 34:10), and he is referred to a number of times as "servant of the Lord" (Num 12:7–8; Deut 34:5; Josh 1:1). In Joshua (8:31) he is called author of the Book of the Law. In Numbers (12:3) his humility and selflessness are praised, and this is echoed in later Jewish tradition where Moses is known as "the humblest of men."

The NT contains 80 references to Moses, most frequently as lawgiver (e.g., Matt 19:7; Mark 10:3ff; John

---

From the Words of Moses

The Lord, the Lord, mighty, merciful and gracious, long-suffering, and abundant in love and truth, keeping troth to thousands, forgiving iniquity, and transgression, and sin, but who will by no means clear the guilty; punishing the iniquities of the fathers on the children, and on the children's children, to the third and fourth generation

(Ex 34:6–7).

Wherefore it shall come to pass, if you harken to these judgments, and keep, and do them,- that the Lord your God shall keep unto you the covenant which he swore to your fathers: and He will love you, and bless you, and multiply you: and will bless the fruit of your womb, and the fruit of your land, your corn, and your wine, and your oil, the increase of your cattle, and the flocks of your sheep, in the land which he swore to your fathers to give you. You shall be blessed above all peoples: there shall not be a male or female barren among you, or among your cattle. And the Lord will take away from you all sickness, and will put none of the evil diseases of Egypt, which you know, upon you; but will lay them upon all those who hate you. And you shall consume all the peoples which the Lord your God shall deliver to you; your eye shall have no pity on them: neither shall you serve their gods; for that will be a snare to you

(Deut 7:12–16).

Give ear, O heavens, and I will speak;
And hear, O earth, the words of my mouth.
My doctrine shall drop as the rain,
My speech shall distil as the dew,
As the small rain upon the tender herb,
And as the showers upon the grass:
For I will call on the name of the Lord:
Ascribe greatness to our God.
He is the rock, His work is perfect:
For all His ways are justice

(Deut 32:1–4).

The Tablets of the Law carved in stone.

7:22ff). Although Moses is credited with delivering the law, it remained for Jesus to bring grace and truth (John 1:17). Moses' contribution is praised, but that of Jesus is superior. Moses is the prophet who pointed the way to Jesus (Luke 24:27, 44; John 5:45ff; Acts 3:22, 26:22). At the transfiguration, Jesus stands flanked by Moses, who represents the law, and Elijah who represents prophecy. Jesus is considered the fulfillment of both (Matt 17:1–8; Mark 9:2–8; Luke 9:28–36). Matthew 5:17ff quotes Jesus as granting full recognition to the law of Moses, which he (Jesus) has come not to change but to fulfill.

It was under Moses' stewardship that the monotheism of the Patriarchs became the religion, indeed the culture, of an entire people, thus laying the foundation for Christianity and Islam as well as Judaism. The story of Moses is contained in the books of Exodus, Leviticus, Numbers, and Deuteronomy.

The Ten Commandments

1. You shall have no other gods before me.
2. You shall not make for yourself any carved image, or any likeness of anything that is in heaven above, or that is in the earth beneath, or that is in the water under the earth; you shall not bow down to them nor serve them. For I the Lord your God am a jealous God, visiting the iniquity of the fathers on the children to the third and fourth generations of those who hate me, but showing mercy to thousands, to those who love me and keep my commandments.
3. You shall not take the name of the Lord your God in vain, for the Lord will not hold him guiltless who takes his name in vain.
4. Remember the Sabbath day, to keep it holy; six days you shall labor and do all your work, but the seventh day is the Sabbath of the Lord your God. In it you shall do no work: your, nor your son, nor your daughter, nor your manservant, nor your maidservant, nor your cattle, nor your stranger who is within your gates. For in six days the Lord made the heavens and the earth, the sea, and all that is in them, and rested the seventh day. Therefore the Lord blessed the Sabbath day and hallowed it.
5. Honor your father and your mother, that your days may be long upon the land which the Lord your God is giving you.
6. You shall not murder.
7. You shall not commit adultery.
8. You shall not steal.
9. You shall not bear false witness against your neighbor.
10. You shall not covet your neighbor's house; you shall not covet your neighbor's wife, nor his manservant, nor his maidservant, nor his ox, nor his donkey, nor anything that is your neighbor's. (Ex 20:2–17)

III.26 THE JUDGES

The period of the Judges is the name given to the era between the conquest of the Land of Canaan by the Israelites under Joshua and the establishment of the monarchy under Saul, covering some three centuries up to the 11th century BC. The period is characterized by the emergence of local leaders who led the emerging nation into battle against their enemies. These figures were known as "judges," but those mentioned in the Book of Judges were not judges in the legal sense, with the exception of Deborah. They were military heroes, who as charismatic figures exerted great influence on the people. Nevertheless, it appears that no single judge achieved the support of all the tribes. The Book of Judges lists 13 judges, to whom Samuel, the last of the judges, should also be added.

The period of the Judges was one of consolidation of

the initial territorial conquests begun under Joshua. The neighboring states, unaccustomed to the existence of the new Israelite entity, exploited Israel's loose tribal structure to extend their own influence in the region. Simultaneously, the emergence of the Philistines as a new local power added to the ongoing series of wars and uprisings.

The period is portrayed at times as one of anarchy: "in those days, when there was no king in Israel" (Judg 17:6; 18:1; 19:1; 21:25); not only does the Book of Judges record the battles which took place between the Israelite tribes and their neighbors, but also the intertribal fighting common at the time, culminating in the near destruction of the tribe of Benjamin (Judg 17:1–21:25). It has therefore been suggested that the Book of Judges was written in order to justify the recently emergent monarchy. In fact, one of the judges, Gideon, was offered the monarchy. He rejected it, however, declaring that neither he nor his son was fit to rule over the tribes but that "the Lord shall rule over you" (Judg 8:23). His son, Abimelech, tried later to establish himself as king, but the people rejected his claim (Judg 9).

The Book of Judges opens with an account of the Israelite conquest of the Land of Canaan (Judg 1:1–2:5), attributing the conquests to the individual tribes whose territory was concerned. In spite of the military success of the nation, the people are depicted as falling into the snares of idol-worship (Judg 2:6–3:6). God punishes the tribes by making them subject to the surrounding nations, and sends judges to rescue them. Shortly after the death of each judge, however, the nation returns to its past ways, and the cycle repeats itself.

See also III 21, Books of the Old Testament: Judges.

THE JUDGES

Othniel. First of the judges, led Israel in battle against Cushan-Rishathaim, king of Aram-Naharaim, who had subjugated Israel for eight years. Othniel's victory led to 40 years of peace for the tribes (Judg 3:7–11).

Othniel is referred to as both "the son of Kenaz, the brother of Caleb" (Josh 15:17) and "the son of Kenaz, Caleb's younger brother" (Judg 1:13), leaving it unclear whether Othniel was the brother of Caleb or Kenaz (of the tribe of Judah). For his conquest of the Judean town of Debir, he was given Achsah, the daughter of Caleb, in marriage (Judg 1:12–13). In Chronicles, Othniel is recorded as having had two sons, Hathath and Meonothai (I Chr 4:13–14). Heldai the Netophite, a descendant of Othniel, is mentioned as having commanded a division in the army of David (I Chr 27:15).

Ehud. Son of Gera, from the tribe of Benjamin, the second of the judges. A deception by Ehud led to the Israelite victory over Eglon, king of Moab. Chosen to bring the tribute of Israel to Eglon, Ehud hid a double-edged sword in his cloak. He requested a private audience with the king in which he informed Eglon that he bore a message for the king from God. As Eglon rose to receive the message, Ehud stabbed him to death, and escaped from the palace before the assassination was detected. Ehud then assembled the people, leading them in battle against Moab. His victory brought 80 years of peace to the land (Judg 3:12–30).

Shamgar. All that is known about the third judge, Shamgar, son of Anat, is that he fought against the Philistines, slaying 600 men with an ox goad (Judg 3:31).

JUDGES OF ISRAEL			
JUDGE	YEARS OF REIGN	MAIN ACCOMPLISHMENT	SOURCE (BOOK OF JUDGES)
Othniel	40	Conquered Debir	1:12-13, 3:8-11
Ehud	80	Defeated Moabites	3:12-30
Shamgar		Battled Philistines	3:31
Deborah	40	Defeated Canaanite general Sisera	4-5
Gideon	40	Defeated Midianites	6-8
Abimelech	3	Proclaimed self king	9
Tola	23	Protected Israel	10:1-2
Jair	22	Protected 30 towns	10:3-5
Jephthah	6	Defeated Ammonites	11:1-12:7
Ibzan	7	Protected Israel	12:8-10
Elon	10	Protected Israel	12:11-12
Abdon	8	Protected Israel	12:13-15
Samson	20	Battled Philistines	13-16

Deborah. Wife of Lapidoth, and unique among the women of the Bible in that she served not only as a judge and prophetess, but also as a military leader.

Deborah acted as a local judge in the territory of the tribe of Ephraim. The loose confederation of Israelite tribes in her time was subject to Jachin, king of Hazor. Deborah called on the warrior, Barak son of Abinoam, to lead an uprising against Jachin according to the military strategy she had received from God. Barak refused to go to war without Deborah, causing her to declare that the outcome of the battle would be decided by a woman. Leading an army composed of soldiers from the tribes of Naphtali and Zebulun, Barak crushed the opposing general, Sisera, at the Kishon River. Although Sisera managed to escape, he was later killed by Jael, fulfilling the prophecy of Deborah (Judg 4). The victorious "Song of Deborah" (Judg 5) is counted among the most ancient of the biblical songs. Although it differs somewhat in its account of the battle from the preceding chapter, it nonetheless portrays Deborah as a prominent leader among the early Israelite tribes.

Gideon. The lengthiest account of a leader in the Book of Judges is that accorded to Gideon. The son of Joash from the town of Ophrah in the territory of Manasseh, Gideon had 70 sons from his many wives and concubines. One son, Abimelech, was judge following him. Gideon was offered the monarchy but rejected it (Judg 8:22-23).

Baal worship was prevalent among the tribes at the time of Gideon and was perceived as the cause of their subjugation to Midian (Judg 6:1). Having received

The Spring of Harod, at the foot of Mount Gilboa, where Gideon selected his best men to fight the Midianites.

from an angel his calling to lead the tribes to victory against Midian, Gideon destroyed an altar erected to Baal as a cultic center. This action earned him the name Jerubaal, meaning, "let Baal contend" (Judg 6:24-32). Gideon was later reaffirmed in his task by a sign from God in which a fleece left out overnight was covered with dew while the surrounding area remained dry (Judg. 6:36-40).

Out of 22,000 volunteers, Gideon selected a small force for battle consisting of a mere 300 men. After defeating Midian in a surprise attack under the cover of darkness, Gideon beheaded the captive Midianite princes, Zeeb and Oreb. He continued pursuit of the kings, Zebah and Zalmunna, until they, too, were captured and put to death (Judg. 7:3-8:21).

Gideon's sortie against the enemies of Israel was not supported by the bulk of the people of Israel. The elders of Succoth and Penuel both refused to feed Gideon's troops as they went to battle. After his victory over Midian, Gideon returned to these two cities, and, in retribution, tortured the elders of Succoth with thorns, and destroyed the fortifications of Penuel (Judg 8:5-17). Gideon then continued to govern the tribes until his death. He was buried in his hometown of Ophrah (Judg 8:29-32).

Abimelech. Born in Shechem to the concubine of Gideon. After his father's death Abimelech attempted to seize power in Shechem, but was blocked by a coalition of Gideon's 70 sons. Supported by his mother's family, Abimelech then attacked Ophrah, his family home, and slaughtered his half-brothers, thereby becoming Gideon's sole heir. Abimelech had governed Shechem as king for three years when it was discovered that Jotham, the youngest son of Gideon, had survived the massacre. With Abimelech's authority threatened, the local populace conspired against him. Abimelech suppressed the revolt and entered Shechem, massacring the inhabitants, razing the cultic center, and "sowing the city with salt" (Judg 9:45). Continuing his conquests, Abimelech next besieged the neighboring city of Thebez, where a woman, standing on the ramparts, flung a flagstone at him and mortally wounded him. Rather than suffer death at the hands of a woman, Abimelech ordered his arms-bearer to kill him, ending the first attempt to establish a monarchy among the tribes (Judg 9).

Tola. Son of Puah, who judged Israel for 23 years following the death of Abimelech. He belonged to the tribe of Issachar and was buried in Shamir (Judg 10:1-2).

Jair. Originating from the region of Gilead, Jair ruled Israel as judge for 22 years following the death of Tola. He had 30 sons, and ruled directly over thirty villages in a stretch of land called Havoth Jair. Jair was buried in the town of Kammon (Judg 10:3-5).

Jephthah. The judge Jephthah is said to have governed Israel for six years, but it is more likely that he was merely a local chieftain in the Gilead area. The son of a prostitute, Jephthah was forced by the legitimate sons of his father to leave his homeland. Exiled, he established himself as the leader of a gang of outlaws in the land of Tob (Judg 11:1-3).

Because of his military prowess, the tribal leaders appealed to Jephthah to lead them in battle against Ammon, agreeing, in return, to appoint him tribal leader (Judg 11:4-11). Having accepted, Jephthah first requested of Ammon to enter into a peace treaty with Gilead, but his offer was rejected and so he prepared for war. Jephthah attempted to appease God by vowing as a burnt-offering the first thing to greet him should he return home victorious. After his victory it was his daughter who led the procession to greet him on his return, and he was obliged to fulfill his vow (Judg 11:12-40).

The tribe of Ephraim, offended at not being asked to take part in the battle against Ammon and therefore unable to partake of the spoils of war, attacked Gilead. Jephthah once again led the inhabitants of Gilead to victory. However, the fighting brought to a peak the intertribal warfare preceding the monarchy (Judg 12:1-7).

Ibzan. Ibzan judged Israel for seven years. He had 30 sons and 30 daughters, all of whom married outside his clan. Nothing else is known of him except that he was buried in his hometown of Bethlehem (Judg 12:8-10).

Elon. Elon, from the tribe of Zebulun, judged Israel for ten years following the death of Ibzan. He was buried in the town of Aijalon (Judg 12:11-12).

Abdon. Abdon, son of Hillel, lived in the town of Pirathon in the territory of the tribe of Ephraim. He judged Israel for eight years following the death of Elon. Abdon was apparently a wealthy man and is recorded as having 40 sons and 30 grandsons who rode on 70 asses. He was buried in his hometown of Pirathon (Judg 12:13-15).

Samson. Samson, son of Manoah, last of the Israelite judges in the Book of Judges, came from the town of Zorah in the territory of the tribe of Dan. Although he is known mainly for his physical prowess, Samson was a man of God who was dedicated, even before his birth, as a Nazirite (Judg 13:3-5). It was his dedication to God, rather than his locks of hair, that served as the source of his immense strength. Samson is also perceived as a miracle-worker. When he found himself near death after battling the Philistines, a rock gushed forth as a spring to revive him in answer to his prayer (Judg 15:18-19).

Samson was particularly attracted to Philistine women. Three such love affairs are recorded in the Book of Judges (Judg 14:1; 16:1; 16:4), each occasion leading to his rejection and disgrace at the hands of the Philistines, and each leading to his ensuing revenge. Because of the apparent apathy of his countrymen, Samson carried out his vengeance alone, armed only with his remarkable strength. This had appeared at an early age; while still young, he slew an attacking lion unarmed (Judg 14:6). He later killed a thousand men with the jawbone of an ass (Judg 15:15) and carried the gates of the city of Gaza to Hebron (Judg 16:3). He destroyed the Philistine harvest by attaching torches to the tails of foxes and releasing the foxes in the Philistine fields (Judg 15:4-5).

Although Samson's attraction to Philistine women led to his defeating the Philistines, it also led to his own downfall. He fell in love with Delilah, a woman whom the Philistines used to discover the source of his strength. After misleading Delilah three times, Samson was finally induced to reveal to her the secret of his prowess, which he identified as his hair. Delilah

Samson killing Philistines with the jawbone of an ass. Detail from the marble-inlaid floor of Siena Cathedral, Italy.

immediately informed the Philistine nobility who sheared his locks and carried him blinded to Gaza. Samson was imprisoned and forced to work a millstone. However, his hair slowly began to grow back. Brought to the Temple of Dagon, he was chained between two pillars to endure taunting by the Philistine aristocracy. Calling on God to restore his strength, Samson toppled the pillars, causing the temple to crash down both on the Philistines and on himself (Judg 16:23-31). He had judged Israel for 20 years.

III.27 THE KINGS OF JUDAH AND ISRAEL

KINGSHIP

The rule of kings was the established form of government for the people of Israel immediately preceding and throughout the First Temple Period. Before the establishment of the monarchy, during the period of the Judges, the people of Israel was a loosely-knit confederation of tribes without any central authority. In times of war, a military leader would arise to lead the tribes involved in battle. Rarely, however, was this authority extended to more than those tribes immediately involved in the battle, and as the danger passed, the leader would pass into obscurity. Legal issues were determined by local elders who often, like Samuel, roamed a designated area mediating disputes (I Sam 7:16).

The first mention of the establishment of a monarchy appears in Deuteronomy (17:14-15), where it is offered as a possibility to the tribes rather than as a positive commandment. Debate existed among the people as to the desirability of a monarchy. Whereas some of the people saw a monarchy as a means of uniting the tribes into a common front capable of overcoming common problems, others saw a monarchy as a rebellion against the divine authority and kingship of God.

Several attempts to establish a monarchy failed. On one occasion, Gideon was offered the kingship, but he refused, saying that only God was the king of Israel (Judg 8:22-23). His son, Abimelech, attempted to have himself proclaimed king but was rejected by the people after ruling for three years (Judg 9). Following the anointment of the first king, Saul, by Samuel, a lottery was held in which Saul was confirmed in his position by heavenly mandate (I Sam 10:20-24).

The system of succession to the throne evolved throughout the period of the monarchy, and it appears that a conflict existed between the traditional manner of appointing a leader, based on ability and charisma, and the later system of dynastic rule. After the death of Saul, attempts were made to appoint his son as king in his stead. He was rejected, however, by the tribe of Judah who favored the more capable David (II Sam 2). Later, the concept of the Davidic dynasty as the sole royal dynasty was accepted only by the tribe of Judah. In the Northern Kingdom, dynasties were constantly being usurped by individuals who deemed themselves more competent to fill the role of king. Primogeniture did not always play a decisive role in the choosing of an heir to the king. The position of the prince's mother in the royal court was also an important factor. Bathsheba was able to sway David to appoint Solomon his heir despite the claims of the older Adonijah (I Kgs 1).

The investiture ceremony was held in the presence of the elders of the nation. Two accounts exist of coronation ceremonies: that of Solomon took place at the spring of Gihon (I Kgs 1:38-40), but once the Temple was built, all investitures took place there. Rehoboam, however, is recorded as having had a separate coronation at Shechem (I Kgs 12:1), although this was apparently for the benefit of the elders of the Northern tribes who could not make the journey to Jerusalem and were in the throes of a growing secessionist movement.

Common to all accounts of the coronation was the forging of a tripartite covenant among the king, God, and the people (II Kgs 11:17). After the anointing of the king, the people shouted, "Long live the king!" (II Kgs 11:12), and the elders submitted to the royal authority. The king often received a new name upon his assuming the throne, as is recorded with the later kings of Judah (II Kgs 23:34; 24:17) and with Solomon, who was originally named Jedidiah (II Sam 12:25). Also upon investiture, the king obtained the symbols of his royal authority: the crown and armlet (II Sam 1:10), the throne (II Sam 14:9), and the scepter (Ps 45:6). Control of the harem was also seen as a sign of royal authority, and Adonijah's attempt to gain possession of his father's concubine, Abishag, was taken by Solomon as a sign of rebellious intentions (I Kgs 2:13-22).

The position of king included various responsibilities of both a temporal and a religious nature. The king was the supreme military leader and the highest court of appeal. In many cases, he was a religious authority, but the powers invested in the king as such remain unclear. Jehoshaphat, Hezekiah, and Josiah stood at the center of successful religious reformations (II Chr 17:7-9; II Kgs 18:3-4; II Kgs 22:3-20). On the other hand, Uzziah's attempt to transfer the Temple ritual from the priesthood to the monarch failed (II Chr 26:16-21). Nor was the king above the civil laws of the state. He had neither the power to expropriate property (I Kgs

			KINGS OF JUDAH AND ISRAEL		
DATE (BC)	JUDAH	ISRAEL	DATE (BC)	JUDAH	ISRAEL
1020	Saul (1026–1004)		730	Ahaz	
1000	David (1004–965)			(regent 743–733;	Pekah (735/4–733/2)
990		United		king 733–727)	Hoshea (733/2–724)
980		Kingdom		Hezekiah (727–698)	
970		of Israel	724	(Fall of the Northern	
960	Solomon (965–928)			Kingdom of Israel)	
950			720		
940			710		
930	Rehoboam (928–911)	Jeroboam I (928–907)	700	Manasseh (698–642)	
920			690		
910	Abijah (911–908)	Nadab (907–906)	680		
	Asa (908–867)	Baasha (906–883)	670		
900			660		
890			650		
880		Elah (883–882)	640	Amon (641–640)	
		Zimri (882/1)		Josiah (639–609)	
		(Tibni 882/1–878)	630		
		Omri (882/1–871)	620		
870	Jehoshaphat	Ahab (regent 873–871;	610	Jehoahaz (609)	
	(regent 870–867;	king 871/0–852/1)		Jehoiakim (608–598)	
	king 867–846)		600	Jehoiachin (597)	
860				Zedekiah (596–586)	
850	Jehoram	Ahaziah (852/1–851/0)	586	(Fall of Jerusalem;	
	(regent 851–846;	Jehoram (851/0–842)		Babylonian Exile)	
	king 846–843)				
840	Ahaziah (843–842)				
	Athaliah (842–836)	Jehu (842–814)			
	Jehoash (Joash)				
	(836–798)				
830					
820					
810		Jehoahaz			
		(regent 817–814;			
		king 814–800)			
800	Amaziah (798–769)	Jehoash (800–784)			
790					
780		Jeroboam II			
		(regent 789–784;			
		king 784–748)			
770	Uzziah (Azariah)				
	(regent 785–769;				
	king 769–733)				
760	Jotham				
	(regent 758–750;				
	king 750–743)				
750		Zechariah (748/7)			
		Shallum (748/7)			
		Menahem (747/6–			
		737/6)			
740		Pekahiah (737/6–			
		735/4)			

Painted sherd, depicting a (royal?) figure seated on a throne, from Jerusalem, dating to the 7th century BC.

Nor was the king above the civil laws of the state. He had neither the power to expropriate property (I Kgs 21) nor to execute his subjects at whim (II Sam 11). As the monarchy became established, the king assumed the power of taxation. No evidence exists that either Saul or David taxed their subjects, being content with either their own means or the spoils of conquest. Taxation, in the form of both produce and forced labor, began in the reign of Solomon (I Kgs 4:7-19; 5:13-16).

In order to govern effectively, the king was surrounded by advisors and elders who composed the royal court consisting of: the commanders of the royal bodyguard and army, scribes and secretaries (II Sam 8:18), the chief administrator over the local administrators, the palace administrators, and royal friends (I Kgs 4:5-6), among other officials responsible for the running of the kingdom. The religious leaders of the state, including priests and prophets, were also attached to the royal court (I Sam 22:6; II Sam 7:2; I Kgs 4:4). By the time of the fall of Judah to Babylonia, the monarchy had become so entrenched in the consciousness of the people that the Messianic period was later foreseen as the re-establishment of the Davidic dynasty over an independent Jewish state.

KINGS OF THE UNITED KINGDOM

Saul (1026-1004). Saul son of Kish from the tribe of Benjamin was the first king of Israel. Before his anointing as king, the tribes were plagued by recurring Philistine invasions, leading the people to believe that only a strong central authority would be able to unite the tribes and marshal sufficient power to counter the Philistine threat. His election as king is presented in parallel narratives, reflecting both a pro-monarchic (I Sam 9:1-10:16) and an anti-monarchic account (I Sam 8; 10:17-27, 12). Saul began his reign by defeating the Ammonites besieging Jabesh-Gilead (I Sam 11).

As a result of continuing Philistine incursions into the territory of the tribes (I Sam 13:3), Saul prepared for war. His son, Jonathan, killed the Philistine commander at Geba, signaling the beginning of the uprising. The two armies met at Michmash, on opposite sides of a steep ravine. On the night preceding the battle, Jonathan entered the enemy camp, killing 20 soldiers. This demoralized the Philistine troops, and the next day they were defeated. Though forced to retreat into their own territory, the Philistines continued to plague the tribes throughout Saul's reign (I Sam 13-14). Saul attempted to unite the tribes under his central authority, and to liquidate all foreign enclaves within Israelite territory. He expelled the Moabites and Ammonites to Transjordan, and even massacred the Gibeonites, despite the treaty made between them and Joshua (Josh 9).

In fulfillment of the biblical precept, Saul fought and annihilated the Amalekites. He did, however, spare Agag, their king, thereby incurring the wrath of the prophet Samuel. Samuel himself killed Agag, but Saul's disobedience to the divine commandment opened the rift between Samuel and Saul (I Sam 15).

The split between the two caused Saul severe depression; he was often overcome by fits of anguish, and suspected his entourage of plotting against him. Since music brought Saul relief from his depression, David, a skilled musician, entered Saul's service in order to help the king during his fits of melancholy (I Sam 18:10). By slaying the Philistine champion, Goliath, David became a hero among the people of Israel. Saul became jealous of David's popularity, and on two occasions attempted to kill him (I Sam 18:10-11; 19:9-10). Saul even attempted to kill his own son and heir, Jonathan, because of the deep friendship that existed between him and David (I Sam 20:33). David was forced to flee the palace, and Saul, seeing in David a rival for his throne, pursued him throughout the remainder of his reign, slaying all, including the inhabitants of the priestly city of Nob, who supported David (I Sam 22:17-18). Saul's intense hatred of David only increased the distance between himself and the people, who began to view Saul as unfit for the kingship. The biblical text records that Saul lost the mandate from God to continue as king (I Sam 28:6).

Faced with battle against the Philistines at Mount Gilboa, Saul, who no longer had the support of the priesthood and therefore could not make use of the priestly oracle, asked a witch in the town of Endor to raise the prophet Samuel from the grave, that he might inform Saul of the outcome of the battle (I Sam 28:7-8). Samuel's spirit, after remonstrating with Saul for resorting to witchcraft, predicted Saul's defeat. Saul's forces were not suitably prepared for battle and were unable to match the Philistine armaments, which included war-chariots, an innovation in the region. The armies of Saul were crushed by the Philistines, and Jonathan and two other sons of Saul were killed in the battle. Saul himself was mortally wounded.

Unable to face the prospect of defeat, Saul commanded his arms-bearer to slay him. When the arms-bearer refused, Saul committed suicide by falling on his sword (I Sam 31:4). In another version of the story, an Amalekite youth claimed to have killed Saul (II Sam 1:6-10). The next morning, Philistine troops found the dead body of Saul; they beheaded it, and hung the corpse on the walls of the city of Beth Shean (I Sam 31:8-10). The inhabitants of the neighboring town of Jabesh-Gilead, indebted to Saul for saving them several years earlier from the Philistines, came at night and removed the body to their own town where they burned it so as to protect it from the ravages of the Philistines (I Sam 31:12). In another version, the inhabitants of the town did not burn the body but gave it an honorable burial (I Chr 10:12).

David (1004-965). No other king played as pivotal a role in the history of Israel as David. He came from the town of Bethlehem in the territory of the tribe of Judah. He was the youngest of the eight sons of Jesse (I Sam 16:11-12) and a descendant of Boaz and Ruth (Ruth 4:17). Whereas David spent his early years as a shepherd, once he became king, he brought Israel to the pinnacle of its military power. David established an empire with borders extending over virtually the entire territory promised to the Patriarchs, from Mesopotamia in the north to Egypt in the south. In addition to being a king and military leader, David was also a musician and poet, with many of the Psalms attributed to him.

David is first mentioned when, still a youth and a shepherd, he was anointed by Samuel as King Saul's successor (I Sam 16:13). He was invited by Saul to court both because of his musical skills and his reputation as a warrior (I Sam 16:17-23). He began his rise to power when, as a youth, he slew the Philistine champion, Goliath (I Sam 17:38-51). David held two positions at court; he was an army commander (I Sam 18:5) and a royal musician (I Sam 16:14-23). Only the tunes of David could bring Saul out of his increasing melancholy. Saul initially felt a strong attachment to David, and even gave him his daughter Michal in marriage (I Sam 18:27). David's greatest companion in the court, however, was Saul's son and heir, Jonathan, who "loved him as his own soul" (I Sam 18:1).

David's immense popularity among the people eventually aroused Saul's bitter jealousy, and Saul began to realize that he was a potential rival to Jonathan for succession to the kingship. After Saul had

Samuel anointing David. Wall painting from Dura-Europos synagogue; 3rd century.

twice attempted to murder him (I Sam 18:10-11; 19:9-10), David was forced to flee the royal court. Whereas Saul continued to pursue David, Jonathan remained loyal to his friend (I Sam 18-20). During his wanderings, David obtained the support of his tribesmen in Judah (I Sam 23:1-5), as well as that of the Philistines, who saw in him an ally in their fight against Saul (I Sam 27:2-12).

After Saul had been killed in the battle of Gilboa, David was anointed king of the tribe of Judah in the city of Hebron (II Sam 2:4). David was not, however, accepted as king by the other tribes who, at the instigation of Saul's general Abner, had anointed Saul's son Ishbosheth as king. Upon the defeat of Ishbosheth, David was proclaimed king of all the tribes (II Sam 4:4-5:3).

After eight years of ruling the nation from Hebron, David decided to confirm his authority over the semi-autonomous tribes by establishing a United Kingdom. David chose the Jebusite enclave of Jerusalem, straddling the border between the tribe of Judah and the Northern tribes, to be the new capital of the country. After conquering Jerusalem (II Sam 5:6-10), David brought the Ark of the Covenant to the city (II Sam 6), thereby establishing Jerusalem as the religious as well as the political center of Israel.

As head of a unified nation, David renewed the struggle against the Philistines. The Philistines were defeated at Emek Rephaim (II Sam 5:22-25), and forced to retreat to the coastal plain, where they no longer posed a threat (II Sam 8:1).

David continued to expand his realm, conquering the remaining Canaanite enclaves in the north. At the same time, the nation acquired new techniques in metallurgy, enabling the forging of better weapons, and increasing the kingdom's military might (II Sam 10:7-19). David used this new strength to subdue the Moabites (II Sam 8:2), Edomites (II Sam 8:14), and Ammonites (II Sam 12:26-29), gaining access to the Red Sea port of Ezion-Geber and new trade routes.

Having consolidated his control over the areas immediately surrounding his kingdom, David captured the Aramean states of Damascus and Aram Zobah, thereby extending his authority to the banks of the Euphrates (II Sam 8:3-8).

David's court was not free of intrigues. While his armies were engaged in their campaign against the Ammonites, David ascended the roof of his palace from which he noticed Bathsheba, the wife of Uriah the Hittite, one of his military commanders. David immediately fell in love with Bathsheba, and committed adultery with her. When it became known to David that Bathsheba had become pregnant by him, he plotted to kill her husband by sending him to the front lines of battle. Uriah was killed, and David married Bathsheba (II Sam 11). The prophet Nathan condemned David for his murder, foretelling: "The sword

David playing the harp, depicted on the mosaic floor of the 6th-century synagogue in Gaza.

shall never depart from your house" (II Sam 12:10). David repented and the sentence was revoked, but the first son born to Bathsheba died as a punishment for David's sin (II Sam 12:13-19).

David was also faced with several revolts. The Northern tribes, led by Sheba son of Bichri, rejected the authority of the tribe of Judah over the remaining tribes. David succeeded in crushing the revolt (II Sam 20).

Perhaps the most painful revolt to David was that of his son Absalom. After Absalom's sister, Tamar, had been raped by her half-brother, Amnon, Absalom killed Amnon. David exiled Absalom from the court, and although the two were later reconciled, Absalom rebelled against his father. At first the people sided with Absalom and the revolt went in his favor; David was forced to flee the capital. Events turned, however, and in a fierce battle the forces of Absalom were defeated. Absalom tried to flee the site of the battle, but his long locks became tangled in the branches of an oak tree and he was killed (II Sam 13-18).

As David lay upon his death-bed, his son Adonijah had himself proclaimed king. Since David had previously sworn to Bathsheba that her son, Solomon, would succeed to the throne, Bathsheba, after taking counsel with the prophet Nathan, approached David and reminded him of his promise. David declared that Solomon was, indeed, his heir, and had him anointed (I Kgs 1).

The reign of David was marked by far-reaching reforms in the administration of Israel. David declared the Israelite religion as the official state religion, and even planned to construct a Temple, a task he was forbidden by God to carry out, but he did purchase the land for the construction of the Temple (II Sam 24:18-25). He reorganized the priesthood, making the High Priest a member of the royal court (II Sam 8:17-18). He also divided the country into regions, ignoring the earlier tribal divisions and creating the structure of a unified realm. The country was run by a bureaucracy headed by the king, and a period of unprecedented cultural achievement began. In later Jewish tradition, David's rule is considered the epitome of Jewish political and religious independence that will remain unequaled until the coming of the Messiah, himself a descendant of David.

These messianic traditions are expressed in the gospels in the person of Jesus, who was descended from David (Matt 22:41-46; Mark 12:35-37; Luke 20:41-44; John 7:42) and born in Bethlehem, David's hometown.

David's Chief Officials

Secretary (Recorder): Jehoshaphat son of Ahilud
Scribes: Seraiah, Shavsha, Sheva
Priests: Zadok, Abimelech, Abiathar
Army commander: Joab
Responsible for forced labor: Adoram
Supervisor of the Cherethites and Pelethites: Benaiah son of Jehoiada
Advisors: David's sons, Hushai, Ira the Jairite
   (II Sam 8:15-18; 20:23-26; I Chr 18:14-17).

Solomon (965-928). Solomon, the third and last king of the United Kingdom of Israel, was the son of David and Bathsheba. Solomon is widely remembered for his wisdom, wealth, and wives. As king, he presided over an era of unparalleled glory for Israel, with his kingdom a central focus of trade and culture in the ancient world. The biblical text records that God appeared to Solomon, and offered to grant him anything that he might desire. Solomon requested that God give him "an understanding heart to judge Your people, that I may discern between good and evil" (I Kgs 3:9). Pleased at Solomon's request, God promised that there would be "none like you before you, nor after you shall any arise like you" (I Kgs 3:12). It is reported that Solomon wrote 3,000 proverbs and 1,005 songs, and was deemed the wisest of all sages (I Kgs 5). His wisdom is exemplified in his astute ability in rendering judgment (I Kgs 3:16-28) and in his political acumen.

Solomon ascended the throne prior to his father's death after his half-brother, Adonijah, had tried unsuccessfully to seize the throne (see above, under David). In order to establish his authority after David's death, Solomon executed Adonijah and all the royal officials implicated in Adonijah's plot (I Kgs 2:13-46).

The decline of both Assyria and Egypt left Solomon with an empire stretching from Egypt to the Euphrates, making Israel the outstanding power in the region at that time. Although there were a few abortive attempts at rebellion against Solomon's authority, no record exists of any significant military encounters during his reign. By diplomatic means, he was able to extend the borders of his kingdom, and annexed the northern territory of Hammath (II Chr 8:3-4). Solomon cemented his ties with the neighboring states through a series of political marriages, including his marriage to the daughter of the Pharaoh of Egypt (I Kgs 3:1; 11:1). He is said to have had 700 wives and 300 concubines (I Kgs 11:3), a fact later condemned by the author of the Book of Kings (I Kgs 11). In addition to political treaties with the surrounding states, Solomon also forged economic treaties. His fame reached the shores of the distant kingdom of Sheba (in the southern part of the Arabian peninsula), whose queen came to visit him in Jerusalem, apparently in the interest of forging closer economic ties (I Kgs 10). Solomon also befriended Hiram, king of the Phoenician city of Tyre, and the latter helped Solomon in the establishment of a merchant fleet in the southern port of Ezion-Geber (I Kgs 10:11-12). Tribute from subject states and control of the major arteries of international traffic filled the coffers of the kingdom (I Kgs 5:1; 10:15,28-29).

Solomon embarked on various building projects, fortifying existing cities and building new ones, as well as constructing 4,000 stables for his cavalry (II Chr

king Solomon, maybe we could consider joint custody?

9:25). His royal palace was an architectural wonder, taking 13 years to complete (I Kgs 7:1-12). Solomon also built a palace for the daughter of Pharaoh (I Kgs 7:8), and pagan temples for his other wives (I Kgs 11:7-8).

His greatest accomplishment was the construction of the Temple. The work lasted seven years, and the edifice is described in great detail in I Kings 6-7. In order to build the temple, Solomon imported materials at great cost from Hiram, King of Tyre; taxes raised (I Kgs 4:7-19) to pay for the construction of the Temple and other building projects of Solomon strained the national treasury. The forced labor imposed on the people, involving one month in three (I Kgs 5:13-14), caused a decline in Solomon's popularity. Jeroboam, one of Solomon's ministers, rebelled against the king (I Kgs 11:26-28), and although the revolt was quelled, it laid the foundation for the secession of the Northern tribes after Solomon's death.

Solomon is described as having "loved the Lord, walking in the statutes of David his father" (I Kgs 3:3). Later tradition credits Solomon with the authorship of the books of Proverbs, Song of Songs, and Ecclesiastes.

Solomon's Chief Officials

Priests: Zadok and Abiathar
Scribes: Elihoreph and Ahijah sons of Shisha
Secretary (Recorder): Jehoshaphat son of Ahilud
Army commander: Benaiah son of Jehoiada
Supervisor of the prefects: Azariah son of Nathan
King's companion: Zabud son of Nathan the priest
Palace supervisor (vizier): Ahishar
Responsible for forced labor: Adoniram son of Abda

(I Kgs 4:1-6)

KINGS OF JUDAH

Rehoboam (928-911). Rehoboam, son of King Solomon and the Ammonite princess, Naamah, succeeded to the throne of Israel on the death of his father. The nation had suffered under Solomon because of the excessive taxes and forced labor he imposed on the people in order to build the Temple and support his extensive empire. Upon his death, the elders of the nation demanded of his heir, Rehoboam, that he lower taxes. After taking counsel with his advisors, the new king responded, "My father made your yoke heavy, and I will add to your yoke; my father chastised you with whips, but I will chastise you with scorpions" (I Kgs 12:14). Rehoboam's response led to the secession of the Northern tribes, with only Judah and Benjamin remaining loyal to the Davidic dynasty. A state of war existed between the two kingdoms throughout the reign of Rehoboam (I Kgs 12; 14:30).

Archaeological evidence corroborates the biblical account of the Egyptian invasion of Shishak in the fifth year of the reign of Rehoboam (I Kgs 14:25-26), in response to which Rehoboam fortified 15 Judean cities (II Chr 11:5-12). He began his reign by supporting the predominance of the Israelite religion in the kingdom. As his reign progressed, however, he became more lax in the defense of the religion, and permitted pagan practices to flourish (II Chr 12:1-2). Rehoboam had 18 wives and 60 concubines, by whom he fathered 28 sons and 60 daughters (II Chr 11:21). He is mentioned in the genealogy of Jesus in the Gospel of Matthew.

Abijah (Abijam) (911-908). Although Rehoboam's successor Abijah is condemned for tolerating the idolatrous practices begun under his father, he is praised for his victory in battle against Jeroboam. Abijah succeeded in weakening the Northern Kingdom by conquering extensive territories along the border with Israel, including the cultic center at Bethel (II Chr 13).

Abijah married 14 wives who bore him 22 sons and 16 daughters (II Chr 13:21-22; 14:1). He is mentioned in the genealogy of Jesus in the Gospel of Matthew.

Asa (908-867). Asa, who succeeded his father, Abijah, was a religious reformer who "took away the male prostitutes out of the land, and removed all the idols his fathers had made" (I Kgs 15:12), going so far as to remove his mother from her privileged status, "because she had made a monstrous image for an Asherah" (I Kgs 15:13).

The first ten years of Asa's reign were peaceful, allowing him to fortify the border cities and establish an army of some 580,000 troops (II Chr 14:5-8). These preparations were responsible for Asa's victory over Zerah the Cushite at Mareshah (II Chr 14:9-13). Asa also fought against Baasha, king of Israel, losing the strategic Judean town of Ramah, six miles (9 km) north of Jerusalem. In order to alleviate his loss, Asa entered into a pact with Ben-Hadad, king of Aram, and the latter attacked the northern cities of Israel (I Kgs 15:16-22).

In his old age, suffering from a leg ailment, Asa called on doctors to heal him instead of calling on God, an act for which he was condemned by the prophet Hanani. Asa is mentioned in the genealogy of Jesus in the Gospel of Matthew.

Jehoshaphat (regent 870-867; king 867-846). Jehoshaphat, son of Asa, seems to have served as regent during his father's final illness (II Chr 17:1). A great reformer, Jehoshaphat contributed to the welfare of Judah in many fields. He wiped out all traces of idolatry in the kingdom and sent priests throughout the country to teach the Law to the common people (II Chr 17:7-9). He also reorganized the judicial system by establishing courts throughout the country and creating a supreme court of appeals in Jerusalem (II Chr 19:4-11). He fortified the cities, established outposts in Ephraim, built storage centers and granaries, and expanded the army (II Chr 17:1-19).

Jehoshaphat was also the first king to make a treaty with the Northern Kingdom. In order to strengthen the tie, Jehoshaphat wed his heir, Jehoram, to Athaliah, daughter of Ahab of Israel (I Kgs 22:44). The treaty enhanced the military capabilities of Judah and led to the subjugation of Moab, Philistia, and Edom (II Chr 17:10-11; I Kgs 22:47). The new-found prosperity enabled Jehoshaphat to co-operate with Israel in the construction of a fleet in Ezion-Geber (II Chr 20:35-36). He is mentioned in the genealogy of Jesus in the Gospel of Matthew.

Jehoram (Joram) (regent 851-846; king 846-843). Jehoram ruled Judah for eight years following the death of his father, Jehoshaphat (II Kgs 8:17). His marriage to Athaliah, daughter of King Ahab of Israel by Ahab's Tyrian consort, Jezebel, led to the reintroduction of Baal worship to Judah (II Kgs 8:18). Jehoram was a weak king. Under his rule, Edom and Libnah both managed to reassert their independence from Judah (II Kgs 8:22). Jehoram also lost control of the highways to the west and was cut off from access to the copper mines in the south. Because of his weakness, Jehoram, fearing that his brothers would depose him, had them all murdered (II Chr 21:4).

Jehoram was defeated in battle by a coalition of the Philistines and various Arab tribes. His wives and sons, excepting the youngest, were taken into captivity, and his treasuries were sacked (II Chr 21:16-17).

He is mentioned in the genealogy of Jesus in the Gospel of Matthew.

Ahaziah (843-842). Ahaziah, son of Jehoram and Athaliah, ruled Judah for one year following the death of his father. He permitted idolatry to continue under his rule (II Chr 22:3-4).

Ahaziah supported his cousin, Jehoram, king of Israel, in his unsuccessful war against Hazael of Aram. While Ahaziah was visiting his wounded cousin in Jezreel, Jehu, an army commander instigated by the prophet Elisha, launched a rebellion. Jehoram was killed in the ensuing battle at Ramoth Gilead, and Ahaziah fled to the ascent of Gur where he, too, was injured. Although Ahaziah managed to escape capture, he died of his injury in Megiddo (I Kgs 9:14-27).

Athaliah (842-836). Athaliah, the only queen to rule

over Judah, was the daughter of Ahab and Jezebel of Israel. She was wed to Jehoram of Judah as part of a political treaty between her father and King Jehoshaphat (I Kgs 22:44). Following the death of her son Ahaziah, Athaliah usurped power in Judah and slaughtered all claimants to the throne, except for her grandson, Joash, who was rescued by his aunt, Jehosheba (II Kgs 11:1–3). When Joash reached the age of seven, Jehoiada the High Priest declared him to be the true king in place of Athaliah. Athaliah rushed to the Temple to suppress the coup and was killed upon the orders of Jehoiada (II Kgs 12:13–18).

Joash (Jehoash) (836–798). The son of King Ahaziah, Joash's rule began with Athaliah's death (see above). Throughout the life of Jehoiada, Joash supported the priesthood by eradicating Baal worship in the kingdom (I Kgs 12:7–16). After Jehoida's death, however, Joash rejected his pact with the priesthood and restored the worship of Baal. Jehoiada's son Zechariah opposed the introduction of Baal worship into the country, and this opposition led to his eventual murder by order of Joash (II Chr 24:17–22).

During his reign, the Arameans made several successful attacks on Judah, including the conquest of Gath, and prepared to march on Jerusalem. Joash succeeded in averting the attack by bribing the Aramean king, Hazael, with the treasures of the Temple (II Kgs 12:17–18).

Joash was assassinated by two of his servants (II Kgs 12:20–21).

Amaziah (798–769). Following the assassination of his father, Joash, Amaziah ascended the throne at the age of 25. After establishing his authority, his first act was the execution of the murderers of his father; the Bible commends him for sparing their families (I Kgs 14:1–6).

He attempted to restore Judah's sovereignty over Edom, attacking that nation with an army of 300,000 men from the tribes of Judah and Benjamin, and 100,000 mercenaries from the Northern Kingdom. Although he conquered Sela, killing 10,000 Edomites, the prophets condemned Amaziah's co-operation with the Kingdom of Israel, forcing him to send the mercenaries home. Enraged at their treatment, the mercenaries plundered Judah on their way back to Israel (II Chr 25:5–13). Amaziah then decided to declare war on Israel. Although Joash, king of Israel, warned Amaziah of the outcome of such a battle. Amaziah ignored the warning, and attacked. Following his defeat at Beth Shemesh, Amaziah was taken captive; Joash then entered Jerusalem and plundered the city and the Temple treasure (II Kgs 14:8–14).

Because of Amaziah's idolatry, a plot was formed to depose him. He fled to Lachish where he was murdered (II Kgs 14:19).

Tablet recording the reburial of the remains of King Uzziah, between the 1st century BC and the 1st century AD.

Uzziah (Azariah) (regent 785–769; king 769–733). Uzziah ascended the throne of Judah at the age of 16 upon the assassination of his father, Amaziah. He came into conflict with the priesthood for his attempt to usurp the priestly duties in the Temple. Upon entering the Temple to offer incense, a right reserved solely for the priests, Uzziah was smitten with leprosy (II Chr 26:16–21). He was unable to govern the country, and his son, Jotham, was made regent. It is assumed that the 52 years accredited to Uzziah's reign include the years that Jotham and Ahaz (at the end of the reign) ruled as regents.

During his long and generally successful rule, Uzziah reorganized the army and fortified Jerusalem and its environs. He expanded the extent of his authority as far as the Red Sea, and rebuilt the port of Elath. He then fortified the routes southward against incursions of nomadic Arab tribes. He also extended his borders northward into Israel and subjugated the Ammonites, and westward into Philistia where he captured Ashdod and gained control over the main trade route to Egypt (II Chr 26). Uzziah's defeat at the hands of Tiglath-pileser III of Assyria marked the beginning of the decline of the Kingdom of Judah. Due to his disease, Uzziah was buried outside the crypt of the kings (II Chr 26:33). A tablet discovered on the Mount of Olives in Jerusalem and dated between the 1st century BC and the 1st century AD, records the reburial of the bones of King Uzziah. He is mentioned in the genealogy of Jesus in the Gospel of Matthew.

Jotham (regent 758–750; king 750–743). Jotham began his rule during the life of his father Uzziah who was incapacitated with leprosy. He continued Uzziah's programs, expanding the latter's building projects (II Chr 27:3–4); among the structures listed as having been built by Jotham was the upper gate of the Temple (II

Kgs 15:35). Jotham also continued the war with Ammon, and succeeded in reducing that nation to a tributary state of Judah (II Chr 27:5). He is mentioned in the genealogy of Jesus in the Gospel of Matthew.

Ahaz (regent 743-733; king 733-727). Aged 20, Ahaz inherited the throne of Judah from his father, Jotham, and reigned for 16 years. He restored idolatry to Judah and even sacrificed his own son to Moloch (II Kgs 16:3-4).

Judah was attacked by Pekah, king of Israel, and Rezin, king of Aram, after Ahaz's refusal to enter into a coalition with them against Assyria. The objective of the invasion was to replace Ahaz as king in order to form an anti-Assyrian alliance (II Chr 28:5-8; Is 7:6). Ahaz was defeated at the outset, and many captives were exiled to Samaria. Only the intercession of the prophet Oded enabled the prisoners to return to Judah (II Chr 28:5-15).

With Judah weakened, Edom managed to conquer Elath while the Philistines occupied the southern and western regions of the country. Important cities were lost to the invaders (II Kgs 16:6). Although the prophet Isaiah attempted to console Ahaz, informing him that God would not allow Judah to fall, Ahaz was unconvinced, and entered into a pact with Assyria (Is 7:1-17; II Kgs 16:7-8). This treaty resulted in the emergence of Judah as a vassal state of Assyria. Ahaz traveled to Damascus in order to submit to Tiglath-pileser III, and while there was attracted to Assyrian idolatry. He built a pagan altar in Jerusalem based on an Assyrian model and sacrificed upon it (II Kgs 16:10-13).

Ahaz was buried in the city of David, but because of his idolatry, his body was not placed in the crypt of the kings (II Chr 28:27). He is mentioned in the genealogy of Jesus in the Gospel of Matthew.

Hezekiah (727-698) Hezekiah acceded to the throne following the death of his father, Ahaz. Five years before, Assyria had conquered Aram, and ten years later, in the fifth year of Hezekiah's reign (722 BC), the Northern Kingdom, too, fell to Assyria and its inhabitants were exiled. The fall of the Northern Kingdom paved the way for Assyrian expansion into Judah. This threat, coupled with the constant danger of Philistine and Edomite incursions into the southern regions of the country, placed the kingdom in a precarious situation. In addition, the levy demanded by the Assyrians in order to maintain peace with Judah brought the kingdom to the brink of economic collapse. Hezekiah realized that without far-reaching political and religious reforms, Judah was headed for disaster.

With the support of the prophet Isaiah, Hezekiah eradicated all idolatrous centers in Judah, purified the Temple, and restored the traditional rites and ceremonies, such as Passover, that had fallen into disuse (II Kgs 18:3-4; II Chr 29-30). Hezekiah next strengthened

The Pool of Hezekiah which collected the water coming from a spring outside the city.

the army and in a series of battles, conquered the surrounding areas, including Philistia (I Chr 4:34-43). Feeling able to assert himself, Hezekiah revolted against Assyrian domination in the year 701 BC (II Kgs 18:7). In preparation for the Assyrian attack, Hezekiah fortified Jerusalem, and built the Siloam tunnel to provide Jerusalem with water in the event of siege (II Kgs 20:20). Sennacherib, king of Assyria, besieged Jerusalem, but the city was spared destruction when, according to the biblical account, a plague broke out among the Assyrian troops and Sennacherib was forced to retreat (I Kgs 19:35). It does appear, however, that Hezekiah did, in fact, pay a heavy tribute to Sennacherib in return for the latter's lifting the siege.

In order to strengthen his regional position, Hezekiah entered into treaties with the rulers of the surrounding states, including Egypt (II Kgs 18:21) and Babylonia (II Kgs 20:12-16).

Hezekiah is listed in the genealogy of David in the Gospel of Matthew.

Manasseh (698-642). Manasseh succeeded his father, Hezekiah, when he was aged 12 and ruled for 55 years, the longest period of any monarch of Judah or Israel. Manasseh did not continue his father's traditions, and his reign saw the decline of Israel in all areas. During his reign, Judah remained an Assyrian province and Manasseh annulled his father's religious reforms and permitted the reinstitution of Baal and Asherah worship. He allowed the establishment of the cult of Moloch, which demanded the regular sacrifice of children, and even offered his own son as a sacrifice (II Kgs 21:1-9). Manasseh was condemned by the prophets, and in response, he persecuted them along with anyone else who dared question his authority.

The Bible tells little of Manasseh's political history. Assyrian sources refer to him as a loyal vassal of King

Esarhaddon. He also mobilized a contingent to fight alongside Ashurbanipal in his campaign against Egypt. However, the Book of Chronicles records that Manasseh was led to Babylon in chains by the Assyrians. While in Babylonia, he repented his rebellion, and as a result, his kingdom was restored (II Chr 33:11-20). No historical evidence other than the account in Chronicles exists to verify this event.

Manasseh is mentioned in the genealogy of Jesus in the Gospel of Matthew.

Amon (641-640). Amon followed in the ways of his father, Manasseh, and this may have been responsible for his assassination at the hands of his servants. The people, however, rejected the attempted coup, and crowned Amon's son, Josiah, as king (II Kgs 21:18-19).

Josiah (639-609). A strong leader, Josiah returned Judah to its former glory. He was also a religious reformer who restored the Israelite religion to its past pre-eminence, following many years of neglect. The changes he made in the kingdom's society were effected in stages. In the eighth year of his reign, Josiah rejected the pagan practices of his Assyrian overlords, calling for a return to the religion of David (II Chr 34:3). Four years later, Josiah destroyed all the cultic centers in Judah, eventually expanding the scope of this activity to the territory of Ephraim, Manasseh, and the surrounding areas, formerly under the control of the Northern Kingdom. This was done after Josiah had managed to exert his influence on these areas following the death of the Assyrian emperor, Ashurbanipal (II Chr 34:3-7).

Josiah's most important reform occurred during the 18th year of his reign (621 BC). During the cleansing of the Temple, an unknown scroll of the Torah, apparently the Book of Deuteronomy, was found by the priest Hilkiah. The prophetess Huldah confirmed the authenticity of the scroll, and warned that ignoring the scroll would lead to national disaster. Josiah responded by immediately enforcing the authority of the text, making Jerusalem the sole center of religious worship (I Kgs 22:3-20).

Following the Babylonian attack on Assyria, Josiah led his troops to the aid of Assyria. They were attacked at Megiddo by Egyptian troops led by Pharaoh Necho II, and Josiah was fatally wounded in the battle (609 BC; II Kgs 23:29-31; II Chr 35:20-25). He is mentioned in the genealogy of Jesus in the Gospel of Matthew.

Jehoahaz (609). Jehoahaz became king of Judah at the age of 23, following the death of his father, Josiah. Jehoahaz is called Shallum by the prophet Jeremiah (Jer 22:11), and it is most likely that this was his original name before he assumed his throne-name. Although crowned by the people (II Kgs 23:30), Jehoahaz succeeded in ruling for only three months, after which he

was deposed by Pharaoh Necho II of Egypt, who eventually exiled him to Egypt where he died (II Kgs 23:30-34).

Jehoiakim (608-598). Jehoiakim was declared king by Pharaoh Necho of Egypt following the exile of his brother, Jehoahaz. Upon coronation, his name was changed from Eliakim to Jehoiakim (II Kgs 23:34).

Jehoiakim was a puppet ruler, with real authority invested in Necho. Egypt taxed Judah heavily, and Jehoiakim raised the tribute to Egypt by taxing all land in the kingdom.

After the defeat of Necho by Nebuchadnezzar of Babylonia in the battle of Carchemish (605 BC), Judah became a vassal state of Babylonia. Jehoiakim acquiesced at first, but rebelled three years later. Nebuchadnezzar sent troops to Judah to quell the revolt (II Kgs 24:2); these sacked the Temple and exiled a part of the population to Babylon (597 BC). According to the Book of Kings, Jehoiakim died peacefully (II Kgs 24:6), but Chronicles records that he was taken in fetters to Babylon (II Chr 36:6).

Jehoiachin, also called Jeconiah and Coniah (597). Jehoiachin succeeded Jehoiakim when he was 18. He and his court were also exiled to Babylonia three months after his accession to the throne, and he was succeeded by his uncle, the puppet-king Zedekiah (II Kgs 24:8-14).

Even after his exile to Babylonia, it was believed by the common people that Jehoiachin would eventually return to Judah to re-establish his rule. The Jews in Babylon even reckoned dates from the exile of King Jehoiachin (Ezek 1:2).

Jehoiachin remained in prison throughout the life of Nebuchadnezzar, but with the accession of Evil-Merodach to the throne of Babylonia, he was released from prison and invited to live in the Babylonian court (II Kgs 25:27-30). Babylonian tablets record that Jehoiachin, called "king of Judah," and his five sons were treated as royal pensioners, receiving daily rations from the court. He is mentioned in the genealogy of Jesus in the Gospel of Matthew.

Zedekiah (596-586). Zedekiah, whose original name was Mattaniah, youngest son of King Josiah (II Kgs 24:17-18), was the last king of Judah. He inherited the throne after his nephew, Jehoiachin, had been exiled to Babylonia, and served as a puppet-king for the Babylonians. The people did not recognize his authority and continued to see in Jehoiachin the rightful king of Judah (Ezek 1:2). Zedekiah was unable to withstand domestic pressure for rebellion against Babylonia, and therefore, entered into an anti-Babylonian confederation with Edom, Moab, Ammon, Tyre, and Sidon (Jer 27:3). This confederation was condemned by the prophet Jeremiah, who was consequently branded a traitor (Jer 37:9-21). Nonetheless, Zedekiah frequently took counsel with Jeremiah (Jer 37:17-18). As the confederation crumbled, Zedekiah attempted to appease the Babylonian king and sent messengers to him (Jer 29:3). After Nebuchadnezzar demanded that Zedekiah himself appear before him, the king had to journey to Babylon to assure Nebuchadnezzar of his fealty (Jer 51:59). Nevertheless, when the Egyptians in an anti-Babylonian move succeeded in conquering the Phoenician cities, Zedekiah immediately aligned himself with the Egyptians, and once more revolted against Babylonia. Nebuchadnezzar set out to crush this new threat to his authority aided by all the former members of the anti-Babylonian front, excepting Judah and Tyre, and when Tyre fell, Judah was left alone to face the Babylonian onslaught. Zedekiah attempted to make religious reforms in the hope that God might help the people of Judah in their battle against the Babylonians, and in doing so, freed all slaves in Judah (Jer 34:8-10). Babylonia lifted its siege of Jerusalem in order to meet an Egyptian advance intended to relieve Judah. Feeling themselves saved, the Judean aristocracy resubjugated the emancipated slaves (Jer 34:11). The Egyptians were defeated by the Babylonians, and the siege of Jerusalem was restored.

Although Nebuchadnezzar had originally intended to blockade the city and starve its inhabitants, Jerusalem held out for one and a half years, frustrating the original intentions of Nebuchadnezzar, and forcing him to carry out a frontal attack. He broke through the walls of Jerusalem and destroyed the Temple. Zedekiah and his court managed to flee but were later captured on the Plains of Jericho (Jer 39:4-5). Zedekiah was taken to the encampment of Nebuchadnezzar at Riblah where he was forced to witness the execution of his own sons. Afterward, he was blinded and taken to prison in Babylonia, where he died in captivity (II Kgs 24:17-19; 25:1-7).

THE NORTHERN KINGDOM

Jeroboam (928-907). Jeroboam son of Nebat, from the tribe of Ephraim, led the secessionist movement of the Northern tribes which resulted in the establishment of the Northern Kingdom of Israel. Although, under Solomon, Jeroboam held the prestigious position of manager of labor for the tribes of Ephraim and Manasseh, he rebelled against Solomon's authority (I Kgs 11:26-28). The prophet Ahijah the Shilonite foretold to Jeroboam that, at the death of Solomon, he would be made king of ten of the twelve tribes. Upon hearing this, Solomon attempted to murder Jeroboam, who managed to escape to Egypt to await Solomon's demise (I Kgs 11:29-43). After Solomon's death, his son Rehoboam acceded to the throne. His refusal to lower the taxes imposed upon the kingdom by his father led

to the secession of the Northern tribes, who proclaimed Jeroboam as their ruler, and he was anointed king in Shechem (I Kgs 12:20). Although Jeroboam forged the Northern Kingdom into a viable nation-state, the feud between him and Rehoboam persisted throughout his reign, causing perpetual war and bloodshed (I Kgs 14:30).

Jeroboam was a great builder; apart from fortifying the new capital of Shechem, he built the city of Penuel in Transjordan and eventually moved his capital to the city of Tirzah. He also established cultic centers at Bethel and Dan to vie with the Temple in Jerusalem. The golden calves erected in these new centers, as well as the changing of the date of the Feast of Tabernacles (I Kgs 12:25-33) earned Jeroboam the wrath of the prophets, and he became a symbol of the corruption of the Northern Kingdom (II Kgs 13:2 et al). Jeroboam was attacked by the Egyptian king, Shishak, and although he retained his throne, the kingdom was destroyed. The weakened Jeroboam was then attacked by Abijah, king of Judah, and much of the territory of southern Ephraim was lost (II Chr 13:3-19).

Nadab (907-906). Nadab, son of Jeroboam I, ruled Israel for two years following the death of his father. He continued his father's evil ways and, in the words of the Bible, "made Israel to sin." His assassination brought to an end the dynasty of Jeroboam I (I Kgs 15:25-28).

Baasha (906-883). Baasha son of Ahijah from the tribe of Issachar declared himself king of Israel following his killing of Nadab, during the siege of the Philistine stronghold of Gibbethon. Upon ascending the throne, he slaughtered all the descendants of Jeroboam I, thereby ending the hegemony of the tribe of Ephraim over the Northern Kingdom. After the signing of a treaty between Israel and Ben-Hadad I, king of Damascus, Baasha went to war against the Kingdom of Judah, and was able to conquer the city of Ramah before Ben-Hadad was bribed by Asa, king of Judah, to invade the northern region of Israel, and force Baasha's surrender. The prophet Jehu son of Hanani foretold the downfall of the house of Baasha, attributing it to the continuation of the evil ways of Jeroboam I, i.e., the toleration of idolatry (I Kgs 15:27-16:7; II Chr 16:1-6).

Elah (883-882). Elah was king of Israel for two years following the death of his father, Baasha. Elah was assassinated while drunk, by Zimri, a commander in his army (I Kgs 16:6-14).

Zimri (882/1). Zimri, "captain of half the chariotry" (I Kgs 16:9) declared himself king of Israel, following his assassination of Elah. He killed all the males of the family of Baasha, father of Elah, in order to secure his position as monarch. However, when word reached Omri, commander of the army, he immediately left his encampment at Gibbethon, and besieged Tirzah, the capital. Rather than fall captive to Omri, Zimri barricaded himself in the palace and set it afire, perishing in the flames. He had reigned for seven days (I Kgs 16:9-20).

Omri (882-871). Omri ruled the Northern Kingdom of Israel for twelve years. After the suicide of Zimri (see above), no male issue of the royal family of Baasha remained, and the army chose Omri as king, but his claim to the throne was threatened by Tibni son of Ginnath, who claimed the throne for himself. A civil war, lasting four years, ended with the death of Tibni and the consolidation of power by Omri (I Kgs 16:16-22). Omri moved the Israelite capital from Tirzah to his newly built city of Samaria (I Kgs 16:24-25). He subdued both Moab and Medeba. The marriage of his son Ahab to the Phoenician princess, Jezebel, was part of a treaty made by Omri with the Phoenicians in order to stem the growing influence of Assyria. The treaty with the Phoenicians caused an influx of foreign culture to the Northern Kingdom, which was later condemned by the prophets Elijah and Elisha. Prophetic disapproval led to an undervaluation of his achievements. Bible historians have concluded that he was one of the strongest rulers of the Northern Kingdom, which was known to the Assyrians by his name long after after his death.

Ahab (regent 873-871; king 871/0-852/1). Ahab son of Omri, and his Phoenician wife, Jezebel, were perhaps the most infamous rulers of the Kingdom of Israel. Under the influence of Jezebel, Ahab introduced the pagan practices of Phoenicia, with Ahab himself erecting an altar and temple for the worship of Baal (I Kgs 16:32-33). Official sanction was given to 450 prophets of Baal and 400 prophets of Asherah (I Kgs 18:18-19). In response to Israelite opposition to these pagan practices, Jezebel ordered the destruction of the altar of God and the murder of the Israelite prophets. However, a court official, Obadiah, was able to save 100 prophets by hiding them in caves and providing them with sustenance (I Kgs 18:3-4,13).

Ahab and his court were constantly under attack from the prophet Elijah. Elijah warned the king of an ensuing drought and famine that would be sent by God as punishment for his sins. As the drought began, Elijah fled the wrath of the king who held him personally responsible for the famine. After three years, Elijah reappeared, and although the king condemned him for the sufferings of the people, the prophet reversed the blame, citing the sins of Ahab (I Kgs 17:1-7; 18:1-10,18). This led to the confrontation between Elijah and the prophets of Baal at the summit of Mount Carmel (I Kgs I 18:20-40). Although the victory of Elijah led to the execution of the priests of Baal, and the end of the drought, Jezebel, incensed at the massacre of her priests, attempted to take vengeance on Elijah, who was again forced to flee the country (I Kgs 19:1-2).

Queen Jezebel had an enormous influence on Ahab, not only in religious spheres, but also in the day to day running of the state. Ahab coveted the vineyard of Naboth, and when the latter refused to sell him the property, Jezebel arranged for false witnesses to testify that Naboth had blasphemed. After his execution, the property was seized by the royal court and became the possession of Ahab. The prophet Elijah condemned the seizure and foretold the impending fall of the house of Ahab as punishment (I Kgs 21).

In spite of the excesses of his reign, Ahab was an adept statesman and ruler. Continuing the policies of his father, Omri, Ahab maintained a state of peace with

Site of Samaria, the capital of the kings of Israel, where Ahab built himself a palace known as the House of Ivory.

his neighbors, Phoenicia and Judah. His daughter, Athaliah, wed the son of King Jehoshaphat of Judah, and she herself eventually assumed the throne of Judah (II Kgs 8:18). Ahab was a great builder, completing the construction of the new capital of Samaria, and fortifying other cities, such as Jericho. He was fond of exhibiting his wealth and built for himself a new palace, the House of Ivory, in Samaria (I Kgs 22:39).

Ahab was threatened by the rise to power of Aram. On three occasions, Aram went to war with Israel. On the first occasion, they managed to besiege the royal city of Samaria. Ahab united the people and fought back the Aramean threat (I Kgs 20:3-21). A year later, Ben-Hadad of Aram again attacked the Kingdom of Israel and was again defeated. Ahab negotiated a treaty with Aram, returning all territories previously lost to Aram to Israelite control, and granting market rights for Israelite merchants in Damascus (I Kgs 20:34). This treaty made Israel a regional power which participated in a coalition of twelve kings against Shalmaneser III of Assyria (853 BC) in the indecisive battle fought at Karkar in Syria. Ahab sought to regain the Gilead region still under Aramean domination and, in league with the Judean king, Jehoshaphat, attacked Aram. Ahab was severely wounded in the onslaught, and demanded of the driver of his chariot to remove him from the battlefield, but his request went unheeded. He died that evening as a result of his wound.

Ahaziah (852/1-851/0). Ahaziah, son of Ahab and Jezebel, carried on his father's tradition by worshiping the Phoenician gods introduced by his mother (I Kgs 22:40, 52-53). The death of Ahab prompted the tributary state of Moab to rebel against the authority of Israel, and Moab's king, Mesha, refused to pay the yearly tribute demanded of his kingdom (II Kgs 1:1; 3:4-5). Possibly because he had been injured in an accident in the palace when he fell from the second storey (II Kgs 1:2), Ahaziah was unable to enforce the collection of the tribute, and thus weakened Israel's position in the region. Following his injury, Ahaziah sent messengers to the Philistine city of Ekron to inquire of the oracle of the god, Beelzebub, whether he would recover. On their way, the messengers encountered the prophet Elijah who castigated them with the words, "Is it because there is no God in Israel, that you go to inquire of Beelzebub, god of Ekron?" (II Kgs 1:3). Elijah informed the messengers that Ahaziah was destined to die. Upon hearing the prophecy of Elijah, Ahaziah sent a detachment of men to arrest him. Elijah accompanied the men to the king and repeated his prophecy (II Kgs 1:2-16)

Ahaziah attempted to forge a naval pact with Jehoshaphat, king of Judah, but was rebuffed. Upon sailing from the southern port of Ezion-Geber, Ahaziah's fleet was wrecked. He died, as Elijah had prophesied, after a two-year reign.

Jehoram (851/0-842). Jehoram, son of Ahab and Jezebel, was the last member of the dynasty of Omri to rule over Israel, succeeding his childless brother, Ahaziah. Although he is recorded in Chronicles (II Chr 21:5) as having ruled for twelve years, other texts, particularly the Assyrian tablets of Shalmaneser III, state that he reigned for a shorter period. Jehoram limited the extent of the Baal worship initiated by his mother, but he did not eradicate the practice entirely, and its influence was still felt in the royal court (II Kgs 3:2). With the help of the Kingdom of Judah, Jehoram was able to suppress the Moabite uprising (II Kgs 3:4-27). He was not, however, as successful in his handling of the threat from Aram, and was wounded in an encounter with Hazael, king of Aram (II Kgs 8:28-29). He was sent for recuperation to Jezreel, where he was assassinated by Jehu (II Kgs 9:16-26).

Jehu (842-814). Jehu acceded to the throne of the Kingdom of Israel after his assassination of Jehoram. Previously, he was commander of Israel's army. His rebellion enjoyed the support of the prophet Elisha, who had him anointed (II Kgs 9:1-13) as well as of the Rechabites (II Kgs 10:15-16), both of whom opposed the idolatrous practices of the preceding dynasty. Jehu also received the support of the commanders of the army and other interested groups in the kingdom who were dissatisfied with the military and economic affairs of the state (II Kgs 9:14).

After his assassination of Jehoram, Jezebel, and Ahaziah, king of Judah (II Kgs 9:21-27, 31-35), Jehu liquidated the remainder of the house of Omri, to strengthen his grasp on the kingdom (II Kgs 10:1-11). He also destroyed the remaining priests of Baal (II Kgs 10:18-28).

Jehu's bloody rise to power caused the severing of Israel's ties with Judah and Phoenicia. Without the support of its allies, Israel succumbed to an Aramean invasion and lost the territory of Gilead (II Kgs 10:32-33). Jehu reigned for 28 years and was buried in Samaria.

Jehoahaz (regent 817-814; king 814-800). Jehoahaz son of Jehu ruled over the Kingdom of Israel following the death of his father. During his reign, the Aramean armies, commanded by King Hazael and his son Ben-Hadad, invaded Israel and destroyed its army. Jehoahaz turned to God who sent "a deliverer," probably in the form of Adad-Nirari III, king of Assyria. Although the Assyrian subjugation of Aram brought relief to Israel, Jehoahaz had turned his land into a vassal state of Assyria (II Kgs 13:1-5).

Jehoash (800-784). Jehoash succeeded his father, Jehoahaz, and at the outset of his reign, the country was subjected to three hostile fronts: Assyria, to whom Israel owed tribute; Aram, which had succeeded in

King Jehu (or his ambassador), prostrate at the feet of Shalmanezer III; detail from "The Black Obelisk," an Assyrian limestone monument of the 9th century BC.

conquering the northern region of Israel during the reign of Jehoahaz, and Moab, whose regular attacks on Israel had weakened the Israelite army. With the advice of the prophet Elisha, Jehoash was able to overcome the Arameans and restore to Israel its lost territory. Having strengthened his domain, he attacked Amaziah, king of Judah, after the latter challenged his authority. Jehoash destroyed a section of the wall surrounding Jerusalem, and looted the Temple and the royal palaces.

Jeroboam II (regent 789-784; king 784-748). Jeroboam II reigned over Israel following the death of his father, Jehoash.

He attacked Aram, the enemy of the Kingdom of Israel, which had been weakened following the attacks of Adad-Nirari III and Shalmaneser IV, kings of Assyria (II Kgs 14:23-28). The military success of this campaign extended the borders of Israel to Hamath, including the Aramean capital of Damascus, immediately transforming Israel into a regional power.

The Northern Kingdom experienced a period of peace throughout the long reign of Jeroboam II, and the cordial relations that existed between Israel and Judah prompted the two kingdoms to conduct a joint census of the inhabitants of Transjordan (I Chr 5:17). The new-found wealth created an upper class among the residents of Israel, which, because of the oppression of its poor, led to the harsh condemnations of the prophet, Amos.

Zechariah (748/7). Zechariah, son of Jeroboam II, was the last king of Israel from the house of Jehu. He ruled for only six months before he was assassinated by Shallum son of Jabesh (II Kgs 14:29; 15:8-11).

Shallum (748/7). Shallum son of Jabesh ruled Israel as king for one month following his assassination of King Zechariah. He was murdered, in turn, by Menahem son of Gadi (II Kgs 15:10,13-15).

Menahem (747/6-737/6). Menahem son of Gadi was probably an officer in the Israelite army when he seized the throne by assassinating King Shallum. He destroyed the city of Tiphsah in revenge for its support of Shallum and in general suppressed opposition to his reign, which was plagued throughout by the westerly expansion of the Assyrian Empire under Tiglath-pileser III. Upon the arrival of the Assyrian forces in Samaria, Menahem paid a tribute of 1,000 talents of silver to the Assyrians, rendering Israel a vassal state. He is condemned by the Bible for reviving the ways of Jeroboam (i.e., tolerating idolatry), while the heavy taxation he imposed made him unpopular with his people (II Kgs 15:17-22).

Pekahiah (737/6-735/4). Pekahiah son of Menahem ruled Israel for two years following the death of his father. Like his father, "he did evil in the sight of the Lord." He was then assassinated by Pekah, apparently a military commander from the region of Gilead, probably for his pro-Assyrian orientation (II Kgs 15:22-26).

Pekah (735/4-733/2). Pekah son of Remaliah seized power following his assassination of Pekahiah. In an attempt to lessen the Assyrian influence on Israel,

Pekah entered into a treaty with Rezin, king of Aram, directed against Assyria. He attempted to bring Judah into this treaty as well, but Ahaz, king of Judah, refused to renege on the pact he had made with Assyria. Pekah, enraged at this, encouraged the two vassal states of Philistia and Moab to rebel against Judah, and he and Rezin advanced on Jerusalem. Ahaz was forced to enter into a pact with Tiglath-pileser III in order to save himself. The Assyrians conquered Aram and went on to besiege Israel, exiling many of its inhabitants to Assyria and leaving Pekah only the hill country of Samaria. Pekah, who had brought on this disaster, was assassinated by Hoshea (II Kgs 15:25–16:5).

Hoshea (733/2–724/3). Hoshea son of Elah was the last king of the Northern Kingdom of Israel. After his assassination of Pekah, he acceded to the throne of a largely truncated kingdom, which was, in effect, merely a province of the Assyrian Empire, with his authority extending only to the mountains of Ephraim. In the annals of Tiglath-pileser III, Hoshea is mentioned as a vassal placed upon the throne by the Assyrian king. Wtih the support of Egypt, however, Hoshea revolted against the Assyrian Empire. The failure of the revolt led to the capture of Hoshea, the siege and fall of Samaria, and the exile of the inhabitants of Israel to Assyria (722 BC; II Kgs 15:30; 17; 18:9–12).

III.28 PROPHETS AND PROPHECY

The prophets of the Bible were charismatic individuals who received and imparted messages revealed to them by God. Although the Pentateuch is also held to be prophetic, and contains numerous instances of God's revelation to individuals (especially to Moses, considered "the greatest of the prophets" in Jewish tradition), it is the second part of the Old Testament that is known as "The Prophets."

The Nature of Prophecy. The biblical conception of prophecy presumes that God makes his will known to a succession of individuals. The mission of the prophet is not primarily the popular concept of foretelling future events. It is rather the transmission of the word of God to his people (whether they wish to hear it or not). The prophet does not choose his career; the prophet is chosen.

Those chosen for prophecy, although overwhelmed by their experience of God, do not merge with the divine or lose their individual identity. The knowledge they are granted is not about God. It is about God's actions in history, and in discharging his mission, the prophet must translate this knowledge into the contemporary idiom of his people. As God's spokesman on earth, the prophet, more often than not, finds himself in the role of radical iconoclast, chastising the people and challenging them to obedience to the divine will.

The True Prophet. Jeremiah's condemnation of the false prophets of his generation suggests a concise description of the true prophet (Jer 28: the confrontation with Hananiah son of Azzur; see also Jer 6:14; 8:11; 14:14; 23:17).

Jeremiah declares that the false prophets, who betrayed the people by lulling them into a false sense of security, had not been sent by God, had not been

> ### The False Prophet
>
> If there arise among you a prophet, or a dreamer of dreams, and he give you a sign or a wonder, and the sign or the wonder come to pass, of which he spoke to you, saying, let us go after other gods, which you have not known, and let us serve them; you shall not harken to the words of that prophet, or that dreamer of dreams: for the Lord your God puts you to the proof, to know whether you love the Lord your God with all your heart and with all your soul. You shall walk after the Lord your God, and fear Him, and keep His commandments, and obey His voice, and you shall serve Him, and hold fast to him. And that prophet, or that dreamer of dreams, shall be put to death; because he has spoken to turn you away from the Lord your God, who brought you out of the land of Egypt and redeemed you out of the house of bondage, to thrust you out of the way which the Lord your God commanded you to walk in. So shall you put the evil away from the midst of you   (Deut 13:1–5).

admitted into the divine council, and did not intercede with God in behalf of Israel. He who has in fact been admitted to the divine council will indeed act, at times, as intercessor for his people before God. Nevertheless, the primary task of the prophet is to serve as God's messenger and spokesman, holding Israel responsible for its deeds. No level of society or personage is spared from being the object of the prophet's righteous anger as he castigates evil in all its manifestations. Many of the true prophets accepted their mission only with the greatest reluctance (Is 6:5; Jer 1:6; Jonah 1:1–3). Their burden was difficult to bear, and their lives filled with frustration, rejection, and, at times, persecution. The false prophet, not sent by God and not admitted to his council, neither intercedes on behalf of his people nor exposes its members to the divine imperative.

Former and Latter Prophets. Traditionally, the Prophetic section of the Old Testament is divided into Former and Latter Prophets. Included among the Former Prophets are the books of Joshua, Judges, Samuel, and Kings. The books of the Latter Prophets consist of Isaiah, Jeremiah, Ezekiel and the twelve short books: Hosea, Joel, Amos, Obadiah, Jonah, Micah, Nahum, Habakkuk, Zephaniah, Haggai, Zechariah, and Malachi. These are the classical literary prophets.

While the books of the Former Prophets primarily narrate biographies and historical information, the books of the Latter Prophets consist mainly of their namesakes' prophecies. Isaiah, Jeremiah, and Ezekiel became known as "major prophets," with all others being classed as "minor prophets."

The Uniqueness of Classical Prophecy. The classical prophets who flourished for some 300 years from the middle of the 8th century BC to the mid-5th century, represent a new phenomenon in the history of religion. For the first time in human history, they interpreted the most momentous geopolitical events in light of their own religious outlook, showing how the God of Israel was the moving force behind these great happenings, all of which were seen to focus upon his people Israel. Classical prophecy supplied the reasons for Israel's punishment, the destruction of its Temple, and its exile as well as predicting and providing the formula for the future restoration.

The Word of the Prophet. The prophetic demand of moral perfection grew in the face of the human tendency to appease God and conscience with ritual and sacrifice. Amos and others who emphasized the centrality and supremacy of the moral law (eg. Amos 5:21–24; Hos 6:6; Mic 6:6–8) did not, however, wish to eradicate the sacrificial cult. What they found objectionable was the substitution of ritual for right behavior and obedience to the will of God. Sacrifices brought by those guilty of moral corruption were not only unacceptable but offensive to God — an abomination.

Such views often placed the prophets at odds with the priests and Temple establishment.

Moral behavior and decency, moreover, were decisive in determining the fate of the nation, which enjoyed the right to continued existence only insofar as its members conducted themselves with rectitude and integrity.

God and Man

What does the Lord ask of you but to do justice, love mercy, and walk humbly with your God   (Mic 6:8).

Repentance and Redemption. The people were exhorted to abandon their immoral practices. Sincere repentance and righteous behavior, it was said, had the power to evoke divine forgiveness and mercy (Jer 18:7–8; Amos 5:15; Jonah 3:8–10). Some prophets introduced the idea that God Himself might compensate for man's feelings to repent, ultimately initiating the return that would culminate in a "new covenant." God would replace man's heart of stone with a heart of flesh, filling his entire being with the "knowledge of God" that would render him incapable of rejecting the divine imperative. This new covenant, engraved upon the heart of man, would herald the final Redemption (Is 11:9; 55:3; Jer 31:31–33; 32:38–41; Ezek 34:25–31; 36:26–38). When this happens, the remnant of Israel that will survive the Day of the Lord, will live in peace (Is 2:1–4; 11:1–9; 60:5–16; 61:4–9; Hos 2:21–23; Mic 4:3–4). All peoples of the world will cast off idolatry and worship the one God (Is 19:18–25; Zech 14:16–21), and Israel will become a light unto the nations (Is 42:6).

Prophecy in the New Testament. Both John the Baptist and Jesus were considered to be prophets (Matt 21:11,25–26,46; Mark 6:15, 8:28; Luke 7:16, 24:19; John 4:19, 9:17). Jesus apparently accepted the title (Matt 13:57; Luke 13:33). He is sometimes presented in a state of spiritual exaltation (Luke 10:21). Some of his teachings may have derived from prophetic experiences (Mark 1:9–11). Since Jesus and his church were perceived as the fulfilment of the eschatological hope of the Old Testament, the New contains numerous references to the prophets. The prophecies of the Old Testament provided a conceptual framework for the early Christians to understand contemporary history as well as offering hope, since not everything that had been predicted had yet come to pass. The New Testament conception of the End of Days (Eschaton) called for an outpouring of the Spirit including an extension of the gift of prophecy (Joel 2:28–32; Num 11:29), and the events of Pentecost (Acts 2:14–21) were believed to verify this. Paul often speaks of charisms or *charismata*, usually translated as "spiritual gifts." Prophecy was included as one of these gifts (I Cor chaps. 12–14; I Thes 5:20). These charisms were exercised in liturgical contexts, among others, to encourage, edify, and comfort the believer (I Cor 14:3–4). They also had a missionary dimension (I Cor 14:24–25). Some recipients of charisms attained authority in the churches. At times they developed into a more or less stable grouping within the church (Acts 13:1; Eph 4:11).

THE PROPHETS

Ahijah. A prophet from Shiloh during the reigns of Solomon, Rehoboam, and Jeroboam. He prophesied to Jeroboam that the kingdom of Israel would be divided and that Jeroboam would become king. To symbolize this, the prophet tore Jeroboam's new garment into 12 pieces, saying: "Take for yourself ten pieces; for thus says the Lord God of Israel: 'Behold, I will tear the kingdom out of the hand of Solomon and will give ten tribes to you" (I Kgs 11:29-37). When Abijah was old and blind, Jeroboam sent his wife in disguise to inquire about their son's illness. The prophet recognized her and predicted the death of their child and the doom of Jeroboam's house because of the sins of the king (I Kgs 14:1-18).

Amos. A herdsman and dresser of sycamore trees (Amos 7:14) from the Judean town of Tekoa, 9 miles (16 km) southeast of Jerusalem. Amos prophesied against the corruption prevalent in the Northern Kingdom of Israel in the middle of the 8th century BC. Under King Jeroboam II, the Northern Kingdom had achieved wealth and military power unrivaled since the days of Solomon. Amos decried the growing oppression of the poor, claiming that it was the source of this new-found wealth. Land was expropriated for the use of the nobility, and as a result, the masses slowly starved as the elite grew wealthy. Amos denounced the upper classes for their excesses, and declared that their immoral behavior would ultimately be the cause of their own downfall. Amos' harsh attacks led to his denunciation to the king as a conspirator by Amaziah, priest of Bethel (7:10-17). Amaziah demanded that Amos return to Judah where he could continue his prophetic mission freely. Enraged, Amos replied that he was not a prophet by choice but rather a messenger sent by God to fulfill a task (cf. 3:8).

Amos was the first of a line of prophets who emphasized moral behavior over ritual observance, thereby shaping the religious nature of the people for the coming three centuries. See also: III.21, Books of the Old Testament.

> Seek good and not evil, that you may live: and so the Lord, the God of hosts, shall be with you, as you have spoken. Hate the evil, and love the good, and establish justice in the gate.
> (Amos 5:14-15).

Deborah. See III.26, Judges.

Elijah. Elijah the Tishbite ranks as one of the most intriguing of biblical figures. His stories contain numerous miracles which in many cases parallel those of Moses, and even physical objects associated with Elijah, such as his mantle, were attributed with extraordinary powers. On the other hand, little is known of Elijah's personal history; his life and death are shrouded in mystery. Although he is referred to as being from the town of Tishbi in Gilead, Elijah is presented as a wanderer, roaming the kingdoms of Israel, Judah, and beyond in defense of God and his Law. Elijah's zeal made him a scourge to the rulers of the Northern Kingdom of Israel and several times he found himself fleeing for his life. God, however, protected Elijah, sustaining him miraculously.

Elijah prophesied during the reigns of Ahab, Ahaziah, and Jehoram, but Ahab and his Phoenician wife Jezebel were clearly his greatest adversaries. Elijah condemned Ahab relentlessly for the excesses committed by both him and his wife. Instigated by the episode of the vineyard of Naboth (I Kgs 21) Elijah foretold Ahab's impending doom. The climax of Elijah's prophetic career was his contest with 850 priests of Baal on the summit of Mount Carmel (I Kgs 18). Although the victor, Elijah was forced to flee the country to the wilderness of Mount Horeb where God revealed him-

Ascension of the Prophet Elijah; detail from the Verdun altar; 1180.

self to the prophet (I Kgs 19). God allotted to Elijah three final tasks, after which his mission would be complete: the anointing of Jehu as king to replace the dynasty of Ahab, the anointing of Hazael as king of Aram, and the anointing of Elijah's own disciple, Elisha, as his successor. Returning to Israel, Elijah succeeded only in anointing Elisha before being taken bodily to heaven.

Elijah's death is not recorded in the Bible. After having appointed Elisha as his successor, Elijah walked with him to the Jordan. After handing his miraculous mantle to Elisha, an act symbolizing the transmission of Elijah's prophetic mission, Elijah was transported to heaven by a fiery chariot led by fiery horses (II Kgs 2:11) leaving Elisha to continue his work.

The biblical account of Elijah's unique end stimulated the development of various Jewish traditions (Malachi 4:5-6) concerning Elijah's return as the herald of the Messiah. Elijah, it was believed, would settle all controversies and bring peace.

The NT contains a number of instances of identification of John the Baptist with Elijah (Luke 1:17; John 1:21). Some identified Jesus with Elijah (Matt 16:14; Mark 6:15, 8:28; Luke 9:8,19), but this was rejected by Jesus, who confirmed the identification with John the Baptist (Matt 11:14, 17:11ff; Mark 9:12ff). At the Transfiguration (Matt 17:3; Mark 9:4; Luke 9:30), Jesus was attended by Moses and Elijah.

Elisha. The prophet Elisha, from the town of Abel-Meholah, prophesied during the reigns of Jehoram, Jehu, Jehoahaz, and Jehoash of the Northern Kingdom.

The central theme of his prophecies was the ongoing war between Aram and Israel; however, as the disciple and heir of Elijah, Elisha was also an accomplished worker of miracles.

After Elijah had handed over his mantle, a symbol of authority, to Elisha, Elisha was recognized by the prophets of his time as the leader of the prophetic guild with supreme authority on all matters.

Many miracles are attributed to the prophet Elisha. He often used his powers to aid the poor and was particularly concerned with the fate of widows. He healed the sick and even raised the dead son of a Shunammite widow (II Kgs 4:8-37). When Naaman, general of the king of Damascus, was stricken with leprosy, Elisha cured him (II Kgs 5:20-27). Elisha showed skill as a military tactician. In spite of his hatred for Jehoram son of Ahab, he assisted him and King Jehoshaphat of Judah in their battle against Moab (II Kgs 3:15-24).

Elisha continued the mission of Elijah, and anointed Jehu as king in place of Jehoram (II Kgs 9:1-13). Elisha is also attributed with the anointing of Hazael as king of Aram (II Kgs 8:7-15).

Ezekiel. The prophet Ezekiel son of Buzi is classed

Ezekiel's vision of the dry bones. Wall painting from the synagogue of Dura-Europos; 3rd century.

with Isaiah and Jeremiah as one of the three Major Prophets. Little is known of his life, although it appears that he was a member of the priestly family of Zadok.

The Divine Chariot

And I looked, and, behold, a storm wind came out of the north, a great cloud, and a fire flaring up, and a brightness was about it, and out of the midst of it, as it were the color of electrum, out of the midst of the fire. Also out of the midst of it came the likeness of four living creatures. And this was their appearance; they had the likeness of a man. And every one had four faces, and every one had four wings. And their feet were straight feet; and the sole of their feet was like the sole of a calf's foot: and they sparkled like the color of burnished brass. And they had the hands of a man under their wings on their four sides; and as for their faces and their wings (of those four) their wings were joined one to another; they turned not when they went; they went everywhere straight forward. As for the like of their faces, they had the face of a man, and they four had the face of a lion on the right side: and they four had the face of an ox on the left side; they four also had the face of an eagle   (Ezek 1:4-10).

And above the firmament that was over their heads was the likeness of a throne, in appearance like a sapphire stone: and upon the likeness of the throne was the likeness of the appearance of a man, above upon it
          (Ezek 1:26).

Ezekiel was exiled to Babylonia with the court of King Jehoiachin in 597 BC, and he settled, along with other exiles, in the town of Tel Abib. The symbolism he used throughout his prophecies is unique, and many of his legal prescriptions seem to contradict earlier rulings of the Pentateuch. Therefore, at first, the rabbis sought to suppress the Book of Ezekiel. Only after much struggle and debate was it finally canonized.

Many of the theological ideas of Ezekiel differ from those of his predecessors. He states that only members of the Zadok family are fit for the priesthood, directly contradicting the biblical injunction that all descendants of the family of Aaron may administer in the Temple. He also views the redemption of Israel as being not for the benefit of the people but rather for the glorification of God. The nations mock God for having chosen a people whom he is constantly punishing. Only the redemption of undeserving Israel can enhance the majesty of God throughout the world. Nonetheless, Ezekiel stresses the element of repentance. Not only will the people not be punished for the sins of their forefathers, as had been formerly accepted, but the penitent will be cleansed of all their sins and be spared the suffering of the redemption process. See also: III.21, Books of the Old Testament.

Gad. The prophet Gad was one of King David's leading advisors. Even before David had established his monarchy, Gad supported him in his struggle with Saul, advising the fleeing David to return to Judah (I Sam 22:5). After David had established himself in Jerusalem, Gad counseled him to erect an altar to God at the threshing-floor of Araunah the Jebusite in order to halt a plague among the people (II Sam 24:18). Gad is last mentioned as organizing the Levitical choir in the Temple (II Chr 29:25).

Habakkuk. Little is known about the prophet Habakkuk, whose book is the eighth of the twelve Minor Prophets. He prophesied during the period of the Chaldean rise to power in 612 BC. His prophecies contain two main themes: 1) a series of five oracles concerning Judah and the Chaldeans; 2) a song of praise for God. See also: III.21, Books of the Old Testament.

Haggai. The Bible furnishes no information at all on the life of Haggai. In contrast, the period of his calling is well-documented, since Haggai records the specific dates of each of his four prophecies, all in the year 520 BC.

He prophesied during the period of the reconstruction of the temple after the work had long been interrupted, and blamed the people themselves for waiting for an opportune time to commence work. The people heeded Haggai, and three weeks later construction was resumed. The poverty of the returning exiles, however, prevented them from building an elaborate structure, but Haggai consoled the people, promising that their edifice would be even more magnificent than the Temple of Solomon (2:9), while reminding them that the Temple, if not coupled with moral behavior on behalf of the people, is meaningless. See also: III.21, Books of the Old Testament.

Hanani. Hanani prophesied during the reign of Asa, King of Judah. He condemned the treaty made by Asa with Aram, and implored the king to put his faith in God alone. Infuriated, Asa imprisoned the prophet (II Chr 16:7-10). Hanani is commonly identified with the father of the prophet Jehu (I Kgs 16:1).

Hosea. Son of Beeri, whose book is the first of the twelve Minor Prophets. The bulk of his prophecies are to be dated to the time of Jeroboam II of Israel, i.e., the latter half of the 8th century BC.

In the first three chapters, Hosea compares Israel's worship of Baal to the unfaithfulness of a woman to her husband. To symbolize this harlotry, Hosea was commanded by God to marry Gomer, a prostitute, and had with her three children. He then befriended a second woman who, by consorting with other men, dramatized Israel's consorting with other gods. He commanded her to have no dealings with men over a lengthy period of time, symbolizing Israel who, as punishment for its iniquity, will be left without king or ritual centers. By remaining faithful throughout this period, Israel shall be forgiven (Ch. 3).

Chapters 4-14 do not mention the prophet by name. Israel is castigated for its sins, which the prophet delineates as moral perversity: dishonesty, corruption, and sexual excesses all coupled with idolatry. The prophet, clearly reiterating the centrality and primacy of moral behavior, declares that God will not be appeased by ritual acts (6:6); Israel must follow the ethical code as brought down in the Decalogue (4:1-2,6; 5:4; 6:3-6). Foreign treaties will not spare Israel (5:13; 7:11; 12:1; 14:4). He still claims God's love for his people (Ch. 11), and calls for them to repent, with a promise of a blissful future (Ch. 14). See also: III.21, Books of the Old Testament.

> And I will betroth you to me for ever; and I will betroth you to me in righteousness, and in judgment, and in loyal love, and in mercies. And I will betroth you to me in faithfulness: and you shall know the Lord   (Hos 2:19-20).
>
> For I desired loyal love, and not sacrifice; and the knowlege of God more than burnt offerings   (Hos 6:6).

Huldah. Huldah wife of Shallum, keeper of the wardrobe (II Kgs 22:14), is one of five women prophets mentioned in the Bible. During the restoration of the Temple, undertaken in the 18th year of the reign of King Josiah, a scroll of the Law was discovered by Hilkiah the High Priest. The scroll, which has been identified by scholars as the Book of Deuteronomy, suggested that neither national nor religious affairs were being conducted in accordance with the will of God. When King Josiah prompted Hilkiah to ascertain the veracity of the scroll, he turned to Huldah. Huldah affirmed its contents, stating that neglect of the Law and rampant idolatry had provoked God to punish the people. Upon hearing this, King Josiah wept bitterly, and Huldah responded that God would accept the penance of King Josiah and suspend the decree until after Josiah's death (II Kgs 22:14-20). This prompted Josiah to make sweeping reforms (as described in II Kgs 23:1-25; cf. II Chr 34:29-33), effectively eradicating idolatrous practices in Judah.

Iddo. Iddo the Seer prophesied during the reigns of Solomon, Rehoboam and Abijah, kings of Judah. His prophecies were recorded in the now-lost "Words of Shemaiah the Prophet and Iddo the Seer" (II Chr 9:29; 12:15; 13:22).

Isaiah. Isaiah son of Amoz is classified as one of the three Major Prophets. His prophetic activity spanned the reigns of Uzziah, Jotham, Ahaz, and Hezekiah, kings of Judah. Since the prophecies recorded in the

Miniature showing King Hezekiah, hearing Isaiah's prophecy of his death. Miniature from the Paris Psalter; 10th century.

> And it shall come to pass in the last days, that the mountain of the Lord's house shall be established on the top of the mountains, and shall be exulted above the hills; and all the nations shall flow unto it. And many people shall go and say, Come, and let us go up to the mountain of the Lord, to the house of the God of Jacob; and He will teach us of His ways, and we will walk in His paths: for out of Zion shall go Jerusalem. And He shall judge among the nations, and shall decide among many people: and they shall beat their swords into plowshares, and their spears into pruning hooks: nation shall not lift up sword against nation, neither shall they learn war any more
>
> (Is 2:2-4).
>
> The wolf also shall dwell with the lamb, and the leopard shall lie down with the kid; and the calf and the young lion and the fatling together; and a little child shall lead them. And the cow and the bear shall feed; their young ones shall lie down together: and the lion shall eat straw like the ox. And the suckling child shall play on the hole of the cobra, and the weaned child shall put his hand on the viper's nest. They shall not hurt nor destroy in all my holy mountain: for the earth shall be full of the knowlege of the Lord, as the waters cover the sea
>
> (Is 11:6-9).

Book of Isaiah extend over a much longer period of time, however, including the post-destruction period and the time of Cyrus, King of Persia, modern scholars maintain that only the text of chapters 1-39 is the original work of the prophet Isaiah from Jerusalem, the remainder being the work of a later prophet who lived in Babylon, known in critical circles as Deutero-, or Second, Isaiah.

Isaiah was an extremely influential prophet and was surrounded by disciples (8:16). His wife is also referred to as a prophet (8:3). Yet in spite of his influence and power, Isaiah originally believed himself unfit to fulfill the tasks imposed upon him (6:5) and only through a spiritual "cleansing" (6:6-7) was he purged of his inadequacies and capable of fulfilling his divinely-appointed mission.

Isaiah's mission began in the last year of the reign of Uzziah, and the ensuing years of his activity were turbulent ones in the region. Assyrian expansion prompted the Northern Kingdom of Israel to ally itself with the neighboring nation of Aram. Judah was implored to join this coalition. However, Isaiah, an interpreter of the workings of God in history, perceived the root of danger to the kingdom as corruption within Judah rather than any external enemy. Isaiah counseled against participation in an attack against Assyria, but his appeal was rejected by King Ahaz. This led to an attack on Judah by Israel and Aram. Two sons were born to Isaiah at this time; the first he named Shear Jashub, "a remnant shall return," in order to inform the king that Judah would survive the attack (Ch. 7). The second was named Maher-Shalal-Hash-Baz, "the spoil speeds, the prey hastens," implying that both Aram and the Northern Kingdom would fall to the Assyrians (8:3-4), as they did: Aram in 734 BC and Israel in 722. Isaiah used these events in order to convince Judah to mend its ways lest it, too, suffer a similar fate (9:8-10:4). His call, however, went unheeded.

In the meantime, Assyrian expansion reached the gates of Jerusalem in 701 BC and the royal court debated an alliance with Egypt to counter the Assyrian threat. Isaiah once again counseled against foreign alliances (30:1-7) and encouraged the king to return to God. The prophet himself recounts the miraculous lifting of the siege of Jerusalem (36-39), a sign of God's acceptance of Hezekiah's repentance. See also: Book of Isaiah, III.21, Books of the Old Testament.

Jehu. Son of Hanani. Prophet during the time of Baasha, king of Israel, and Jehoshaphat, king of Judah (I Kgs 16:1,7,12). He prophesied the end of Baasha's dynasty and censured Jehoshaphat for allying his army with that of King Ahab of Israel in the attack against the Arameans in Ramoth Gilead (II Chr 19:2-3). See also: III.27, Kings of Judah and Israel.

Jeremiah. Jeremiah is the second of the Major Prophets. Perhaps no other prophet lived as turbulent a life. He not only prophesied unpopular prophecies but witnessed the destruction of Judah in 586 BC. His warnings went unheeded, but many of his contemporaries viewed him as a traitor.

Jeremiah was born in the small village of Anathoth, near Jerusalem. It is uncertain just when Jeremiah first received his calling to prophecy but the text indicates that it occurred at an early age (1:6). Most accounts date this first calling around 626 BC, the year of the conquest of Babylonia by Nabopolassar, the founder of the Neo-Babylonian Empire. Jeremiah witnessed a dramatic succession of events as the Babylonians under Nebuchadnezzar twice conquered the rebellious kingdom of Judah, and foretold its consequences. In one of his earliest visions, he saw a boiling cauldron, symbolic of the disaster which was about to overcome the nation from the north (Jer 1:13). He issued his warnings through his visions, as well as the many symbolic acts which he performed: he was commanded to remain unmarried, symbolizing the estrangement of Judah from God (16:1-13), he wore a yoke to represent the impending yoke of captivity (chs.

27-28), he shattered vessels, implying the imminent shattering of the people (ch. 19). His unpopular views led to attempts to kill him (11:19), he was considered a madman (29:26ff.), and several times he was imprisoned and beaten (chs. 37, 38). Once in prison, he was moved to a dank cistern and only at the intervention of an Ethiopian eunuch was he rescued and transferred to house arrest (38:6ff.). The priest Pashhur beat him mercilessly for his denunciation of the Temple (ch. 20), and the prophet Hananiah broke Jeremiah's yoke (ch. 29). Jeremiah's prediction regarding the destruction of the Temple brought the prophet close to execution for blasphemy; it was only after a court official, Ahikam, recalled a similar pronouncement by the prophet Micah that Jeremiah was spared (ch. 26).

Like other prophets, Jeremiah castigated the people for their sinfulness and called upon them to repent. He did not foresee an early redemption from the Babylonians and counseled the king to pay the tribute demanded by Babylonia and to submit to contemporary political realities.

After twenty years of prophesying orally, Jeremiah commissioned the scribe Baruch to copy his words on a scroll to be presented to the king. King Jehoiakim promptly destroyed the scroll and sought to kill Jeremiah (ch. 36). Jeremiah survived the destruction of Jerusalem in 586 BC and relocated to the court of the governor Gedaliah at Mizpah where he continued his calling (ch. 39-40). The assassination of Gedaliah led to Jeremiah's exile to Egypt where he continued his prophecies, unheeded, until his death (ch. 43-44). See also: III.21, Books of the Old Testament.

> Woe to him that builds his house by unrighteousness, and his chambers by injustice; that uses his neighbor's service without wages, and gives him not for his hire; that says, I will build me a wide house with large upper chambers, and he cuts out windows; and it is covered with rafters of cedar, and painted with vermillion. Shall you reign because you compete in cedar? did not your father eat and drink, and do judgment and justice, and it was well with him? He judged the cause of the poor and needy; then it was well with him: was not this to know Me? says the Lord. But you have eyes and heart only for your dishonest gain, and for shedding innocent blood, and for oppression, and for practicing violence
>
> (Jer 22:13-17)

Joel. Joel son of Petuel is the second of the Minor Prophets. No information is given in the Book of Joel regarding the prophet or the period of his prophetic activity. Although the Greeks were known to Joel, they

The prophet Joel. From the ceiling fresco by Michelangelo in the Sistine Chapel in the Vatican, Rome.

are depicted as a distant power, and as Joel mentions the Temple as being governed by a hierarchy of priests and elders, scholars have suggested that the text was written while Israel was under Persian domination, in the Second Temple oeriod. See also: III.21, Books of the Old Testament.

Jonah. Jonah son of Amittai, from the town of Gath-Hepher in the territory of the Tribe of Zebulun, is mentioned in II Kings (14:25) as prophesying during the reign of Jeroboam II and foretelling the return of all territories lost by Israel to Aram. The Book of Jonah consists of a narrative containing only one prophecy: "Forty more days, and Nineveh will be destroyed" (3:4). God directs Jonah to journey to Nineveh in order to warn the inhabitants of impending doom should they not repent their sinful ways. Rejecting God's command, Jonah sails westward to Tarshish. During this journey, a great tempest arises at sea, and the sailors, fearful for their lives, cast lots to determine who is responsible. The lot falls upon Jonah, and as the sailors cast him into the sea (at Jonah's instruction), the storm subsides. Jonah survives the ordeal by being swallowed by a great fish. After three days and nights in the belly of the fish, Jonah prays to God to rescue him and is cast up on the coast. Once again, God appears to Jonah, and commands him to warn Nineveh of the impending disaster. His warning has great impact on the city; led by the king, the inhabitants fast and pray for 40 days and disaster is averted. Jonah then complains to God, claiming that he, in his great mercy, would have spared the city even had Jonah not pleaded for repentance. Jonah flees to the desert and awaits

death. God spares Jonah, however, by providing a castor oil plant (a "gourd" is the familiar translation) to supply him with shade. After three days, a worm destroys the plant, and Jonah prays for his own death. God responds, "You are concerned about the castor oil plant ...and should I not be concerned about Nineveh."

The message of the book, that any prophecy of doom can be overcome through repentance, warranted its inclusion among the prophetic texts. See also: III.21, Books of the Old Testament.

Malachi. Malachi, Hebrew for "my messenger," may not be the prophet's given name but rather a term denoting his calling. Malachi is the last of the prophetic books and deals with the restoration of Judah prior to the time of Ezra and Nehemiah. The book contains numerous references to the laws and duties of the Pentateuch, giving rise to the suggestion that Malachi may have been a religious reformer at the time of the restoration. Malachi views the events of his time not as the final Redemption but as a stage which will eventually lead to the messianic age. In this same connection, Malachi originated the notion that the messianic era would be heralded by the prophet Elijah (4:5). Malachi saw the impending messianic era in the most universal of terms, as a time when all the nations of the earth will recognize the dominion of God. See also: III.21, Books of the Old Testament.

> Have we not all one father? Has not one God created us? Why do we deal treacherously every man against his brother, to profane the covenant of our fathers? (Malachi 2:10)
>
> Behold, I send my messenger, and he shall clear the way before Me: and the Lord, whom you seek, shall suddenly come to his Temple; and the messenger of the covenant, whom you delight in, behold He shall come, says the Lord of hosts. But who may abide the day of his coming? and who shall stand when He appears? for He is like a refiner's fire, and like the washers' soap: and He shall sit as a refiner and purifier of silver: and He shall purify the sons of Levi, and purge them like gold and silver, that they may offer to the Lord an offering in righteousness
>
> (Malachi 3:1–3).

Micah. The prophet Micah, from the town of More-sheth-Gath in Judah, prophesied during the reigns of kings Jotham, Ahaz, and Hezekiah of Judah. He directed his prophesies at both Judah and the Northern Kingdom of Samaria. He perceived himself as fully capable of his calling, declaring himself "full of power, by the spirit of the Lord" (3:8). Micah was the first prophet to predict the downfall of Jerusalem (3:12). See also: III.21, Books of the Old Testament.

Micaiah. Son of Imlah. Micaiah prophesied during the reigns of Ahab, king of Israel and Jehoshaphat, king of Judah (I Kgs 22:8-28; II Chr 18:7-27). Before going to battle to recapture Ramoth Gilead from the Arameans, Ahab, at the request of his ally Jehoshaphat, gathered 400 prophets in consultation. They all predicted that Ahab would be victorious. Jehoshaphat, however, was not satisfied, and insisted on further consultation. Micaiah, who had not been called with the other prophets because of the king's hatred toward his unfavorable prophecies, was summoned. At first he repeated the favorable oracle of the other prophets, but Ahab was suspicious and demanded the truth. Micaiah then warned that Israel would be scattered on the mountains as sheep that have no shepherd, and he went on to discredit the other prophets. One of these, Zedekiah, struck Micaiah on the cheek and Ahab ordered Micaiah imprisoned until his return (I Kgs 22:17-28; II Chr 18:1-27). Micaiah's prophecy came true when Ahab was killed in battle (I Kgs 22:35; II Chr 18:34).

Miriam. Miriam, sister of Moses and Aaron, was one of the five women prophets mentioned in the Bible. Miriam watched over the fate of the infant Moses after he had been placed in the bulrushes of the river (Ex 2:4-8). She later became a leader of the people in her own right, and is recorded as having led the women of Israel in singing and dancing at the crossing of the Red Sea (Ex 15:20-21).

Feeling themselves competent to take a larger role in the governing of the people, Miriam and Aaron complained about the authoritarian leadership of Moses, noting both the marriage of Moses to a Cushite woman and their own prophetic ability. God intervened, inflicting Miriam with leprosy which only the prayer of Moses could cure (Num 12:1-15). Miriam died in the desert and was buried in Kadesh Barnea (Num 20:1).

Moses. See III.25.

Nahum. No biographical details exist about the prophet Nahum, and although he prophesied about the welfare of Jerusalem and the downfall of Nineveh (612 BC), it is impossible to date the prophecies precisely. See also: III.21, Books of the Old Testament.

Nathan. Nathan was a central figure in the life of King David, serving not only as a prophet but also as a faithful courtier, who influenced the king on a number of occasions.

Nathan is first mentioned in the royal court after David had established himself in Jerusalem. David complained that whereas he, as king, lived in a magnif-

icent palace of cedar-wood, the Ark of the Covenant remained in a tent. At first, Nathan agreed to the king's plan to build a temple, but then God appeared to Nathan in a dream and informed him that not David but David's son would build the Temple (II Sam 7). Because of the sincerity of David's request, however, God would establish the Davidic dynasty for all time (I Chr 17:1-15).

After David's sin with Bathsheba, Nathan castigates him for his actions. David is warned of the results of his sin: His sons will be slain, and his wives abused. Only after David repents does Nathan inform him that God has lessened his punishment; only the son born of the adulterous liaison with Bathsheba will die (II Sam 12:1-15).

Nathan last appears to David when the latter is on his deathbed. After Adonijah had proclaimed himself king during his father's final days, Nathan persuades Bathsheba to approach David and remind him of his promise that Solomon should be his heir. David proclaims Solomon king in his stead (I Kgs 1). Nathan is last mentioned with his contemporary, Gad, as a choirmaster in the Temple (II Chr 29:25). It appears that his prophecies were recorded in the no longer extant work, the "Book of Nathan the Prophet" (I Chr 29:29).

Noadiah. One of the five women prophets in the Bible. She castigated Nehemiah for rebuilding the walls of Jerusalem (Neh 6:14). Noadiah is the last prophetic figure mentioned in the Bible.

Obadiah. The prophet Obadiah foretold the Temple's destruction and castigates Edom for its active role in support of the Babylonian conquest of 586 BC (1-16) Final justice for the sins of Edom will, however, be realized at the end of days, when Judah, under the guidance of God, will occupy the country. See also: III.21, Books of the Old Testament.

Oded. The prophet Oded was active in Samaria during the reign of Pekah, king of Israel. He persuaded the Israelites to repatriate their 200,000 Judean prisoners (II Chr 28:9-15).

Samuel. Samuel, last of the Judges, was the son of Elkanah and his wife Hannah of the tribe of Ephraim. Hannah had been childless for many years. Humiliated by Peninah, the fertile second wife of Elkanah, Hannah appealed to God to grant her a son. In her petition, Hannah vowed that her son would be a Nazirite, dedicated to the service of God. The prayer of Hannah was answered, and Samuel was born. After his weaning, Samuel was taken to the tabernacle at Shiloh to be raised by Eli the High Priest (I Sam chap. 1).

Samuel began prophesying at a young age. His prophecy concerned the termination of the line of Eli and its fulfilment elevated Samuel's stature in the eyes of the people (I Sam 3:10-14). In time, he was revered not only as a prophet, but also as a priest, judge, and military leader. Samuel made his home in Ramah but traveled throughout the country to judge the people, frequenting the religious centers of Bethel, Mizpah, and Gilgal (I Sam 3:20).

Although Samuel's sons also judged the people, they were widely recognized as corrupt and dishonest officials (I Sam 8:1-3). The people begged Samuel to establish a monarchy so as to create order in the land. Samuel initially rejected the idea, and only after consulting with the elders at Mizpah did he acquiesce, appointing Saul as king (I Sam chap. 10).

Saul disappointed and angered Samuel by attempting to seize power reserved for the priests (I Sam 13:9-14) and by sparing the life of Agag, king of Amalek, sworn enemy of Israel (I Sam 15:1-23). Although Saul later expressed his contrition (I Sam 16:4-13), Samuel rejected him as unsuitable for the monarchy and appointed David in his stead. When Saul pursued David as a traitor, the latter took refuge in Samuel's home (I Sam 19:18-23).

In spite of his rejection of Saul, Samuel felt an affinity for him. Even after Samuel's death, Saul attempted to communicate with the prophet's spirit, which at the coaxing of the witch of Endor appeared one last time, informing Saul of his impending defeat at the hands of the Philistines (I Sam 28:3).

In the NT he is listed both among the prophets (Acts 3:24; 13:20) and the judges (Heb 11:32). See also: III.21, Books of the Old Testament.

Shemaiah. The prophet Shemaiah lived during the turbulent years following the death of King Solomon. He was consulted by King Rehoboam as to how Judah should respond to the secession of the northern tribes of Israel. Shemaiah counseled against war, declaring the secession to be the will of God (I Kgs 12:22). After Rehoboam had established his reign, he again consulted Shemaiah when threatened by Shishak, King of Egypt (II Chr 12:5). Shemaiah held that by permitting idolatry to flourish during his reign, Rehoboam had incurred God's wrath and was thus responsible for the threat. The repentance of Rehoboam and his court mitigated God's decree; although Shishak succeeded in looting the palace and Temple, total destruction was averted (II Chr 12:7-12).

Wife of Isaiah. Although she is not mentioned by name, the wife of Isaiah is called a prophet. She is recorded as having borne two sons to Isaiah, Shear-Jashub and Maher-Shalal-Hash-Baz (Is 8:3).

Zechariah. Zechariah son of Berachiah son of Iddo prophesied during the restoration of Judah. A contemporary of Zerubbabel, Joshua the High Priest, and the prophet Haggai, his first recorded prophecy

occurred in the second year of the reign of Darius I (520 BC). See also: III.21, Books of the Old Testament.

> These are the things that you shall do; speak every man the truth to his neighbor; execute the judgment of truth and peace in your gates: and let none of you devise evil in your heart against his neighbor; and love no false oath: for all these are things that I hate, says the Lord
>
> (Zech 8:16-17).

Zephaniah. Zephaniah prophesied during the reign of King Josiah of Judah. The Bible (Zeph 1:1) is very specific in listing the genealogy of Zephaniah, referring to him as the "son of Cushi, son of Gedaliah, son of Amariah, son of Hezekiah." If the Hezekiah referred to here is King Hezekiah, Zephaniah was distantly related to King Josiah. Zephaniah directed much of his prophecies against the indulgences of the ruling classes, and if indeed he belonged to the royal classes, his stature would have granted him a certain measure of immunity. Zephaniah apparently lived in Jerusalem; his detailed descriptions of the city (1:10-11) have served scholars as an important source of information on the structure of the city in the 7th century BC.

Zephaniah decried the assimilationist trends prevalent in Judah. Judah had adopted the dress of the Philistines and many of their customs and superstitions, e.g., skipping over the threshold. Adoption of these customs was at the root of the idolatrous practices spreading throughout the nation and provoking God to anger. Zephaniah is often designated the "Prophet of the Day of the Lord" for his detailed description of impending tragedy should these customs not be abandoned (1:2-18).

Zephaniah called the nation to repentance; only by a return to God can the nation be spared catastrophe and see the destruction of its enemies (presumably Assyria; 2:1-15). He foresees that the people's sinfulness will bring on a catastrophe which only the righteous of Israel will survive and then, joined by the returning exiles, they will build a just, new Israel (3:14-20). See also: III.21, Books of the Old Testament.

JACK CORBOR © 82

Aaron Son of the Levite Amram and Jochebed; brother of Miriam and Moses, and the first high priest of Israel. He was appointed by God to be Moses' spokesman and received the staff given by God to Moses to bring on three of the ten plagues (Ex 7:19-20; 8:1-2, 12-13). Aaron's leadership role continued after the Exodus, and when Moses was on Mount Sinai, Aaron incurred God's wrath because of his decisive role in making the golden calf (Ex 32:1-6). In contrast with the rest of the people, Aaron was never punished; not even when he and his sister publicly doubted Moses' authority, and Miriam was stricken with leprosy. His sincere repentance and ardent plea on Miriam's behalf, however, brought about a reconciliation and Moses' petition to God for his sister's recovery (Num 12:1-13).

Aaron and his four sons were anointed and consecrated as priests by Moses at God's command (Ex 28:1). Eleazar and Ithamar co-officiated faithfully with their father in the tabernacle at Moses' side, but Nadab and Abihu were punished with death for offering an inappropriate sacrifice with "a strange fire" (Lev 10:1-2).

Aaron pours oil into the candlestick as described in Exodus 37:23. Miniature from a manuscript; France c.1280.

זה המערה ואהרן העת שמן כנירות

Aaron's support of Moses throughout Korah's revolt led to accusations by the Israelites against both of them of destroying the people of God (Num 16:3, 17:6). It was Aaron's incense offering that finally placated God and led to the end of the punitive plague that ensued (Num 17:9-15), after which his priesthood was divinely reconfirmed when his staff blossomed with almonds (Num 17:16-26)

Aaron was implicated in his brother's sin of hitting the rock with his staff instead of speaking to it, and he was likewise prohibited from ever reaching the promised land (Num 20:7-13). He died on Mount Hor at the age of 123, his priestly authority and garments having been passed on to Eleazar (Num 20:22-29).

Aaron's role as a lover and pursuer of peace is preserved throughout Jewish tradition. In contrast, the Apostolic Writings portray him in an imperfect light in comparison to Jesus, the perfect priest (Heb 7:11).

Abdon Minor judge. See III.26, Judges.

Abed-Nego Babylonian name given to Azariah, one of the administrators of the province of Babylon appointed at Daniel's request. Together with Meshach and Shadrach (in Hebrew, Mishael and Hananiah), Abed-Nego was educated at Nebuchadnezzar's court and remained faithful to the God of Israel, even when thrown into a fiery furnace after refusing to bow down to the gods of the Babylonians. Their miraculous emergence unharmed from the flames brought the king to praise the God who redeemed them for their unswerving trust. Their story is related in the Book of Daniel.

Abel Second son of Adam and Eve. He was a shepherd whose offerings to God were favored, whereas those of his farmer brother Cain were rejected. Cain's jealousy overcame him and led to the world's first fratricide (Gen 4:1-8).

Abel appears in the Apostolic Writings as an example of an innocent, righteous man senselessly victimized, and his blood is compared to that of Jesus as having atoning value (Heb 11:4).

Abiathar ("the father excels") Son of the high priest Ahimelech. He witnessed the mass murder of his family and neighbors from Nob by Doeg, ordered by Saul for their support of David (I Sam 22:18-20). As the only priest to escape, and for his loyal service, David on ascending the throne appointed Abiathar's son high priest, together with Zadok (II Sam 8:17). Abiathar became David's trusted advisor, especially during Absalom's revolt (II Sam 15:35; 17:15; 19:12-14), but supported Adonijah rather than Solomon for the royal succession (I Kgs 1:7). Upon Solomon's accession, Abiathar was stripped of his priestly authority, exiled to his hometown of Anathoth, and replaced by Zadok (I Kgs 2:26-27).

The apostle Mark refers to Abiathar as offering David refuge in his flight from Saul (Mark 2:25-26).

Abida, Abidah ("father of knowledge") Son of Midian and the grandson of Abraham through his second wife, Keturah (Gen 25:4).

Abidan ("my father judged") A leader of the Benjamites, mentioned in the census ordered by Moses (Num 1:11), as a tribal representative at the dedication of the tabernacle and as having led his clan's march out of Sinai (Num 7:60-65, 10:24).

Abiel ("my father is God") Of the tribe of Benjamin, a grandfather (or great-grandfather) of Saul; son of Zeror, and father of Kish (I Sam 9:1).

Abiezer ("my father is [my] help") Patriarch of one of the most important families in the tribe of Manasseh (Josh 17:2). The judge Gideon was an Abiezrite (Judg 6:11).

Abiezer was also the name given to a Benjamite from Anathoth who served as one of David's "thirty mighty men" in charge of 24,000 servants (II Sam 23:27).

Abigail Name of David's sister or stepsister (II Sam 17:25) and of his wife. The latter's first husband, Nabal, died on hearing of Abigail's loyalty to David after Nabal himself had rejected him (1 Sam 25). As David's wife, she accompanied him on his journeys (I Sam 27:3; 30:5), attended his coronation at Hebron (II Sam 2:1-4), and bore him an heir, Chileab, also called Daniel (II Sam 3:3).

Abihu ("my father is he", or "He [God] is my father"). Second son of Aaron and Elisheba (Ex 6:23), who together with his brothers Nadab, Eleazar, and Ithamar served as a priest with his father (Ex 28:1). Abihu and his brother Nadab, accompanied their father at Mount Sinai where they saw the God of Israel. Later they were consumed by fire during the ceremonies for the dedication of the tabernacle after offering up a "strange fire" to the Lord (Lev 10:1-2). Leaving no progeny, their priestly line became extinct (Num 3:4).

Abijah ("God is my father") Name of nine different personalities in the Bible, both male and female. Prominent among them were: Samuel's corrupt son (I Sam 8:3); a descendant of Aaron who led the eighth division of service in David's sanctuary (I Chr 24:10). Among the descendants of this Abijah was John the Baptist's father (Luke 1:5); a king of Judah (see III.25, Kings of Judah); the son of King Jeroboam of Israel, whose early death was punishment for his father's idolatry (I Kgs 14:1-18); and the wife of the Judean king, Ahaz, the mother of King Hezekiah (II Kgs 18:2).

Abimelech ("the father is king", or "Melech is father"). King of Gerar who entered into peace covenants with Abraham and Isaac (Gen 21:27-32; 26:1-31). He took Sarah for himself after Abraham introduced her as his sister, but restored her immediately following a dream that revealed her true status as Abraham's wife (Gen 20:1-18).

Another Abimelech was Gideon's cruel son, ruler of the city of Shechem during the period of the judges, who massacred all possible fraternal rivals (70 in number) except for his youngest brother Jotham who escaped. See III.24, Judges.

Abimelech was also the name of a Philistine king in David's time (Ps 34:1).

Abinadab ("my father is generous" or "noble"). A resident of Kirjath Jearim, in whose home the ark of the covenant rested from the time of its return by the Philistines until David took it up to Jerusalem 20 years later (I Sam 7:1-2).

Abinadab was also the name of a brother of David, a son of Saul (I Sam 31:2), and of a son-in-law of Solomon (I Kgs 4:7-11).

Abiram ("father of pride"). Of the tribe of Reuben: a ringleader of Korah's revolt against Moses' authority in the desert. God punished Abiram and his brother and fellow-rebel Dathan by having the earth swallow them up together with their families (Num 16).

Another Abiram was the firstborn son of Hiel of Bethel who rebuilt the city of Jericho. Abiram died (I Kgs 16:34), in fulfillment of Joshua's curse, "Cursed be the man before the Lord who rises up and builds the city Jericho; he shall lay its foundation with his firstborn" (Josh 6:26).

Abishag Girl from Shunem who cared for King David in his last days (I Kgs 1:1-4). After David's death, his son Adonijah wished to marry Abishag, but King Solomon, interpreting this as a claim to the throne, had him killed (I Kgs 2:13-25).

Abishai David's nephew by his sister, Zeruiah, and the brother of Joab and Asahel, whose loyalty to his uncle was as steadfast as it was ruthless. Although on several occasions David restrained him from impulsive manslaughter, Abishai did succeed in avenging his brother Asahel's death and killing Abner, Saul's commanding officer who had sided with David (II Sam 3:30). As one of David's "mighty men," Abishai exhibited great prowess and courage against the Edomites and Ammonites and in a battle with the Philistines, saved David's life from a giant (II Sam 21:15-17).

Abital ("my father is dew"). One of the six wives of King David when he ruled from Hebron; mother of Shephatiah (II Sam 3:4).

Abner ("my father is Ner" or "father of light"). Uncle King Saul and commander of his army (I Sam 14:50). He fought against the Philistines and pursued David until Saul's death. Thereafter he proclaimed Saul's son, Ishbosheth, king at the same time that David was crowned king in Hebron (II Sam 2:8-9). Abner was defeated in the ensuing battle between the two armies (II Sam 2:17) and fled, only to be pursued by Asahel, the brother of David's commander Joab. Abner killed Asahel in self-defense (II Sam 2:18-23), and begged Joab to cease the bloodshed (II Sam 2:26). Abner turned his loyalty to David by recognizing him as king of a reunited monarchy (II Sam 3:12-13). Although David

Left: The Philistines returning the ark of the covenant which was then placed in the house of Abinadab at Kirjath Jearim. Wall painting from the synagogue of Dura-Europos. Right: The monument in Jerusalem known as Absalom's tomb.

sent Abner from Hebron in peace (II Sam 3:21), Joab invited him back and killed him in revenge for his brother's murder (II Sam 3:23-30). David's sorrow over this loss of "a prince and a great man" (II Sam 3:38) was so great that he charged Solomon with taking revenge on Joab for this murder (I Kgs 2:5).

Abraham. The first patriarch of Israel. See III.23, Patriarchs.

Absalom (Also **Abishalom**) ("father of peace"). Third son of King David, by the Geshurite princess, Maacah (II Sam 3:3). The rape of his sister, Tamar, by his half-brother, Amnon, prompted Absalom to have Amnon killed, after which he sought asylum with his grandfather, Talmai, king of Geshur (II Sam 13). David's army commander, Joab, secured his return after three years, but could not persuade David to receive his son until another two years had passed, when Absalom was fully pardoned (II Sam 14).

Absalom later led a rebellion against his father with the help of the king's advisor Ahithophel (II Sam 15), forcing David to flee over the border. Absalom rejected Ahithophel's counsel to attack in favor of Hushai's advice to wait and lead the troops himself, without realizing that David had sent Hushai as a spy (II Sam 16:15-17:14). Absalom lost the eventual battle (II Sam 18:6-7) but, in spite of David's orders to spare his son, Joab killed Absalom as he hung from a tree, his long hair tangled in its branches (II Sam 18:5-15). David's public grief over the death of his son cast a pall over his army's victory feast until Joab convinced him of its demoralizing effect, claiming that Absalom would have killed them all (II Sam 19:1-9).

Absalom had three sons (II Sam 14:27), who apparently did not survive him, since he built a memorial to himself in his lifetime (II Sam 18:18). The existing monument in the Kidron Valley in Jerusalem called Absalom's tomb dates only from a thousand years later but was popularly associated with Absalom.

Achan (or **Achar**) Israelite of the tribe of Judah who disobeyed the order against the taking of booty during Joshua's capture of Jericho. As a result, the Israelites were defeated in their attack on Ai. After his public admission of the sin, he and his family were stoned to death (Josh 7:1, 18-24).

Achbor An advisor to King Josiah. He was sent to the prophetess Huldah to inquire about the scroll of the Law found in the Temple by the high priest Hilkiah (II Kgs 22:12-14). He is also referred to as Abdon (II Chr 34:20) and had a son, Elnathan, who served in King Jehoiakim's court (Jer 26:22; 36:12).

Achish Philistine king of Gath. When finally convinced that David could be trusted, he gave David, who was hiding from Saul, refuge for more than a year (I Sam 21:11-15) and appointed him his personal bodyguard in preparing to attack Saul's army (I Sam 28:1-2). However, when it came to the battle, he responded to his officers' suspicions of David's motives and dismissed David and his men from battle with the Israelites (I Sam 29:1-11).

Achsah Caleb's daughter, whom he gave as wife to his nephew, Othniel, as a reward for capturing the city of Debir. She received from her father wells and property in the Negeb (Josh 15:15-19; Judg 1:12-15).

Adah ("ornament"). One of the wives of Lamech, the other being Zillah. She bore Lamech two sons, Jabal and Jubal (Gen 14:19-21). Adah is also the name of the wife of Esau, and mother of Eliphaz. She was the daughter of Elon the Hittite (Gen 36:2,4).

Adaiah ("ornament of God"). The father of Maaseiah, one of the officers involved in the plot of Jehoiada the priest to overthrow Queen Athaliah. The coup's success allowed Joash to ascend the throne of Judah (II Chr 23:1).

Adam ("man"). The first man, formed on the sixth day of creation (Gen 1:26). A possible etymology (Gen 2:7) for the name is the Hebrew word *adamah*, meaning earth, the substance from which Adam was formed. Adam was placed in the Garden of Eden where he was to rule over the beasts (Gen 2:15, 19–20). Out of Adam's rib, God created Eve, the first woman, to serve as Adam's companion (Gen 2:21–23). Following their sinful partaking of the forbidden fruit, the couple was expelled from Eden (Gen 3). Eve bore Adam three sons: Cain, Abel and Seth (Gen 4:1–2; 5:3). Adam died at the age of 930 (Gen 5:3–5).

The New Testament contrasts Adam, who committed the first sin, bringing death to mankind, with Christ who brought forgiveness and life (Rom 5:12–17).

Addar (or **Ard**). Son of Bela and grandson of Benjamin. Addar accompanied Jacob into Egypt (Gen 46:21; I Chr 8:3).

Adin ("voluptuous"). Founder of a family which returned from exile with Zerubbabel. Conflicting accounts are given regarding the size of the returning family. Ezra records that it numbered 454 (Ezra 2:15), Nehemiah, 655 (Neh 7:20). An additional 51 members of the family later returned with Ezra. The family supported Nehemiah's call to cut themselves off from idolators (Neh 8:6; 10:1–16).

Adino Another name for Josheb-Bashebeth the Tachmonite, leader of David's heroes. He is said to have killed 800 men in one battle (II Sam 23:8).

Adnah Officer in Saul's army, coming from the tribe of Manasseh. He deserted to join David at Ziklag (I Chr 12:21).

Adoni-Bezek ("lord of Bezek" or "lord of lightning"). Canaanite king, defeated by the tribes of Judah and Simeon at Bezek. He once boasted that 70 kings with their thumbs and big toes cut off had served him. Upon his capture, he was similarly mutilated (Judg 1:1–7).

Adonijah ("God is my Lord"). Son of David and Haggith, and fourth in line to the throne (II Sam 3:4). After his older brothers' deaths, Adonijah regarded himself as heir, and as David was dying, had himself proclaimed king. His attempted coup was thwarted when David proclaimed Solomon his heir. On ascending the throne, Solomon pardoned Adonijah, but this pardon was later rescinded when the latter sought to marry David's concubine, Abishag. Solomon interpreted this as an attempt to seize the throne, and had Adonijah executed (I Kgs 1–2).

Adonikam ("my Lord has risen"; also called **Adonijah**). Head of a family of 666 or 667 members that returned from exile with Zerubbabel. He was a signatory of Nehemiah's "covenant of reforms" (Ezra 2:13;).

Adoniram (**Adoram, Hadoram**) ("the Lord is exalted"). Son of Abda; official under David and Solomon in charge of forced labor. Adoniram oversaw the laborers in Lebanon who were sent to supply materials for the Temple. He was later dispatched by Rehoboam to pacify the rebellious northern tribes, but was killed by a mob in Shechem (II Sam 20:24; I Kgs 4:6; II Chr 10:16–19).

Adoni-Zedek ("Zedek is lord" or "my lord is righteousness"). King of Jerusalem, and leader of an Amorite coalition opposing Joshua. Following their unsuccessful siege of the Gibeonites, allies of the Israelites, the coalition's five kings escaped, finding refuge in a cave at Makkedah. Upon capturing the kings, Joshua had them executed (Josh 10).

Adrammelech Son of the Assyrian king, Sennacherib. Adrammelech (which was the name of an Assyrian god) and his brother Sharezer assassinated Sennacherib in Nineveh following their father's failure to conquer Jerusalem. The brothers then fled to Ararat (II Kgs 19:37).

Adriel ("God is my help"). Son of Barzillai from the town of Meholah. Saul gave his daughter Merab to Adriel despite his promise to give her to David (I Sam 18:17–19). Adriel's sons were later handed by David to the Gibeonites for execution in reparation for Saul's massacre (II Sam 21:8–9).

Agag Amalekite king defeated but spared by Saul despite Samuel's order to destroy all the Amalekites. Saul's mercy towards Agag incurred Samuel's wrath and caused the rift between prophet and king. Agag was hacked to death by Samuel at Gilgal (I Sam 15).

Agur Son of Jakeh, otherwise unknown sage attributed with the authorship of Proverbs 30.

Ahab Son of Omri, king of Israel. See III.27, Kings of Israel and Judah.

Another Ahab was the son of Kolaiah, a false prophet who lived among the Babylonian exiles. Jeremiah foretold his execution by Nebuchadnezzar as punishment for misleading the people (Jer 29:21–22).

Ahasuerus Biblical name of Persian kings.

1. Father of Darius the Mede, commonly identified with Cyaxares who conquered Nineveh c.612 BC (Dan 9:1).

2. The son of Darius I (Ezra 4:1) in whose reign the events of the Book of Esther took place. He is said to have ruled over 127 provinces "from India to Ethiopia" (Est 1:1–2). Ahasuerus celebrated the third year of his reign with an elaborate feast and ordered that his consort Vashti appear. Her refusal resulted in her deposition as queen. After searching his kingdom for a new consort, Ahasuerus finally selected the beautiful Esther, who was Jewish but hid her origins from the king. At the same time, the king promoted Haman to be his chief advisor. Haman was unable to coerce Mordecai, uncle of Esther, to bow before him. Seeking revenge, Haman persuaded Ahasuerus to consent to a massacre

of all the Jews in the kingdom. Mordecai informed Esther of Haman's intentions, and she foiled the plot. Haman was executed and replaced by Mordecai as Ahasuerus' advisor (Ezra 4:6; Esther). The Book of Esther portrays Ahasuerus as a weak king, easily influenced by his advisors.

Ahaz King of Judah. See III.27, Kings.

Ahaziah King of Israel. See III.27, Kings.

Ahiezer ("my brother is help"). A leader of the tribe of Dan who led his clan's march in the wilderness of Sinai (Num 1:12; 2:25; 7:66-71 10:25).

Ahijah ("God is my brother"). Son of Ahitub and descendant of Eli the High Priest. Ahijah served as priest in the Shiloh sanctuary during the reign of Saul, and was responsible for bringing the Ark of the Covenant into battle (I Sam 14:3, 18).

Another Ahijah was a prophet active during the final years of Solomon. See III.28, Prophets.

Ahikam ("my brother has risen"). Son of Shaphan and father of Gedaliah. As an official in the court of King Josiah, Ahikam was a member of the delegation sent to consult the prophetess Huldah about the authenticity of the new-found Book of the Law. Ahikam later protected Jeremiah from King Jehoiakim (II Kgs 22:8-14; Jer 26:22-24).

Ahimaaz Son of the High Priest Zadok. Ahimaaz remained loyal to David throughout Absalom's rebellion, and was one of the priests who carried the Ark of the Covenant out of Jerusalem when David fled the city. He later served with his brother Jonathan as a messenger commissioned to bring Hushai's report of Absalom's plans to David. Although detected, they managed to hide in a well from which they escaped to rejoin David (II Sam 15:36, 17:17-21). Ahimaaz was one of the messengers who informed David of Absalom's defeat. He omitted, however, to mention that Absalom had been killed, fearing that David might have the bearer of this news killed (II Sam 18:19-31).

Ahiman Descendant of Anak and brother of Sheshai and Talmai. His family inhabited Hebron at the time of the Israelite conquest, but they were dispossessed and killed by Caleb (Josh 14:10-15; 15:14).

Ahimelech ("my brother is king"). High priest of Nob. He gave sanctuary to David as he fled from Saul, feeding him the showbread and arming him with Goliath's sword. Doeg the Edomite informed Saul, who ordered him to kill the 85 priests of Nob. Only Ahimelech's son Abiathar escaped the ensuing massacre (I Sam 21,22). Abiathar's son, also called Ahimelech, served as a priest in the days of David (II Sam 8:17).

Ahinoam ("my brother is joy"). Second wife of David and mother of Amnon; she came from Jezreel. She was captured by the Amalekites at Ziklag but was quickly rescued by David (I Sam 25:43; 30:1-18; II Sam 2:1).

Ahio ("his brother"). Ahio and his brother, Uzzah, accompanied the Ark of the Covenant from their father's home to Jerusalem (II Sam 6:2-4).

Ahira Leader of the tribe of Naphtali, mentioned in the census ordered by Moses, at the dedication of the tabernacle. He led his clan as they marched in the wilderness of Sinai (Num 1:15; 2:29; 7:78-83; 10:27).

Ahithophel ("brother of folly"). Father of David's hero Eliam and grandfather of Bathsheba. He came from Giloh in Judah. Ahithophel was an important advisor to David but later turned against the king and supported Absalom in his rebellion. Ahithophel advised Absalom to kill David before he could muster his forces, saying that only David's death would assure Absalom's acceptance among the nation. Ahithophel's advice was rejected in favor of that of Hushai, who was secretly waiting for David and who advised Absalom to wait until the entire nation could be brought to oppose David. Regarding his rejection as a portent of defeat, Ahithophel committed suicide (II Sam 16,17).

Aholiab Craftsman of the tribe of Dan, son of Ahisamach. He assisted Bezalel in the construction of the tabernacle and its vessels in the wilderness (Ex 35:30-36:2).

Amalek Grandson of Esau and a leader in the land of Edom. Eponymous ancestor of the Amalekites (Gen 36:12).

Amasa David's nephew. He defected to the rebellious Absalom who appointed him commander of the army in place of Joab who remained loyal to David (II Sam 17:25). Despite Amasa's defeat, David, angered that Joab had ignored his order to spare Absalom, convinced the elders of Judah to replace Joab with Amasa as commander of the army (II Sam 19:14). When Sheba son of Bichri later rebelled, Amasa was given three days to gather troops loyal to David. Joining the forces at Gibeon, he was murdered by Joab (II Sam 20). Amasa's murder was later avenged by Solomon (I Kgs 2:5-6).

Amaziah ("God is strong"). King of Judah. See III.27, Kings. Another Amaziah was a priest at Bethel who attempted to stop Amos from prophesying. Amos rebuked Amaziah, foretelling the end of his family (Amos 7:10-17).

Ammiel ("my kinsman is God"). Spy from the tribe of Dan sent by Moses to Canaan (Num 13:12).

Ammiel is also the name of the father of Machir of Lo Debar in whose home Mephibosheth son of Jonathan was hidden (II Sam 9:1-5). Ammiel later helped David at Mahanaim during the latter's flight from Absalom (II Sam 17:27-29).

Amminadab ("my kinsman is generous"). Father of Nahshon, leader of Judah (I Chr 2:10), and of Elisheba wife of Aaron (Ex 6:23). Amminadab is later listed as an ancestor of both David (Ruth 4:19-22) and Jesus (Matt 1:4,16; Luke 3:23, 33).

Ammon Child of Lot's incestuous union with his daughter; eponymous ancestor of the Ammonites (Gen 19:38).

Amnon ("faithful"). Firstborn son of David and Ahinoam of Jezreel (II Sam 3:2). Amnon fell in love with his half-sister, Tamar. Feigning sickness, he called his sister to his chamber to prepare him food. After an unsuccessful attempt to seduce Tamar, Amnon raped her. David's inaction following Amnon's deed prompted Tamar's full brother, Absalom, to avenge his sister. Two years after the incident, Absalom invited Amnon and all his brothers to a sheepshearing ceremony at Baal Hazor, where he feasted them with wine. As Amnon became drunk, Absalom ordered his servants to kill him, and fled to Geshur to escape David's wrath (II Sam 13).

Amon King of Judah. See Chapter III.25, Kings. Another Amon was governor of Samaria during the reign of Ahab. He imprisoned the prophet Micaiah son of Imlah for predicting Ahab's defeat at Ramoth Gilead (I Kgs 22:26-27).

Amos Prophet from the town of Tekoah. See Chapter III.26, Prophets.

Amram ("kinsman exalted") Father of Moses, Aaron, and Miriam. He was the son of Kohath son of Levi. His wife, Jochebed, was also his aunt (Ex 6:18,20).

Amraphel King of Shinar who, as a member of a coalition of four kings, waged war against five other kings of the Valley of Siddim, conquered Sodom, and took Lot captive. Amraphel was later pursued and defeated by Abraham who came to rescue Lot (Gen 14:1-17). Some scholars identify Amraphel with Hammurabi, but this, however, appears unlikely.

Anah Son of Seir, chief of the Horites. He discovered water in the wilderness when he pastured his father's donkeys (Gen 36:24).

Anak Son of Arba, eponymous ancestor of a nation of giants who inhabited the southern region of Canaan, including the city of Hebron. Three descendants of Anak, Ahiman, Sheshai, and Talmai, inhabited Hebron at the time of Joshua, but were driven out of the hill-country by Caleb (Josh 15:13-14).

Aner Amorite chief of Hebron, who with his brothers, Eshcol and Mamre, helped Abraham in his battle with the four kings who had taken Lot captive. As Abraham did not partake of the spoils of battle, Aner and his brothers shared the spoil among themselves (Gen 14).

Aram Fifth son of Shem, eponymous ancestor of the Arameans. Aram was either the father (Gen 10:22-23) or the brother (I Chr 1:17) of Uz, Hul, Gether and Mash.

Another Aram was the son of Kemuel and grandson of Abraham's brother Nahor (Gen 22:21). The patriarchs maintained marital ties with his descendants.

Araunah (also **Ornan** in I Chr 22:15 ff) (Hittite: "noble"). Jebusite citizen of Jerusalem who owned a threshing floor on Mount Moriah. It was on this spot that God restrained the angel from destroying Jerusalem following David's census (II Sam 24:16). David regarded the land as a fitting place to erect the Temple. Araunah was prepared to offer both the threshing floor and his oxen to David as a gift, but David insisted on paying him 50 silver shekels (II Sam 24:17-25). In one instance, the name Araunah follows the definite article (II Sam 24:16), leading scholars to conjecture that a title preceding the name was omitted. It has been suggested that Araunah was the last Jebusite king of Jerusalem.

Arba ("four"). Citizen of Hebron, called the "greatest of the Anakim" (Josh 14:15), at the time of the Israelite conquest. As Hebron was also called Kirjath Arba ("city of Arba"; Josh 15:13), he may have been regarded as one of its founders.

Arioch King of Ellasar who, as a member of a coalition of four kings, waged war against five kings of the Valley of Siddim, conquered Sodom, and took Lot captive. He was later defeated by Abraham who came to rescue Lot (Gen 14:1-17).

Arioch was also the name of Nebuchadnezzar's captain of the guard who was instructed to kill all the wise men of Babylonia for their failure to explain the king's dream. He avoided this by bringing Daniel to Nebuchadnezzar to interpret the dream (Dan 2:12-16).

Arphaxad (**Arpachshad**) Son of Shem and grandfather of Eber (Gen 10:22-24), born two years after the Flood (Gen 11:10-13). Arphaxad lived 438 years.

Artaxerxes ("kingdom of righteousness" in Old Persian). Name of three Persian kings. Scholars are uncertain of the precise identity of the Artaxerxes mentioned in the Books of Ezra and Nehemiah (Ezra 7; Neh 2:1-8). Some scholars identify him with Artaxerxes I Longimanus, son of Xerxes I. Unrest in the Empire, particularly Egypt, during his reign would account for the temporary work stoppage on the reconstruction of the Temple (Ezra 4:7-23). Other scholars identify the king with Artaxerxes II Mnemon, son of Darius II, whose reign was also plagued by a number of rebellions, notably one by his brother Cyrus. Artaxerxes II is sometimes identified with Ahasuerus of the Book of Esther.

Arza Royal steward, in whose house King Elah of Israel was assassinated by Zimri (I Kgs 16:8-10).

Asa King of Judah. See III.27, Kings.

Asahel ("God has made"). Nephew of David and brother of Joab. One of David's heroes, noted for his speed. He commanded 24,000 men who served David. Following Abner's defeat at Gibeon, Asahel pursued him, but Abner, being a superior soldier, killed him. Later, Joab, seeking to avenge his brother, killed Abner (II Sam 2:17-23; 3:22-30).

Asaiah Member of the delegation sent by King Josiah to the prophetess Huldah to ascertain the authenticity of the new-found "Book of the Law" (II Kgs 22:12-14).

Asaph Musician, son of Berachiah from the tribe of Levi. Asaph, Ethan, and Heman accompanied the Ark of the Covenant as it was taken from the house of Abinadab to Jerusalem (I Chr 15:17). He later accompanied the Ark from the City of David to Solomon's Temple (II Chr 5:2,12). His descendants were prominent Temple musicians. Asaph is attributed with the authorship of Psalms 50 and 73-83.

Asenath (Egyptian: "she belongs to [the goddess] Neit"). Wife of Joseph and mother of Manasseh and Ephraim. She was the daughter of Potipherah, priest of On (Gen 41:45, 50–52; 46:20).

Asher ("happy"). Eponymous ancestor of the tribe of Asher See also III. 22, The Twelve Tribes.

Asshur Son of Hezron and grandson of Judah, born after his father's death. His two wives, Helah and Naarah, bore him seven sons. He was said to have founded the city of Tekoa (I Chr 2:24–25).

Athaliah Daughter of Ahab and Jezebel, wife of King Jehoram of Judah, and later queen of Judah. See III.27, Kings.

Azariah ("God has helped"). Name of 28 people in the Bible, among them prophets, priests and kings (see III.28, Prophets, III.27, Kings). One Azariah was the companion of Daniel who received the name Abed-Nego (Dan 1:7).

Azgad Ancestor of a family of 2,322 members who returned from the Babylonian Exile with Zerubbabel (Neh 7:17). Later, 110 members of the family returned to Judah with Ezra (Ezra 8:12). A representative of the family was among the signatories of Nehemiah's covenant (Neh 10:15).

Baal-Hanan ("the Lord was compassionate"). Seventh king of Edom, son of Achbor (Gen 36:38–39).

Baalis King of Ammon who planned the murder of Gedaliah, governor of Judah, in an attempt to increase his influence over Judah. The assassin, Ishmael, later received sanctuary in Ammon (Jer 40:14–41:15).

Baanah Benjamite captain of troops loyal to Ishbosheth, son of Saul. Baanah and his brother Rechab sought to appease David by murdering Ishbosheth. David responded by having them executed (II Sam 4:4–12).

Baasha King of Israel. See III.27, Kings.

Baalam Seer from Pethor summoned by Balak king of Moab to curse the Israelites. Balaam, regarding the Israelites as blessed, originally refused to comply with Balak. Only after Balak sent him a second delegation did Balaam, with permission from God, accept. God cautioned Balaam to say only what He would put in his mouth. Balaam set out for Moab, but God sent an angel to block his way. Balaam did not notice the angel; his ass, however, did and refused to continue. Balaam beat the beast until it spoke, asking why it was being beaten. Only then did Balaam notice the angel. Arguing that God had granted him permission, Balaam continued to Moab. Upon arrival, Balaam overlooked the Israelite encampment and attempted to curse them. All his attempts were unsuccessful. Each utterance became a blessing for the Israelites and a curse for Moab and the surrounding nations. Unable to perform Balak's commission, Balaam left Moab (Num 22–23). He travelled to Midian, where he induced the Israelites to worship Baal. In the ensuing battle, Balaam was killed (Num 31:8, 16; Josh 13:22).

Balaam appears three times in the New Testament as a symbol of avarice and apostasy (II Pet 2:15; Jude 11; Rev 2:14).

An angel appearing before Balaam, who rides an ass. Miniature from an Armenian Bible; Constantinople, 17th century.

From The Blessings of Balaam

How lovely are your tents, O Jacob!
Your dwellings, O Israel!
Like valleys that stretch out,
Like gardens by the riverside,
Like aloes planted by the Lord,
Like cedars beside the waters,
He shall pour water from his buckets,
And his seed shall be in many waters.
His king shall be higher than Agag,
And his kingdom shall be exalted.

(Num 24:5–7).

Baladan ("follower of Baal"). Babylonian king whose son, Merodach-Baladan, corresponded with King Hezekiah (II Kgs 20:12).

Balak Son of Zippor, king of Moab. He attempted to halt the Israelite advance across the plains of Moab by employing Balaam to curse the Israelites (Num 22–23).

Barak ("lightning"). Israelite commander who defeated the Canaanite general, Sisera. Barak, son of Abinoam from Kadesh-Naphtali, was summoned by Deborah to lead the tribes into battle. He agreed, provided that Deborah accompany him. She foretold Barak's victory, but declared that because he lacked faith in his own capability, Sisera would be slain by a woman. Barak brought together an army of 10,000 men from the tribes of Naphtali and Zebulun, and defeated Sisera at Mount Tabor. Sisera escaped the field of battle but was killed by Jael (Judg 4).

Baruch ("blessed"). Scribe and companion to Jeremiah. Baruch, son of Neriah, came from a distinguished family. His brother Seraiah served in the royal court (Jer 51:49). Following Jeremiah's imprisonment, Baruch relayed the prophet's oracles to the people. He later recorded and publicized Jeremiah's prophecies. Jehudi son of Nethaniah read one of his scrolls to King Jehoiakim who burnt it and had Jeremiah and Baruch arrested. Despite the loss of the original scroll, Jeremiah dictated an expanded version of its contents to Baruch (Jer 36). Baruch served Jeremiah not only as scribe but as secretary and companion as well. He witnessed the prophet's purchase of his ancestral property in Anathoth and stored the deeds away (Jer 32:12–14). Baruch followed Jeremiah into exile in Egypt. He was accused by the leading exiles of inciting Jeremiah against them (Jer 43:2–3). Nothing is known of his later fate.

One oracle of Jeremiah was directed to Baruch (Jer 45). Baruch was later pseudepigraphically attributed with the authorship of several apocryphal books, including the Book of Baruch, which appears in the Vulgate after the Book of Jeremiah.

Barzillai Wealthy resident of Gilead who supported David in his flight from Absalom by providing food and drink to the encampment of Mahanaim (II Sam 17:27–29). Following Absalom's defeat, David asked Barzillai to join his court in Jerusalem, but Barzillai declined because of his advanced age (he was 80). He sent his son Chimham in his stead (II Sam 19:31–40). David never forgot the kindness shown him by Barzillai and commended Barzillai's son to Solomon in his will (I Kgs 2:7). Barzillai is sometimes identified with the ancestor of a family who returned to Judah after the Babylonian Exile. The family was disqualified from the priesthood because of their questionable lineage (Ezra 2:62).

Basemath ("perfume") Wife of Esau and mother of Reuel (Gen 26:34; 36:4). One text states that Basemath was the daughter of Elon the Hittite (Gen 26:34), while another text calls her the daughter of Ishmael (Gen 36:4). Another Basemath was a daughter of Solomon who married Ahimaaz, governor of Naphtali (I Kgs 4:15).

Bathsheba Wife of David and mother of his heir, Solomon. Bathsheba was married to Uriah the Hittite when David, looking from the roof of his palace, first saw her bathing. He seduced her, and she became pregnant. David then ordered his military commander, Joab, to station Uriah so that he would be killed in battle, allowing David to marry Bathsheba. The prophet

"David espies Bath Sheba at the bath." In the lower section David is shown praying to God. Miniature from the Saint Louis Psalter.

Nathan rebuked David harshly for his adultery in a parable comparing the king to a thief who had stolen the sole sheep of a pauper. Bathsheba's son died as a punishment for David's behavior, but she soon gave birth to a second son, Solomon (II Sam 11–12). Bathsheba later bore David three more sons, Shimea, Shobab, and Nathan (I Chr 3:5).

Bathsheba was instrumental in bringing Solomon to the throne. As David lay on his deathbed, his eldest surviving son, Adonijah, had himself proclaimed king. Bathsheba and Nathan the prophet successfully petitioned David to act upon his earlier promise to make Solomon heir (I Kgs 1). After Solomon's accession to the throne, Adonijah requested Bathsheba to obtain Solomon's permission for the right to marry Abishag, David's concubine. Bathsheba approached Solomon, and was treated with the greatest respect. Solomon, however, rejected the petition and had Adonijah executed for treason (I Kgs 2).

Bathsheba is mentioned in the genealogy of Jesus as the "wife of Uriah" (Matt 1:6).

Bathshua ("daughter of Shua"). Canaanite wife of Judah whom he met at the house of Hirah the Adullamite. Bathshua bore Judah three sons: Er, Onan, and Shela (Gen 38:1–5).

Belshazzar (Babylonian: "O Bel [lit. 'lord', epithet of Marduk] protect the king"). Eldest son of King Nabonidus of Babylonia. Nabonidus is commonly confused with Nebuchadnezzar, and Belshazzar therefore, wrongly referred to as the son of Nebuchadnezzar. Belshazzar reigned as regent during his father's sojourn in Arabia. At a great feast, Belshazzar served wine from golden vessels plundered from the Temple. A message, interpreted by Daniel as foretelling the fall of Belshazzar, appeared on the wall of the palace, written by a mysterious hand. That night, Belshazzar was slain, and Darius the Mede became king (Dan 5).

Belteshazzar (Babylonian: "protect the life of the king"). Name given to Daniel in Babylonia (Dan 1:7).

Benaiah ("God has built"). One of David's heroes, commander of Solomon's armies. Various heroic acts are attributed to Benaiah: he killed two "lion-hearted men" from Moab; he killed a lion in a pit during the snow; and he killed an Egyptian with his own spear. Benaiah's great prowess earned him important rank among David's 30 "mighty men". He was commander of David's guard, possibly the Cherethites and Pelethites (II Sam 23:20-23), and served as commander of the army in the third month (I Chr 27:5). Benaiah later supported Solomon against his brother Adonijah. When Solomon became king, Benaiah executed several individuals regarded as endangering Solomon's reign, including Adonijah, Joab, and Shimei (I Kgs 2:22, 34, 46). After the death of Joab, he was appointed commander of the army (I Kgs 2:35).

Ben-Ammi ("son of my kinsman"). Son of Lot by an incestuous union with his daughter. Ben-Ammi was the ancestor of the Ammonites (Gen 19:31-38).

Ben-Hadad Name of three kings of Aram.

Ben-Hadad I, although an ally of King Baasha of Israel, supported Asa in his war against the Northern Kingdom by occupying Gilead and parts of western Galilee (I Kgs 15:16, 20).

Ben-Hadad II waged three wars against Ahab, king of Israel. Although defeated twice and taken captive (I Kgs 20), Ben-Hadad concluded a treaty with Ahab, returning all occupied territory. He then expanded the treaty to include the king of Phoenicia in a pact to fight Assyria. The alliance attacked Shalmeneser III at Karkar in 853 BC, but was dissolved three years later. Ben-Hadad was then attacked by a new alliance of Ahab and Jehoshaphat king of Judah. Ben-Hadad was victorious, and Ahab was killed (I Kgs 22). Shortly after his victory, Ben-Hadad was assassinated by Hazael who took his throne (II Kgs 8:7-15).

Ben-Hadad III was the son of Hazael. He occupied large sections of Israel during the reigns of Jehoahaz and Joash. His oppressive rule was broken by the Assyrian king Adad-Nirari III in 802 BC (II Kgs 13:3-5).

Ben-Hail Member of the court of King Jehoshaphat, appointed to teach the law to the inhabitants of Judah (II Chr 17:7).

Ben-Hesed Appointed by Solomon governor over a district including Arubboth, Sochoh, and Hepher, Ben-Hesed provided the royal household with provisions during one month of the year (I Kgs 4:10).

Benjamin ("son of my right hand"). Eponymous ancestor of the tribe of Benjamin. See III.21, The Twelve Tribes.

Ben-Oni ("son of my sorrow"). Name given by Rachel to Benjamin at birth (Gen 35:18).

Bera King of Sodom. Bera formed an alliance with the other kings of the Valley of Siddim. They were defeated by an alliance led by Chedorlaomer king of Elam (Gen 14:1-10).

Beriah Son of Asher, father of Heber and Malchiel. Beriah and his sons accompanied Jacob into Egypt (Gen 46:17). Beriah was the ancestor of the Beriites (Num 26:44-45).

Bethuel Son of Abraham's brother Nahor, father of Rebekah and Laban (Gen 24:15).

Bezalel, Bezaleel ("in God's shadow"). Craftsman commissioned by Moses in the wilderness to construct the tabernacle, its vessels and the priestly garments. Bezalel son of Uri is described as a skilled artisan in metals, precious stones, and wood (Ex 31:1-11). Although the tabernacle was later destroyed, some utensils made by Bezalel, notably the brass altar, were still used in Solomon's day (I Kgs 3).

Bigthan, Bigthana Royal chamberlain who planned to assassinate King Ahasuerus. Mordecai uncovered the plot, and Bigthan and his accomplice Teresh were hanged (Est 2:21-23).

Bigvai Head of a Levite family who returned from the Babylonian Exile with Zerubbabel (Ezra 2:14; Neh 7:19). Two additional sons of Bigvai later returned with Ezra (Ezra 8:14). Bigvai was a signatory of Nehemiah's covenant (Neh 10:16).

Bilhah Maidservant of Rachel, given as a concubine to Jacob. Bilhah bore Jacob two sons, Dan and Naphtali (Gen 30:1-8). Later, she had relations with Reuben (Gen 35:22).

Birsha King of Gomorrah and member of an alliance with the other kings of the Valley of Siddim. They were defeated by an alliance led by Chedorlaomer king of Elam (Gen 14:1-10).

Boaz Kinsman of Naomi from Bethlehem who married Ruth. Ruth met Boaz while gathering grain in his field. Enchanted by her, Boaz ordered his servants to allow her to take more than the permitted allotment for the poor. After Ruth's kinsman declined to contract levirate marriage with her, Boaz, although only a distant relation, agreed to marry Ruth. He also bought Elimelech's field, ensuring that the property would remain in the family. Ruth bore Boaz a son, Obed, who was grandfather of David (Ruth 4:17) and an ancestor of Jesus (Matt 1:5; Luke 3:32).

Cain First murderer; eldest son of Adam and Eve. Cain was an agriculturalist; his brother Abel was a shepherd. The two sacrificed to God from their produce, Cain bringing the first fruits, and Abel, the first-born of his flocks. Cain's jealousy was aroused when God accepted Abel's sacrifice but rejected Cain's. In his anger, Cain slew his brother. God punished Cain by making him a nomad. God then marked Cain, but the mark is explained as a protection rather than as a punishment. Cain settled in the land of Nod where he built a city, Enoch, the name of his son (Gen 4).

In the New Testament, he is condemned for his lack of faith (Heb 11:4), and heretics are said to walk in the way of Cain (Jude 11).

Caleb Spy from the tribe of Judah, dispatched by Moses to Canaan. Of the 12 spies who were sent, only Caleb and Joshua returned with favorable reports about Canaan, advising its immediate conquest. The other ten reported that the indigenous inhabitants of Canaan were stronger than the Israelites. The people accepted the report of the majority, and asked to return to Egypt. God punished the Israelites by declaring that all those over the age of 20 would be barred from entering Canaan. Caleb was exempted from punishment because of his positive report (Num 13-14).

He conquered Hebron from the sons of Anak, and was given the region as an inheritance (Josh 14:6-14). He promised to marry his daughter Achsah to anyone who would conquer Debir. This was accomplished by Othniel son of Kenaz, Caleb's brother. The Negeb was given to Achsah as a dowry (Judges 1:12-13).

Carmi Son of Reuben who accompanied Jacob into Egypt (Gen 46:8-9). Carmi was the ancestor of the Carmites (Num 26:6).

Chedorlaomer King of Elam, leader of an alliance of four kings who fought the five kings of the Valley of Siddim, including the kings of Sodom and Gomorrah. Chedorlaomer's alliance ruled the valley for 12 years until an unsuccessful revolt was waged against them. The revolt was crushed, and prominent citizens, including Lot, were taken hostage. Abraham waged war against the alliance in order to rescue Lot. He defeated Chedorlaomer outside Damascus (Gen 14:1-15).

Chenaniah Chief Levite musician in the time of David. He is described as wearing "a robe of fine linen" (I Chr 15:22, 27).

Chilion Son of Elimelech and Naomi. Chilion, together with his parents and his brother, migrated to Moab to escape famine in Judah. He married Orpah, a Moabite woman, but died childless after ten years (Ruth 1:1-4).

Chimham Member of the courts of David and Solomon. Chimham's father, Barzillai, was invited to join David's court in recognition for the services he rendered the king at Mahanaim. Barzillai declined, but sent his son instead (II Sam 19:32-38). In his will, David told Solomon that Chimham should always be cared for by the king (I Kgs 2:7).

Coniah Name used by Jeremiah for King Jehoiachin (Jer 22:24).

Cush Son of Ham and grandson of Noah. He was the father of Nimrod the hunter and the ancestor of the Cushites. Apart from Nimrod, Cush had five sons (Gen 10:6-8).

Cain and Abel offering their sacrifices to God; from a stone relief in the Cathedral of Pistoia, Italy; 13th century.

Cyrus Founder and emperor of the Persian Empire. In 538 BC, he issued an edict permitting the Jews to return to Judah from exile in Babylonia and rebuild the Temple (Ezek 1:2-4; 6:3-5; II Chr 36:23). Isaiah regards Cyrus as a savior, referring to him as the "anointed of God" (Is 45:1). Cyrus rose to power by assassinating his grandfather Astyages of Media in 550 BC. As king, he extended his authority by conquering Lydia and Babylonia (the latter in 539 BC). He ruled over the largest empire known to man up to that time. His policies towards the Jews were part of a larger policy of respect for all conquered nations.

Dan ("to judge"). Eponymous ancestor of the tribe of Dan. See III.22, The Twelve Tribes.

Daniel ("God is my judge"). A prophet. See III.28, Prophets.

Dara, Darda Sage, son of Zerah from the tribe of Judah. He is counted among the sons of Mahol, apparently a musician's guild. Solomon's wisdom is compared to that of Dara, among others (I Kgs 4:31).

Darius Name of three biblical kings of Persia.

Darius I the Great (Hystaspis) succeeded Cambyses II. His rise to power was marked with bloody rebellion, led by an usurper on the throne claiming to be the son of Cambyses. While still in the throes of civil upheaval, Darius allowed the reconstruction of the Temple in Jerusalem to continue, as permitted by Cyrus. He ruled Persia from 522-486 BC.

Darius II (Nothus) (442-404 BC) may be the king mentioned in the Book of Nehemiah (Neh 12:22).

Darius III (Codomanus) (336-330 BC), the last king

*Left: The Cyrus Cylinder, which tells how Cyrus captured Babylon and how he returned the former inhabitants to their cities; 538 BC.
Right: The tomb of Cyrus II the Great.*

of Persia, has been identified with the fourth king of Persia mentioned in Daniel 11:2.

Darius the Mede, son of Ahasuerus (Dan 9:1) who cast Daniel into the lion's den (Dan 6) has not been identified by scholars. The text states that he succeeded Belshazzar and preceded Cyrus as king of Babylonia (Dan 5:30–31; 6:28). Attempts have been made to identify him with contemporary figures, notably the son of Cyrus, but none is satisfactory.

Dathan Leader of a rebellion against Moses. Dathan and his brother, Abiram, from the tribe of Reuben sided with Korah's rebellion, complaining that Moses had taken the Israelites out of Egypt to die in the desert, and had usurped power for himself and members of his family. The rebellion failed, and Dathan, Abiram, and their families were swallowed up by the earth (Num 16).

David King of Judah and Israel. See III.27, Kings.

Deborah ("bee"). Prophetess and judge. See III.26, Judges).

Deborah is also the name of Rebekah's nurse, who died in Bethel and was buried under the "oak of sorrow" (Gen 35:8).

Delilah Mistress of Samson. Delilah spied for the Philistines by seducing Samson to determine the source of his super-human strength. Once Samson revealed that it lay in his uncut locks of hair, Delilah cut them off and delivered him to the Philistines (Judg 16).

Dinah Daughter of Jacob and Leah, raped by Hamor, prince of Shechem. Hamor agreed to marry Dinah and had himself and all his subjects circumcised. Dinah's brothers, Simeon and Levi, took advantage of the ailing Shechemites by entering the city and slaughtering its inhabitants to avenge Dinah's rape (Gen 34).

Ebed-Melech ("servant of the king"). Ethiopian eunuch in King Zedekiah's court who persuaded Zedekiah to release the prophet Jeremiah from his imprisonment in a cistern. As a reward, Ebed-Melech was spared the destruction of Jerusalem (Jer 38:7–13; 39:15–18).

Eber ("Hebrew"), Great-grandson of Shem son of Noah; father of Peleg and Joktan. Eber lived 464 years (Gen 10:24–25; 11:16–17). Genesis 10:21 refers to another Eber as the eponymous ancestor of the Hebrews. He is mentioned in the genealogy of Jesus in Luke (3:35).

Eglah ("heifer"). A wife of David; mother of his son, Ithream (II Sam 3:5).

Eglon ("calf"). Moabite king who conquered and controlled Israel for 18 years. While bringing the Israelite tribute, Ehud, son of Gera, told the king that he had a message from God which must be relayed privately. Eglon, described as exceedingly fat, dismissed his courtiers and rose from his throne to hear the prophecy. Ehud then stabbed the king with a dagger and escaped the palace. Eglon's death brought eight decades of peace for the Israelites (Judg 3:12–30).

Ehud A Benjamite and military hero who led the Israelites in battle against the Moabites after assassinating their oppressive king, Eglon, with his hand-made double-edged dagger (Judg 3:15–30).

Another Ehud was a judge of Israel. See III.26, Judges.

Elah King of Israel. See III.27, Kings.

Eldad Elder who, along with Medad, began to prophesy in the wilderness. When Joshua wanted to have them silenced, Moses reacted by saying, "Oh, that all the Lord's people were prophets" (Num 11:26–29).

Eleazar ("God has helped"). Son of Aaron and his successor in the priesthood (Num 20:24–28). He was associated with Moses and then with Joshua in the division of the Land of Canaan (Num 34:17; Josh 14:1). The priestly line of Zadok traced its ancestry to Eleazar.

Elhanan ("God was merciful"). Son of Dodo; one of David's heroes (II Sam 23:24); possibly identical with the Elhanan son of Jair who is credited with killing Goliath (II Sam 21:19) or Goliath's brother (I Chr 20:5).

Eli ("The Lord is exalted"). Priest of the sanctuary of Shilo for 40 years. He received Samuel for service in the sanctuary (I Sam 2:11). He was threatened by a prophet with the end of his house because of the wickedness of his sons, Hophni and Phinehas (I Sam 2:27-36), and indeed, they were killed in battle. On hearing the news of the death of his sons and the capture of the Ark by the Philistines, Eli, then aged 98, fell and died (I Sam 4:11-18).

Eliab ("God will provide"). Leader of the tribe of Zebulun in the wilderness (Num 10:12, 16).

Another Eliab was the son of Jesse and the eldest brother of David. Samuel first selected him to succeed Saul as king, but he was turned down by God (I Sam 16:4-7). Later, when serving in Saul's army, he was incensed at David's leaving his flocks to take part in a battle (I Sam 17:28).

Eliakim ("God will set up"). Son of Hilkiah; master of King Hezekiah's household who was warmly praised by Isaiah (Is 22:20-25). He was one of those who negotiated the surrender of Jerusalem with Sennacherib, and became involved in a dispute with the Assyrian envoy (II Kgs 18:37).

Another Eliakim was renamed Jehoiakim and was king of Judah. See III.27, Kings.

Eliasaph ("God has added"). A leader of the tribe of Gad in the wilderness (Num 10:12-20).

Eliel ("the Lord is my God"). Head of a family of the tribe of Manasseh who, because of his unfaithfulness to God, was exiled to Assyria (I Chr 5:23-26).

Eliezer ("God is my help"). Eleven men are called by this name in the Old Testament. One was Eliezer of Damascus, Abraham's servant (Gen 15:2). Another, the second son of Moses, was the ancestor of a levitical family (I Chr 23:15-17).

Elihu ("God is the one"). Son of Barachel the Buzite; he argued with Job, defending God's ways (Job 32-33).

Elijah ("Yah is my God"). A prophet. See III.28, Prophets.

Elimelech ("God is my king"). Husband of Naomi, who took his family from Bethlehem to Moab to escape famine. He died in Moab (Ruth 1:1-3).

Eliphaz Eldest son of Esau, and ancestor of several Edomite clans (Gen 36:9ff). Another Eliphaz (of Teman) was one of Job's three friends (Job 2:11).

Elisha ("God is my salvation"). A prophet. See III.28, Prophets.

Elishama ("God heard"). Ephraimite who assisted Moses in taking the census in the wilderness. He led his tribe out of the Wilderness of Sinai (Num 10:22).

Elishaphat ("God has judged"). Son of Zichri, captain of the army. Elishaphat took part in the coup deposing Athaliah and installing Joash on the throne of Judah (II Chr 23:1).

Elisheba Wife of Aaron; mother of his four sons, Nadab, Abihu, Elazar, and Ithamar. Elisheba was the daughter of Amminadab and the sister of Nahshon, leader of the tribe of Judah (Ex 6:23).

Elizaphan (**Elzaphan**) ("God has protected"). Leader of the Levite family of Kohath in the wilderness (Num 3:30). Elizaphan and his brother Mishael removed the

bodies of Nadab and Abihu from the Tabernacle (Lev 10:4).

Elizur ("my God is a rock"). Son of Shedeur; leader of the tribe of Reuben, mentioned in the census ordered by Moses at the dedication of the Tabernacle, and as having led his clan's march out of Sinai (Num 1:5; 2:10; 7:30-35; 10:18).

Elkanah ("God has created"). Father of the prophet Samuel. Elkanah had two wives, Peninnah, who bore him children, and Hannah, who was barren. Hannah accompanied Elkanah on his yearly pilgrimage to Shilo and vowed that if she would have a son, he would be dedicated to the service of God. Within a year she bore Elkanah a son, Samuel (I Sam 1).

Elnathan ("God has given"). Son of Achbor; prince in the court of King Jehoiakim sent by the king to bring the prophet Uriah from Egypt for execution (Jer 26:22). Elnathan later begged Jehoiakim not to destroy the scroll containing the prophecies of Jeremiah (Jer 36:25). Elnathan may have been the father of Jehoiakim's wife, Nehushta (II Kgs 24:8).

Elon A judge. See III.26, Judges.

Emmanuel See Immanuel.

Enoch Son of Cain; father of Irad. Cain built a city in the Land of Nod named for Enoch (Gen 4:17-18). Another Enoch was the son of Jared and father of Methuselah. Enoch is described as having "walked with God and he was not, for God took him" (Gen 5:24). This obscure description caused Jews and Christians to regard Enoch as a predecessor of the prophet Elijah who, because of his intimate relationship with God, was gathered up to heaven while still alive (Heb 11:5). Enoch lived 365 years. He is mentioned in the genealogy of Jesus (Luke 3:37).

Enosh (**Enos**) Son of Seth, father of Cainan. Enosh lived 915 years (Gen 5:6-11). It was in the days of Enosh that mankind began to worship God (Gen 4:26).

Ephraim Son of Joseph; eponymous ancestor of the tribe of Ephraim. See III.22, The Twelve Tribes.

Ephron Hittite living in Hebron who sold Abraham the Cave of Machpelah as a burial place for Sarah. Ephron was willing to give the site to Abraham, but Abraham insisted on paying him 400 silver shekels (Gen 23).

Er ("watchful"). Son of Judah; husband of Tamar. Er, described as being "wicked in the sight of the Lord" (Gen 38:7), died childless (Gen 38:1-7).

Esarhaddon ("[the god] Asshur has given a brother"). Son of Sennacherib; king of Assyria c.680-669 BC. Esarhaddon ascended the throne following his brother's assassination of their father (II Kgs 19:37). Esarhaddon's empire extended to Egypt. Archaeological evidence shows that King Manasseh of Judah was a vassal of Esarhaddon.

Esau ("hairy"?). Firstborn son of Isaac and Rebekah; twin brother of Jacob. Esau was also called Edom because of his ruddy complexion at birth, and was

The stories of Jacob and Esau. From the doors of the Baptistery of San Giovanni, Florence; sculpture by Vittorio Ghiberti.

regarded as the ancestor of the Edomites (Gen 25:25). Esau was born with Jacob holding his heel, foreboding the fulfillment of a prophecy told to Rebekah while pregnant that the elder son would serve the younger (Gen 25:22-23). Esau, the favorite son of Isaac, grew up to be a hunter. He sold his birthright to his brother Jacob for a bowl of lentils (Gen 25:27-34). When Isaac prepared to bless his sons, Jacob tricked Isaac into giving him the blessing reserved for the firstborn. Esau was later blessed by Isaac that he and his descendants would dwell in the wilderness, live by the sword, and serve the descendants of Jacob (Gen 27). Esau plotted to kill Jacob (Gen 27:41), but the two brothers were later reconciled (Gen 33:1-17).

Esau married two Hittite women, Judith and Basemath (Gen 26:34), also called Adah and Aholibamah (Gen 36:2). Isaac was displeased by Esau's marrying outside the confines of the clan, so Esau also married Mahalath daughter of Ishmael (Gen 28:6-9). In Jewish and Christian tradition, Esau symbolizes materialism and immorality (Heb 12:16). His destruction is prophesied in Jeremiah (Jer 49:7), Malachi (Malachi 1:2), and the Book of Obadiah.

Esh-Baal Another name for Ishbosheth son of Saul (I Chr 8:33).

Eshcol ("cluster of grapes"). Brother of Aner, chief of Hebron. Eshcol and his brothers helped Abraham defeat the four kings who had taken Lot captive. As Abraham did not partake of the spoils of battle, Eshcol and his brothers shared the spoils among themselves (Gen 14).

Esther Queen of the Persian emperor Ahasuerus; heroine of the Book of Esther. Esther the daughter of Abihail lived with her cousin Mordecai. When she was

chosen to be Ahasuerus' queen in place of Vashti, Esther did not reveal to Ahasuerus that she was Jewish until the king's advisor Haman persuaded Ahasuerus to consent to a massacre of the Jews. Esther was coaxed by Mordecai to intervene with the king, thereby annulling the decree.

Although Esther is the name most commonly used for the queen, it appears that she only adopted the name (perhaps related to the Persian godess, Ishtar) after becoming Ahasuerus' consort. Her original name was Hadassah, Hebrew for myrtle (Est 2:7).

Ethan ("strong one"). Putative author of Psalm 89; son of Zerah; grandson of Judah and Tamar. Ethan's wisdom was surpassed only by Solomon's (I Kgs 4:31; I Chr 2:6-8).

Eve First woman; wife of Adam and mother of Cain, Abel and Seth. Eve was created as a companion to Adam, and formed from one of his ribs. She was persuaded by the serpent to eat the forbidden fruit of the Tree of Knowledge, and persuaded Adam to do the same. God punished Eve with the pains of childbirth and the subjugation of women to their husbands (Gen 2-3). Eve is mentioned in the New Testament as an example of woman's vulnerability (I Tim 2:11-15; II Cor 11:3).

Evil-Merodach Son of Nebuchadnezzar; King of Babylonia. Evil-Merodach ascended the throne in 562 BC following the death of his father. He released King Jehoiachin of Judah from captivity and invited him to partake of the royal table (II Kgs 25:27-30). Evil-Merodach was assassinated by his brother-in-law, Neriglassar, after a two-year rule.

Ezekiel ("may God strengthen"). A prophet. See III.28, Prophets.

Ezra ("[God] helps"). Scribe; leader of the Jews who returned from the Babylonian Exile to Jerusalem during the reign of Artaxerxes I in 458 BC. Ezra stemmed from a priestly family (Ezra 7:1-5). He served as the spiritual leader of the returnees. In 444 BC during the Feast of Tabernacles, he convened the Jews of Jerusalem for an assembly in which they renewed their covenant with God (Neh 8:1-12). He later urged the people to divorce their foreign wives (Ezra 10:18-44). Ezra's memoirs covering the first year of his mission are recorded in the Book of Ezra. See III.21, Books of the Old Testament.

Gaal Son of Ebed; leader of the Shechemite rebellion against the self-imposed monarchy of Abimelech son of Gideon. Gaal was forced out of Shechem by Zebul (Judg 9:26-41).

Gad ("good fortune"). Son of Jacob and Zilpah; eponymous ancestor of the tribe of Gad (see III.22, The Twelve Tribes). Gad is also the name of a prophet who served in David's court. (see III.28, Prophets).

Gaddiel ("my happiness is God"). Spy from the tribe of Zebulun sent by Moses to Canaan (Num 13:10).

Gamaliel Son of Pedahzur; leader of the tribe of

Manasseh mentioned in the census ordered by Moses, at the dedication of the Tabernacle, and as having led his clan's march out of Sinai (Num 1:10; 2:20; 7:54-59; 10:23).

Gedaliah ("God is mighty"). Babylonian-appointed governor of the province of Judah; son of Ahikam. Gedaliah came from a family of court officials. After the destruction of Jerusalem in 586 BC, Gedaliah chose Mizpah as the administrative capital of the province. Among his acts was an amnesty granted to the survivors of the Judean army. Baalis king of Ammon provoked Ishmael son of Nethaniah to assassinate Gedaliah. The murder caused numerous Jews to flee to Egypt, and brought about the end of Jewish autonomy in the Babylonian Empire (II Kgs 25:22-26).

Gehazi Servant of the prophet Elisha. Gehazi advised Elisha to reward the Shunammite woman with the birth of a son. Gehazi later attempted to resurrect the boy from the dead by placing Elisha's staff on his face. However, the cure did not work and it was left to Elisha himself to save the boy (II Kgs 4:1-37).

Having cured Naaman of his leprosy, Elisha refused to take any payment. Gehazi followed Naaman and told him that the prophet had changed his mind and would accept a reward for the cure. Elisha cursed Gehazi with leprosy for his lie (II Kgs 5:20-27). Gehazi last appears informing King Jehoram of the miracles his master had performed (II Kgs 8:4-5).

Gemariah ("God has accomplished"). Son of Shaphan; father of Michaiah. Baruch read the prophecies of Jeremiah in Gemariah's chamber at the entry of the Temple (Jer 36:10). Gemariah later begged Jehoiakim not to destroy the scroll containing Jeremiah's prophecies (Jer 36:25).

Gershon (Gershom).Eldest son of Levi (Gen 46:11). His descendants, the Gershonites, were responsible for carrying the curtains and coverings of the tabernacle in the wilderness (Num 3:25-26; 4:24-26).

Another Gershon (Gershom) was the eldest son of Moses, born to Zipporah in Midian (Ex 2:22). His descendant Jonathan headed a family of priests in the cultic center at Dan (Judg 18:30).

Geshem ("the Arab"). Opponent, with Sanballat the Horonite and Tobiah the Ammonite, of Nehemiah's project to rebuild the walls of Jerusalem (Neh 6:1-6). Archaeologists have identified Geshem with the king of the North Arabian state of Kedar.

Gideon ("he who casts down"). A judge. See III.26, Judges.

Gilead Son of Machir, after whom the Land of Gilead was named (Num 26:29-30).

Gog King of the nations of Meshech and Tubal in the Land of Magog. Ezekiel prophesied that Gog will lead an army to attack Israel's northern border. His defeat by Israel will usher in a new era when Israel and all the nations of the world will recognize God, and God, in turn, will help Israel overcome any difficulties (Ezek 38-39). According to the New Testament, Gog and Magog will lead Satan's army against God's chosen people (Rev 20:7-9).

Goliath Philistine giant from Gath sent to taunt the Israelites. Despite the giant's fearful appearance, David slew Goliath with a slingshot (I Sam 17). Goliath's sword was placed in the sanctuary of Nob, from where it was given to David as he fled from Saul. In II Samuel 21:19, it is stated that Goliath was killed by Elhanan of Bethlehem. The apparent contradiction is resolved by a verse in Chronicles (I Chr 20:5) stating that Elhanan killed Goliath's brother Lahmi.

Gomer Eldest son of Japheth son of Noah; father of Ashkenaz, Riphath, and Togarmah (Gen 10:2-30). Ezekiel foretells that the descendants of Gomer will form an alliance with Gog in the battle of the End of Days (Ezek 38:6). Scholars identify the descendants of Gomer with the Anatolians, known in Greek as the Cimmerians. Another Gomer, daughter of Diblaim, was a harlot whom God commanded the prophet Hosea to marry. Their marriage symbolized the unfaithfulness of the people of Israel to their covenant with God. Gomer bore Hosea three children: Jezreel, Lo-Ruhamah and Lo-Ammi, whose names, possibly like that of their mother, symbolically represent God's temporary rejection of Israel (Hos 1-2).

Habbakuk A prophet. See III.28, Prophets.

Hadad, Hadar The eighth king of Edom, whose reign preceded the establishment of the monarchy in Israel. His capital was Pau (Gen 36:31-39).

David brandishing Goliath's head. From the candelabrum at the Israel parliament, Jerusalem, by Benno Elkan.

Haman leading Mordecai through the streets of Susa. Wall painting of the synagogue of Dura-Europos, 3rd century.

Hadadezer ("Hadad is help"). King of Zobah who was defeated by David on three separate occasions (II Sam 8:3-8; 10:6-11:1).

Hadassah ("myrtle"). Hebrew name of Esther (Est 2:7).

Hadoram See Adoniram.

Hagar Egyptian handmaid to Sarah. After ten years of barrenness, Sarah gave Hagar to Abraham as a concubine, as was the custom. After Hagar conceived, Sarah jealously regretted her action and expeled Hagar from her home. In the wilderness, an angel appeared to Hagar telling her to return and prophesying an important future for the son she would bear. On her return, Hagar gave birth to a son, Ishmael (Gen 16). In time, Sarah bore Isaac. In a disagreement between the two women over Ishmael's inheritance, Sarah made Abraham cast Hagar out for a second time, this time with her son. Before she left, God promised Abraham, "I will make a nation of the son of the slave woman" (Gen 21:1-21).

In the New Testament, Paul argues from the relations of Abraham, Sarah, and Hagar to show the freedom of Christians from the obligations of the Law (Gal 4:24-25).

Haggai A prophet. See III.28, Prophets.

Haggith Wife of David and mother of his son, Adonijah (II Sam 3:4).

Ham One of Noah's three sons (Gen 6:10) who, together with their families, escaped the Flood. Ham was cursed for seeing his father's nakedness while Noah was drunk (Gen 9:18-25). He was the father of Cush, Mizraim, Put, and Canaan (Gen 10:6).

Haman Son of Hammedatha the Agagite; chief minister at the court of Ahasuerus, ruler of the Persian Empire (Est 3:1). He devised a plot to destroy the Jews, whom he hated, and built a gallows for Mordecai, a Jew who refused to bow down to him (Est 3:5-7). The plot, however, turned full circle on Haman, and he was himself hanged on the same gallows (Est 7:5-10).

Hammedatha Father of the notorious Haman who was chief minister to King Ahasuerus (Est 3:1).

Hamor Father of Shechem and ruler of the town of that name. His son was enamored of Dinah, the daughter of Jacob, and took her by force. Shechem and Hamor were later killed in revenge by Jacob's sons, Levi and Simeon (Gen 34).

Hamutal or **Hamital** Daughter of Jeremiah of Libnah; queen to King Josiah and mother of Jehoahaz and Zedekiah (II Kgs 23:31; 24:18).

Hanameel Son of Shallum; a close relative of Jeremiah the prophet to whom he sold his field for 17 shekels (Jer 32:7-12).

Hanani A seer who rebuked Asa, king of Judah, for his lack of faith in God. He was imprisoned for his outspokenness (II Chr 16:7-10).

Another Hanani was a relative of Nehemiah who was given the task of overseeing the reconstruction of Jerusalem (Neh 7:2).

Hananiah ("the Lord has been gracious"). Son of Azur; a Benjamite of Gibeon. Under Zedekiah, king of Judah, Hananiah publicly argued against Jeremiah the prophet, falsely prophesying that within two years, all the exiles, including Jeremiah, would return to Jerusalem and the land of their forefathers (Jer 28).

Hannah ("grace"). Favorite wife of Elkanah of Ephraim. Greatly suffering from her barrenness, Hannah vowed in the sanctuary that if God would grant her a son, she would dedicate him as a Nazirite. She gave birth to Samuel, and when he was three, she took him to the sanctuary to be cared for and taught by the priest, Eli (I Sam 1).

Hanun Son and successor of Nahash, king of Ammon. After an incident in which men sent to him in peace by King David were insulted, his nation became involved in a war that spelled disaster for both Hanun and Ammon (II Sam 10).

Haran Youngest son of Terah, of Ur of the Chaldees; brother of Abraham and Nahor. His children were Lot, Milcah, and Iscah. Haran died in Ur before the family migrated to Haran (Gen 11:26-28).

Harbona, Harbonah Eunuch serving at the court of King Ahasuerus who informed the king of the gallows Haman had built for Mordecai (Est 1:10; 7:9).

Hazael ("God sees"). King of Damascus who reigned for some 45 years at the time of Athaliah, Jehoahaz, and Joash, rulers of Judah, and Jehu and Joram, kings of Israel. He had turned against his master, Ben-Hadad, killed him, and usurped the throne. As king, he made aggressive forays into Israel, and stopped short at the borders of Judah only when King Joash bribed him to retreat (II Kgs 12:18–19).

Hazarmaveth ("the court of the Lord of Death"). Son of Joktan (Gen 10:26).

Heber Husband of Jael who killed Sisera, the captain of Jabin's army. Heber dissociated himself from the Kenite clan to which he belonged, and lived in Galilee. He was descended from Hobab, Moses' father-in-law (Judg 4:11).

Hegai Eunuch at the court of King Ahasuerus who advised Esther (Est 2:8,15).

Heman ("faithful"). A Levite of the family of Kohath; son of Joel, and a grandson of Samuel. He was in charge of the music and musicians at the services in the House of the Lord during the reign of David (I Chr 15:16–22).

Another Heman, son of Mahol, was noted for his wisdom (I Kgs 4:31). He may be the Heman to whom Psalm 88 is ascribed.

Henadad ("favored by Hadad"). head of a family of Levites who, together with his sons, Bavai and Binnui, played an important role in the rebuilding of the Temple (Ezra 3:9; Neh 3:18–24).

Heth Son of Canaan; eponymous ancestor of the Hittite nation (Gen 10:15; 25:10).

Hezekiah ("God is my strength"). King of Judah. See III.27, Kings.

Hiel Man of Bethel. He rebuilt Jericho during the reign of Ahab, in defiance of the ban issued by Joshua (Josh 6:26). Joshua's curse was fulfilled when Hiel's eldest son died as the foundations were laid, and his youngest son died as the gates were installed (I Kgs 16:34).

Hilkiah Son of Shallum and, according to Ezra 7:1, an ancestor of Ezra. As high priest, he discovered the Book of the Law of Moses during a renovation of the Temple, and brought the book to King Josiah (II Kgs 22).

Hiram King of Tyre (961–936 BC). He provided craftsmen and materials for both David's palace (II Sam 5:11) and Solomon's Temple (I Kgs 5:21–25). He felt genuine friendship for David (I Kgs 5:15), and made trade and peace treaties with Solomon. In keep-

The sarcophagus of Ahiram (Hiram), king of Tyre, found in his tomb at Byblos, Lebanon.

ing with these treaties, he shared profits with Solomon from ships trading in the Red Sea (I Kgs 5:26–28).

Another Hiram was a Tyrian bronzesmith sent by King Hiram to Jerusalem to make artifacts for the Temple (I Kgs 7:13–14). He was the son of a resident of Tyre and an Israelite woman (II Chr 2:13).

Hobab Son of Reuel. The theory that he was the brother-in-law of Moses is derived from Numbers 10:29, where Reuel is identified with Jethro, father of Moses' wife, Zipporah. In that verse, however, Hobab himself is called the father-in-law of Moses. Moses asked Hobab for his assistance in leading the Children of Israel through the wilderness (Num 10:29–31).

Hoglah ("partridge"). One of the five daughters of Zelophehad. Like her sisters, she married a relation so that her father's inheritance would remain in the tribe (Num 26:33; 36).

Hoham King of Hebron and an ally of the five Amorite kings. The coalition was defeated by Joshua at Gibeon and Beth-Horon (Josh 10).

Hophni Son of Eli the priest; brother of Phinehas. Both priests served in the sanctuary but abused their office (I Sam 2:12–17). The people regarded them with horror, and they were cursed by Samuel (I Sam 3:11–18). They both died at an early age in a battle with the Philistines (I Sam 4:10–11).

Hophra ("the heart of the god Ra endures"). King of Egypt from 588–568 BC. Despite Jeremiah's warning, King Zedekiah signed a treaty with him, thus annulling all allegiance to Nebuchadnezzar king of Babylonia. Hophra's army set out to honor the treaty and aid Zedekiah against Nebuchadnezzar's siege of Jerusalem but retired across the border before the battle began (Jer 37). Hophra was killed by a member of his family, who then assumed the throne (Jer 44:33).

Hosea ("may the Lord save"). A prophet. See III.28, Prophets.

Hoshea Joshua's original name which was changed by Moses (Num 13:8, 16). Another Hoshea was the last king of Israel (see III.27 Kings).

Huldah ("weasel"). A prophetess. See III.28, Prophets.

Hur He helped Aaron support Moses' upraised arms at the battle with Amalek at Rephidim (Ex 17:10–12). When Moses ascended Mount Sinai, Hur remained with Aaron in charge of the Israelites (Ex 14:14).

Hushai An Archite, a family of the tribe of Benjamin. A friend of David (I Chr 27:33), he spied for him in the camp of Absalom before the latter's rebellion (II Sam 15:32–37; 16:16–19). He succeeded in counteracting the sound advice given to Absalom by Ahithophel (II Sam 17:7–14).

Ibzan A minor judge. See III.26, Judges.

Ichabod Son of Phinehas the priest and grandson of Eli. The name, taken to mean "the glory is degraded," was given to him by his mother who was dying in childbirth, after hearing that her husband had been killed in battle with the Philistines (I Sam 4:21).

Iddo A minor prophet or seer in the reigns of Solomon, Rehoboam, and Abijah (II Chr 9:29) (See III.28, Prophets). He seems to have been the author of a chronicle concerning the acts and sayings of Abijah the prophet (II Chr 13:22) as well as a book on genealogies which incorporated the activities of Rehoboam (II Chr 12:15).

Immanuel (Emmanuel) ("God is with us"). Symbolic name given by Isaiah to an infant shortly to be born to a young woman. He would be a sign that God would deliver King Ahaz and the people of Judah from their enemies (Is 7:14, 8:8). In the New Testament, the prophecy was taken as applying to the virgin birth of Jesus and to his future mission (Matt 1:23).

Isaac The second patriarch of Israel. See III.23, Patriarchs.

Isaiah ("God is salvation"). A prophet. See III.28, Prophets.

Ish-Baal See Ishbosheth.

Ishbi-Benob Philistine giant who was killed by Abishai for attacking David (II Sam 21:16–17).

Ishbosheth (originally Ish-Baal, "man of Baal," but the name of the heathen god Baal was altered to *bosheth*, "shame"). Saul's youngest son and successor. After Saul's death, David was made king of Judah, but Abner (Saul's cousin and commander-in-chief of his army) proclaimed Ishbosheth king of Israel at Mahanaim. He reigned only two years, as war broke out between Israel and Judah, and Ishbosheth was defeated (II Sam 2:8–3:11). In revenge for a past crime of Saul, wherein he had claimed the lives of men from Gibeon, two of their kinsmen killed Ishbosheth and presented his head to David as a tribute. David's anger at the murder of an innocent man resulted in their execution (II Sam 4:5–12).

Ishmael, Ishmaelites ("may God hear"). Son of Abraham and Hagar, Sarah's Egyptian handmaiden. He was born when his father was 86 (Gen 16:15–16). Ishmael was circumcised at the age of 13 (Gen 17:23–25), and was expelled a few years later from Abraham's household with his mother by Abraham's jealous wife, Sarah, who had meanwhile given birth to Isaac. After wandering with his mother in the wilderness around Beersheba, Ishmael married an Egyptian girl who bore him twelve sons and a daughter (Gen 21:9–21; 25:13–15). These children were to be the founders of the Arab nation, the Ishmaelites. To Abraham's consolation, God blessed Ishmael, saying, "I will make him a great nation" (Gen 17:20) and "I will multiply your descendants exceedingly, so that they shall not be counted for multitude" (Gen 16:10). He joined his brother Isaac in burying Abraham and lived to the age of 137 (Gen 25:17).

Another Ishmael was the son of Nethaniah and one of the killers of Gedaliah. He belonged to the royal house of Judah. After the destruction of Jerusalem in 586 BC, the Babylonians made Gedaliah governor of Judah. Ishmael assassinated Gedaliah and a number of his supporters at Mizpeh. He took the citizens of Mizpeh captive, but they were rescued by Johanan, "the captain of the forces." Ishmael himself escaped to Ammon (Jer 40:13–41:18).

Israel Name given to Jacob by the angel with whom he had wrestled all night at Penuel, near the ford of Jabbok. It is explained as meaning, "You have struggled with God" (Gen 32:29).

Issachar Eponymous ancestor of the tribe of Issachar. See III.22, The Twelve Tribes.

Ithamar Youngest of Aaron's four sons. As a priest, he and his brother Eleazar succeeded to the holy office of their elder brothers, Nadab and Abihu, when they died (Lev 10). He supervised the construction (Ex 38:21) and transportation (Num 4:28, 33) of the ark in the wilderness. His descendants became priests of the house of Eli (I Sam 14:3; 22:9; I Chr 24:3).

Ittai A man of Gath; Philistine soldier in David's army who refused to abandon David when Absalom rebelled, and commanded the troops in the subsequent battle (II Sam 15:19–22).

Jaakan Probably the forefather of the sons of Jaakan mentioned in Deuteronomy 10:6. He was the son of Ezer the Horite (I Chr 1:42).

Jabal Brother of Jubal and son of Lamech and Adah. He was considered the father of all nomadic shepherds (Gen 4:19-20).

Jabin King of Hazor. He was head of a coalition formed to resist the invading Israelites, but was defeated by Joshua (Josh 11:1–12). The army of another Jabin, also king of Hazor, was defeated by Barak (Judg 4:7, 15).

Jacob A patriarch. See III.23, Patriarchs.

Jaddua ("he is known" [to God]). Son of Jonathan; last of the high priests named in the Bible (Neh 12:11,22).

Jael ("mountain goat"). Wife of Heber the Kenite. After Barak had defeated Jabin's army, its commander, Sisera, fled and took refuge in the tent of Jael. While he was asleep, she drove a tent peg through his temple (Judg 4:17–21).

Jahaziel ("God will see"). Son of Zechariah; a Levite. He had a vision before King Jehoshaphat and all the people foretelling Judah's triumph in battle against the Ammonites (II Chr 20:14–17).

Jair ("may [God] give light"). Son of a Judahite man and a Manassite woman, he defeated and partitioned a group of villages in the region of Gilead. He called the villages Havvoth-Jair (Num 32:41). Another Jair was a minor judge. See III.26, Judges.

Japheth Third son of Noah (Gen 6:10) who, with his family, was saved from the Flood in the ark built by Noah (Gen 9:18). He and his brother Shem were blessed when they covered their father's nakedness after he became drunk (Gen 9:23–27). The descendants of Japheth spread to the "isles of the Gentiles" (Gen 10:5), usually identified as Anatolia and the Greek coastlands.

Jael killing Sisera. Pen drawing after the Master of Flemalle; c.1430.

Jared Son of Mahalaleel, father of Enoch, and one of the earliest patriarchs of the line of Seth (Gen 5:15–20).

Jashobeam First among the mighty men of David, famous for killing as many as 300 men in one day (I Chr 11:11).

Javan Son of Japheth; father of Elishah, Tarshish, Kittim, and Dodanim (Gen 10:2–4). The connection with Genesis 10:5 and Japheth's descendants points to the name Javan as being representative of the Ionians (it is the same word).

Jeconiah Alternate name for King Jehoiachin of Judah (see III.27, Kings).

Jedidah ("God's friend" or "friendly", "beloved"). Daughter of Adaiah of Boseath. She married Amon of Judah and became his queen. She was the mother of Josiah who succeeded his father (II Kgs 22:1).

Jeduthun Levite who was a musician in the time of David. He had six sons and, although in I Chronicles (16:42) they are referred to as "keepers of the gate," it is obvious that they, too, were musicians (I Chr 25:1–6), and either played or sang with their father at the dedication of Solomon's temple.

Jehoahaz ("God has held firmly"). Alternative name for Ahaziah king of Judah. Name of a king of Judah and a king of Israel. See III.27, Kings.

Jehoash, Joash ("God has bestowed/donated"). Father of Gideon; a member of the family of Abiezer of the tribe of Manasseh. His son was commanded by God to destroy the altar that Joash had built to Baal, but when the people of Ophrah became angry at Gideon and called for his death, Joash defended him (Judg 6:11–32).

Another Joash was the son of King Ahab of Israel. The prophet Micaiah was sent to Joash by his father to be imprisoned for prophesying the defeat of Ahab at Ramoth Gilead at the hands of the Syrians. The prophecy was later fulfilled (I Kgs 22:26).

Joash is also the name of a king of Judah. See III.27, Kings.

Jehoiachin ("God will establish"). King of Judah. See III.27, Kings.

Jehoiada Priest and brother-in-law of King Ahaziah of Judah. When Ahaziah was killed by Jehu, his mother, Athaliah, ascended the throne, first making sure that all the legal heirs were killed. However, the king's son, Joash, was hidden by Jehoiada and his wife for six years, and finally restored to his rightful place on the throne after ordering the killing of Athaliah and the destruction of the temple of Baal. As long as Joash was a minor, Jehoiada served as regent (II Kgs 11:1–12:3). After Joash's ascension, Jehoida influenced him to repair the Temple. He died at the age of 130 (II Chr 24:15–16).

Jehoiakim ("God will arise"). King of Judah. See III.27, Kings.

Jehonadab, Jonadab ("God has donated"). Son of David's brother, Shimeah. He helped his friend, David's son Amnon, organize the rape of Tamar (II Sam 13:3–5).

Another Jehonadab was the son of Rechab the Kenite (I Chr 2:55). Brought up in nomadic ways, Jonadab imposed austere measures upon his family and all the people of his tribe, thus enabling them to uphold the traditions of their forefathers (Jer 35). He conspired with Jehu against the worshipers of Baal, killing many of them and destroying their idols and temples (II Kgs 10:23).

Jehoram, Joram ("God is high"). King of Israel. See III.27, Kings.

Jehoshabeath, Jehosheba Daughter of King Jehoram and wife of Jehoiada who hid Joash, the king's son, from Athaliah, who had usurped the throne (II Kgs 11:2–3).

Jehoshaphat ("God has judged"). Son of Ahilud; recorder in the court of David and Solomon (I Chr 18:15; I Kgs 4:3).

Another Jehoshaphat was king of Judah. See III.27, Kings.

Jehozabad, Jozabad ("God has given" [a child]). Son of Shomer (in II Chronicles 24:26, son of Shimrith, a woman of Moab). A servant who killed his master, King Joash, as he lay in bed (II Kgs 12:21).

Jehu A prophet (see III.28, Prophets) and a king of Judah (see III.27, Kings).

Jehuval (Jucal) ("God will show his ability"). Son of Shelemiah. He was sent with Zephaniah by King Zedekiah to Jeremiah the prophet, to ask him to pray for Jerusalem against imminent attack by the Chaldean armies (Jer 37:3).

Jehudi ("Jew," or "a man of Judah"). Son of Nethaniah. He was sent by King Jehoiakim to Baruch, Jeremiah's scribe, to ask him to bring the scroll of Jeremiah which Jehudi read out loud (Jer 36:14, 21).

Jephthah ("God will open"). A judge. See III.26, Judges.

Jeremiah A prophet. See III.28, Prophets.

Jeroboam ("may the people grow numerous"). Name of two kings of Israel (see III.27, Kings).

Jerubbaal (interpreted as "let Baal contend against us"). Name given to Gideon after he had destroyed the altar of Baal belonging to his father, Joash, after which Joash relented and renounced the worship of Baal (Judg 6:25-32).

Jeshua (alternatively, "Joshua"; also a contraction of "Jehoshua"). Son of Jozadak, born in Babylonia; first high priest after the return of the exiles to Zion (Ezra 2:2). He participated in the rebuilding of the altar and the Temple, and the restoration of important Temple rites (Ezra 3:2-9; 5:2). He appears in two visions of Zechariah (Zech 3:1-10; 6:11), representing the survival of the priesthood: "a brand plucked from the fire."

Jesse Son of Obed and father of David. He was a Judahite from Bethlehem (Ruth 4:18-22). He had eight sons (I Chr 23:13-15; 27:18). When the rift between David and Saul was at its height, David had his parents placed temporarily in the care of the king of Moab (I Sam 22:1-4).

Jesse is named in the genealogy of Jesus (Matt 1:56; Luke 3:32). The messianic king is called "the root of Jesse" (Is 11:1,10).

Jether Eldest son of Gideon who could not, because of his youth, bring himself to kill the Midianite rulers, Zebah and Zalmunnah, who had murdered his relatives (Judg 8:20).

Another Jether (or Ithre) was the father of Amasa, commander of Absalom's army. He was an Ishmaelite (II Sam 17:25; I Chr 2:17).

Jethro Moses' father-in-law, a Midianite priest (also called Reuel in Ex 2:18, and Hobab in Num 10:29). When Moses fled from Egypt he found refuge with Jethro and married his daughter, Zipporah (Ex 2:15-22). After the Exodus, Jethro joined Moses in the wilderness and shared with him his knowledge of the land through which they passed. He instructed Moses in establishing a judicial system (Ex 18).

Jetur A son of Ishmael; ancestor of a clan in Transjordan (Gen 25:12-15; I Chr 1:31).

Jezebel Queen of Ahab, king of Israel, and mother of Ahaziah, Athaliah, and Joram. She was a Phoenician princess who brought the worship of Baal to Israel. She sought the elimination of the prophets of the God of Israel, including Elijah. She persuaded Ahab to confiscate the vineyard of Naboth by organizing his death.

For this, she and Ahab were condemned by Elijah, who foretold her grisly death (I Kgs 21:20-33). Jezebel was killed by Jehu in a conspiracy. She was pushed to her death out of a palace window (II Kgs 9:30-34). Jezebel's name is traditionally used as a byword for a wicked woman (cf. Rev 2:20).

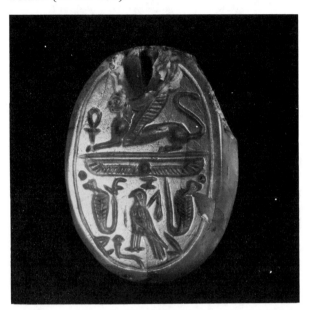

Opal Phoenician seal with symbols, and inscribed "izbl," the Phoenician form of the name Jezebel; 9th-8th century BC.

Jezreel Eldest son of the prophet Hosea by Gomer (Hos 1:4). The name was given to symbolize the future punishment of Jehu, who had spilled blood in the towns of Jezreel.

Joab Son of Zeruiah; David's nephew; commander-in-chief of David's army. After David's ascent to the throne, Joab's younger brother was killed by Abner in a battle led by Joab against Saul's son, Ishbosheth. The rancor Joab felt for Abner after this action finally exploded when the latter was pardoned by David and won over to his cause. Joab jealously connived against him and murdered him (II Sam 3:27).

Joab was faithful to David throughout the latter's lifetime, and fought as his general in all his wars. In domestic matters, he was also David's friend, and organized the death of Uriah the Hittite (II Sam 11:1-25). He was instrumental in the reconciliation between David and Absalom after the latter's banishment (II Sam 14:21-33), but when Absalom rebelled against David, Joab had no compunction in killing him out of loyalty to David (II Sam 18:14-17).

Joab favored Adonijah over Solomon as David's successor, but once on the throne, Solomon sent Benaiah to kill Joab, who died holding on to the horns of the altar in the tabernacle (I Kgs 2:28-34).

Job Ancient worthy mentioned, along with Noah and Daniel, in Ezekiel 14:14, 20. He is the central figure of the Book of Job (see III.21, Books of the Old Testament), in which he is singled out by Satan to challenge his piety, and made to undergo a series of personal tragedies to test his faith in God. Through a series of conversations, four of his friends (Eliphaz, Bildad, Zophar, and Elihu) maintain that, as suffering must be the result of sin, Job must have done wrong, a charge which he adamantly rejects. Eventually, God speaks to him out of a whirlwind, affirming divine omnipotence which is inscrutable to man. Finally, Job is rewarded for his steadfastness by the restoration of his fortunes.

In the New Testament, Job is cited as a paradigm of faith (James 5:11).

Jochebed ("God is glory"). Daughter of Levi who married her nephew, Amram. She was the mother of Moses, Aaron, and Miriam (Ex 2:1; 6:20; Num 26:59).

Joel ("Yah is God"). Son of the prophet Samuel; a judge in Beersheba. See III.26, Judges.

Various other Bible figures were called Joel, including the head of the levitical family of Gershon in the time of David (I Chr 15:7).

Another Joel was a prophet (see III.28, The Prophets).

Johanan ("God has been gracious"). Son of Kareah; an army captain who remained in Judah after the destruction of Jerusalem by the Babylonians in 586 BC. He pursued Ishmael, the murderer of the Babylonian-appointed governor, Gedaliah, killed two of his men, and released all the captives Ishmael had taken. Still afraid of the Babylonian reaction, and contrary to Jeremiah's opinions (Jer 42:9-22), Johanan led the Jews remaining in Judah into Egypt (Jer 43:5-7).

Joktan Son of Eber and brother of Peleg (Gen 10:25). He was the founder of the Joktanite tribes who occupied most of the south and south-west Arabian peninsula (Gen 10:30).

Jonah ("dove"). A prophet. See III.28, Prophets, and III.21, Books of the Old Testament.

Jonathan ("God has given"). Eldest son of King Saul. A distinguished warrior, he first proved himself in the battle against Michmash, going out alone with his armorbearer and making a surprise attack on the Philistines. Saul later joined him in the attack, thoughtlessly cursing anyone who would eat before evening. Jonathan, unaware of the curse, ate some honey in the woods as they passed through. Saul would have killed him for this insubordination had not the soldiers, assured of their victory, spoken on his behalf (I Sam 14).

Jonathan became firm friends with David after the victory over Goliath, for which he admired him greatly, and their lifelong friendship became proverbial. When Saul's anger caused David to flee the court, Jonathan intervened on his behalf (I Sam 19:1-7).

In the battle of Gilboa, Jonathan died at the hands of the Philistines, alongside his father and two brothers (I Sam 31:2). David composed a moving lament: "Saul and Jonathan were lovely and pleasant in their lives,

and in their death they were not divided: they were swifter than eagles; they were stronger than lions" (II Sam 1:17-27).

Joseph ("may [God] increase"). Son of Jacob and Rachel. His brothers were jealous of the favoritism he received from his father. The tensions were compounded when Joseph told his brothers of his dreams, which indicated his superiority (Gen 37:5-11). When he was 17 years old, Joseph was sent by his father to report on the whereabouts of his brothers who were tending the flocks. His brothers decided to kill him there, but Reuben remonstrated with them and they put Joseph in a deep pit, first divesting him of his garment, a "coat of many colors" which he had received from Jacob. Later, they sold him to a passing caravan of tradesmen and returned home with Joseph's

Joseph forced into a pit by his brothers. On the right, the brothers bargain the sale of Joseph. Miniature from a psalter, France

soiled tunic and a concocted story in which he had supposedly been killed by a wild animal (Gen 37:29-36).

Joseph was taken to Egypt and sold to an Egyptian officer called Potiphar. He proved a successful servant, and Potiphar put him in charge of his household. He was falsely accused, however, by Potiphar's wife who had tried in vain to seduce him, leaving Potiphar no choice but to throw Joseph into prison. There, Joseph's accurate interpretations of the dreams of various imprisoned members of Pharaoh's household brought him to the attention of Pharaoh, who summoned him to interpret his own dream. Pleased by Joseph's interpretation that Egypt would experience seven years of plenty followed by seven years of famine, Pharaoh appointed Joseph governor over all Egypt. Joseph managed Egypt's affairs well, stockpiling against the seven years of famine to come.

When the famine came, it also struck Canaan, causing Jacob to send his sons to buy corn in Egypt. They did not recognize their brother who was by now completely Egyptian in education and speech. Joseph recognized them, but treated them as strangers. He hid valuables among their belongings and accused them of robbery and spying. When they had become thoroughly frightened, Joseph relented, but insisted that they bring his full brother Benjamin who had been left behind in Canaan. On their return, Joseph first, through a ruse, pretended that Benjamin was a thief, but soon there was a tearful reunion in which he revealed his true identity. Eventually, Jacob was brought to Egypt, and the family was reunited (Gen 42-45).

When Jacob died, Joseph took him back to Canaan for burial (Gen 50:12-13) and left similar instructions for his own burial (Gen 50:25). Moses took his bones along through the wilderness, and after the arrival in Canaan, Joseph was buried in Shechem (Josh 24:32).

Joshua ("God is salvation"). Son of Nun of the tribe of Ephraim (originally called Hoshea/Oshea until changed by Moses; Num 13:8,16); successor of Moses; conqueror of Canaan. He led the Israelite army at Rephidim, where the Israelites defeated the Amalekites (Ex 17:11-12). Joshua was one of the two scouts sent to spy out the Land of Canaan who returned with positive accounts regarding its conquest (Num 13-14). He attended on Moses and guarded the tabernacle (Ex 33:11).

Joshua was solemnly commissioned to succeed Moses and to lead the Israelites into Canaan (Deut 1:3-8; Josh 1:1-5). Under his military leadership, most of the land was captured and divided into areas for the different tribes. He ensured that the laws given to Moses were upheld, including the circumcision of the people and the keeping of Passover. He died at the age of 110, and was buried at Timnath Serah (Josh 24:29-30). His life is recounted in the Book of Joshua. See also III.21, Books of the Old Testament.

Josiah ("may God give"). King of Judah. See III.27, Kings.

Jotham ("may God complete"). Youngest of Gideon's 70 sons; sole survivor of a tribal massacre by Abimelech, who later took over the throne of Shechem. In his anger, Jotham spoke out against the people at Mount Gerizim, making the point by telling a parable. After cursing the people, he fled (Judg 9:7-15).

Another Jotham was king of Judah (see III.27, Kings).

Jubal Son of Lamech and Adah; brother of Jabal. He was considered the father of "those who play the harp and the flute" (Gen 4:19,21).

Judah Eponymous ancestor of the tribe of Judah (see III.22, The Twelve Tribes).

Keturah ("incense"). Abraham's second wife (named "concubine" in Genesis and Chronicles) whose children Zimran, Jokshan, Medan, Midian, Ishbak, and Shuah became the progenitors of various tribes in Arabia (Gen 25:1-2; I Chr 1:32-33).

Kish Landowner of the tribe of Benjamin; father of King Saul (I Sam 9:1-3). His home was in Gibeah, and he was buried in Zela together with his son and his grandson, Jonathan (II Sam 21:14).

Kohath The second son of Levi (Gen 46:2). He was father to Amram, Izhar, Hebron, and Uzziel and the grandfather of Aaron, Moses, and Miriam (Ex 6:18). He founded the Kohathite clan.

Korah Esau's youngest son, who held a high position in Edom (Gen 36:5).

Another Korah led a revolt against his cousins, Moses and Aaron. He and 250 others challenged Moses' leadership. God sent down a fire which destroyed the conspirators while Korah was swallowed up by the earth (Num 16). Korah's sons were spared and several Psalms were attributed to "the sons of Korah."

Laban ("white"). Called Laban the Aramean of Haran, he was the son of Bethuel, brother of Rebekah and uncle of Jacob. He received Abraham's servant and agreed to send back his sister to marry Isaac (Gen 24). When Jacob fled the wrath of his brother, Esau, he escaped to Laban in Padan Aram. Laban had two daughters, Leah and Rachel. Aware of Jacob's love for Rachel, Laban forced him by trickery to work in his service for 14 years, marrying the elder daughter Leah first before he could marry his beloved Rachel. Jacob used his cunning to make himself wealthy at his uncle's expense, but before Jacob returned to Canaan with his wives and sons, Laban made a covenant with him (Gen 30-31).

Lamech Descendant of Cain and son of Methushael (Gen 4:18-19). He had two sons, Jabal and Jubal, by Adah, his first wife, and one son, Tubal-Cain, a blacksmith, and a daughter, Naamah, by his second wife, Zillah. Lamech's song to his wives is one of the earliest poems in Hebrew literature, although its exact meaning is not clear. He lived to the age of 777 (Gen 4:16-24).

Leah ("wild cow"). The third matriarch of the Jewish people. See III.24, Matriarchs.

Lemuel King of Massa, known for his mother's words of good advice on how to govern and on the dangers of licentiousness and drunkenness (Prov 31:1–9).

Levi Eponymous ancestor of the Levites. See III.22, The Twelvev Tribes.

Lo-Ammi Son of Hosea the prophet and his wife, Gomer. The name, meaning "not my people," refers to the Lord's rejection of Israel for worshiping Baal (Hos 1:9).

Lo-Ruhamah Daughter of Hosea the prophet and his wife, Gomer. The name, meaning "not accepted," refers to the Lord's rejection of Israel for worshiping false gods (Hos 1:6).

Lot Son of Haran, brother of Abraham. After Haran died, Lot accompanied his grandfather, Terah, and Abraham on their journey from Ur of the Chaldees to Haran. When God called Abraham to go to Canaan, Lot accompanied him as he did again subsequently on a journey to Egypt in time of famine. Strife between the herdsmen of Abraham and Lot forced them to agree to part, and Lot chose to settle in the lush Jordan Valley (Gen 11–14). When an invading coalition of kings captured Lot, he was rescued by Abraham.

On the road to Sodom, a rock formation known as Lot's Wife.

When the cities of Sodom and Gomorrah were destroyed for their wickedness, Lot and his family were saved, but his wife disregarded the command not to look back and was turned into a pillar of salt. The incestuous union of Lot with his daughters produced children who became the progenitors of the Moabite and the Ammonite tribes (Gen 19).

In the New Testament, reference is made to the story of Lot in illustration of Jesus' teaching (Luke 17:28–32); and Lot is cited as a "righteous man" in the Second Epistle of Peter (II Pet 2:7).

Lud Son of Shem (Gen 10:22; I Chr 1:17), traditionally identified as the eponymous ancestor of the Lydians, settlers in Asia Minor.

Machir Son of Manasseh and grandson of Joseph (Gen 50:23); father of Gilead (Josh 17:1).

Another Machir, son of Ammiel, assisted King David in Mahanaim at the time of Absalom's revolt (II Sam 17:27–29).

Magog Second son of Japheth whose seven sons represented peoples living in the Fertile Crescent. Magog was also the name of a people and land, cf. "Gog in the land of Magog" (Ezek 38:2). It was believed that destruction would come from the north after which Magog would be punished by fire (Ezek 39:6). In Revelations 20:9, Magog is seen as joint leader of Satan's armies gathered against God's people for the eschatological battle.

Maher-Shalal-Hash-Baz (literally, "speed the spoil, hasten the prey"). Son of Isaiah the prophet. The symbolic name refers to the anticipated speedy end of the enemies of Judah (Is 8:3–4).

Mahlah Eldest of the five daughters of Zelophehad. On their father's death, they received a ruling from Moses that in the absence of a son, daughters would inherit their father's property on condition that they marry within the tribe (Num 27).

Mahlon Son of Elimelech and Naomi. Famine forced the family to leave Bethlehem and move to Moab where Mahlon married Ruth the Moabite. After Mahlon's death, Ruth insisted on accompanying her mother-in-law back to Judah (Ruth 1).

Malachi A prophet. See III.28, Prophets.

Malchishua ("my king is noble"). Son of King Saul and Ahinoam. Together with other male members of the family, he was killed by the Philistines in a battle on Mount Gilboa (I Sam 14:49; 31:2).

Manasseh Eponymous ancestor of the tribe of Manasseh (see III.22, The Twelve Tribes), and a king of Judah (see III.27, Kings).

Manoach ("contented"). Father of Samson; a Danite from Zorah. An angel announced to his barren wife that she would conceive and bear Samson (Judg 13:24).

Medad ("beloved"). One of the 70 Israelites chosen to assist Moses in the desert. Together with Eldad, he received the gift of prophecy from God (Num 11:26–27).

Melchizedek ("righteous king"). King of Salem (Jerusalem); a Gentile and priest of "God most High." Abraham, on his return from his victorious battle with Chedorlaomer, was received by him with bread, wine, and a blessing. Melchizedek, in turn, received a tithe of the booty taken in the war (Gen 14:18). In the Dead Sea documents, Melchizedek is declared "an angel" and in the Epistle to the Hebrews (Heb 5:1–8:2), he is said to be like "the son of God" and a forerunner of Jesus.

Menahem ("comforter"). King of Israel. See III.27, Kings.

Mephibosheth Son of Jonathan, grandson of King Saul. The name was probably originally Merib-Baal (I Chr 8:34; 9:30) but later "Baal" (a pagan name) was replaced by *bosheth*, "shame". When he was five years

Melchizedek, king of Salem, welcomes Abraham. Reconstruction after archaeological finds.

old his leg was badly injured when he was dropped by a nurse who was fleeing after hearing of the death of his father and grandfather, leaving him with a permanent limp (II Sam 4:4). Because of an oath he had made to Jonathan, David spared the life of Mephibosheth, gave him a respected place at court, and restored his property and steward, Ziba. In Absalom's revolt, Ziba sided with David but Mephibosheth remained with Absalom. Mephibosheth subsequently recanted his role in the rebellion and David forgave him, but insisted that he divide his property between himself and Ziba (II Sam 19:24–30). Mephibosheth's son Micha founded a distinguished clan (I Chr 8:35; 9:41).

Merab Elder daughter of King Saul. She married Adriel the Meholothite although initially she was promised to David (I Sam 18:17–21). Her five sons were given by David, with other offspring of Saul, to the Gibeonites for execution to atone for Saul's slaughter of the Gibeonites (II Sam 21:8–9 says that these were the sons of Michal, but this seems to be a confusion).

Merari Third son of Levi and head of the Merarites, a Levitical family entrusted with carrying components of the tabernacle in the desert (Num 26:57).

Merib-Baal Another name for Mephibosheth, the son of Saul. In various such names, "Baal" (the Canaanite god) was replaced by *bosheth*, "shame," as in Ishbosheth, Jerubosheth, and "prophets of shame" for "prophets of Baal" (I Kgs 18:19, 25).

Merodach (from Akkadian "calf of the sun god Utu"). Hebrew form of "Marduk," a Mesopotamian god, chief god of Babylonia, later called "Bel" (or Ba'al). Merodach signifies the divine element in the Hebraicized

version of Babylonian names such as Evil-Merodach and Merodach-Baladan, and some have seen a connection with Mordecai. Marduk is mentioned in Hammurabi's legal judgments (c.1750 BC).

Merodach-Baladan (Marduk-apla-iddina II). Ruler of Bit-Yakin near the Persian Gulf in the Chaldees. In 741 BC he captured Babylon and made himself king, retaining the throne for 11 years until he was toppled by Sargon II of Assyria. After hiding in Bit-Yakin, he again gathered his forces, sent a dispatch to King Hezekiah of Judah (Is 39:1), and entered Babylon to become king for the second time. After nine months he was ousted, this time by Sennacherib of Assyria. Bit-Yakin was overrun, and Merodach-Baladan was forced to flee to Elam where he subsequently died.

Mesha King of Moab in the time of Kings Ahab and Jehoram of Israel and Jehoshaphat of Judah. The Bible (II Kgs 3) relates that Mesha revolted against Jehoram, to whom he had been tributary. Jehoram, supported by Judah and Edom, invaded and devastated Moab but at the siege of the town of Kir Hareseth, Mesha sacrificed his eldest son on the city wall to his god Chemosh and the Israelites withdrew in horror. An alternative account of events was discovered in 1868 on the Moabite Stone (now in the Louvre) containing Mesha's own version which describes his triumph over the Israelites and his magnificent reign. See also I.1, Peoples of the Ancient Near East.

The Moabite Stone inscribed with King Mesha's version of his victories over the Israelites.

Meshach Originally called Mishael. Young man of Judah imprisoned with Daniel and two other friends in Babylon by Nebuchadnezzar. They miraculously escaped unscathed from "a fiery furnace" (Dan 3).

Methuselah Son of Enoch, grandfather of Noah (Gen 5:21–22). His life span was 969 years, the longest of any person in the Bible.

Micah ("who is like God"). A prophet. See III.28, Prophets.

Another Micah, who came from Mount Ephraim, is mentioned in the Book of Judges (ch.17). He built a shrine, placing into it cultic objects and images. A Levite priest who was invited by Micah to take over the priesthood of the shrine was subsequently persuaded by members of the tribe of Dan to leave, and they looted the objects of cult worship from the shrine.

Micaiah ("who is like God"). A prophet. See III.28, Prophets.

Michael ("who is like God"). Patron angel of Israel, called "one of the chief princes" (Dan 10:3). Michael is destined to punish the sinners and praise the righteous in the End of Days (Dan 12:1–3). In the New Testament Michael is depicted struggling with Satan over the body of Moses (Jude 9; Rev 12:7).

Michal Saul's youngest daughter, who married David instead of Merab after he had killed 200 Philistines as a brideprice (I Sam 18:20–27). Through her resourcefulness, she saved him when Saul attempted to kill him (I Sam 19:11–17). She remained childless as a punishment from God for disapproving of David dancing in ecstasy before the Ark of the Lord as they brought it to Jerusalem (II Sam 6:16–23).

Midian Son of Abraham and Keturah. He was sent away by Abraham with his brothers to live in the east (Gen 25:1–6). He was the eponymous ancestor of the Midianites.

Milcah ("queen"). Daughter of Abraham's brother, Haran. She married Nahor, another brother of Abraham, and was the grandmother of Rebekah (Gen 11:29). Another Milkah was one of the daughters of Zelophehad (Num 26:33).

Miriam Daughter of Amram and Jochebed, sister to Moses and Aaron. See III.28, Prophets.

Mishael ("who belongs to the Lord"). One of Daniel's three friends who was imprisoned with him by the Babylonians and miraculously rescued from the fiery furnace. His name was changed to Meshach (Dan 1).

Another Mishael, son of Uzziel the Levite, joined his brother Elzaphan in removing the bodies of Nadab and Abihu from the camp after they had been killed for offering strange fire before the Lord (Lev 10:4).

Mithredath ("given by Mithra" — the Persian god). Treasurer at the court of Cyrus, King of Persia, who was responsible in 536 BC for returning to Sheshbazzar, prince of Judah, those holy artifacts that had been stolen from the Temple in Jerusalem by Nebuchadnezzar (Ezra 1:8).

Another Persian official of that name interrupted the rebuilding of Jerusalem by complaining about it in a letter to Artaxerxes (Ezra 4:7).

Moab Son of Lot by an incestuous union with his daughter (Gen 19:30–38); eponymous ancestor of the Moabites.

Mordecai (possibly connected to the Babylonian divine name "Marduk"). Cousin of Esther whom he encouraged to become queen of Persia by marrying Ahasuerus. When he refused to bow before the vizier, Haman, the latter planned to have Mordecai and all the Jews of the kingdom killed. Mordecai and Esther plotted to turn the tables on Haman who was hanged instead of Mordecai, and Mordecai inherited Haman's functions at court. The story of Mordecai and Esther is told in the Book of Esther.

Tomb of Esther and Mordecai at Susa, Iran.

Moses Greatest of the prophets (see III, 25, Moses).

Naamah ("pleasant"). Daughter of Lamech and Zillah, sister to Tubal-Cain (Gen 4:22). Another Naamah was a wife of Solomon and mother of Rehoboam the king (I Kgs 14:21).

Naaman Commander of the army of Aram. He was afflicted by leprosy and turned for help to the prophet Elisha who cured it by having him bathe in the Jordan. In gratitude, Naaman praised the God of Israel as the one true God (II Kgs 5). He was cited by Jesus as an example of God's concern for the non-Israelite (Luke 4:27).

Nabal ("vile"). Husband of Abigail and a wealthy resident of Judah who pastured his flocks in the Judean desert. When David sent messengers to Nabal to demand payment for protection of his flocks from thieves, he was answered with insults. In anger David's men marched on Nabal but were intercepted by Abigail bearing food and wine. Nabal was humiliated by his wife's action, suffered a stroke, and died ten days later (I Sam 25). Subsequently, David married Abigail (II Sam 2:2; 3:3).

Naaman bathing in the Jordan; enamel plaque, 12th century.

Naboth A Jezreelite, owner of a vineyard adjacent to the palace of King Ahab. Refusing Ahab's offer for the land, for it was the inheritance of his sons, Naboth was unjustly sentenced for blasphemy and stoned to death through legal trickery perpetrated by Jezebel, Ahab's wife. When Ahab took possession of the vineyard, Elijah confronted him, accused him of the crime, and prophesied that as Naboth had died a bloody death so would Ahab. The king repented and God withheld punishment during his lifetime (I Kgs 21).

Nachon ("straight"). Owner of a threshing-floor near Jerusalem in the place where Uzzah was struck dead when he put out his hand to steady the Ark of the Lord (II Sam 6:6).

Nadab Eldest son of Aaron and Elisheba, mentioned as present with Moses and the elders on Mount Sinai. He later became a priest and with his brother Abihu was struck dead when he offered "strange fire" on the altar in the House of God (Lev 10:1–7; Num 26:61).

Another Nadab was king of Israel (see III.27, Kings.)

Nahash ("serpent"). Ruler of the Ammonites who attacked the city of Jabesh Gilead under Saul's rule (I Sam 2–12) but was defeated. He was friendly with David and may have sheltered him when he fled from Saul (II Sam 10:2; I Chr 19:2).

Nahor Son of Terah, brother of Abraham and Haran. He married Milcah, his niece, who bore him eight children (Gen 22:20–22).

Nahshon Son of Amminadab, of the tribe of Judah. He was the brother-in-law of Aaron (Ex 6:23), and was selected to assist Moses in taking a census of the Israelites. He was appointed head of his clan and was the first to offer a sacrifice in the tabernacle (Num 7:12). He is listed in the genealogy of Jesus (Matt 1:4; Luke 3:32).

Nahum ("comforted"). A prophet. See III.28, The Prophets.

Naomi ("delight"). Mother of Mahlon and Chilion and wife of Elimelech. The family left Bethlehem for Moab in time of famine during the period of the Judges. Naomi became a widow and her sons married the Moabite women, Orpah and Ruth. When her sons died also, Naomi decided to return to her own people and her daughter-in-law Ruth insisted on returning with her.

By virtue of her sad life Naomi later wished to be called "Marah" (bitter). Afterward, however, Ruth married Naomi's kinsman Boaz and bore Obed, in whom Naomi rejoiced (Ruth 1–4).

Naphtali Eponymous ancestor of the tribe of Naphtali (see III.22, The Twelve Tribes).

Nathan ("He [God] has given"). A prophet. See III.28, The Prophets.

Nathan was also the name of David's son, probably by Bathsheba, and therefore Solomon's brother (II Sam 5:14). He is listed in the genealogy of Jesus (Luke 3:31).

Nebuchadnezzar Babylonian ruler, historically the second of this name. He succeeded his father, Nabopolassar, to the throne and ruled from 605–562 BC. He commanded the Babylonian army in battle against the Assyrians, defeated Necho II and the Egyptians (II Kgs 23:29; II Chr 35:20) at the battle of Carchemish in 605 BC and fought in Syria and Palestine (II Kgs 24:7). In his campaign against Egypt in 601 BC, he received the submission of King Jehoiakim of Judah. In 598/7, he moved against Jerusalem and removed King Jehoiakim who had withheld tribute, appointing Zedekiah in his place. However, Zedekiah rebelled against Babylon and Nebuchadnezzar was forced to wage war with Judah for a second time. Holding out for more than a year and a half, the city of Jerusalem was finally sacked in 586 BC, and Zedekiah was blinded and taken a prisoner to Babylon. The Temple was destroyed, its sacred vessels looted, and 10,000 captives were deported to Babylon (II Kgs 24,25). By virtue of his military successes Nebuchadnezzar expanded the Babylonian empire extensively and was responsible for building, fortifying and restoring temples and public buildings throughout his empire. The events in the first chapters of the Book of Daniel are ascribed to the court of Nebuchadnezzar where Daniel was an interpreter of dreams.

Nebushasban (Nebushazbar) ("[The god] Nabu save me"). Babylonian officer (according to the most familiar translation, a eunuch) who helped to rescue the prophet Jeremiah from prison (Jer 39:13–14).

Nebuzaradan Babylonian officer at the court of Nebuchadnezzar. He was present at the sacking of Jerusalem in 587 BC, where he was in charge of firing the city and of the deportation to Babylon of many citizens of Judah. On Nebuchadnezzar's order he freed Jehoiakim (II Kgs 25:8–17; Jer 52:30).

Necho (II) Egyptian pharaoh, who succeeded his father, Psammetichus I, and ruled c.610/9–595 BC. Most of his rule was spent in fighting the Babylonians. Eventually he was forced to abandon parts of his empire to the Babylonians but still retained his place on the Egyptian throne. After his defeat at the hands of Nebuchadnezzar at the battle of Carchemish (Jer 46:2), Necho turned his attention towards home and the prosperity of Egypt within its borders. He oversaw the cutting of a canal between the Nile and the Red Sea, afterwards completed by Darius the Persian.

Nehemiah Son of Hacaliah; cup-bearer to King Artaxerxes II of Persia (465–424 BC). On hearing of the ruined condition of Jerusalem, he requested permission to go there and the king sent him there to rebuild the city and gave him building materials and an armed guard. Nehemiah's rebuilding of the walls of Jerusalem was opposed by a group centered around Samaria, including Sanballat and Tobiah (Neh 2:17–20; 6:1–14). Nevertheless, Nehemiah and the Jews managed to complete rebuilding the walls within 52 days (Neh chaps. 3–4; 6:15–19). By instituting laws, he assisted in the repopulation of Jerusalem and also introduced various reforms in religious and legal matters. He was particularly concerned about the avoidance of intermarriage with foreign wives (Neh 10). After returning to Persia, he again visited Jerusalem, expelled Tobiah from the Temple, and made further laws to ensure Sabbath observance, prevent intermarriage, and strengthen the unity of his people with their God (Neh 13:4–27). See also III. 21, Books of the Old Testament.

Nergal-Sharezer (Nergal-Sarezer) Senior officer in Nebuchadnezzar's army, who participated in the sacking of Jerusalem in 586 BC (Jer 39:1–8).

Nimrod Son of Cush. Known as "Nimrod the mighty hunter before the Lord" (Gen 10:8–12; I Chr 1:10), he was a warrior living in Babylonia. He is said to have founded the cities of Nineveh and Calah in Assyria and the land adjoining Assyria became known as the "land of Nimrod" (Micah 5:6).

Noadiah ("the Lord has arranged an encounter"). A prophet. See III.28, Prophets.

Noah releasing a dove from the ark. Detail of a mosaic on the ceiling of St. Mark's Cathedral, Venice; 13th century.

Noah Hero of the Flood epic. A righteous man who "walked with God" (Gen 6:9), Noah was selected by God to survive the Flood and continue humankind. He was instructed to build an ark and to make provision for his family and a representation of animals (Gen 6:13–22). After the Flood, God made a covenant with Noah, setting a rainbow in the sky as a token of remembrance and a promise that the catastrophe would not recur. Noah turned to husbandry and planted a vineyard, and an incident is recounted when he was inebriated (Gen 9). Noah is known as one of the three "righteous" men alongside Job and Daniel (Ezek 14:14, 20) and his righteousness is also mentioned in the New Testament (Heb 11:7; II Pet 2:5).

Obadiah ("servant of God"). A prophet. See III.28, Prophets.

Obed-Edom Man from Gath in whose house David placed the ark of the Lord before it was moved to Jerusalem. It remained there for three months, and the members of the household became blessed by its presence (II Sam 6:10–12).

Og King of Bashan; ruler of many towns in Transjordan. He is portrayed as being of the race of the Rephaim, giants of whom the Israelites were in fear. After their success in battle with the Canaanite king Sihon, Moses and the Children of Israel went on to defeat Og and his kingdom, a victory which became proverbial (cf. Ps 135:11; 136:20). Og's giant bed, made of black basalt, was captured by the Ammonites and displayed at Rabbath-Ammon (Deut 3:2; Josh 12:4–6; 13:12).

Omri King of Israel. See III.27, Kings.

Onan Son of Judah (Gen 38:4). When his elder brother Er died, he was expected by law to marry his brother's widow. Onan refused to consummate the union and "spilt his seed upon the floor" (presumably coitus interruptus), whereupon God, in anger, struck him dead (Gen 38:4–10).

Oreb ("raven"). Midianite prince defeated by the tribe of Ephraim. His head was brought to Gideon (Judg 7:25).

Orpah Moabite woman who married one of Naomi's two sons, the other marrying Ruth. When Naomi decided to return to her people Ruth accompanied her but Orpah followed Naomi's request and stayed behind in Moab. (Ruth 1:14–15).

Osnapper (Asnapper) Assyrian king (possibly Ashurbanipal) who settled peoples from Mesopotamia in Samaria (Ezra 4:10).

Othniel Son of Kenaz; first of the judges (see III.27, Judges).

Pagiel Son of Ocran of the tribe of Asher who assisted Moses in taking the first census of the Children of Israel. He led the armies of the tribe of Asher in the wilderness (Num 10:26).

Palti (Paltiel) ("God is my advisor"). Son of Laish of the tribe of Benjamin. When David fled from Saul (I

Sam 25:44), Palti was given David's wife, Michal, but later she was taken back.

Pashhur (**Pashur**) Son of Malchijah; father of Jeroham (I Chr 9:12). When Nebuchadnezzar attacked Jerusalem, Pashhur was sent with Zephaniah by Zedekiah the king to ask for a prophecy from Jeremiah (Jer 21:1-2). Jeremiah foresaw the triumph of Nebuchadnezzar (Jer 38:2-3).

A contemporary also called Pashhur was a priest in the Temple who had Jeremiah punished for foretelling the destruction of the Temple. Jeremiah predicted his exile to Babylon (Jer 20:1-6).

Pekah ("[God] has opened [his eyes]"). King of Israel. See III.27, Kings.

Pekahiah ("God has opened [his eyes]"). King of Israel. See III.27, Kings.

Pelatiah ("God rescued"). A Levite who signed the covenant, a detailed agreement not to break God's laws and not to "forsake the house of our God" after all the former wickedness in the land in the time of Nehemiah (Neh 10).

Another three men with this name are mentioned in the Bible: a Simeonite who battled with the Amalekites and occupied their land when King Hezekiah ruled in Judah (I Chr 4:42); a member of the family of David, son of Hananiah; and a son of Benaiah, a leader of the people in the time of Ezekiel. While Ezekiel was prophesying, Benaiah fell dead as a punishment for his heathen ways (Ezek 2:1,13).

Peninnah One of the wives of Elkanah. She bore many children while her co-wife, Hannah, was barren (I Sam 1:4).

Statue of Rameses II, thought to be the Egyptian Pharaoh of the Exodus.

Perez ("breach"). One of the sons born to Judah and Tamar. He was the eponymous ancestor of the family of Perezites (Num 26:20).

Pharaoh (Egyptian for "great house"). Title of Egyptian kings. The Pharaoh of the Exodus was probably Rameses II.

Phicol Commander of army of Abimelech, king of Gerar (Gen 21:22,32; 26:26).

Phinehas Son of Eleazar the priest and grandson of Aaron the high priest (Ex 6:25; I Chr 6:3-4,50; Ezra 7:1-5). During the lapse into heathenism among the Israelites at Shittim, he slew a man who lay with a Midianite woman. For his zeal, God rewarded him and his descendants with an abiding priesthood (Num 25:1-15).

He took part in Moses' war against the Midianites and was given the privileged position of attending to the sacred vessels of worship and of sounding the alarm trumpet (Num 31:6).

Another Phinehas was the son of Eli the priest. He and his brother Hophni abused the office of priesthood and their death in the battle of Aphek was seen as punishment for their sins (I Sam 4).

Potiphar ("he whom [the sun god] Re has given"). An officer of Pharaoh and captain of the guard who purchased Joseph from the Midianites (Gen 37:36). He imprisoned Joseph following his wife's accusation against him (Gen 39:7-20).

Poti-Phera ("he whom [the sun god] Re has given"). Priest of On. Joseph married his daughter Asenath (Gen 41:45, 50).

Puah ("young woman"). A midwife who refused to abide by Pharaoh's cruel decree whereby all Hebrew new-born males were to be killed (Ex 1:15-22).

Pul See Tiglath-pileser.

Rabshakeh Assyrian official sent by King Sennacherib at the head of a delegation to persuade King Hezekiah of Judah to surrender (II Kgs 18).

Rachel ("ewe"). Matriarch. See III.24, Matriarchs.

Rahab A prostitute of Jericho who sheltered two of Joshua's men sent to spy out the land. When the King of Jericho sent to arrest them, she made possible their escape by letting down a scarlet cord from her roof where she had hidden them. When the Israelites conquered Jericho, she and her family were spared (Josh 2, 6:22-25). She is listed as an ancestor of Jesus (Matt 1:5) and praised in the New Testament (Heb 11:31; James 2:25).

Rebekah Matriarch. See III.24, The Matriarchs.

Rechab A Benjamite who, with his brother, killed Saul's son Ishbosheth while he was sleeping and brought his head to David. David punished them both for their treachery with death (II Sam 4:1-9).

Also the eponymous ancestor of the nomadic clan of Rechabites (probably Kenites in origin), who adopted an ascetic lifestyle which forbade them to own land, grow vines, drink wine, or live in houses (Jer 35).

Rehoboam King of Judah. See III.27, Kings.

Reuel ("friend of God"). Son of Esau and Basemath (Gen 36:4,10,17; I Chr 1:35).

Reuel is also one of the names of Moses' father-in-law (also called Jethro) (Ex 2:18; Num 10:29).

Rezin ("man of favor"). King of Damascus who, with his ally Pekah of Samariah, led an attack on King Ahaz of Judah when the latter refused to join them in an anti-Assyrian front. Rezin was killed in the victorious attack on Damascus (II Kgs 16:9).

Rezon ("favor"). Ruler of Aram-Damascus during the reign of Solomon (I Kgs 2:23-24).

Rizpah ("glowing coal"). Daughter of Aiah; concubine of Saul, who bore him two sons, Armoni and Mephibosheth (II Sam 21:8). After Saul's death, Abner, hoping to succeed to the throne, took Rizpah for himself, but Saul's son Ishbosheth disapproved of the union (II Sam 3:7). David later surrendered her two sons to the Gibeonites as atonement for Saul's crimes against them, and they were hanged. Rizpah sat day and night by the unburied corpses allowing no creature near them until David, learning of her vigil, saw to their proper burial (II Sam 21:1-14).

Ruth A Moabite woman living in the time of the Judges. When Naomi came to Moab with her family from Judah in time of famine, Ruth married Mahlon, one of her two sons. After Naomi and Ruth were both widowed, she insisted on accompanying Naomi to Bethlehem. In Bethlehem, Naomi sent her to glean in the fields of her husband's relative, who was attracted to her and eventually married her. Their son was Obed the grandfather of David (I Chr 2:12) and an ancestor of Jesus (Matt 1:5). The story is to be found in the Book of Ruth. See III.21, Books of the Old Testament.

Samson ("little sun"). A judge. See III.26, The Judges.

Samuel A prophet. See III.28, Prophets.

Sanballat ("Sin [the moon god] gave life [to him]"). Governor of Samaria under the Persians in the time of Nehemiah. He was hostile to the Jerusalem community and opposed Nehemiah's plans to rebuild the walls of Jerusalem (Neh 2:10,19; 4:1-2; 6:6-7). His daughter married a priest in Jerusalem whom Nehemiah expelled (Neh 13:28).

Sarah (Sarai, "princess"). The first matriarch of the Jewish people. See III.24, The Matriarchs.

Sargon ("the king is legitimate"). Name given to several Mesopotamian kings. The name, openly declaring the legitimacy of the monarch, implies that he was actually an usurper of the throne.

The first Sargon, who is not mentioned in the Bible, is known only from cuneiform texts. The history of this Sargon parallels the Moses story at the beginning of Exodus. Sargon II of Assyria (721-705 BC) was originally the general who conquered Samaria, the capital of the Northern Kingdom, and exiled its inhabitants (II Kgs 17). He later took the throne in a coup against Merodach-Baladan and declared himself king of Baby-

lonia. Sargon II was killed in battle against the Cimmerians; his remains were never recovered from the battlefield, prompting his successor, Sennacherib, to initiate a commission of inquiry to determine what sin Sargon had committed to warrant this ignominious death. This may have inspired the prophet Isaiah to declare that the sins of Sargon were arrogance and brutality (Is 14:20-21).

Sargon II, king of Assyria.

Saul First king of Israel. See III.27, Kings.

Segub The younger son of Hiel of Bethel who rebuilt the city of Jericho. He died in fulfillment of Joshua's curse (I Kgs 16:34) that the sons of the man who rebuilt Jericho would die (Josh 6:26).

Sennacherib King of Assyria (705-681 BC). His first campaign involved an attack on a rebellion in Babylonia, the leader of which, Merodach-Baladan, had requested the support of King Hezekiah of Judah (II Kgs 20:12-19; Is 39). After suppressing the revolt in Mesopotamia, Sennacherib turned his attention to the east where an anti-Assyrian coalition was being created by Egypt. Sennacherib soon defeated these peoples, including various city-states in Palestine, and eventually besieged Jerusalem (701 BC). However, for some reason (the Bible says a plague broke out in his camp) he had to break off the siege and return to Babylonia (II Kgs 19:35). He was assassinated by his sons while he was worshiping, apparently shortly after his return to his capital, Nineveh (II Kgs 19:37).

Seraiah Son of Azariah; high priest in Jerusalem dur-

Sennacherib, king of Assyria seated on his throne. From a stone relief; 8th century BC.

ing the Babylonian siege in 586 BC which culminated in its destruction. Seraiah was taken prisoner and executed by Nebuchadnezzar (II Kgs 25:18–21).

Another Seraiah, son of Tanhumeth, was an army officer who remained in Judah at the time of the exile by Nebuchadnezzar, and joined Gedaliah whom Nebuchadnezzar had made governer of Judah. After Gedaliah had been murdered, Seraiah and his other supporters fled to Egypt (II Kgs 25:22–25).

Seth Third son of Adam and Eve, father to Enosh, who lived to the age of 912. Seth's birth, coming as it did after the killing of Abel, was considered by Eve as a God-given consolation (Gen 4:25).

Shadrach Babylonian name given to Hananiah, one of the administrators of the province of Babylon appointed at Daniel's request (Dan 2:49). Together with Meshach and Abed-Nego (in Hebrew, Mishael and Azariah) and Daniel, Shadrach was educated at Nebuchadnezzar's court (Dan 1:3–7) and remained faithful to the God of Israel (Dan 1:8–16), refusing to bow down to the gods of the Babylonians and being thrown into a fiery furnace. Their miraculous survival brought the king to praise the God who redeemed them for their unswerving trust (Dan 3:1–30).

Shallum A king of Israel. See III.27, Kings.

Shalman Identity uncertain. The name could be a contraction of Shalmaneser (V) the Assyrian king, or may be Salamanu King of Moab. He is reported by Hosea the prophet to have besieged and destroyed Beth-Arbel (Hos 10:14).

Shalmaneser Name of several Assyrian kings. Shalmaneser V (727–722 BC) besieged Samaria for three years. It fell to his successor, Sargon II.

Shamgar A judge. See III.26, Judges.

Shammah Brother of David. He was one of the sons of Jesse whom Samuel passed over in favor of David in anointing Saul's successor (I Sam 16:9).

Two other men of the same name were among David's 30 chosen warriors (II Sam 23:11,25,33).

Shaphan ("rock badger"). Scribe of King Josiah sent to the Temple to take money for the workmen. While he was there, Hilkiah the high priest showed him the "Book of the Law" that had been found. After reading it, Shaphan took it to the king. The latter, moved by its contents, sent Shaphan and his son, Ahikam, to Huldah the prophetess for advice (II Kgs 22:3–14).

Sharezer One of the sons of King Sennacherib of Assyria who killed their father while he was praying (I Kgs 19:37; Is 37:38).

Shear-Jashub ("the remnant will return"). Symbolic name given by the prophet Isaiah to one of his sons to symbolize his belief in God's mercy (Is 7:3).

Sheba Son of Bichri of the tribe of Benjamin, who led an unsuccessful revolt of the men of Israel against David and the people of Judah. He and his men were pursued and Sheba was beheaded (II Sam 20:1–22).

Sheba, Queen of Sabean queen who, laden with riches, traveled to Jerusalem to test King Solomon's wisdom. Scholars have surmised that the real purpose of the visit was to arrange a trade agreement between the two countries (I Kgs 10). In the New Testament, Jesus refers to her as the queen "from the south" (Matt 12:42).

Shebna Minister, secretary, and treasurer to King Hezekiah of Judah. Isaiah prophesied that the ostentatious tomb built by Shebna for himself would be his downfall and that he would die in a strange land (Is 22:15–19).

Shechem Son of Hamor, king of the city of Shechem. Shechem's rape of Jacob's daughter, Dinah, resulted in her brothers, Simeon and Levi, massacring the inhabitants of the city in revenge (Gen 34).

Shelumiel ("the Lord is my peace"). Son of Zurishaddai of the tribe of Simeon. He was chosen by God through Moses as captain or representative of his tribe and assisted in the census taken of the Children of Israel in the wilderness (Num 1:2–6). He later made the offering in the tabernacle on behalf of his tribe (Num 7:36–41).

Shem ("renown"). Eldest son of Noah who, together with the rest of Noah's family, survived the Flood. Shem and his brother Japheth covered their father's nakedness when he became drunk and received a blessing (Gen 9:18–27). Traditionally, he is the ancestor of the Semites.

Shemaiah ("God listened"). Of the 28 individuals called Shemaiah mentioned in the Bible, one was a prophet (see III.28, Prophets).

Shemeber King of Zeboiim, one of the five Canaanite kings attacked and defeated by Chedorlaomer of Elam in the valley of Siddim by the Dead Sea (Gen 14:2).

Shemer Man from whom Omri king of Israel bought the hill on which Samaria was built (I Kgs 16:24).

Sheshbazzar ("Sin [the moon god] guard the father"). Governor of Judah under Cyrus king of Babylon, given the important mission of returning to Jerusalem the holy vessels taken from the Temple by Nebuchadnezzar after the sacking of the city in 586 BC. With Cyrus' protection, financial help, and encouragement, Sheshbazzar helped to lay the new foundations of the temple at Jerusalem (Ezra 5:13-17). He was succeeded by his nephew, Zerubbabel.

Shimei ("[God] has heard"). Son of Gera, of the tribe of Benjamin. A relative of Saul, he bore bitter feelings toward David whom he called "a man of blood" (II Sam 16:5ff), and whom he cursed openly. Although David forgave him at the time, he ordered his successor, Solomon, to punish him. When Solomon became king he forbade Shimei ever to leave the city of Jerusalem. He was killed returning from a trip to Gath some years later by Solomon's men (I Kgs 2:36-48).

Shiphrah ("beautiful"). Midwife who refused to accept the law made by Pharaoh whereby all males born to the Hebrews should be killed (Ex 1:15-22).

Shishak Libyan founder of the 22nd Dynasty in Egypt. He reigned as Pharoah Sheshonk I for 21 years. After Solomon's death he attacked Judah and Israel, destroying many towns and leaving behind many signs of his occupation, the severity of which is confirmed by present archaeological discoveries: fragments of inscriptions, fires, massive destruction, etc. (II Chr 12).

Shobach, Shophach Aramean general under King Hadadezer when Aram was at war with Ammon. He was killed by David's men in a battle with the Israelites at Helam in Transjordan (II Sam 10:16-18).

Shobi An Ammonite prince of the house of King Nahash. Shobi provided refreshment and a haven for David and his men when they were hiding at the time of Absalom's revolt (II Sam 17:27).

Sihon Amorite king who refused to allow the Israelites free passage through his country. Moses led his army against Sihon and killed him at Jahaz. The territory subsequently occupied became that of the tribes Gad and Reuben (Deut 3:12).

Simeon Eponymous ancestor of the tribe of Simeon. See III.22, The Twelve Tribes.

Sisera Commander of the army of Jabin, king of Canaan (Judg 4). He oppressed Israel for 28 years until defeated by the Israelite army led by Deborah and Barak. Fleeing the battlefield, he took refuge in the tent of Jael, who killed him by driving a tent peg through his skull (Judg 4).

So King of Egypt (II Kgs 17:4) with whom Hoshea conspired to rebel against Assyria, thereby bringing the wrath of the Assyrian enemy upon Israel. Scholars are undecided in identifying So as a king or as a somewhat lesser army commander (II Kgs 17:4).

Solomon Third king of Israel. See III.27, Kings.

Talmai Aramean king of Geshur, whose daughter Maacah married David and bore Absalom (II Sam 3:3). After killing his brother Amnon, Absalom fled to the court of Talmai where he stayed for three years (II Sam 13:37).

Tamar ("date palm"). Canaanite woman who married Judah's son Er, and after Er's death, married his brother, Onan. When Onan died, Judah felt she was bringing his sons bad luck and did not let his third son, Shela marry her, whereupon she disguised herself as a prostitute, seduced Judah himself, and bore him twin sons, Perez and Zerach. Judah admitted that she had been in the right (Gen 38). She is mentioned in the genealogy of Jesus (Matt 1:3).

Tattenai Persian governor of the region beyond the Euphrates under Darius, the Persian king (Ezra 5:3; 6:6, 13).

Terah Son of Nahor. Father of Abraham and his brothers Nahor and Haran. Terah journeyed with his family from Ur of the Chaldees to Haran, where he died (Gen 11:24-32). Joshua called him an idolator who worshiped "other gods" (Josh 24:2).

Tibni Son of Ginath, rival of Omri for the Israelite throne. In a long war between the two men and their followers, Tibni was killed and Omri gained the throne (I Kgs 16:21-23).

Tiglath-pileser III (referred to as Pul in I Chr 5:26). Assyrian king, the son of Adadnirari III, who ruled Assyria in 745-727 BC. He brought pressure to bear upon the North Syrian states which were later made provinces of Assyria, and he received tribute from Rezin of Damascus, Menahem of Samaria, and many other rulers.

Against Israel's advice, Ahaz of Judah, who also paid tribute, asked him for assistance to withstand attacks on Judah by an Israel-Aramean coalition (II Chr 28:17-18; II Kgs 16:17). In 733 BC the Assyrians attacked Damascus and within a year had defeated the remainder of their allies, including Israel, whose territories were annexed and from which many were exiled to Assyria (II Kgs 15:29).

Tirhakah Ethiopian king of Egypt (approximate reign 690-664 BC) who, according to the Bible (II Kgs 19:19; Is 37:9) attacked Sennacherib, king of Assyria, in 701 BC. From other historic sources it appears that he cannot have been more than army commander at the time, and the biblical title of "king" appears anticipatory.

Tobiah ("Yahweh is good"). An Ammonite who together with Sanballat actively opposed and made repeated attempts to foil Nehemiah's project to rebuild the walls of Jerusalem (Neh 2:10-20; 6:1-14).

Toi King of Hamath who sent David gifts after the latter's defeat of Hadadezer, king of Jobah (II Sam 8:10).

Tola Judge. See III.26, Judges.

Tubal-Cain Son of Lamech and Zillah; a metal worker seen as the father of metallurgy (Gen 4:22).

Uriah ("God is my light"). Name of several individuals in the Bible including: 1) a Hittite, one of David's "mighty warriors" and the husband of Bathsheba with whom David committed adultery. When Bathsheba became pregnant, David deliberately sent Uriah to fight at a dangerous area in the front where he was killed (II Sam 1-24). 2) Priest who was most likely one of the witnesses when Isaiah wrote his prophecy on Samaria (Is 8:2). He aided King Ahaz in replacing the Temple altar with an altar on an Assyrian model (II Kgs 16:10-16). 3) a prophet in the time of Jeremiah. His prophecies angered King Jehoiakim and Uriah fled to Egypt but was brought back by the king's men and summarily executed (Jer 26:10-24).

Uzza, Uzzah Son of Abinadab, a Levite. He was struck dead when he put out his hand to steady the ark which was in danger of falling as it was brought from his father's house at Gibeah on its way to the City of David (II Sam 6:6-7).

Uzziah King. See III.27, Kings.

Vashti Consort of King Ahasuerus. When summoned before the king's guests at a banquet in his palace at Shushan to display her beauty, she refused to appear. Angered, Ahasuerus deposed her as queen and banished her from the palace (Est 1:10-22).

Zabad ("gift"). Son of Shimeath, a woman of Ammon. Servant at the court of King Joash of Judah. Zabad, together with another servant, slew the king as he lay sick in bed, to avenge the death of Zechariah, son of Jehoiada the priest, who was stoned to death at the command of the king for speaking of the transgressions of his people and of their forsaking the House of God (II Chr 24:20-26).

Zadok ("righteous"). Son of Ahitub; a priest at the court of David. He took part in the selection and accounting of Solomon as successor to David, and he and his descendants were chief priests in the Temple until its destruction (I Kgs 1:7, 39).

Zalmunna King of Midian who oppressed the land of Israel. He was killed by Gideon in revenge for executing his brothers (Judg 8:4-21).

Zebulun Eponymous ancestor of the tribe of Zebulun. See III.22, The Twelve Tribes.

Zechariah ("God has remembered"). Son of Jehoiada the priest. He was stoned to death in the Temple court at the orders of King Joash for scolding the people for their sins against God (II Chr 24:20-23).

Zechariah is also the name of a prophet (see III.28, Prophets) and of a king of Israel (see III.27, Kings).

Zedekiah ("God is [my] righteousness"). One of 400 prophets at the court of King Ahab who joined in falsely prophesying the victory of the king at the battle of Gilead against the Arameans. Micaiah, who predicted the opposite, was struck by Zedekiah on the cheek (I Kgs 22:13-28; II Chr 18:12-27).

Another Zedekiah, son of Maaseiah, and a contemporary of Jeremiah, was also a false prophet who lied to the exiles in Babylon about an imminent return to the homeland. Jeremiah severely reprimanded him for his immoral life and predicted his death at the hand of Nebuchadnezzar, which prophecy was duly realized when Zedekiah was roasted alive (Jer 29:21-23).

Zedekiah is also the name of a king; see III.27, Kings.

Zelophehad Father of five daughters and no sons. When he died his daughters claimed his inheritance, which was awarded to them by Moses, thus originating the law whereby inheritance from a man who has no male heirs goes immediately to his daughters with the proviso that they do not marry out of the tribe (Num 27:8; 36:1-9).

Zephaniah ("God has hidden away"). Son of the priest Maaseiah. He was sent by King Zedekiah to ask Jeremiah to pray for deliverance of Jerusalem from the Babylonian siege. After the fall of Jerusalem, Zephaniah, who was deputy high priest, was among those whom Nebuzaradan exiled to Riblah where they were killed by the king of Babylon (II Kgs 25:18).

Another Zephaniah was a prophet of Judah; see III.28, Prophets.

Zerah ("shining"). Ethiopian army commander who led the Egyptian forces invading Judah and was repelled by King Asa and his army at Mareshah, driven back, and finally defeated at Gerar (II Chr 15:10-19).

Zerah was also one of the twin sons born to Tamar and Judah (Gen 38:18,30). His descendants were the clan of Zarhites (Num 26:20).

Zeresh Wife of Haman, who encouraged him to build a lofty gallows on which to hang Mordecai. After Esther denounced him, Haman himself was hanged on those gallows (Est 5:14; 6:13; 7:10).

Zerubbabel ("seed of Babylonia"). Grandson of King Jehoiakim (Ezra 3:2). In 520 BC Zerubbabel laid the foundations for the rebuilding of the Temple. He refused permission for the residents of the land to participate in the construction, leading to the schism with the Samaritans (Ezra 4). Both Haggai (Hag 2:21-23) and Zechariah (Zech 4:6-10) imply that messianic hopes were placed in him. He is mentioned in the genealogy of Jesus (Matt 1:12; Luke 3:27).

Ziba Slave of Saul who informed David that Mephibosheth, the lame son of Jonathan, had survived. David charged him with the care of Mephibosheth. During Absalom's revolt, when David was forced to go into hiding, Ziba brought him food. He falsely alleged that Mephibosheth had turned against the king, and David, believing him, made over the property of Mephibosheth to him. When the truth was revealed, David decided to divide the property between the two since, despite Ziba's lies, David was indebted to him for his loyalty during the revolt (II Sam 9:9–21; 19:24–29).

Zilpah Slave of Jacob's wife Leah, who gave her to Jacob as his concubine. She bore him two sons, Gad and Asher (Gen 30:11–15).

Zimri King. See III.27, Kings.

Zipporah Wife of Moses; daughter of Jethro, the Midianite priest. When Moses' life was endangered, Zipporah was convinced that the circumcision of her son Gershom, which she had previously opposed, would appease God and thereby save her husband's life. She perfomed the operation herself, and Moses remained unharmed (Ex 4:24–26). She had a second son named Eliezer.

GIANTS

Whereas it is conjectured that the average height of a man in the biblical world was about five feet, certain individuals and races mentioned in the Bible attained a height considerably greater. These people included the Nephilim, thought to be among the original inhabitants of Canaan (Gen 6:4). Their abnormal stature earned them the status of demigods, comparable to the Titans of ancient Greek mythology. Upon bringing back their report to Moses, the spies reported about the Nephilim that "we were in our own sight as grasshoppers, and so we were in their sight" (Num 13:33). Most of the early giants in the Bible are said to be descended from Anak (Deut 9:2), whose name apparently denotes anyone of an abnormally large size (Num 13:28). Giants were frequently used as warriors, and their great height was often enough to scare off their opponents (I Sam 17:1–11).

Ahiman, Sheshai, Talmai Sons of Arba who inhabited Hebron at the time of the Israelite conquest. They were defeated by Caleb (Josh 15:13–14).

Anak Son of Arba (Josh 15:13; 21:11); progenitor of a nation (Deut 9:2) inhabiting the area around Hebron (Num 13:22). Though they were driven out by Caleb (Josh 15:13–14), a remnant of them remained in the Philistine cities of Gath, Gaza, and Ashdod (Josh 11:21–22).

Arba Related to Anak and regarded as the greatest hero of the Anakim. Hebron, the city in which Arba lived, was also called Kirjath Arba (Josh 14:15).

Goliath Most famous of the biblical giants, slain by David at the behest of Saul (I Sam 17). In another version of the story, Elhanan of Bethlehem was credited with slaying Goliath (II Sam 21:19).

Ishbi-Benob Philistine giant defeated by Abishai son of Zeruiah, one of David's 30 heroes (II Sam 21:16–17).

Lahmi Philistine giant, brother of Goliath, killed by Elhanan of Bethlehem (I Chr 20:5).

Og King of Bashan in Transjordan, defeated by Moses (Deut 3:1–13). Og was reputed to have in Rabbath-Ammon an iron bedstead nine cubits long and four cubits wide (Deut 3:11).

Philistine Giant Inhabitant of Gath, noted for having six fingers on each hand and six toes on each foot. The giant was slain by David's nephew, Jonathan (I Chr 20:6–8).

Sippai, Saph Philistine giant slain by Sibbechai the Hushathite, one of David's 30 heroes (II Sam 21:18; I Chr 20:4).

Mycenean warrior carrying a shield and a spear, and wearing a horned helmet and leather body armor, as in the biblical description of Goliath; from the "Warrior's Vase," Greece.

The Temple was the central sanctuary of the Israelite religion in ancient times. It stood on Mount Moriah in Jerusalem, traditionally identified as the site of the binding of Isaac. Although land for the Temple was originally purchased by King David for the purpose of building a central religious edifice, God forbade David to erect the structure, as his hands were bloodied by war. David did take part in the planning, but construction was carried out by his son Solomon.

The Temple of Solomon was dedicated c.960 BC and remained standing until the Babylonian conquest in 586 BC. With the return of the Jews to Judah from exile in Babylon, work was begun on a Second Temple, which was dedicated in 520 BC. Although this second structure was, at first, less impressive than the original, in time it was expanded and enriched. The height of the Second Temple's glory was reached in approximately 20 BC when Herod the Great began to refurbish the existing structure, making the Temple the gem of the Near East. The rabbis of the day declared: "One who has not seen the Temple of Herod has never seen a beautiful building." Contemporary Roman authors also declared the Temple to be one of the wonders of the ancient world. It was destroyed in AD 70 by a Roman army putting down the Jewish revolts against Roman rule.

FIRST TEMPLE

The First Temple was erected by King Solomon on a stretch of land overlooking the Jebusite city of Jerusalem. Work on the Temple was begun in the seventh year of Solomon's reign (964 BC) and lasted seven years. Solomon made every effort to ensure that the building would be a masterwork, enlisting his ally, Hiram, king of Tyre, to assist in planning and construction. Hiram supplied Solomon with cedar, cypress wood, and gold, as well as skilled craftsmen.

The Temple itself stood in a royal compound containing Solomon's palace, a palace for Solomon's wife, the daughter of Pharaoh, the harem, a Hall of Judgment, and a Hall of Cedars. The Temple was a stone building overlooking the remainder of the compound. It was 60 cubits (90 ft) long and 20 cubits (30 ft) wide; its height was 30 cubits (45 ft). In front of the Temple was a square patio of 10 cubits (15 ft) on which were situated two bronze pillars called Jachin and Boaz. Surrounding the main edifice was a building three storeys in height, containing storerooms for the Temple treasures. This was in turn surrounded by a courtyard, delineating the actual Temple compound, and containing the main altar.

The main building of the Temple consisted of two rooms. The first, a hall of 20 by 40 cubits (30 by 60 ft), had ten golden candelabra, a gold-plated altar for incense, and a gold-plated table for the showbread. The chamber was paneled with cedar wood and decorated with carvings inlaid in gold; the floor of the hall was set with cypress wood. A door led from the hall to the Holy of Holies, the Temple's most sacred sanctuary, entered by the High Priest only on the Day of Atonement. The Holy of Holies was a square chamber measuring 20 by 20 cubits (30 by 30 ft). It too was paneled with cedar wood and inlaid with gold. Unlike the main hall, however, its floor was also made of cedar wood and gold plated. The Holy of Holies contained the Ark of the Covenant, bearing the Tablets of the Law of Moses. Two wooden cherubs 10 cubits (15 feet) in height spread their wings as a canopy over the Ark.

In the surrounding Temple compound were three courtyards: the priestly court where the sacrificial rite was performed, an enclosure for the male worshipers, and an enclosure for female worshipers. Apart from the main sacrificial altar of bronze, the priestly court also contained an immense bronze water basin known as the "sea," resting on the backs of 12 bronze oxen. In the courtyard were also ten smaller wheeled basins with which the priests could perform ritual ablutions prior to offering sacrifices. These basins stood opposite the entrance of the sanctuary, five to the north of the portal and five to the south.

Throughout the Temple's existence, its centrality in Israelite culture varied significantly. In Solomon's period, it was the focal point of all religious activity for the United Kingdom. However, when the Northern tribes seceded, they built their own cultic centers in Dan and Bethel. In the four centuries of the Temple's existence, several renovations were made. Prominent among these was the work done by King Joash, who ordered that money brought to the priests be used to refurbish worn implements (II Kgs 12). The religious reforms of King Josiah gained momentum on the discovery of a previously unknown book of the Law (identified as Deuteronomy) as the Temple was being purified. Other kings, notably Manasseh and Amon, achieved notoriety for introducing pagan rituals into the Temple.

Sacrifices were offered in the Temple on behalf of both the individual and the community. Individual sacrifices were offered as both a means of atoning for sins and a sign of thanksgiving to God upon momentous occasions. The daily ritual of the Temple included sacrifices offered regularly on behalf of the nation, such as the morning and afternoon sacrifices, and the special sacrifices offered on Sabbaths, festivals, and the New Moon (Num 28-29). On the eve of Passover, the most important of the pilgrimage festivals, the entire nation would gather around the Temple compound to offer the Paschal lamb. Other rituals in the Temple included the offering of the Omer (the first measure of barley) on the second day of Passover, the bringing of the first fruits on Pentecost, and the water libation on Tabernacles. In time, the Temple ritual became increasingly complex, and achieved a certain level of pageantry. Musicians and singers accompanied the sacrificial rite and many of the Psalms were composed for use in the Temple. They were sung by a choir of Levites, the tribe dedicated to the Temple service and responsible for its administration, judicial office, and keeping of the gates.

The First Temple was destroyed during the Babylonian conquest of Jerusalem in 586 BC. A description of the First Temple is given in I Kings ch.6-8.

SECOND TEMPLE

Reconstruction of the Temple was enabled by King Cyrus of Persia, who issued a decree in 538 BC allowing Jews to return to Judah from Babylonian exile. The construction of the Second Temple was marked by controversy with the local Samaritan population, which attempted to thwart the returning exiles' efforts. Construction was even halted for a short period, and only recommenced as a result of the exhortations of the prophets Haggai and Zechariah. Upon completion and dedication of the Temple in 520 BC, the office of High Priest was conferred upon Joshua, a descendant of Zadok, High Priest in Solomon's time. Two accounts are given in the Bible of the reaction of the people of Judah to the new Temple. Whereas the younger returnees rejoiced at the re-establishment of Jewish sovereignty represented by the Temple, the older returnees grieved that the new structure was a poor imitation of Solomon's Temple.

With the return of Ezra and Nehemiah to Jerusalem, approximately 70-80 years after its dedication, the Temple's central position in Jewish life was restored. Among the reformations carried out by Ezra was the verification of the genealogy of priests and Levites and the redistribution of Temple tasks among them.

The centrality of the Temple was reaffirmed by the Seleucid monarch, Antiochus III (223-187), who issued a decree ensuring the sanctity of the Temple and its adjoining areas, and forbade the introduction of unclean animals into Jerusalem. With the advent of his successor, Antiochus IV (Epiphanes; 175-164), the Temple was defiled, with Antiochus IV and a faction of Hellenized Jews converting it into a center for pagan worship. The brutal repression suffered by the Jews at the hands of Antiochus sparked the Hasmonean revolt, which succeeded in driving the Seleucids from Judah. With the fall of Jerusalem to Judah Maccabee, leader of the

Model showing how the Temple looked from a southeastern angle.

Stone inscribed "to the place of trumpeting," found on the Temple Mount.

revolt, the Temple was rededicated, and Jewish ritual restored in 164 BC. The day of the rededication of the Temple, 25 Kislev, is celebrated by Jews to this day as the Feast of Hanukkah.

Coin of the time of Bar Kokhba showing the façade of the Temple; 2nd century.

Upon their assumption of power, the Hasmonean family united the roles of High Priest and king, thereby ending the 800-year dynasty of the House of Zadok. The first Hasmonean High Priest was Jonathan, who assumed the post in c.150 BC. His descendants continued to function as priest-kings for approximately 100 years, until the appointment of Herod as ruler of Judea. Under Herod, the office of High Priest became politicized, with High Priests appointed and deposed at Herod's whim. Herod also introduced sacrifices on behalf of the Roman emperor, a practice which continued until the outbreak of the Jewish war in AD 66. Roman armies destroyed the Temple in AD 70 and carried its treasures and sacred vessels to Rome.

Structure. Nothing is known of the structure of the early Second Temple except that it was but a pale reflection of the First. Herod undertook a massive renovation of the Temple. All existing descriptions of the Second Temple, as found in the Talmud and Josephus, refer to Herod's edifice.

Herod began his renovations in the year 20 BC and conducted a dedication one and a half years later. The actual work continued for decades, and recent archaeological evidence indicates that it was never actually completed. Herod increased the size of the Temple Mount which he surrounded with massive fortifications. This created a huge outer forecourt, surrounding the smaller Temple courtyard, which was accessible via a flight of stairs. Around the inner court was a railing posted with signs in Greek and Latin, warning that entry into the inner court was forbidden to non-Jews on pain of death.

The inner courtyard of the Temple contained sev-

The monumental stairway leading up to the Temple Mount, dating from Second Temple times.

eral structures, notably the House of the Sanhedrin, the supreme Jewish religious and legislative body, and a synagogue. The Temple stood in the center of the inner court. The structure was plated with gold, causing it to reflect the sun's rays and dazzle onlookers. The design of the Second Temple was similar to that of the First, except that the Ark of the Covenant, lost during the Babylonian conquest, was lacking, so that the Holy of Holies remained an empty chamber.

Ritual. Ritual in the Temple was conducted by the priests, aided by the Levites. Supreme authority in the Temple belonged to the High Priest, who was assisted

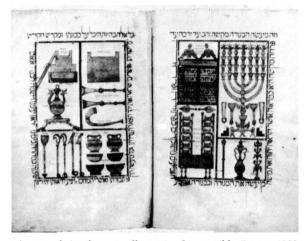

The Temple implements. Illustration from a Bible; France, 1299.

by a captain in charge of the compound. Other officers included Temple treasurers, a physician, choirmasters, and the keeper of the priestly vestments. These were assisted by additional, lower ranking officers.

Sacrifices were offered daily on behalf of the nation. These were performed by the priests, assisted by a group of lay Israelites representing the people. Passover, Pentecost, and Tabernacles were pilgrim festivals, when the entire populace was instructed to appear at the Temple. On festivals, the priestly shifts were increased to serve the vast multitudes of worshipers.

In the Second Temple, the ritual was expanded to include prayers and biblical readings accompanied by music. Music in the Temple was the dominion of the Levites, who formed orchestras and choirs. A psalm was recited by the Levites for each day of the week and on festivals. Interspersed in the ritual was the sounding of silver trumpets, upon which the congregation would prostrate themselves in adoration of God. Service in the Temple concluded with the priestly benediction of the assembly.

In the New Testament Jesus was first brought to the Temple as a child (Luke 2:41–51), and visited the Temple several times during his ministry. It appears that he approved of the rituals performed there but condemned the corruption prevalent among the upper echelons of the Temple administration and foretold the destruction of the Temple as a result. In the future, his body would replace the Temple as the place of encounter between God and man (Mark 14:58; John 2:18-22).

The early disciples of Jesus continued to frequent the Temple and participate in its rituals (Acts 21:26) while developing the concept of the community as a spiritual temple. In the latter books of the New Testament, the Temple is transferred to Heaven where it serves as a celestial sanctuary (Heb 9:11; Rev 5:6-14).

The Garments of the Priests in the Temple

The High Priest wore eight garments: four undergarments and four outer garments. Ordinary priests wore special undergarments but not the outer garments.

The High Priest's four undergarments were a tunic, a sash, a headdress, and breeches. The tunic was woven from linen and wool and, unlike those of the ordinary priests, was fringed. The sash went around the tunic: that of the High Priest was woven from fine linen and dyed wools, while those of the regular priests were fashioned from fine twined linen only. The turban of the High Priest was a miter, while ordinary priests wore "decorated turbans for headgear."

The four rich and splendid outer garments were worn only by the High Priest. They were made of a mixture of dyed wool and fine linen. Another characteristic of these garments was the interwoven threads of pure gold and the gold filaments.

The four outer garments were the ephod, the breastplate, the robe of the ephod, and the plate (crown) hanging in front of the miter (turban). These outer garments had the character of royalty since they were woven from gold, blue, and purple wool. When the High Priest wore all these garments along with the miter, and was in full dress, he was the picture of royalty.

The ephod was worn over the blue tunic, secured by two shoulder straps and a belt in the middle. The straps bore two onyx stones with the names of the 12 sons of Jacob (six on each stone). The front of the ephod carried the breastplate, which was either a square tablet or pouch, and which was made of gold, various fibers, and wool On it were placed the Urim and Thummim, which the High Priests used as oracles for purposes of divination.

The robe of the ephod was worn under the ephod and was therefore longer than the ephod and extended below it. This garment was entirely made of blue wool, and on its hem hung bells of gold and pomegranate shapes made from wool and linen.

The plate, sometimes known as a crown, hung on a blue thread in front of the miter. Fashioned from pure gold, it had on it the words 'Holy to the Lord'. During the Second Temple period, only the name of God was inscribed on the plate.

In contrast to the regal attire worn the rest of the year, on the Day of Atonement the High Priest wore garments made of ordinary linen; a tunic, breeches, sash, and miter. The ordinary priest wore breeches of regular linen when he ascended the steps of the outer altar to remove the ashes that were left from the sacrifice.

The Sabbath. The word Sabbath comes from the Hebrew *shabbat*, "to cease, desist" (i.e., from work). The weekly Sabbath was the most important of the ancient Hebrew holy days. It is first mentioned in the creation story (Gen 2:1-3) and reappears constantly throughout both the Old and the New Testaments. It is the only holy day mentioned in the Ten Commandments (Ex 20:8-11; Deut 5:12-15). The importance of the Sabbath was such that Jeremiah foresaw that its neglect could result in the destruction of Jerusalem (Jer 17:27). Conversely, the reward for observance of the Sabbath was Israel's dominion over the Land of Israel (Is 58:13-14).

The purpose of the Sabbath was twofold; it was a celebration of God's creation of the world (Ex 20:11), and a reminder of the Israelites' liberation from Egypt (Deut 5:15). As a commemoration of creation, the Sabbath had a universal aspect. Even Gentiles residing in the Land of Israel were required to observe the Sabbath (Ex 20:10; Deut 5:14), and its observance was a fundamental commitment to be taken by Gentiles who wished to tie in their lot with the people of Israel.

The Sabbath was considered a day of rest. The primary commandment of the Sabbath was abstinence from work (Ex 23:12; 34:21; 35:2; Lev 23:3; Deut 5:14), and animals also had to be allowed to rest. Among the labors particularly forbidden on the Sabbath were: the gathering and preparation of food, travel (Ex 16:23-30), agricultural work (Ex 34:21), the kindling of fire (Ex 35:3), and the hauling of burdens (Jer 17:21-27). Later Rabbinic exegesis added several other prohibitions to the list of chores forbidden on the Sabbath.

The Sabbath was a day for special sacrifices (Num 28:9-10) and for pilgrimages to the prophet (II Kgs 4:23) or the Temple (Is 1:13). By New Testament times, additional rituals were performed on the Sabbath, including readings from the Pentateuch and Prophets followed by a sermon (Matt 4:23).

Jesus regarded the Sabbath as important, but noted that "the Sabbath was made for man, not man for the Sabbath" (Mark 2:27). He further reasoned that since work was permitted in the Temple on the Sabbath, and he was more exalted than the Temple, his followers would be permitted to work on the Sabbath (Matt 12:1-8).

Some scholars have sought to trace the origins of the Sabbath to Babylonian "days of ill luck." This hypothesis is, however, incorrect, since those days do not correspond with the weekly Sabbath. It has also been related to *shapattu*, the Babylonian day of the full moon, the 15th day of the month, which was a day to "pacify the heart of the god." However, there was no resemblance between this concept and the Sabbath, "a holy day until the Lord." Another perceived parallel is that the Babylonian god rested after creating humans, but even here the motivation is quite different. Others have suggested a connection between the resting of the gods after the creation of man in the Babylonian epic and the similar sequence of events in Genesis: first the creation of the first human couple and then God's cessation from labor.

The Sabbath as a day of rest seems to have been an original Israelite contribution which became universally adopted because of the influence of the Bible on Christianity, Islam, and Western civilization. The meticulous observance of the Sabbath, while sometimes condemned by critics of the Israelite religion as a source of idleness (see Tacitus: Histories, The Jews: 5), was regarded by the Jews as a "delight" (Is 58:13).

New Year (Hebrew *Rosh ha-Shanah*). The New Year was celebrated on the first day of the seventh month (in post-biblical times called the month of Tishri). Although the day appears in the Bible as a separate holiday, it is not identified as the New Year, but rather as "a sabbath, a memorial of blowing of horns, a holy gathering" (Lev 23:24). Work was forbidden on the day, and special sacrifices were offered in the Temple. Rams' horns were blown, aside from the trumpets sounded on all New Moons. As the day is not recorded among the pilgrimage festivals, it has been suggested that the rituals of the day were limited to the Temple, and did not include the common people.

Day of Atonement (Hebrew *Yom Kippur*). The Day of Atonement, on the tenth day of the seventh month, was the most solemn of the biblical festivals. It was a day of fasting and repentance for the sins of the nation, and involved a complex Temple ritual known as the *Avodah*, or service. All work was forbidden on the Day of Atonement, which is referred to as a "sabbath of solemn rest," and a day when the people are commanded to "afflict your souls" (Lev 23:26-32).

In biblical times, the sins of the people were perceived as polluting the sanctity of the Temple, which then required purification. Not only did the altar upon which the sacrifices were regularly offered become unclean, but even the Holy of Holies, to which entry was forbidden to everyone except the High Priest, required appropriate cleansing to purify it of the sins of the people. The rites performed on the Day of Atonement purified not only the Temple but also the people (Lev 16). For seven days prior to the Day of Atonement, the High Priest resided in his chamber in the Temple where he was twice purified by the ashes of the red heifer and rehearsed the ritual.

At dawn on the Day of Atonement, the High Priest performed the regular Temple duties of the day. Upon their completion, he immersed himself and exchanged his normal vestments for garments of white linen. He then approached a young bull situated between the Sanctuary and the altar, laid his hands upon its head, and confessed the sins of his household. Next he drew two lots: on one was inscribed "for God" and on the other "for Azazel." The lots were placed on two male goats. The goat upon which the lot "for God" fell was brought to the slaughtering area, while the goat designated "for Azazel" was marked with a crimson strand. The High Priest returned to the bull, and once again confessed upon it, this time for the sins of the priests. The animal was slaughtered and its blood was collected in a basin and handed to another priest who stirred it so that it would not clot. Ashes from the outer altar were mixed with incense and brought by the High Priest into the Holy of Holies, the only occasion during the year that the inner sanctuary was entered. There he offered prayers for the people during the forthcoming year. Leaving the Holy of Holies, the High Priest offered a short prayer. He then took the basin of bull's blood and sprinkled it eight times in the Holy of Holies. The goat selected "for God" was then slaughtered and its blood, too, sprinkled in the Holy of Holies. The remainder of the blood of the bull and the goat was then sprinkled on the screen separating the Sanctuary from the Holy of Holies, and on the altar of the incense. Any remaining blood was spilt. The High Priest confessed the sins of the people upon the head of the goat designated "for Azazel," which was then led off to escape in the wilderness: the (e)scapegoat. According to later rabbinic custom, the goat was cast off a cliff.

Pilgrimage Festivals. This was the name given to the three festivals, Passover, Pentecost, and Tabernacles, on which the people were required to journey to the Temple in Jerusalem in fulfillment of the biblical precept: "Three times in the year all your males shall appear before the Lord God" (Ex 23:17). Apart from the particular sacrifices of the festival, the pilgrim was required to bring a sacrifice, "as he is able" (Deut 16:17), and the tithes that were to be eaten in Jerusalem (Deut 26:13). On the week-long Tabernacles, when the harvest was completed, the pilgrims were commanded to remain in Jerusalem the entire length of the holiday, but as Passover, also week-long, occurred in the middle of the agricultural season, the requirement to be in Jerusalem covered only the first day of the festival (Deut 16:7). Pentecost was only a one-day festival. All three festivals had both an agricultural and a historical significance.

Passover (Hebrew *Pesah*). The spring festival of Passover, beginning on the eve of the 15th day of the first month (Nisan), is the first of the three pilgrimage festivals. It celebrates the Exodus of the Israelite tribes from Egypt and the beginning of the barley harvest. Before leaving Egypt, on the eve of the 15th day of the first month, Moses commanded the Israelites to gather in their homes and slaughter a lamb. The blood of the lamb was then smeared upon the doorposts of the houses. As God passed over Egypt, slaying the firstborn, all houses so marked were spared.

Moses commanded the people to repeat the sacrifice each year, in commemoration of the Exodus miracle. In addition to eating the Passover sacrifice, the Israelites were commanded to eat unleavened bread, symbolic of the haste with which they left Egypt (Ex 12:34) and of the poverty they endured there (Deut 16:3). The people were also commanded to eat bitter herbs, which tradition linked to the bitterness of the enslavement (Ex 1:14), and, at the same time, to relate the story of the Exodus to their children in order that God's wondrous deeds as well as the origins of Jewish nationhood not be forgotten (Ex 12:14-27).

The name Passover (God "passed over" the homes of the Israelites) was applied to the yearly sacrifice (the "paschal lamb"), while the seven days are referred to as the "Feast of Unleavened Bread." Some scholars have suggested that, in fact, these names refer to two separate festivals, predating the Exodus, which were combined into a single festival only at a later date. Each time the laws of the Festival of Unleavened Bread are mentioned, however, they are described as a continuation of the festival of the Passover offering. Apart from the particular commandments relating to the Exodus, the second day of Passover was set aside for the offering of the first sheaves of the barley harvest to the priests (Lev 23:9-14).

Passover was probably the most important of the pilgrimage festivals, and many accounts of its celebration are given throughout the Bible (Josh 5:10-12; II Kgs 23:21-23; Ezra 6:19). Its significance was such that those unable to make the pilgrimage on the 14th of the first month were given another opportunity to offer the Passover sacrifice on the 14th of the second month (Num 9:1-14).

Multitudes made the Passover pilgrimage to Jerusalem in Second Temple times. It was customary for families to partake together of the Passover meal in Jerusalem and a service emerged for the occasion which was further developed in post-Temple Jewish custom. Jesus' wish to share a Passover meal with his disciples is stated in all four Gospels (Matt 26:2-19; Mark 14:1-16; Luke 22:1-15; John 11:55-12:2) which identify the Last Supper with the Passover meal (although John 18:28, 19:14 says otherwise). This was celebrated and commemorated as a thanksgiving (Greek, *eucharistia*, festival), with the unleavened bread and wine of the Passover ritual and Last Supper represented by the wafer and the communion wine. The Last Supper thus became the new feast marking the deliverance effected by Christ. Christ is called "our Passover" in I Cor 5:7, and in the same context Paul used the removal of leaven as symbolizing new life and joy.

Pentecost (Hebrew *Shavu'ot*). Pentecost was the second of the pilgrimage festivals. The name Pentecost (Greek "fiftieth") stems from the fact that the Bible gave no set date for the festival, but rather described it as falling after the counting of seven weeks (the Hebrew name *Shavu'ot* means "weeks") following the bringing of the barley offering, with Pentecost on the fiftieth day (Lev 23:15-20). The counting is to start on the "morrow of the sabbath, from the day that you brought the sheaf of the wave offering" (Lev 23:15). In the Second Temple period the ambiguity of this verse gave rise to a bitter disagreement between the Pharisees and the Sadducees as to the actual date of the beginning of the counting; the Pharisees began from the second day of Passover, whereas the Sadducees counted from the day following the intermediate Sabbath of Passover. Agriculturally, Pentecost celebrated the completion of the barley harvest and the beginning of the wheat harvest. Two loaves were offered in the Temple (Lev 23:17-20), as were the first fruits of the harvest, which were brought to Jerusalem in a joyful procession. Historically, later tradition, by virtue of calculations based on Exodus 19:1-2, associated Pentecost with the giving of the Law at Mount Sinai.

Pentecost was celebrated in New Testament times and came to have a special meaning for Christians.

Pilgrims bringing baskets of the first fruits to the Temple at the festival of Pentecost; 19th-century engraving.

Paul states that he intends to remain in Ephesus "until Pentecost" (I Cor 16:8). The key reference is in Acts 2 where Pentecost is associated with the very birth of the Church. The apostles and others assembled in Jerusalem on the first feast of Pentecost shortly after Jesus' death and resurrection. The Lord sent the Spirit, and the apostles began to speak in other tongues. The apostle Peter interpreted this as the fulfillment of the prophecy of Joel 2:8-32 and three thousand of those present became believers in Jesus.

Tabernacles (Hebrew *Sukkot*). The third of the pilgrimage festivals, Tabernacles is an autumn festival, beginning on the 15th day of the seventh month and lasting seven days. The eighth day, i.e., the day following the last day of Tabernacles, is a separate holiday called "a solemn assembly" (Lev 23:36). On the first and eighth days, work is forbidden.

Like the other pilgrim festivals, Tabernacles has both agricultural and historical significance. The different aspects of the festival are reflected in its different names: Tabernacles, or the Feast of Booths, "that your generations may know that I made the children of Israel dwell in booths when I brought them out of the land of Egypt" (Lev 23:43), and the "Feast of the Ingathering, which is at the end of the year, when you have gathered in your labors out of the field" (Ex 23:16).

Various commandments are attached to Tabernacles, including dwelling in booths during the festival (Lev 23:42-43), and the taking of the four species, a citron, a palm frond, a willow branch, and a branch from a myrtle (Lev 23:40). Individuals brought to the Temple baskets of harvest fruits as well as animal sacrifices. In addition, 70 bulls were offered during the holiday (Num 29:12-34). Rabbinic tradition states that these represent the nations of the world for whom Tabernacles would become a festival in the Messianic Era.

On the festival of Tabernacles following a sabbatical year, the entire nation would gather in Jerusalem to hear the Pentateuch read by the king (Deut 31:10-11). Jesus went secretly to Jerusalem to observe the festival (John 7).

New Moon. The feast of the New Moon is celebrated in biblical times upon the first appearance of the new moon, which was counted as the beginning of the new month. The day had special significance and had all the trappings of a holiday (Hos 2:11). No work was done (Amos 8:5), special sacrifices were offered (Num 28:11-15), and trumpets were blown (Num 10:10). It was customary to celebrate the day with feasting (I Sam 20:5) and pilgrimages to the prophet (II Kgs 4:23) and Temple (Is 1:13-15).

In Second Temple times, the New Moon festival lost much of its importance and was treated as a semi-holiday, when necessary work was permitted. Eventually it became a regular working day, marked only by liturgical additions.

Fasts. Fasts in the Bible were proclaimed for several reasons: 1) As a sign of mourning: David fasted on being informed of the deaths of Saul and Jonathan (II Sam 1:12). 2) To prevent impending disaster: the people of Nineveh fasted that God might spare their city (Jonah 3:7). 3) As part of the Day of Atonement ritual (Lev 23:27).

Communal fasting in response to circumstances was generally at the instigation of the king or a prophet in times of trouble such as a famine, and was binding on the entire nation. Instances also occur of individuals fasting in the face of disaster, as did David when his son by Bathsheba became ill (II Sam 12:22-23). Fasting was never considered sufficient in itself, atonement being effected only by complete repentance. The prophet Zechariah hints that fasting without remorse for sins led to the destruction of the First Temple and the exile of the people. During the Babylonian exile, the religious authorities proclaimed four fasts mourning the events leading up to the exile. "The fast of the fourth month, and the fast of the fifth, and the fast of the seventh, and the fast of the tenth" (Zech 8:19) were proclaimed in commemoration of: 1) the breaching of the walls of Jerusalem; 2) the destruction of the Temple; 3) the assassination of the governor Gedaliah son of Ahikam; and 4) the beginning of the siege of Jerusalem. The prophet declares that these fasts are of a temporary nature, and "shall become times of joy and gladness, and cheerful feasts to the house of Judah" (Zech 8:19). These fasts are still observed today by Orthodox Jews.

Fasting was a central feature of Jewish ascetic and messianic sects of the late Second Temple period and the practice is frequently mentioned in the New Testament, notably among the followers of John the Baptist (Mark 2:18).

While Jesus fasted in preparation for his healing activities and at times of crisis, he also warned against fasting merely to win admiration (Matt 6:16-18). Like the prophets, he stressed true contrition as an essential to fasting.

Purim. The holiday of Purim celebrates the salvation of the Jews of the Persian Empire from destruction at the hands of the vizier Haman, as recorded in the Book of Esther. Purim is the last of the festivals recorded in the Bible, but its celebration may not have been universally accepted until later. (The Book of Esther is the only biblical text not found in the Dead Sea Scrolls.)

Christian festivals grew out of events recorded in the New Testament, including: Christmas, to recall the birth of Jesus (Luke 2:1-20); Epiphany, the appearance of the Magi (Matt 2:1-12); Lent, Jesus' temptation in the wilderness (Matt 4:1-11; Luke 4:1-12); Easter, the resurrection (Mark 16:1-8); Ascension Day, Jesus' ascent into heaven (Acts 1:9-10); and Pentecost (see above).

Greek Orthodox bishops and priests awaiting the start of the Christmas procession into the Church of the Nativity, Bethlehem.

III.32 FAMOUS QUOTATIONS AND PHRASES

The extent to which biblical idiom has influenced our daily speech is not generally appreciated. Beginning with the Greek Septuagint and Jerome's Latin Vulgate, this process was accelerated by the work of Bible scholars and translators throughout Europe during the Reformation. German, French, English, and other European languages thus absorbed hundreds of given

("Christian") names, place names, and untranslatable Hebrew terms (e.g., *Amen, Baal, Cherub, Hallelujah, Messiah, Sabbath, Satan*), as well as coining their own equivalents of biblical Hebrew concepts: "angel," "bless," "curse," "holiness," "idolatry," "Lord," "prophet," "psalm," "righteousness," and so forth.

Even more important, however, was the naturaliza-

tion of essentially Hebraic phrases, idioms, and proverbial expressions, thanks to the impact of Luther's
German Bible, for example, or of the English King
James (Authorized) Version. So quickly and easily
were these expressions absorbed that they have become
an integral part of the English language and, in many
cases, their biblical origin is never even realized.
Although the following list does include some of the
most familiar examples, it cannot pretend to be
exhaustive. An asterisk placed before the source reference indicates that the phrase in question is based on,
rather than a literal quotation of, the Scriptural text.

Pentateuch

Let there be light! (Vulgate: *Fiat lux!*)	Gen 1:3
In the image of God	Gen 1:27
The breath of life	Gen 2:7
The Garden of Eden	Gen 2:8
The Tree of Life	Gen 2:9
Eating forbidden fruit	*Gen 2:17
It is not good that man should be alone	Gen 2:18
A helpmate	*Gen 2:18
Bone of my bones, and flesh of my flesh	Gen 2:23
By the sweat of one's brow	*Gen 3:19
To return to the dust	*Gen 3:19
Am I my brother's keeper?	Gen 4:9
The mark of Cain	*Gen 4:15
The land of Nod	Gen 4:16
As old as Methuselah	*Gen 5:27
Mighty men of old, men of renown	Gen 6:4
To go the way of all flesh	*Gen 6:12
Whoever sheds man's blood, by man shall his blood be shed	Gen 9:6
The Cities of the Plain	Gen 13:12
A good old age	Gen 15:15
Every man's hand against him	Gen 16:12
The Promised Land	*Gen 17:8
Selling one's birthright for a mess of pottage	*Gen 25:34
The voice is the voice of Jacob, but the hands are the hands of Esau	Gen 27:22
The house of God	Gen 28:17
Behold, this dreamer cometh	Gen 37:19
Lean years	*Gen 41:27
Corn in Egypt	Gen 42:1
Bring down my gray hairs with sorrow to the grave	Gen 42:38
The fat of the land	Gen 45:18
Fallen by the wayside	*Gen 45:24
A new pharaoh who knew not Joseph	*Ex 1:8
A stranger in a strange land	Ex 2:22
A land flowing with milk and honey	Ex 3:8
The great I Am	*Ex 3:14
Signs and wonders	Ex 7:3
Let My people go!	Ex 7:16
To harden one's heart	Ex 7:22
Spoiling the Egyptians	*Ex 12:36

The house of bondage	Ex 13:14
To make one's exodus	*Ex 13
The Lord shall reign for ever and ever	Ex 15:18
The fleshpots of Egypt	Ex 16:3
The bread of heaven	*Ex 16:4
On eagles' wings	Ex 19:4
A kingdom of priests and a holy nation	Ex 19:6
I am the Lord your God	Ex 20:2; cf. Deut 5:6
An eye for an eye and a tooth for a tooth	Ex 21:24
Worshiping the Golden Calf	*Ex 32:4
A stiff-necked people	Ex 33:3
Strange fire	Lev 10:1
To find a scapegoat	*Lev 16:7ff.
Imitatio Dei	*Lev 19:2
Loving one's neighbor as oneself (the Golden Rule)	*Lev 19:18
An eye for an eye, a tooth for a tooth	Lev 24:20
Proclaim liberty throughout the land	Lev 25:10
In the wilderness	Num 1:1
To spy out the land	Num 13:16
A people that shall dwell alone	Num 23:9
With the edge of the sword	Num 21:24
How goodly are your tents, O Jacob, your dwellings, O Israel!	Num 24:5
Be sure your sin will find you out	*Num 32:23
Man does not live by bread alone	Deut 8:3
The wife of your bosom	Deut 13:7
The apple of his eye	Deut 32:10
Jeshurun waxed fat, and kicked	Deut 32:15

Prophets

Hewers of wood and drawers of water	Josh 9:21
I am going the way of all the earth	Josh 23:14
The stars in the courses (fought against Sisera)	Judg 5:20
A shibboleth	Judg 12:6
Smiting the enemy hip and thigh	*Judg 15:8
From Dan to Beersheba	Judg 20:1
To arise as one man	*Judg 20:8
The good and the right way	I Sam 12:23
A man after his own heart	I Sam 13:14
Like David and Jonathan	*I Sam 18–20
The Lord's anointed	I Sam 16:6, 24:7
How are the mighty fallen!	II Sam 1:25
The poor man's lamb	*II Sam 12:3
A judgment of Solomon	*I Kgs 3:28
Every man under his vine and under his fig tree	I Kgs 4:25
To your tents, O Israel!	I Kgs 12:16
He slept with his fathers	I Kgs 14:20
Halting between two opinions	*I Kgs 18:21
A still small voice	I Kgs 19:12
The mantle of Elijah	*I Kgs 19:19
To draw a bow at a venture	*I Kgs 22:34

Is thy servant a dog?	II Kgs 8:13
(Jehu)... drives furiously	II Kgs 9:20
A broken reed	II Kgs 18:25
The ox knows his master and the ass his master's crib	Is 1:3
Seek justice, relieve the oppressed, judge the fatherless, plead for the widow	Is 1:17
Beating swords into plowshares and spears into pruning-hooks	*Is 2:4
To grind the faces of the poor	*Is 3:15
The wolf shall dwell with the lamb and the leopard shall lie down with the kid	Is 11:6
To move heaven and earth	*Is 13:13
Watchman, what of the night?	Is 21:11
The desert shall rejoice and blossom as the rose	Is 35:1
A broken reed	*Is 36:6
To set one's house in order	*Is 38:1
A voice crying in the wilderness	Is 40:3
All flesh is grass	Is 40:6
A drop from a bucket	*Is 40:15
A light to the nations	Is 42:6
There is no peace for the wicked	Is 48:22
Seeing eye to eye	*Is 52:8
A man of sorrows and acquainted with grief	Is 53:3
Like a lamb to the slaughter	Is 53:7
	Cf. Jer 11:19
Rise and shine!	*Is 60:1
Saying, Peace, peace, when there is no peace	Jer 6:14
Balm in Gilead	Jer 8:22
Like a gentle lamb that is led to the slaughter	Jer 11:19
Can the leopard change his spots?	Jer 13:23
False prophets	*Jer 29:9
Sour grapes	Jer 31:29
Teeth set on edge	Jer 31:29
Wheels within wheels	*Ezek 10:10
The Valley of Dry Bones	*Ezek 37
To sow the wind and reap the whirlwind	
	*Hos 8:7
A brand plucked from the burning	Amos 4:11
	(See Zech 3:2)
Every man under his vine and under his fig-tree	Mic 4:4
To do justly, and to love mercy, and to walk humbly with your God	Mic 6:8
Woe is me!	Mic 7:1
The just shall live by faith	Hab 2:4
Prisoners of hope	Zech 9:12
Have we not all one father? Has not one God created us?	Malachi 2:10

Writings

The seat of the scornful	Ps 1:1
In an uproar	Ps 2:1
Out of the mouth of babes and sucklings	Ps 8:3
What is man, that You are mindful of him?	Ps 8:5
You have made him but little lower than the angels	Ps 8:6
Fire and brimstone	PS 11:6
	(see also Gen 19:24)
The fool has said in his heart there is no God	Ps 14:1
The heavens declare the glory of God and the firmament shews His handiwork	Ps 19:1
The Lord is my shepherd; I shall not want	Ps 23:1
Green pastures	Ps 23:2
The valley of the shadow of death	Ps 23:4
The sins of one's youth	*Ps 25:7
In the land of the living	Ps 27:13
Seek peace, and pursue it	Ps 34:15
Deep calls unto deep	Ps 42:7
Whiter than snow	Ps 51:9
A broken and a contrite heart	Ps 51:19
O for the wings of a dove!	*Ps 55:7
We took sweet counsel together	Ps 55:14
To lick the dust	Ps 72:9
A stubborn and rebellious generation	Ps 78:8
This vale of tears	*Ps 84:7
To go from strength to strength	Ps 84:8
From everlasting to everlasting	Ps 90:2
Threescore years and ten	Ps 90:10
Teach us to number our days	Ps 90:12
The fowler's snare	*Ps 91:3
Bless my soul!	*Ps 103:1
As for man, his days are as grass	Ps 103:15
Wine makes glad the heart of man	Ps 104:15
At death's door	*Ps 107:18
They that go down to the sea in ships	Ps 107:23
At their wit's end	Ps 107:27
The fear of the Lord is the beginning of wisdom	Ps 111:10
	cf. Prov 1:7
Not to believe the evidence of one's own eyes and ears	*Ps 115:5–6
All men are liars	Ps 116:11
A lamp unto my feet	Ps 119:105
Like a lost sheep	Ps 119:176
I am all peace; but when I speak, they are for war	Ps 120:7
They that sow in tears shall reap in joy	Ps 126:5
Except the Lord build the house, they labor in vain that build it	Ps 127:1
Out of the depths (Vulgate: De profundis)	Ps 130:1
His mercy endures for ever	Ps 136:1
By the rivers of Babylon, there we sat down, yea, we wept, when we remembered Zion	Ps 137:1
We hung our harps upon the willows	Ps 137:2
If I forget you, O Jerusalem, let my right hand forget its cunning	Ps 137:5
Put not your trust in princes	Ps 146:3
Hallelujah. Praise the Lord	Ps 148:1
Whom the Lord loves, he reproves	Prov 3:12
A crown of glory	Prov 4:9
The path of the righteous	Prov 4:18

Go to the ant, you sluggard; consider its ways and learn wisdom	Prov 6:6
Wisdom is better than rubies	Prov 8:11
A wise son makes a glad father	Prov 10:1
The memory of the righteous is blessed	Prov 10:7
Hope deferred makes the heart sick	Prov 13:12
Spare the rod and spoil the child	*Prov 13:24
A soft answer turns away wrath	Prov 15:1
Better a dinner of herbs where love is, than a stalled ox and hatred therewith	Prov 15:17
A word in season	Prov 15:23
Man proposes, God disposes	*Prov 16:9
Pride goes before a fall	*Prov 16:18
Train up a child in the way he should go	Prov 22:6
Answer a fool according to his folly	Prov 26:5
As a dog returns to its vomit	Prov 26:11
Wise in his own conceit	*Prov 26:12
The way of a man with a maid	Prov 30:19
A woman of valor who can find? Her price is far above rubies	Prov 31:10
Grace is deceitful, and beauty is vain; but a woman that fears the Lord shall be praised	Prov 31:30
The Lord gave and the Lord has taken; blessed be the name of the Lord	Job 1:21
There the wicked cease from troubling and there the weary be at rest	Job 3:17
Man is born unto trouble	Job 5:7
Job's comforters	*Job 16:2
To escape by the skin of one's teeth	*Job 19:20
I know that my redeemer liveth	Job 19:25
The roots of the matter	Job 19:28
He was righteous in his own eyes	Job 32:1
The Great Unknown	*Job 36:26
The voice out of the whirlwind	*Job 38:1
Who is this that darkens counsel by words without knowledge?	Job 38:2
Thus far, and no further (Vulgate: *Non plus ultra*)	*Job 38:11
Black, but beautiful	Song 1:5
A rose of Sharon, a lily of the valleys	Song 2:1
For lo the winter is past.. the voice of the turtle is heard in our land	Song 2:11–12
Many waters cannot quench love	Song 8:7
Your people shall be my people, and your God my God	Ruth 1:16
Vanity of vanities, all is vanity	Ecc 1:2
All the rivers run into the sea, yet the sea is not full	Ecc 1:7
There is nothing new under the sun	Ecc 1:9
To everything there is a season	Ecc 3:1
A time to be born, and a time to die	Ecc 3:2
A time to keep silent, and a time to speak; a time to love and a time to hate; a time for war, and a time for peace	Ecc 3:7–8
The sleep of the just	Ecc 5:11
You can't take it with you	*Ecc 5:14

One man in a thousand	Ecc 7:28
There's no discharge in the war	Ecc 8:8
Eat, drink and be merry	*Ecc 8:15
Better a living dog than a dead lion	Ecc 9:4
The race is not to the swift, nor the battle to the strong	Ecc 9:11
A fly in the ointment	*Ecc 10:1
A little bird told me	*Ecc 10:20
Cast your bread upon the waters	Ecc 11:1
The dust shall return to the earth as it was and the spirit shall return to God who gave it	Ecc 12:7
Of making many books there is no end; and much study is a weariness of the flesh	Ecc 12:12
Like the laws of the Medes and Persians	*Est 1:19
To every people after their language	Est 1:22
And if I perish, I perish!	Est 4:16
What shall be done to the man whom the king delights to honor?	Est 6:6
Feet of clay	Dan 2:33–4
The burning fiery furnace	Dan 3:6
The writing on the wall	*Dan 5
You are weighed in the balance, and found wanting	Dan 5:27
In the lion's den	*Dan 6:17ff.
To cast oneself on the mercy of the four winds	*Dan 7:2
Our days on earth are as a shadow	I Chr 29:15
He died in a good old age	I Chr 29:28
Drew a bow at a venture	II Chr 18:33

Apocrypha

Great is truth, and it shall prevail (Vulgate: *Magna est veritas et praevalet*)	I Esd 4:41
He that touches pitch will be defiled	Eccl 13:1
A stain on one's honor	*Eccl 33:22
A friend in name only	Eccl 37:1
Let us now praise famous men, and our fathers that begot us	Eccl 44:1
At his last gasp	*II Macc 7:9

JERICHO

DICK CAPORO 80

Map and guide, courtesy of Lottie and Moshe Davis. Illustrated by Charles Harper.

III. 33 U.S. Towns with Old Testament Names

GUIDE TO PLACES ON MAP AND ILLUSTRATIONS

(Lake) **Aaron**, Douglas, Minnesota; *Aaron lighting the lamps (Num 8:3).*

Ai, Fulton, Ohio; *The battle at Ai (Josh 8:18).*

Bethel, Roosevelt, New Mexico; *Bethel: Jacob's dream (Gen 28:12).*

Bethlehem, Barrow, Georgia; *Bethlehem: David the shepherd (I Sam 16:11).*

Boaz, Marshall, Alabama; *Ruth and Boaz (Ruth 2:10).*

Canaan, Seminole, Florida; *Canaan: Report of Joshua and Caleb (Num 13:27).*

Damascus, Faulkner, Arkansas; *Wares from Damascus (Ezek 27:18).*

Ebenezer, Acadia, Louisiana; *Ebenezer: The stone of help (I Sam 7:12).*

Eden, Graham, Arizona; *Eden: The Lord planted a garden (Gen 2:8).*

Edray, Pocahontas, West Virginia; *Edrei: King Og (Deut 3:1).*

Egypt, Wharton, Texas; *Egypt: Building Pithom and Raamses (Ex 1:11).*

Eleazer, Randolph, North Carolina; *Eleazar, son of Aaron (Num 20:28).*

Elim, Nemaha, Nebraska; *Elim: springs and palm trees (Ex 15:27).*

Elisha, Little Compton, Newport, Rhode Island; *Elisha: Chariot of fire (II Kgs 2:11).*

Ephraim; Manassa, Conejos, Colorado; *The blessings of Ephraim and Manasseh (Gen 48:20).*

Gaza, Belknap, New Hampshire; *Gaza: Samson carrying city gate (Judg 16:3).*

Genesis Bay, Cape May, New Jersey; *Genesis: "and behold, it was very good" (Gen 1:31).*

Gideon, Cherokee, Oklahoma; *Gideon selects his soldiers (Judg 7:7).*

Gilboa, Schoharie, New York; *Gilboa: "In their death they were not divided" (II Sam 1:23).*

Gilead, Branch, Michigan; *Gilead: The pact of Laban and Jacob (Gen 31:48).*

Goshen County, Wyoming; *Goshen: Jacob and Joseph united (Gen 46:29).*

Havilah, Kern, California; *Havilah: Land of gold (Gen 2:11).*

Hebron, Jackson, Colorado; *Hebron: A city of refuge (Josh 20:7).*

(Mt.) **Hermon**, Santa Cruz, California; *"Hermon shall rejoice in thy name" (Ps 89:12).*

Jericho, Grant, Washington; *At the walls of Jericho (Josh 6:20).*

(Lake) **Jerusalem**, California; *Jerusalem: Solomon's Temple (I Kgs 6:12).*

Jonah, Williamson, Texas; *Prayer of Jonah (Jonah 2:2).*

Joppa, Cullman, Alabama; *Jonah sailed from Joppa (Jonah 1:3).*

Jordan, Salt Lake, Utah; *Crossing of the Jordan (Josh 3:17).*

Joshua, San Bernardino, California; *Joshua: "Sun, stand thou still" (Josh 10:12).*

Kedron, Cherokee, Oklahoma; *Kedron: The pyre of idols (II Kgs 23:4).*

Lebanon, Boone, Indiana; *Cedars of Lebanon (I Kgs 5:6).*

Mamre, Kandiyohi, Minnesota; *Mamre: The tent of Abraham (Gen 13:18).*

Mizpah, Elko, Nevada; *Mizpah: Jephthah's daughter (Judg 11:34).*

(Lake) **Moses**, Douglas, Minnesota; *Moses: The child wept (Ex 2:6).*

Mt. Ararat, Eldorado, California; *Mt. Ararat: "And the ark rested..." (Gen 8:4).*

Mt. Carmel, Cavilier, North Dakota; *Mt. Carmel: Elijah's contest with idolators (I Kgs 18:24).*

Mt. Horeb, Marion, Oregon; *Mt. Horeb: "The bush was not consumed" (Ex 3:2).*

Mt. Moriah, Van Buren, Iowa; *Mt. Moriah: They walked together (Gen 22:8).*

Mt. Olive, Izard, Arkansas; *Mt. Olive: David flees Absalom (II Sam 15:30).*

Mt. Tabor, Multnomah, Oregon; *Barak at Mt. Tabor (Judg 4:6).*

Nimrod, Wadena, Minnesota; *Nimrod, mighty hunter (Gen 10:9).*

Nineveh, Leon, Texas; *Nineveh; The king repents (Jonah 3:6).*

Ophir, Montgomery, North Carolina; *Gold from Ophir (I Kgs 9:28).*

Pisgah, Cooper, Missouri; *Pisgah: "and the Lord showed him all the land" (Deut 34:1).*

Rehoboth, McKinley, New Mexico; *Rehoboth: the well of Isaac (Gen 26:22).*

Salem, Utah, Utah; *Salem: a feast of peace (Gen 14:18).*

Samaria, Oneida, Idaho; *The siege of Samaria (II Kgs 18:9).*

Sharon, Barber, Kansas; *Rose of Sharon (Song 2:1).*

Shiloh, Clebourne, Arkansas; *Shiloh: "For this child I prayed" (I Sam 1:27).*

Sinai, Brookings, South Dakota; *Sinai: "All that the Lord has spoken we will do" (Ex 19:8).*

Sodom, Trumbull, Ohio; *Sodom: Lot's wife (Gen 19).*

Solomon, Mills, Iowa; *Solomon: "She is the mother" (I Kgs 3:27).*

Tekoa, Whitman, Washington; *Tekoa: The vision of Amos (Amos 9:13).*

Zarephath, Somerset, New Jersey; *Zarephath: Bread for Elijah (I Kgs 17:15).*

Zion, Towner, North Dakota; *David prays for Zion (Ps 51:18).*

Zoar, Tuscarawas, Ohio; *Escape to Zoar (Gen 19:22).*

IV. THE INTERTESTAMENTAL PERIOD

IV.34 THE APOCRYPHA

The Apocrypha ("hidden" books) is a term used to denote 13 books included in the Septuagint (the first Greek translation of the Bible) and in Jerome's Latin translation (the Vulgate), which were incorporated in the Catholic and Greek Orthodox canons but not in the Hebrew or Protestant Bibles. It contains intertestamental (i.e., between the Old and New Testaments) historical works, additions to various canonical books, devotions, and apocalypses. The books were composed c.300 BC-AD 70, and most were written in either Hebrew or Aramaic. The Catholic Church, which declared these books to be authoritative Scripture at the Council of Trent (1546), included them in their Bible.

THE BOOKS OF THE APOCRYPHA

The Letter of Jeremiah (c.300 BC). Short work attributed to Jeremiah in which the prophet exhorts the people to abandon the worship of idols. The book is based on Jeremiah 10:1-6, and is often added to the Book of Baruch (see below).

Tobit (500-400 BC). Story of Tobit from the tribe of Naphtali who is exiled to Assyria where, despite his righteousness, misfortune befalls him. The book ends with Tobit's son Tobias rectifying the wrong done to his father. The allegorical message of the book is that despite the suffering of the Children of Israel, God "will scourge us for our iniquities, and will have mercy again, and will gather us out of the nations, among whom he has scattered us" (Tobit 13:5).

Judith (c.150 BC). Story of Judith, a widow, who seduced Nebuchadnezzar's general Holofernes, plied him with drink, and slew him, thereby lifting the siege of her city. The book is important for its description of Judith's meticulous observance of various religious laws.

I Esdras (**III Esdras**) (150-100 BC). Addition to the books of Ezra and Nehemiah (also known as I and II Esdras), incorporating elements from those books and II Chronicles 35-36 as well as some original material. Esdras is the Greek form of Ezra. The book contains historical material which formed the basis of Josephus' description of the exiles' return to Zion from Babylonia (*Ant.* 11:1-158). One point of departure from standard Scripture is the book's account of the origins of Zerubbabel, depicted as a bodyguard of Darius I. At a banquet, he engages in debate as to which is stronger: wine, king, woman, or truth. When Zerubbabel wins the debate by advocating the ascendancy of truth, Darius agrees to grant his request to permit the Jews to rebuild Jerusalem (I Esdras 3-4).

II Esdras (IV Esdras) (c.AD 70). Apocalyptic work attributed to Ezra, concerning the destruction of Jerusalem as a result of the sins of Israel. After a period in which Israel will be cleansed of its sinfulness, Jerusalem will be rebuilt under a reconstituted Davidic dynasty. The book remains faithful to rabbinic thought of the messianic age.

Prayer of Manasseh (c.100 BC). Penitential Psalm attributed to King Manasseh of Judah who, according to II Chronicles 33:12-13, repented his sinfulness.

Additions to Esther (2nd century BC). Six passages appended to the Greek translation of the Book of Esther. Their intention was to create an underlying religious theme to the Book of Esther where God is nowhere mentioned.

Prayer of Azariah and Song of the Three Young Men, Susannah and the Elders, Bel and the Dragon

Susannah and the Elders; painting by Tintoretto (1518-1594).

The three young men in the furnace; fresco, Rome, 3rd century.

(c.165–100 BC). Three additions to the Book of Daniel. The Prayer of Azariah and the Song of the Three Young Men were originally inserted into the Greek translation of Daniel between verses 3:23 and 3:24. They recount the prayers of Shadrach, Meshach, and Azariah, uttered while in the fiery furnace. These prayers center on the misfortunes encountered by Jews despite God's covenant with them.

Susannah and the Elders is an attempt to explain the high regard given Daniel by the Babylonians. The book recounts how Daniel saved Susannah from a false charge of adultery, prompted by her rejection of the advances of two elders. Daniel's interrogation of the elders proved that they were lying.

Bel and the Dragon contains two stories in which Daniel proves the fraudulence of the idols worshiped by the Babylonians. In the first story, Daniel proves to King Cyrus that the priests are the ones eating the food offered to the god Bel. Daniel then succeeds in poisoning a dragon regarded by the Babylonians as a god. The Babylonians coerce Cyrus to cast Daniel into a den of lions where he is miraculously preserved while fed by the prophet Habakkuk.

Baruch (c.2nd-1st century BC). Book attributed to Baruch, scribe of the prophet Jeremiah. The theme of the book is the Babylonian exile as a punishment for Israel's sins, and it foretells the return to Zion. In the Vulgate, the book also contains the Letter of Jeremiah.
Ecclesiasticus (Wisdom of Jesus ben Sirach, or Sira) (c.180 BC). Apocryphal book of the Wisdom Literature containing poems and proverbs similar to the Book of Proverbs. The author intended the book as a critique of the predominant Greek culture and as a defense of Judaism. The book can be divided into eight sections, each preceded by a poem in praise of wisdom. Among the themes discussed are the oneness of God and the reverence demanded by the Torah and the Temple.
I Maccabees (c.110 BC). Book detailing the events of the Hasmonean revolt, from the conquest of Alexander the Great. The book is the primary source for information regarding events celebrated on the festival of Hanukkah.
II Maccabees (c.110-70 BC). Apocryphal book based on a larger Greek work written by Jason of Cyrene on the Hasmonean revolt. II Maccabees differs from I Maccabees in its stress on the underlying religious motifs of the Hasmonean revolt, rather than merely serving as a historical account of the events. Among the prominent religious themes of the book is the concept of martyrdom.
Wisdom of Solomon. Pseudepigraphic work possibly dating from the 1st century BC. It may have been written in Greek, and reflects both rabbinic and Hellenistic thought. Its object is to strengthen the faith of believing Jews in the face of the temptations of Greek culture. It consists of three parts: an eschatology, depicting the ultimate fate of the righteous and the wicked; a "wisdom" section, maintaining that God is close to the Jews when they adhere to the values created by wisdom; and a homily on the Book of Exodus.

IV.35 THE SECOND TEMPLE ERA

Persian Period. The famous edict of Cyrus in 538/7 BC (II Chr 36:22-23; Ezra 1:1-4) marked the dawn of a new era in Jewish history. The proclamation, which permitted the exiled Jews of the now defunct Babylonian empire to return to their ancestral home and way of life, was similar in character to other proclamations of the Persian ruler elsewhere in former Babylonian-ruled territories. For the Jews of the time, however, the royal decree meant a sudden reversal of their situation. Some 40,000 Jews took advantage of the opportunity to return to Zion, but they were apparently only a minority of those living in Babylonia.

Three personages stand out from among the initial exile groupings to leave Babylon for the satrapy known as "Across the River" of which Judah was a subdivision: Sheshbazzar, "Prince of Judah"; Zerubbabel, who was, like Sheshbazzar, a scion of the royal line of David; and the High Priest, Joshua son of Jozadak.

The newcomers were from the outset greeted with a decided lack of enthusiasm by the indigenous populace, perhaps even including those of Israelite origin. This initial cold welcome soon turned into outright hostility. Certain elements, most notably from the area of Samaria, and perhaps with the connivance and even encouragement of the local Persian officialdom, attempted to thwart the efforts of those Jews who wished to reestablish the Temple and their Mosaic traditions.

Two prophets, Haggai and Zechariah, with their words of encouragement and optimism in this early, bleak period, provided the necessary impetus toward implementing the first stages of the work and the resultant Temple dedication some 20 years after Cyrus' proclamation.

Almost nothing is known of subsequent developments until the arrival of Ezra from Babylonia sometime in the mid-5th century. His partnership with Nehemiah, who came some years later, marks a decisive turning point in the history of the Jewish people. Ezra was primarily concerned with the spread and practice of the Law of Moses. He worked with Nehemiah to get the Judahites to put away their pagan wives and the two initiated a renewed covenant between the Jews and the divine Law. In all likelihood the Pentateuch acquired its canonical imprimatur at this time. Jews enslaved by their landowning compatriots were released and their masters severely chastised. The sanctity of the Sabbath day was rigorously enforced. In order to increase Jerusalem's meager Jewish population, Nehemiah set quotas for resettlement from the outlying areas. Much attention was paid to reestablishing the Temple organization and service on a sound footing.

Little is known of the next 70 years until the arrival in the Near East of Alexander the Great in 333 BC, which ushered in the Hellenistic era.

Hellenistic Period. The Land of Israel was for Alexander just another province which he conquered. His death in 323 BC ushered in the period of the wars of the successors. The Near East was divided up between two of his generals, Ptolemy I and Seleucus I, with Seleucus controlling, in the main, northern Syria and parts far to the east and Ptolemy as new ruler of southern Syria (including the biblical Land of Israel), Egypt and other domains.

In 200 BC, the Seleucids under Antiochus III ("The Great") took over the country with some Jewish logistic and perhaps military support. A shortlived political and social calm prevailed in the country for some years thereafter, as may be gleaned in part from the book of Ecclesiasticus.

Next to occupy the Seleucid throne was Seleucus IV. Pressed for money, and instigated by certain Jewish hellenizing elements, he attempted to plunder the Temple treasury in Jerusalem, but was foiled.

Antiochus IV (Epiphanes), who ascended the Seleucid throne in 175 BC, was warmly greeted by some of Judah's aristocratic circles. Jason, brother of the High Priest, Onias III, offered the Seleucid monarch a large sum in return for his being awarded the high priest-

hood. Antiochus, like his predecessors in dire need of money to repay a huge war indemnity to Rome, and planning his own military campaigns, accepted with alacrity and appointed Jason High Priest of the Jews.

The process of Hellenization now grew rapidly, largely among sectors of the wealthy upper-crust of Jewish society. Even the priesthood was not immune; many of its members abandoned their official Temple duties in order to participate in the activities of the pagan gymnasia. Antiochus Epiphanes, who had suffered an ignominious political defeat by Rome, now did something virtually unheard of in the ancient world. In 168 or 167 BC, the Jerusalem Temple was converted into a pagan sanctuary, as the Seleucid sovereign issued a string of decrees designed simultaneously to prevent the Jews from practicing their age-old faith, and to enforce the Greek-pagan way of life.

The Jews refused to accept these measures. The entire people now engaged in acts of mass martyrdom, choosing torture and death rather than embrace paganism. Things came to a head when Mattathias, the aged head of a respected priestly clan, the Hasmoneans, struck down both the royal representative and a Jew preparing to offer pagan sacrifice in Mattathias' native village, Modi'in. The elder's five sons embarked upon a guerrilla campaign against both Greek forces and renegade Jews. At Mattathias' death, his son Judah the Maccabee assumed leadership of the revolt. In quick succession he defeated a series of Seleucid commanders. His brilliant campaigns, waged at the outset with inferior numbers and equipment, made him one of the outstanding military leaders of antiquity.

Within three years (in 164 BC) he recaptured Jerusalem, and purified and rededicated the Temple. This is the origin of the Hanukkah festival celebrated to this day. Judah's political acumen was evident in the way he exploited both Seleucid intra-dynastic strife and the political situation of the region. He was the first of the Hasmonean leaders to conclude a friendship pact with Rome, the up and coming superpower. The anti-Jewish decrees were rescinded by the Seleucids.

When Judah fell in battle in 160 BC, he was succeeded by his brother Jonathan (the first of the Hasmonean dynasty to attain the high priesthood). The treaty with Rome was renewed and a covenant of friendship concluded even with Sparta. On Jonathan's death in 142 BC, leadership passed to his capable brother, Simon, who in seven or eight years cleared a path toward control of the coast; demolished the citadel in Jerusalem, thereby removing the last overt vestige of Seleucid domination there; and reestablished Jewish sovereignty for the first time since the fall of the monarchy of Judah almost four and a half centuries earlier.

Next in the Hasmonean line was Simon's son, John Hyrcanus I, who enjoyed the lengthiest rule of any in the Hasmonean dynasty (down to 104 BC). The real

Ancient stone lamp, used at the Festival of Hanukkah instituted by Judah Maccabee.

causes of the Pharisee-Sadducee schism (see IV.37, Jewish Sects) during his tenure are not too clear, but the wealthier, upper-crust Sadducees now became increasingly influential in Jewish, and later to some extent in Roman, policymaking circles. Among Hyrcanus' important military and political accomplishments were his capture and destruction of Samaritan Shechem, and his thrust southward into the ancient Edomite region whose inhabitants were converted en masse to Judaism.

Alexander Jannaeus (Yannai) ascended the throne in 103 BC. He was the first of the Hasmonean line to be crowned king, and his 27-year reign was marked by military expansion in all directions, making the borders of the Land of Israel the most extensive since the days of David and Solomon.

Pompey, the Roman conqueror of Jerusalem, in 63 BC.

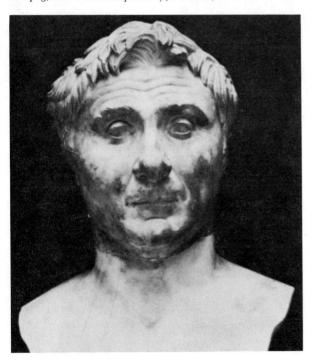

The nine-year reign of Queen Salome Alexandra, beginning in 76 BC, was generally tranquil. Pharisee rabbis frequented her court and she kept a firm hand on political affairs. On her death in 67 BC, however, a clash erupted between the brothers, Aristobulus II and Hyrcanus II. The more forceful Aristobulus swiftly established himself on the Hasmonean throne. But in 64 BC, the Roman general, Pompey, annexed Syria as a Roman province, and a year later placed Jerusalem and all of Judea under Roman rule.

Roman Period. Within a few years Gabinius, Pompey's lieutenant and governor of the area, had divided the Hasmonean kingdom into several administrative districts, with pagan control reallotted over several of them. The Hasmonean descendants made strenuous efforts to reassert Jewish statehood, but a pro-Roman element entered the scene in the person of Antipater, a high-ranking official who was of Edomite ancestry. Antipater got himself appointed regent of Judea by the Romans, and his sons, Herod and Phasael, were made administrators of Galilee and Judea respectively.

Herod soon proved himself eager to do Rome's bidding, and brutally suppressed Jewish attempts to assert independence. In 37 BC he sat on his vassal throne in Jerusalem, thanks to the backing of Mark Antony and massive intervention by Roman forces.

Herod's rule, which lasted until 4 BC, was cruel and repressive. He not only executed untold numbers of the general populace, but also several members of his own family. At the same time, he sought to win the sympathies of the Jews, most spectacularly in his immense building projects, notably the vastly enlarged and magnificent reconstruction of the Jerusalem Temple which earned unstinting praise even from the rabbis. Herod's manifold building projects in Jerusalem (many of these intended for pagan use) were instrumental in enhancing the special fame of Jerusalem among the cities of the east. Yet despite Herod's innumerable construction projects, both inside his country and outside, he did not win the hearts of his own people.

The physical and economic difficulties of Jewish life, as well as the loss of sovereignty and the alien Roman rule, led to the growth of messianism and sectarian groupings such as the Essenes. The bulk of the population, however, regarded the Pharisees as expressing the Judaism that satisfied them. Herod's death was the signal for uprisings across the land. His son Archelaus (ethnarch of Judea) emulated his father, reacting to the violent outbursts with attempts at brutal suppression, and continuing the policy of changing high priests at whim. In AD 6, the Roman emperor deposed him, banishing him to Gaul. His brother, Herod Antipas (ruler in Galilee) who had John the Baptist put to death, was to follow suit, being himself banished there some three decades later.

Facade of the Herodian Temple. Part of a scale-model of Jerusalem in Second Temple times.

Archelaus' deposition was followed by a development dire in its consequences: the establishment of Judea as a Roman province with a procuratorial regime. The Roman governor Quirinius' population census at this stage, intended for taxation purposes, fueled an immediate flareup, which was exacerbated by the Roman procurators in the country, whose almost unrelieved rapacity, a common enough feature of Roman governors under the empire, coupled with the existing tax load, made life ever more unendurable for an already overburdened Jewish peasantry and town proletariat. As a matter of policy, Rome strove to avoid undue clashes with the Jewish faith and its traditions, but these positive steps were far outweighed by the procurators' harshness. Added to this was their

continued practice of arbitrarily switching high priests. Although many members of the priestly aristocracy were intensely disliked by the people, the pagan administration, it was felt, should have no say in this internal matter affecting Jewish law and tradition.

In AD 41 the unbalanced emperor Caligula decreed that a statue of himself as a divinity be displayed throughout the empire, including the Temple in Jerusalem. The Jews once again showed themselves prepared for mass martyrdom rather than comply with this unbearable edict. Only a providential coup at court, ending with Caligula's assassination, put an end to his scheme.

The overall picture, however, was not one of unrelieved misery and gloom. Pontius Pilate, the executioner of Jesus, was recalled to Rome after a series of acts which flagrantly flouted the feelings of both Jews and Samaritans. Agrippa I, Herod's grandson, ruled over a great part of the country between AD 37 and 44, the last years as a vassal king, and displayed deep concern for Jewish feelings.

The Great Revolt against Rome broke out in AD 66. After initial successes, the rebels were beaten by the Roman armies. The climax came with the long and bloody siege of Jerusalem which ended in 70 when the Roman troops under Titus captured the city, destroying it and the Holy Temple by fire.

Coin after the fall of Judea. Obverse: Emperor Vespasian. Reverse: Captive Jew, mourning woman, and legend "Judaea capta."

The Jews of the Diaspora. The first Jewish exile dates from 720 BC, when the Ten Tribes of the Northern Kingdom of Israel were forcibly transplanted to Assyrian-controlled territories in the east. Their subsequent history was the subject of legends, but these were no more than unsubstantiated conjecture. Not long afterward Egypt became home for individuals and small groups of Jews who were either forcibly transferred there as war captives, or else came seeking their economic fortunes as private individuals or as mercenary soldiers. It was only after the destruction of the first Temple in Jerusalem that there is specific mention of a group of Jews, fleeing Babylonian wrath, going down to Egypt and forcing the prophet Jeremiah to accompany them (Jer 42:5-7). Large numbers of Jews had shortly before been removed to Babylon by Nebuchadnezzar after his two victorious assaults against Judah (597, 586 BC). This was the actual beginning of the Babylonian exile and of what was to become a powerful rooted Jewish community.

Archaeological finds dating from the latter half of the 5th century at Elephantine (Yeb) in southern Egypt and the Murashu archive in Babylonia both indicate established and even thriving Israelite communities, the former consisting of garrison settlers and the latter of royal officialdom, tenant farmers, and even landowners. The finds are also instructive in portraying only an insignificant degree of assimilation into the pagan surroundings. The Elephantine community in particular is distinctive for its temple service on foreign soil (despite the existence of the Jerusalem Tem-

ple), and the ties it maintained with the Jews of Judah.

Many Jews were taken captive to Egypt by Ptolemy I during his conquest of Judah shortly before 300 BC. Others made their way to the Land of the Nile, Cyrenaica, and Libya, some as soldier-settlers. Jewish soldier-colonists were transplanted from Babylonia to the areas of Lydia and Phrygia in 210 BC, this time by the Seleucid monarch, Antiochus III. No less than 2,000 Jewish families were brought to the region as garrison soldiery to contain rebellious elements there. Soon all of Asia Minor was a thickly populated area of Jewish settlement.

Jews were living on the Greek mainland as early as the mid-3rd century BC. Still farther west, in Italy, early non-Jewish literary sources point to Jews engaging in religious propaganda and being expelled from Rome in 139 BC. Here, too, the Jewish community grew by leaps and bounds. The Jews of Italy had made their presence especially strongly felt by the time of Julius Caesar and Pompey in the mid-1st century BC. Jewish settlements also existed as far north as the Caspian Sea region (perhaps as early as the 4th century BC) and Armenia.

Meanwhile, the Jewish population of Syria was growing apace as a natural adjunct to the Land of Israel to

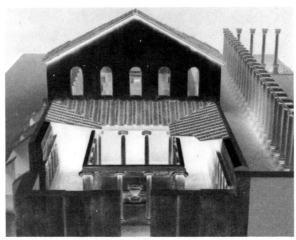

Model of the 1st century synagogue of Sardis, Turkey.

the south. So contiguous were these two lands, both demographically and geographically, that they were often regarded by the rabbis as one entity for purposes of Jewish law.

By the 1st century AD, the New Testament (Acts 2:9-11; notably the journey of Paul) and the Jewish philosopher-statesman Philo of Alexandria, attest to the spread of the Jews throughout every region of the inhabited world in Europe, Asia, or Libya. No reliable figures exist of the numerical strength of the Jews in the Roman Empire outside the confines of Judea. It is apparent, however, that the Jewish homeland, certainly toward the end of the Second Temple era in the 1st century, contained only a minority of the Jews of the inhabited world.

IV.36 THE BEGINNINGS OF THE SYNAGOGUE

How and when the synagogue came into being is a subject for speculation and scholarly dispute. The most accepted theory is that it emerged during the Babylonian exile. There the Jewish exiles from the kingdom of Judah found themselves cut off from the focus of their cult, the Temple with its elaborate ritual, and lacked any accepted format of worship. The solution may have come from grassroots, from the people, or it may have been inspired from the top, perhaps from the prophet Ezekiel or the author of the second part of the Book of Isaiah. It has been suggested that the exiles convened informally on the Sabbaths and festivals. Perhaps on these occasions they visited the prophets and other religious leaders who offered them words of consolation ('Comfort ye, comfort ye, my people') and buoyed up their hopes for a return to their homeland. Perhaps here too, the people listened to expositions of the Bible, especially the Pentateuch which had been accepted as holy. Prayers may have been formulated for the ordinary man to recite, with expressions of confession and repentance and petitions to God to bring the exiles back to their own land where they could rebuild the destroyed Temple. Jews later thought that Ezekiel's reference to "a little sanctuary" (11:16) referred to these incipient synagogues.

However, not all scholars accept this theory. Some have placed the origin of the synagogue already in the period before the destruction of the First Temple. Indeed, such a belief was held in ancient times, as attested by Acts 15:21: "For from early generations Moses has had in every city those who preach him, for he is read every Sabbath in the synagogues." Scholars he is read every Sabbath in the synagogues."

Scholars have theorized that when pilgrims traveled to Jerusalem on the pilgrim festivals, many others remained behind and must have had alternative ways to express themselves religiously. In this case, the exiles to Babylonia would have carried with them the seeds of community worship expressed in the synagogue. When the exiles returned to Judah they would have brought their experience of community prayer, while the activities of Ezra and Nehemiah would have encouraged the establishment of local centers for prayer and study. Other scholars, however, are concerned by the absence of any mention of synagogues at this time and insist that they emerged at a much later period.

The earliest concrete information on a synagogue comes from an inscription found near Alexandria, Egypt, in the 3rd century BC. It commemorates the dedication to the Egyptian monarch of a Jewish place of prayer. Another inscription from the same period shows that a synagogue in Lower Egypt had been given the right of asylum. The synagogue as a focus of com-

Columns in the synagogue at Masada; the steps in the background were the seats for the congregants. Roman period.

munity worship must have appeared revolutionary (or eccentric) at a time when pagan temples were regarded as the habitation of the deity and when shrines could be entered only by priests, and worship was confined to sacrifice.

The word "synagogue" comes from the Greek for "place of gathering." This corresponds to the Hebrew term and indicates that it was a multi-purpose institution, serving as a community center as well as a place of worship. Jews established synagogues throughout their Diaspora, as emerges most clearly from Paul's account of his travels. As soon as he arrived in any city he made a point of visiting its synagogue. There as a guest, he would be invited to preach. In most places he was favorably received but in some places his words culminated in quarrels, and even in violence. He first preached in a synagogue in Damascus and continued in Salamis in Cyprus, in Antioch of Pisidia, Iconium, Thessalonica, Berea, Corinth, and Ephesus (in today's Greece and Turkey).

In the late Second Temple period, the synagogue spread rapidly not only in the Diaspora but also in Palestine. Here the Temple and synagogue coexisted, with a division of functions. The Jew went to the Temple to seek forgiveness for his sins; he went to the synagogue to offer up his personal supplications and to listen to expositions of the sacred scriptures. Synagogues flourished in Jerusalem, even on the Temple Mount where there was a synagogue connected to the Temple. Sacrifices were offered in the Temple; prayers were recited in the synagogue. Striking evidence of the provincial synagogues is to be found in the Gospels which relate that Jesus gave regular addresses in the

Greek inscription on the remnant of a synagogue in Jerusalem built by Theodotus prior to the destruction of the Temple.

synagogues of Galilee, especially on the Sabbath. Jesus often began by reading the Bible and the homily, which gave him the opportunity to propound his message (see Luke 4:15–21). Luke 7:5 mentions that the synagogue at Capernaum, where Jesus preached, was built thanks to a sympathetic Roman centurion.

Archaeologists have discovered the remains of a number of ancient synagogues in the Holy Land dating from prior to the destruction of the Second Temple. In Jerusalem an inscription states that one Theodotus constructed a synagogue for reading the Bible, teaching its commandments, and also to serve as a hospice. The remains of three synagogues have been uncovered: one in Herod's desert retreat, Masada, dating from the 1st century BC and comprising an entrance hall and a sanctuary; one in another of Herod's desert strongholds, Herodion, not far from Jerusalem; and a third at Gamla on the Golan Heights.

The synagogue was central to the development of Christianity. Early Jewish Christian communities called their assembly a synagogue (James 2:2). The Christian worship, changed from Saturday to Sunday, was based on the synagogue prayer form and the reading of the Bible, to which Christians added the celebration of the religious meal (the *agape*) and the Eucharist. This became the essence of the Mass. The church too was indebted to the synagogue both for its concept and its hierarchy.

IV.37 THE JEWISH SECTS

In the latter centuries of the Second Temple period, various parties and sects emerged among the Jews in Palestine. The two main groups were the Pharisees and the Sadducees, the former emerging largely from the lower and middle classes guided by what was to become the rabbinical tradition, the latter from the aristocratic and priestly elite centered around the Temple. There were also many smaller groups such as the ascetic Essenes and the nationalistic Zealots. These groupings evinced considerable rivalry and even physical hostility, culminating in fighting in Jerusalem during the Roman siege (AD 67–70).

Following are the best-known sects and parties.

Pharisees. The spiritual leaders of the Jewish people in the Land of Israel during the latter part of the Second Temple era, and subsequently of the far-flung Jewish Diaspora. Whatever their actual historical origins, the Hebrew title *perushim* ("separated ones", "those set apart") is in odd contrast to their intimate involvement with both the spiritual and the political development of the Jewish people.

It is commonly believed that the Pharisees' spiritual roots go back to the days of Ezra and Nehemiah (during the latter part of the 5th century BC) and the Men of the Great Assembly, teachers and legislators.

The Pharisees make their first recorded appearance during the Hasmonean era, in all likelihood in the reign of John Hyrcanus (135/4–104 BC). The Jewish historian of antiquity, Josephus Flavius, relates that in Hyrcanus' days a schism developed between the latter and the Pharisee members of his intimate circle. The Pharisees emerged victorious in their struggle with the Sadducees some decades later when the powerful Hasmonean king, Alexander Yannai (Jannaeus), made his deathbed behest in 76 BC to his wife, Queen Salome Alexandra, to restore the Pharisees to their former status and influence.

The Pharisee world is known basically through its academies of learning. The famed schools of Hillel and Shammai were already flourishing in the Land of Israel in the 1st century AD. To the Pharisees, the Law was not confined to the Written Law of the Bible, but was also to be found in an ancient oral tradition which sought to adopt the ancient legislation to changing situations. These teachers and leaders were far from concerning themselves only with the minutiae of Jewish law. Readily evident in their literature are the sages known for the humble trades from which they derived their livelihood; the simplicity of their ways; concern for their fellows; their belief in man's freedom of choice and concomitant responsibility for his actions; the respect in which they held their elders, and which they demanded in man's relationship toward his fellows; and, in general, the humane spirit which infused their legal decisions. It was the Pharisee tradition which laid the groundwork upon which the Jews, both in the Land of Israel and in the Diaspora, were to build the edifice of post-exilic Judaism.

The Pharisee and the publican. Mosaic at Apollinari in Classe, Ravenna, Italy; 5th century.

Although they were criticized by Jesus for their insistence on legalistic interpretations and their hypocrisy, he was himself raised in a Pharisaic framework and remained close to their doctrines, from which he derived many of his teachings. Paul expressed his pride at being raised at the feet of the Pharisee leader, Rabbi Gamaliel (Acts 22:3).

Sadducees. An important politico-religious party in the Land of Israel during the Second Temple period. Although their origins remain obscure, their Hebrew title (*Zadokim* or *Zedukim*) and their indisputable links with the high priesthood indicate a connection with the Zadokite high priestly line (originating with the High Priest Zadok at the time of Solomon). Like the Pharisees, they first spring to historical prominence during the 2nd century BC reign of John Hyrcanus the Hasmonean leader, when the Pharisee-Sadducee cleavage is supposed to have occurred. The Sadducees, although assuming a position of political priority vis-a-

vis the Pharisees at this stage, had henceforth to contend with the latter's mass popular backing and popularity for the remainder of the Second Temple period.

An incontrovertible fact is the close relationship of the Sadducees and the oligarchic upper crust of Jewry in the country, and their representation among the high priestly aristocracy. Yet another important feature is the Saducee involvement in the country's political affairs: the high priests were not only political appointees during the last century of the Temple's existence (from the days of King Herod onward), but had been inevitably involved in affairs of state for at least two centuries previously. The close connections with the wealthy business interests of their people (and perhaps of the general populace as well), were an added factor necessitating heightened political concern.

Such Sadducee "worldliness," however, in no way mitigated the party's theological and general spiritual outlook. Aside from the fact that in Judaism the spiritual and temporal go hand-in-hand, the very intimate relationship of the Sadducee grouping and the Temple priesthood made religious interest mandatory. There were Sadducee extrabiblical religious decrees, while instances of Sadducee interpretation of biblical laws may be found.

Pharisee rabbinical opposition to Sadducee religious practice extended to the various Sadducee high priestly incumbents, and in the latter decades of the Second Temple there would be a Pharisee deputy at the Sadducee High Priest's side at all times to prevent possible deviations from Pharisee Temple legislation and practice. Such surveillance was deemed necessary to prevent incidents such as that indicated in the Talmud story of a Sadducee who poured the water of the libation ceremony at his feet, instead of on the altar, and the populace pelted him with their citrons.

Sadducean theology maintained that divine fate had no place in the general scheme of things; that man is totally free in his choice of good or evil; that there were neither angelic nor demonic spirits in the universe; and that there was no after-life, the last a cornerstone of Pharisaic belief. Josephus speaks of Sadducee rigidity in applying Jewish law, especially in the realm of capital punishment (citing, as an example, their haste in executing Jesus' brother, James).

The Sadducees never gained a foothold among the broad mass of the Jewish people of their day and age. Unlike the Pharisees, they could not cope with the Temple's disappearance in the year AD 70 and were no longer heard from thereafter.

In the New Testament, Sadducces and Pharisees alike were condemned by John the Baptist as a "generation of vipers" (Matt 3:7), and Jesus also grouped the two together in his denunciations (Matt 16:6, 11ff).

Zealots. A group (or groups) of Jewish activists who banded together in the Land of Israel to fight Roman domination, between the latter half of the 1st century BC and the seventies of the 1st century AD. With the destruction of the Jerusalem Temple in AD 70, this rebel grouping even attempted to provoke Jewish anti-Roman rebellions outside the confines of the Holy Land.

The fall of the Dead Sea bastion of Masada to the Roman legions in the year 73/74 marks the termination of the Zealots' organized activities on Holy Land soil, as far as can be determined from historical sources. It may well be, however, that the two-year long revolt against Roman rule by Diaspora Jewry in 115–117 during the rule of the Emperor Trajan, and perhaps even the great rebellion of Bar-Kokhba in Palestine a decade and a half later, had its root, in part at least, in Zealot-oriented elements.

The main source of knowledge of the Zealots lies with the historian Josephus, whose writings are pro-Roman and often anti-Zealot. Josephus also mentions another Jewish element, the Sicarii, as active in the struggle against Rome and on behalf of Jewish independence during the same period. The latter, in addition to constituting a fighting opposition to Roman rule, are depicted simultaneously as active in doing away with Jewish pro-Roman collaborators (for which purpose they employed the dagger, or *sica* in Latin, hence their name), and in the taking of hostages to secure the release of their comrades in Roman hands.

Neither the Zealots nor the Sicarii emerged full-blown on the historical scene with the Jewish opposition to the census in Judea in the year AD 6 conducted by Quirinius, the Roman legate of Syria. They were successors to a long line of Jewish freedom fighters harking back at least to the days of Hezekiah of Galilee (c.40 BC), when bitterness against Herod's fierce pro-Roman approach burst to the fore.

What motivated the Zealots and their Sicarii counterparts? Did they have a strong ideological underpinning or were they no more than "brigands" or "revolutionaries" (a Roman term of opprobrium), as Josephus calls them? This latter description does not square with the fact of a century-long line of freedom fighters. Josephus himself elsewhere refers to the Zealot group as a "philosophical school," more precisely as the "fourth philosophy" numbered among such other respectable schools as the Pharisees, Sadducees, and Essenes. Indeed, on several occasions he depicts the Zealots as having an "almost unconquerable passion for liberty," regarding only God as their master (*Antiquities*, 18:23–24). He also refers to their messianic beliefs. Menahem, one of the early leaders of the Great Revolt against Rome in AD 66, may have had messianic pretensions as, it would seem, did his father. This is not surprising; although the Zealots/Sicarii were political parties, Jewish political views, especially among the highly ideological Zealots, had strong religious underpinnings. No fighter for Jewish independence and sovereignty could possibly fail to equate these aims with a belief in the ultimate messianic age.

Essenes. A Jewish sect originating apparently in the 2nd century BC and extending down to the 1st century AD, located in various areas of Palestine.

The name (*Essaioi* in Greek) has been given various connotations: "holy ones," "the pious," and more recently, "healers." The sect's actual historical origins remain obscure, despite all that has been written about them by the Jewish historian, Josephus; by the ancient Jewish thinker, Philo; by the Roman writer on natural history, the elder Pliny; and by Eusebius, one of the Church Fathers. The sensational discoveries in the Judean Desert since 1947 of the Dead Sea Scrolls, seem to have added to knowledge of this group, although some scholars are still uncertain as to the actual identity of the authors of these scrolls.

Life in the Essene community was generally that of a reclusive monastic order, although there was at least one offshoot sect of an urban, semi-monastic character. Josephus himself spent several years among them, while the Roman writer, Pliny, refers to them as "remarkable beyond all the other tribes in the whole world" (*Natural History,* 15:73). It would appear that during the early 1st century AD, the Essenes numbered 4,000 members.

How did the community live? From the information available, the following general pattern emerges. The community was organized in the form of an order with superiors to whom members were bound in utter obedience. Candidates for the order were required to undergo a three-year probationary period, at the end of which they took an oath of communal loyalty and sect secrecy toward outsiders. The main branch of the sect apparently accepted only adult males as a general rule, with some exceptions for children who were to be indoctrinated with the ideals of the community. Although the order as a whole rejected marriage and women, Josephus knew of a branch of the Essenes which permitted marriage. The sect engaged in agriculture and crafts. A striking group feature was the commonly-held property, wages, food stocks, and clothing, all these items being apportioned by elected officials. Daily meals, apparently of a sacral character, were taken in common. Personal modesty, physical cleanliness, and ritual purity were stressed.

Unlike the Pharisees, the Essenes believed in an unalterable destiny, thereby eliminating the element of free will. They were rigidly observant of the Sabbath, again in contradistinction to the more considerate Pharisaic law. The Jewish scripture was read and expounded among them, although they possessed sacred writings of their own.

The sect was of a marked eschatological nature, that is, it had an emphatic "end of days" outlook. They gave special prominence to the messianic concept as such, and developed a dual (and perhaps even triple) notion of the Messiah to come. The Essenes spoke not only of a royal or Davidic Messiah and a prophet Messiah, but also of a priestly Messiah.

Despite their self-regard as an anti-mainstream elite, Essenes were to be found in Jewish fighting ranks during the Great Revolt against Rome (AD 66–70). Yet the Essenes, fringe group that they were, disappeared from history upon culmination of the revolt and destruction of the Jerusalem Temple.

Dead Sea Sect. See IV.38, Dead Sea Scrolls (The Sect).

IV.38   THE DEAD SEA SCROLLS

Discovery and Importance. In the early summer of 1947, two Bedouin shepherds, grazing their flock on the northwestern shore of the Dead Sea, 8 miles (13 km) south of Jericho, came across a rocky cave which excited their curiosity. The area, known as Qumran, was one of the more desolate sectors of the the barren Dead Sea region. Stones were thrown into the cave and the sound rebounded of the shattering of an object. Upon further investigation, the shepherds discovered eight unbroken earthenware jars inside the cave. One of the jars contained some bound leather packets. These were to be the first of the famed Dead Sea finds, later to become known the world over as the Dead Sea scrolls.

After several unsuccessful attempts had been made to sell their curious finds (of whose importance the Bedouin had not the slightest inkling), a Bethlehem antique dealer purchased the scrolls, only to resell them to the head of the Syrian Orthodox monastery of St. Mark in Jerusalem, Mar Athanasius Samuel. The documents were scrutinized by several scholars who passed judgment that they were worthless. The first person to realize the true significance of the manuscripts was Prof. Eliezer Sukenik, of the Department of Archaeology at the Hebrew University in Jerusalem (and father of Yigael Yadin who was later to occupy the same chair and devote a major portion of his time to the study of the scrolls).

Three of these Jewish-authored scrolls, depicting fascinating aspects of the life and beliefs of a Jewish sect in the Land of Israel some 2,000 and more years before, were acquired by Prof. Sukenik on behalf of the University on November 29, 1947, the day of the United Nations vote on the Partition Resolution, which recognized a Jewish State in that very land, the first one since AD 70 when the sect had disappeared.

The scrolls acquired at the time were: The War of the Sons of Light Against the Sons of Darkness; The Book of Isaiah scroll (incomplete); and hymns reminiscent of biblical psalms. Four other scrolls were taken by the Syrian patriarch to the United States. He advertised them for sale in the "Wall Street Journal" seven years later. The notice came to the attention of Yadin, who arranged for their purchase on behalf of the State of Israel, and took them to Jerusalem. All seven scrolls are housed today in the Israel Museum's Shrine of the Book in Jerusalem, built for that purpose. The four scrolls bought in the U.S. are: the Manual of Discipline; a complete Isaiah scroll; a commentary on the Book of Habakkuk; and what has been called the Genesis Apocryphon.

All this, however, was to be but the beginning of excavations and finds in the area. From 1949 until digging and searches ended in the vicinity and actual site of Qumran in the Dead Sea region, hundreds of manuscript fragments and many lengthier documents came to light. Later on, two archaeological expeditions under Yadin unearthed still more scroll fragments at the site of Masada, the forbidding cliff fortress in the Dead Sea area.

The importance of these discoveries is enormous. They are fascinating not only from the aspect of sheer bulk (fragments are numbered in the thousand), but even more so for the variety of their contents, ranging from Bible and apocrypha-related writings to documents outlining the life, beliefs, and expectations of the Qumran community. These manuscripts have thrown a blaze of light on the history and literature, beliefs and practices of a Jewish ideological fringe group in the last two or three centuries of the Second Temple era and have uncovered the earliest Bible manuscripts yet known. For many, the documents are of inestimable value for the history of early Christianity, which may have a connection with the ideology and religious life of the sect.

The Sect. The prevailing, though by no means universal, view today is that the sectarian group indicated in the bulk of the Dead Sea documents belonged to the sect of the Essenes.

The Dead Sea group may have originated as early as 200 BC, if not somewhat earlier. This seems to emerge from the atmosphere of Jewish-Hellenistic crisis delineated in some scrolls, and from the expression "age of wrath" allied with the name of King Antiochus, referring perhaps to the wicked Seleucid ruler in the immediate pre-Maccabean or early Maccabean era. Archaeological evidence at Qumran itself points to the mid-2nd century establishment of the site. As the documents contain various allusions to what appears to be the Roman imperial epoch, and since according to archaeological findings, the group seems to have disappeared from the place in the year AD 68, we have something like a 250-year history for this sect.

The members of the group, generally speaking, lived a rigorously monastic existence, far from populated areas and mainly, as already indicated, in the barren, forbidding Dead Sea wastes. Marriage, children, and personal wealth were taboo. Yet in all these areas there were exceptions, or perhaps there existed splinter

Meals were taken in common and in an atmosphere of strict silence. Ritual purity of foods and utensils were far more rigorous than in the Jewish community at large under Pharasaic leadership. Personal hygiene was stringently enjoined on all, and here too ritual purity prevailed. According to the scroll texts, supreme authority was in the hands of the community priesthood or, in the absence of the latter, invested in the Levites. The Messianic Rule and the War Rule, however, mention lay heads, while the eventual Messianic ruler of Israel (the Messiah of Israel) is referred to not as "king" but as "prince," in line with Ezekiel 34:24.

Left: Clay jars in which the first seven Dead Sea Scrolls were discovered in a cave, in 1947. Right: General view of Qumran in the Judean Desert, where the Dead Sea Scrolls were found.

groupings with somewhat more modified views. Thus, one of their documents speaks of groups living a village existence, although still set apart from their fellow Jews and pagan neighbors. Some were married, reared children, employed servants (also frowned upon in other documents), and even engaged in commerce.

A person desiring to join the sect remained on probation for two and perhaps even three years or more. This seems to have been a two-stage process: entrance into the Covenant of Moses as interpreted by the community, and acceptance into the "Holy Congregation." The application for membership handed over to the congregation his money and belongings, these becoming the common property of the community upon his final acceptance.

Members of the sect generally spent most, or a good deal of, their waking hours in study and prayer, and the group's leader, the Teacher of Righteousness, would reveal the true, hitherto hidden, significance of biblical prophecy. The prophets, in fact, were regarded as guides along the road to the Messianic era. Although it saw itself as the elect of Israel, the sect was keenly aware of the sin of hubris, and in various hymns stresses the need for God's continuous support for perseverance in the way of holiness.

Another of the congregation's striking differences was its use of a solar calendar, as against the lunar calendar of normative Judaism. The community reckoned according to 52 seven-day weeks, making for a 364-day year. This led to religious festival observance being at variance with that of the bulk of Jewry in the Land of Israel. The biblically ordained Temple and its ritual presented a severe problem to the sect which refused to recognize the validity of the existing Jerusalem Temple. The contradiction was apparently resolved through the community's belief that its daily worship of God through prayer and study would suffice until the future rededication of the sacred Temple.

Two other important aspects of the sect's ideological world were its concept of a final all-out war before ultimate victory, and its messianic views. On the first score, they believed that they, the Sons of Light, would eventually engage in a 40-year war against the Sons of Darkness and, of course, emerge triumphant. On the Messianic level, the Essenes and/or their contemporary offshoots seem to have conceived of two and maybe even three such Messiahs: a lay Messiah (a kingly figure); a priestly Messiah; and a prophet Messiah, perhaps harking back to the portrayal of Elijah as harbinger of the Messiah (Malachi 3:23,24). A striking point about the Essene community is that there were members of this supposedly highly reclusive sect among the active participants in the Great Revolt against Rome which broke out in 66.

The Scrolls. The scroll literature covers varied fields: depictions of sect life, practices and ideology or religious outlook; biblical excerpts and sectarian commentaries on these and other biblical passages; excerpts of apocryphal (non-canonical) literature, perhaps the most famous of these being the fragments of the Hebrew original of the Book of Ecclesiasticus.

Special mention must be made of the two Isaiah scrolls, one being a complete, virtually identical copy of the biblical book. These and other biblical excerpts in various manuscripts represent types of biblical texts that circulated in Israel in the century before and after the turn of the era. They bear witness to the interesting fact that there existed a variety of textual traditions which were current contemporaneously. Excerpts from all books of the Bible have been unearthed in the Dead Sea region, with the sole exception of the Book of Esther.

The main scrolls are:

1. The Damascus Rule: also known as the **Damascus Covenant** or **Zadokite Document.** This document previously surfaced in the form of two medieval manuscripts found at the end of last century. Several Qumran caves have yielded manuscript fragments which appear to correspond to parts of the medieval document. An exceptionally odd (and thus far unresolved) feature is a reference to the faithful of the covenant who left Judea for the "Land of Damascus." It is still unclear whether this latter is a geographical description or intended to indicate an ideological transformation of some sort. This document consists of assurances to the faithful, the followers of the sons of Zadok, as they are called, that the Almighty would ultimately reward their fidelity. There is sermonic material and legal and moral precepts to fortify the group in its separatist ways.

2. Manual of Discipline or **Community Rule** outlines the community's organization and practices until the advent of the Messianic age.

From the Zadokite Document

All that enter the covenant with no intention of going into the sanctuary to keep the flame alive on the altar do so in vain. They have as good as shut the door.

In an era of wickedness, they must take heed to act in accordance with the explicit injunctions of the Law;
to keep away from men of ill-repute;
to hold themselves aloof from ill-gotten gain;
not to defile themselves by laying hands on that which has been vowed or devoted to God or on the property of the sanctuary;
not to rob the poor of God's people;
not to make widows their prey or murder the fatherless;
to distinguish between unclean and clean and to recognize holy from profane;
to keep the sabbath in its every detail, and the festivals and fasts in accordance with the practice laid down originally by the men who entered the covenant in the "land of Damascus";
to pay their required dues in conformity with the detailed rules thereof;
to love each man his neighbor like himself;
to grasp the hand of the poor, the needy, and the stranger;
to seek each man the welfare of his fellow;
to cheat not his own kin;
to abstain from whoredom, as is meet;
to bring no charge against his neighbor except by due process, and not to nurse grudges from day to day;
to keep away from all unclean things, in accordance with what has been prescribed in each case and with the distinctions which God himself has drawn for them;
not to sully any man the holy spirit within him.

From the Manual of Discipline

This is the procedure which all members of the community are to follow in all dealings with one another, wherever they dwell.

Everyone to obey his superior in rank in all matters of work or money. But all are to dine together, worship together, and take counsel together.

Wherever there be ten men who have been formally enrolled in the community, one who is a priest is not to depart from them. When they sit in his presence, they are to take their places according to their respective ranks; and the same order is to obtain when they meet for common counsel.

When they set the table for a meal or prepare wine to drink, the priest is first to put forth his hand to invoke a blessing on the first portion of the bread or wine.

Similarly, wherever there be ten men who have been formally enrolled in the community, there is not to be absent from them one who can interpret the Law to them at any time of day or night, for the harmonious adjustment of their human relations.

The general members of the community are to keep awake for a third of all the nights of the year reading books, studying the Law, and worshiping together.

3. War Scroll more popularly referred to as **The War of the Sons of Light against the Sons of Darkness.** Describes the 40 years of armed struggle before the Sons of Light (i.e., members of the sect) emerge victor-ious against their enemies. This is an unusual type of composition for a group whose basic ideology was that of a monastic or semi-monastic existence based on study and prayer.

From The War of the Sons of Light against the Sons of Darkness.

When they come up from gathering in the fallen and return to the camps, they shall all of them sing the hymn of return. Next morning, they shall launder their garments and wash themselves clean of the blood of the guilty corpses and return to their assigned positions at the place where the line was drawn up before the slain of the enemy fell. And there they shall all of them bless the God of Israel and extol his name together in joy and take up word and say:

"Blessed be the God of Israel
Who keeps the loyalty of his covenant
and constantly evinces salvation

to the people whom he redeemed.
He has summoned those that were stumbling
but has gathered the horde of the heathen
for extermination without survival,
exalting the melting heart by his justice,
opening the mouth of the dumb for joyful song,
endowing with strength hands that were slack,
teaching them arts of war;
giving firm stance to tottering knees
and vigor to the shoulders of the bowed;
All wicked nations are come to an end
and all their heroes have no standing."

4. Thanksgiving Psalms. Scroll containing dozens of psalms (some incomplete) praising God for saving mankind. These psalms are a major source for understanding the theology of the sect.

A Psalm of Thanksgiving

I give thanks unto Thee, O Lord,
for Thou has wrought a wonder with dust
and hast shown forth Thy power
in that which is molded of clay.
For Thou hast made me to know Thy deep, deep truth,
and to divine Thy wondrous works,

and hast put in my mouth the power to praise,
and psalmody on my tongue,
and hast given me lips unmarred
and readiness of song,
that I may sing of Thy lovingkindness
and rehearse Thy might all the day
and continually bless Thy name.

Part of the Thanksgiving Scroll containing psalms praising God for saving mankind; one of the Dead Sea Scrolls found at Qumran.

5. Copper Scroll. This scroll has fired popular imagination with its list of real or imaginary treasures (64 caches of gold and silver, among other items). Claimed by some scholars as a fictional account, while others think these were actual riches hidden away either by the Essenes or the Zealot defenders of Jerusalem during the revolt against Rome (66–70).

6. Temple Scroll. This is a highly odd scroll, even for an unusual sectarian group such as the Essenes.

It contains strict rules and regulations concerning worship in the Jerusalem Temple, laws on the purity of the cities of the Land of Israel, celebration festivals, and laws pertaining to the kingly office and the royal army.

7. Genesis Apocryphon. Aramaic Midrash and embellishment of parts of the Book of Genesis. The main portion of the scroll depicts the trials and tribulations of Abraham and Sarah.

Another literary genre represented by the scrolls are midrashic biblical commentaries, two of which stand out among the few possible sources of historical information on the sect:

1. Commentary (Heb. *Pesher*) **on Nahum:** Considered as highly instructive for the history of the sect, with its mention of the (Seleucid) kings Antiochus and Demetrius, and a Jewish sovereign who "hangs men alive." Some have interpreted the latter remark as a reference to Alexander Jannaeus' crucifixion of his Jewish opponents.

2. Commentary on Habakkuk. Regarded as another principal source of information on the first two chapters of the prophet Habakkuk.

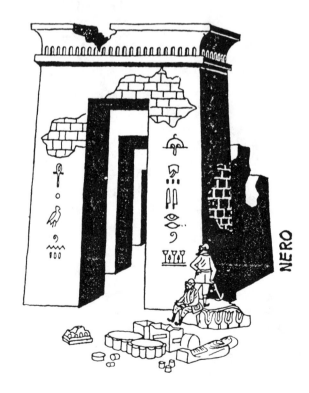

As far as I can make out, Norman, it says 'What! Make bricks without straw?'

V. THE NEW TESTAMENT

V.39 THE PEOPLES OF NEW TESTAMENT TIMES

Greeks. This nation inhabits the islands and peninsulas of the western Mediterranean and the Aegean, possessing a common language, religion, and culture. According to Jewish tradition, the Greeks were descended from Javan, the fourth son of Japheth son of Noah (Gen 10:2-4). The early Greeks were merchants (Ezek 27:13) and slave-traders (Joel 4:4-6) who plied the Mediterranean in search of new commercial venues.

The Greek empire under Alexander the Great (356–323 BC) subjugated the entire eastern Mediterranean basin and Persia. The Greeks insisted on a policy of cultural colonization, called Hellenization, which affected the Jewish aristocracy of Judea. The territory itself was a point of contention between two domains of the Greek empire, the Seleucids of Syria and the Ptolemies of Egypt. The ensuing tensions led to a Jewish revolt headed by the Hasmonean family. The rebels eventually managed to achieve limited independence from both kingdoms (Book of Maccabees). Nevertheless, Greek culture continued to dominate much of the population of Palestine up to and including the Roman period. Hellenism was particularly influential among the Gentile peoples of the region, and the term "Greek" came to denote all Gentiles, and was so used by Paul. Paul characterized the Greeks with the pursuit of wisdom (meaning philosophy), as opposed to the Jewish pursuit of miracles and divine signs (I Cor 1:18-2:16). In Romans, he declared that teachings of Christ could lead to the salvation of the Greeks as well as the Jews (Rom 10:12).

Hellenism dominated the rise of the early Church. Since Hebrew was unfamiliar to even the Jewish inhabitants of the region, the Greek translation of the Old Testament, known as the Septuagint, was an authoritative religious text. The New Testament, as well as various apocryphal and pseudepigraphical writings, was written mostly in Greek, and the language was used by the church until the 2nd century AD. Much of the early missionary work mentioned in the New Testament was carried out by Hellenized Christians (Acts 8:1-3). Paul himself often used terms reminiscent of Greek philosophy. In his Epistle to Philemon, Paul uses the Platonic expression "form" in describing Jesus (Philem 1:6-7). Nonetheless, most scholars agree that the influence of Greek philosophy on the early Church was minimal.

Nabateans. People who inhabited the southern Transjordan and Negeb regions of Palestine from the 4th century BC. The Nabateans originated in Arabia, but, impelled by hunger, broke northwards out of the Arabian peninsula. They infiltrated Moab and Edom and other areas in the region. Their language was a dialect of Aramaic, which replaced the proto-Arabic they had spoken in Arabia. The Nabateans left no inscriptions until the 2nd century BC, and all knowledge of them prior to that period is based on Greek and Roman writings.

The Nabatean capital was situated at Petra, sometimes identified as the biblical town of Sela (Judg 1:36). The city served as a major regional trading center. The Nabateans were highly accomplished in commerce, engineering, and art. They were known for advanced and imaginative systems of desert agriculture and for their daring raids on travelers in the vicinity of their towns. These raiding excursions developed into wars of conquest, and the Nabateans eventually built an empire

Main street at Nabatean Petra, Jordan.

extending as far as Damascus. Tensions developed between the Jews and Nabateans for hegemony over the region. The extent of contacts between the two cultures is indicated by the fact that Herod's mother was Nabatean. The Nabateans were subdued by Rome in AD 106, but managed to maintain their own culture until the rise of Byzantine Christianity.

The Nabatean king Aretas IV is mentioned in the New Testament as having appointed a governor over Damascus from whom Paul escaped (II Cor 11:32).

Parthians. This people inhabited the Seleucid Greek province of Parthia in Persia. The Parthians revolted against the Seleucids, establishing an empire of their own which rivaled Rome. They invaded the Province of Judea in 40 BC, but their increasing strength was finally curbed by Mark Antony. Josephus states that many of the Israelites deported by Babylonia were resettled in Parthia; it is possible that these Jewish exiles formed the core of learned Parthians who settled in Jerusalem (Acts 2:9).

Romans. This was originally the name of Latin-speaking inhabitants of the Tiber River region. By 265 BC, the Romans had gained supremacy in the affairs of the entire Italian peninsula and set off on a course of conquest, creating an empire unparalleled in human history. When the Hasmonean kingdom of Judea was torn by a power struggle between Hyrcanus and Aristobulus II, the two sons of Queen Salome Alexandra, the Roman general Pompey was asked to mediate and took advantage of the situation by declaring Judea a Roman protectorate (63 BC). The Jews were regarded favorably by the Romans because of the support they had offered Julius Caesar during the civil war. In return, they were granted certain privileges, including religious freedom, but at the same time, Hasmonean rule was abolished. Antipater, an Edomite (Idumean), was appointed regent of Judea (47 BC). In 40 BC, his son Herod was chosen by the Senate to succeed him as King of Judea.

Herod proved to be an unpopular king, and his son and successor Archelaus proved even more unpopular. The Roman authorities replaced him with an official called a procurator.

The Jews were increasingly angered by the excesses of Roman rule in Palestine, and various nationalist and messianic movements arose. The Jews found Roman rule so harsh that eventually a Jewish revolt broke out against Rome (AD 66). After impressive initial successes, the Jews were beaten back by the Roman forces who, after a lengthy siege, recaptured Jerusalem and destroyed the Temple (AD 70).

Jews were living in Rome from the 2nd century BC, and there is evidence of a Christian community there soon after Jesus' death. In AD 50, Emperor Claudius expelled the Jews from Rome; two Christians, Aquila and Priscilla, are noted among the refugees (Acts 18:2).

Paul journeyed to Rome, where he was imprisoned (Acts 19:21, 28:16). His Epistles to the Romans were directed to the Church in Rome, and it is thought that several other epistles were written while Paul was imprisoned there. Church tradition asserts that the apostle Peter served as bishop of Rome, and that he was martyred there with Paul. The Book of Revelation compares the evil of Rome with that of Babylon (Rev 18). Roman persecution of the Christians intensified during the reign of Diocletian (AD 284–305). In AD 313, however, Christianity was recognized as a legitimate religion by the Edict of Milan. In AD 381, Constantine declared Christianity the official religion of the Roman empire.

Samaritans. These were residents of the district of Samaria. When Samaria (the Northern Kingdom of Israel) was conquered by Assyria in 721 BC, its Israelite inhabitants were exiled. In keeping with Assyria's policy of population transfers, the territory was resettled by peoples from far-flung regions of the Assyrian Empire. Although the deportees to Samaria were pagan they were rapidly assimilated into the predominantly Israelite culture. Their religious conversion was not total, however, and pagan customs infiltrated their worship, causing the ethnically pure inhabitants of Judah to despise the Samaritans (II Kgs 17:24–41). The Samaritans came to consider themselves Israelites and even offered to help in the reconstruction of the Tem-

Scythian horseman; felt cloth from frozen burial chambers in the Altai Mountains in Central Asia; 300 BC.

ple. The inhabitants of Judah rejected these advances, and in the ensuing hostility between the two groups, the Samaritans made several efforts to hinder the rebuilding of both the walls of Jerusalem and the Temple (Ezek 4; Neh 6).

The breach between the Judeans and the Samaritans intensified, and by the 4th century BC, the Samaritans were clearly recognizable as a separate sect. They claimed descent from the tribes of Ephraim and Manasseh, and regarded Mount Gerizim as the sacred mountain chosen by God. The Jews were perceived as schismatics who, they claimed, had transferred the cultic center from Shiloh to Jerusalem. Samaritans accepted only a modified version of the Pentateuch as canonical, and regarded Moses not only as the supreme prophet but as the Messiah. A temple was erected on Mount Gerizim near Shechem, in fulfillment of the tenth commandment of the Samaritan Pentateuch. Jews rejected Samaritan religious innovations, and referred to the Samaritans as "that foolish people that dwells in Shechem" (Eccl 50:25-26). The Samaritan Temple was destroyed in 128 BC by the Hasmonean monarch, John Hyrcanus.

The attitude towards the Samaritans in the New Testament is ambiguous. Jesus warned his disciples to distance themselves from the people (Matt 10:5-7) and their religious practices (John 9:52). At the same time, he was in contact with Samaritans, often to the amazement of his disciples (John 4). Perhaps the most famous of Jesus' parables is that of the "good Samaritan" (Luke 10:33-37). Samaritans were among the first people to accept the gospel (Acts 8:5-25).

Approximately 500 Samaritans still inhabit the cities of Shechem and Holon.

Scythians. They were a nomadic tribe which inha-

Samaritan high priest holding the scrolls of the Samaritan version of the Pentateuch.

bited the Caucasus region of the present-day Soviet Union. The Scythians were a war-like tribe, whose southernmost conquests extended to the Philistine cities of Ashdod and Ashkelon c.600 BC. They were allied with the Assyrians against the expansion of Medea. Although the Scythians had already disappeared from Palestine by Roman times, the city of Beth Shean was renamed Scythopolis (i.e. City of the Scythians). Paul considered the Scythians to be barbarians, but noted that since the coming of Jesus, they too were capable of achieving grace (Col 3:11). Christian tradition asserts that the apostle Andrew spent his final years preaching to the Scythians.

V.40 TEXT AND CANON

FORMATON OF THE NEW TESTAMENT CANON

The canon of the New Testament consists of 27 books arranged in the familiar order. First come the gospels of Matthew, Mark, Luke, and John, being four different accounts of the life of Jesus. They are followed by the Acts of the Apostles, a book that presents itself as the continuation of Luke's Gospel; it starts with the ascension of Jesus to heaven and recounts events from the first three decades of the subsequent activity of his followers. Next come the Epistles of Paul, the leading personality in much of Acts, which fall into two groups. Romans, I and II Corinthians, Galatians, Ephesians, Philippians, Colossians, and I and II Thessalonians are

addressed to those geographically located early Christian churches. I and II Timothy, Titus, and Philemon are addressed to associates of Paul; the first three are commonly called the Pastoral Epistles. The Epistle to the Hebrews ends in Pauline fashion, but does not explicitly claim to come from Paul. There follow the Catholic Epistles, named after their proclaimed authors: James (the half-brother of Jesus), I and II Peter, I, II, and III John, and Jude. They are called Catholic, or General, Epistles because they are not addressed to individual churches. The last book is known as the Apocalypse of John or the Revelation to John.

At the end of the 1st century AD, the Scriptures of the Christian communities were still the Scriptures of their Jewish contemporaries. A century later, however, almost all of the above books had become established as the additional Scriptures of Christians. Also the claims of other books to become Christian Scriptures, the so-called "apocryphal" New Testament books, had been largely rejected. Only one of these apocrypha continued to have considerable influence in Christian tradition, while never becoming fully canonized: the Protevangelium of James, which recounts the childhood of Mary, the mother of Jesus. Even the accepted order of the New Testament books was well on the way to becoming fixed. How did this development come about in that specific short period?

It is instructive to contrast the attitudes of two important Christian figures of the period, Papias (c.60-c.130) and Origen (c.185-c.254). Papias composed five books of "Expositions of the Oracles of the Lord" in which he drew upon various gospels and other New Testament writings. Yet he also explicitly stated that he preferred not to rely upon books but upon what he had heard from people who had personally known the first followers of Jesus. Barely a century later, Origen was writing systematic commentaries on both the Jewish Scriptures (the "Old Testament" of Christians) and the New Testament books, treating them as a single body of authoritative Scripture. Also the term "New Testament" was already used to designate the specifically Christian Scriptures from at least the time of Tertullian (c.160-c.220).

Three factors promoted the emergence of the New Testament as Christian Scripture in the 2nd century. One was the fact that the final canon of Jewish Scripture was itself decided only in that period. Another was the need to determine an authoritative interpretation of that Scripture for Christians. The third was the attempt of Marcion, an early Christian heretic, to establish his own canon of authoritative Christian literature, excluding the Jewish Scriptures. More basic than all these reasons was the ongoing worship and prayer life of the early Christian communities, which required suitable reading for church services.

1. The early writings of rabbinic Judaism show that the inclusion of certain books in its canon, notably Esther, the Song of Songs, and Ecclesiastes, was not finally decided before the early 2nd century AD. The Talmud records discussion from that period about whether these three books were written "in the Holy Spirit" and whether they "soil the hands" like other books of Scripture. It also indicates that some rabbis of the period regarded Ben Sira (Ecclesiasticus) as authoritative, even as Scripture, although this book was expressly excluded from the rabbinic canon. The discovery of the Dead Sea Scrolls has confirmed that in the preceding century some Jews had regarded several other books as scriptural.

Precisely because the Jewish canon of Scripture was still partly open, there was room for Christians to

decide that they could augment Scripture with writings that were becoming crucial for their faith. All the more so, since the mainly Greek-speaking Christians of the 2nd century had as their Jewish Scriptures not the rabbinic canon but rather the collection of translations into Greek, together with some original Greek works, commonly known as the Septuagint. This collection, begun in the pre-Christian era, contains extra books as well as additions to and different versions of the books of the rabbinic canon. Indeed, arguments about whether the rabbinic canon or the Septuagint more faithfully represented ancient scriptural tradition played a major role in the early disputes between Jews and Christians. The arguments already appear in the Christian author Justin Martyr (c.100-c.165) and were the stimulus prompting Origen to begin his systematic study of the divergences between the Hebrew and various Greek versions of Jewish Scripture.

To this day, the Greek Orthodox and Roman Catholic Bibles contain these extra books. Protestants excluded them, but nevertheless retained the non-Jewish order of earlier Christian Bibles. The Jewish Bible starts from the Pentateuch, whose primary focus is not history but the divine commandments embedded in the historical narrative, and descends to two lesser classes: the Prophets, which echo the commandments, and the Writings, whose main role is liturgical. The Old Testament of Christians, and especially of Protestants, is introduced by Histories, ascends through the Psalms and Wisdom Literature, and climaxes in the Prophets, regarded as the anticipators of the Coming of Christ. Thus the ritual commandments, such as the dietary laws, lie at the heart of the Jewish Bible but are merely archaic details for most Christians. Jews include Ruth and Esther among the Writings, Christians place them among the Histories.

It all illustrates how the canonical order, no less than the canonical choice of books, can embody a theological attitude. The message of the traditional order of the New Testament, too, is clear enough: the Gospels proclaim the teaching of Jesus and the promise of salvation given through him, Acts and the Epistles deal with the dissemination of the faith throughout the world, while Revelation foretells how it will all end in the Second Coming of Christ.

2. This leads to the second factor mentioned: the earliest Christians, who were all Jews, saw in the ministry of Jesus the culmination of all the anticipations and promises of salvation to Israel that were contained in their Jewish Scriptures. It promoted the emergence of those authoritative Christian interpretations of Jewish Scripture which are found in the New Testament books. Eventually these books became at least as authoritative as the ones that they interpreted; they, too, were regarded as divinely inspired and thus as constituting Scripture. Almost at the same time, a similar development took place among Jews through

which the Mishnah and Talmud became their own authoritative interpretation of Scripture.

3. As for Marcion, a contemporary of Justin, his canon was not expansive but rather highly restrictive. In an attempt to separate Christianity totally from Judaism, he denied any authority to the Old Testament and set up his own canon of Scripture consisting of a few books already important to Christians, namely, Luke's Gospel and Paul's Epistles. Since even these were too Jewish for his taste, he made only a selection from Paul and severely edited Luke.

This posed a severe challenge to Christian writers of his time. They responded by undertaking two major tasks. The first and more urgent was to demonstrate that their Old Testament validated Christianity not as a variant of Judaism, but rather over and against Judaism, regarding this as the best manner of proving it to be truly Christian Scripture. With this tactic, they sowed the seeds of much of later Christian anti-Jewish polemics. The other task was to define what already existing specifically Christian books, besides those picked out by Marcion, would become authoritative for Christians.

All the New Testament books were written in Greek. Even the versions of the Syriac-speaking churches appear to go back to those Greek originals rather than to any anterior texts in a Semitic language. Classicists have often disparaged the language of the New Testament, even calling it the language of the market place, but unjustly. It is in fact much closer to Classical Attic than is the archaic language of Homer. The books are written in several significantly distinct but unquestionably literary styles. Much of the Gospel of Luke and the early chapters of Acts are written in the "translation Greek" of the Septuagint, which systematically reproduced the Hebrew syntax and diction of the sacred text. The remainder of Acts and some of the Epistles, especially Hebrews, are in an elevated Hellenistic prose. Much of the Pauline writings is in a consciously epistolary style, just as Cicero used in his letters a style different from that of his treatises. John's Gospel is in a simple but always very correct prose.

Modern scholars have questioned the traditional authorship of many of the books, especially of the Gospels, Acts, and Catholic Epistles. Of the Epistles of Paul, only Romans, I and II Corinthians, Galatians, and Philemon are universally regarded as genuinely Pauline; most regard the Pastoral Epistles as by an associate or imitator of Paul. In recent years, however, there have been attempts to reestablish traditional authorships. Since Paul explicitly mentions that he dictated his letters, divergences in style may reflect not different authors but his use of different scribes. Use of a gifted scribe has likewise been proposed as an explanation for the excellent Greek of the Epistles of Peter, the Galilean fisherman. Few scholars today, in contrast to many in the last century, would date much of the New Testament beyond the end of the 1st Christian century. Some now suggest that almost all of it antedates the destruction of the Second Temple.

Similar questions occupied those writers of the 2nd and subsequent Christian centuries who established the traditional authorships, which served as a criterion for including books in the canon. They were concerned to determine the connection between such books and those first followers of Jesus, including Paul, who gained the title of being his apostles. The "apostolicity" of such books, however, was understood in two not wholly distinct senses. On the one hand, Christian writers wished to determine whether a given book had been written by an apostle or at least accurately reflected an apostle's personal testimony (compare John 21:24). On the other hand, they tested the authenticity of the books against the teachings handed down to them by tradition from the apostles, who in this sense were treated as a collective rather than as individuals.

On its own, however, the second sense of apostolicity did not suffice to make a book into Scripture. For example, the epistle known as 1 Clement, whose author became Bishop of Rome in the late 1st century, quickly gained high prestige and authority. Yet it was never a candidate for canonization, since it clearly did not record the testimony of an apostle. Likewise, even down to the 4th century, there was resistance to including Hebrews and Revelation in the canon because their apostolic authorship was in doubt.

Nevertheless, the conception of the apostles as a collective authority was highly important for how the churches saw the New Testament as a collection of Scripture. The canon was not merely a list of books; even their canonical order could imply a theological viewpoint. All the more important was the way in which books were interpreted collectively in the light of one another.

For instance, the New Testament contains two versions of when Jesus ascended to heaven: either immediately after his resurrection from the dead (Luke 24:51 in almost all manuscripts) or 40 days later (Acts 1:9). There are also two versions of how the original apostles received the Holy Spirit: either from Jesus himself (John 20:22) or after his ascension (Acts 2:4). In both cases, the second version became authoritative in Christianity, so much so that most Christians never notice the alternative even when they read the verses concerned. This illustrates how the New Testament came to be read as an integrated account of the origins and basis of faith in Christ, drawing here upon one book and there upon another. The process was well under way when Tatian composed his Diatessaron (c.150), a composite account excerpted from the four canonical Gospels; indeed this, rather than its sources, was the dominant form of the Gospel in Syriac-speaking churches until the 5th century.

It was the integrated story, as much as the individual books, that constituted the scriptural canon. There could be variants in the manner of integrating the story, but then there were also variant manuscripts of the books. One of the causes of the great doctrinal dissensions in the Church during the 4th and 5th centuries, which led to the first of the schisms that have persisted until today, was that the different New Testament books reflect different theological outlooks as well as different details of fact. The Nicene Creed, more properly the creed promulgated by the Councils of Constantinople (381) and Chalcedon (451), integrated in an authoritative manner several of those outlooks. It united most of the Church, but its promulgation was accompanied by the schisms mentioned.

It is widely held by scholars that the different groups of New Testament books, such as the Pauline writings, the Johannine writings, Luke-Acts or Matthew's Gospel, originated in different Christian communities founded in the age of the apostles. The Mother Church, until it fled Jerusalem shortly before AD 70, may have provided a central focus of allegiance (compare Acts 15 and Gal 2). The few writings known from Christian authors of the period immediately following suggest that there continued to be distinct churches expressing a variety of theological outlooks.

In 1 Clement, for example, several Pauline epistles are used, but there is no sign of the Pastoral Epistles or even of II Corinthians, although 1 Clement itself is addressed to the church in Corinth. Much use, however, is made of I Corinthians, and also of Hebrews. The author quotes sayings of Jesus that are found in the Gospels of Matthew and Luke, yet not with the same wording.

By contrast, from what is known about the lost works of Papias, it seems that he paid no attention at all to the Pauline writings. He discussed the Gospels of Matthew and Mark, while also using John's Gospel, I Peter, and I John. The teaching of the Revelation of John was highly esteemed by him.

Intermediate in time between 1 Clement and Papias are Ignatius (c.35-c.107) and his follower Polycarp (c.69-c.155). Both use most of the Pauline epistles and I Peter; they know sayins found in Matthew and Luke. Polycarp even uses the Pastoral Epistles; he treats 1 Clement as an authority alongside the other books mentioned. Yet both of them, too, show no knowledge of II Corinthians. Since scholars have good reason to regard this book as a composite of two or more writings by Paul, it may not yet have come into circulation.

These examples show that well before Marcion most of the New Testament books were being used as authorities, while much less regard, if any, was paid to New Testament apocrypha. Yet different writers treated different groups of books as authorities. Moreover, among those authorities were already books whose inclusion in the canon was long resisted (Hebrews,

Revelation), and a book that was never a candidate (1 Clement). None of these books, however authoritative, was yet treated as Scripture. If Scripture is regarded as literature written "in the Holy Spirit," then it required a further working of the Holy Spirit among the communities that possessed those books before they perceived them as thus inspired.

Most intriguing is the relationship of Christian writers of this early period to the Gospels of Matthew, Mark, and Luke, which scholars call the "Synoptic Gospels" because of their similarities. Papias made a famous comment whose literal meaning would seem to be: "Matthew compiled the oracles in the Hebrew language, and everyone translated them as best he could." The implication is that Matthew's Gospel was the first, but written in Hebrew, while others, including the authors of gospels in Greek, made translations from what they found in it. So Papias was indeed understood by later Christian writers down to Origen and Jerome (c.342-420), both of whom knew Hebrew and claimed to have seen that original Hebrew text of Matthew, since lost.

As most scholars in the 20th century have held that Mark's Gospel was the first and was a major source of Matthew's and Luke's Gospels, they have sought to reinterpret Papias' statement, suggesting that he meant not Hebrew but Aramaic or even a Hebraizing style of Greek. They also argue that Papias meant a list of Jesus' sayings by Matthew's compilation of the "oracles." This collection of Jesus' sayings, first in Aramaic, later in Greek, is called Q by scholars, an abbreviation for Logien-Quelle or Sayings source. This lost document is reconstructed by listing the 200-230 verses common to Matthew and Luke and absent from Mark, all of which turn out to be sayings or teaching material. This source would have been compiled by Matthew as early as AD 45-50 or even earlier. But a list of sayings did not adequately reflect the full figure of Jesus and his activities. The early Christians were not satisfied with this document, important as it was.

Mark, then, on the most common hypothesis, was the first to put together a *narrative* of the story of Jesus, especially of his death and resurrection, but omitting most of his teaching since this was available in Q. Soon this solution was also found to be inadequate because it involved two separate documents. So both Matthew and Luke undertook to rewrite the gospel story, this time combining Q and Mark, inserting Q into the Marcan story-line, and adding other material as they went along. Matthew wrote for a more Jewish-Christian community, Luke for a Gentile-Christian community. In their present Greek forms, these gospels date from AD 80-90.

Other traditions already established in the 2nd Christian century are that Luke accompanied the apostle Paul, writing down his testimony, and that Jesus' "beloved disciple" whose testimony underlies

John's Gospel (21:20,24) was indeed John the son of Zebedee. By the end of the century, it was widely accepted that there were only four authoritative gospels, although others were sometimes quoted by the most orthodox of Christians. Indeed, the canonical list was complete apart from some of the Catholic Epistles and the continuing hesitations about Hebrews and Revelation.

Tying up those loose ends, however, took much longer. It had to wait until the Church emerged from persecution by the Roman Empire and sought to define its doctrinal foundations in universal councils of bishops, starting with the Council of Nicaea (325). Only in the late 4th century was the definitive list of New Testament books being promulgated, with the term "canon" being used to denote it.

THE SYNOPTIC PROBLEM

The word "synoptic" is derived from a Greek word meaning "to view together." The Gospels according to Matthew, Mark, and Luke are known as the synoptic Gospels because they present a similar view of the same series of events: the deeds and sayings of Jesus.

These books date from the 1st century AD and were written in Greek, although the syntax and vocabulary of the texts suggest that the material originally existed in written form in either Hebrew or Aramaic. To date, scholars have collated more than 1,000 Greek manuscripts containing portions of one or more of the synoptic Gospels.

None of the synoptic Gospels gives the name of its author. The attribution of authorship to Matthew, Mark, and Luke is a Christian tradition dating to the late 2nd century AD. The first Gospel may have been ascribed to Matthew because of the tradition that the disciple Matthew wrote a gospel in Hebrew (which was translated into Greek). For example, Papias, the bishop of Hierapolis in Asia Minor in the mid-2nd century AD, wrote that "Matthew put down the words of the Lord in the Hebrew language, and others have translated them, each as best he could" (Eusebius, *Ecclesiastical History* III 39, 16).

The Problem. The "synoptic problem" concerns the order in which Matthew, Mark, and Luke were written, and the literary sources they may have used. Although the many similarities among the synoptic Gospels suggest an interdependence, there are also differences. For example, according to Luke 4:22, after Jesus spoke in his hometown synagogue in Nazareth, the people said, "Is not this Joseph's son?" According to Mark 6:3 they said, "Is not this the carpenter, the son of Mary...?" However, Matthew 13:55 recounts, "Is not this the carpenter's son? Is not his mother called Mary?"

Jesus' foretelling of Peter's denial appears in all three Gospels (Matt 26:34; Mark 14:30; Luke 22:34). In Matthew and Luke, Jesus says that Peter will deny him three times before the cock crows, whereas according to Mark, Jesus says that Peter will deny him three times before the cock crows twice.

In a saying that appears only in Matthew and Luke, Jesus says: "What man of you, if his son asks him for bread, will give him a stone? Or if he asks for a fish, will give him a snake?" (Matt 7:9-10); "What father among you, if his son asks for a fish, will instead of a fish give him a snake; or if he asks for an egg, will give him a scorpion?" (Luke 11:11-12).

For the past 200 years, scholars have been trying to determine the significance of such similarities and differences. It appears that the writers of the synoptic Gospels borrowed from each other or shared common sources, or both. But it is still unclear who borrowed from whom, and which variants are the most accurate and original.

Solutions to the Problem. The earliest known theory of the synoptic relationship was proposed in *De Consensu Evangelistarum I* by Augustine, bishop of Hippo from AD 396-430. Augustine held that the synoptic Gospels were written in the same order in which they appear in the New Testament, with Mark using Matthew's account, and Luke referring to Matthew and Mark. This view, which is accepted for a long time by the Roman Catholic Church, held sway until about 1790, and has been revived by B.C. Butler (*The Originality of St. Matthew*, 1951). See Diagram I.

The oldest modern, critical, theory is that Matthew was the first Gospel written and was used by Luke, with Mark writing last and copying from both Matthew and Luke. This was first proposed in 1764 by Henry Owen, but has been called the Griesbach Hypothesis because it was advocated by Johann J. Griesbach in 1789. It was the dominant theory among scholars from about 1790 to 1870, and has been brought into currency again by William R. Farmer (*The Synoptic Problem*, 1964). See Diagram 2.

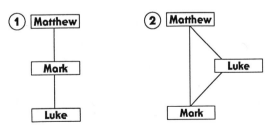

The most widely accepted synoptic theory today is the Two-Document Hypothesis which was proposed by Heinrich J. Holtzmann in 1863 and given its classic statement in 1924 by Burnett Hillman Streeter in *The Four Gospels*. According to this theory, Mark wrote first and was used independently by Matthew and Luke. In addition to Mark's document, Matthew and Luke also worked from a non-canonical document consisting mostly of sayings of Jesus. This second source is a hypothetical text referred to by scholars as "Q," thought to be an abbreviation of the German word *Quelle*, meaning source. See Diagram 3.

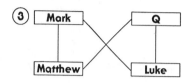

Robert L. Lindsey has argued that Luke was written first and was used by Mark, who in turn was used by Matthew. This theory postulates two non-canonical documents that were unknown to the synoptist (a Hebrew biography of Jesus and a literal Greek translation of that original) and two other non-canonical sources known to one or more of the writers. According to Lindsey, Matthew and Luke and perhaps Mark as well were acquainted with an anthology of Jesus' sayings taken from the Greek translation of the Hebrew biography. Luke alone was acquainted with a second source, a Greek biography which attempted to reconstruct the story order of the original Hebrew text. Mark used Luke while only rarely referring to the anthology, while Matthew used Mark and the anthology. Luke and Matthew did not know each other's Gospels, but independently used the anthology (Diagram 4).

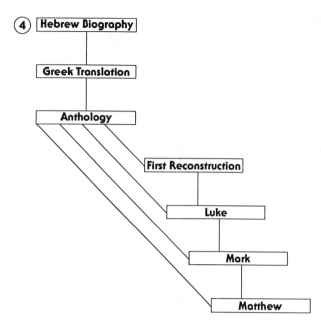

Importance of Hebrew. A number of scholars in Israel, most prominently David Flusser of the Hebrew University, have espoused Lindsey's source theory. These scholars, now collaborating as the Jerusalem School of Synoptic Research, believe that a Hebrew *Vorlage* lies behind the Greek texts of the Gospels. By translating the Greek texts back into Hebrew and interpreting how this Hebrew text would have been understood by 1st-century readers, one gains a fuller understanding of the text's original meaning.

V.41 THE BOOKS OF THE NEW TESTAMENT

THE GOSPELS

Matthew. The Gospel according to Matthew is generally listed as the first book of the New Testament. About half the text contains favorite discourses of Jesus such as the Sermon on the Mount (5-7), the missionary address to the apostles (10), the seven parables of the Kingdom of Heaven (13) and the eschatological discourses (23-25). Matthew also contains the Lord's Prayer (6:9-14), which later became the basis of most Christian services. Like the other gospels, the book is primarily an account of the birth, ministry, death, and resurrection of Jesus.

Scholars are uncertain as to when the book achieved its final form. They have suggested that the discourses and parables are part of an older tradition called Q which Matthew shares with Luke, which was possibly recorded by the apostle Matthew, an eyewitness to Jesus' ministry. A final author would have edited the material, adding an introduction and conclusion, and some explanatory material of his own. Since the book was probably intended originally for a primarily Jewish audience, it is thought that its earliest draft may have been composed in Aramaic, the Jewish lingua franca.

Important themes in the book include: the prominent role played by the disciples, especially Peter, in continuing the ministry of Jesus (13:51; 16:18-19), and the importance of the Church as a body. Matthew is the only gospel to mention the word "Church" (16:18; 18:17), and the book contains important information regarding Church authority. Great attention is paid to the role of angels, particularly in ushering in Jesus' ministry.

Little is known about the author. Matthew is described as a tax-collector (9:9; 10:3), but he certainly had a well-grounded Jewish education, as is exhibited by his mastery of scripture and legal matters. No evidence

Entrance to the Syrian Orthodox Church of St. Mark, Jerusalem, built on the traditional site of Mark's house.

St. Matthew portrayed as a scribe holding a parchment scroll. Miniature from a Byzantine manuscript.

is given regarding the identity of the author of the book's final draft. It is assumed to have been compiled between AD 75 and AD 90, possibly in Antioch or in Caesarea Maritima, where Jerome claims to have seen the original text in Aramaic.

The message of the Gospel according to Matthew is straightforward: Jesus Christ is the promised Messiah of biblical prophecy, come to lead all humanity toward salvation.

Mark. The Gospel of Mark, the second book of the New Testament, was often considered the least important of the synoptic gospels (the others being Matthew and Luke) because of the sparsity of the teachings of Jesus recorded and its apparent lack of narrative cohesiveness. In modern times, the book has been rediscovered. It is now considered by many to be the oldest gospel, from which both Matthew and Luke borrowed extensively.

Mark is primarily a narrative of the ministry of Jesus. The narrative is, however, seemingly abrupt, with certain important details merely alluded to. Noticeably lacking is an account of Jesus' continuing ministry following the resurrection. Three women enter Jesus' tomb where they are visited by a man in a white robe who informs them that Jesus has risen from the dead. The book ends with the women running away in fear. Whereas some ancient manuscripts continue the story, others do not. Today it is thought that the the shorter ending was intentional; this curt conclusion serves to stress to the believer the importance of looking forward to Christ's return or *parousia*. The literary climax of the book can be seen as Jesus dies on the cross; the Temple curtain is ripped, and a centurion exclaims, "Truly, this was the Son of God" (15:38–39).

The author believes that God's presence can be seen in the suffering of Jesus which heralds the impending Kingdom of God. Jesus, described in Mark as the Son of Man, and his death as a sacrifice, lie at the very basis of Christianity. The author does not support the apostolic claim as heirs to the legacy of Jesus, and portrays the apostles in a rather negative light. The apostles cannot comprehend the suffering of the Son of Man, a primary creed of the text (8:27–33; 9:9–13; 10:35–45), despite its being stated "plainly" to Jesus' intimate followers (8:32), nor can they follow the Mystery of the Kingdom of Heaven (4:11–13).

The Gospel of Mark contains two main themes: the immediacy in which Mark sees the arrival of the Kingdom of Heaven is best illustrated in Jesus' own declara-

ing presence of the eternal Kingdom of God. The immediacy in which Mark sees the arrival of the Kingdom of Heaven is best illustrated in Jesus' own declaration to his followers at the Last Supper, "Assuredly, I say to you, I will not longer drink of the fruit of the vine until that day when I drink it new in the Kingdom of God" (14:25). Even in his absence, Jesus will continue to attend to his followers. In Mark's accounts of the feedings of the multitudes (6:30–44; 8:1–10), a great amount of food is left over, implying that Jesus the shepherd will continue to feed his flock despite his corporeal absence as he declares in the Last Supper that the bread he breaks and blesses is symbolic of his own body; the wine is symbolic of his blood. Although he will no longer be there in person, his spirit will continue to grant them divine life and nourishment (14:22).

Many scholars hold that the gospel was written some years after the destruction of the Temple in Jerusalem in AD 70. Others claim that the book was written earlier, following the Great Fire in Rome in AD 64. Since early Christians in Rome suffered under Nero's harsh persecution, the author felt that an eye-witness account of Jesus' ministry would confirm their faith. This assumption would mean that the gospel was originally intended for Gentile Christians, a tradition supported by Clement of Alexandria (c.150–c.213), who states that the Gospel was composed to support the teachings of Peter in Rome. Christian tradition states that Peter dictated the content of the book to John Mark, accounting for the book's canonization on the grounds of apostolicity; however, most scholars point to the text's antagonism to the apostles as making such a hypothesis unlikely.

The message of Mark is that Jesus, Son of Man, died as a sacrifice to atone for man's sins. Only through his death can mankind be redeemed. Since the crucifixion, man's redemption is imminent.

Luke. This is the first part of a larger historical work, containing both the Gospel according to Luke and the Book of Acts. The two, written by the physician Luke, a companion of Paul, were the first attempt at creating a purely Christian historiography. Whereas the other gospels sensed the immediacy of the Kingdom of God, and therefore believed that history had come to its conclusion, Luke responded to the growing lack of faith in the Christian communities resulting from the delay in the promised return of Jesus Christ. He regarded the coming of Jesus as only one, albeit the central, episode in human history. He regarded the Church as a new historical order that inherited the previous order of the Law and the prophets. Jesus begins his ministry not by announcing the imminent coming of the Kingdom of Heaven, but rather the presence of the Holy Spirit working through him (4:14) and ushering in this new era. Instead of a didactic

Two pages from the Gospel of St. Luke. From an Armenian Book of the Four Gospels; 12th century.

following of the old Law, what is significant to this new period is an emulation of the life of Jesus and his disciples. As such, it was deemed important to produce a book that depicted their lives in a manner worthy of emulation.

According to Luke, history can be divided into three periods: a) the Israelite period from Adam to John the Baptist: "The law and the prophets were until John" (16:16). Luke places great emphasis on the role of John the Baptist as the bridge between this first period and the succeeding period. With the birth of Jesus, humanity entered a new, universal period. Jesus is depicted as a savior for all humankind, not only the Jewish people. As opposed to Matthew, who traces Jesus' genealogy to Abraham, forefather of the Jewish people, Luke traces the genealogy to Adam (3:23–38), forefather of all humankind. Unique to Luke's account of the Nativity is the declaration of the heavenly host, "Glory to God in the highest, and on earth peace, goodwill toward men" (2:14). Jesus is the redeemer of the second epoch of history. Unlike Matthew, Luke holds that Jesus does not bring a new law to the Jews, but merely expands the tradition to include Gentiles as well. Unlike Mark, Luke claims that Jesus is not the sacrifice come to redeem mankind. Mankind can be redeemed through faith in God as expounded by Jesus, and by loving one's neighbor (10:27).

This explains the importance placed by Luke on emulating the lives of Jesus and the apostles. Luke places particular emphasis on issues such as prayer. Other Gospels refer to prayer only in reference to Jesus' passion; Luke presents Jesus praying in six specific instances: baptism (3:21); retiring into the wilderness after healing a man (5:16); choosing the apostles (6:12); ministering (9:18); upon his transfiguration (9:28–29); and teaching how to pray (11:1).

Luke's third epoch is the period of salvation. Following his resurrection, Jesus calls upon the apostles and Paul to preach salvation throughout the world as is portrayed in the Book of Acts.

The Gospel according to Luke was written to counter those who believed "that the Kingdom of God would appear immediately" (19:11). Only when the Gentiles have accepted Christ will the End of Days arrive.

John. The Gospel according to John, the fourth book of the New Testament, is very different from the three preceding, synoptic gospels (Matthew, Mark, and Luke). Although the author was apparently familiar with the sources used to compose Matthew and Luke and with the Gospel of Mark, only about a tenth of the passages of John have parallels in those texts. Particularly conspicuous is the theological perspective of the book, which also differes vastly from its predecessors. One instance can be seen in the author's attitude toward the Jews; whereas the other gospels regard the Jews as rival claimants to divine authority, John clearly depicts them as enemies of the one true Church (e.g., 8:44).

In writing his gospel, the author intended to clarify for lay people those signs communicating knowledge

St. John the Evangelist. Miniature from the Lambeth Bible.

of Jesus as the Christ. Those who are prepared for a higher spiritual existence will have no need for such signs (6:1-59; 20:24-29). The term for sign, *semeion*, used by John is particular to his gospel. It has the special connotation of a sign which leads to belief.

One prominent sign is Jesus' very incarnation. Jesus is simultaneously a human being and the "only begotten son" of God, the Father. Time and eternity are in him joined; the divine light, the divine word, and truth have, in him, entered human existence. John uses the Greek term *logos*, "the divine Word," to define the nature of the essential reality of existence: "the Word became flesh and dwelt among us" (1:14). The transcendence or sacred otherness of God includes the divine nearness in Christ and in creation as a whole. Only through symbols and through participation in the divine reality that Jesus claims for himself and his followers can one adequately speak of and comprehend the incarnation of God in Jesus (see 17:20-21). Jesus is the human incarnation of the Son of God, a concept that can only be grasped by true believers. Jesus supplants earlier Jewish savior figures such as the Patriarchs or Moses.

Little is known about the authorship of John. It is possible that the numerous references to the "beloved disciple" (13:23, 19:26, 20:2, 21:20, 24) allude to the author, although some scholars have suggested that the term represents an allegorical figure, possibly the future church.

ACTS

The Book of Acts is a continuation of the Gospel of Luke, with which it once formed a single text. Whereas Luke concerns itself with the life, teachings, and death of Jesus, Acts continues the story by documenting the rise of the early Church.

Two theories exist regarding the structure of the Book of Acts. The first states that the text is primarily a historical document, concerned with the development of early Church leadership. The first 12 chapters of the book are concerned with the ministry of Peter, mentioned in Luke as heir to Christ's legacy (Luke 22:31-32). Chapters 13-28 concern themselves solely with the mission of Paul. This hypothesis does not, however, account for the narrative regarding Stephen contained in chapters 6 and 7. Another theory states that the text records the expansion of the Church from Jerusalem throughout the Roman Empire. The book closes with an account of Paul's arrival in Rome (28:16-31) depicted as the climax of Paul's mission to the Gentiles. Accordingly, the message of the book can be summarized in the verse, "You shall be my witnesses in Jerusalem and in all Judea and Samaria and to the ends of the earth" (1:8). The first seven chapters focus on the Church of Jerusalem; chapter 8 tells of the spread of the gospel to Samaria; chapter 9 deals with missionary activity in Syria and Judea. Beginning with chapter 10, the text records the missions and journeys throughout the Roman Empire: Cyprus and Galatia (13-14), Philippi, Thessalonica, Corinth (16-18), Ephesus and the surrounding areas (19), and finally Rome (27-28).

The book documents the rise of the early church from a sect of Jewish Christians (sometimes called "the brethren," "the way," or "the Nazarenes"), one of the many contemporary Jewish sects, to a distinct religion whose adherents were primarily Gentile. The mission of Paul, accounting for over half the text, was to the main towns of Europe and Asia Minor, and concludes in Rome, the capital of the Empire. The author of Acts makes particular efforts to demonstrate the compatibility of the Church with Rome. In Corinth, Paul assures the faithful that the Gentile Church will receive the same privileges accorded to Judaism (18:12, 19:31-35). It therefore appears that the book was written primarily for Gentile converts to Christianity, synthesizing the teachings of the Church with Roman traditions. At the same time, Paul does not reject the Jewish roots of the fledgling Church. The author constantly mentions that whenever Paul arrived at a new town, he preached first at the local synagogue.

The Book of Acts contains two central themes: the ascendancy of the belief in Jesus' resurrection, and the unique role played by the Holy Spirit as the guiding force behind the Christian community. Some commentators renamed the book "The Acts of the Holy Spirit."

The Book of Acts is invaluable as a source for the continuing apostolic tradition following the ascension of Christ.

EPISTLES

Romans. The longest of the Pauline Epistles. The letter was composed by Paul in Corinth, before he had visited Rome. It has been questioned whether the final chapter, containing a list of greetings, was part of the original content of the letter.

Paul composed the epistle in order to record the message of the new Church and to justify his position regarding the Jewish religion, particularly after his decision that circumcision was no longer obligatory for Gentile converts. Paul defends his own belief that with the coming of Jesus, the age of ceremonial law had come to its conclusion. He explains the rite of baptism as a means by which the lives of the baptized are incorporated into Christ; his death and resurrection have liberated the baptized from sin since they are now beyond the confines of the Law (6:3-11).

The concept of a life of the spirit superseding a life based on the commandments given in the Old Testament is essential to Paul's letter. In chapter 13, he

repeats the Ten Commandments as binding on Christians, but comments that they can be summarized in the one Christian commandment, "Love your neighbor as you love yourself" (13:8-10). Yet despite his break with Jewish tradition, Paul sees no reason for hating the Jewish people. The Jews have served and have yet to serve an important role in God's scheme, and it is not for mankind to judge them for their rejection of Christ (9-11).

The book is sometimes divided into three sets or diptychs of contrasting panels, the first depicting human sin, and the second, its remedy in Christ. In the first set, Paul states categorically that the sins of both the Jews and the Gentiles are idolatry and hypocrisy (1:18-3:20). He responds that only by faith in Christ can man achieve salvation (3:21-4:25). Paul then discourses on the original sin of Adam (5), which can only be overcome by dying and rising through baptism, incorporated in the body of Christ. In the third diptych, Paul declares that the old law encourages the sin of concupiscence; those in whom the Holy Spirit dwells are guided by a new principle (*nomos*) of life.

Although the book discusses such important themes as the atonement achieved through Christ's death (3:24ff.), grace through baptism (6:1-11), and the gifts of the spirit (8), the Epistle is by no means exhaustive. Several themes central to other Pauline epistles are conspicuously lacking, notably the church, the eucharist, and the resurrection of the body. Some scholars, wondering what lay behind Paul's writing so lengthy a discourse on his personal theology, have suggested that the epistle was originally intended as Paul's final testament. Paul would have viewed the Church of Rome, capital of the Empire, as crucial in spreading the new faith. By preparing his own mission to Rome, he was laying the foundation for a universal Church.

I & II Corinthians. The two Pauline Epistles to the Corinthians make up the seventh and eighth books of the New Testament. References in the text indicate that Paul wrote at least two additional letters to the Church at Corinth, the Previous Letter (I Cor 5:9) and the Sorrowful Letter (II Cor 2:4). The Second Epistle to the Corinthians is generally thought by scholars to contain at least two disconnected epistles (II Cor 1-9; 10-13), and as many as five (II Cor 1:1-2:13 with the inclusion of 7:5-16; 2:14-7:4 deleting verses 6:14-7:1, which are sometimes assumed to be a later insertion; 8; 9; 10-13). All the known epistles illuminate the problems faced by the early Church as its nucleus moved from Jerusalem toward Europe, and from being a primarily Jewish sect to an essentially Gentile religion.

The Church at Corinth was composed of both Jews and Gentile converts. Prominent in the religious life of Corinth was the cult of Aphrodite, goddess of love, whose sensuous rituals influenced even the most devout Jews and Christians. Among the devout Christians in Corinth was Chloe (I Cor 1:11). Alarmed at the increasing vices exhibited by Church members, she wrote to Paul complaining about their behavior and seeking advice on how her household should counter the problem. Paul's first letter to Corinth, the otherwise unknown "Previous Letter," may have been an initial attempt to stem the penetration of unscrupulous elements into the Church (I Cor 5:9).

The impact of the "Previous Letter" was limited. Incidents of incest, prostitution, and homosexuality were known among believers; people were participating in pagan rituals and using the pagan legal system. There were even groups who denied such fundamental Christian creeds as the Resurrection. The questions asked by the devout community at Corinth reflected the deep-rootedness of this sinful behavior. Rather than discuss these crucial issues with Paul, they brought his attention to questions pertaining to particular legalistic matters such as divorce, the eating of meat from pagan rituals, and tithes. Paul does not censure the Corinthians. He attempts, rather, to encourage them, and begs them to adhere to the authentic Christian doctrine which he goes on to expound. Having no authentic Christian tradition to guide them, Paul advises his readers of the importance of love as the greatest gift of the spirit (I Cor 13:13).

Paul visited Corinth sometime in AD 54. In one instance he was insulted by the community who had not defended him from abuse by non-believers. In his "Sorrowful Letter," Paul expresses his despair at not having received the support of the community and informs them that he will not return to the city on his way to Judea as previously promised. The repentance of the community was later reported to Paul by Titus, and inspired the composition of Paul's fourth epistle, II Corinthians 1-9, in which Paul reconciled himself with the Corinthians (6:11-7:16) and explained his mission to them (1:12-6:10).

In Paul's final epistle to Corinth, he rebukes the Corinthians for hearkening to heresies that had been introduced by spurious younger preachers, sarcastically referring to them as "most eminent apostles" (II Cor 11:5). Paul exhorts his listeners to test themselves, to determine whether they are in fact living in faith (II Cor 13:5). By asserting his authority Paul paved the way for his final visit to Corinth, where he hoped to be greeted by a Church united under his guidance.

Galatians. This Pauline Epistle was sent to the region of Galatia in Asia Minor. It is a monograph addressed to the Gentile residents of the area, concerning the question of whether they were obligated by Jewish ceremonial law, particularly circumcision. Paul answers an emphatic "No," in keeping with his personal philosophy as well as the rulings of the Jerusalem Council of AD 49 (Acts 15). After establishing his own authority to answer these questions with a lengthy autobiographi-

Aramaic text of Paul's Epistle to the Galatians; from a 7th-century manuscript at St. Mark's monastery, Jerusalem.

cal sketch (1:10-2:21) in which he claims that his authority comes from a direct revelation from Jesus, Paul declares that "if righteousness comes through the Law, then Christ died in vain" (2:21).

Paul teaches by historical example that the essence of a righteous life is faith in Jesus rather than the performance of the Mosaic law. In chapter 3, he reminds his readers that Abraham attained grace before the Law was given. The Law was only given to guide those participating in God's particular covenant with Abraham, and obligates only Abraham's descendants. Any person can attain grace through faith alone. Paul continues by depicting various pairs to illustrate the two covenants coexisting: two wives of Abraham, Hagar the slave girl representing the old covenant of Mount Sinai, and Sarah the free woman whose children represent the new covenant of the heavenly Jerusalem (4:21-31). Paul takes the opportunity of the pairs to bring his discussion to the topic of the Flesh and the Spirit, the last major theme of the epistle (5).

Some debate exists as to the date of the letter's composition and to the region of Galatia to which it was sent. Until the 19th century, it was generally accepted that the letter was addressed to the inhabitants of northern Galatia, but it has more recently been supposed that the letter was addressed to southern Galatia. Paul is not supposed to have traveled north on his first missionary voyage, and the letter must therefore be dated after his second voyage in AD 50. On the other hand, Paul makes no mention of the Jerusalem Council of AD 49 that would have confirmed his assertions, and this therefore suggests an earlier date of composition. Galatians may be the earliest of Paul's epistles. It has always been regarded as one of the more important Pauline Epistles, and is classified as one of the four "capital epistles," the others being Romans and I and II Corinthians.

Ephesians. Letter attributed to Paul, sent to the Church he had established at Ephesus several years earlier. The epistle differs from Paul's other letters by not referring to specific individuals or to controversies relating to that particular Church. Some scholars suggest that the epistle was composed by one of Paul's disciples who attempted to summarize his master's teachings. Others, noting that some early manuscripts do not contain the opening words "in Ephesus," propose that the letter was in fact written by Paul, but not to the Church of Ephesus in particular. It is claimed that the letter was actually sent to several cities, of which Ephesus was one. Marcion refers to the letter as the "Epistle to the Laodiceans."

Much of the letter reads as a hymn in praise of Christ. The text is divided into two messages, one concerning doctrine (1-3) and the other, an appeal for morality (4-6). It pleads for the unity of all Christians in the Church, represented as the body of Christ. Only in the Church can Jews and Gentiles attain true unity (1:15-2:22). Reflections on the mystery of the Church (3:1-13) indicate that the letter was composed comparatively late in Church history, after the break with Judaism had been complete.

The epistle goes to great lengths to stress the importance of the bond of love that should exist between Christians, particularly emphasizing the love that should exist between man and wife. The letter is significant in tracing the theological development of the Pauline churches.

Philippians. This epistle was sent by Paul to the first European Church, established at the Greek city of Philippi during Paul's second voyage (Acts 16:9-40) and was apparently written during Paul's imprisonment in Rome, c.AD 62. In it, Paul expresses his wish to return to Philippi, and informs the inhabitants that in the meanwhile he hopes to send them Timothy (2:19-24). Paul thanks the Philippians for the money they had sent him (4:10-19) and promises to keep them informed of his circumstances (1:12).

In the letter, Paul shares with the Philippians the self-contentment he has found in the service of Christ. A common theme in the epistle is joy. Paul even sets himself as an example of one who can rejoice in any circumstances, describing himself as a man who has "learned in whatever state I am, to be content" (4:12) and encourages the Philippians to emulate him in this (4:8-9).

The letter also contains a hymn known as the Carmen Christi, praising the exaltation of Christ (2:5-11), which is considered to be among the oldest Church hymns.

The tone of the epistle changes radically in the beginning of chapter 3, as Paul gives a brief testimony of the trials of his own life (3:1-14). The letter as a whole is important for its teaching that all situations, no matter how difficult, must be faced joyfully in the service of Christ.

Colossians. Epistle attributed to Paul. The epistle itself says that Paul wrote it while imprisoned (4:3,10), but some scholars question the Pauline authorship. Traditional Pauline concepts such as righteousness and law are lacking, while others are presented in a manner dissimilar to standard Pauline manner. Alternatively, it is possible that changing circumstances in the Church induced Paul to adopt a style similar to that of the Church's adversaries.

The traditional Pauline themes of the epistle are given new meaning. The typical depiction of Christ as the image of God and of the Christian community as the Body of Christ is restated in the belief that all things are created in and for Christ, giving the doctrine of Christ's reconciliation a cosmic relevance.

Paul bases his epistle on a baptismal hymn (1:13-20) which he expands. The epistle is an exhortation to combat heresies prevalent at the time. It appears that the false teachings intended were Jewish in origin, but their esoteric nature, including the worship of angels (2:18) seems to point in the direction of the Essenes or some other Gnostic sect. The epistle stresses that holiness is not achieved by asceticism but by total devotion to the will of Christ (2:6-23). Paul also stresses the importance of baptism (3:1-17) and prayer (4:2-4) as a means of bringing about salvation.

I Thessalonians. Paul's First Epistle to the Thessalonians may be the earliest of the Pauline epistles, depending on the date of Galatians. Although Paul had managed to plant the seeds of a new Church in Thessalonica during his second missionary voyage (AD 49-50), he was oppressed by the Jewish inhabitants of the city and forced to leave the town (Acts 17). It appears that some degree of persecution continued to plague Christian converts in the city, and combined with Paul's hasty departure, many issues remained unresolved. Being unable to return (I Thes 2:18), Paul resorted to sending a letter to the faithful to clarify problematic points that had arisen.

The theological discussion is concerned with the future train of events facing the Church. Paul declares that the "dead in Christ" will rise from their graves to greet the risen Christ, who will come unexpectedly.

II Thessalonians. Paul's Second Epistle to the Thessalonians was composed shortly after the first epistle and continues its message, clarifying some points that may have been misunderstood. Certain Thessalonians had interpreted Paul's assertion that Christ would come unexpectedly as an indication of the immediacy of the Second Coming. Many had abandoned their work in anxious expectation of Christ's arrival. Paul castigates such behavior, regarding it as laziness, and says that those who remain voluntarily unemployed should not be fed by the community (II Thes 3:10).

He explains that the Second Coming must be preceded by certain events including an abandonment of faith and the appearance of "the man of sin" (II Thes 2:1-12). Dark days still lie ahead for the faithful, but Paul urges the Thessalonians to utilize the remaining time to the best of their ability.

I Timothy. This Epistle was sent by Paul to his disciple Timothy who headed the Church at Ephesus. The three Epistles (I and II Timothy and Titus) sent to individuals rather than to communities are commonly referred to as the "Pastoral Epistles" because they contain advice for church leaders or pastors. The Pastoral Epistles may have been written by a disciple of Paul to apply his message to a later time.

The first Epistle to Timothy may have been written to establish the young Timothy's authority over the Ephesian Church. The letter contains much information about the organization of the Church, including a strategy for the salvation of humanity (I Tim 2:1-7). Paul advises Timothy on the treatment of various people connected with the Church, such as elders (I Tim 5:17-22) and widows (I Tim 5:3-16). The author also sets standards for both the lay members of the Church (I Tim 2:8-15) and for its elders (I Tim 3:1-13).

II Timothy. This is the second epistle addressed to Timothy, in which he is recalled to Rome, apparently in order to be made Paul's successor. The letter is the most personal of the Pastoral Epistles, providing much information on Timothy and the elderly Paul. Paul expresses disappointment that as he nears the end of his life he has been deserted by many of his former companions (II Tim 1:15; 4:10,14-16) and is writing the letter from prison (II Tim 1:8,17). He predicts that the Church will still face many difficult times, continuing the difficulties he had faced in his mission (II Tim 3:1-12). Paul looks forward to his impending death as the crowning conclusion of a life dedicated to Christ.

The letter contains more biographical information about Timothy than any other book in the New Testament, but the central character of the epistle is Paul himself, ever optimistic, despite his many disappointments. "I have fought the good fight, I have finished the race, I have kept the faith. Finally, there is laid up for me the crown of righteousness, which the Lord, the righteous judge, will give to me on that day" (II Tim 4:7).

Titus. This Pastoral Epistle was sent by Paul to Titus exhorting him to serve as an example of the "godly life." This short book stresses the importance of goodly works in bringing about salvation, but notes that "not by works of righteousness that we have done, but according to His mercy, He saved us" (3:5).

Paul wrote this epistle to Titus, a Gentile convert to the new faith (Acts 16:1-3), to instruct him in the establishment of the Church in Crete. The bulk of the letter's content tells Titus how to enhance the Church's position, and points out desired traits for Church members (1:5-9; 2:1-10). Paul summarizes the basic creeds of the Church, particularly on grace, explaining how these creeds can be taught to the different congregations (2:15-3:3). He also points to those differences between Christians and pagans that lead to Christian salvation (2:11-14; 3:3-7). He warns Titus of false teachers, apparently referring to various factions that stressed the Jewish roots of Christianity (1:10-16; 3:9-11).

Paul's exhortation to forsake worldly passions in favor of a godly life has served as a basic tenet for devout Christians throughout the ages.

Philemon. This short epistle was written by Paul, who apparently met and converted Philemon on one of his journeys. Philemon's slave Onesimus ran away from him and sought Paul out in Rome. Paul succeeded in winning over the slave and convinced him to return to his master, and sent this letter to persuade Philemon not to be harsh with Onesimus. Although, characteristically, Paul does not condemn the practice of slavery, he points out to Philemon that since he and Onesimus share a brotherhood in Jesus, he should treat his slave as "more than a slave, as a beloved brother in Christ" (1:16).

Hebrews. This "word of exhortation" was only attributed to Paul at the end of the 2nd century. In recent times scholars have questioned the Pauline authorship of this epistle, noting that Paul's name does not appear once in the text. There are other indications, notably vocabulary and subject matter, which suggest that the text may not have been composed by Paul. If the author was not Paul, he must have been a close disciple and supporter.

More than any other New Testament book apart from the Gospels, Hebrews centers on the personality of Jesus as the hub of all creation and the purpose of God's relationship with humanity. The book opens with a statement of Jesus' superiority to the prophets (1:1-3). His stature is later compared favorably with the angels (1:4-14), Satan (2:14), and Moses (2:17-3:6). Jesus is defined as the God through whom creation came about and has been sustained. His death is described as the supreme sacrifice, by which all people can receive Divine forgiveness. As such, there is no longer a need for the Temple sacrifices to continue after Jesus' death (10).

The first known mention of the Epistle to the Hebrews is in a letter by Clement of Rome dated AD 95.

Although the book is commonly referred to as the Epistle to the Hebrews, the text does not have the qualities of an epistle apparent in other New Testament books. Some references are made to the readers (5:11-12; 6:9; 10:32; 13:3,7,18-24), but there is no introductory greeting nor is the author's name mentioned. It is therefore suggested that the letter was intended as a written sermon, rather than an epistle (13:22).

James. This Epistle is generally attributed to James, brother of Jesus, who was martyred in Jerusalem in AD 62. The letter was apparently composed in Palestine, and is often thought to be the oldest of the New Testament books. It is addressed to "the twelve tribes that are scattered abroad" (1:1), and calls on these apparently Jewish-Christians to let their faith guide their daily lives, in veneration of Christ.

The Epistle of James emphasizes the importance of good works, as opposed to Paul's stress on faith. Nonetheless, faith, too, plays an important role in the letter and appears as a concept no less than in any other epistle. One apparent contradiction between James and Paul is the Pauline assertion that no man is justified by works (Rom 3:28; Gal 2:16), which seems to differ from James' contention that by actions a person can be put right with God (2:24). The contradiction can be resolved, however, by explaining the Pauline verses as referring to the *initial* reception of justification, which can only be brought about through faith in Christ, whereas James alludes to the *continuing* lifestyle of the faithful.

The epistle is a practical guide for Christian living. "True religion" is defined as visiting orphans and widows (1:27). James stresses the importance of keeping all the Law (2:10-13) and exhorts his readers to guard their tongues from evil (3; 4:6-17; 5:12). The wealthy are warned that their riches will not save them from the Lord's judgment. A life of faith must be accompanied by a life of good works involving the physical as well as the spiritual needs of man. James complements the doctrine of a life of faith by teaching that such a life must be accompanied by personal holiness as achieved through good works.

I Peter. This epistle was apparently written by Peter while in Rome. It is addressed to the "strangers," probably Jewish and Gentile (I Pet 2:9-10) converts to Christianity who resided in Asia Minor. Peter exhorts his readers to remain faithful to their beliefs despite persecution, and calls on them to apply Jesus' teachings to their daily lives. I Peter often echoes other New Testament writings, particularly the epistles of Paul, but the letter also contains several doctrines unique to Peter, notably a rationale for the persecutions suffered by Christians. Peter states emphatically that present suffering is merely a prelude to future glory on "the day when Jesus Christ is revealed" (I Pet 4:13).

Peter wrote the epistle in Rome, which he refers to as "Babylon" (I Pet 5:13). His authorship of the letter is not generally questioned, although some scholars, noting its articulate Greek, have suggested that Silvanus, described as the letter's bearer and scribe (I Pet 5:12)

had considerable input in editing and revising the original text.

It has also been suggested that the first part of the epistle (1:3-4:11) was originally intended as a baptismal sermon. The epistle opens with a prayer (1:3-21) and continues with exhortations and instructions (1:22-4:11). However, others point out that the term "baptism" only appears once in the letter, and even there incidentally. Moreover, the book is clearly an epistle, and no satisfactory explanation has been offered as to why such a sermon would be incorporated into the body of a letter.

II Peter. This epistle is ascribed to Peter. In it he entreats Christians to beware the false teachings invading the Church (II Pet 2). Peter counsels his readers to follow the teachings of the scriptures to contest these heresies (II Pet 1:19-21; 3:14-16).

The second letter of Peter is similar to the Epistle of Jude. Peter's canonical authority could then be attested by the fact that Jude drew upon the earlier letter to compose his own epistle. This would justify the inclusion of this letter in the canon, which was only fully accepted in the 4th century. Most scholars, however, are of the opinion that this letter depends on the letter of Jude, which implies that II Peter would have been composed somewhat later than the lifetime of Peter; the opening verse attributing the letter to Simon Peter would then represent pseudonymity. The letter aimed at filling its readers with hope, declaring that the delay in Christ's return is intended to allow for all sinners to repent so that they are not destroyed for their sins (II Pet 3:9).

II Peter differs from the preceding book both in style and in theological outlook. The differing theological outlooks of the letters can be reconciled by recognizing the target populations of both epistles. II Peter is clearly an attempt to strengthen the faith of believers disappointed by the delay of Jesus' return. One particular heresy combated in the letter may have been an early form of Gnosticism. The author would then use the terminology of the Gnostics in challenging their heresies, further explaining the peculiarities of the letter, particularly in relation to I Peter.

I John. Epistle traditionally attributed to the apostle John, exhorting Christians to live in fellowship with God and His Son, while being wary of false teachings (I John 2:18-23). Jesus' commandment to "love your neighbors" is particularly prominent in the epistle. It is generally thought the epistle was composed in Ephesus toward the end of the 1st century.

The letter was apparently written to counter the heresies of the Gnostics who taught that their adherents had received a unique revelatory knowledge by which they had achieved a state of sinlessness. Gnostics denied the notion that Jesus had become incarnate as man, since it opposed their own philosophy rejecting the material world. John declares that people who accepted this teaching were endowed with the "spirit of the Antichrist" (I John 4:3).

John stresses that all men sin, but since the death of Christ to atone for man's sins, forgiveness can be attained by confession (I John 1:5-2:2). However, he does not regard confession as a justification for continuing to lead a sinful life. He declares that true Christians must surmount their propensity to sin. Through rebirth in Christ, the Divine in man, not the physical life, must dominate the true believer (I John 2:14-17; 3:3-10; 4:4). Like James, John enunciates the need for good works to accompany faith. One who does not actively love his brother cannot be said to love God (I John 4:7-21).

II & III John. These two short epistles were composed by someone who referred to himself simply as the "elder." The epistles are generally attributed to John, the author of the preceding epistle. The letters are uniquely personal for New Testament literature, addressed to the Lady and her children (II John 1:1), sometimes thought to represent a specific Church and its members, and to Gaius (II John 1:1), both of whom are otherwise unknown. The author notes the good deeds of the recipients that have caused him great pleasure. He states his intention of visiting them soon, thereby accounting for the briefness of the epistles. The author looks forward to an opportunity when he can express himself face-to-face.

Apart from the general discussion of Christian love, the letters briefly address the problems of heresies which have entered the Church. II John counters these heresies in more general terms, while III John is more specific.

Jude. One of the General Epistles addressed to all Christians. Scholars are unsure of the identity of its author, being uncertain of the identity of the James referred to by Jude as his brother (1:1). Some scholars identify James as the brother of Jesus, meaning that the author is himself the brother of Jesus. His reference to himself as the "bondsman of Jesus Christ" (1:1) would therefore simply indicate the humility of Jude before his more illustrious brother. Both James (Gal 1:19) and Jude (Matt 13:55) are named brothers of Jesus. Another possibility is that Jude is the apostle Jude, son of James (Luke 6:16; Acts 1:13).

The epistle urges Christians to distance themselves from false teachers, apparently a warning against the Gnostics. Gnostics taught that since all matter is evil and only the spiritual is good, any indulgences are to be overlooked as inconsequential. Jude goes as far as to compare these false teachers with Satan (1:9). The author attacks these heretics in the harshest possible terms.

The epistle of Jude was only added to the canon in the 2nd century AD. It was written as early as AD 60 or possibly around the year AD 80.

REVELATION

This work is known as "The Book of the Revelation to John," "The Book of the Apocalypse," and "The Apocalypse of St. John the Divine." An account of the End of Days, it was written by John, sometimes identified as the author of the fourth Gospel and the Johannine Epistles, although this identification is uncertain. The author composed the book on the island of Patmos, where he had been imprisoned for missionizing (1:9-10). This allusion to official persecution of Christians may indicate that the text was composed during the reign of the emperor Domitian (AD 81-96).

The term "revelation" is a Latin translation of the Greek *apo-kalypsis*, which means "unveiling." This would reflect the nature of the text, which reveals those future events leading to the return of Jesus Christ. The description of future events is allegorical, causing the book to be considered one of the most enigmatic of

The Apocalypse; miniature from the Bible of the Poor.

biblical books. The author was influenced by the Book of Daniel and the apocalyptic descriptions contained in the prophetic books of Isaiah, Ezekiel, and Zechariah.

Revelation describes Jesus as the fulfillment of biblical prophecy. More than any other book, it makes use of Old Testament imagery, particularly as related to the Exodus. Jesus is often compared to the paschal lamb, and his death is depicted as a fulfillment of all Old Testament prophecy. Certain uniquely Christian rituals receive their first mention in the Book of Revelation, among these the celebration of the Lord's Day on Sunday rather than on Saturday (1:10), and various references to the celebration of the Eucharist.

One stylistic device particular to the author of Revelation is the extensive use of numbers and colors as symbols; 3 (God), 4 (the world), 7 (completeness), 12 (God's chosen, both the tribes and the apostles), 1,000 (a multitude of people), and 666 (the beast). Earthly judgments are represented by different colored horses (6:2–8). Jesus himself rides a white horse (19:11). The Roman Empire is referred to as the "whore of Babylon" (17–18) because of the idolatrous worship offered to the emperor. It is possible that the author made such an extensive use of symbolism to veil the precise meaning of a book that would otherwise have been considered seditious.

Despite the pessimistic description of the trials and tribulations to face the faithful before Christ's Second Coming, Revelation is optimistic in its account of the final judgment, in which the truly righteous will be saved. The author is certain that Christ will soon return to improve the fate of humanity. The book closes with a cry of hope: "Come, Lord Jesus!" (22:20).

V.42 JESUS OF NAZARETH

Historical Sources. Information concerning the historical figure of Jesus is derived primarily from the New Testament, though early non-Christian references are found in the Roman writers, Tacitus and Suetonius. Another passage about Jesus attributed to the Jewish historian, Josephus Flavius, is dubious and probably the product of a later Christian hand. The four gospels are devoted almost entirely to Jesus' life and teachings. In addition, details concerning his life are mentioned in the Book of Acts and the New Testament epistles. Later apocryphal writings about the life of Jesus are less reliable and have inherited a great deal of legendary material.

Birth and Early Life. The exact date of Jesus' birth is not known with any certainty. The accounts given by Matthew and Luke indicate that he was born near the end of the reign of Herod the Great (37–4 BC). Matthew (1:18–25) and Luke (2:1–14) preserve independent traditions of the birth but both relate that Jesus was born in Bethlehem of a virgin and without an earthly father. Mary, instead, conceived through the miraculous intervention of the Holy Spirit.

Joseph and Mary, obeying the angelic decree (Luke 1:31), named their son Jesus, whose Hebrew equivalent, Joshua, means "he will save" or "God saves" (Matt 1:21). The New Testament records that Jesus (Luke 2:21) and his cousin John (Luke 1:59), were publicly named at the time of their circumcision.

Jesus was raised in Nazareth, a small Galilean village overlooking the Jezreel Valley. His parents were religiously observant and they presented him at the Temple in Jerusalem (Luke 2:22ff.) according to the biblical injunction (Lev 12:2–4). The family made their annual pilgrimage to the Temple in Jerusalem at Passover (Luke 2:41) in accord with religious custom. Joseph is not mentioned during the time of Jesus' ministry and may have already died before his son's baptism by John the Baptist at the age of 30. Mary, on the other hand, is numbered among those who followed Jesus (Luke 8:20–21) and was present with him at his crucifixion (John 19:25).

Ministry and Teachings. The synoptic Gospels depict Jesus' ministry as lasting not more than a year, while John's Gospel leaves the impression that it lasted two to three years. After being baptized by John the Baptist in the Jordan River, Jesus returned to Galilee. His ministry apparently was not received by the inhabitants of Nazareth (Luke 4:16–30), and he subsequently

The Adoration of the Kings by Hans Süss von Kulmbach.

The Genealogy of Jesus Christ

Jesus and his ancestry, shown on the mosaic ceiling of Kariye Church in Istanbul, Turkey.

The genealogy of Jesus is essentially an abstract of the Old Testament, continuing the line of David up to the New Testament times. It is divided into three periods: from Abraham to David, from David to the Babylonian Exile, from the Babylonian Exile to Jesus. In sum, there are forty-two generations from Abraham to Jesus.

The genealogy of Jesus in Matthew begins with Abraham and presents Jesus as King, descendant of Abraham, the father of the called race, and not Adam, the father of the created race. The Gospel of Luke, on the other hand, goes all the way back to Adam, in order to show that Jesus was a man.

Luke gives the genealogy of David's son Nathan, who was Mary's forefather. In Matthew, David's son Solomon is given as the forefather of Joseph. Thus both Mary and Joseph were descendants of David, and Jesus may be counted as the descendant of David through both Solomon and Nathan. Actually, Solomon was not a direct forefather of Jesus, and his relation to Jesus is indirect through Joseph's marriage to Mary.

There are several omissions in the genealogy of Jesus. Three generations, the descendants of Joram, given in the Old Testament, are left out from the genealogy of Jesus, most likely due to Joram's marriage to the daughter of Ahab and Jezebel, which corrupted Joram's descendants (II Chronicles 21:5; 22:1-4). Such an omission of three generations is in line with Exodus 20:5. Another generation — Jehoiakim — is also omitted from the genealogy of Jesus possibly because Jehoiakim was made king by Pharaoh and collected taxes for him (II Kings 23:34-35).

Representation of Jesus from the 6th century. It is the oldest hand-painted icon in the world and is believed to have been inspired by the Holy Shroud of Edessa.

The Lord's Prayer

Our Father in heaven,
Hallowed be Your name.
Your kingdom come.
Your will be done
On earth as *it is* in heaven.
Give us this day our daily bread.
And forgive us our debts,
As we forgive our debtors.
And do not lead us into temptation,
But deliver us from the evil one.
For Yours is the kingdom and the
     power and the glory forever.
     Amen.

Matt 6:9–13

The Lord's Prayer inscribed in over fifty languages at the Pater Noster Church, Jerusalem.

moved to Capernaum, concentrating his work in the region of the northern shore of the Sea of Galilee. During the course of his ministry, which involved teaching and healing (Matt 4:23), he acquired a group of disciples, twelve of whom are named in the Gospels (Mark 3:13–19).

Much of the ethical and religious teachings of Jesus parallel what is known of the teachings of some of his contemporaries. The tension between Jesus and the Pharisees has sometimes been misunderstood in Christian thought by a lack of familiarity with the warp and woof of Jewish argumentation in didactic circles of the time. Jesus' criticisms echo sentiments directed at the Pharisees heard from the Essenes, the Sadducean king Alexander Yannai, and even in the Talmud, itself a product of Pharisaic Judaism. While Jesus challenged the duplicity of the Pharisees, he upheld their authority to expound the scriptures (Matt 23:2–3). Tensions between Jesus and the Pharisees may reflect Jesus' affinity with another stream of Jewish piety, the Hasideans ("the pious ones"), which at times also challenged Pharisaic Judaism. It has also been suggested that he was influenced by the thinking of the Dead Sea Sect.

Jesus also exhibits similarities with other streams of Jewish religious thought. He appears to have crystallized elements from the fabric of Jewish religious thinking and from these formed his own movement. Many of his teachings are akin to those of the rabbinic school of Hillel, which emphasized love of God and neighbor. The heart of his public message was the proclamation of the nearness of the *kingdom of heaven*. The ethical content of this kingdom was that God's will would be done on earth as it is in heaven (Matt 6:10). God's will is for justice (Matt 6:33) and peace (Rom 14:17). The beatitudes of Luke 6:20–21 are based on Isaiah 61:1–4.

The question of Jesus' self-understanding of his role in God's redemptive activity is a matter of scholarly debate. John the Baptist anticipated that Jesus would fulfill the role of the eschatological Son of Man (Luke 3:16-17). At times Jesus voices a similar understanding of himself (Luke 12:49-53). Jesus never explicitly calls himself the Messiah. He does, however, affirm the profession of one of his disciples when Peter identifies Jesus as the Messiah (Matt 16:16-17). His response to the high priest also alludes to his self-understanding in messianic terms (Luke 22:69). That messianic expectations were attached to Jesus is also bolstered by the political charges brought against him by the Sadducean priesthood (Luke 23:2) and the Roman sign hung in mockery on his cross which read "King of the Jews" (Mark 15:26).

Arrest and Crucifixion. At the close of his ministry Jesus took his disciples and went up to Jerusalem for the feast of Passover. All of the Gospels indicate that Jesus understood that he would die in Jerusalem (Luke 9:44), "for it cannot be that a prophet should perish away from Jerusalem" (Luke 13:33). His popularity in Galilee preceded him to Jerusalem and upon his arrival in the city he was greeted by crowds who were expecting the arrival of a messianic deliverer.

In the following days Jesus found himself at odds with the religious establishment centered in the Temple. His action in the Temple (Mark 11:15-19), as a reflection of his preaching of the Kingdom, alarmed the authorities.

Jesus was not alone in his criticism of the corruption and complicity of the Sadducean priesthood. Yet, his challenge of their authority together with their fear that the messianic fervor of the crowds would incite rebellion and Roman reprisals, prompted the ruling priests to take action.

On the eve of Passover, after sharing the paschal meal, Jesus and his disciples went out of Jerusalem to the Mount of Olives. He was there apprehended by the Temple guards and taken to the high priest, Caiaphas. The following morning after a brief interrogation by the leaders, he was handed over to Pontius Pilate, the Roman procurator, on the charge of sedition.

Pilate sentenced Jesus to death by crucifixion. He was forced to carry his own cross, helped by Simon of Cyrene, and was crucified between two brigands outside the walls of Jerusalem. He died at three o'clock in the afternoon and was buried just before the beginning of the Sabbath. Because of insufficient time to prepare the body, the women who had accompanied him from Galilee had to return to the grave with spices after the Sabbath ended.

Resurrection. The Gospel accounts differ as to whether an angel or Jesus himself announced his resurrection to the women (see Matt 28:2-10; John 20:14-18). Nevertheless, the Gospels and the Book of Acts recount that Jesus appeared to his disciples on that day (Luke 24:13-35) and subsequent occasions for the next 40 days (Acts 1:3). Shortly before the Jewish Feast of Weeks (Pentecost) Jesus ascended to heaven. From that time the Church has awaited the *parousia* or Jesus' second coming when, it is believed, he will come again as the eschatological Judge and establish his eternal kingdom.

The Last Supper. Carved marble plaque formerly over the portal of the Church of the Holy Sepulcher, Jerusalem.

V.43 THE APOSTLES

The term refers principally to the twelve closest disciples whom Jesus chose to send out to preach as his representatives. "He called his disciples to him, and from them he chose twelve whom he named apostles. These were: first Simon, who is called Peter, and Andrew his brother; James the son of Zebedee, and John his brother; Philip and Bartholomew; Thomas and Matthew the tax collector; James the son of Alphaeus, and Lebbaeus, whose name was Thaddeus; Simon the Canaanite; and Judas Iscariot who also betrayed Him" (Luke 6:13-16). Because he betrayed Jesus, Judas Iscariot was replaced immediately (Acts 1:23) at Peter's suggestion. The names of Barsabbas and Matthias were put forward and lots were drawn. Matthias was selected and thereafter "numbered with the eleven apostles" (Acts 1:23-26). It seems, therefore, that the number twelve was not chosen at random. Perhaps it was meant to symbolize the kingdom of heaven, including all twelve tribes of Israel restored (Matt 19:28; Luke 22:30; Rev 21:10-14). Jesus told them that they would "sit upon twelve thrones, judging the twelve tribes of Israel."

The Twelve are indicated in the gospels of Matthew, Mark and Luke, with some variations as to the order in which they are listed (Matt 10:2-4; Mark 3:13-19; Luke 6:14-16).

Peter, James, and John formed the "inner circle" who alone witnessed certain events, including the raising of Jairus' daughter; the transfiguration; and the agony in the Garden of Gethsemane. Peter was recognized as the leader. He had received the promise of the keys of the kingdom of heaven.

The Twelve were constant companions of Jesus and received his teachings. Jesus sent them two by two to preach the kingdom of God and to heal the sick (Mark 6:7). He instructed them: "Do not go into the way of the Gentiles, and do not enter a city of the Samaritans. But go rather to the lost sheep of the house of Israel. And as you go, preach, saying: The kingdom of heaven is at hand. Heal the sick, cleanse the lepers, raise the dead, cast out demons... Provide neither gold nor silver, nor copper in your moneybelts, nor a bag for your journey, nor tunics, nor sandals, nor staffs; for a worker is worthy of his food..." He foresaw hardship and persecution for the apostles: "I send you as sheep in the midst of wolves. Therefore be wise as serpents and harmless as doves. But beware of men, for they will deliver you up to councils and scourge you in their synagogues..." He recommended boldness: "Whatever I tell you in the dark, speak in the light; and what you hear in the dark preach on the housetops..." (Matt 10:5ff).

After the resurrection, Jesus instructed the eleven for the last time in Galilee: "Go and make disciples of

Enamel plaque representing Pentecost, showing apostles receiving "divided tongues of fire" (Acts 2:1-4). Verdun Altar.

all the nations, baptizing them in the name of our Father and Son and of the Holy Spirit, teaching them to observe all things that I commanded you" (Matt 28:20).

THE TWELVE APOSTLES

Andrew (Greek: "manly"). Son of Jonah (John) and brother of Simon Peter, Andrew was a fisherman, native of Bethsaida in Galilee, but lived in Capernaum. He was first a disciple of John the Baptist. When he heard John introduce Jesus as the "Lamb of God," he followed Jesus to Bethany and was soon convinced that he was the Messiah. He then led Simon Peter to Jesus. They returned to their fishing, but a few years later, after John the Baptist's death, Jesus bid them follow him and become "fishers of men," along with James. They left their nets and gave all their time to their new task (Matt 4:18; Mark 1:14-29). Andrew was present when the crowd, assembled at Tiberias to hear Jesus preach, had to be fed, and tried to find a solution to the problem.

Andrew is always listed among the first four in the apostolic lists (Matt 10:2; Mark 3:18; Luke 4:14). With Peter, James, and John, he was present at the Mount of Olives with Jesus when he predicted the destruction of the Temple.

Eusebius writes in the 4th century that Andrew preached to the barbarians of Scythia. According to a legend, Andrew was imprisoned in Achaia and crucified at Patras. He is said to have remained alive on the cross for two days, preaching to the onlookers.

Bartholomew. A man of Cana, he is often identified with Nathanael. He met Jesus through his friend Philip who invited him to "come and see the Messiah," to which Nathanael replied: "Can anything good come out of Nazareth?" (John 1:47). However, he responded to the invitation and when Jesus saw him approach, he remarked: "Behold an Israelite in whom there is no guile." After talking to Jesus, Nathanael became a disciple (John 1:45-51). Jesus assured him that he would see great things, and Nathanael saw Jesus resurrected (John 21:2). He appears as one of the Twelve in the Gospels of Matthew (10:3), Mark (3:18), Luke (6:14), and in the Acts (1:13).

James. Son of Alphaeus (Matt 10:3; Mark 3:18; Luke 6:15; Acts 1:13). His mother was Mary, one of the women who was present at the crucifixion. He is also sometimes called James the less (Mark 15:40). He may have been the brother of Matthew (Levi) and Joses (Mark 2:14; 15:40).

Mary holding James' head after he was decapitated. Embroidered drape at the Armenian Cathedral of St James, Jerusalem

James. Son of Zebedee, brother of John. James and his brother were working at their father's fishing business on the shore of the Sea of Galilee when Jesus called them, as well as two associates, Andrew and Peter, to be his disciples and "fishers of men." Peter, James, and John are often mentioned together in Jesus' company. They were the only ones present at the Transfiguration (Matt 17:1-2), the only ones to witness the resurrection of the daughter of Jairus (Luke 8:51) and, with Andrew, were close to Jesus while he was praying on his last night at Gethsemane. James and John were very keen to occupy a prominent place in the Kingdom at the right and left hand of Jesus, to the point of requesting their mother to intervene in their favor (Matt 20:20-24; Mark 10:35-41).

James was beheaded by King Herod Agrippa (c.44). He was the first of the Twelve to die a martyr (Acts 12:1-3).

John. Son of Zebedee and brother of James. The two brothers became known as "Boanerges," i.e., "sons of thunder," implying vehemence, zeal, and intensity (Mark 3:17). Like James and Simon (Peter), John abandoned the family fishing business on the shore of the Sea of Galilee to follow Jesus. It is thought that John was the "beloved disciple" who leaned on Jesus' shoulder at the Last Supper (John 13:23). Jesus chose him to take care of his mother Mary after the crucifixion (John 19:26ff). He was one of the first to reach the empty tomb (John 20:2-5). He witnessed the resurrection with Peter and the others and was the first to

Jesus and St John; detail from the Last Supper by Andrea del Sarto.

recognize Jesus in the dim form that appeared to them at the Sea of Galilee (John 21:7). Whenever John's name appears in the gospels it is associated with Peter. John and Peter were active in Jerusalem after the resurrection and played an important part in the early history of the Church.

Judas Iscariot. One of the Twelve chosen by Jesus, later replaced by Matthias after he betrayed Jesus. He is sometimes called "the son of Simon" (John 12:4), or "Iscariot" in the three Synoptic Gospels (Matt 10:4; Mark 3:19; Luke 6:16). In the list of the Twelve Apostles wherever he is mentioned, it is indicated that he was the betrayer. He was the only one of the Twelve not to be a native of Galilee (his name Iscariot implying that he was from the Judean town of Kerioth). Judas was responsible for the common finances of Jesus and the apostles (John 12:6). John refers to his greed for money. Judas offered to deliver Jesus to the priests for 30 silver pieces. At the Last Supper Jesus foretold Judas' betrayal (Matt 26:23-25), and when Judas and the other apostles were in the Garden of Gethsemane, Judas identified Jesus to the Roman soldiers by kissing him, a pre-arranged sign, and Jesus was arrested (Matt 26:47ff; Mark 14:43ff; Luke 22:47-48). After Jesus' arrest, Judas felt the enormity of his guilt and returned the money, with which a piece of land was bought, known as Akeldama ("Field of Blood"). According to Matthew, Judas hanged himself in remorse (Matt 27:3-5). According to Acts (1:16ff) Judas bought the land himself, then fell down "headlong, he burst open in the middle and all his entrails gushed out" (Acts 1:18-19).

Matthew. Writer of the Gospel according to Matthew. Known also as Levi (Mark 2:14; Luke 5:27), he was a tax collector before becoming one of Jesus' disciples (Matt 9:9, 10:3; Mark 2:14). Matthew was from Capernaum or the vicinity. Jesus saw him at his tax office during his travels in Galilee and ordered him to leave everything behind. He rose and followed Jesus. Matthew gave a feast which Jesus attended as did other tax collectors and "other sinners," arousing criticism from the Pharisees (Matt 9:10; Mark 2:15-16; Luke 5:27-30). Matthew was one of the Twelve chosen by Jesus (Matt 10:3; Mark 3:18; Luke 6:15; Acts 1:13). He witnessed the resurrection. After the apostles returned to Jerusalem, he was with them in the "upper chamber" (Acts 1:1-13). According to Eusebius, Matthew preached in various places outside the Holy Land.

Peter (Simon). Leader of the Twelve following the crucifixion. Simon, as he was first known, was Andrew's brother. Originally from Bethsaida, he lived with his family at Capernaum. Jesus called Simon and Andrew, who were fishermen, to become "fishers of men." Simon was then given the additional name of "Cephas," i.e., "stone" or "rock" in Aramaic, or "Petros" in Greek, hence Peter.

Peter, like James and John and sometimes Andrew, was present at important moments of Jesus' ministry: he witnessed the transfiguration (Mark 9:2-13). He heard Jesus predict the coming events and the End of the Age (Mark 13:2ff); and he was present at the Garden of Gethsemane on the night of the agony. Peter was one of the early disciples and witnessed the miraculous

The Handing of the Keys to St Peter; fresco by Perugino in the Sistine Chapel, Rome.

Paralytics waiting to be healed; 14th-century mosaic. Turkey.

catch of fish (Luke 5:1-11); he was the first to say to Jesus at Casaerea Philippi: "You are the Christ (messiah), the son of the living God," whereupon Jesus said to him: "You are Peter, and on this rock I will build my Church... and I will give you the keys of the kingdom of heaven" (Matt 16:13-23).

Peter, however, argued with Jesus on several occasions, even rebuking him when Jesus predicted his imminent death (Matt 16:21-22). Together with John, he was entrusted with the preparations for the Passover (for what was to be the Last Supper). Jesus predicted Peter's threefold denial. Peter also protested at Jesus' washing the disciples' feet and then asked that Jesus wash his hands and head also since this would bring him closer to Jesus (John 13:6-9). Peter's denial of Jesus occurred only a few hours later near the house of the high priest in Jerusalem where Jesus was detained, and afterwards "he wept bitterly" (Matt 26). After the crucifixion, John was the first to reach the empty sepulcher, but Peter was the first to enter the burial chamber. As Jesus had predicted, after the ascension Peter took the leadership and became the spokesman of the disciples. Peter also saw Jesus resurrected in Galilee before appearing to the other apostles (Luke 24:34: I Cor 15:5).

It was Peter who suggested a replacement for Judas Iscariot and who was the first of the apostles to perform miracles in the name of Jesus, healing a paralytic and raising Tabitha from the dead (Acts 3:1-8; 5:15; 9:32-41), and punishing offenders by death (Ananias and Sapphira; Acts 5:1-10). He converted and baptized Cornelius the Roman centurion (although he was a Gentile) and his household at Caesarea (Acts 10:34-38). Peter was imprisoned by Herod Agrippa but was miraculously freed by an angel (Acts 12:3-11). His ministry was not confined to the Holy Land: he journeyed to Antioch (Gal 2:11) and to other places in Asia Minor, later traveling to Rome (I Pet 5:13).

Peter is said to have been martyred during Nero's persecutions of the Christians in AD 64. He was crucified, and requested that it be done head down. St Peter's Basilica in Rome on Vatican Hill was built on a site venerated since the year 160 as the burial place of the apostle. The Tempietto in Rome, designed by Bramante, was built on the site where, according to tradition, Peter's crucifixion took place.

Philip. Apostle from Bethsaida in Galilee, like Andrew and Peter, and, like them, one of the early disciples of Jesus. Jesus met him in Galilee and Philip answered his call: "Follow me" (John 1:43). Philip introduced his friend Nathanael to Jesus (John 1:45-51). He was with Jesus at the multiplication of the loaves and fishes (John 6:5-7). When he asked Jesus to reveal the father, he received the reply: "Have I been with you so long, and yet you do not know me, Philip? He who has seen me has seen the Father" (John 14:8-9). After the ascension of Jesus, Philip was present in the "upper room" where the apostles Peter, James, John, Andrew, and Thomas were staying (Acts 1:13-14). In the gospels of Matthew, Mark, and Luke, Philip is only mentioned in the list of the Twelve Apostles.

Simon the Zealot. Apostle called also Simon the Canaanite (erroneously) or Simon the Canaanean. He may have been a member of the Zealot party whose members were fanatic nationalists and violently opposed Roman rule. The epithet "Zealot" may simply refer to his religious zeal. He received the authority to cast out evil spirits and to heal (Matt 10:1-4: Mark 3:14-18: Luke 6:15).

Thaddeus. One of the Twelve, according to Matthew (10:2) and Mark (3:18). In Luke (6:16), he is called "Jude the son of James," and not mentioned as an apostle. In some translations he is called Lebbaeus.

Thomas. Apostle, called "the Twin" in Matthew 10:3. On several occasions he openly expressed his doubts regarding some of Jesus' actions, and after hearing of Jesus' resurrection, Thomas said:" Unless I see in his hands the print of the nails and stick my hand into his side, I will certainly not believe." Whether Thomas actually felt the wounds is not clear, but when Jesus appeared again he was finally convinced. Jesus reproved him, saying: "Happy are those who do not see and yet believe" (John 20:24-29). The episode gave rise to the expression "doubting Thomas."

Achaicus. A Christian who visited Paul in Philippi and to whom Paul sent greetings in his First Epistle to the Corinthians (I Cor 16:16-18).

Agabus. A Christian prophet who, when visiting Antioch, foretold that a famine would take place in the reign of Claudius "throughout the world." When Paul was in Caesarea, Agabus was also there and foretold his arrest if he went to Jerusalem (Acts 11:27-28; 21:10-12).

Agrippa. See Herod Agrippa.

Alexander (man's defender). The name of two men from Ephesus: a Jew designated by his coreligionists as spokesman to plead with the mob during the riot caused by Demetrius the silversmith (Acts 19:24-41); a Christian accused by Paul that his faith had "suffered shipwreck" (I Tim 1:18-20).

Amplius (Ampliatus). A Christian of Rome to whom Paul sent greetings (Rom 16:8).

Ananias. A disciple in Jerusalem, who sold his property for the benefit of the church but kept back a part of the proceeds of the sale while affirming that he was giving all to the apostles. Peter denounced the deceit, and Ananias and his wife Sapphira were struck dead (Acts 4:32-5:10).

Another Ananias was a Christian of Damascus who, after receiving a vision, explained to Paul his experience on the road to Damascus, helped him regain his sight, and predicted that he would become a preacher of the Gospel (Acts 9:10-19: 22:12-17).

Ananias was also the name of a high priest in Jerusalem who opposed Paul; when Paul appeared before the Sanhedrin after he was arrested, Ananias struck him (Acts 23:1-10); later he gave evidence against him at Caesarea (Acts 24:1-19).

Andrew (Greek: "manly"). See V.43, Apostles.

Andronicus. A kinsman of Paul in Rome. A Christian even before Paul, he had been imprisoned (Rom 16:7).

Anna. A devout old woman who was present when the infant Jesus was presented at the Temple (Luke 2:36-38).

Annas (Greek abbreviation of the Hebrew *Hananiah*, "The Lord has been gracious"). Jewish high priest; the first to hear Jesus after his arrest. He then sent him bound to his son-in-law Caiaphas (Matt 26:57; John 18:13).

Antipas. A martyr of the church of Pergamum (Pergamos) (Rev 2:13).

Apollos. An Alexandrian Jew who "had been instructed in the way of the Lord," but "knew only the baptism of John." At Ephesus, where he resided and preached, he was further enlightened by Priscilla and Aquila, and subsequently preached the Gospel in Achaia and Corinth (Acts 18:24-26; I Cor 1:12; 3:5-10; Titus 3:13).

Aquila. A Jew who had taken up residence at Corinth following Claudius' decree banishing the Jews from Rome. On his first journey to Corinth, Paul, who practiced the same trade of tentmaking as Aquila, stayed at his house and they became close friends. Aquila and his wife Priscilla accompanied Paul to Ephesus where they too preached the Gospel (Acts 18:24-26). The couple seem to have returned to Rome, since Paul sends them greetings in his Epistle to the Romans (Rom 16:3-5).

Archippus. A Christian living in Asia Minor, saluted by Paul as a "fellow soldier" in his Epistle to Philemon (2). In the Epistle to the Colossians Paul urges him to fulfill his mission (Col 4:17).

Aretas. The name of four Nabatean kings. The one mentioned in the Epistle to the Corinthians is Aretas IV, the father-in-law of Herod Antipas. At the time that Paul was in Damascus, the city was under his control (II Cor 11-32).

Aristarchus. A Thessalonian who traveled with Paul on his third missionary journey and was arrested with him at Ephesus during the riot caused by Paul's preaching there (Acts 19:29). They again traveled together when Paul returned to Rome (Acts 27:1-2). In two of his epistles Paul conveys Aristarchus' greetings (Col 4:10; Philem 24).

Artemas. One of Paul's companions whom he wanted to send to Cyprus to replace Titus (Titus 3:12).

The Roman emperor Augustus (44 BC–AD 14).

Augustus. Title given to the first Roman emperor Gaius Octavius (Octavian) in 27 BC. Octavian was educated and adopted by his uncle Julius Caesar who made him his heir. He was sole ruler of the Roman empire from 44 BC until his death in AD 14. His policy was to avoid intervention in the government of the provinces, and his main achievement was that, for some time, peace and security were restored throughout the Empire. He favored the ruler of Judea, Herod, who was a loyal vassal, and even added to Herod's territories. According to Luke 2:1, Augustus ordered a census of the population for tax collection purposes which brought Mary and Joseph to Bethlehem. The title Augustus was assumed by the Roman emperors who succeeded him.

Barabbas ("son of Abbas"). A robber who was arrested for murder during an insurrection. When Jesus was tried, Pontius Pilate released Barabbas at the request of the crowd instead of releasing Jesus as he had proposed to do (Mark 15:7; Luke 23:11-18; John 18:39-40).

Bar-Jesus ("son of Jesus"). A magician attached to the court of the proconsul of Cyprus, Sergius Paulus, at Paphos. He tried to turn his master away from Paul's and Barnabas' preaching. In a later encounter with Paul, he was struck blind temporarily (Acts 13:6ff). Bar-Jesus is also designated as "Elymas," i.e., "sorcerer" (Acts 13:8).

Barnabas. An Apostle (Acts 14:4) and a devout, generous man; a Levite of Cyprus. His original name was Joses or Joseph, but the apostles surnamed him Barnabas, popularly explained as "son of comfort." To come to the aid of the apostles he sold his property.

Barnabas was closely associated with Paul. When Paul returned to Jerusalem after his conversion, Barnabas persuaded the church in Jerusalem to accept Paul as a sincere believer. The church leader sent Barnabas to Antioch to superintend the Christian community there, and he called Paul, who was then in Tarsus, to assist him. They were entrusted with the financial aid contributed by the community to the Christians in Jerusalem, which they took to the Holy City during the famine (Acts 11:22-30). They were both chosen to visit various places and preach in the synagogue, traveling to Seleucia and Cyprus. They were expelled from Antioch of Pisidia by some Jews who were envious of their success, and returned to Antioch, then to Jerusalem to clarify the question of the obligation of circumcision for the non-Jewish converts to Christianity. They then returned to Antioch to prepare Paul's second missionary journey. Paul objected to taking Mark with them, and as a result they went separate ways: Paul took Silas and traveled through Syria and Cilicia, while Barnabas and Mark went to Cyprus (Acts 13-15). No more is known of his career. Tertullian suggested that Barnabas was the author of Hebrews.

Barsabbas ("son of Sabba"). Surname of the apostle Joseph Barsabbas (see V.43, Apostles) and of Judas Barsabbas, a member of the Jerusalem church who had the gift of prophecy. He and Silas were chosen to accompany Paul and Barnabas as delegates of the Jerusalem church to inform the Gentile converts at Antioch of the decree of the apostles of Jerusalem concerning circumcision (Acts 15:22-23).

Bartholomew. An Apostle. See V.43, Apostles

Bartimaeus ("son of Timai"). A blind beggar who was cured by Jesus at Jericho (Mark 10:46-52). In the Gospel of Luke (18:35-43) the miracle is described without mentioning the name of the blind man. John cites Bartimaeus as an example of those who "have not seen and yet have believed" (John 20:29).

Bernice (Berenice). Jewish princess. She was first married to her uncle Herod of Chalcis, brother of King Herod Agrippa I. When her husband died she lived with her brother Agrippa II, and they were present when Paul was tried by Festus in Caesarea (Acts 25; 26:30). She later became the mistress of the future emperor Titus and went with him to Rome.

Blastus. The chamberlain of Herod Agrippa I who intervened in behalf of the people of Tyre and Sidon (Acts 12:20).

Boanerges. Nickname meaning "sons of thunder" applied by Jesus to James and John, the sons of Zebedee, because of their impetuosity (Mark 3:17).

Caiaphas. Son-in-law of the high priest, Annas, with whom he worked in close cooperation. He later succeeded him and was high priest from AD 18 to 36. He was at the trial of Jesus and was also a member of the court which tried Peter and John after they cured a crippled man in the name of Jesus (Matt 26:3,57: Luke 3:2; John 11:49; Acts 4:6).

Claudius. Roman emperor, mentioned (Acts 11:28) in connection with Agabus, who had predicted a famine, which actually did strike Palestine and Syria during the reign of Claudius (AD 41-54). He is again mentioned in connection with the decree he issued banishing all Jews from Rome (Acts 18:2).

The Roman Emperor Claudius (AD 41-54).

Cleopas. Disciple who encountered the risen Jesus in Emmaus (Luke 24:18). Cleopas may be the same person as Clopas, the husband of Mary, one of the women who stood at the foot of the cross with the mother of Jesus (John 19:25).

Cornelius. The first Gentile to be baptized by Paul. He was a Roman centurion of the Italian cohort stationed at Caesarea, a man "who feared God and gave alms generously" (Acts 10:1ff).

Damaris. Athenian woman who turned to Christianity after she heard Paul speak at the Aeropagus (Acts 17:22–34).

Demas. A co-worker and companion of Paul during his first imprisonment at Rome. He later deserted him, preferring "this present world" (Col 4:10–14; II Tim 4:10; Philem 24).

Demetrius. A silversmith in Ephesus who stirred up a riot against the Christians through fear that Paul's preaching was going to harm his business, as he made shrines for the goddess Artemis (Acts 19:24,38).

Dorcas. Also known as Tabitha; a Christian woman from Joppa, renowned for her good deeds, which including making clothes for the poor. When she died, the apostles sent for Peter who was at the neighboring town of Lydda. The apostle hurried to Joppa and through his prayers brought her back to life (Acts 9:36–40).

Elizabeth (Elisabeth; "my God has sworn"). Wife of the priest Zacharias and mother of John the Baptist. She conceived after being barren for many years following the prediction of an angel to her husband. During her pregnancy, she was visited by her cousin, Mary of Nazareth (Luke 1:5ff).

View of Ein Karem where, according to tradition, Elizabeth lived and was visited by Mary of Nazareth.

Epaphroditus ("charming"). A native of Philippi, one of Paul's esteemed fellow workers. While in Rome he fell ill, presumably from overwork, and almost died. Paul had to send him back home (Phil 2:25–30)

Eunice ("victorious"). Timothy's mother, from whom he inherited his "genuine faith" (II Tim 1:5).

Euodia. A Christian of Philippi who disagreed with her fellow worker, Syntyche. Paul urged them both to compose their differences (Phil 4:2).

Eutychus ("fortunate"). A young man of Troas who fell asleep during a long discourse of Paul's, and fell from a window-seat on the third storey of the house where they were assembled. He "was taken up dead," but Paul restored him to life (Acts 20:6–12).

Felix. Roman procurator of Judea from AD 52 to c.60, who presided over Paul's trial at Caesarea. He kept him two years in prison, trying in vain to obtain a bribe from him (Acts 24).

Festus. Procurator of Judea after Felix was recalled to Rome in c.60. Paul was still in prison at Caesarea and requested permission to appeal to Caesar. Festus accepted and sent him to Rome (Acts 25:12ff).

Gaius. A Macedonian who traveled with Paul and was with him during the riot at Ephesus (Acts 19:29). Another Gaius, or perhaps the same one, was baptized by Paul at Corinth (Rom 16:23; I Cor 1:14). The addressee of the Third Epistle of John is also called Gaius.

Gallio. Roman proconsul of the province of Achaia. When the Jews of Corinth, the capital, had Paul arrested, the prisoner was brought before Gallio, but Gallio dismissed the case as a dispute between Jews (Acts 18:12–17).

Gamaliel. Known as Gamaliel the Elder, a Pharisee, a renowned teacher of the law. Paul was one of his students (Acts 22:3). He was a tolerant man and advised the Sanhedrin against persecuting the early Christians in Jerusalem (Acts 5:33–40).

Herod (The Great). Son of Antipater, an Idumean, who was appointed governor of Judea in 47 BC, and

Head found in Egypt and supposed to represent Herod the Great.

king under Augustus. His mother, Cypros, was a Nabatean of noble descent.

Although of Jewish faith, Herod and his family were considered aliens. He had secured his throne after the overthrow and execution of the Hasmonean king, and, furthermore, he was a friend of Rome. For these reasons, Herod was greatly resented by his subjects. His reign was bloody and filled with court intrigues, which he resolved by executing the parties involved, including his own wife (Mariamne) and his children. The emperor Augustus is said to have remarked that he would rather be Herod's pig than his son: since Herod was an observant Jew and did not eat pork, the pig had a better chance of surviving. His suspicious nature and cruelty is illustrated in the New Testament when Herod orders the slaughter of the infants of Bethlehem (Matt 2), an episode known from no other source.

Herod reigned for 33 years. In spite of his outrages, his cruelty, and his lust for power, he became known as "Herod the Great." He was a resourceful politician, a good administrator, and a great builder, constructing whole cities, erecting theaters, strongholds, and palaces, and rebuilding the Temple in Jerusalem. But he was hated by the Jews for promoting Hellenization in the country, restricting the power of the Sanhedrin, and imposing heavy taxation. Order was maintained by oppression. He was loyal to Rome and promoted the cult of the Emperor in the non-Jewish parts of his kingdom, but he finally succeeded in alienating Augustus by his brutality and aggressive policy against the Nabatean kingdom. After his death in 4 BC, his kingdom was divided between his sons Archelaus, Antipas, and Philip.

Herod Agrippa I (called Herod in the Acts of the Apostles). Son of Berenice and Aristobulos, grandson of Herod the Great, he was four years old when his grandfather executed his father. Agrippa was brought up in Rome at the imperial Court with Claudius and Drusus. Tiberius had him thrown in prison where he remained until Caligula's accession in AD 37. The new emperor granted him additional territories and the title of king. Agrippa successfully sought the favor of his Jewish subjects. Possibly in light of this, he had James the son of Zebedee put to death, and imprisoned Peter (Acts 12:1-10). In AD 44, while attending games held in honor of the Emperor at Caesarea, he was taken with violent pains in the stomach and died a few days later (Acts 12:21-23).

Herod Agrippa II (called Agrippa in the Acts of the Apostles). Son of Herod Agrippa I, he was 17 when his father died, and considered too young to rule. Judea was ruled by Roman procurators, but not long after, Emperor Claudius gave him the kingdom of Chalcis and transferred to him the tetrarchies formerly held by Philip and Lysanias, with the title of king. Agrippa was at Caesarea with Bernice, his sister, when Paul appeared before Festus. After Paul had presented his case in a

Coin of Herod the Great.

Portrait of Agrippa II on a coin struck at Caesarea.

Coin of Herod Antipas struck at Tiberias.

long tirade, Agrippa said to him: "You almost persuade me to become a Christian" (Acts 26:1ff). In AD 66 Agrippa tried to prevent the Jewish revolt against powerful Rome, but in vain. He remained loyal to Rome and after the war he resumed his kingship until AD 100.

Herod Antipas (called King Herod in the Gospels and the Acts of the Apostles). Youngest son of Herod the Great by his Samaritan wife Malthace. He inherited Galilee and Perea from his father's kingdom and inherited also his father's cunning. He had John the Baptist imprisoned and beheaded (Mark 6:14-28). Jesus referred to him as "that fox" (Luke 13:32). When he was sent to Herod Antipas, Jesus refused to answer his questions, whereupon "Herod and his men of war treated him with contempt and mocked him and sent him back to Pilate" (Luke 23:1ff). He spent his last years in exile in Gaul.

Herod Archelaus. Son of Herod the Great and Malthace. Like his brother Antipas, he was brought up in Rome. He ruled over Judea with the title of ethnarch from 48 BC. At that time, Joseph and Mary returned to Judea with Jesus, but hearing that Archelaus ruled there, they settled in Galilee (Matt 2:19-22). In c.AD 6, Archelaus' subjects complained to Rome about his tyranny and Herod Agrippa I accused him of plotting against the empire. He was banished to Gaul.

Herodias. Granddaughter of Herod the Great and Mariamne, she married Herod Philip and had a daughter, Salome. She divorced Philip and married her uncle, Herod Antipas. John the Baptist condemned the marriage, which was against the law (Matt 14:3ff; Mark 6:17ff).

Jairus. Leader of a synagogue on the shores of the Sea of Galilee, who appealed to Jesus to save his dying daughter. Jesus went to the house where the child was already dead and brought her back to life (Mark 5:21-43, Luke 8:40-56).

Jambres and Jannes. Egyptian magicians from the time of Moses mentioned by Paul (II Tim 3:8), as an example of those who resist the truth.

James. Name of two apostles, the sons of Zebedee and of Alphaeus (see V.43, Apostles). Another prominent James in the NT is the brother of Jesus, Joses, Simon and Judas, the sons of Mary (Matt 13:53; Mark 6:3; Gal 1:19). He was the first bishop of the Church of Jerusalem. The Church Fathers, teaching that Mary died a virgin, suggested that he may have been Jesus' cousin or half-brother. James became a believer after he witnessed the resurrection of Jesus in Galilee (John 7:5; I Cor 15:7). The Epistle of James is usually attributed to him (see V.41, Books of the New Testament).

Jannes. See Jambres.

Jason (popular Greek name adopted by Hellenized Jews instead of Joshua or Jesus). Paul's host in Thessalonica, who was arrested with him on the accusation of lese majesty against Caesar (Acts 17:5-9). He may be the same Jason who conveys greetings to the Christians of Rome through Paul (Rom 16:21).

Jesus. See V.42, Jesus of Nazareth.

Joanna. Wife of Chuza, an official in the household of Herod Antipas, tetrarch of Galilee. She was one of the women healed by Jesus and among those who attended to his needs during his ministry. She was present when the tomb where Jesus had been laid after the crucifixion was found empty, and was among the women who announced the resurrection to the apostles (Luke 8:1-3; 24:1-10).

John the Baptist dressed in goatskin, with a lamb in a medallion. Carved ivory, 6th century.

John. See V.43, The Apostles.

John the Baptist. Prophet who taught the approach of the Last Judgment. His father, Zacharias, was a priest who was offering incense at the altar when an angel foretold the birth of a son to his elderly barren wife, Elizabeth. John was ordained to be a Nazirite from birth. He grew up in the wilderness of Judah, wearing a garment of camel's hair and eating locusts and wild honey. He preached repentance and baptized his followers in the river Jordan to symbolize their purification from their past sins, "for the kingdom of heaven is at hand," instructed them in moral duties, and urged them to fast. His ascetic life and his prediction attracted many followers.

Jesus came from Galilee to be baptized, and upon seeing him the Baptist exclaimed: "Behold the Lamb of God who takes away the sin of the world" (John 1:29). In the eyes of Jesus, John was more than a prophet, he was the forerunner of a messianic age (Matt 11:9-15).

Herod Antipas imprisoned John the Baptist for denouncing the tetrarch's marriage to his brother's wife Herodias (Luke 3:19-20). During a feast at Herod's palace, Herodias' daughter requested John the Baptist's head. Unwillingly Herod agreed, as he had promised before witnesses to fulfill the young girl's wish if she agreed to dance before him. John was executed and his head brought on a platter before the assembled guests (Matt 14:1-13; Mark 6:14-29).

Joseph ("may God increase"). Carpenter of Nazareth, husband of Mary mother of Jesus. The Gospel of Matthew traces his lineage to the house of David and back to Abraham (Matt 1). Jesus was conceived by the Holy Spirit when Joseph was betrothed to Mary but before "they had come together" (Matt 1:18; Luke 1:27). Joseph and Mary went to Bethlehem as was required by the census ordered by the governor of Syria, Quirinius, and Jesus was born there. Fearing Herod's persecution, Joseph fled to Egypt with his family where they remained for a while, and then returned to Nazareth. Joseph took his family to Jerusalem on two occasions: to present the infant Jesus at the Temple and for the Passover pilgrimage when Jesus was twelve years old (Matt 1 and 2; Luke 2; 4:22). The gospels do not mention Joseph after this.

Joseph Barsabbas. See Barsabbas.

Joseph of Arimathea. A wealthy disciple of Jesus. After the crucifixion he obtained permission from Pontius Pilate to bury the body of Jesus in a tomb that he owned (Matt 27:57ff; Mark 15:43).

Judas. One of the brothers of Jesus (Matt 13:55; Mark 6:3).

Judas. Son of James, one of the Twelve Apostles in Luke 6:16 and Acts 1:13. He is not mentioned among the Twelve in Matthew and Mark. He may be the same person as Jude, the author of the Epistle of Jude, although Jude identifies himself at the beginning of the epistle as "the brother of James." John (14:22) refers to "Judas (not Iscariot)" who asks Jesus how he will manifest himself.

Judas the Galilean. He led a nationalist rebellion at the time of the census ordered by Quirinius. He was mentioned by Gamaliel in his address to the Sanhedrin in connection with the persecution of the apostles (Acts 5:37).

Jude. See V.41, Books of the New Testament.

Julius. Centurion responsible for bringing Paul safely

The tomb of Joseph of Arimathea in the crypt of the Church of the Holy Sepulcher, Jerusalem.

St. Luke. Sculpture by Nanni di Banco (1384-1424).

The resurrection of Lazarus; carved marble formerly on the lintel of the portal of the Church of the Holy Sepulcher, Jerusalem.

to Rome during the voyage from Caesarea (Acts 27).

Junia. Recipient of special greetings from Paul in his Letter to the Romans (16:7). Junia and Andronicus are referred to as "my kinsmen and fellow prisoners." They had become believers in Christ long before Paul himself.

Lazarus. Brother of Martha and Mary of Bethany, who was resurrected by Jesus. He is mentioned only in the Gospel of John (11).

Levi. Son of Alphaeus, a tax collector who became a follower of Jesus (Mark 2:14; Luke 5:27).

Luke. Referred to as the Evangelist. Traditionally accepted as the author of the Gospel of Luke and the Acts of the Apostles. A physician, he became a faithful traveling companion of Paul, who refers to him as "the beloved physician" and "fellow worker." Luke was with Paul at Troas on his second journey and from there went with him to Philippi on the third missionary journey. He accompanied him back to Jerusalem (Acts 20:6ff) and was with him in Rome on his last journey. Paul wrote to Timothy: "Luke alone is with me" (II Tim 4:11).

Lydia. Jewish proselyte from Thyatira in Asia. She came to Philippi to sell purple-dyed goods and heard Paul preach. Eventually he baptized her and her household. She gave Paul and Silas hospitality in her home (Acts 16).

Lysinias. Tetrarch of Abilene when Herod Antipas was tetrarch of Galilee. Luke mentions him to indicate the time when John the Baptist began preaching in the wilderness (Luke 3:1).

Lysias, Claudius. Roman centurion stationed in Jerusalem who rescued Paul from the mob in the Temple area on Paul's last visit to Jerusalem. During his interrogation of Paul, Lysias discovered that he was a Roman citizen, and sent him to Felix, the governor of Caesarea (Acts 23:26–30).

Malchus. Servant of the high priest. Peter cut off his ear when Jesus was arrested in the Garden of Gethsemane. The story is given in all four gospels, but only John mentions the name of the man (John 18:10).

Mark. Evangelist, companion of Paul, whose full name was John Mark, the son of Mary of Jerusalem, whose house served as a meeting place for the early Christians (Acts 12:12).

After Paul and Barnabas (Mark's cousin according to Col 4:10) had completed their relief mission in Jerusalem, Mark accompanied them as their assistant on their first missionary journey, but for some unknown reason, he left them and returned to Jerusalem (Acts 13:5,13). When Paul set out on his second journey, he refused to take Mark along. Barnabas disagreed and "the contention became so sharp that they parted from one another": Barnabas sailed for Cyprus, taking Mark with him. Some years later, however, Mark was with Paul in Rome as "his fellow laborer" (Philem 24). John

Mark was also associated with Peter in Rome. Peter calls him "Mark, my son" (I Peter 5:13).

Martha. Sister of Lazarus and Mary of Bethany. When Jesus visited them, Martha served him with devotion (Luke 10:38ff; John 11).

Mary. Mother of Jesus (the "Virgin Mary"). She was betrothed to Joseph, a carpenter from Nazareth, when Jesus was conceived by the Holy Spirit (Matt 1:18-20; Luke 1:35). Joseph married her after an angel appeared to him. Towards the end of Mary's pregnancy, she and Joseph went to Bethlehem because of the requirements of the population census ordered by Quirinius, and Jesus was born there (Luke 2:1-20). The family returned to Nazareth after a stay in Egypt to which they had fled, in fear of Herod's persecution (Matt 2:14-22; Luke 2:39). The last mention of Mary in the gospels is at the crucifixion of Jesus, when she was at the foot of the cross. During his last moments, Jesus entrusted his mother to the care of John, who took her to his home (John 19:25-27).

Five other Marys are mentioned in the NT: (1) Mary Magdalene, one of the most devoted of the Galilean followers of Jesus after he had healed her from evil spirits (Matt 27:56,61; 28:1; Luke 8:2; 24:10). She was the first to see that the tomb where Jesus had been put after the crucifixion was empty, and the first to whom the risen Jesus appeared (John 20). (2) Mary of Bethany, the sister of Martha and Lazarus, who anointed Jesus' feet and wiped them with her hair (Luke 10:39-42; John 11; 12:3). (3) Mary, the mother of James (Matt 27:56; Mark 15:40) whom Matthew calls "the other Mary." She was with the women of Galilee who were present at the crucifixion (Matt 27:61; Mark 15:47; Luke 24:10). (4) Mary, the mother of Mark (Acts 12:12). (5) A woman of the Christian congregation of Rome saluted by Paul for her achievement (Rom 16:16).

The three Marys (the mother of Jesus; Mary Magdalene; the mother of James), painting by Annibale Caracci.

Matthew. See V.41, Books of the NT; V.43, Apostles.

Matthias ("Gift of the Lord"). Apostle chosen by Jesus to replace Judas (Acts 1:23,26). See V.43, Apostles.

Nathanael ("God has given"). Man of Cana, often identified with Bartholomew, one of the Twelve Apostles. See V.43, Apostles.

Nicanor ("conqueror of man"). One of the seven worthy deacons chosen to assist the apostles in Jerusalem and to make distributions to the needy Christians of Jerusalem, including Greek widows (Acts 6:5).

Nicodemus ("conqueror for the people"). Pharisee and probably a member of the Sanhedrin, "who came to Jesus by night" to hear more about his teaching. When Jesus was arrested, he protested that it was unjust to condemn a prisoner before hearing him. After the crucifixion, he openly brought spices for Jesus' burial. He is mentioned only in the gospel of John (3:1-21; 7:50-51; 19:39).

Nicolas ("conqueror for the people"). One of the seven deacons chosen to assist the apostles in the distribution of food to the needy Christians of Jerusalem. He was a Greek from Antiochus who had converted to Judaism before becoming a Christian (Acts 6:5).

Onesimus ("profitable, useful"). Runaway slave belonging to Philemon, whom Paul met in Rome. After converting him, Paul sent him back to his master with a letter in which he pleads with Philemon to receive him "no longer as a slave but more than a slave, as a beloved brother...both in the flesh and in the Lord" (Philem 8-16).

Onesiphorus ("profit-bearing"). Christian from Ephesus: Paul praises his household for their generosity and devotion (II Tim 1:16; 4:19).

Paul (Saul). The details of his life are known from the Acts of the Apostles and the Pauline Epistles. Paul was born in the Asia Minor city of Tarsus (c.AD 10), where he spent his childhood. His Jewish parents were Roman citizens. Later, he lived in Jerusalem where he received a Jewish education as a student of a leading Pharisaic rabbi, Gamaliel the Elder. He was a tentmaker by profession. Paul, or Saul as he is first called in the New Testament, was an enthusiastic Pharisee and became an agent of the Sanhedrin in its efforts to suppress the nascent Christian church. He applied himself to the task with great zeal (Acts 7:58). After Stephen's death, "still breathing threats and murder" (Acts 9:1) against the disciples, he was sent to Damascus. Not far from the city, he had a strange experience: He heard Jesus saying to him: "Saul, Saul, why are you persecuting me...I am Jesus, whom you are persecuting." Following this vision Paul was struck blind for three days until he was healed by Ananias, a Christian of Damascus, who also baptized him (Acts 9).

Paul began immediately to preach his new faith in the synagogue but soon had to flee the city because the Jews wanted to kill him, and they enlisted the support of the governor of Damascus, who ordered his arrest.

His disciples helped him out of the city by letting him
down over the city wall in a basket at night since the
gates were guarded (II Cor 11:32ff). Paul returned to
Jerusalem but the Christians there were skeptical
about his conversion in spite of Barnabas' sponsorship.
He returned to his native town, where he remained for
several years until Barnabas came to Tarsus. Together,
they journeyed to Antioch where many Christians of
Jerusalem had taken refuge following Stephen's execution. Paul and Barnabas preached there for a whole
year, returning to Jerusalem to bring assistance to the
Christians in need following the famine that had
struck the country (Acts 11:27–30). Having accomplished this mission they returned to Antioch, bringing with them Mark, and embarked on the first missionary journey: to Cyprus, where Paul converted
Sergius Paulus, the governor, then to Pergamos and
Antioch in Pisidia where they preached for the first
time to the Gentiles; then to Iconium, Derbe, and
Lystra, where Paul healed a cripple and was almost
killed by the Jews because of his preaching; finally
they returned to Antioch in Syria. Wherever they went,
they appointed elders to carry on their work and spread
the Gospel (Acts 13, 14).

After some time in Jerusalem, where the preaching
of the Gospel to the Gentiles was approved by the

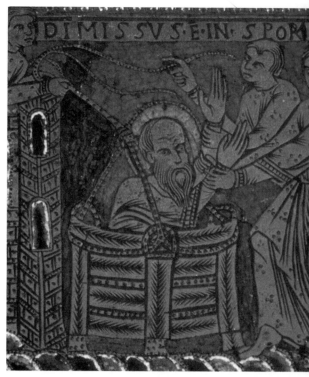

*To escape arrest, Paul is let down in a basket over the walls of
Damascus. Enamel plaque of the 11th century.*

The journeys of Paul.

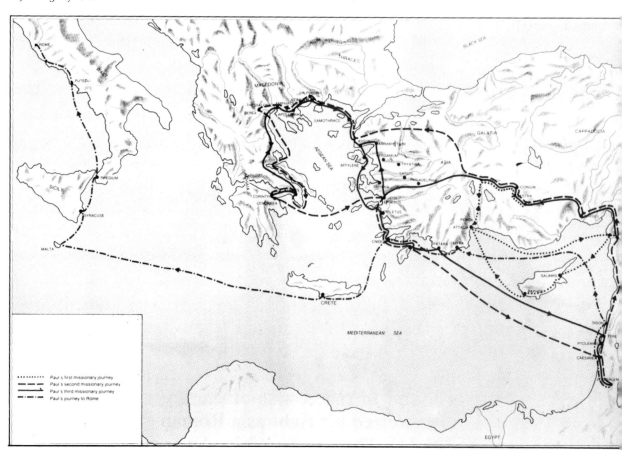

Church Council (Acts 15), Paul embarked on a second missionary journey, accompanied this time by Silas. The two traveled through Syria and Cilicia, Phrygia, Galatia, and then Troas, where Luke joined them. They sailed together to Samothrace, landed on the continent at Neapolis and then journeyed to Philippi where they were faced again with hostility, and were imprisoned. Leaving Luke in Philippi, Paul and Silas traveled through Amphipolis and Apollonia and stopped at Thessalonika and Beroea, encountering hostility in both places.

Paul then proceeded to Athens and addressed the people at the Aeropagus, but in spite of his eloquence, he made but few converts. Again, in Corinth Paul had little success with the Jews and warned them: "Your blood be upon your heads; I am clean. From now on I will go to the Gentiles" (Acts 18:6). He did as he said and preached in the house of Justus, a proselyte. At the instigation of his Jewish enemies, Paul was summoned before Galio, the proconsul, who refused to interfere in a religious dispute, and Paul was able to remain some time longer in Corinth unmolested before returning to Jerusalem "for a festival."

He did not remain long in Jerusalem; he returned to Antioch, and undertook his third missionary journey. Traveling overland, he proceeded to Galatia and Phrygia, and then to Ephesus, where he spent two eventful years. Because of the hostility of some of the Jews there, he gave up attending synagogue and met with the believers in the Gospel in another place ("the school of Tyrannus"). Paul triumphed over the attraction of the people to magical arts, but his preaching provoked disturbances led by a silversmith, Demetrius, who made shrines for the worship of the goddess Artemis.

Paul went to Macedonia and then Corinth and Greece where he stayed for three months (Acts 20:2-3), continuing to Miletus, Tyre, Ptolemais, Caesarea, and back to Jerusalem. This was to be his last visit to the holy city where he was already famous for his successful preaching throughout the Roman provinces and had aroused the enmity of the Jews. Paul was arrested and sent to Caesarea to be tried by Felix, the Roman governor, since he claimed Roman citizenship and as such his right to appeal to Caesar. Felix kept him in prison for two years, hoping to receive a bribe. The new procurator Festus sent Paul to Rome with other prisoners. They boarded a ship sailing round the eastern Mediterranean coast. After stopovers at Tyre and Myra, they sailed on a large ship along the south coast of Crete. The ship was driven off course by a storm and shipwrecked on Malta. After three months they were able to sail to Puteoli, via Syracuse in Sicily and Rhegium (Reggio) in Italy, from where they walked to Rome.

Paul was allowed to rent a house in Rome and to receive visitors, but was under house arrest for two years. Here he wrote the so-called captivity letters, the Epistles to the Colossians and to the Ephesians, and the Epistle to Philemon.

It is not clear whether Paul ever fulfilled his wish to go to Spain (Rom 15:24). It is possible that he revisited Asia, Achaia, and Macedonia and was arrested at Troas, as implied in his second letter to Timothy.

Paul's personality and the hardships he endured emerge through the Acts and Epistles. He first appears as a young man at whose feet the people who stoned Stephen laid their outer garments. Not only did he approve of Stephen's execution but, because of his zeal for tradition, he began a campaign of persecution against Jesus' followers. He extended his action outside Jerusalem and received written authorization to look out for other disciples as far as Syria; he was mandated to bring them back as prisoners to be tried in Jerusalem by the Sanhedrin (Acts 8:1: Gal 1:13). His vision on the road to Damascus changed him from a fierce persecutor of the Christians to a fanatical believer in Jesus whose sole aim was now to disseminate Jesus' teachings in spite of many hardships. "Three times I have been beaten with rods: once I was stoned. Three times I have been shipwrecked: a night and a day I have been adrift at sea; on frequent journeys in danger from my own people, danger from Gentiles: danger in the city, danger in the wilderness, danger at sea, danger from false brethren" (II Cor 11:24-26). In spite of all obstacles, aggravated by poor health, he was sustained by his passionate faith: "I take pleasure in my infirmities, in reproaches, in needs, in persecutions, in distresses, for Christ's sake. For when I am weak, then I am strong" (II Cor 12:7-10).

It is not related how and when Paul died. Tertullian, of the African Church, wrote in the 2nd century that Paul was beheaded. Later historians record that the site of his execution was on the left bank of the Tiber, outside Rome. The place became known as "Three Fountains" as legend holds that at the spots where his head bounced three times a spring appeared. Eusebius, the bishop of Caesarea (4th century), writes that Paul was taken back to Rome and killed during Nero's persecutions of the Christians.

Peter (Simon). See V.43, Apostles.

Philemon. Citizen of Colossae, converted by Paul. Recipient of Paul's Epistle to Philemon, which requests him to receive back his runaway slave, Onesimus, who had become a Christian.

Philip. See V.43, Apostles

Philip. Son of Herod the Great and Mariamne. His wife Herodias, the mother of Salome, left him to live with Herod Antipas, his half-brother (Matt 14:3; Mark 6:17; Luke 3:19).

Philip the Evangelist. One of the seven deacons chosen by the apostles to look after the widows, orphans, and needy Christians (Acts 6:1-6). When the persecutions scattered all the Christians of Jerusalem with the exception of the apostles, Philip went to preach in Samaria and performed miracles. Many were baptized, including Simon the magician (Acts 8:4-13). Later, "an angel of the Lord spoke to Philip" telling him to go to Gaza. On his way south he met an Ethiopian in the service of Candace, the queen of Ethiopia, whom he converted and baptized. Later he lived in Caesarea where he gave hospitality to Paul (Acts 21:8).

Philip the tetrarch (4 BC-AD 34). Son of Herod the Great and his fifth wife, Cleopatra of Jerusalem. He inherited the territories of Iturea and Trachonitis (Luke 3:1), which he administered efficiently. He founded the town of Caesarea Philippi. Philip married Salome, the daughter of Herodias, but had no children. At his death his territory was given to Herod Agrippa.

Phoebe ("radiant"). Deaconess of the church of Cenchrea. Paul recommends her warmly in his Epistle to the Romans which he sent with her from Corinth (Rom 16:1).

Pilate (Pontius Pilatus). Procurator of Judea at the time of Jesus' ministry. He was appointed by Tiberius in AD 26, when Herod Antipas was king, and ruled the province for ten years. The official residence of the Roman ruler was in Caesarea but Pilate went to Jerusalem with military reinforcements for the Passover festival. Herod Agrippa sent Jesus to Pilate to judge him. Jesus was accused by "the chief priests and the scribes" of blasphemy, of subversion by inciting people not to pay their taxes, and of making himself a king rivaling the Emperor. Pilate was not convinced that Jesus was guilty of a crime meriting death and asked the crowd that he be released in place of Barabbas, a prisoner, condemned to death but due to be freed, as it was customary to release a prisoner at each festival. The crowd shouted and became unruly, crying out for the release of Barabbas. Pilate then sentenced Jesus to death, at the same time taking water and "washing his hands before the multitude, saying, 'I am innocent of the blood of this just person. You see to it" (Matt 27:1-26; Mark 15:1-15: Luke 23:1-25; John 18:28-40). Non-Scriptural sources describe him as obstinate, harsh, and violent.

Stone inscription found at Caesarea in which Pontius Pilate commemorates the erection of a building in honor of Tiberius.

Priscilla (Prisca). Wife of Aquila, who gave hospitality to Paul in Corinth (Acts 18:1-3). She and her husband had a church in their home (Rom 16:3).

Publius. Wealthy resident of Malta, in whose house Paul stayed for three days, during which he cured Publius' sick father (Acts 28:7-8).

Quirinius. According to Luke 2:1-2, he was Roman governor of Syria at the time of the census ordered by the Roman emperor that led to the visit of Mary and Joseph to Bethlehem, where Jesus was born. According to Josephus, he took the census in AD 6/7.

Rhoda ("rose"). Servant in the house of Mary, Mark's mother. After his miraculous release from prison, Peter went to Mary's house. Rhoda recognized his voice through the closed door but was so surprised that instead of letting him in, she ran to tell the others the good news (Acts 12:13).

Salome. Wife of Zebedee and mother of the apostles James and John. She was one of the women who witnessed the crucifixion of Jesus and came on the third day after his death to prepare the body for burial (Mark 15:40).

Sapphira ("beautiful"). Wife of Ananias, a disciple in Jerusalem. She conspired with her husband to defraud the church, resulting in their death (Acts 5:1).

Sergius Paulus. Roman proconsul of Cyprus when Paul was there on his first missionary journey. He summoned Barnabas and Paul to "hear the word of

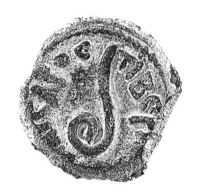

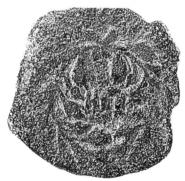

Bronze coin issued by Pontius Pilate, with the symbol of his office, and the name of Tiberius Caesar.

God." In spite of the opposition of a magician called Elymas or Bar-Jesus, he was converted (Acts 13:7-12).

Silas. Leading member of the early church of Jerusalem, called by the Roman name Silvanus in Paul's Epistles. He was a Roman citizen. He and Barnabas were chosen to accompany Paul to Antioch to convey the decision of the council of Jerusalem regarding circumcision (Acts 15:22,30-32). He was Paul's companion during his second missionary journey and is said to have "exhorted the brethren with many words and strengthened them" (Acts 15:32). He traveled with Paul through Syria, Asia Minor, Macedonia, and Thessalonica. When Paul left for Athens, Silas stayed at Berea and then joined him at Corinth (Acts 16 and 18). He was associated with Paul in his epistles written from Corinth (1 Thes 1:1; II Thes 1:1).

Silvanus. See Silas.

Simeon. Pious man who was in the Temple when Joseph and Mary presented the infant Jesus. He had received a revelation that he would not die before seeing the Messiah. When he saw Jesus he pronounced a hymn of praise, later known in Christian liturgy as the *Nunc Dimittis*: "...For my eyes have seen Your salvation which you have prepared before the face of all peoples, a light to bring revelation to the Gentiles, and the glory of Your people Israel" (Luke 2:25-32).

Simon ("[God] has heard"). Apostle, to whom Jesus gave the name Peter. See V.43, Apostles.

Simon the zealot, one of the Twelve Apostles. See V.43, Apostles.

Simon. Brother or kinsman of Jesus (Matt 13:55; Mark 6:3).

Simon the leper. When Jesus visited him in Bethany, one of the women present anointed Jesus' feet with costly oil (Matt 26:7; Mark 14:3). When Simon objected to this because the woman was "a sinner," Jesus related a parable about forgiving sinners.

Simon of Cyrene. A Jew forced by the Romans to help Jesus carry the cross (Matt 27:32; Mark 15:21).

Simon. Father of Judas (Iscariot) who betrayed Jesus.

Simon the tanner. A Christian of Joppa (Jaffa) in whose house Paul was staying when he received a message from Cornelius the centurion (Acts 9:43; 10:1-8).

Simon the magician (Simon Magus). Considered to have great power by the people of Samaria. Seeing the miracles performed by Philip, he was converted, but later, noticing that John and Peter imparted the holy spirit to the believers by the laying on of hands, offered money to "buy" that power. Peter was so angered that he cursed him. Simon was frightened and begged the apostles to pray that he would not receive the punishment with which he was threatened (Acts 8:9-24). The word "simony" is derived from this incident.

Sosthenes ("the strong one"). Leader of the synagogue at Corinth at the time of Paul's visit. He was assaulted when the proconsul Gallio refused to hear the charges of the Jews against Paul because they were of a religious nature (Acts 18:12-17).

Stephanas. First person of Achaia to be converted by Paul. He and his household were Paul's "first fruits"

The house believed to be that of Simon the tanner in Jaffa (Joppa).

there. Later, Stephanas visited Paul at Ephesus (I Cor 17:15,17).

Stephen ("crown"). First Christian martyr. He was an outstanding personality "full of faith and power who did great wonders among the people," and one of the seven deacons chosen by the disciples to give assistance to the needy among the Christian community of Jerusalem. Stephen was accused of blasphemy and brought to trial before the Sanhedrin. He replied by giving a summary of the history of the Jews and attacking them for being "stiff-necked and uncircumcised in heart and ears" and for resisting the Holy Spirit and killing the messiah. The infuriated crowd cast him out of the city and stoned him to death (Acts chap.7).

Susanna ("lily"). One of the women who provided for Jesus during his preaching tour in Galilee (Luke 8:3).

Synthyche ("happy event"). Woman of the church of Philippi. In his Epistle to the Philippians (4:2) Paul urges her and Euodia to compose their differences.

Tabitha. See Dorcas.

Tertius ("third"). Unknown scribe who wrote the epistle of Paul to the Romans. He inserted his own greetings in the letter. He is the only "secretary" of Paul mentioned by name (Rom 16:22).

Tertullus. Roman professional advocate appointed to

present the case against Paul to the governor Felix at Caesarea. Tertullus first praised Felix and spoke favorably about Paul, and then presented him as a troublemaker (Acts 24:1ff).

St. Stephen's Gate in Jerusalem. Stephen is said to have been stoned to death nearby.

Thaddeus. One of the Twelve Apostles. See V.43, Apostles.

Theophilus ("friend of God"). Otherwise unknown person to whom Luke dedicates his Gospel and the Acts of the Apostles (Luke 1:3–4; Acts 1:1).

Theudas. Jewish rebel who started an insurrection against Rome. Gamaliel cites him (along with Judas the Galilean) to the Sanhedrin as an example of a movement that ceased to cause trouble after the death of its leader, and as an argument not to take any notice of the Christian congregation after Jesus' death (Acts 5:34–40). Josephus (*Ant* 20,97–99) describes Theudas as a magician who led many followers to the Jordan, asserting that the river would divide at his command. They were attacked by the Roman cavalry and Theudas' head was brought to Jerusalem.

Thomas ("twin"). One of the Twelve Apostles. See V.43, Apostles.

Timon. One of the seven deacons appointed by the apostles to see to the needs of the Christians in Jerusalem (Acts 6:1–6).

Timothy ("one who honors God"). Son of a Greek father and a Jewish Christian mother, Eunice, a native of Lystra. As a child, he was taught the Scriptures by his mother, and perhaps also by his grandmother, Lois, who knew Paul. It is not clear when he became a Christian. Paul chose Timothy, still a very young man, as a traveling companion when Barnabas and Mark left him, and to avoid the hostility of the Jews, he allowed him to be circumcised (Acts 16:3). When Paul had to leave Berea, he left Timothy behind as his representative (Acts 17:13–15). He later sent him to visit Thessalonica, Corinth, Ephesus, and Macedonia to encourage and strengthen the faith of the brethren (Acts 19:22; I Cor 16:10; II Cor 1:19). Timothy was imprisoned with Paul, either at Rome or elsewhere, and was released (Heb 13:23).

Timothy appears to have been a shy young man. Paul writes to the Corinthians: "When Timothy comes, see that you put him at ease" (I Cor 16:10–11). But he was an able representative, trusted and greatly esteemed by Paul, who writes to the church in Philippi: "I have no one like-minded, who will sincerely care for your state...you know his proven character that as a son with his father served me in the gospel" (Phil 2:19–22). Two of the Pastoral Epistles were addressed to him.

Titus. Christian associated with Paul for many years. He was a Greek convert from paganism whom Paul did not allow to be circumcised (Gal 2:1–3). During his third missionary journey, while at Ephesus, Paul delegated Titus to deal with the difficult situation of the Corinthian church at the time, and he won Paul's praise for his good work there (II Cor 2:13). In Achaea he was entrusted with the collection for the poor Christians of Judea (II Cor 8–23). Paul sent him on other missions: to Nicopolis (Titus 3:12), and to Dalmatia (II Tim 4:10). Titus then went to Crete to organize the church; Paul's advice for this work is the subject of his Epistle to Titus.

Trophimus. Christian Ephesian who accompanied Paul to Jerusalem after the riot at Ephesus. When Paul went to the Temple with several other companions, Asian pilgrims who recognized Trophimus and thought that Paul had brought him, a Gentile, to the Temple, provoked a riot and Paul's arrest (Acts 21:27ff). Later when traveling with Paul, he fell ill and had to remain in Miletus (II Tim 4:20).

Tryphena ("dainty"). Christian woman in Rome praised for her good work by Paul in his letter to the Romans (16:12). She is mentioned together with Tryphosa, who may have been her sister.

Tychicus. One of Paul's faithful fellow-workers from Asia, and his traveling companion for a time. While Paul was in prison in Rome, he sent Tychicus to Colossae and Ephesus with letters in which he wrote that Tychicus would give the church there further details of the situation. When Paul was imprisoned in Rome for the second time, he entrusted Tychicus with a similar mission (Col 4:7; Eph 6:21; II Tim 4:12).

*Zacharias inscribing the name of his newborn son on a tablet.
Armenian miniature, 1335.*

Urbanus. Christian in Rome to whom Paul sent greetings (Rom 16:9).

Zacchaeus. Tax collector in Jericho. As he was a short man, he climbed on a tree to be able to see Jesus over the crowd when Jesus came to visit the town. Jesus invited himself to stay at the tax collector's house. Zacchaeus promised to distribute to the the townspeople half of his wealth in compensation for overtaxing the poor (Luke 19:1-10).

Zacharias ("God has remembered"). Elderly priest, father of John the Baptist. While he was offering incense in the Temple, the angel Gabriel appeared to him, announcing that his wife, Elizabeth, barren for many years, would bear him a son to be named John. The priest was struck dumb until the circumcision of his son when he indicated in writing that he should be called John. Immediately his power of speaking was restored and the speech he uttered is known as the "Benediction" (Luke 1:5-20).

Zebedee ("gift of God"). Father of the apostles James and John. His two sons worked with him as fishermen on the northern shore of the Sea of Galilee (Matt 4:21; Mark 3:17; Luke 5:10).

V.45   PARABLES

The word "parable" comes from the Greek *parabole*, literally "throwing alongside," and is applied to fictitious moral narratives, commonly used as teaching devices in the Bible. These short stories are taken from familiar everyday life and imply a spiritual message. They have been called "an earthly saying with a heavenly meaning." In the Bible, they usually convey a single idea and are characterized by brevity and simplicity.

The boundary between the parable on the one hand, and the allegory, fable, simile, or metaphor on the other, is not always well-defined, so that lists of biblical parables differ. Some cite nine parables in the Old Testament, others only two, saying that the others belong to different categories. It is in the teachings of Jesus that the parable really plays a central role and is the chief method of instruction. Indeed, according to Matthew 13:34 and Mark 4:33, Jesus' sole means of communication to the crowds was through parables. Scholars have discerned between 27 and 72 parables in the Synoptic Gospels. Differences between the versions in these Gospels have led some modern scholars to the conclusion that the parables were adapted by the early Church to its own homiletic requirements and this led to the different formulations.

The scholar Herman Joachim Jeremias has distinguished eight major themes in the New Testament parables:

1. The assurance of the imminence of the kingdom of God;
2. The arrival of a New Era;
3. Divine mercy for sinners;
4. The early approach of judgment;
5. The requirement for an immediate personal response;
6. The essential elements of discipleship;
7. The passion;
8. The fulfillment.

Some Parables of the Old Testament

The ewe lamb (II Sam 12:1-14);
The two brothers and the avenger (II Sam 14:1-11);
The escaped captive (II Kgs 20:35-40);
The vineyard (Is 5:1-7);
The eagle and the vine (Ezek 17:3-10);
The lion whelps (Ezek 19:2-9);
The vine (Ezek 19:10-14);
The forest fire (Ezek 21:1-15);
The boiling post (Ezek 24:3-5).

THE PARABLES OF JESUS

	MATTHEW	MARK	LUKE
The sower	13:3–8	4:3–8	8:5–8
Seed growing		4:26–29	
The mustard seed	13:31–32	4:30–32	13:18–19
The vineyard	32:33–44	12:1–12	20:9–18
The budding fig tree	24:32–33	13:28–29	21:29–31
The doorkeeper		13:34–36	12:35–38
Going before the judge	5:25–26		12:58–59
Two houses	7:24–27		6:47–49
Children in marketplace	11:16–19		7:31–35
Return of unclean spirit	12:43–45		11:24–26
Wheat and weeds	13:24–30		
The leaven	13:33		13:20–21
Treasure	13:44		
The pearl of great price	13:45–46		
The net	13:47–50		
The lost sheep	18:10–14		16:4–7
The unmerciful servant	18:23–35		
Laborers in the vineyard	20:1–16		
The father and two sons	21:28–32		
The marriage of the King's son	22:1–14		14:16–24
The thief in the night	24:43–44		12:39–40
The faithful servant	24:45–51		12:42–46
The wise and foolish bridesmaids	25:1–13		
Pounds and talents	25:14–30		19:12–27
The sheep and goats	25:31–46		
The two debtors			7:36–50
The good Samaritan			10:29–37
The friend at midnight			11:5–8
The rich fool			12:16–21
The steward on trial			12:42–48
The barren fig tree			13:24–30
The narrow door			13:6–9
Places of honor at a feast			14:7–11
The tower and the king to war			14:28–32
The lost coin			15:8–10
The prodigal son			15:11–32
The unjust steward			16:1–13
The rich man and Lazarus			16:19–31
The master and servant			17:7–10
The unjust judge			18:1–8
The Pharisee and the publican			18:9–14
The pounds			19:12–27

V.46 FAMOUS QUOTES AND PHRASES

As in the case of the Old Testament, many New Testament phrases and expressions became an integral part of English and other European languages by way of the Vulgate, and, more especially, through the work of Reformation scholars and translators. Once again, a few technical terms were borrowed directly from Hebrew or from Aramaic, the regional vernacular spoken in the time of Jesus and his disciples: *Abba, Armageddon, Corban, Hosanna, Mammon,* and *Rabbi.* Others, such as "charity," "Christ," "faith," and "Son of man," are Jewish religious concepts in popular (Greco-Latin) form.

The following list of examples does not include Old Testament echoes and citations, of which Matthew's gospel contains a goodly share. An asterisk placed before the source reference indicates that the phrase in question is based on, rather than a literal quotation of, the New Testament text. The quotation refers to the first citation in the New Testament; some are repeated in other books.

The Gospels

Blessed are the meek, for they shall inherit the earth	Matt 5:5
The salt of the earth	Matt 5:13
The light of the world	Matt 5:14
Hiding one's light under a bushel	*Matt 5:15
Not one jot	Matt 5:18
To turn the other cheek	*Matt 5:39
Let not your left hand know what your right hand does	Matt 6:3
Our Father which art in heaven	Matt 6:9
(Vulgate: *Pater noster*)	cf. Luke 11:2
No man can serve two masters	Matt 6:24
You cannot serve God and Mammon	Matt 6:24
Consider the lilies of the field.. they toil not, neither do they spin	Matt 6:28
Sufficient unto the day is the evil thereof	Matt 6:34
Casting pearls before swine	*Matt 7:6
Seek, and you shall find; knock and it shall be opened to you	Matt 7:7
Do as you would be done by	*Matt 7:12
A wolf in sheep's clothing	*Matt 7:15
By their fruits you shall know them	Matt 7:20
Building a house upon the sand	*Matt 7:26
Weeping and gnashing of teeth	Matt 8:12
The foxes have holes and the birds of the air have nests	Matt 8:20
Let the dead bury the dead	Matt 8:22
New wine in old bottles	Matt 9:17
He that is not with me is against me	Matt 12:30
A prophet is not without honor, save in his own country	cf. Luke 11:23 Matt 13:57
The blind leading the blind	*Matt 15:14
A sign of the times	*Matt 16:3
The keys of the kingdom	Matt 16:19
Get thee behind me, Satan!	Matt 16:23
Taking up the cross	*Matt 16:24
What shall it profit a man if he gain the whole world and lose his own soul?	Matt 16:26 cf. Mark 8:36
If your eye offend you, pluck it out	Matt 18:9
Whom God has joined together, let no man put asunder	*Matt 19:6
It is easier for a camel to go through the eye of a needle than for a rich man to enter the kingdom of God	Matt 19:24

Many that are first shall be last and the last shall be first	Matt 19:30
A den of thieves	Matt 21:13
Many are called but few are chosen	Matt 22:14
Render unto Caesar the things which are Caesar's; and unto God the things that are God's	Matt 22:21
To strain at a gnat	Matt 23:24
A whited sepulchre	*Matt 23:27
Well done, good and faithful servant	Matt 25:23
Dividing the sheep from the goats	*Matt 25:32
Thirty pieces of silver	Matt 26:15
All they that take the sword shall perish with the sword	Matt 26:52
To wash one's hands of a matter	*Matt 27:24
The sabbath was made for man, not man for the sabbath	Mark 2:27
A house divided cannot stand	*Mark 3:25
Their name is legion	*Mark 5:9
Suffer the little children to come unto me	Mark 10:14
The widow's mite	*Mark 12:42
The poor are always with us	*Mark 14:7
No room at the inn	*Luke 2:7
Peace on earth and goodwill toward men	*Luke 2:14
Let your servant depart in peace	Luke 2:29
Physician, heal thyself	Luke 4:23
The laborer is worthy of his hire	Luke 10:7
Fallen among thieves	*Luke 10:30
Go, and do likewise	Luke 10:37
The poor, the halt, and the blind	*Luke 14:21
The prodigal son	*Luke 15:11ff.
Killing the fatted calf	*Luke 15:23
Father, forgive them, for they know not what they do	Luke 23:24
In the beginning was the word	John 1:1
Whose shoe's latchet I am not worthy to unloose	John 1:27
The wind bloweth where it listeth	John 3:8
To be a shining light	*John 5:35
Search the Scriptures	John 5:39
Not to judge by appearances	*John 7:24
Casting the first stone	*John 8:7
The truth shall make you free	John 8:32
Jesus wept	John 11:35
In my Father's house are many mansions	John 14:2
Greater love hath no man than this	John 15:13
They hated me without a cause	John 15:25
Whither goest thou? (Vulgate: *Quo vadis?*)	John 16:5
Behold the man! (Vulgate: *Ecce homo!*)	John 19:5
Touch me not! (Vulgate: *Noli me tangere*)	John 20:17
A doubting Thomas	*John 20:24-9

Remainder of the New Testament

Breathing fire and slaughter	*Acts 9:1
Kick against the pricks	Acts 9:5
No respecter of persons	Acts 10:34
But Gallio cared for none of these things	Acts 18:17

It is more blessed to give than to receive	Acts 20:35	To work out one's own salvation	Phil 2:12
A citizen of no mean city	Acts 21:39	The peace of God, which passeth all understanding	Phil 4:7
A law to themselves	Rom 2:14	Labor of love	I Thes 1:3
To hope against hope	*Rom 4:18	Filthy lucre	I Tim 3:3
The wages of sin is death	Rom 6:23	Old wives' tales	*I Tim 4:7
Honor to whom honor is due	*Rom 13:7	Use a little wine for your stomach's sake	I Tim 5:23
Eye hath not seen nor ear heard	I Cor 2:9	Money is the root of all evil	*I Tim 6:10
All things to all men	I Cor 9:22	Fight the good fight	I Tim 6:12
To put away childish things	I Cor 13:11	To the pure all things are pure	Titus 1:15
Through a glass darkly	I Cor 13:12	Sharper than a two-edged sword	Heb 4:12
Faith, hope and charity	I Cor 13:13	The patience of Job	James 5:11
In the twinkling of an eye	I Cor 15:52	Let your yea be yea; and your nay, nay	James 5:12
The last trumpet	*I Cor 15:52	Covering a multitude of sins	*I Pet 4:8
O death, where is thy sting? O grave, where is thy victory?	I Cor 15:55	The Devil is a roaring lion seeking whom he may devour	*I Pet 5:8
To suffer fools gladly	II Cor 11:19	Faithful unto death	Rev 2:10
A thorn in the flesh	II Cor 12:7	To rule with a rod of iron	*Rev 2:27
The right hand of fellowship	Gal 2:9	A sting in the tail	*Rev 9:10
Fallen from grace	Gal 5:4	The new Jerusalem	Rev 21:2
Let not the sun go down on your wrath	Eph 4:26	Alpha and Omega, the beginning and the end, the first and the last	Rev 22:13
They two shall be one flesh	Eph 5:31		

V.47 THE BEGINNINGS OF THE CHURCH

The main written sources concerning the expansion of the early Church are the Acts of the Apostles and Paul's letters. The Acts of the Apostles provide an insight into the geographical and theological growth of the Christian Church in the Roman Empire. The first part (1-12) is centered on Peter, the apostle, whom Jesus established at the head of his disciples, and the second part (13-14; 16-28) chronicles the development of the Church outside Palestine under Paul's leadership. Chapter 15 of the Acts deals with the assembly of Jerusalem where the leaders, Peter and Paul, James, and "the apostles and elders" gathered to examine the main problem facing the growth of the Church, the integration into one harmonious fellowship of the Christians of Jewish origin with those coming from the Greek and Roman world. The final editing of the Acts of the Apostles took place around the years 85-90, the result of a combination of a few older documents with at least two former editions. Paul's letters are generally expositions addressed to various churches. Besides these writings, the other books of the New Testament, mainly the Gospels, reflect early Church religious thought and the life of the Christian communities in the third part of the 1st century.

Jesus died most probably on 14 Nisan (7 April) in the year 30. According to Christian tradition and faith, "he was raised on the third day in accordance with the scriptures, and he appeared to Cephas, then to the twelve" (I Cor 15:4-5). The resurrection of Jesus was "the Good News," the foundation of Christian preaching. The disciples very soon began to proclaim Jesus' victory over death and to declare him Christ, Savior, Son of God (cf. Acts 4:23,31).

The Acts of the Apostles show that Jesus' disciples at first continued the kind of life they had led while they were gathered around their Master before his death. They were living in fact according to the rhythm of life customary to the Jews of their time, while continuing their fellowship with Jesus. As they did not have their own places of worship they participated in the cult performed in Jerusalem, "going up to the temple at the hour of prayer" (Acts 3:1). Those Jews who converted to Christianity outside Jerusalem also pursued the same lifestyle they had followed before their adhesion to Jesus, and continued to attend the local synagogues.

Peter emerged naturally as the guide and pastor of the community. During the early days, accompanied by John, he cured a lame man at "the gate of the temple called Beautiful" (Acts 3:1-10) "in the name of Jesus Christ of Nazareth" (3:6). This healing was taken as the sign that a new era had started and that the power of the risen Lord was bringing salvation.

As the community grew, problems of organization and common life became more evident. "The Helle-

St. Peter's Basilica on Vatican Hill, Rome, built on the site venerated since the year 160 as the burial place of the Apostle.

nists murmured against the Hebrews because their widows were neglected in the daily distribution" (Acts 6:1). This reference indicates that there were two important groups among the first Christians of Jewish origin: the "Hebrews," born and raised in Palestine, speaking Aramaic, not very open to Greek culture, and the "Hellenists" who, knowing Aramaic, had adopted a Greek-influenced style of life, either in Palestine under the influence of Hellenism, or most probably in the Diaspora from where they had returned. The motives which brought the two groups into opposition relate to the opening of the Christian faith to "non-Jews." The "Seven" who were chosen to cope with social and charitable needs were "men of good repute, full of the Spirit and of wisdom" (Acts 6:3). They all had Greek names and seem to have been preachers of the Gospel, as the twelve apostles chosen by Jesus were supposed to be. As only the first two of the list of twelve, Peter and John, were shown in activity, so only the first two of the list of seven, Stephen and Philip, are described as exercising a ministry. Philip, to whom the title of "evangelist" was to be attributed (Acts 21:8), went to Samaria (Acts 8:5-6) and was brought to baptize the Ethiopian eunuch "a minister of Candace, queen of the Ethiopians" (Acts 8:27). After that he "was found at Azotus, and

passing on, he preached the gospel to all the towns till he came to Caesarea" (Acts 8:40).

As for Stephen, he preached the gospel in Jerusalem where he was stoned shortly after as a result of a popular riot maliciously fomented against him. Stephen died a true and faithful disciple of Jesus. Like his master, he was a victim of the hatred of some of the Jewish authorities, in this case "the synagogue of the Freedmen" (Acts 6:9). This event should be placed very early in the history of the first Christian community, two or three years after Jesus' death, when the community was still confined to Jerusalem.

It was persecution which impelled the Christians, mainly the "Hellenists," to leave Jerusalem and to preach the gospel to the Jews outside the city, in the Diaspora, and even to non-Jews. The Acts of the Apostles refer to Christians and communities covering ethnic groups and geographical areas without connection with a founder. Very early there were Christians in Damascus (Acts 9:2,10,20; cf Gal 1:17), in Judea, Galilee, and Samaria (Acts 9:31; 11:1; II Thes 1:14), Caesarea (Acts 9:30), Lydda (Acts 9:32), Joppa (Acts 9:36). A church was established in Antioch of Syria (Acts 11:20-21) with its "prophets and teachers" (Acts 13:11). Two of the latter, "Simon who was called Niger," and

"Lucius of Cyrene," originated from North Africa. This church, conducted by the "Hellenists," became missionary and was a base for the first itinerant preachers, Barnabas and Saul (13:2-4). The Acts later mention a certain Apollos, who came from Alexandria where "he had been instructed in the way of the Lord" (18:25), an indication that Alexandria received the gospel very early, as Paul met Apollos at Ephesus during his third journey, in the years 52-56. The first Epistle of Peter (1:1) attests to the existence of churches in Pontus, Asia, and Bithynia (north of Turkey). The Epistle to the Colossians speaks of communities in Laodicea (2:1) and Hierapolis (4:13), and reveals that Paul was in correspondence with some other churches who "had not seen his face" (2:1). The Epistle to the Romans, as well as the end of the Acts of the Apostles, confirms the presence in Rome of a strong church well versed in Christian doctrine before Paul's coming. The existence of Christians in Rome goes back to before Claudius' edict expelling the Christians (49-50, or even 40 according to some specialists). Other communities were established elsewhere, including in the south of Italy (Acts 28:13).

While the "Hellenists" were leaving to carry the "Good News" elsewhere, Peter remained in Jerusalem for a little time. Since the foundation of the Christian community, his role of leadership is well described, for instance in the election of Matthias as "one of the twelve" (Acts 1:15-23), in his long discourse on Pentecost (Acts 2:14-36), in the welcoming of the first converts (Acts 2:37-41) and in the judgment of Ananias and Sapphira (Acts 5:1-11). He also acted as the word-bearer of the Christians and their delegate, together with John, to the new groups, such as the one in Samaria (Acts 8:14-25). Paul referred to him and recognized him in his role (Gal, 1:18; 2:9; Acts 15).

Peter, however, left Jerusalem some time after the "Hellenists." "He came down to the saints that lived at Lydda" (Acts 9:32-34). Like Jesus, he raised up a lame man, an act which "turned to the Lord all the residents of Lydda and Sharon" (Acts 9:35). He also went to Joppa, where, like Jesus, he revived a dead woman, Tabitha. Afterwards he went to Caesarea (Acts 9:43) where he came to understand that God makes no distinction between persons. Consequently he baptized in the Christian faith Cornelius and his family, who were Gentiles. This narrative (Acts 10), as well as the preaching of Barnabas and Paul in Cyprus, Antioch of Pisidia, and Iconium (Acts 13-14) was a preparation for the Jerusalem assembly in 51 (or 49 according to a number of exegetes) where the brethren of Jewish origin ratified and recognized officially that Gentiles could be accepted among the disciples of Jesus.

While Peter was away from Jerusalem, James, the group leader of "the brothers of Jesus", had taken over the leadership of the local community, where he remained until his martyrdom in 62. Peter then moved

to Antioch (cf Gal 2:11), where for the first time (Acts 11:26) the adepts of the "Way" were called "Christians." So they were now distinguished from the Jews and appeared as a new autonomous movement. After that, tradition, attested by the first epistle of Peter (5:13), places Peter in Rome. He faced martyrdom, probably in 64, under Nero's persecution. The context of this persecution is described with horror by Tacitus. Peter was replaced by Linus (64-76), Cletus (76-88) and Clement (88-97).

It was Paul who developed the Church outside the Jewish land. A Pharisee of the strict observance, Paul was born in Tarsus at the dawn of the Christian era. At first, he was a persecutor of the followers of Jesus but around the year 33 he was baptized, following a vision (Acts 9:1-2). Shaken to the core, he became an apostle of Jesus. After his first missionary journey with Barnabas, the Acts mention two other journeys which took him to Galatia, the province of Asia, Mesopotamia, and Greece. He also went to Jerusalem for the assembly where he could have his apostolate recognized by the other leaders of the Church. Some important communities, like those in Galatia, Philippi, Thessalonika, Corinth, and Ephesus, were founded, which became radiating centers of Christian life, thought, and evangelization. On his apostolic journeys, Paul at first found refuge in the Jewish communities. He would then announce Jesus to people of his own Jewish faith. Some among them joined the Christian faith; but others, often the leaders of the synagogue, would not tolerate his activity and Paul would often be sent quickly out of the synagogue, sometimes persecuted. The Christian communities consequently were made up of people of Jewish as well as of Gentile origin. The faithful of Gentile origin would sometimes place a very liberal interpretation on Christian freedom. Disciples of Jewish origin would find difficulty in mixing with those who had not submitted to the Mosaic law. Sometimes Jewish-Christians of strict observance would travel from one community to another, as in Galatia or Corinth, in order to correct Paul's teaching according to their own views and impose Jewish rites, notably circumcision, on Gentile Christians. These tensions and conflicts are reflected in Paul's letters, which at the same time give a general view of the social, liturgical, and charismatic organization of the churches.

During his apostolic journeys, Paul not only founded many churches, but organized them and set up ministers capable of leading them. Paul indeed always knew how to recruit efficient and faithful collaborators, like Timothy, Titus, Silas, Luke, Aquila, and Priscilla. More than 100 names in the Acts of the Apostles and in the Pauline letters are associated with his ministry. He also organized a money collection for the poor of the Jerusalem community, according to the request made at the end of the assembly of AD 51 (cf Gal 2:10). In AD 56 (57 or 58 according to some exegetes) Paul returned to

Jerusalem at Pentecost for the purpose of bringing this collection. In the spring of 57 Paul reached Rome, where he enjoyed relative freedom and could preach Jesus' word. The Acts of the Apostles as well as Paul's letters are silent on what happened to him after that. Either he went to Spain according to his plan alluded to in the Epistle to the Romans (15:28), or more probably he went back to Asia according to the information gleaned from the Second Epistle to Timothy. Christian tradition, attested by the post-apostolic writers, was always convinced that he was beheaded just south of Rome, on the via Ostiensis, near the present Basilica of St. Paul, during Nero's persecution in 64-65.

Meanwhile the Christians were collecting their traditions about Jesus their founder and about their origins, and continued to examine their way of life and their religious expression. For instance, the Epistle to the Hebrews was produced around the year 70 in order to demonstrate that Jesus was a worthy replacement for the High Priest as well as the Temple and its cult. The four gospels received their final touch. The Gospel according to Mark (a little before AD 70) was destined mainly for communities formed by Gentiles in and around Rome. The Gospel according to Matthew (c.80) was drawn up for Christians coming from Judaism in Palestine-Syria. The Gospel according to Luke, who is also the author of the Acts of the Apostles, was finished toward the year 85, for communities largely of pagan origin. The tradition of John started in Palestine, but developed in Asia around Ephesus. Just around the end of the 1st century it produced three letters and the fourth gospel. The Book of Revelation, issued from the same milieu, aimed at reinforcing the hope of Christians who had to face another violent persecution, that of Domitian (91-96), which was followed later by that of Trajan (98-117).

The Church of the Nativity, Bethlehem, built in 326, over the Grotto venerated by the early Christians as the place where Jesus was born.

STATISTICS OF THE BIBLE

OLD TESTAMENT

Books	39
Chapters	929
Verses	23,214
Words (Hebrew)	593,493

NEW TESTAMENT

Books	27
Chapters	260
Verses	7,959
Words (Greek)	181,253

Longest Book	Psalms (150 chaps)
Shortest Book	III John (1 chap; 14 verses)
Longest verse	Esther 8:9 (90 words)
Shortest verse	John 11:35 "Jesus wept"
Middle verse	Psalms 118:8
Most common word (King James Version)	"and"
Most mentioned name	David (1,118 times)
Most common name	Zechariah (31 people)
Longest name	Maher-Shalal-Hash-Baz (Is. 8:4)
Most Prolific Bible author	Paul

VI. THE BIBLE IN CIVILIZATION

VI.48 TRANSLATIONS OF THE BIBLE

Not only is the Bible the world's "number-one best seller," it was probably the first book translated into other languages and, whether in whole or part, translations have continued to appear in virtually all the languages of mankind. Sometimes, only one or two versions in the more obscure dialects have been printed; in English, however, new translations become available almost year by year. Cultural historians point to the fact that the entire development of a "primitive" language, such as Old Church Slavonic, was bound up with the translation of Scripture, for which an alphabet had to be invented and the first dictionaries or grammars were compiled. Often enough, a given language was only written down when some enterprising Bible translator found himself obliged to shoulder that task.

Until at least the period of the First Temple's destruction in 586 BC, Jews spoke only Hebrew and had a sound grasp of their Scripture. During the era of the Second Temple, however, they began speaking other languages: Aramaic in Judea and Greek in the new community of Alexandria. A growing demand for versions of the Hebrew Bible that would be more readily understood led to the appearance of the Septuagint (LXX) or "Translation of the Seventy Sages" in Greek (c. 250–50 BC), and of various Targums ("translations" or paraphrases of Scripture) in everyday Aramaic (c.100 BC to c. AD 700). Both translations were widely used by the Jewish communities around the time of Christianity's first appearance in the Roman Empire.

Since the early Church had its own New Testament in Greek, portions of which may originally have been composed in Aramaic by their Jewish-born authors, it was foreseeable that Christianity would also utilize the Septuagint, which formed the basis of other Christian translations. Further to the west, both Jews and Christians had begun translating parts of the Bible into Latin. This process culminated in Jerome's Latin Vulgate (c. AD 405), which had a threefold significance: it became the "authorized version" of the Western (Roman Catholic) Church; its cultural influence was greater than that of any other Bible translation; and, thanks to Jerome's reliance on the original (Hebrew) language of the Old Testament as well as his use of early rabbinic exegesis, it would later serve as a model for Protestant Bible translators.

Fragment of the Book of Revelation (12:12–13:1), from a Greek papyrus of the 3rd century AD.

The Vulgate's role in subsequent Christian history was a paradoxical one. Firstly, despite Jerome's view of the Apocrypha as non-canonical, these "extraneous books" of the Second Temple era were incorporated in the Latin (as also in the Greek) Bible. Secondly, the Vulgate's authority was resolutely upheld by the Catholic Church during the Reformation, and just as resolutely denied by the Protestant reformers. Thirdly, Jerome's approach to Bible translation lay behind Protestantism's "return to the sources" and its campaign in favor of vernacular Bibles that would make the Scriptures accessible to the ordinary Christian layman.

Thus, from the beginning of the 16th century, Bible translation was a major weapon in the hands of Christian reformers bent on weakening the Vulgate's authority and severing the links between much of Europe's population and the Church of Rome. Having jettisoned a Latin text incomprehensible to the masses, which utilized expository methods first developed by the Septuagint and the Targum, Martin Luther and his successors created a religious revolution with their "open Bible of the Reformation." Hebraic turns of phrase became everyday expressions in German, English, French, Dutch, and other languages; biblical precedents were invoked by social and political, as well as religious, reformers; and the foundations were also laid for a modern, "scientific," and objective type of Bible scholarship.

Since the Reformation, most translations of the Bible have appeared under Protestant auspices, with English and German in the lead. Here, the British and Foreign Bible Society has particularly distinguished itself as the publisher and distributor of Bibles in many tongues. Also active in this field is the American Bible Society. Catholic Bibles still mostly rely on the Vulgate, but their number and scholarly level are on the upgrade. There have also been several Jewish translations of the (Hebrew) Bible into various European languages, the most recent versions in English being sponsored by the Jewish Publication Society of Philadelphia.

ANCIENT TIMES

The Bible in Greek. Although its origins are shrouded in mystery, the Septuagint is undoubtedly the most ancient Bible translation, a product of Hellenistic Alexandria (mid-third cent. BC). Legend has it that 72 Judean elders presented identical Greek texts to the Egyptian ruler, Ptolemy II Philadelphus, after laboring isolated in separate cubicles for 72 days to provide his library with an authentic version of the Pentateuch. Some accounts refer to 70 (rather than 72) elders, hence the name *Septuagint* (Translation of the "Seventy" Sages). Objections were expressed in Palestine to such a translation; more orthodox Jews feared that reading the Bible in any language but Hebrew would imperil Judaism in the Diaspora and Jewish religious unity.

By about 50 BC, however, the Prophets, Hagiographa, and Apocrypha had also been translated into Greek. A comparative study of the Septuagint and the Hebrew Old Testament reveals many textual differences in order, wording, and content. The Septuagint underwent periodical correction, further changes and even interpolations being made after its adoption by the Church. Alarmed by this development, Greek-speaking Jews eventually commissioned new or revised translations of the Hebrew Bible. The first, by Aquila the Proselyte (early second cent.), was a highly regarded, literal version of the Old Testament; the slightly later rendering by Theodotion (a Diaspora Jew who may once have been a Christian) still tried to harmonize the Septuagint with the original Hebrew; while the idiomatic Greek translation by Symmachus (a 3rd-century proselyte of Samaritan or Christian birth), though influenced by rabbinic exegesis, avoided Aquila's literalism.

More scholarly Christians also expressed their dissatisfaction with the Septuagint. As an outstanding Hebraist, the 3rd-century church father Origen of Alexandria was able to discover many corrupt readings in the text, which made the Greek version less reliable than the original. He therefore produced a new dual-language edition of the Old Testament, the *Hexapla* (AD 245), which took its name from six parallel columns running through the work. These supplied the Old Testament in Hebrew, an accurate transliteration of the same in Greek, Origen's edited version of the Septuagint, and the new Greco-Jewish translations by Aquila, Symmachus, and Theodotion. Origen's *Hexapla* was really meant to answer Jewish theological strictures against Christianity, but it also helped to expose textual errors and to establish the Old Testament canon.

The Septuagint formed part of the Greek Orthodox Bible and was also translated into Latin at some early date (thus foreshadowing the Vulgate) and left its impress on the Bibles of three Eastern churches: the Coptic or Egyptian (third cent.), the Armenian (fifth cent.), and the Ethiopic (fifth-sixth cent.). The earliest (ninth cent.) Christian Bible in Arabic likewise bore its stamp.

Aramaic and Syriac. Aramaic, the language which Jews adopted as their vernacular speech after the Babylonian exile, was closely related to Hebrew. Under the Babylonians and Persians, Aramaic had the status of a Near Eastern lingua franca. When the Pentateuch was read "distinctly" and expounded to the people in Ezra's day (Neh 8:8), this may hint at a simultaneous translation of the Five Books of Moses into everyday Aramaic, although many Bible scholars reject that possibility. However, there is reason to believe that an "interpreter" gave Aramaic oral explanations of the Hebrew Bible in Judea, and the Dead Sea Scrolls contain a fragmentary Aramaic text of Job, the earliest known (second-cent. BC) Aramaic translation.

Written in Judea and Babylonia, the Aramaic Targums display contrasting approaches to the transmission of Scripture, literal or paraphrastic and explanatory. The best known example is *Targum Onkelos* to the Pentateuch (second-third cent. AD), and another important literal version is *Targum Yonatan* to the Prophets. The value of these Aramaic translations and paraphrases of Scripture was understood by early Christian scholars, but their exegetical importance only came to be appreciated during the Reformation.

The Samaritans, a dwindling sect now mainly concentrated around Nablus (biblical Shechem), also preserve a translation of the Pentateuch in their ancient Aramaic dialect (the "Samaritan Pentateuch"). Over the past few centuries, however, scholarly attention has also been devoted to the *Peshitta*, a Syriac version of the Old Testament which probably originated among Jews speaking that eastern Aramaic dialect in Roman times. The name *Peshitta* ("straightforward") does suggest that different texts were once available in Syriac, and that this "plain" or "literal" version won

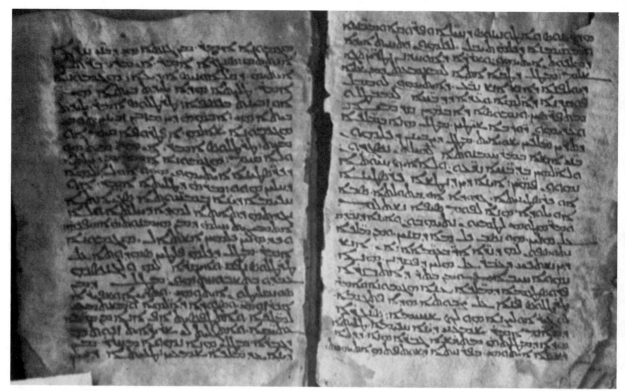

Pages from the Codex Syriacus, including an 8th-century martyrology, a 4th-century biblical script and traces of an earlier manuscript. Santa Caterina Monastery library, Sinai.

general acceptance. At some point between the 3rd and 5th centuries, this version of the Hebrew Bible was appropriated by the Syrian Church, the Jacobite and Nestorian branches of which have slightly differing Bible text traditions.

Jerome's Latin Vulgate. By the end of the 2nd century AD, Latin versions of the Bible were circulating in the Roman Empire. Some Old Testament manuscripts appear to have been based on the Hebrew text and were probably written by Jews, but other manuscripts (including the New Testament portion of the Bible) were verbatim translations from the Greek. Known collectively as the Old Latin Version (*Vetus Latina*), these early texts did not survive for long and can only be identified from marginal notes or citations in other ancient documents. Papal awareness of the many errors that had crept into the *Vetus Latina* explains why the church father Jerome was given the task of producing a more textually accurate Latin Bible for Christians of the West.

Secluded in his monastic retreat near Bethlehem, from the year 386, Jerome brought his great biblical and linguistic talents to bear on that task. Initially, he revised the New Testament and portions of the Old, while checking the Hebrew and Greek originals, but then found so many discrepancies between the Hebrew Bible and the Septuagint that he abandoned the Old Latin and the Septuagint altogether. Finally a com-

pletely new Latin version of the Old Testament emerged from his labors, based on the Hebrew and utilizing not only Origen's *Hexapla* but the rabbinic learning of certain Jews who taught him Hebrew as well. Together with his revised New Testament and Apocrypha, Jerome's original translation of the Old Testament formed the *Vulgata*, or "commonly received" Latin version of the Scriptures, which was completed around 405. Its authority, as the official Bible of the Western Church, was unchallenged before the Reformation; its status, despite the need for some correction, was reaffirmed by the Council of Trent (1545–63); and from it derived the first complete Roman Catholic Bible in English, the so-called *Douay Version* (1582–1610). Even today, most Catholic Bibles remain tied to the Vulgate.

THE MIDDLE AGES

An ever-present fear of heresy determined the general opposition of the Church to unsupervised Bible translation throughout the medieval West. Papal inquisitors blocked most attempts to translate the Bible. For most of Western Christendom, even the Vulgate was not freely available, and popular knowledge of the Bible was limited to the Psalms, the Gospels, and some New Testament epistles.

The first known Bible translator in Europe was an older contemporary of Jerome. Around 370, the missionary bishop Wulfila (Ulfilas) devised a new alphabet for his Gothic translation, which was based on a Latin text predating the Vulgate. Only fragments of that Bible survive in manuscript, but they constitute the earliest prose in any Germanic language. Later German translations include a versified (Old Saxon) Genesis and a 14th-century Old Testament known as the *Wenzel Bible*. One of the very first works to be printed from movable type was Gutenberg's 42-line Bible in Latin (Mainz, 1456), while no less than 14 Bibles in High German and four Low German editions were printed before Luther's new version appeared. The earliest of these, from the Strassburg press of Johann Mentel (1466), has the distinction of being the first Bible printed in any modern language.

Although far less of the Bible was translated into Anglo-Saxon, Caedmon wrote certain paraphrases in verse (c. 670) and Alfred the Great's Anglo-Saxon code of law made liberal use of Old Testament precedents (such as the Decalogue) in the vernacular. Throughout the Middle Ages, Bible translation mainly took the form of interlinear (Latin-English) copying or paraphrasing of the Psalms and Gospels, and it was only with the appearance of Wycliffe's Lollard Bible in the late 14th century that Englishmen began to "search the Scriptures."

Two sectarian movements, the Albigenses and the Waldensians, promoted Bible translation in medieval France. A crusade helped to destroy the Albigensian heresy, but the Waldensians survived in Provence, where they continued to defy Papal authority and re-emerged as Protestants during the Reformation. Not

St Jerome's cell at Bethlehem. He isolated himself here to translate and revise the Bible. The fruit of his labor is the Vulgate.

surprisingly, therefore, even the versified Bible of Herman de Valenciennes (c.1190) gave rise to alarm, yet King Louis IX authorized the preparation of a complete French Bible some 40 years later. A team of scholars from the University of Paris worked on this *Bible Complète*, which did not always reach a high standard, with a mass of scholastic glosses drowning the actual text.

The Vatican maintained a tighter control over Bible translation in Italy and in the Iberian peninsula. Fear of heresy in medieval Spain prompted a decree by Juan I of Aragon (1233) banning translations throughout his realm. This was aimed not only against the Albigensian movement, but also against Castilian versions of the Old Testament by Jewish and Christian scholars who relied on the Hebrew text as well as the Vulgate. A more enlightened attitude prevailed under Alfonso X the Wise of Castile; during his reign (1252–84), the prohibition was set aside and work began on a Spanish translation of the Vulgate. Over the next 200 years, most Bible projects in Spanish were undertaken by professing Jews or enlisted the aid of Jewish converts. A Castilian version of the Old Testament by Moisés Arragel, known as the *Alba Bible* (1422–33), was the outstanding example. With the expulsion of Jews from Spain in 1492, Bible scholarship steadily dwindled, although Catholic and convert humanists remained active until the late 16th century.

Among the Slavs of Eastern Europe, Wulfila's Gothic Bible had its counterpart in the 9th-century Old Bulgarian text of two missionary brothers, Cyril and Methodius. For the new Church which they organized in the Balkans, a translation of the Greek Septuagint had to be prepared and Cyril, a linguist, devised a Slavic alphabet that utilized Hebrew as well as Greek letters. Apart from the Septuagint, Cyril consulted the Hebrew text of the Old Testament when preparing this translation. Its use spread in time, from the Bulgarians and Moravians to other Slavic peoples that adopted the Eastern Orthodox ritual (notably the Serbs, Ukrainians and Russians), but the subsequent development of each language necessitated regional changes in Cyril's version. Responding to the challenge of heretical "Judaizers" in 15th-century Novgorod, Archbishop Gennadi proceeded to revise the Old Bulgarian text, and it was from his manuscript (1499) that the *Ostrog Bible* was first printed in 1581. Largely incomprehensible to the masses even then, it has retained an authority comparable to that of the Vulgate in the Latin (Catholic) Church.

Prior to the 19th century, only one attempt was made to produce a modernized Russian text of the Bible (Prague, 1517–19). Elsewhere, especially in Poland, translations of the Vulgate served the needs of the Catholic Church. The first printed Bibles were chiefly the work of Calvinists (Lutheranism having to contend with anti-German sentiment among the Poles).

RENAISSANCE AND REFORMATION

Two processes gave rise to the Protestant Reformation: humanism, and the first attempts to make ordinary people familiar with Bible teachings in the vernacular. Renaissance scholarship promoted Christian Hebraism and a "return to the sources" of biblical truth.

By the time of Wycliffe, there had been many translations of the Vulgate into modern speech. What chiefly distinguished his English Bible (completed in 1382) was its underlying purpose, to make the Scriptures intelligible and available to unlearned common folk. The Peasants' Revolt of 1381 encouraged Wycliffe in the midst of his campaign to win over the masses. Armed with handwritten copies of the English Bible, his agents scoured the land, teaching the Scriptures and preaching Wycliffe's revolutionary ideas. The Church was scandalized, but the favor which he enjoyed at court made counter-measures impossible until years after his death in 1384.

Wycliffe's influence was not confined to England. A generation later, his teachings were propagated by John Huss throughout Bohemia. Huss created a mass movement which led to the founding of an independent Moravian Church (1457). His other great achievement was a modernized revision of the Old Church Slavonic (Bulgarian) Bible. Unlike Wycliffe's version, this Czech translation had been printed before the century ended.

Catholic initiative was responsible for modern Latin translations of the New Testament by Erasmus (1516) and of the Old Testament by Santes Pagnini (1528), as well as for the earliest polyglot Bible (1514–17). Nominally, at least, Erasmus and Pagnini, together with the pioneering French Bible translator Jacques Lefèvre d'Etaples and others, remained within the Church. However, their work helped to undermine its authority; their successors mostly abandoned Catholicism. In 1522, Martin Luther published his German New Testament (utilizing the version by Erasmus in parallel Greek and Latin columns) while the establishment of his Evangelical (Protestant) Church was already under way. In 1534–5, Sebastian Münster published *Hebraica Biblia*, the first Protestant Old Testament in Latin based directly on the original Hebrew; and Luther issued his complete Bible in German.

A translation that "made history," Luther's German Bible was the first complete version in any modern language to be prepared from the Scriptural (Hebrew and Greek) tongues. It helped to unify spoken German, had an enduring impact on German literature, and made the vernacular Bible an integral part of Christian worship, thus promoting the Reformation. Apart from serving as a model for all future German translations, it also gave shape and majesty to Protestant Bibles in other European languages. Culturally as well as reli-

giously, Luther's Bible exerted an influence similar to that of the *Authorized Version* in English-speaking lands.

In France, numerous editions were printed (chiefly in Lyons and Paris) from the latter half of the 15th century. French Protestantism took its inspiration from the militant Genevan theocracy of Jean Calvin. The Calvinist brand of Protestantism was exported to other European lands, where new vernacular Bibles soon appeared. In Poland, the ostensibly Catholic *Leopolita Bible* (Cracow, 1561) betrayed certain Lutheran features; its Calvinist successors were the *Brzesc* (or *Radziwill*) *Bible* of 1563 and the *Gdansk* (or *Danzig*) *Bible* of 1632, which eventually served all Polish Pro-

Page from the first Latin Bible printed in Europe in 1456.

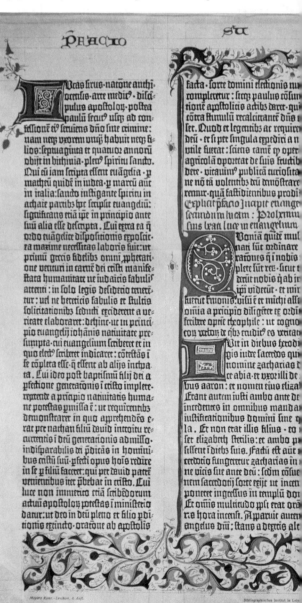

testants. After Janos Erdosi's pioneering edition of the New Testament, Gaspar Karolyi issued the first complete Bible in Hungarian; known as the *Viszoly Bible* (1590), it remained the standard Protestant version until the 1950s. In Holland, each of the Protestant churches favored a different text after the Reformation. As a move toward greater harmony, the Dutch States General commissioned a new translation, the *Statenbijbel* (1637), which was only replaced in 1951.

As compared with the Vulgate, Protestant Bibles arranged the Scriptural books in a different order, had many separate chapter divisions, and (like Jerome) excluded Apocryphal writings from the Bible canon. From Luther's time, this negative attitude to the Apocrypha was motivated by Catholic exploitation of certain "proof texts" drawn from it to justify the requiem mass, praying to Christian saints, and other rites. The Counter-Reformation did succeed in halting Protestantism's onward march throughout the whole of Europe, but it could not avert the far-ranging triumph of the Protestant Bible. Overall, the Catholic response was weak and belated: translations from the Vulgate, often by Jesuits. Amazingly enough, no approved vernacular Bibles were published in Catholic Spain and Italy until the latter half of the 18th century.

The English Bible. Nearly 140 years elapsed between John Wycliffe's death and the preparation of William Tyndale's New Testament, the second milestone in the English Bible's history. At Cambridge, Tyndale was greatly influenced by Erasmus and then resolved to base his version on the Greek text. Fellow churchmen, suspicious of his motives, compelled the translator to seek refuge (and find a publisher) abroad; after visiting Luther in Wittenberg (1524), he declared himself a Protestant. The New Testament portion of his Bible appeared a year later and 3,000 copies were smuggled from Germany over to England, infuriating Henry VIII (still loyal to Rome as "Defender of the Faith") and the Catholic hierarchy. Tyndale, however, followed Wycliffe's inspiring example. "Ere many yeares," he told one vehement critic, "I wyl cause a boye that dryveth the plough shall know more of the Scripture than thou doest." He only managed to issue the Pentateuch and Jonah before someone denounced him as a heretic in Antwerp; he died a martyr in 1536, the remainder of his Old Testament appearing separately a year later.

Down to the *King James (Authorized) Version* of 1611, each "new" English Bible was at least partially based on Tyndale. More a skilled compiler than a translator, Miles Coverdale published his version in 1535, and his more conciliatory approach gained favor at court.

King Henry's chancellor, Thomas Cromwell, and Archbishop Thomas Cranmer were ardent supporters of the Reformation, but also fearful of the unsettled religious climate. Aware that the latest versions of the Scripture (and the marginal notes accompanying

them) were still too advanced for most Anglicans, Cromwell saw the need for a moderate revision and asked Coverdale to prepare it. What finally emerged from the press was in large measure Tyndale's version stripped of his "objectionable" notes. Welcomed even by his former opponents, this *"Great" Bible* (1539) was the Church of England's first "authorized version."

After Thomas Cromwell's political disgrace and execution (1540), there was a long period of religious unrest. English Protestant refugees spent 30 months working on the *Geneva Bible* (1560), a scholarly revision of the *"Great" Bible*. Coverdale was a member of the editorial team headed by William Whittingham, Calvin's brother-in-law. The *Geneva Bible*, dedicated to

Title page of Beza's English translation of the Bible, 1595.

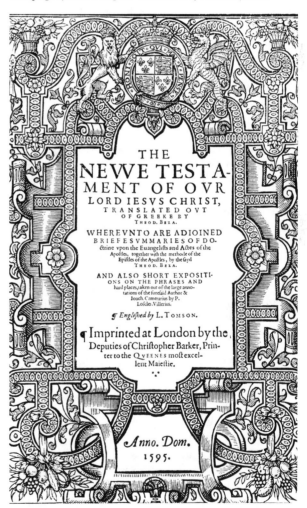

Queen Elizabeth, was an English best-seller from Shakespeare's time down to the Pilgrim Fathers and the Cromwellian era.

The so-called *Bishops' Bible* of 1568 was the second officially approved text ("appoynted to be read in churches"), but lacked wide appeal. Nor was the two-part *Douay Version* (1582–1610) an outstanding achievement: produced in France, it aimed to supply English Catholics with an "authorized" Bible of their own, but over-dependence on the Vulgate and incomprehensible Latinisms in the text reduced its effectiveness. However, even the *Douay Version* and the *Bishops' Bible* had some small role in the process of translation that reached a historic climax with the *King James Version*'s appearance in 1611.

Shortly after James I ascended the throne in 1604, he summoned representative churchmen to a meeting at Hampton Court, where matters of religious interest were discussed. Even Roman Catholics had finally accepted a Bible in the vernacular; yet this Protestant conference displayed no wholehearted enthusiasm for the idea that a new English Bible would be timely. Though no admirer of Puritanism, King James had a practical interest in Bible translation; furthermore, he would not have overlooked the gratifying suggestion that a new Bible might honor the new king. Accordingly, the project went forward.

The translators, laymen as well as Anglican and Puritan clergy, worked in teams and included ranking oriental and Greek scholars of the time. They had all previous translations at their disposal and the most recent biblical apparatus. The *King James Version* took seven years to complete and was also styled the *Authorized Version* (AV or KJV). The first of four early revisions was made in 1615, while many others have been published since the 1880s. Such constant revision proved necessary from the beginning, in view of the *King James Version*'s obsolescent language and the changes that have affected modern spoken English. Nevertheless, through the power and beauty of its expression, the KJV had supplanted all other English Protestant Bibles around 1690. Over the past 300 years, its cultural and psychological impact on the English-speaking peoples has been enormous.

MODERN TRANSLATIONS

From the 17th century until the early 1900s, Bible translation was dominated by the reprinting or revision of popular "classics." Complete Bibles now appeared in modern Greek (NT, 1638; OT, 1840), Romanian (1688), Slovak (1829–32), and more exotic languages such as Chinese (1823), Basque (1859–65), and Japanese (1887). Protestant missionaries, together with the British and Foreign Bible Society, were responsible for most of these wide-ranging translations. An important development, from the mid-19th century onward, was the appearance of modernized translations into the vernacular, usually (though not always) based on previous versions.

Both lay and church-sponsored translation of the Bible has had to consider the implications of 20th-century biblical research and archaeological finds in the Middle East. Apart from heavily annotated critical editions, there are now more popular ones for the informed reader which take account of the latest knowledge and have been translated anew from the Scriptural tongues.

Over the past 200 years, Jewish translators have mainly concentrated on the Pentateuch and its associated weekly readings from the Prophets. Around 1770, however, Moses Mendelssohn began translating the Hebrew Bible into German and, with the help of collaborators, this project was completed in the early 19th century. A celebrated German Jewish enterprise of modern times, by Franz Rosenzweig and Martin Buber, ran to 15 volumes (1925–61). Other versions have included a complete Old Testament in Hungarian (1898–1907); *La Bible du Rabbinat français* (1899–1906) directed by Zadoc Kahn; and an entirely new "Hebraic" translation into French by André Chouraqui (OT and NT, 1974–78).

As in continental Europe, British scholars publishing "new" versions of Scripture were at first tied to the almost sacrosanct (KJV) model. A few tried their hand at an original rendition. Some concentrated on greater textual accuracy, others endeavored to make the *King James Version* more readable, while others again introduced minor changes here and there on religious grounds.

In view of the *King James Version*'s enduring popularity, minimal changes were made in the English *Revised Version* (RV), produced by a team of British and American Bible scholars, which appeared in 1885. The standard English Bible's elegant diction was retained, but the editors sought to eliminate archaisms and to make other overdue improvements on the basis of contemporary research. Differences between U.S. and British usage were chiefly responsible for the appearance of a modified RV, the *American Standard Version* (1901), forerunner of the *Revised Standard Version* (1952), and the *New American Standard Bible* (1971). A similar process of development was to affect *The Holy Scriptures* or "American Jewish Version" of the Old Testament (1917).

Following the RV-ASV example, other revisions of the Bible were published by James Moffatt (1913–24) and Edgar J. Goodspeed, whose paraphrastic New Testament (1923) was later combined with a similar version of the Old Testament by J.M. Powis Smith (1927) to form *The Bible: An American Translation* (1931). In succession to these came a wide range of Bible projects: a new version in "basic English" by S.H. Hooke (1941–49); a fresh translation of the Vulgate for Roman Catholics by Monsignor Ronald Knox (1944–49); Hugh J. Schonfield's *Authentic New Testament* (1955), a best-selling original translation with scholarly notes alluding to rabbinic sources; the *Amplified Bible* (1958–64); and the *Jerusalem Bible* (1966), an English Catholic version of the French *Bible de Jérusalem* of 1956. From

1948, such Bibles tended to reflect the new insights prompted by investigation of the (Qumran) Dead Sea Scrolls, as well as ancient Greek papyri.

Current best sellers are the *New International Version* (1978); *Today's English Version*, marketed as the *Good News Bible* (1976) and deriving from a British translation for Protestant missionaries; the *Revised English Bible* (1989); and, still, the old *King James Version*, which remains the standard against which all other English translations are judged. Interest also attaches to the *Living Bible* (1971), a clear paraphrase originally meant for children; the *New English Bible* (1970), an ecumenical British Protestant revision; and *Y Beibl Cymraeg Newydd* (1988), the latest edition in Welsh. There is a *New Jerusalem Bible* (1985) and a modernized three-volume update of the American Jewish translation (1962-82), called the New Jewish Publication Society of America translation (NJPS).

FAMOUS AND UNUSUAL BIBLES

Wycliffe's Version (1382). First systematic translation of the Bible into English; by John Wycliffe. To further his program of religious enlightenment, he completed the NT in 1380 and the OT in 1382. Over-reliance on the Vulgate was partly corrected by John Purvey's revision (1388), which utilized other sources. Though condemned and burned in 1415, Wycliffe's Version exerted a vast influence until the 16th century and over 170 manuscript copies have survived.

Alba Bible (1422-33). First Spanish translation of the complete OT; prepared by a Jewish scholar, Moisés Arragel, for Don Luis Guzmán, grand master of the Order of Knights of Calatrava. With a Franciscan as his consultant, Arragel based this Castilian version on the Latin text (adjusting it to the Hebrew wherever they diverged), and also supplied a commentary that drew from Christian as well as rabbinic sources. The original manuscript (now in Madrid) was richly illuminated; a new edition appeared in 1920-22.

Gutenberg Bible (1456). First Bible ever printed; by Johann Gutenberg and his associates at their new press in Mainz. Begun in 1452, soon after Gutenberg had perfected his method of printing with movable lead type, this Latin Bible was ready by 1456 and heralded the appearance of other (Hebrew, Greek and vernacular) editions. The text resembles a manuscript: chapters are headed by an illuminated letter, with further decoration at the top and bottom of each page. Less than 50 of the 200 copies printed still exist, enhancing their value.

Gutenberg's Bible. Gutenberg, inventor of printing in Europe, and his associates, worked from 152 to 1456 to produce the first Bible ever printed.

Complutensian Polyglot (1514-17). First complete Bible published in Spain; at Alcalá de Henares. Greek scholars and converted Jewish Hebraists worked on this great project, which drew its title from Alcalá's Latin name (Complutum). It ran to six volumes, all but one (the dictionary "apparatus") including the Hebrew, Greek, Latin and Aramaic texts in parallel columns. The *Biblia Complutensis* marked a revolutionary advance in Christian Bible scholarship. Pope Leo X withheld its license until 1520, and the 600 copies were only printed in 1522.

Tyndale's Bible (1525-31). First original English

A page from the Complutensian Polyglot Bible, first printed in 1522.

translation from Hebrew and Greek; by the reformer William Tyndale. Only the NT (1525), the Pentateuch (1530), and Jonah (1531) appeared in his lifetime; the remainder of his OT was published in 1537, a year after he had died a martyr in Flanders (praying that God might "open the King of England's eyes"). Thousands of copies were printed abroad and smuggled into the kingdom, but few have survived. Nonetheless, Tyndale "fixed the phrases" of Scripture in English and exerted a powerful influence on the King James Version.

Luther's Bible (1534). New High German translation published in Wittenberg; by Martin Luther, the founder of Protestantism. Though a less gifted Hebraist than other reformers of his time, Luther enriched his German OT with insights drawn from Jewish Bible commentary. The six-volume edition set the seal on Luther's revolt against Rome, but its majestic language also had a vast impact on German cultural history. Such

was the popularity of Luther's Bible that it went through 11 successive editions (as well as numerous reprints) during his lifetime, and created the standard for all future German translations.

Coverdale's Bible (1535). First complete printed version of the Scriptures in English; by Tyndale's associate Miles Coverdale. Though published in Zurich, his "Byble" was dedicated to Henry VIII and owed much of its success to the new religious climate in England. No Hebraist, Coverdale relied on earlier Latin and German texts; while borrowing also from Tyndale, he moderated the former's outspokenly Protestant glosses and retained certain well-loved terms of Latin origin.

"Bug" Bible. Early English edition, for which the date of printing is variously given as 1535 or 1551. Its nickname derives from a quaint rendering of Psalm 91:5, "Thou shalt not nede to be afrayed for eny bugges [i.e., bugbears or specters] by night." In the KJV, this archaism had already given way to "terror." Other editions acquired a similar notoriety: the *"Fool's"* Bible, for omitting the word "no" in Ps 14:1; the *"Lions"* Bible, for misspelling "loins" in I Kgs 8:19; the *"Printers"* Bible, which gave the wrong word for "princes" in Ps 119:161; and the *"Vinegar"* Bible (1717), where the same thing happened to "vineyard" in a New Testament parable (Matt 20). Additional examples are cited below.

Serrières Bible (1535). First complete Protestant version in French; by Pierre Robert Olivétan, a relative of Jean Calvin. Financed by the Waldenses, this Bible is linked with Serrières in France, but appeared in the Swiss town of Neuchâtel. An erudite work, based on the Scriptural tongues and laden with Calvin's prefaces, it needed frequent revision because of its awkward style. The Geneva (1553) edition published by Robert Estienne first introduced chapter and verse divisions that have become standard. A more thoroughly revised edition (1588) served as the model for later French Catholic as well as Protestant Bibles.

Great Bible (1539). "Anglican compromise" version entitled *The Byble in Englyshe*; by the industrious Miles Coverdale. Still largely based on Tyndale, it was less of a Protestant work than Coverdale's own (1535) version, thus enabling Thomas Cromwell to gain royal approval for its use as the first English Bible "appoynted to be read in churches." The extra-large sheets which inspired this *"Great"* Bible's name had to be printed in Paris, thanks to an agreement between Henry VIII and François I; after threats to suspend publication there, Cromwell had both the production and the press transferred to London. Within three years the *"Great"* Bible went through six reprints and acquired a long introduction by the Archbishop of Canterbury that gave rise to its other title, *"Cranmer's Bible."*

Gustaf Vasa Bible (1541). First complete edition in Swedish; mainly by Laurentius Petri (Andreae), archbishop of Uppsala, and his brother Olaus Petri, the Stockholm reformer. Since neither had learned Hebrew, they based their OT on the Vulgate and Luther's German Bible. King Gustavus I, for whom the Bible was named, had a copy placed in every Swedish church. This translation remained Sweden's official (Protestant) Bible until 1917.

Geneva Bible (1560). Revised edition of the *"Great" Bible*; published by a group of English Protestants who had taken refuge in Geneva after Mary Tudor's succession to the throne. They intended having copies smuggled into England, but Mary's death and the new Protestant regime of Elizabeth I (from 1558) did away with export barriers. The *Geneva Bible* came out in a popular cheap edition that sold well even after the KJV's appearance. Its nickname, the *"Breeches" Bible*, derives from the translation of Gen 3:7, where Adam and Eve "sewed fig leaves together and made themselves breeches" (i.e., girdles; "aprons" in the KJV).

Radziwill Bible (1563): Second complete edition in Polish, but the first based directly on the original (Hebrew and Greek) texts; a Calvinist enterprise by numerous scholars working for six years under the patronage of Mikolaj Radziwill, a high-born supporter of the Reformation.

Bishops' Bible (1568). Newly revised Anglican text; by an episcopal committee following the directives of Archbishop Matthew Parker (hence its title). Aware that the *"Great" Bible* lagged behind its popular rival, the *Geneva Bible*, Parker borrowed the former's OT and the latter's NT verse divisions and notes, hoping to supersede both of these earlier translations. Ultimately, the *Bishops' Bible* did become England's new "authorized" version, but it never managed to lessen the *Geneva Bible's* appeal. By 1606, however, it had gone through 20 editions, providing a basis for the *King James Version*. Its nickname, the *"Treacle" Bible*, derives from a peculiar rendering of Jer 8:22, "Is there no tryacle in Gilead, is there no phisition there?" In Jer 46:11 and Ezek 27:17, "tryacle" again replaces "balm" or "salve."

Antwerp Polyglot (1568-72). An improved and expanded update of the *Biblia Complutensis*; prepared by French and Flemish scholars working for Christophe Plantin, one of the greatest Christian printers of Hebrew books. Fearing that Spanish repression of heresy in Flanders would uncover his own Protestant involvements, Plantin managed to gain Vatican approval and Philip II's patronage for a "Second Complutensian Bible" that ultimately far outshone its model. The Old Testament (vols. 1-4) comprised amended Aramaic and Latin translations as well as the Hebrew, Septuagint, and Vulgate; the NT (vol. 5) included not only the Greek and Latin texts, but also the Syriac, Hebrew transcription, and a Latin rendering; while newly composed dictionaries and essays figured in the "apparatus" (vols. 6-8). The *Biblia Sacra's* 1,200 sets were published in two editions, one for export to Protestant lands and another (secretly expurgated) for Catholics.

The Bible in the vernacular; woodcut illustrations in a Czech translation of the Bible published in 1489.

Kralice Bible (1579-93). First original Czech translation from Hebrew and Greek; by a panel of Bohemian scholars under the direction of Bishop Jan Blahoslav. Their six-volume work took its name from the castle of a Moravian baron who financed the printing. Sponsored by the *Unitas Fratrum* (United Brethren), a Hussite sect that reemerged as the Moravian Church, this Bible survived the Counter-Reformation to become the standard Protestant version in Czech.

Ostrog Bible (1581). First complete edition in Church Slavonic. Periodical revisions were unavoidable because of Church Slavonic's growing remoteness from spoken Russian. These revised editions appeared under Tsar Alexis I (1663), Peter the Great (1714), and Elizabeth Petrovna (1751). The *Tsarina Elizabeth Bible*, for which the OT Hebrew was first consulted, remains the accepted version of the Russian Orthodox Church.

Vizsoly Bible (1590). First complete text published in

Hungarian: by Gaspar Karoly, a former pupil of the German reformer Philipp Melanchthon. This Bible, translated from the Scriptural tongues as well as the Vulgate, derives its name from the town of Vizsoly (Gonc), where Károly served as the Calvinist preacher. A revision by A. Molnar appeared in the same year as his famous *Psalterium Ungaricum* (1608). This version by Karoly had an enormous impact on the nation's cultural and religious life. Over 100 new editions or revisions had appeared by 1890, yet Hungarian Protestants still cling to the old text.

Douay Version (1582–1610). First complete Bible in English for Roman Catholics; originated by Cardinal William Allen, but largely the work of Gregory Martin, who had also quit Elizabethan England. Realizing that the lack of a "faithful" translation placed English Catholics at a severe disadvantage, Allen began his project in 1578, at the English College in Douai. The NT was published in Rheims, however, after the College had been forced to move there (*Rheims New Testament*, 1582); the OT appeared much later, when the College had returned to its old home (*The Holie Bible*, 1610). It was English Catholicism's official text until the 1940s.

Authorized (King James) Version (1611). Classic and "official" Church of England translation, *The Holy Bible, Conteyning the Old Testament, and the New*; prepared from 1604, at James I's request, by a representative panel of 47 (originally 54) scholars. An ecumenical work, designed to create harmony between the various Protestant churches, it took previous English versions into account but relied mainly on the *Bishops' Bible*. Headlines were introduced, as well as Stephen Langton's chapter divisions (1551) and the verse divisions of Robert Estienne (1553). When establishing their texts, the KJV's translators referred to standard Jewish editions of the OT and to the Greek NT versions published by Erasmus (1516) and Théodore de Bèze (1565). The new Anglican Bible gave rise to the first printed versions in Irish (1685) and Scots Gaelic (1783–1801). Changes in the English language threatened to render the KJV obsolete, four revised editions sppeared, and the familiar present-day wording stems from the revision of 1762. Americans usually speak of the *King James Version*, while the *Authorized Version* (or "AV") is its title in the British Commonwealth.

"He and She" Bible. Nickname given to the first two editions of the *King James Version* (1611 and 1615), in which the sex of a person referred to was confused because of a printer's error. Firstly, in Lev 20:11, a man was forbidden to have relations with "his grandmother's wife" (instead of "his father's"); secondly, in Ruth 3:15, "she [rather than "he"] went into the city."

"Wicked" or "Adulterers" Bible. A London edition of 1632 which omitted the vital "not" in its rendering of the Seventh Commandment ("Thou shalt commit adultery")! As a result, the printers were fined the sum of £500, a crippling amount in those days.

Statenbijbel (1637) Famous Dutch Protestant version, newly translated from the original tongues; commissioned by and named in honor of the States General, it was ten years in the making and appeared at Leiden. The text won popular and official acceptance, and (though often revised) maintained its position until the 1950s. By then, a new Bible in Afrikaans had been adopted by the Netherlands Reformed churches of South Africa.

London Polyglot (1654–57). Multilingual Bible, the outstanding work of its kind, consisting of a variety of Scriptural texts in nine languages: Hebrew, Aramaic, Greek, Latin, two forms of Syriac, Ethiopic, Persian, and Arabic.

Upbiblum God (1663). First Bible published in North America; by John Eliot, a New England missionary who won fame as the "Apostle of the Indians." Convinced that these native Americans were descended from the Ten Lost Tribes of Israel and still followed ancient Hebrew practices, Eliot translated the Scriptures into an Algonquian dialect spoken by the Indian tribes of Massachusetts. His Amerindian text, printed in Cambridge, appeared before any English-language edition of the Colonies.

Biblia lui Serban (1688). First complete Romanian Bible; published in Bucharest and named in honor of Prince Serban Cantacuzino, whose patronage it enjoyed. Based on the Septuagint, this translation was revised in 1795; its influence can be detected in the national culture as well as in later editions of the Romanian (Orthodox) Bible.

Synodal Bible (1860–75). Pioneer Russian Orthodox translation; by scholars under the direction of Metropolitan Vasili Philaret and the Holy Synod. One team concentrated on the ancient Greek texts, revising the NT and Apocrypha; a second team published a complete OT 15 years later, bringing the translation to a successful end in 1875. Long admired for its style and accuracy, the *Synodal Bible* has even been reprinted in the U.S.S.R. (1956).

Revised Version (1885). Updated and modernized text of the *King James Version*: by British and U.S editorial committees. From 1870 onward, while anxious to retain the *Authorized Version's* characteristic flavor, they brought it more into line with spoken English and also made certain changes reflecting biblical and archaeological discoveries. Publication of the revised NT (1881) and OT (1885) was generally welcomed, but differences in spelling and usage necessitated a further revision, the *American Standard Version* (1901), which critics then charged with inept literalism.

American Jewish Version (1917). Revised translation of the Old Testament for English-speaking Jews, *The Holy Scriptures according to the Masoretic Text*; produced by U.S. Bible scholars under the direction of Max L. Margolis and issued in Philadelphia by the Jewish Publication Society of America (JPS). While utilizing

19th-century Jewish Bible commentary and translation, the editors also checked standard Christian versions of the OT in English (from Wycliffe to the RV) so as to "combine the spirit of Jewish tradition with the results of biblical scholarship, ancient, medieval, and modern." This most widely read Jewish translation has now been replaced by a new JPS Bible, *Tanakh: The Holy Scriptures* (1962–82), the product of collaborative effort over 25 years, initially under Harry Orlinsky's editorship. Though still traditionally based, and acclaimed for its elegant modernized diction, the New AJV (the NJPS) has aroused criticism among Orthodox Jews because of its receptiveness to the latest trends in biblical research.

Revised Standard Version (1946–52). New American translation; by a panel of scholars (including a Jew, Harry Orlinsky) working under the auspices of the World Council of Churches. In both content and presentation, this Bible was innovative: splendidly organized, highly readable, textually consistent, yet able to preserve much of the Authorized Version's "timeless English." However, it also provoked controversy on two accounts: the rewording of some favorite biblical passages, and other new readings with "far-reaching theological implications." Nevertheless, the RSV was sufficiently ecumenical in its approach to gain the support of U.S. and British Catholics for a slightly modified edition of their own, the *Oxford Annotated Bible with the Apocrypha* (1965).

New English Bible (1970). One of the most important and authoritative of English translations; sponsored by all the major Protestant churches in Great Britain. Soon after World War II, chaplains who had served in the British armed forces urged that such a Bible was a vital necessity, most soldiers finding even the Revised Version incomprehensible and actually believing that Jesus "spoke like a 17th-acentury Englishman." The NEB's version of the Scriptures was entirely new, designed for the modern reader, and scrutinized by a panel of literary experts. An intended successor, the *Revised English Bible*, was published in 1989.

Bible Translations and Manuscripts

Oldest complete Hebrew Bible manuscript: Leningrad Codex (AD 1008).

Oldest complete New Testament manuscript: Codex Sinaiticus (c. 4th century AD; ends with books of Barnabas and The Shepherd of Hermas which do not appear in most versinos). Now in British Museum.

Earliest illustrated Bible: Produced in England, AD 716. now in Florence.

Number of languages of complete Bible translations today: 314.

Number of languages of partial translations: 1,900.

Most widely translated book: Gospel of Mark.

Longest cable ever sent: Revised Version translation of New Testament, published in full in US newspapers three days after publication in England, 1881.

First modern language English translations: Old Testament — by Helen Spurrell (Britain), 1885.

New Testament — by Ferrar Fenton (Britain), 1895.

First New Testament in America: John Eliot's translation for the Massachusetts Indians, 1661.

Number of Bibles distributed by the American Bible Society in 1975: 2,188,491.

First translation to set poetical parts in verse: The Geneva Bible of 1560.

New International Version (1978). Best-selling U.S. Evangelical text; prepared afresh by scholars under the New York Bible Society's direction. While resembling the Revised Standard Version in many ways, it employed the technique of "dynamic equivalence" rather than conventional translation to impress the full sense of a passage on the reader.

VI.49 THE BIBLE IN ART

A major hindrance to the representation of biblical figures and themes in art was the Second Commandment (Ex 20:4; Deut 5:8), which prohibited all "graven images" and the "likeness" of any creature fashioned by God. Certain items in the Temple of Jerusalem (e.g., the winged cherubim) were exempt from this rule, but an underlying fear of man's tendency to mistake shadow for substance (e.g., in the idolatrous worship of the Golden Calf) pervades the Hebrew Bible and also motivated later Byzantine, Islamic, and Reformation iconoclasm. However, by the 2nd century AD, Rabbinic Judaism had developed a more liberal attitude toward figurative art, enabling biblically-inspired Jewish craftsmen to promote a new artistic tradition. Their stone carvings in Galilean synagogues and Roman catacombs depicted the seven-branched Temple candelabrum and other ritual objects, omitting the human form, although portrayals of men and women were allowed in the mosaic floors of synagogues and in murals.

Perhaps the earliest, and certainly the most comprehensive, biblical tableau of that age has been unearthed in the well-preserved Hellenistic frescoes in a synagogue at Dura-Europos on the Euphrates, dating from about AD 245. An impressive array of Old Testament figures and stories are depicted, within a thoroughly Jewish framework, in which the ancient Israelites are represented in contemporary (Roman or Persian) dress.

Owing to the conflicting pressures of Muslim iconoclasm in the East and Church imagery in the West, synagogue decoration became non-pictorial from around the 6th century. Even among the Church Fathers and in medieval Christendom, there was hesitation (sometimes transformed into firm opposition) over the issue of biblical art. To impress the faithful, convert the unbeliever, and familiarize the illiterate masses with Scriptural history, however, the Church generally promoted all types of religious art. Reverence for the Greek Septuagint no doubt explains the initial (and enduring) popularity of Old Testament and Apocryphal themes.

There was also a theological basis for this choice of subject matter, namely, the doctrine that the Church (as the "New Israel") had brought mankind a New Covenant to replace the Old (Mosaic) Law of the Jews. Christian typology viewed dozens of personalities and events in the Old Testament as "prefiguring" others in the Gospels: Man's fall from grace in Eden thus represented Original Sin; Abraham's dismissal of Hagar symbolized repudiation of the "Old Law"; Elijah stood for John the Baptist; Athaliah's slaughter of the Davidic princes anticipated Herod's Massacre of the Innocents; Bathsheba, Esther, and Judith (among others) prefigured the Virgin; Isaac, David, and Daniel similarly constituted the "type" of Jesus; both the death of Abel and Job's sufferings foreshadowed the Passion; the paschal meal in Egypt was the Last Supper; and even the story of Jonah hinted at the Entombment and Resurrection of Jesus.

Frescoes and mosaics, followed by illuminated manuscripts, gave the earliest expression to Christian art. From Roman times to medieval Kiev and Italy, Old Testament motifs were especially important in the Byzantine tradition, which embraced southwestern Europe as well as the Balkans and Asia Minor. Icons later appeared in lands dominated by the Eastern Orthodox (Byzantine) Church, while carvings and sculpture, tapestry, and stained-glass windows distinguished churches of the Latin (Roman Catholic) West. Statuary was frowned upon in the East, where iconoclasm held sway for more than a century (726–842), but no comparable revolt took place in the West. There,

Ahasuerus and Esther, enthroned, receive a report on the numbers slain in Shushan; fresco from Dura Europos.

effigies of Hebrew kings and prophets or Apocryphal saints often adorned chapels, churches, and cathedrals. The Holy Family or the Virgin (Madonna) and Child were other favorite subjects, legend asserting that St. Luke had painted the first Madonna.

During the Middle Ages, numerous biblical subjects were treated cyclically in the windows of new Gothic cathedrals; episodes involving Hebrew prophets (Augsburg), Judean kings and other Old Testament figures encircling the Virgin and Child (Notre-Dame, Paris), and well-known dramatic incidents such as the destruction of Sodom and Gomorrah, the Judgment of Solomon, or Judith's slaying of Holofernes — all "frozen" in stained glass (Chartres). The same kind of technique had already typified Byzantine manuscript illumination, from the 5th-century *Cotton Genesis* to the 10th-century *Joshua Roll*, in which the conquering Israelites and their general were portrayed as Roman soldiers. With few exceptions, however, medieval Christian artists chose to abandon the realism of classical Greece and Rome for a stiff, almost lifeless formalism. This defect was not rectified until long after the dawn of the Renaissance in 14th-century Florence.

THE GREAT MASTERS

Inspired by classical models and ideals, Florentine painters and sculptors emphasized symmetry, lifelike expression in the human figure, and greater realism in landscape backgrounds. Rejecting medieval convention, they sought to represent this world rather than the next, to portray human activity, light and shade, true-to-life color, and natural poses. Some artists concentrated on themes drawn from both the Old and the New Testament, others on one or the other. Giotto exemplified and pioneered this new individualism with his three-dimensional Christian frescoes: *The Raising of*

Part of the Joshua Roll showing the capture of Jericho. On the left, three priests bearing the Ark; 10th-century illuminated manuscript, now at the Vatican Library.

Lazarus, The Kiss of Judas, The Descent from the Cross (c.1305-9), and related scenes. His visualization of the Second Temple as a structure resembling the Muslim Dome of the Rock in Jerusalem led to widespread use of the same background in *Marriage of the Virgin* paintings by Perugino, Raphael, and Bramante (1504), as well as in other New Testament works by artists such as Brueghel the Elder, Dürer, El Greco, and Veronese.

At the height of the Gothic period, there was also a move away from stylized, conventional portrayal in the round. Working near Dijon, for a Burgundian duke, Claus Sluter freed the statue from its domination by architecture with his animated figures of the Virgin and Child (c.1393), to which he added the brightly colored, vital, life-sized figures of Moses and five other Hebrew prophets in his *Well of Moses* (1397-1402). To the south, in Florence, Lorenzo Ghiberti made use of his training as a goldsmith to inject realistic effects into the biblical reliefs of his magnificent bronze doors for the church of St. John the Baptist (1425-52). However, the outstanding sculptor of the early Renaissance was Ghiberti's pupil, Donatello, who revived Greek use of the nude figure and Roman monumental statuary. Combining grace and vigor, Donatello's masterly works include *Moses, Joshua, Jeremiah,* and *Habakkuk* (the "Bald One"), a famous nude *David* (c.1430), *Judith and Holofernes* (1455-7), and *Mary Magdalen* (c.1457).

All of the leading Florentine painters dealt with biblical themes, beginning with Masaccio, Fra Angelico, and Uccello. Two of Fra Angelico's subjects, *The Annunciation* (c.1437), and the *Adoration of the Magi* (c.1445), long enjoyed popularity; the first inspired other treatments by Leonardo da Vinci (1472-3), Andrea del Sarto, and Titian; the second reappeared in works by Leonardo, Botticelli, Hieronymus Bosch (c.1495), Dürer (1504), and other artists down to Rubens in the 17th century. Uccello's best-known painting was a fresco of *The Deluge* (c.1445); his study of pers-

pective had also gained a most thorough exponent in Masaccio (a friend of Ghiberti and Donatello), whose interest in sculpture gave rise to three-dimensional effects. This can be judged from his *Expulsion of Adam and Eve* (1426-8), *Trinity* (c.1426), and *Rendering of the Tribute Money* (c.1425-8), which are still weighed down by medieval Church symbolism.

Outside Florence, Piero della Francesca, and his fellow Umbrian Perugino, used the new techniques in their biblical representation, the former painting a *Virgin and Child with Two Angels* and the *Visit of the*

The Patriarchs depicted on a stone relief at the 13th-century Cathedral of Amiens, France.

A panel from the Angers Apocalypse tapestry, by Nicolas Bataille, begun in 1377, one of the rare tapestries of that period that have survived.

Adam and Eve. Engraving by Albrecht Dürer (1471-1528).

Queen of Sheba to King Solomon (1452-64). Among the earlier Venetian artists, Giovanni Bellini concentrated on New Testament subjects (e.g., *The Agony in the Garden*, c. 1460), while Mantegna created a sculptured effect in *Samson and Delilah, Judith,* and *Esther and Mordechai* (c. 1495). Both he and Bellini used the domed Temple background for their versions of the *Circumcision* and *Presentation of Jesus*. Realism had meanwhile penetrated the Low Countries, where a Gothic love of the fantastic also characterized paintings by the foremost Dutch artist, Hieronymus Bosch: *The Garden of Eden, Noah Leaving the Ark, John the Baptist in the Desert,* and *The Crucifixion* (1480-1505).

On the threshold of the 16th century, Florence was the training school of exceptionally gifted Renaissance painters and sculptors, who mostly produced their best work elsewhere. Leonardo da Vinci confined his attention to New Testament motifs: outstanding among these is *The Last Supper* (1495-8), an objective portrayal of human nature in all its complexity. Sandro Botticelli dealt with many biblical themes, notably in the series of religious frescoes painted on the walls of the Vatican's Sistine Chapel (1481-2). These include *The Punishment of Korah, Dathan and Abiram,* a specially-commissioned warning against heresy. In his religiously troubled later years, Botticelli executed *The Mystic Nativity* (1500) and ran a workshop for the wholesale production of Madonnas. Raphael, some 30

Madonna del Granduca; painting by Raphael (1483–1520).

Young David; painting by Andrea del Castagno (1423–57).

years younger than Leonardo da Vinci, ranks with him and with Michelangelo as a great creator of the High Renaissance. His *Sposalizio* (1504), *Deposition* and *Entombment* (1504–8), *Sistine Madonna* (c.1513), and Vatican *Stanze* frescoes (1509–14), as well as the *Transfiguration* left unfinished at his death (1520), were of New Testament or Christian inspiration; but he also designed and supervised the painting of Old Testament scenes in the Vatican *Loggie* (c.1513–19).

Outshining all other interpreters of the Bible in art, Michelangelo Buonarroti created immortal works expressing Neoplatonism's love of beauty and perfection, alongside a religious belief far removed from the Catholic Middle Ages. Except for the gigantic classical statue of David (1501–4) in Florence, most of his biblical masterpieces were commissioned in Rome, a famous example being the St. Peter's *Pietà* (c.1499). Another huge statue, that of *Moses* (1513–16), is thought to represent Michelangelo's view of the "Old Covenant"; together with his *Rachel* and *Leah* statues (1542–5), it was designed for the S. Pietro in Vincoli tomb of Pope Julius II. While Raphael was decorating the *Stanze*, Michelangelo spent the years 1508–12 in the Sistine Chapel, painting biblical frescoes on the newly replastered ceiling. Old Testament prophets and ancient sibyls, triumph and tragedy, panel scenes from Genesis including *The Creation of Adam* and *The Flood*, together with the Davidic ancestors of Jesus, form one vast panorama conveying the epic of sacred history and the drama of man's spiritual quest.

Working furiously, atop a scaffold 80 ft high, Michelangelo performed an incredible feat that needed all of his resources as a painter, architect, sculptor, and poet. At the age of 61, he was recalled to depict *The Last Judgment* (1536–41) on the Sistine Chapel's altar wall below. Pope Paul III also commissioned him to execute two other New Testament frescoes, *The Conversion of St. Paul* and *The Martyrdom of St. Peter* (1542–50). Unlike the Old Testament frescoes, *The Last Judgment* was a gloomy, searing vision, overshadowed by political events and Luther's Reformation, which shattered the old innocence, joy, and perspective of the Renaissance.

In Germany, Matthias Grünewald had displayed powerful and terrifying effects in the New Testament scenes of his *Isenheim Altarpiece* (c.1515). Albrecht Dürer, the leading German artist, tried to combine the medieval Gothic and 16th-century Italian traditions; he did succeed in becoming the foremost interpreter of the Renaissance in northern Europe. Dürer painted *Job and his Wife* (c.1504), *Christ among the Doctors* (1505–7), and *The Four Apostles* (1526), but his real strength lay in the woodcut or engraving. A brilliant craftsman, he produced single plates (*Adam and Eve, Samson and the Lion, The Prodigal Son*, etc.) as well as entire series: *The Apocalypse* (1498), *The Great Passion* (1498–1510), and a *Life of the Virgin* (1501–11). Both

The Virgin, St Anne with John the Baptist; drawing by Leonardo. da Vinci.

Mary Magdalene; painting by Titian (c.1489–1576).

Lucas Cranach the Elder and Hans Holbein the Younger were fond of biblical subjects, to which they brought an innovative Protestant approach. Cranach, Luther's close friend and portraitist, specialized in highly erotic female nudes (including Lot's daughters, Delilah, and Bathsheba); Holbein displayed a penetrating realism in subjects like *The Dead Christ in the Tomb* (1521) and executed a series of woodcut illustrations to the Protestant Bible, as did Cranach for Luther's version.

Though influenced by Dürer, the biblical paintings, woodcuts, and engravings of Lucas van Leyden, a Dutchman, were less substantial than the works of his Flemish successor, Pieter Brueghel the Elder, who shared Bosch's satirical manner and demonic fantasies. Apart from his *Fall of the Rebel Angels* and *Massacre of the Innocents*, Brueghel painted a celebrated *Tower of Babel* (1563), viewing the whole vast scene from above. At this latter stage of the Renaissance, however, *Cinquecento* artistry was shifting to a new Italian base in Venice, where Titian, Veronese, and Tintoretto portrayed themes from the Bible in their own individual style.

Titian, the greatest Venetian master, adapted his painting to successive trends in the course of his long career. From *The Assumption* (1518), his subjects ranged to Old Testament drama (Cain and Abel, David and Goliath; 1543–4), *The Fall* (1570), *The Crowning with Thorns* (c.1573–5), and an unfinished *Entombment* (1576). Dynamic and sometimes violent, Tintoretto's work showed less concern for description than for depicting dramatic events in the Scriptures. Examples from his early period include *The Golden Calf, Last Judgment,* and *Presentation of the Virgin in the Temple* (1546), *The Murder of Abel* (in *Stories from the Old and New Testament,* 1550–51), and a voluptuous portrayal of *Susanna and the Elders* (c.1560). Later, as the Counter-Reformation spirit prevailed, Tintoretto painted two cycles from the New Testament only (1564–87) as well as *The Last Supper* (1594). Paolo Veronese endowed his biblical scenes with gorgeous pageantry rather than "sacred" content. He painted *The Finding of Moses* three times, one version clothing Pharaoh's daughter and her retinue in mid-16th-century Venetian dress, while Titian, Tintoretto, Veronese himself, and other artists figure among the musicians depicted in *The Marriage at Cana* (1563). Veronese's execution of *The Last Supper* led to his arraignment before the Inquisition in 1573, on the ground of having taken liberties with this theme through "profane" intrusive details. Despite a vigorous rebuttal, the artist had to modify his painting and rename it *The Feast in the House of Levi!*

El Greco, a Cretan trained in Venice but a Spaniard by adoption, imbued his New Testament works (e.g., the *Descent from the Cross,* 1597; *The Resurrection,* 1600) with a mystical faith and passion that would soon characterize Baroque art. The Roman artist Caravaggio, another stormy petrel, adhered more closely to the

The Parable of the Blind Leading the Blind; painting by Peter Breughel the Elder (1528–69).

Baroque style emerging in Italy with his vivid realism (*The Conversion of St. Paul*, 1600–1; *The Flagellation of Christ*, 1606–1610). With its unidealized naturalism and appeal to the emotions, the Baroque manner suited lands dominated by the Counter-Reformation, particularly Spain, where it influenced the painting of Ribera (*Jacob's Dream*, c.1646) and Murillo (*The Holy Family* or "*Virgin of Seville*," 1670). In France, however, Baroque art's opulent and emotional character was suppressed in favor of a classical serenity amenable to the autocratic regime of Louis XIV. Claude Vignon's romantic individualism (*Christ among the Doctors*, 1623) thus gave way to Poussin's biblical dramas in a rural setting (*Eliezer and Rebekah*, c.1648; *Four Seasons*, 1660–64), and to Claude Lorrain's more poetic landscapes (*The Mill*, 1648; *The Expulsion of Hagar*, 1668), in which the small figures are often contrasted by light and space (*Embarkation of the Queen of Sheba*, 1648).

Amazingly versatile and productive, Peter Paul Rubens was not only the greatest Flemish artist but also the leading exponent of the Baroque in northern Europe. His personal style, vigorous and majestic, finds expression in *The Adoration of the Magi* (c.1616) and two religious masterpieces, *The Raising of the Cross* (1610) and *The Deposition* (1611–14). Old Testament themes gave Rubens more opportunity to exercise his imagination: *Adam and Eve in Paradise*, a glorious woodland scene painted together with Brueghel the Elder; *Bathsheba at the Fountain* (c.1635), an alluring seated nude;

and a powerful, realistic treatment of *Daniel in the Lions' Den* (1618).

If Michelangelo reached the summit of biblical art with his sculptures and frescoes, Rembrandt van Rijn attained similar heights with the oil paintings that contributed to his fame as the preeminent Dutch artist.

There were typically Baroque elements in his earlier work, but they mellowed and gave way to subtler effects lending an air of mystery or compassionate insight, as in the delicate portrayal of *Bathsheba* (1654). Rembrandt was, in any case, an undogmatic Protestant hostile towards the underlying aims of the Catholic Baroque. His originality stems from a bold jettisoning of Christian typology; the universal significance attached to each picture; and, most of all perhaps, an objective use of Jewish models (from the artist's own neighborhood in Amsterdam) rather than the contemporary Europeans or stylized figures portrayed in Bible scenes heretofore. Of Rembrandt's 650 paintings and 2,000 or more etchings and drawings, a considerable number deal with Scriptural (particularly Old Testament) themes. Rembrandt's "Protestant iconography of the Bible" was the work of four decades (1630–1669). Among the oil paintings, there are whole cycles devoted to Joseph, Samson, David, Esther, and the Apocryphal Tobit; etchings or drawings, meant for a less affluent public, sometimes widen the biblical panorama.

Ruth and Naomi by Leonard Baskin, 1984.

LATER WORKS

The decorative Rococo style which eventually superseded the Baroque had its chief exponent in Tiepolo, the last of the great Venetians, who produced some biblical canvases and murals as well as two huge altarpieces, *The Gathering of the Manna* and *The Sacrifice of Melchizedek* (c.1735–40). However, there was a general decline of interest in the Bible among 18th-century artists; even Sir Joshua Reynolds and John Singleton Copley, the pioneers of biblical art work in England, concentrated on the Samuel theme.

Attitudes and fashions soon changed with the upsurge of Romanticism and other movements in Western Europe. The English poet William Blake, who illustrated his own works under supposedly Divine inspiration, devoted many paintings and engravings to the Old Testament, his "great code of art." Foremost among these are color-printed drawings of *Nebuchadnezzar* and *Elijah in the Chariot of Fire*, and his *Inventions to the Book of Job* (1826), a series of 21 watercolors. There was a similar biblical revival in France, with paintings by Corot (*Hagar in the Wilderness*, 1835; *The Destruction of Sodom*, c.1857), Delacroix (*Christ on the Cross, Daniel in the Lions' Den*, 1849), and others. Gustave Doré also executed a long series of dramatic engravings to illustrate the Bible and Apocrypha (1866).

The simplicity and idealism typifying the English

Pre-Raphaelite movement found expression in the biblical subjects of Ford Madox Brown (*The Coat of Many Colours*, 1866), John Millais, Dante Gabriel Rossetti, and William Holman Hunt. Like Rembrandt, Holman Hunt was not satisfied with conventional models and settings; from 1854, he paid a number of visits to Egypt and the Holy Land in search of more accurate local color and ethnic types for his religious paintings (e.g., *The Finding of Christ in the Temple*, 1862).

The great French sculptor Auguste Rodin carved modernistic and challenging studies of *John the Baptist* (1881), *Adam and Eve* (1881–4), and an enormous *Porte d'Enfer* (1880–1917) inspired by Ghiberti's bronze doors in Florence. Kokoschka, Rouault, Salvador Dali, and many other leading 20th-century artists have occasionally dealt with biblical themes. Since 1900, many of the outstanding and original creations have been produced by Jewish painters and sculptors, such as Jacques Lipchitz, Sir Jacob Epstein, and Marc Chagall. As controversial as Rodin in his time, Epstein sculpted *The Burial of Abel* (1938), *Adam* (1939), and a monumental *Jacob and the Angel* (1941). His New Testament subjects, *Ecce Homo* and *Lazarus* (1947), *Madonna and Child* (1953), and *Christ in Majesty* (1959) were designed for British churches.

The Prodigal Son; bronze sculpture by Rodin; c.1889.

Dozens of episodes in the Hebrew Bible, the Apocrypha, and the New Testament lend themselves to fictional treatment in prose, the writer's imagination being called upon to elaborate the narrative, bridge gaps, or sharpen the portrayal of character. Since the last days of the Second Temple, a wealth of other source material embroidering the Scriptures has also been available in the shape of Jewish exposition, commentary, legend, and folklore; early Christian (Patristic) traditions; and tales from the Koran and Islamic legends. Although not written or presented as fiction, many a talmudic or Islamic sidelight on the Old Testament could be placed in the genre of the short story, providing entertainment as well as instruction.

No Western fiction on biblical themes was composed until two German writers, Grimmelshausen and Philipp von Zesen, published romances about Joseph and Asenath in the late 17th century. Thereafter, more than 70 years elapsed before Henry Fielding, in England, parodied the story of Joseph and Potiphar's wife in *Joseph Andrews* (1742). Even so, the Bible's impact on the novel and short story largely dates from around 1850. Thanks to the example of Fielding, such prose works often had a satirical intent; alternately, they have conveyed a national or political message to the reader.

The first 19th-century novel with a biblical setting was William Ware's *Julian: or Scenes in Judea* (1841). The modern Hebrew novelist Abraham Mapu, who lived in Eastern Europe, published *The Love of Zion* in 1853. Successors included two American writers, Joseph Holt Ingram (*The Pillar of Fire*, 1859; *The Throne of David*, 1860), and the pioneer of Reform Judaism in the U.S., Isaac Mayer Wise, whose works included *The Combat of the People; or, Hillel and Herod* (1859) and *The First of the Maccabees* (1860). With *Ben-Hur* (1880) and *The Boyhood of Christ* (1888), Lew Wallace, a former Union general, made his name as the earliest exponent of New Testament fiction. In Europe, Gustave Flaubert mingled realism and sensuality in *Herodias*, the last of his *Trois Contes* (1877); while Pontius Pilate's reminiscences gave an ironical flavor to a later story, *The Procurator of Judea*, by Flaubert's compatriot, Anatole France. The Scots novelist, George Macdonald, published a biblical dream romance (*Lilith*, 1895); Old Testament themes also inspired the Czech writer Julius Zeyer (*Asenat*, 1895), the Polish novelist Boleslaw Prus (*Faraon*, 1895-6), and the Russian story-teller Aleksandr Kuprin. *Josua* (1890) was a characteristic tale by Georg Moritz Ebers, a German Egyptologist who specialized in archaeological romance.

In the early 20th century, Sir Henry Rider Haggard wrote *Moon of Israel*, a Moses tale told from the Egyptian viewpoint. Jewish writers such as Arnold Zweig (*Jerusalem Delivered*, 1910) also made their specific contribution to this new genre. Two works that appeared in 1918 were a Swedish tale (*Jahves eld*) about Moses by Hjalmar Söderberg and Joseph Ponten's early novel, *Der babylonische Turm*, in which the Tower of Babel symbolized the rise and fall of Bismarck's Prussian empire.

Many more novels and stories were written between the two World Wars, nearly all of them on Old Testament themes. They included a Samson novel in German (1928) by Felix Salten, the creator of *Bambi* (it was translated into English by Whittaker Chambers); others on the same theme by the Dutch writer Israel Querido (1927-9) and the Russian Zionist Vladimir Jabotinsky; legendary biographies of Moses and Solomon in French by Edmond Fleg (1928-30); Gala Galaction's Romanian works (e.g., *Roxana*, 1930); novels by two American Jewish writers, Louis Untermeyer (*Moses*, 1928) and Robert Nathan (*Jonah; or the Withering Vine*, 1925); together with those of a Canadian novelist, W.G. Hardy. The Nazi rise to power in Germany left its imprint on Thomas Mann's tetralogy, *Joseph and his Brothers*, on Harald Tandrup's Danish version of the Jonah story, and on Franz Werfel's German novel about Jeremiah, *Hearken unto the Voice* (1937).

The Yiddish writer Sholem Asch wrote two biblical cycles, one on the New Testament and one on the Old. Irving Fineman turned to Old Testament themes (*Jacob*, 1941) in the U.S.A.; Karl Boxler's Swiss-German novel, *Judas Makkabaus* (1943), sub-titled "A Small Nation Fights for its Faith and Homeland," clearly drew a parallel between the struggles waged against their oppressors by the Jews under their Maccabean champions and the Swiss led by William Tell. In Nazi-occupied Europe, the Belgian (Flemish) novelist Ernest André Claes added *Herodes* (1942) to his biblical output, while the Danish anti-Nazi Kaj Munk, best known for his dramas, wrote a collection of *Tales about Jesus* (1943) not long before he was murdered by the Gestapo. *The Robe* (1942), a novel by the American writer Lloyd C. Douglas, portrayed the first impact of Christianity, and Gladys Schmitt wrote *David the King*.

Many postwar biblical novels grappled with the nightmare of Hitlerism in various ways. There was a short-lived "return to the sources" in Communist-ruled Hungary, with works by Geza Hegedus (*The Iconoclasts*, 1945) and Janos Kodolanyi (*The Burning Bush*, 1957), as well as among the defiantly Catholic Poles (e.g., Zofia Kossak-Szczucka, Jan Dobraczynski). Elsewhere, however, feelings of despair or disillusionment with "the gods that failed" were voiced by Lion Feuchtwanger in his American exile and by Stefan

Heym in East Germany, while a skeptical approach to religion or even a complete break with the Christian tradition could be detected in the novels of Marnix Gijsen (Belgium), Robert Graves (*King Jesus*, 1946), Par Lagerkvist (Sweden), and Nikos Kazantzakis (*The Last Temptation of Christ*, 1955). New, if less devastating, insights characterized the Old Testament romances of Frank Slaughter (U.S.A.) and Poul Hoffmann's Danish trilogy about Moses (1958–62). The most determined effort to re-examine questions of human responsibility and moral action, in light of the immediate (Nazi) past, came from younger German novelists such as Alfred Andersch and Stefan Andres (*Die Sintflut*, 1949–59; *Der Mann im Fisch*, 1963).

In addition to the problem of evil, Jewish novelists had to face the whole issue of their people's survival, which was brought into sharper focus once again during and after Israel's War of Independence. In Canada, A ele Wiseman (*The Sacrifice*, 1956) and Charles Israel (*Rizpah*, 1961, found modern relevance in biblical stories, as did the expatriate South African writer, Dan Jacobson (*The Rape of Tamar*, 1970), in Britain. Among those in the U.S. who created a vogue for historical romance with overtones of the Israeli present were Howard Fast and the non-Jewish best-selling writer James Michener. It has been estimated that in the U.S. the flood of novels drawn from Holy Scripture exceeds that from any other source. Over 300 such novels (excluding juvenile books) have appeared in the 20th century.

Knights in search of the Holy Grail; 14th-century miniature. The Holy Grail was believed to be the cup used by Jesus at the Last Supper. It became the subject of many medieval legends and romances.

SOME MAJOR WORKS OF FICTION ON BIBLICAL THEMES

Histori vom Keuschen Joseph (1667). German prose romance by Hans Jakob Christoffel von Grimmelshausen, the first novel on a biblical theme, which made Potiphar's wife a demonic temptress and her niece, Asenath, Joseph's guardian angel. Reworked under a different title in 1671, it was the basis for a more sophisticated novel by Philipp von Zesen (*Assenat*, 1670).

Ahavat Tsiyyon ("The Love of Zion," 1853). Historical novel by Abraham Mapu; not only the first bestseller in Hebrew, but also the first modern romance with a biblical setting. Thanks to its masterly portrayal of Israelite freedom in the days of Isaiah, this novel had a vast appeal to East European Jewry, went through many editions, and had no less than three English translations.

Le Procurateur de Judée. Short story by Anatole France, included in *L'Etui de nacre* (1892). Bearing the mark of this French writer's skepticism and irony, it opens with a now aged Pontius Pilate discussing old times with a close friend. Judea's one-time governor, an inveterate anti-Semite, is asked about a young Galilean who was crucified for some offense, but when the name of Jesus is mentioned he murmurs, "Jesus? I cannot remember such a person."

Moses and Jesus. Short story by the Anglo-Jewish writer Israel Zangwill, included in *Blind Children* (1903). This imaginary encounter between the lawgiver of Judaism and the founder of Christianity, inspired by Zangwill's religio-national outlook, is notable for the bitter remarks which the two protagonists exchange.

Sulamif("Sulamith: A Tale of Antiquity," 1908). Idyllic prose romance by the Russian novelist Aleksandr Ivanovich Kuprin. Taking its inspiration from the Song of Songs, this "hymn to love" tells how Solomon, in his old age, finds contentment, peace of mind, and true affection in the arms of a young girl, whom a jealous rival eventually has put to death.

Joseph und Seine Bruder (1933–42). Old Testament classic by the great German novelist Thomas Mann. A tetralogy begun in the year of Hitler's rise to power, and extending from *The Tales of Jacob* to *Joseph the Provider*, this epic work has been translated into many languages (including English, 1934–44). Noted for its psychological penetration, the novel blends Scriptural history with Jewish and other legendary material, also expressing the author's contempt for Nazi race theories. Together with fellow writers of stature, Mann contributed to a volume entitled *The Ten Commandments: Ten Short Novels of Hitler's War against the Moral Code (1944)*.

Father Abraham (1935). Biblical romance by the Canadian writer and classical scholar William George Hardy. Sarah, portrayed as a Habiru queen, is this tale's real hero; its villains, Hagar and Ishmael, get their just deserts after Isaac nearly falls victim to their murderous ambition. Hardy's other works include a novel about Moses, *All the Trumpets Sounded* (1942).

Profeten Jonas Privat ("Jonah and the Voice," 1937). Novel by the Danish writer Harald Tandrup satirizing the anti-Jewish obsession in Nazi Germany. Johan is an inoffensive little Jew, terrified by the mission entrusted to him; Assyria's king is a bloodthirsty Hitler, capable of uniting street mobs and upper-class "idealists" in one popular rampage. Jonah manages to survive, and then becomes "an untiring questioner" of God's justice.

The Nazarene (1939). Historical novel by the Yiddish writer Sholem Asch; first part of a New Testament cycle that would also comprise *The Apostle* (1943) and *Mary* (1949).

Appearing under the shadow of Hitlerism, it outraged sections of Jewish opinion which charged Asch with "spreading heresy nd preaching conversion." As later in *Moses* (1951) and *The Prophet* (1955), the novelist displayed his creative ability as a story-teller, portrayer of character, and delineator of the ancient world's scenery and religions.

Het Boek van Joachim van Babylon (1947). Flemish romance by the Antwerp scholar and diplomat Marnix Gijsen (Jan-Albert Goris). A postwar bestseller, this pseudo-Apocryphal tale, amplifying what is known about Susanna and the Elders, completely altered the story, with ironical reference to the author's own lapse from Catholicism.

My Glorious Brothers (1948). Epic historical novel by the American Jewish writer Howard Fast, portraying the desperate Maccabean revolt against a pagan oppressor. Like *Spartacus* (1952), it gave voice to the novelist's political beliefs ("that resistance to tyranny is the truest obedience to God"). Fast later published another biblical novel, *Moses, Prince of Egypt* (1958).

Barabbas (1950). Novel by the Swedish writer Par Fabian Lagerkvist which gained him the Nobel Prize for Literature in 1951. One of a series on New Testament themes, written in a "biblical" style but decidedly un-biblical in approach, it had a dubious character as its hero and reflected the author's stand as a "religious atheist" who maintained that Christianity provides no answers to eternal questions.

Sansibar (1956). German novel by Alfred Andersch transposing the Belshazzar's Feast motif to the Nazi era. Throughout that time, Pastor Helander awaits the fiery Writing on the Wall that will proclaim the overthrow of Hitlerism. The letters appear when he falls under a hail of Nazi bullets, and the pastor's dying thought is that retributive justice must follow this signal from God.

The Scarlet Cord (1956). Biblical romance about Rahab, "the woman of Jericho," by the U.S. novelist Frank G. Slaughter. He portrays her as a Habiru priestess devoted to Joshua, who is responsible for every stage of her degradation. Rahab's loyalty to the Israelite cause is finally rewarded by her marriage, not to the boorish Joshua, but to his physician. An earlier novel by the same author was *The Song of Ruth: A Love Story from the Old Testament* (1954).

Jefta und seine Tochter (1957). Last work of the German Jewish novelist Lion Feuchtwanger. By emphasizing the tragic absurdity of Jephthah's sacrifice, Feuchtwanger revealed his own despair over Germany's surrender to the Nazis, Stalinist control of Eastern Europe, and, above all, the nightmare of the Holocaust which had almost engulfed him in 1940.

The Source (1965). Epic historical novel by the U.S. writer James Michener. Its title comes from Makor, a fictitious hill site in northern Israel where an American-backed expedition unearths successive layers of Near Eastern civilization. Within this modern archaeological framework, different stories can be told, shedding light on the biblical past as well as on Jewish ties with the Holy Land down the ages. A sense of historic continuity involving many peoples and three world religions also emerges from *The Source*.

Der Konig David Bericht ("The King David Report," 1972). German novel by Stefan Heym in which the Old Testament serves to disguise a political message. The aged Michal finds that a chronicler's "official" version of David's life and career differs sharply from her own precise recollections: for the powers that be, a glorious feat of whitewashing is all that matters. Heym's disenchantment with Communism (and its rewriting of history) was expressed in this mordant satire, which, though banned in East Germany, gained plaudits in the West.

VI.51 THE BIBLE IN DRAMA

Both the Old and the New Testaments contain an enormous variety of tragic, thrilling or light-hearted motifs, character sketches, dialogue, and episodes that provide all the essential ingredients of drama.

Plays based on biblical themes originated in pre-Christian Hellenistic Alexandria. Over a millennium then elapsed before this type of drama was revived, with the encouragement and supervision of churchmen, in medieval Europe. There, between the 11th and late 15th centuries, a new genre of mystery, miracle, and passion plays came into being, the staging of which provided common folk with religious instruction and no little entertainment. Mysteries portrayed both Old and New Testament figures; miracle plays dealt with the lives of Christian saints; passion plays dramatized the life and death of Jesus.

Whole cycles of Old Testament dramas were eventually performed (often by trade guild members) in English towns; on a larger scale, this process in France gave rise to the collection of 48 plays known as the *Mistère du Viel Testament*, as well as to many New Testament productions; Italy also had its *sacre rappresentazioni*, with analogues as far afield as Crete; while the German-speaking lands also had their New Testament miracle and passion plays. Especially after the inauguration of the feast of Corpus Christi in 1246, biblical play cycles developed, starting with the Creation and ending with the Last Judgment, with the Crucifixion as the climax.

Initially, these religious dramas were staged inside or at the entrance to the churches, and the actors spoke their lines in a Latin incomprehensible to the masses. Old Testament figures and episodes were seen as "prefigurations" of the New Covenant. Later, however, performances were removed to a different setting, away from the local church, with vernacular speech replacing Latin. The Reformation accelerated these changes in order to foster the new translations of the Bible and loosen popular ties with Catholicism. Due to the influence and advocacy of Martin Luther, Old Testament dramas and comedies in German (emphasizing moral rather than purely religious issues) were first written by the Augsburg humanist Sixtus Birck and the Nuremberg mastersinger Hans Sachs.

Others who followed their example included Olaus Petri in Sweden, various Elizabethan playwrights in England, Dutch Protestants, and French Calvinist writers. Before long, this biblical vogue found striking expression in plays by the Dutch ex-Protestant Joost van den Vondel, the Dalmatian humanist Mavro Vetranovic, the Italian Giambattista Andreini, and leading dramatists of the Spanish golden age (Calderon, Tirso de Molina, Gil Vicente, Felipe Godinez). For sheer grandeur alone, the English poet John Milton

(*Samson Agonistes*) and the French dramatist Jean Racine (*Athalie, Esther*) had no rivals.

A specifically Jewish contribution also emerged with the beginnings of a secular biblical drama in Hebrew (Italy) and comedies such as the Purim play (the story of Esther) in Spanish (Amsterdam) and Yiddish (Central Europe). From the late 17th century onward, with the spread of Enlightenment and Rationalism, works on biblical themes often served as a vehicle for political satire (Dryden's *Absalom and Achitophel*, 1681), patriotic sentiment, and suppressed hatred of foreign domination (Alfieri's dramas; Madach's Hungarian *Mozes*, 1860). Christian Weise's Old Testament plays also heralded a revival of the genre and, thanks to Klopstock, a new social message in Germany.

Throughout the 19th century themes drawn from the Bible and Apocrypha were given a variety of interpretations, by the French Romantics (Chateaubriand, Lamartine), German and Austrian Realists (Hebbel, Otto Ludwig), and other European dramatists. Following the subversive lead of Voltaire's mocking tragedy (*Saül*, 1763), and the iconoclasm of Byron's verse play (*Cain*, 1821), however, a number of modern writers have adopted a frankly skeptical attitude toward the Bible (usually the Old Testament), which their works have sometimes sought to debunk. Among the playwrights in this category were George Bernard Shaw (*Back to Methuselah*, 1921), John Masefield (*A King's Daughter*, 1923), and Laurence Houseman (the author of four anti-biblical *Old Testament Plays*, 1950).

A miracle play at Coventry; from an old print.

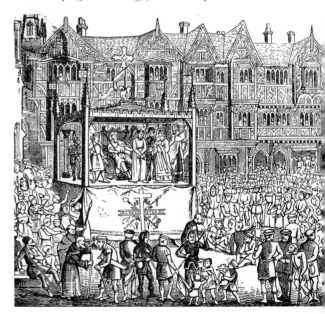

Christ before Pilate. Scene from the Passion Play of Oberammergau, 1922.

On the whole, that approach has not characterized 20th-century biblical drama, although most writers have brought psychological factors and their own modern outlook into play. There were for example, political undertones in the works of Stanislaw Wyspianski (*Daniel*, 1907), a Polish Neo-Romantic, and Leonid Andreyev (*Samson in Chains*, 1923), an anti-Bolshevik Russian emigre. Those who dramatized biblical figures in Germany included Georg Kaiser, Frank Wedekind, and three leading Jewish writers whom the Nazis drove into exile: Stefan Zweig, Franz Werfel, and Richard Beer-Hofmann. In 1911, Kaiser turned the story of Judith into a comedy (*Die jüdische Witwe*); Beer-Hofmann's Old Testament trilogy (*Die Historie vom König David*, 1918–36), written in Vienna, was never completed. Moral issues and modern conflicts also dominated the treatment of Old Testament themes among French playwrights such as André Gide (*Bethsabée*, 1908; *Saul*, 1922), André Obey (*Noé*, 1931), and Jean Giraudoux.

In Britain, James Bridie, Christopher Fry (*The Firstborn*, 1946; *A Sleep of Prisoners*, 1951), and Norman Nicholson (*The Old Man of the Mountains*, 1946; *A Match for the Devil*, 1955) were major exponents of the genre. Bridie's superficial frivolity concealed a serious probing of three tales, while Nicholson's realism led him to set his biblical drama in the north of England. Like Bridie, the U.S. poet and playwright Robert Frost

(*A Masque of Reason*, 1945; *A Masque of Mercy*, 1947) disguised his true purpose with an outwardly humorous approach. Nicholson's way of transposing the ancient scene to modern times was anticipated by Marc Connelly and followed by two other American writers, Archibald MacLeish (*J.B.*, 1958) and Clifford Odets (*The Flowering Peach*, 1954). Since the 1950s, much controversy has been aroused by the biblical and religious dramas of Nikos Kazantzakis (*Sodom and Gomorrah*, 1956).

BIBLICAL DRAMA DOWN THE AGES

Exagoge ("The Departure from Egypt," 2nd cent. BC). Greek verse play by Ezekiel the Poet, a Hellenistic Jew of Alexandria. The surviving fragment, clearly influenced by Greek drama though textually related to the Septuagint, is the earliest known literary work adapted from the Bible.

Jeu d'Adam (12th cent.). Church drama representing the Fall of Man, Cain's murder of Abel, and the Old Testament prophets of the Redemption. Apart from its Latin stage directions, this verse play was the first to be written entirely in (Norman) French.

York Plays (1340–50). Oldest and best-preserved collection of English mystery and miracle plays, dealing with events from the Creation to the Last Judgment, which were meant for performance by trade guilds on improvised stage settings.

The entire cycle of 48 plays, alternately naive and realistic, took several days to perform; the texts were first published in 1548. Chester, Lincoln, and other cycles have also been preserved.

The Historie of Jacob and Esau (1568). English play, attributed to Nicholas Udall, which dates from the reign of Queen Mary but appeared only after her sister Elizabeth's accession to the throne. Underlying the biblical drama is many an incisive and sometimes comic allusion to the religious conflicts of 16th-century England, Jacob (the righteous Hebrew) being represented as a Protestant and Esau (the uncouth pagan) as a no less obvious Catholic.

Sedecie, ou Les Juives (1583). Dramatic masterpiece by Robert Garnier and the outstanding early tragedy in French. With notable power and pathos, it shows how Zedekiah ignored the prophet Jeremiah's warnings and thus brought about his own downfall. A highlight of this play is the cruel treatment to which Nebuchadnezzar subjected Judah's royal family after his capture of Jerusalem.

La Venganza de Tamar (1634). Drama by the prolific Spanish writer Tirso de Molina, its theme being Absalom's vengeful killing of Amnon after the latter had raped his half-sister Tamar. Another Old Testament drama (*La mejor espigadera*), based on the story of Ruth, was published by Tirso in the same year.

Oberammergau Passion Play (1634). Famous German passion play about the life and death of Jesus, staged by the villagers of Oberammergau in Bavaria. During an outbreak of the plague there in 1633, the inhabitants vowed to have it performed if the epidemic would end; this duly occurred, and since then performances have been given every ten years, with breaks in the 18th century and in 1940–50. It lasts for several hours and a cast of 1,200 villagers is required. On the recommendation of Church authorities, this passion play's text was modified in 1969 and 1989, to remove certain offensively anti-Jewish stereotypes.

La Cena de Baltasar ("Belshazzar's Feast," c.1634). Outstanding biblical *auto* (sacred drama) written by Pedro Calderón de la Barca, one of Spain's most eminent playwrights. An important feature of this work is the combination of poetic grandeur with excellent stagecraft.

He Thysia Tou Abraam ("The Sacrifice of Abraham," 1635). Greek drama by the Cretan epic poet Vitzentzos Kornaros. Drawing some of his inspiration from a 12th-century miracle play, he portrayed Abraham realistically as a man torn between love for his son and loyalty to his God.

El Macabeo (1638). Baroque masterpiece by Miguel de Silveyra, an emigre Portuguese of Jewish ancestry who wrote in Spanish. Though rather bombastic, this dramatic portrayal of Judah Maccabee and his valiant struggle is the oldest known treatment of the theme in world literature.

Joseph in Egypten (1640). One of the many biblical dramas written by Joost van den Vondel, a preacher of religious tolerance and the greatest Dutch poet of the classical age.

Samson Agonistes (1671). Last major work by John Milton, the greatest of all biblical dramas in English. Taking Greek tragedy as its model, and giving an important role to the chorus, it portrays the final hours of Israel's stricken judge, "Eyeless in Gaza at the mill with slaves," and reaches a climax with his triumph over the Philistines offstage. In this idealized figure of Samson one glimpses Milton's view of himself: blind, lonely, and chagrined after the return of the Stuarts.

Athalie (1691). Classic French tragedy by Jean Racine, originally written for performance by the young ladies of Madame de Maintenon's convent school at Saint-Cyr. Often regarded as the dramatist's outstanding work, with powerful characterization and many biblical echoes, it portrays the frantic efforts made by Judah's idolatrous Queen Athaliah to kill the child Joash, true heir to the throne. Outwitted by the high priest, she is finally dragged out of the Temple precincts to her death. Racine's other biblical tragedy was *Esther* (1689).

Der tod Adams (1757). Tragedy on the Fall of Man theme by Friedrich Klopstock, best known for his Christian epic *Der Messias*. As the leading precursor of German Romanticism, he gave expression in this drama to a Rousseau-esque yearning for an imagined Golden Age.

Saul (1782). Classic tragedy by Vittorio Alfieri, the greatest Italian dramatist of his time, portraying Israel's first king as a man of defiant grandeur who tries to impose his will on friend and foe alike. The hatred of tyranny and longing for freedom voiced here make the Old Testament a vehicle for Alfieri's Italian patriotism.

Cain (1821). Romantic English verse play by Lord Byron. Shattering all literary and religious conventions, it sought to present the first murderer as a hero, denied the benevolence of God, and was therefore condemned as sacrilegious.

Herodes und Mariamne (1850). Dramatic masterpiece by Friedrich Hebbel, a leading Realist and the greatest German tragedian of the 19th century. With its subtle dialogue and penetrating insight into character, this Apocryphal tragedy contains all the elements that distinguished Hebbel's earlier play, *Judith* (1841).

Az Ember Tragediaja ("The Tragedy of Man," 1862). Philosophical magnum opus of the Hungarian playwright Imre Madach. A dream sequence, in which Lucifer shows Adam the many pitfalls awaiting his descendants, enables Madach to establish the framework for his analysis of the eternal conflict between good and evil, and of man's struggle with his own shortcomings. In *Mózes* (1860), the dramatist had reinterpreted the Exodus from Egypt in terms of the Hungarian fight for national liberation.

Salome (1894). Oscar Wilde's daring comedy about John the Baptist, originally written and performed in French. The text served Richard Strauss as a libretto for his opera. Owing to censorship laws, an English version of the play could not be staged in Britain until 1931.

Jeremias (1918). Powerful anti-war drama by Stefan Zweig, which had its premiere in Zurich while the European conflict was still raging and the author was attached to Austria's war ministry in Vienna. Zweig's play drew universal significance from the Old Testament theme and Jewish history to convey its pacifist message.

The Green Pastures (1930). Pulitzer Prize winning play by Marc Connelly, based on Roark Bradford's *Ol' Man Adam an' His Children*, which was later filmed in the U.S. It broke new ground by dramatizing Afro-American concepts of God and the Old Testament.

Noé (1931). French drama by André Obey, according to which man alone is responsible for the evils afflict-ing the world. In line with the new tendency to debunk sacred literature, Obey pictures the Flood as it could have been seen by those inside the Ark, while God and Noah communicate by telephone.

Tobias and the Angel (1931). One of three works on biblical or Apocryphal themes, combining humor and realism, by the Scots playwright James Bridie. It was followed by *Jonah and the Whale* (1932), with *Susannah and the Elders* (1931) turning the virtuous heroine into a mischievous coquette.

Der Weg der Verheissung (1935). Biblical pageant-play by the Czech-born Austrian writer Franz Werfel. An English-language version, *The Eternal Road*, was later staged in New York by Max Reinhardt with "synagogue music" composed by Kurt Weill. The religious doubts that beset Werfel's last years could already be glimpsed in *Paul Among the Jews* (1926), a dramatization of the conflict between Rabbinic Judaism and early Christianity.

The Man Born to be King (1943). Sequence of New Testament plays for radio by Dorothy L. Sayers, renowned for her detective novels. First produced by

Athaliah's Downfall; painting by Antoine Coypel, 1692, based on Racine's tragedy, Athalie.

the British Broadcasting Corporation (December 1941-October 1942), *The Man Born to be King* aroused controversy through its unconventional portrayal of Jesus and use of colloquial modern English, but the series attracted many listeners and has often been repeated.

Sodome et Gomorrhe (1943). Drama by the eminent French writer Jean Giraudoux, the last to be staged in his lifetime.

Conceived during the Nazi occupation of France, this brilliant play highlighted the author's view of incomprehension and comity between the sexes. In place of the Bible's ten righteous human beings, one couple only will avert God's wrath from the Cities of the Plain if they preserve a harmonious sexual relationship. Their inability to do so brings about the final catastrophe.

J.B. (1958). Pulitzer Prize-winning by Archibald MacLeish, whose earlier verse play, *Nobodaddy* (1926), had advanced modern unconventional arguments to vindicate the Creator. Transposed to 20th-century America, Job (alias J.B.) is a successful executive who has to endure one misfortune after another. Rejecting the conventional approach once again, MacLeish allows the three modern comforters to exonerate J.B., who nevertheless insists on blaming himself for all the disasters.

VI.52 THE BIBLE IN POETRY

Practically all verse forms are discernible in the Old Testament: epic poetry in the Songs of Moses and Deborah, for example, meditative verse in Psalms, love lyrics in the Song of Songs, elegiac verse in Lamentations and elsewhere. Their impact on early European literature was considerable, in the shape of biblical paraphrases, religious verse, and also a few epic works. From the 16th century, however, what gave the strongest impetus to biblicism in poetry was the Reformation, accompanied by new (chiefly Protestant) translations of the Scriptures and followed by the devastating Wars of Religion. Throughout Europe, for generations to come, biblical themes and idioms would find a profound echo in man's everyday language; while a host of biblical epics often expressed a nation's longing for independence or a downtrodden minority's hope for religious freedom.

One of the very first literary treatments of a biblical theme was *Heliand* ("The Savior"), an Old Saxon epic in 6,000 alliterative verses dealing with the life and death of Jesus. Composed around 830 by an unidentified Rhenish churchman, it portrayed Jesus as a Teutonic king surrounded by warlike apostles. The epic retained an essentially Christian spirit, however, giving emphasis to the Sermon on the Mount. Despite the hymns and religious influence of Luther and Zwingli, German verse displayed scant Biblicism until the Baroque period of Martin Opitz and Christian Knorr von Rosenroth. Thereafter, Friedrich Klopstock's Christian epic, *Der Messias* (1748-73), heralded the appearance of similar works, on themes drawn from Genesis, by Johann Bodmer (*Noah*, 1750; *Die Synd-Flut*, 1751) and Salomon Gessner (*Der Tod Abels*, 1758). In different ways both Gessner's epic and the pioneering research of a great Bible scholar, J.G. Herder (*The Spirit of Hebrew Poetry*, 1782-3), were to have a major impact on 19th-century English writers. Transcending all boundaries, the lyrical genius of Heinrich Heine continues to influence other poets down to our own day.

In French poetry, the Bible has had a far greater and more consistent role to play. Centuries before new Protestant and Catholic Bibles made their appearance, Herman de Valenciennes wrote a metrical version of the Scriptures (c. 1190); while Clément Marot's *Pseaulmes de David* (1541-3) created a vogue for psalm-singing at the French court. Other poets of the age who followed his example included Jean-Antoine de Baif, Philippe Desportes, and François de Malherbe, was well

---

William Drummond: "Saint John Baptist"
(early 17th century)

The last and greatest Herald of Heaven's King,
Girt with rough skins, hies to the deserts wild,
Among that savage brood the woods forth
  bring,
Which he more harmless found than man,
  and mild.

His food was locusts, and what there doth
  spring
With honey that from virgin hives distill'd;
Parch'd body, hollow eyes, some uncouth
  thing
Made him appear, long since from earth
  exiled.

There burst he forth: "All ye whose hopes rely
on God, with me amidst these deserts mourn;
Repent, repent, and from old errors turn!"
Who listen'd to his voice, obey'd his cry?

Only the echoes, which he made relent,
Rung from their flinty caves "Repent! Repent!"

as Guy Le Fèvre de La Boderie, whose Biblical and Rabbinic erudition left its stamp on everything he wrote. Major religious epics were the work of two Huguenots, Salluste Du Bartas and Agrippa d'Aubigne. In succession to the former's *Judith* (1573) came *La Semaine ou Création du monde* (1578) and an unfinished *Seconde Semaine* (1584-1603), translations of which influenced Milton and Goethe. Amid echoes of the Psalms and Lamentations, D'Aubigne (in *Les Tragiques*, 1616) conjured up a series of apocalyptic visions invoking God's punishment of Babel (Roman Catholic tyranny) and defense of Zion (the persecuted Calvinists). Lesser epics were written by Antoine de Montchrétien (*Susane*, 1601), a Protestant, and Antoine Godeau (*Saint Paul*, 1654), a Catholic.

French Romanticism reflected the exotic, revived interest in the Bible. Poets who dealt with biblical or pseudo-biblical themes included Alphonse de Lamartine (e.g., "Le Crucifix," 1823; *La Chute d'un ange*, 1838); Alfred de Vigny, whose Old Testament heroes (Moses and Samson) portrayed some of his own lonely stoicism, and Victor Hugo, whose treatment of biblical motifs (in *La Légende des siècles* 1859) displayed great insight and lyrical or epic power. Leconte de Lisle, however, the Parnassian movement's standard-bearer, injected a bitter atheistic tone into his miniature epos, *Qain* (1859). The approach of some 20th-century writers, notably Oscar Milosz and Paul Claudel, has been decidedly religious or even mystical.

On a smaller scale, this upsurge of Biblicism in the 16th century, reawakening in the 19th, can be detected elsewhere, from Holland to Eastern Europe. The process begins with Lutheran or Calvinist editions of the Bible, generally followed by the Reformation psalters that appeal to the masses. Such verse translations often marked the real birth of a modern literature, as in Poland and Hungary. Next, long poems and epics on Old Testament themes were usually written, such as Jan Kochanowki's Polish *Threny* (1580) and Ferenc Apati's Hungarian *Cantilena* (c. 1523). Like the French Huguenots, Calvinists in other parts of Europe tended to cast themselves in the role of latterday Israelites facing assorted oppressors. A parallel was thus drawn between Holland's Protestant champion, William of Orange, and Israel's King David in the Dutch national anthem; while the loyally Catholic Marko Marulic, in his epic *Judita* (1521), made Holofernes resemble a Turkish general butchering the Croatians.

Here and there, exceptions to the overall pattern can be found. During the early Middle Ages, for example, Creation epics were written in 9th-century Bulgaria by Ioan the Exarch, and in 13th-century Denmark by Anders Suneson. Moreover, apart from Jewish refugees whose literary medium was Spanish, no biblical poetry of consequence appeared in Holland until the 1800s. Since then, exponents of the genre have emerged in 20th-century Poland (Julian Tuwim), Hungary (Endre

Ady, Attila Jozsef), Russia (Anna Akhmatova, Semyon Kirsanov), and South Africa (Totius, i.e., Jacob Daniel du Toit). Ferenc Kolcsey's *Hymnus* (1823), inspired by a passage in Jeremiah (32:21-29), became the Hungarian national anthem; and Kornel Ujejski's *Skargi Jeremiego* (1893) was an elegiac tribute to Mickiewicz and other Polish heroes.

South of the Alps and the Pyrenees, where Catholicism was never seriously challenged, Biblical poetry took different forms. In Italy, its zenith was reached during the Middle Ages, initally with the *Cantico delle creature*, an adaptation of Psalm 148 by St. Francis of Assisi which marked the beginning of genuine Italian verse. A century later (1307-21), Dante carried this process a stage further in his *Divine Comedy*, which abounds in Scriptural figures and expressions derived from his reading of the Latin Vulgate. Spanish Biblicism can be seen in the translations of Luis de Léon, the mystical verse of San Juan de la Cruz, the "State Poems" of Fernando de Herrera, and other 16th-century works.

Old Testament motifs and echoes have naturally dominated post-biblical Hebrew literature, from the religious poetry and liturgical verse of medieval times onward. Modern Yiddish poetry has also been inspired by biblical themes.

Some of the earliest biblical paraphrases in English verse date back to Caedmon in Anglo-Saxon times (c. 670); and even before the King James (Authorized Version) made its appearance in 1611, Thomas Sternhold's metrical English psalter (1551) had endowed the nation's poetry with Hebrew idiom. Continuing with two Scots poets, William Dunbar and William Drummond, the Anglican John Donne (*Holy Sonnets*), Francis Quarles (*A Feaste for Wormes*, 1620; *Job Militant*, 1624), and George Herbert (*The Temple*, 1633), this process attained its zenith in the works of John Milton. One of his sonnets, "On the Late Massacre in Piedmont" (1655), a masterpiece of biblical anguish and reproach, led Cromwell to defend the persecuted Waldenses through action that would later be called gunboat diplomacy. Of Milton's two great biblical epics, *Paradise Lost* (1667) was a Puritan view of creation and the Fall of Man, lending grandeur to Satan but emphasizing human freedom and responsibility. *Paradise Regained* (1671) was a more explicitly Christian work, based on the Temptation in the Wilderness.

Biblical echoes and allusions also abounded in 18th-century verse (e.g., that of the Scots poet Robert Burns) and Christian hymns (Charles Wesley), while Robert Lowth's pioneering *Lectures on the Sacred Poetry of the Hebrews* (1789), originally published in Latin (1753), anticipated Herder's German work and had a similar impact. This can be gauged from an upsurge of Biblicism among the English Romantics: John Keats, Thomas Moore, William Wordsworth, Samuel Taylor Coleridge, and (especially) William Blake (*The Everlasting*

Gospel, c. 1818), Lord Byron, Robert Browning, and Lord Tennyson (*In Memoriam*, 1850). Byron's *Hebrew Melodies* (1815), set to music by Isaac Nathan, are justly famous, but a more distinctly biblical and Hebraic color is visible in Blake's epic poetry (e.g., *Milton*, 1804; *Jerusalem*, 1804–18), while Browning, who actually learned Hebrew, also showed a positive interest in Jewish themes. Since the appearance of Kipling's "Recessional" (1897), patriotic sentiment has often been expressed in biblical terms, as in Laurence Binyon's much quoted poem "For the Fallen."

One of the early North American poets, Timothy Dwight, adopted this approach in *The Conquest of Canaan* (1785), an epic alluding to the U.S. War of Independence that equated Joshua with George Washington. Old Testament idiom and New Testament creed were later mingled in Julia Ward Howe's *Battle Hymn of the American Republic* (1862), the great marching song of the North during the Civil War. Biblical and Apocryphal subjects chiefly recur in the poems of John Greenleaf Whittier and Henry Wadsworth Longfellow, the former specifically acknowledging his debt to "the Book our mothers read" in a poem entitled "Miriam" 1870). Longfellow's debt was greater and far more extensive, ranging in time from "A Psalm of Life" (1838) to his verse tragedy *Judas Maccabaeus* (1871). It also found expression in the humanitarian *Poems on Slavery* (1842), "The Jewish Cemetery at Newport" (1852), and "Sandalphon" (1857), as well as

the reworked Judaic legends set forth in *Tales of a Wayside Inn* (1863–73). A proto-Zionist note was struck by Emma Lazarus in her *Songs of a Semite* (1882), while Afro-American Bible preaching was imitated in Vachel Lindsay's *The Daniel Jazz* (1920).

Lord Byron: "Oh! Weep for Those" (*Hebrew Melodies*, 1815)

Oh! weep for those that wept by Babel's stream,
Whose shrines are desolate, whose land a dream.
Weep for the harp of Judah's broken shell;
Mourn — where their God hath dwelt the Godless dwell!

And where shall Israel lave her bleeding feet?
And where shall Zion's songs again seem sweet?
And Judah's melody once more rejoice
The hearts that leap'd before its heavenly voice?

Tribes of the wandering foot and weary breast,
How shall ye flee away and be at rest!
The wild-dove hath her nest, the fox his cave,
Mankind their country — Israel but the grave!

VI.53 THE BIBLE IN MUSIC

Psalm-singing by a choir of Levites, with instrumental accompaniment, was one of the distinctive features of Temple worship in Jerusalem. From Psalm 137 it is clear that these singers and their repertoire were widely famed in antiquity. After the Second Temple's destruction by the Romans in AD 70 , however, that musical service could scarcely have survived, although a residue may have found its way into the prayer modes and biblical cantillation of the synagogue, and perhaps even into the "plain chant" (Ambrosian and Gregorian) of the early church. On the Jewish side, an ancient origin has been claimed for settings of the *Kaddish* doxology and other prayers, as well as for "traditional" Ashkenazi tunes that probably date only from the Middle Ages. On the Christian side, musical parallels exist in the Old Testament *Miserere* (Ps. 51), "Triple Sanctus" (Is 6:3), and *Jubilus* (a wordless, melismatic rendition of *Alleluiah*), as well as in the New Testament *Kyrie eleison*, *Ave Maria* and *Magnificat*.

Interreligious musical borrowings no doubt occurred over the centuries, an Arab or Moorish influence creeping into the Eastern Jewish tradition. Among the Jews of northern Europe, an old setting of the *Ma'oz Tsur* (Hanukkah) hymn can be traced to a medieval German air; while many recent synagogue compositions have owed a great deal to Protestant anthems and chorales. A trend in the opposite direction led to Meyer Leon's *Yigdal* tune reappearing as *The God of Abraham Praise*, an English hymn by Thomas Olivers, to Ravel's adaptation of the *Kaddish*, and to the utilization of *Kol Nidre* by several Western composers (Beethoven, Bruch, Ketelbey, and Resnicek).

With the arrival of polyphony during the later Middle Ages, a revolutionary change also took place in sacred music. From the early 1500s, this process was accelerated by Lutheranism, which fostered congregational singing of new hymns and psalm settings in the vernacular. As the Reformation swept through Europe, its musical demands were answered by composers such as Claude Le Jeune, Clemens non Papa, and even William Byrd, a Catholic who wrote for the Anglican church. At the same time, innovative religious music was also developed for loyal Catholics, by Palestrina and Monteverdi in Italy, Josquin Després and Orlando di Lasso in Flanders. The "new style" had a Jewish exponent in Salamone de' Rossi, Monteverdi's fellow composer in Mantua; his unaccompanied "Songs of Solomon" (1622-3), Italian music in Hebrew dress, aimed at a modern revival of Temple psalmody.

Oratorio and Opera. If Claudio Monteverdi was the father of opera, Giacomo Carissimi pioneered the oratorio and cantata, several of his works being devoted to biblical themes. His pupils and successors included G.P. Colonna, Giovanni Battista Bononcini (*Il Giosuè*, 1688), Alessandro Scarlatti (*La Guiditta vittoriosa*, 1695), Antonio Vivaldi, and Antonio Caldara, whose Old Testament compositions extended to opera as well as oratorio (e.g., *Giuseppe*, 1722). Among the earliest exponents of the genre were Marc-Antoine Charpentier in France, together with Heinrich Schütz, Johann Mattheson, and Johann Sebastian Bach in Germany. Schutz excelled in the field of New Testament subject matter, his *Christmas Oratorio* (1664) and three works on *The Passion* (1665-72) anticipating those of Bach.

The same Apocryphal motif inspired Thomas Arne's *Judith* (1761) and Mozart's *Betulia liberata* (1771; using Metastasio's famous text). Almost at the end of the 18th century, Joseph Haydn contributed *The Return of Tobias*, (1774-5; text by Giovanni Boccherini) and *The Creation* (1798). It was in England, however, that the biblical oratorio attained unrivaled heights in the many works of George Frederick Handel. They include *Esther* (1732), *Deborah* (1733), and *Athalia* (1736); *Saul* (1739), which contains the *Dead March* often played at state funerals; *Israel in Egypt* (1739); *Messiah* (1742); *Samson* (1743) and *Joseph* (1743); *Belshazzar* (1744); *Judas Maccabaeus* (1747) and *Alexander Balus* (1748); *Joshua* (1748); *Solomon* (1749), *Susanna* (1749), and lastly *Jephtha* (1752). Earlier, in 1727, Handel had written his famous coronation anthem, *Zadok the Priest*.

Heading the 19th-century oratorio composers were Beethoven, Meyerbeer, Rossini, and Mendelssohn, whose *Athalie* (1845), based on Racine's French drama, includes a celebrated *War March of the Priests*. Berlioz, Anton Rubinstein, César Franck, and Gounod likewise wrote biblical oratorios, as did the British composer Sir Hubert Parry. Among their successors, from 1900, were Jules Massenet, Sir Edward Elgar, the U.S. composer Frederick Shepherd Converse, Arthur Honegger, Sir William Walton, Mario Castelnuovo-Tedesco, and Arnold Schoenberg.

One of the first opera composers outside Italy, Johann Philipp Krieger, wrote a comic *Singspiel* about Rachel and Leah entitled *Von Jacobs doppelter Heyrath* (1700). Three other pioneers of the genre were Caldara, Michel de Monteclair (*Jephté*, 1732), and the French Revolutionary composer Etienne Méhul, whose *Joseph* had a successful premiere in 1807. Just as the greatest

oratorios emerged in the 18th century, so did the outstanding biblical operas make their appearance in the 19th, thanks to Rossini (*Moïse*), Verdi (*Nabucco*), and Saint-Saens (*Samson et Dalila*). Operatic versions of the Queen of Sheba were written by Charles Gounod (1862) and Karl Goldmark (1875), while Anton Rubinstein handled the less familiar Maccabean theme.

Though not quite as impressive, 20th-century biblical operas have had an even wider range. Their composers include Carl Nielson (*Saul og David*, 1902), Richard Strauss (*Salome*, 1905), Vittorio Rieti (*L'Arca di Noè*, 1922) and Ildebrando Pizzetti (*Débora e Jaele*, 1922), Randall Thompson (*Solomon and Balkis*, 1942), Bernard Rogers (*The Warrior*, 1947), Arnold Schoenberg, Darius Milhaud, and Sir Arthur Bliss (*Tobias and the Angel*, 1960). Operas on Apocryphal themes have enjoyed much popularity, with Judith and Holofernes inspiring Resnicek (1923) and Honegger (1926), and Susanna and the Elders attracting Paul Hindemith (1922) and Carlisle Floyd (1956).

Cantatas and Choral Works. Old Testament motifs dominated the pioneering works in this genre, by Franz Schubert (*Miriams Siegesgesang*, 1828), Carl Gottfried Loewe (*Die eherne Schlange*, 1834), Saint Saëns, and Mussorgsky. For *Moïse sauvé des eaux* (1851), Saint-Saëns made use of a text by Victor Hugo, while Mussorgsky's *Iyssus Navin* ("Joshua bin Nun," c. 1864) was apparently inspired by traditional Jewish melodies that he heard in St. Petersburg. Franz Liszt wrote two biblical works for choir in 1879, *Ossa arida* on the Valley of Dry Bones theme and *Via Crucis*, a New Testament cantata on the Stations of the Cross.

Major 20th-century compositions have been written by Zoltan Kodaly, Igor Stravinsky, Ralph Vaughan Williams, and Benjamin Britten. Others include Louis Gruenberg's *The Daniel Jazz* (1923; after Vachel Lindsay); works on the prophecies of Isaiah by Granville Bantock (1927) and Bohuslav Martinu (1963); and an "advanced" *Song of the Three Holy Children* (1956), with electronic effects, by Karlheinz Stockhausen. Like Gruenberg, several modern composers working in this field have been Jewish: Bernard Rogers, Lazare Saminsky, Darius Milhaud, and Leonard Bernstein, together with a number of Israelis such as Josef Tal, Paul Ben-Haim (*Three Psalms*, 1952; *Hymn from the Desert*, 1962), and Ben-Zion Orgad.

Music for Orchestra. Perhaps the earliest examples of "illustrative music," non-vocal works alluding to Scripture, are Johann Kuhnau's *Biblische Sonaten* (1700) and Haydn's *"Lamentation" Symphony No. 26* (c. 1765), which contains motifs resembling Catholic plainsong. In the same category are two 19th-century compositions: Robert Schumann's fanciful *David-sbundler-Tanze* for piano (1837) and *Ein deutsches Requiem* by Johannes Brahms, a work for soloists and chorus as well as orchestra, the Protestant spirit of which is emphasized by texts from Luther's Bible. Among the 20th-century composers who wrote music of this type were Jean Sibelius (*Belshazzar's Feast* suite, 1906), Ernest Bloch, Vaughan Williams, Leonard Bernstein, Aaron Copland, and Darius Milhaud.

Ballet and Stage Music. Only a few European ballets have dealt with Old Testament themes, *Die Josephslegende* (1914) by Richard Strauss being probably the first example. Others have since been composed by Respighi (*Belkis, Regina di Saba*, 1923), Vittorio Rieti, Marc Blitzstein (*Cain*, 1930), Vaughan Williams, and Werner Josten. In Israel, however, there have been many dance theater productions on biblical themes.

The medieval Yiddish Purim-play, with its often comic song accompaniment, is the earliest example of stage music on biblical themes. Some 20th-century composers who wrote stage music of this type were Kurt Weill, Arno Nadel, and Arthur Honegger (for André Gide's *Saül* and Jean Giraudoux's *Sodome et Gomorrhe*). Two Israeli stage productions of 1965 belong to this category: Alexander (Sasha) Argov wrote the music for *King Solomon and the Cobbler*, while Dov Seltzer did the same for Itzik Manger's play, *The Megillah*.

Folk-Song. Whereas the oratorio gave expression to religious piety and the opera sometimes reflected patriotic sentiment, two varieties of folk-song (Jewish and Black American) have expressed yearning for redemption in vividly biblical terms. Jewish folk-song traditions range over many periods, countries, and languages. Modern Hebrew (Israeli) folk-songs, based especially on verses from Psalms, the Song of Songs, and the Major Prophets, are secular compositions by well-known musicians.

By contrast, the "Negro spiritual" written in the Deep South of the U.S. was invariably an anonymous composition. Its inspiration came from Protestant evangelism and from the Black slave's identification with the Israelites languishing under their Egyptian bondage. Like the Hebrews of old, enslaved Blacks awaited a deliverer who would lead them over the Jordan to the Promised Land, where they would be free to live and worship as they pleased. Some familiar examples of the spiritual are *Go Down, Moses, Joshua Fit de Battle of Jericho, Deep River, Ezek'el Saw de Wheel, Dry Bones*, and *Swing Low, Sweet Chariot*. A considerable number of these Black American folk-songs are now popular classics.

GREAT MUSICAL COMPOSITIONS ON BIBLICAL THEMES.

Jephte (c. 1648). Oratorio in Latin, for six voices, organ, and narrator, by Giacomo Carissimi. One of the first oratorios to be written, it displayed Carissimi's imaginative use of the Vulgate and was his most famous composition.

Zadok the Priest (1727). Anthem for chorus, organ, and orchestra, the first of a series of four by George Frederick Handel, written to mark the coronation of George II. This celebrated musical description of King Solomon's enthronement has been performed, ever since Handel's time, at the coronation of British monarchs in Westminster Abbey.

St. Matthew Passion (1729). Oratorio for solo voices, two choirs, and orchestra by Johann Sebastian Bach, first performed in Leipzig. It largely reproduces Matthew's account of the crucifixion and the death of Jesus, using Luther's German text, and ranks as the foremost *Passion* oratorio. Bach's *St. John Passion* had been written earlier (in 1724). A centenary performance of the *St. Matthew Passion*, conducted by Felix Mendelssohn (Berlin, 1829), led to a worldwide revival of interest in Bach's works.

Christmas Oratorio (1734). Oratorio for soloists, chorus, and orchestra by J.S. Bach, with the text based on (Matthew's and Luke's) gospel accounts of the Nativity. Including a famous *Sinfonia*, this "oratorio" actually comprises six cantatas linked together by unifying chorales; each section was to be performed in turn from Christmas Day through Epiphany.

Messiah (1742). One of Handel's outstanding oratorios, with text by Charles Jennens, written for soloists, chorus, and orchestra. Composed in less than a month, it was first performed in Dublin. Handel made liberal use of Old Testament sources seen as foretelling the coming of Jesus. The *Hallelujah Chorus* (at the end of Part 2) is often performed as a separate concert work.

Judas Maccabaeus (1747). Oratorio by Handel, for soloists, chorus, and orchestra, with text by the Rev. Thomas Morell (after I Maccabees and Josephus). Written to celebrate the Duke of Cumberland's victory over the Jacobites at the battle of Culloden Moor (1746), it was first performed at London's Covent Garden Theater. Like Handel's *Messiah* and *Israel in Egypt*, this oratorio has remained an enduring favorite with concertgoers. *"See, the Conquering Hero Comes"* (in Part 3) is an exultant chorus that has even found a place in Jewish religious music.

The Creation (1798). Oratorio for soloists (the archangels Gabriel, Uriel, and Raphael), chorus, and symphonic orchestra by Joseph Haydn. Linley's English text (after Genesis and Milton's *Paradise Lost*) had supposedly been meant for Handel, who died before he could make use of it. While visiting England in 1791, Haydn was given the libretto and then had it revised and translated into German by Baron Gottfried van Swieten. After setting this text to music, Haydn conducted the first performance of his oratorio in Vienna. Ever since then, *The Creation* has been one of the most popular and successful oratorios.

Christ on the Mount of Olives (1803). Oratorio by Ludwig van Beethoven, with German text written by F.X. Huber, first performed in Vienna. There were loud protests in Victorian England about the "objectionable nature of the German libretto," which was therefore replaced by a more religiously acceptable English text and setting: *Engedi; or David in the Wilderness.*

Moses in Egypt (1818). Opera in three acts by Gioacchino Rossini, with libretto by A.L. Tottola, first staged in Naples. Rossini later expanded the work into a four-act grand opera, with new music, a French libretto, and a ballet sequence, under the title of *Moïse* (Paris, 1827). Grafted onto the biblical story is an invented romance linking Pharaoh's son (Aménophis) with Moses' niece (Anaïde). Rossini also composed a biblical oratorio, *Saul* (1834).

Nabucco (1842). Opera in four acts by Guiseppe Verdi, with libretto by Temistocle Solera, first staged at La Scala, Milan. Solera's text, evoking Nebuchadnezzar's enslavement of the Jews and their exile in Babylon, had fired Verdi's dormant patriotism.

When completed, his opera had strong political undertones, hinting at Italy's own subjection to a foreign (Hapsburg) oppressor. *"Va, pensiero, sull' ali dorate"* ("Fly, thought, on golden wings"), the moving Chorus of the Hebrew Slaves in Act 3, aroused vast enthusiasm, audiences hearing in it the lament of political exiles, although a more universal significance was later given to the words and music.

Elijah (1846). Oratorio for soloists, chorus, and orchestra by Felix Mendelssohn, premiered at the Birmingham Festival in England. It is the one 19th-century oratorio that secured a place in the modern repertoire. A decade earlier, Mendelssohn had written another biblical work, *St. Paul* (Düsseldorf, 1836). *Elijah* is thought to be a symbolic reflection of the composer's Jewish birth, *St. Paul* alluding to his childhood acceptance of Christianity.

The Maccabees (1875). Opera by the Russian pianist and composer Anton Grigoryevich Rubinstein, with libretto (after Otto Ludwig's German drama) by S.H. Mosenthal, first staged in Berlin. Though himself a converted Jew, Rubinstein endeavored to strengthen the Jewish element in his opera, which created a very favorable impression in Eastern Europe. He also wrote several biblical oratorios.

Samson and Delilah (1877). Opera in three acts by Camille Saint-Saëns, with libretto by Ferdinand Lemaire, first staged (in German) at Weimar. *Samson and Delilah* was the French composer's only enduring stage success, thanks mainly to its combination of fine music and lavish spectacle. Well-loved features of this opera are the choruses in Act I; Delilah's aria, *Softly Awakes My Heart,* in Act II; and the oriental *Bacchanale* in Act III. Saint-Saëns wrote a number of other biblical works, including the oratorio *Le Déluge* (1876).

Shulamis ("The Shulammite," 1880). Romantic oper-

etta by Abraham Goldfaden, "father of the Yiddish theater," who wrote the music as well as the libretto. Based on the Song of Songs, it told of King Solomon's infatuation with a beautiful country girl. Filmed in 1931, *Shulamis* also turned a Yiddish lullaby, *Rozhinkes mit Mandlen* ("Raisins and Almonds"), into a popular hit.

The Apostles (1903). Oratorio by Sir Edward Elgar, premiered at the Birmingham Festival in England. The composer had planned a New Testament trilogy, but only one sequel (*The Kingdom,* 1906) was ever written. Musical features of *The Apostles* include some "authentic Hebrew melodies, harmonized in the Western fashion," and the simulated blast of a *shofar* (ram's horn).

Salome (1905). Opera in one act by Richard Strauss, first staged in Dresden, utilizing Hedwig Lachmann's German translation of the play Oscar Wilde wrote in French.

This morbid tale of lust, culminating in the execution of both John the Baptist and his depraved admirer, was heightened by the composer's sensual music, notably Salome's *Dance of the Seven Veils.*

Jerusalem (1916). "Unison chorus" by Sir Hubert Parry, which transformed the ironical words of Blake's poem into a rousing hymn of faith ("Till we have built Jerusalem/ In England's green and pleasant land"). Once regarded as a second national anthem, *Jerusalem* is nowadays sung by all present at the end of a promenade concert season in London's Royal Albert Hall. Parry also wrote three biblical oratorios: *Judith* (1888), *Job* (1892), and *King Saul* (1894).

Shelomo (or Schelomo, 1916). "Hebrew rhapsody" for cello and orchestra by the Swiss-born composer Ernest Bloch, first performed in the U.S. Like Bloch's *"Israel"* Symphony (1912–16) and *Sacred Service* (1932–4), *Shelomo* is less indebted to Jewish musical tradition than to the composer's own "intuitive feeling." Its inspiration came from Solomon and Ecclesiastes, but it is also said to reflect the human misery engendered by World War I.

Psalmus Hungaricus (1923). Work for tenor, mixed chorus, organ, and orchestra by Zoltan Kodaly. Written to mark the 50th anniversary of the unified twin cities (Buda-Pest), and first performed there, this "Hungarian Psalm" greatly enhanced Kodaly's musical reputation. The text (Ps 55) was chosen from a 16th-century Calvinist paraphrase of the Bible that has great national importance for the Magyars.

Judith (1926). Opera in three acts by the French-born Swiss composer Arthur Honegger, expanding the music he had written one year earlier for a play by René Morax staged in Monte Carlo. The Apocryphal theme had inspired many works from Scarlatti's time onward, but Honegger's *Judith* was a vehicle for his declamatory style, already pronounced in *Le Roi David* (1921; text by Morax), an anti-Romantic oratorio with spoken narration which he called a "dramatic psalm."

Symphony of Psalms (1930). Work in three movements by Igor Stravinsky, for chorus and orchestra (excluding violins and violas), using a Latin text of the Psalter. "Composed to the glory of God and dedicated to the Boston Symphony Orchestra," it heralded a series of biblical compositions by Stravinsky. They include his *Babel* cantata (Los Angeles, 1945); *Threni* (Venice, 1958), a cantata setting of Lamentations; *The Flood* (CBS, 1962), a dance-drama for television based on the York and Chester miracle plays; and *Abraham and Isaac* (1964), a "sacred ballad" with Hebrew text first performed in Jerusalem.

Belshazzar's Feast (1931). Oratorio for baritone, chorus, and orchestra by Sir William Walton, using a text by Osbert Sitwell (after the Bible). Often styled a cantata, it had notable predecessors in Handel's *Belshazzar* oratorio, (1744) and a non-vocal suite by Sibelius (1906). Walton's oratorio, first performed at the Leeds Music Festival in England, is the outstanding composition on this biblical theme and has entered the modern choral repertoire.

Job (1931). Ballet or "masque for dancing" by Ralph Vaughan Williams, the decor and movements following Blake's *Illustrations to the Book of Job*. Composed for the Ballets Rambert and first staged in London, it engendered *The Voice out of the Whirlwind* for choir and organ. Vaughan Williams wrote several other biblical works, including *Flos Campi*, (1925), a "Rose of Sharon" suite for viola, small orchestra, and wordless chorus.

"Jeremiah" Symphony No. 1 (1944). Orchestral work by Leonard Bernstein, first performed in Pittsburgh. The last movement, "Lamentation," contains a part for mezzo-soprano, using a Hebrew text from the Book of Jeremiah. *Symphony No. 3: Kaddish* (1963), which Bernstein first conducted in Tel-Aviv, was written for mezzo-soprano, two choirs, and orchestra, introduced a speaker, and was dedicated "to the beloved memory of John F. Kennedy." His *Chichester Psalms* for mixed chorus, boys' choir, and orchestra (1965), written for an English cathedral, aroused special interest because of the composer's stipulation that the text be sung only in Hebrew.

David (1954). Opera in five acts by Darius Milhaud, with libretto by Armand Lunel (after the Bible). Notable features are the exceptionally large vocal ensemble, and the inclusion of modern Israeli as well as ancient Israelite figures in the cast. Specially commissioned for the 3,000th anniversary of Jerusalem's establishment as the City of David, Milhaud's opera was first staged there.

Moses and Aaron (1954). Opera by Arnold Schoenberg, who wrote the three-act libretto and music for the first two acts (1932), but never completed the third. Schoenberg's reversion to Judaism under the impact of Hitler's rise to power may well be reflected in this philosophical opera, which dramatizes the conflict between Moses, the prophet of an invisible God, and his priestly brother Aaron, who yields to the demand for some visible object of worship. Originally broadcast by Hamburg radio in 1954, *Moses und Aron* was first staged three years later in Zurich.

Noye's Fludde (1958). Operatic cantata for church performance by Benjamin Britten. First performed at Orford in Suffolk, this musical interpretation of the Deluge story utilized a text based on the Chester miracle play. Another of this English composer's works, *The Burning Fiery Furnace* (1966), is a "parable" likewise intended for staging in churches.

VI.54 THE BIBLE IN MOTION PICTURES

From the early period of silent films, motion picture studios were quick to exploit the Bible's money-making appeal to cinema audiences. Old Testament themes especially lent themselves to dramatic screen portrayal, but few of the many biblical movies that have been produced would rank as classic examples of the cinematic art. Even where an effort was made not to "improve on" the Scriptural narrative, costumes and decor often lacked authenticity; in other cases, the dialogue proved inept, screenwriters injected a gratuitous "love interest," or the creation of spectacular effects overshadowed the Bible's religious message.

SILENT MOVIES

Within the space of one decade, more than two dozen silent films were inspired by the Old Testament alone. About half of these came from pioneer French studios, including titles such as *Abraham's Sacrifice* (1912), *Belshazzar's Feast* (Gaumont, 1913), *Esther and Mordecai* (Gaumont, 1910), *Jephthah's Daughter* (1910), *Joseph's Trials in Egypt* (Pathe, 1914), two *Cain and Abel* productions (1910, 1911) and two more about *Saul and David* (1911, 1912). Some U.S. movies of the same period were another *Cain and Abel* (1911), *David and Goliath* (Kalem, 1908), *The Deluge* (Vitagraph, 1911), *Esther* (Eclectic, 1914), *Joseph in the Land of Egypt* (Thanhouser Studios, 1913; starring James Cruze), *The Life of Moses* in five episodes (Vitagraph, 1909–10), as well as an American version of *Saul and David* (1909).

D.W. Griffith, a pioneer of the "epic" in films such as *The Birth of a Nation*, chose an Apocryphal tale for his

Judith of Bethulia (Biograph, 1914), which starred Lillian Gish in the title role. Two other major productions were *Samson* (Universal, 1914) starring J. Warren Kerrigan and Mayme Kelso, with Harold Lloyd among the supporting actors; and *Joseph and His Brethren* (Dormet, 1915) "adapted from the $100,000 spectacular stage show" of the same title. *The Fall of Babylon* (Biograph, 1919), another biblical movie directed by D.W. Griffith, was actually extracted from his mammoth *Intolerance*, filmed three years earlier; though technically far in advance of its time, that production had been a failure at the box office.

After World War I, a new range of silent "epics" converted the motion picture industry into big business. *The Queen of Sheba* (Fox, 1921), directed by J. Gordon Edwards, starred Fritz Leiber, Betty Blythe (in the title role), and George Siegmann; anachronistic chariot-races featured in this Hollywood spectacular. Beginning his career in Austria, Michael Curtiz directed *Sodom and Gomorrah* (Sascha Films, 1922), which had Lucy Doraine, George Reimers, and a very young Walter Sleazak as its stars; this proved to be one of the most costly films ever made in Austria, and the full version has been restored only latterly from material in East European archives. Where biblical film "epics" are concerned, however, the outstanding producer and director was Cecil B. DeMille, whose first (silent) version of *The Ten Commandments* (Paramount, 1923)

Babylon: Scene from Intolerance; *silent picture directed by David W. Griffith in 1916.*

cost an unprecedented $1,400,000, shattered all box office records, and also boosted many Hollywood careers.

The first half, starring Theodore Roberts (as Moses), Charles de Roch (Pharaoh), and Estelle Taylor (Miriam), had a "cast of thousands" that filled the screen when the Israelites made their departure from Egypt. Special effects included the parting of the Red Sea for the Israelites and an awesome return of the waters to drown Pharaoh's pursuing host. The second half of *The Ten Commandments*, starring Richard Dix (amongst others), was an earnest sequel portraying 20th-century Americans who flout the Mosaic laws and then have to bear the consequences. Never averse to peppering his films with a dash of sex or even sadism, DeMille ("a warm-hearted sentimental salvationist," according to Graham Greene) treated Scriptural texts as ready-made scenarios for one movie after another. "Give me any couple of pages from the Bible," he reputedly said, "and I'll give you a picture."

Two early New Testament movies, both French, were *The Kiss of Judas* (1909) and *The Life of Christ* (Pathé, 1910). Predictably, however, Christian audiences, both Protestant and Catholic, often objected to seeing Jesus portrayed by some far from saintly actor on the movie screen. To avoid trouble, therefore, especially after U.S. church groups began "censoring" New Testament pictures, the film-makers sometimes gave only a hint of Jesus' presence by showing a hand, cloak or shadow, for example, or (later) by making use of a disembodied voice. Nevertheless, from the silent period onward, not a few movie actors did portray Jesus, beginning with Robert Henderson in *From the Manger to the Cross* (1913), George Fisher in *Civilization* (1916), and Howard Gaye in one sequence from D.W. Griffith's *Intolerance* (1916). Grigori Khmara later played the same role in a German production, *I.N.R.I.* (Naumann Films, 1923), directed by Conrad Wiene, which also starred Henry Porten, Werner Kraus, Asta Nilsen, and Alexander Granach. Most impressive of all was *The King of Kings* (Pathé 1927), DeMille's New Testament "epic," which starred H.B. Warner (as Jesus), with Rudolph and Joseph Schildkraut in supporting roles. Filmed partly in color, it was destined to be seen by 800 million people over the next three decades.

However, the majority of New Testament pictures dealt with figures such as John the Baptist or with the infant Christian church. There were several movies of the first type, all based on Oscar Wilde's play and entitled *Salome*, including an early U.S. production (Vitagraph, 1908) and an Italian film (1913), as well as a better known Hollywood version (Fox, 1918) starring Theda Bara in the title role and Albert Roscoe. Thanks to its reliance on Aubrey Beardsley's illustrations, the *Salome* directed by Charles Bryant (United Artists, 1922) had a *succès de scandale*, public attention focusing on the performances of Alla Nazimova (who played

Salome and also produced the film) and Nigel de Brulier (John the Baptist).

An even larger number of silent pictures evoked the heroes and martyrs of early Christianity. No less than five, including one Italian-U.S. co-production, all entitled *The Last Days of Pompeii*, were made in Italy between 1908 and 1926; while two versions of *Quo Vadis* (1912, 1924), based on the Polish novel by Henryk Sienkiewicz and dealing with the Emperor Nero's campaign of persecution, also emerged from Italian studios. Lew Wallace's famous American historical novel likewise inspired the first screen version of *Ben Hur* (Kalem, 1907), directed by Frank Oakes Rose and Sidney Olcott. Filmed partly in color, the second *Ben Hur* (MGM, 1926), directed by Fred Niblo Sr., was a Hollywood "epic" costing nearly four times as much as DeMille's (silent) *Ten Commandments*. It starred Ramon Novarro, Francis X. Bushman, May McAvoy, Carmel Myers, and Betty Bronson; needed 42 cameramen to film the spectacular chariot-race; and took three years to produce.

SOUND FILMS

The advent of sound (1927), followed by other improvements such as full-color photography, theme music, and wide-screen processes (after World War II), gave much more scope to biblical films, but technical advances were no guarantee of success. *Noah's Ark* (Warner Brothers, 1929), directed by Michael Curtiz, starred George O'Brien and Noah Beery, as well as a host of animals, but proved a financial disaster in the year of the Wall Street Crash. Three extras were drowned and several others hospitalized while filming the Flood sequence, and Darryl F. Zanuck (the movie's producer), by attempting to keep the calamity under wraps, only made matters worse.

Cecil B. DeMille was more fortunate with *The Sign of the Cross* (Paramount, 1932), his first biblical talkie, which had Fredric March, Claudette Colbert, and Charles Laughton in the star roles. A new (sound) version of *The Last Days of Pompeii* (RKO, 1935), directed by Ernest Schoedsack, turned out to be a resounding flop at the box office, despite actors such as Preston Foster, Basil Rathbone, and Dorothy Wilson. Moviegoers had obviously become more sophisticated and discriminating; they were now less inclined to accept what one writer has called "eye-filling and often erotic costume extravaganzas masquerading as history."

Green Pastures (Warner Brothers, 1936), where the scenes alternated between heaven and earth, brought a refreshingly different approach. Directed by William Keighley and based on Marc Connelly's Pulitzer Prize-winning play, this motion picture dramatized key episodes from the Old Testament in line with the Black American's anthropomorphic concept of God and had its setting in the Deep South of the U.S.A. Closer to the "epic" tradition was *Golgotha* (Ichtys, 1935), a French movie directed by Julien Duvivier, which starred Robert Levigan (as Jesus) with Harry Baur (Herod) and Jean Gabin (Pontius Pilate).

World events switched the attention of film-makers away from biblical productions until 1949, when Cecil B. DeMille packed movie theaters once again with *Samson and Delilah*, a typical Paramount spectacular. This colorful romp through the Book of Judges starred Victor Mature and Hedy Lamarr in the title roles, with George Sanders, Angela Lansbury, and Henry Wilcoxon among the suppporting cast.

The 1950s marked a high point of the Hollywood-style biblical "epic." Old Testament productions included three different films with similar titles: *David and Bathsheba* (20th Century-Fox, 1951), a Scriptural romance directed by Henry King, which starred Gregory Peck and Susan Hayward, with Raymond Massey, James Robertson Justice, and other supporting actors; a new Italian version of *The Queen of Sheba* (Oro Films, 1952), with a cast headed by Gino Dervi, Leonora Ruffo, and Gino Leurini; and *Solomon and Sheba* (United Artists, 1959), filmed in CinemaScope and directed by King Vidor, which had Yul Brynner and Gina Lollobrigida in the title roles, as well as George Sanders in the supporting cast. These were followed by another CinemaScope romance, *The Story of Ruth* (20th Century-Fox, 1960), in which the heroine was portrayed as a Moabite priestess whose love for Naomi's ill-fated son Mahlon results in her sincere conversion from paganism. Directed by Henry Koster, this film starred Peggy Wood (as Ruth), Stuart Whitman, and James Mitchell.

No biblical movie of that time, however, could rival DeMille's remake of *The Ten Commandments* (Paramount, 1956). Filmed in Technicolor and VistaVision, it ran for nearly four hours and was entirely devoted to the Exodus story. Research and documentation on a characteristically massive scale went into this second version. Bible land sequences were shot on their historical locations, from the western bank of the Nile to Jebel Musa and beyond, the Tablets of the Covenant being carved in red granite hewn from the top of Mount Sinai and engraved in a suppposedly authentic "pre-Canaanite" script. Headed by Charlton Heston (Moses), Anne Baxter (Princess Nefretiri), and Yul Brynner (Rameses II), the star-studded cast included Yvonne de Carlo (as Zipporah), John Derek (Joshua), Sir Cedric Hardwicke (Sethi I) and Edward G. Robinson (Dathan). Elmer Bernstein wrote the musical score, while DeMille's associate producer, Henry Wilcoxon, also played one of the supporting roles (as he had in *Samson and Delilah*). However inflated some of DeMille's religious claims may have been (he declared, for example, that his biblical productions "greatly influenced youth to better moral living"), it is a fact that both versions of *The Ten Commandments* were seen by hundreds of millions throughout the world.

Gina Lollobrigida and Yul Brynner in Solomon and Sheba, *directed by King Vidor in 1959.*

New Testament themes also inspired the movie-makers. In its American sound version, *Quo Vadis* (MGM, 1951) was a lavish spectacular "with a cast of thousands and a well-drilled squad of Christian-gorging lions." Directed by Mervyn LeRoy, it starred Robert Taylor and Deborah Kerr as the leading victims of a depraved Nero (played somewhat tongue in cheek by Peter Ustinov). Several noted British actors (Leo Genn, Finlay Currie, Felix Aylmer, and Abraham Sofaer) appeared in subordinate roles. Directed by Henry Koster, *The Robe* (20th Century-Fox, 1953) was the first motion picture to be filmed in CinemaScope. Based on a novel by Lloyd C. Douglas, it told the story of a Roman soldier's conversion after winning the cloak of Jesus at dice. Victor Mature, Richard Burton, Jean Simmons, and Michael Rennie played the star roles, with Cameron Mitchell in a speaking part only (as the voice of Jesus).

The Prodigal (MGM, 1955), directed by Richard Thorpe, with Lana Turner, Edmund Purdom, and James Mitchell heading the cast, and *The Last Days of Pompeii* (RKO, 1959), yet another remake, directed this time by Mario Bonnard in Italy, made less of an impact. MGM's second version of *Ben Hur* (1959) was, however, even more spectacular than the first, moviegoers being thrilled in particular by the chariot-race that pitted Charlton Heston (Ben Hur) against his rival, Jack Hawkins (Messala). William Wyler directed this remake, for which Miklos Rozsa composed the musical score; Hugh Griffith, Stephen Boyd, Martha Scott, Sam Jaffe, and Haya Harareet played supporting roles. This was the only instance to date of a biblical (or semi-biblical) "epic" and its film director gaining Academy Awards. *Esther and the King* (1960) directed by Raoul Walsh, with Joan Collins as Esther, quickly dropped out of sight.

In *The Private Lives of Adam and Eve* (Universal International, 1960), co-directors Albert Zugsmith and Mickey Rooney tried to exploit the vogue for biblical movies, portraying a group of couples on their way to the Reno divorce court who find themselves obliged to spend the night in a secluded Nevada church. There, the Eden story is retold in a dream sequence, with the various 20th-century partners doubling in Scriptural roles. There was an immediate hostile reaction to this picture, the U.S. Legion of Decency castigating its "blasphemous, pornographic, and sacrilegious" nature, which set alarm bells ringing in the major Hollywood studios. For the next few years, at least, movie-makers exercised greater care in their handling of biblical themes.

The King of Kings (MGM, 1961), a new (sound) version directed by Nicholas Ray, had Jeffrey Hunter in the key role alongside Robert Ryan and Siobhan McKenna. The same New Testament motif, though from a different angle, appeared in Richard Fleischer's movie, *Barabbas* (Columbia, 1962), which starred Anthony Quinn, Silvana Mangano, and Arthur Kennedy. A more novel and highly spectacular biblical movie, directed by Robert Aldrich, was *Sodom and Gomorrah* (20th Century-Fox, 1963), where the cast included Pier Angeli, Stanley Baker, and Stewart Granger. In George Stevens' film *The Greatest Story Ever Told* (United Artists, 1965), Max von Sydow's portrayal of Jesus gained high ratings and there were many talented actors in the supporting cast. Because of its diffident approach, however, as well as the publicity explaining why Stevens had decided to film the movie in Utah (where the scenery was "more like Palestine than Palestine"), this biblical colossus was less than a success. It was said to have inspired a paperback edition of the Bible marketed as "the book of the film." Equally ambitious, was the film project which Dino de Laurentiis originally conceived as a mammoth nine-hour biblical "epic" with a star-studded cast. Finally entitled *The Bible... In the Beginning* (20th Century-Fox, 1966), this particular motion picture faded into "a slow plod through Genesis" with John Huston as the narrator.

RECENT TRENDS AND PRODUCTIONS

One sign of changing tastes was the transposition from stage to screen of the pop-operas *Godspell* and *Jesus Christ Superstar*, both in 1973. *Godspell*, a Columbia film production directed by David Greene, had a musical score composed by Stephen Schwartz and cheerfully dispensed with "big name" stars, Victor Garber, David Haskell, and Jerry Sroka heading the cast. *Jesus Christ Superstar*, a Universal International movie directed by Norman Jewison "starring" Ted Neeley, Carl Anderson, and Yvonne Elliman, was unusual for those movies in being filmed in the Holy Land.

During the 1970s, Hollywood and other studios were increasingly forced to compete with television, and many leading film companies established TV subsidiaries of their own. One outcome of this process was the television "docudrama," which also adopted an innovative approach to biblical themes. The initiative of Britain's Lord (Lew) Grade was partly responsible for two such productions, each comprising half a dozen parts of several hours' duration. *Moses the Lawgiver* (CBC-CBS, 1975), directed by Gianfranco di Bosio with Lord Grade as the co-producer, starred Burt Lancaster (as Moses), Anthony Quayle (Aaron), Irene Papas (Miriam), and a mixed Italian-Israeli cast of supporting actors. This series was later condensed into a single two-hour feature film. It had a sequel in *Jesus of Nazareth* (ITC, 1977), directed by Franco Zeffirelli, with an international cast headed by Anne Bancroft, Ernest Borgnine, Claudia Cardinale, Oliva Hussey, Robert Powell (in the title role), Sir Laurence Olivier, and Anthony Quinn.

In response to the challenge posed by television, some motion picture companies opted for a bolder and more original approach to the Scriptures. One example was *The Passover Plot* (1977), a Golan-Globus production directed by Michael Campus, with Zalman King (as Jesus), Donald Pleasance, and Hugh Griffith heading the cast. Based on a work by Hugh J. Schonfield, this brought a controversial analysis of Jesus and some little-known aspects of his messianic initiative.

Monty Python's Life of Brian (1979), starring John Cleese, was a biblical parody which was widely condemned for bad taste but won a cult following. Willem Dafoe made another unconventional attempt to portray Jesus in *The Last Temptation of Christ* (Universal International, 1988). This New Testament film succeeded in arousing even greater controversy than the Greek novel, by Nikos Kazantzakis, on which it was based. Christians of every denomination expressed their outrage over *The Last Temptation*'s allegedly sacrilegious character; Martin Scorsese, the picture's director, was singled out for attack. No other film of the type had ever provoked such worldwide campaigns in and out of movie theaters, demanding its boycott, ban, or even destruction.

VI.55 BIBLICAL THEMES ON STAMPS

THE OLD TESTAMENT

The ever-increasing number of Old Testament themes on stamps find their way there principally in two ways. The first is direct: stamps devoted to religious holidays, mainly Christmas and Easter in Christian countries

and Jewish festivals in Israel (Moslem holiday stamps do not choose Bible themes). The second way is indirect: through art. Countries wish to honor artists, particularly on an anniversary (e.g., the 500th anniversary of Michelangelo's birth in 1975, the 100th of Chagall's birth in 1987), by reproducing their pictures or sculptures on stamps, and frequently select some of their numerous creations on biblical subjects. But this is not limited to anniversaries. Pictures are reproduced on stamps because they illustrate a theme a country wishes to promote, or simply for their beauty.

There are also other ways, though occurring far less frequently. Biblical themes are used in performing arts, thought worth depicting on stamps (e.g., a play called *Genesis* in Kenya, a ballet of the same name in Cuba, Saint Saëns' opera *Samson and Delilah* in Monaco and Israel). Biblical names are adopted for geographic descriptions (e.g., Adam's Peak in Ceylon, Mount Elias in Alaska, the Bay of Jeremiah in Haiti); they are used for fountains (Rebecca Fountain in Bogota, Samson Fountain in Budovice in Czechoslovakia, Adam and Samson Fountains in Russia); there is a Bathsheba railway station in Barbados, a Jacob's Staff in the Netherlands; and even ships (Nimrod, Rebecca), airplanes (Nimrod, Elijah), and railway engines (Samson in Canada) are sometimes named after Old Testament figures. When these appear on stamps, it is usually only the name that creates a biblical link.

Lastly, stamps often use Old Testament quotations, mostly without a corresponding picture. For instance, there are 38 stamps with different quotations from the Psalms, not counting Israeli stamps. Israel has biblical quotations on the tabs of most of its stamps, if not on the stamp itself.

The most popular Old Testament themes are Adam (29 different issues), Eve (16), the two together and the Expulsion from Paradise (46), Abraham (21), Noah (14), Moses (40), The Ten Commandments (31), Elijah (19), David (50), and Bathsheba (16). We find Adam and Eve depicted by Cranach, Dürer, Titian, Rubens, Michelangelo, Tintoretto, Mabuse, Rafael, Madenielo, Van der Goes, Chagall, and Rodin, as well as on icons and in coconut carving.

This survey does not include three themes which are used out of their biblical context: Noah's Dove, treated as a symbol of peace (although the biblical allusion is often emphasized by adding the olive branch and the rainbow); the Cedars of Lebanon, used on many Lebanon stamps; and the Tree of Life.

Not surprisingly, the country with the most Old Testament stamps is Israel. Moslem countries, if including Old Testament themes at all, present mainly Adam, Eve, and Abraham, while Yemen has a beautiful set on the Queen of Sheba and her visit to King Solomon.

Samson and Delilah, by Michele Rocca. Hungary.

David playing the Harp. Ethiopia.

Belshazzar's Feast, by Rembrandt. Spain, 1969.

First U.N. stamp with a biblical inscription (Isaiah 2:4); 1967.

Rebecca giving a drink to Eliezer, by Murillo. Rwanda.

Jacob's Dream. Yugoslavia.

Adam and Eve. 14th century icon. Czechoslovakia.

Illustration of Isaiah 2:4 U.S.S.R.

Moses receiving the Law. Ethiopia.

THE NEW TESTAMENT

Over 4,500 stamps directly illustrate the New Testament. The two most popular themes are the Nativity (approx. 550 issues) and the visit of the Wise Men (approx. 660 issues). The most common source of New Testament themes on stamps is art. Reproductions of the works of artists such as Dürer, El Greco, Murillo, Raphael, Rembrandt, Rubens, and Titian, to name a few, grace hundreds of stamps. New Testament stamps are primarily issued to commemorate the celebration of Christmas, Easter, and other significant Christian events, such as the Oberammergau passion play in Bavaria.

It is usually the less commonly illustrated New Testament themes which provide collectors with the greatest sense of achievement, whether it be the Temptation of Christ (five issues), Healing Two Blind Men (three issues), the Conversion of Saul (two issues), or the Parable of the Blind Leading the Blind (one issue).

A major sub-topic of the New Testament on stamps is that of New Testament quotations (collecting stamps which depict an actual passage of the New Testament scripture in any language). The earliest stamp to contain a New Testament quotation (issued in 1895) was that of British Central Africa (Nyasaland), where the inscription "Light In Darkness" (John 1:5) can be seen under the coat-of-arms. New South Wales (a colony of Australia) was the next to issue a stamp depicting a New Testament quotation. This was the 1897 charity stamp bearing the inscription "But the greatest of these is charity" (I Cor 13:13).

The New Testament quotation most commonly depicted on stamps is taken from Luke 2:14: "Glory to God in the Highest, and on Earth Peace, Goodwill Toward Men." This text is depicted on at least 86 stamps in various languages.

A stamp issued in Israel in 1958 has the greatest number of languages quoting a New Testament quotation. The inscription is from Matthew 5:43 and is in English, Hebrew, French, Spanish, Russian, and Chinese. (This quotation is also found in the Old Testament.)

Many stamps also depict Christian symbols. The Greek monogram for Christ, IHS, appears on at least 26 different stamps, the earliest of these being the very rare Swiss stamp of 1843 depicting the Geneva coat-of-arms.

Note: All numbers are approximate and probably conservative, as they do not take into account most recent issues.

Christ with a crown of thorns, by Dürer. Mali.

St. Peter sinking in water. Stained glass window. France, 1963.

The Four Horsemen of the Apocalypse. Spain, 1975.

Pentecost, by El Greco. Vatican City, 1975.

Jesus anointed by Mary at Bethany. Bophuthatswana 1982.

Quotation from John (20:27). Uganda, 1985.

Jesus stilling the sea. Surinam, 1973.

Quotation from Matthew 1:23. Nauru.

VI.56 WHAT THEY SAID ABOUT THE BIBLE

The Bible is like an old Cremona; it has been played upon by the devotion of thousands of years until every word and particle is public and tunable.

Emerson

The Jews trudged around with the Bible all through the Middle Ages as with a portable fatherland.

Heine

The Bible in its various transformations is the great book of consolation for humanity.

Renan

The greater the intellectual progress of the ages, the more fully will it be possible to employ the Bible not only as the foundation but as the instrument of education.

Goethe

I am convinced that the Bible becomes ever more beautiful the more it is understood.

Goethe

In the Old Testament of the Jews, the book of Divine righteousness, there are men, events and words so great that there is nothing in Greek or Indian literature to compare with it.

Nietzsche

The Bible is for the government of the people, by the people, and for the people.

Wycliffe

Written in the East, these characters live for ever in the West; written in one province, they pervade the world; penned in rude times, they are prized more and more as civilization advances; product of antiquity, they come home to the business and bosoms of men, women and children in modern days.

R.L. Stevenson

How many ages and generations have brooded and wept and agonized over this book! What untellable joys and ecstasies, what support to martyrs at the stake, from it! To what myriads has it been the shore and rock of safety — the refuge from driving tempest and wreck! Translated into all languages, how it has united this diverse world! Of its thousands there is not a verse, not a word, but is thick-studded with human emotion.

Walt Whitman

Within this awful volume lies
The mystery of mysteries:
Happiest he of human race
To whom God has given grace
To read, to fear, to hope, to pray,
To lift the latch, and learn the way;
And better had he ne'er been born
Who reads to doubt, or reads to scorn.

Sir Walter Scott

The Bible has been the Magna Charta of the poor and of the oppressed. Down to modern times no State has had a constitution in which the interests of the people are so largely taken into account, in which the duties so much more than the privileges of rulers are insisted upon, as that drawn up for Israel in Deuteronomy and Leviticus. The Bible is the most democratic book in the world.

T.H. Huxley

Holy Bible, book divine
Precious treasure, thou art mine;
Mine to teach me whence I came,
Mine to teach me what I am.

John Burton

In the poorest cottage is one Book, wherein for several thousands of years the spirit of man has found light and nourishment, and an interpreting response to whatever is Deepest in him.

Carlyle

A glory gilds the sacred page,
Majestic like the sun,
It gives a light to ev'ry age,
It gives but borrows none.

Cowper

The Scriptures, though not everywhere
Free from corruption, or entire, or clear,
Are uncorrupt, sufficient, clear, entire
In all things which our needful faith require.

Dryden

Brown bread and the Gospel is good fare

Puritan saying

The English Bible, a book which, if everything else in our language should perish, would alone suffice to show the whole extent of its beauty and power.

Macaulay

The Bible is a book of faith, and a book of doctrine, and a book of morals, and a book of religion, of special revelation from God; but it is also a book which teaches man his own individual responsibility, his own dignity, and his equality with his fellow-man.

Daniel Webster

The Scripture, in time of disputes, is like an open town in time of war, which serves indifferently the occasions of both parties.

Swift

On Bible stilts I don't affect to stalk,
Nor lard with Scripture my familiar talk.

Hood

And he who guides the plough, or wields the crook,
With understanding spirit now may look
Upon her records, listen to her song.

Wordsworth ('Translation of the Bible')

The devil can cite Scripture for his purpose.

Shakespeare ('The Merchant of Venice')

Say what you will about the Ten Commandments, you always come back to the pleasant fact that there are only ten of them.

H.L. Mencken

The Bible is the epic of the world. It unrolls a vast panorama in which the ages move before us in a long train of solemn imagery from the creation of the world onward. We see the rise and fall of empires, we see great cities, now the hive of busy industry, now silent and desolate--a den of wild beasts. All life's fever is there, its hopes and joys, its suffering and sin and sorrow.

Sir James Frazer

Behold the works of our philosophers; with all their pompous diction, how mean and contemptible they are by comparison with the Scriptures! Is it possible that a book at once so simple and sublime should be merely the work of man?

Rousseau

We search the world for truth; we cull
The good, the pure, the beautiful
From graven stone and written scroll,
From all old flower-fields of the soul;
And, weary seekers of the best,
We come home laden from our quest,
To find that all the sages said
Is in the Book our mothers read.

Whittier

Homer and the Bible — the only two books which the poet need study. In a sense one finds in them the whole of creation from a dual aspect: the genius of man in Homer, the spirit of God in the Bible.

Victor Hugo

What a book! Great and wide as the world, rooted in the abysmal depths of creation and rising aloft into the blue mysteries of heaven... Sunrise and sunset, promise and fulfillment, birth and death — the entire human drama —everything is in this book. It is the Book of Books, Biblia.

Heine

You can take any fifty pages of the Bible and make a good picture.

Cecil B. DeMille

No public man in these islands ever believes that the Bible means what it says; he is always convinced that it means what he says.

George Bernard Shaw

We were talking about the Bible, and I always read the King James Version, not one of those damn new translations that they've got out lately. I don't know why it is when you've got a good thing, you've got to monkey about changing it. The KJV of the Bible is the best there is or ever has been or will be, and you get a bunch of college professors spending years working on it, and all they do is take the poetry out of it.

President Harry S. Truman

ACKNOWLEDGMENTS

The Publishers have attempted to observe the legal requirements with respect to copyright. However, in view of the large number of illustrations included in this volume, the Publishers wish to apologize in advance for any involuntary ommissions or errors, and invite persons or bodies concerned to write to the Publishers.

p.12 Left: Archaeology Museum Amman. Photo N. Garo; (right) Israel Museum. Moshe Dayan Collection. Photo IMJ/Zev Radovan; p.13, 14, 17, 18 Musee du Louvre Paris; p.20 (left) Vorderasiatisches Museum, Berlin; p.21 Oriental Institute, University of Chicago; p.22 Israel Antiquities Authority; p.23 British Musuem London; p.25 (left) Photo A.van der Heyden; (right) Photo Erich Lessing; p.27 Photo JPH/D.Harris; p.28 British Museum London; p.29 Photo Courtesy B. Rothenberg; p.31 (left) Archaeology Museum Amman. Photo N. Garo; (right) Musee du Louvre. Photo Erich Lessing; p.32 Oriental Institute, University of Chicago; p.33 (left) Israel Antiquities Authority. Photo D. Harris; (right) Oriental Institute, University of Chicago; pp 34, 35, 36 Israel Antiquities Authority.Photo D. Harris; p.37 Israel Antiquities Authority/ Israel Museum; p.38 (left): Israel Museum. Photo Erich Lessing; p.39 Musee du Louvre Paris. Cliche Musees Nationaux; p.39 Photo B. Brendl; p.40 (left): Centre Franco-Egyptien, Karnak. Photo Erich Lessing; (right) Israel Antiquities Authority. Photo IMJ/D. Harris; p.41,42 (top right: Israel Antiquities Authority; p.43 Turino Museum; p.43 Reproduction Israel Museum. Photo IMJ/ D. Harris; p.43 Israel Museum. The Shrine of the Book, Jerusalem; pp.44-54 Photos Azaria Alon; p.55 Photo JPH/D.Harris; pp.56-60 Photos Azaria Alon; p.61 Photo Z. Radovan; p.62 Israel Antiquities Authority/Israel Museum; p.63 (left) Photo D. Harris; (right) ourtesy G. Wigoder; p.64 Photo Erich Lessing; p.65 Israel Museum Jerusalem p.66 Photo D. Harris; p.67 British Museum London; 68 (top) Photo A. van der Heyden; p.68 Israel Antiquities Authority/Photo D. Harris; p. 69 Photo A. van der Heyden; p.70 Photo N. Garo; p.71 Israel Antiquities authority; p.72 (top) Photo Azaria Alon; pp.72, 74, 78 Israel Antiquities Authority; p.73 Photo Erich Lessing; p.75 Photo N. Garo; pp. 76, 77 Photos A. van der Heyden; p.79 JHP/D.Harris; pp.80, 82, 84, 89 Photos A. van der Heyden; p. 81 Photo Werner Braun; p.83 Photo Z. Radovan; p.85 Photo Erich Lessing; p.86,88 (top) Photo JPH/D. Harris; p.90 Photo N. Garo; p.91 Ministry of Tourism, Turkey; pp. 92,93 Photos D. Harris; p.94 Israel Antiquties authority; p.95 Left: Photo D. Harris; p.95 Right: Photo Z. Radovan; pp.97, 98, 100 Photos JPH/D. Harris; p.106 (top) Israel Antiquities Authority/Photo Z. Radovan; p. 106 bottom: Israel Museum, Jerusalem; p.107 Photo Z. Radovan; pp.108, 109, 110, 111 (right) Israel Antiquities Authority; p.111 (left) Photo A. van der Heyden; p. 112 Ketef Hinnom Excavations; p.113 Photo N. Garo; p.114 (right) Photo A. van der Heyden; (left) Photo JPH/D. Harris; p.115 Israel Antiquities Authority; p. 118 Courtesy G. Wigoder; p.119 Israel Museum Jerusalem; Photo IMJ. D.Harris; p.120 (right) Israel Antiquities Authority; (left) Photo Z. Radovan; p.122 British Museum; p. 123 Cairo Museum; pp.128, 129 Israel Antiquities Authorities; p.132 (right)Glass Museum, Tel Aviv; p.132 (left)British Museum; pp.134, 135 Israel Museum; p.136 Photo Erich Lessing; p.142 (left) Photo A. van der Heyden; Right: Israel Antiquities Authority; p.143 Left: Photo JPH/Moshe Caine; pp.143 (right), 144 Photo A. van der Heyden; p.156 British Museum; pp.157, 158, 159 Photo A. van der Heyden; p.170 Musee du Louvre; Photo Erich Lessing; p.171 Belgrade Museo Nazionale. Photo Erich Lessing; p.172 Ashmolean Museum; p.173 Photo JPH/D.Harris; pp.174, 181 Photo A. van der Heyden; p.182 Israel Antiquities Authority; p.183 Museo della Renania, Treviri. Photo Erich Lessing; p.184 p.Israel Exploration Society. Photo Z. Radovan; p.185 Israel Museum Jerusalem; p.193 Israel Antiquities Authority. Photo Z. Radovan; p.195 Left: Israel Museum Jerusalem. Photo IMJ/D. Harris; p.195 right: Photo JPH/D.Harris; p.197 Photo Azaria Alon; p.198 Israel Antiquities Authority; p.199 Photo A.van der Heyden; p.201 Israel Antiquities Authority. Photo A.van der Heyden; p.202 Photo Azaria Alon; pp.203, 205 Y. Meshorer; p.204 Photo D. Harris; p.205 Y. Meshorer; p.206 Photo Erich Lessing, Vienna; pp.208, 209, 212 Photo Azaria Alon; p. 213 Israel Museum Jerusalem; p.213 Cartoon; Courtesy of Dick Codor, New York; 219 left: Courtesy of G.Wigoder, right: Wolfson Museum, Hechal Shlomo Jerusalem. Photo D. Harris; p.220 Museum of Jewish Art Jerusalem. Photo D. Harris; p.221 The Jewish and National University Library; p.222 Schocken Library Jerusalem; p.223 Elsevier Publishing Projects, Amsterdam; p.224 Nationalbibliothek, Vienna; p.234 Photo Fratelli Alinari, Florence; p.236 Jewish National and University Library. Photo D. Harris; p.238 British Museum, London; p.240 (top) Israel Museum, The Shrine of the Book, Jerusalem; (bottom) Bibliotheque Nationale, Paris; p.242 Library of the Armenian Patriarchate, Jerusalem; p.243 Elsevier Publishing Projects, Amsterdam; p.244 Photo Quesada, Madrid; p.246 (top) Biblioteca Nacional de Lisboa, Portugal; bottom: Israel Museum Jerusalem/Photo IMJ. Hillel Burger; p. 249 Embroidery by Vida Simons. Photo D. Gutrie; p.251 Photo Moshe Caine; p. 253 Photo A. van der Heyden; p. 254 (top) Photo Erich Lessing, Vienna; (bottom) Sculpture by Benno Elkan, Photo A. van der Heyden; p.255 Staatliche Museum, Berlin; p.259 (top) Photo JPH/Moshe Caine; (bottom) Galleria dell Accademia, Florence; p.261 Photo JPH/Moshe

Caine; p.263 Photo D. Harris; p.264 Photo Fratelli Alinari, Florence; p.268 JPH/Phto Moshe Caine; p. 269 Photo Museum for Music and Ethnology, Haifa; p.270 Cartoon: Courtesy of Dick Codor, New York; p.272 Israel Museum Jerusalem. Photo IMJ/Z. Radovan; p.273 Photo A.van der Heyden; p.276 Photo D.Harris; p.278 The British Museum, London; p.281 Photo Erich Lessing, Vienna; p.282 JPH/Photo Moshe Caine; p.284 Bibliotheque Nationale, Paris (Ms Gr.139, fol 446v); p.286 Photo Fratelli Alinari, Florence; p.280 Caricature: Courtesy of Dick Codor, New York; p.289 The British Library (Add.1139, fol.114); p.290 (left) JPH/Photo Moshe Caine; (right) JPH/Photo D.Harris; p.295 Armenian Patriarchate Library (Ms 1297, fol 84v); p.296 Bibliotheque Nationale, Paris; p.298 Photo Erich Lessing, Vienna; p.301 Photo Scala, Florence; p.302 Sculpture by Benno Elkan. Photo A. van der Heyden; p.303 JPH/Photo Moshe Caine; p.306 Herzog Anton Museum, Brunswick, Germany; p.307 Israel Antiquities Authority. Photo D.Harris; p.308 Bibliothelque Nationale Paris; Photo JPH; p.311 top: Tower of David Museum of the History of the Jewish People. Photo A. van der Heyden; bottom: Musee du Louvre, Paris. Cliches Musees Nationaux; p.312 Photo Baruch Blendl; p.313 British Museum London; p.314 Photo Erich Lessing, Vienna; p.315 The Oriental Institute, University of Chicago; p.317 British Museum, London; p.320 Archaeological Receipts Fund. Ministry of Science, Greece; p.322 Israel Antiquities Authority; p.323 Bibliotheque Nationale Paris; p.324 Rheinisches Bildarchiv; p.327 Israel Museum Jerusalem; p.328 Photo A. van der Heyden; p.332 Courtesy of Moshe and Lotte Davis, Jerusalem; p.334 Kunsthistorishes Museum, Vienna; 335 Photo Erich Lessing, Vienna; p.337 (top) Israel Museum; (bottom) Photo Fratelli Alinari, Florence; p.338 Photo JPH/D. Harris; p.339 Y. Meshorer; p.340 Photo A.van der Heyden; p.341 Rockefeller Museum, Jerusalem. Israel Antiquities Authority; p.342 Photo Erich Lessing, Vienna; p.345 Photo JPH/D.Harris p.348 Israel Museum. The Shrine of the Book, Jerusalem. p.348 Caricature: Courtesy of Nero (Harry Blackman), London; p.349 Photo A. van der Heyden; p.350 Hermitage, Leningard. Photo Erich Lessing, Vienna; p.351 Photo JPH; p.357 Photo A. van der Heyden; p.358 Hromka Library Jerusalem. Photo A. van der Heyden; p.359 Photo Elsevier Publishing Projects, Amsterdam; p.361 St Mark's Monastery, Jerusalem. Photo A. van der Heyden; pp.366-367 Elsevier Publishing Projects, Amsterdam; p.367 Photo Erich Lessing; p.368 (top) Photo A. van der Heyden; (bottom) Photo Zev Radovan; p.370 Photo Erich Lessing, Vienna; p.371 Left: Armenian Church of St James. Photo A. van der Heyden; (right) Photo Elsevier Publishing Projects, Amsterdam; p.372 Galleria degli Uffizzi, Florence; p.373 Photo Erich Lessing, Vienna; p.374 Fratelli Alinari, Florence; p.375 Photo Erich Lessing, Vienna; p.376 (left) JPH/Photo Moshe Caine; (right) Fratelli Alinari, Florence; p.377 Y. Meshorer; pp.378, 379 (left) Photo Erich Lessing; p.379 (right) Fratelli Alinari, Florence; p.380 Rockefeller Museum, Israel Antiquities Authority. Photo Z. Radovan; p.382 Photo Erich Lessing; p. 384 Photo courtesy Y.Meshorer; p.385 Photo A. van der Heyden; p.386 Photo JPH/D.Harris; p.387 Photo D. Harris; p.391 Elsevier Publishing Projects, Amsterdam; p.393 Photo D. Harris; p.395 Chester Beatty Library; pp.396, 397 Photos A. van der Heyden; p.399 British Library, London; p.400 Photo Elsevier Publishing Projects, Amsterdam; pp.402, 403 British Library, London; p.406 Photo JPH/Moshe Caine; p.407 (top) Vatican Library (MS Pal. Gr.431, fol 6); bottom: Chartres Cathedral, France; p.408 Top: Musee des Tapisseries, Angers; pp.409 (top), 410, 411 Photos Elsevier Publishing Projects, Amsterdam; p.412 (top) Israel Museum Jerusalem (Gift of Rebecca Shulman, New York. Photo IMJ; Bottom: From "Rodin Sculptures," published by Phaidon Press, Oxford; p.414 Photo Elsevier Publishing Porjects, Amsterdam; p.416 Fratelli Alinari, Florence; p.419 Musee du Louvre; cliche Musees Nationaux; p.427 Courtesy Steven Spielberg Jewish Film Archive, Hebrew University Jerusalem; p.431 Top: G. Wigoder collection; pp.431 (bottom), 432, 433 (left) Museum of the Diaspora Tel Aviv, Stephen Roth collection; p.433 (right) Courtesy Darryl Kibble, Redbank, Australia.

Color illustrations: p.225 (top) Photo D. Harris; (bottom) Photo Werner Braun; pp.226-227 Photo Ivo Moretti, Rome; pp.228-229 Photo Elsevier Publishing Projects, Amsterdam; p.230 (bottom) Photo D. Harris; p.231 Photos Erich Lessing; p.232 (top) Photo A. van der Heyden; (bottom) Photo N. Garo.

Typesetting: Yael Kaplan Typesetting Ltd.
Paging: Margalit Bassan

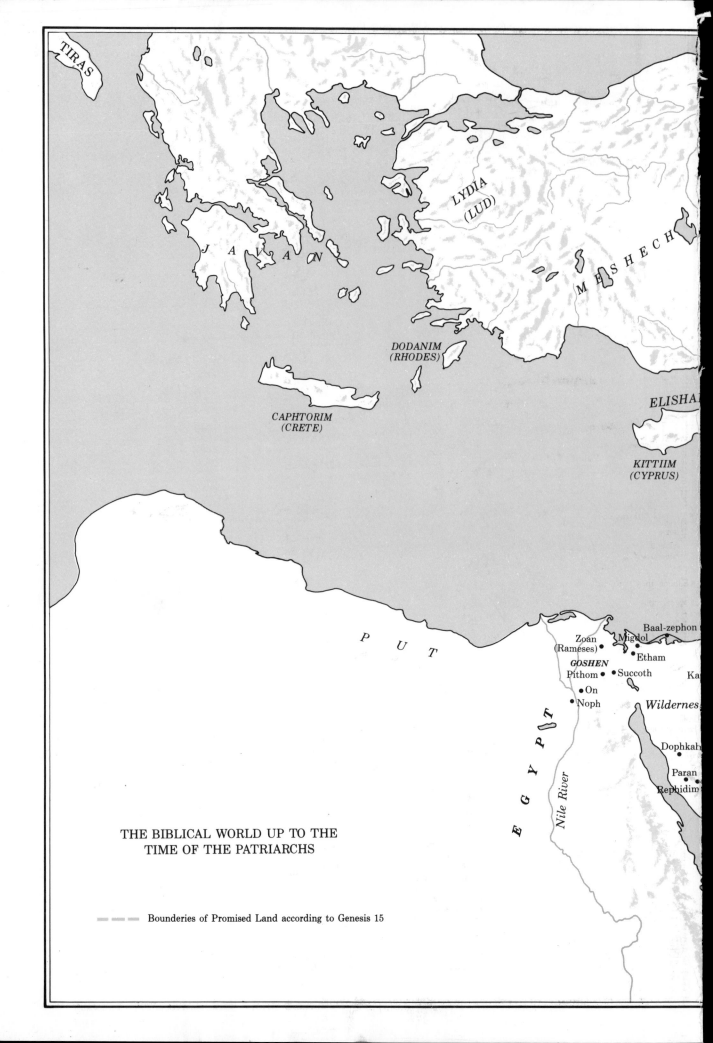

TIRAS

LYDIA
(LUD)

M E S H E C H

J A V A N

DODANIM
(RHODES)

ELISHA

CAPHTORIM
(CRETE)

KITTIIM
(CYPRUS)

P U T

Baal-zephon
Zoan   Migdol
(Rameses) •
     • Etham
GOSHEN
Pithom •   • Succoth   Ka

• On   *Wildernes*
• Noph

E G Y P T

Nile River

Dophkah

Paran •
Rephidim •

THE BIBLICAL WORLD UP TO THE
TIME OF THE PATRIARCHS

━ ━ ━ ━ ━   Bounderies of Promised Land according to Genesis 15